Hands-On Data Science with SQL Server 2017

Perform end-to-end data analysis to gain efficient data insight

Marek Chmel
Vladimír Mužný

BIRMINGHAM - MUMBAI

Hands-On Data Science with SQL Server 2017

Commissioning Editor: Sunith Shetty
Acquisition Editor: Tushar Gupta
Content Development Editor: Snehal Kolte
Technical Editor: Dharmendra Yadav
Copy Editor: Safis Editing
Project Coordinator: Manthan Patel
Proofreader: Safis Editing
Indexer: Mariammal Chettiyar
Graphics: Jisha Chirayil
Production Coordinator: Deepika Naik

First published: November 2018

Production reference: 1281118

Published by Packt Publishing Ltd.
Livery Place
35 Livery Street
Birmingham
B3 2PB, UK.

ISBN 978-1-78899-634-1

www.packtpub.com

Mapt

Contributors

About the authors

Marek Chmel is an IT consultant and trainer with more than 10 years' experience. He is a frequent speaker, focusing on Microsoft SQL Server, Azure, and security topics. Marek writes for Microsoft's TechnetCZSK blog and has been an MVP: Data Platform since 2012. He has earned numerous certifications, including MCSE: Data Management and Analytics, EC Council Certified Ethical Hacker, and several eLearnSecurity certifications.

Marek earned his MSc (business and informatics) degree from Nottingham Trent University. He started his career as a trainer for Microsoft server courses. Later, he joined AT&T, as a principal database administrator specializing in MSSQL Server, Data Platform, and Machine Learning.

I would like to thank my family— my wife and son, for their understanding and support during the time spent working on this book.

Vladimír Mužný has been a freelance IT consultant, developer, and Microsoft data platform trainer since 2000. He is also a frequent speaker on local events in Czech Republic and Slovakia. His most favorite topics are not only MS SQL Server, but also data integration, data science or NoSQL topics. During his career, Vladimír has earned certifications such as MCSE: Data Management and Analytics, MVP: Data Platform and MCT.

Nowadays, Vladimír is a data science enthusiast and works on data migration/integration projects also with output to machine learning models.

I wish to thank my colleague, Marek, my friend, and coauthor; without him, this book would never have been written. I would also like to thank all the team members behind this book for their never-ending passion.

Last but not least, I would like to say thank you to my family for their support, not just during the writing of this book, but also throughout my career.

About the reviewers

Sahaj Pathak has more than 4 years of experience in IT industry with architecting giant products. He has been involved with the design workflow for the frameworks and applications. He is a strong team player, speedy and versatile. He has developed several financial web applications with cutting edge technologies.

He has mastered all the stages of software development. He can interpret the business and client requirements and helped team to build scalable technical solution. His expertise involved in both front end and back end technologies such as Java, Spring, Hibernate, AngularJs, Node.js, and JavaScript.

He is also good at delivering training on latest technologies and server-based solutions.

> *I would like to express my heartfelt thanks to Packt Publishing for giving me this opportunity. Also I would like to thank my parents and friends for supporting me unconditionally.*

Subhash Shah works as a Head of Technology at AIMDek Technologies Pvt. Ltd. He is an experienced solutions architect with over 12 years of experience. He holds a degree in Information Technology from a reputable university. He is an advocate of open source development and its use to solve critical business problems at reduced cost. His interests include micro-services, data analysis, machine learning, artificial intelligence, and databases. He is an admirer of quality code and TDD. His technical skills include translating business requirements into scalable architecture, designing sustainable solutions and project delivery. He is a co-author of *MySQL 8 Administrator's Guide* and *Hands on High Performance with Spring 5*.

Packt is searching for authors like you

If you're interested in becoming an author for Packt, please visit `authors.packtpub.com` and apply today. We have worked with thousands of developers and tech professionals, just like you, to help them share their insight with the global tech community. You can make a general application, apply for a specific hot topic that we are recruiting an author for, or submit your own idea.

Table of Contents

Preface

SQL Server is a relational database management system that enables you to cover end-to-end data science processes using various inbuilt services and features.

Hands-On Data Science with SQL Server 2017 starts with an overview of data science with SQL so that you understand the core tasks in data science. You will learn intermediate to advanced level concepts so that you can perform analytical tasks on data using SQL Server. The book has a unique approach, covering best practices, tasks, and challenges to test your abilities at the end of each chapter. You will explore the ins and outs of performing various key tasks, such as data collection, cleaning, manipulation, aggregations, and filtering techniques. As you make your way through the chapters, you will turn raw data into actionable insights by wrangling and extracting data from databases using T-SQL. You will get to grips with preparing and presenting data in a meaningful way using Power BI to reveal hidden patterns. In the concluding chapters, you will work with SQL Server integration services to transform data into a useful format, and delve into advanced examples covering machine learning concepts such as predictive analytics using real-world examples.

By the end of this book, you will be ready to handle growing amounts of data and perform everyday activities in the same way as a data science professional.

Who this book is for

Hands-On Data Science with SQL Server 2017 is intended for data scientists, data analysts, and big data professionals who want to master their skills learning SQL and its applications. This book will be helpful even for beginners who want to build their career as data science professionals using the power of SQL Server 2017. Basic familiarity with SQL language will aid with understanding the concepts covered in this book.

What this book covers

`Chapter 1`, *Data Science Overview*, covers what the term data science means, the need for data science, the difference compared with traditional BI/DWH, and the competencies and knowledge required in order to be a data scientist.

`Chapter 2`, *SQL Server 2017 as a Data Science Platform*, explains the architecture of SQL Server from a data science perspective: in-memory OLTP for data acquisition; integration services as a transformation feature set; reporting services for visualization of input as well as output data; and, probably most importantly of all, T-SQL as a language for data exploration and transformation and machine learning services for making models themselves.

`Chapter 3`, *Data Sources for Analytics*, covers relational databases and NoSQL concepts side-by-side as valuable sources of data with a different approach to use. It also provides an overview of technologies such as HDInsight, Apache Hadoop, and Cosmos DB, and querying against such data sources.

`Chapter 4`, *Data Transforming and Cleaning with T-SQL*, demonstrates T-SQL techniques that are useful for making data consumable and complete for further utilization in data science, along with database architectures that are useful for transform/cleansing tasks.

`Chapter 5`, *Data Exploration and Statistics with T-SQL*, takes a deep dive into T-SQL capabilities, including common grouping and aggregations, framing/windowing, running aggregates, and (if needed) features such as custom CLR aggregates (with performance considerations).

`Chapter 6`, *Custom Aggregations on SQL Server*, explains how to create your own aggregations in order to enhance core T-SQL functionality.

`Chapter 7`, *Data Visualization*, explains the importance of visualizing data to reveal hidden patterns therein, along with examples of reporting services, PowerView, and PowerBI. By way of an alternative, an overview of R/Python visualization features is also provided (as these languages will play a vital role later in the book).

`Chapter 8`, *Data Transformations with Other Tools*, explains how to use integration services, probably R or Python, to transform data into a useful format, replacing missing values, detecting mistakes in datasets, normalization and its purpose, categorization, and finally data denormalization for better analytic purposes using views.

`Chapter 9`, *Predictive Model Training and Evaluation*, concerns a wide set of predictive models (clustering, N-point Bayes machines, recommenders) and their implementations via Machine Learning Studio, R, or Python.

`Chapter 10`, *Making Predictions*, explains how to use models created, evaluated, and scored in previous chapters. We will also learn how to make the model self-learning from the predictions made.

`Chapter 11`, *Getting It All Together – a Real-World Example*, demonstrates how to use certain features to grab, transform, and analyze data for a successful data science case.

`Chapter 12`, *Next Steps with Data Science and SQL*, summarizes the main points of all the preceding chapters and concludes outcomes. The chapter also provides ideas of how to continue working with data science, which trends are probably awaited in the future, and which other technologies will play strong roles in data science.

To get the most out of this book

Prior knowledge of SQL Server 2017 (Evaluation Edition) is required, as is an understanding of SQL Server Management Studio (version 17.7 was used at the time of writing as the latest edition).

Download the example code files

You can download the example code files for this book from your account at `www.packt.com`. If you purchased this book elsewhere, you can visit `www.packt.com/support` and register to have the files emailed directly to you.

You can download the code files by following these steps:

1. Log in or register at `www.packt.com`.
2. Select the **SUPPORT** tab.
3. Click on **Code Downloads & Errata**.
4. Enter the name of the book in the **Search** box and follow the onscreen instructions.

Once the file is downloaded, please make sure that you unzip or extract the folder using the latest version of:

- WinRAR/7-Zip for Windows
- Zipeg/iZip/UnRarX for Mac
- 7-Zip/PeaZip for Linux

The code bundle for the book is also hosted on GitHub at `https://github.com/PacktPublishing/Hands-On-Data-Science-with-SQL-Server-2017`. In case there's an update to the code, it will be updated on the existing GitHub repository.

We also have other code bundles from our rich catalog of books and videos available at `https://github.com/PacktPublishing/`. Check them out!

Conventions used

There are a number of text conventions used throughout this book.

`CodeInText`: Indicates code words in text, database table names, folder names, filenames, file extensions, pathnames, dummy URLs, user input, and Twitter handles. Here is an example: "The same sample query using the `OPENQUERY` function."

A block of code is set as follows:

```
SELECT * FROM REMOTESRV..Enums.Accounts
```

Any command-line input or output is written as follows:

```
sudo apt-get update
sudo apt-get install mssql-tools unixodbc-dev
```

Bold: Indicates a new term, an important word, or words that you see on screen. For example, words in menus or dialog boxes appear in the text like this. Here is an example: "Its correct name is added to the **Local Login** column."

Warnings or important notes appear like this.

Tips and tricks appear like this.

Get in touch

Feedback from our readers is always welcome.

General feedback: If you have questions about any aspect of this book, mention the book title in the subject of your message and email us at `customercare@packtpub.com`.

Errata: Although we have taken every care to ensure the accuracy of our content, mistakes do happen. If you have found a mistake in this book, we would be grateful if you would report this to us. Please visit `www.packt.com/submit-errata`, selecting your book, clicking on the Errata Submission Form link, and entering the details.

Piracy: If you come across any illegal copies of our works in any form on the internet, we would be grateful if you would provide us with the location address or website name. Please contact us at `copyright@packt.com` with a link to the material.

If you are interested in becoming an author: If there is a topic that you have expertise in, and you are interested in either writing or contributing to a book, please visit `authors.packtpub.com`.

Reviews

Please leave a review. Once you have read and used this book, why not leave a review on the site that you purchased it from? Potential readers can then see and use your unbiased opinion to make purchase decisions, we at Packt can understand what you think about our products, and our authors can see your feedback on their book. Thank you!

For more information about Packt, please visit `packt.com`.

1
Data Science Overview

SQL Server is far more than a regular database management system. It's a huge ecosystem of different services that work together to provide very complex data platform management tasks. With the addition of numerous features in the version of SQL Server 2016 and SQL Server 2017, the capabilities of the system have enlarged again toward modern ways of working with data such as big data, machine learning and data science. You're about to enter a new world with this book, which will allow you to grasp the data-related tasks from a different point of view and get more insight into your data.

Introducing data science

Data science is a modern term that covers a large amount of different disciplines. We can think of data science as a field that uses various tools, processes, methods, and algorithms to extract knowledge and insights from data, which can be stored in a structured and unstructured manner. In one view, we can see data science as being quite similar to data mining.

Data science as a field includes everything that is associated with data manipulation—cleansing, preparation, analysis, visualization, and so on. Data science combines numerous skills that can be used for working with data such as programming, reasoning, mathematical skills, and statistics.

Data science is frequently mentioned together with other buzzwords such as big data, machine learning, and so on. As a matter of the fact, projects working with machine learning and big data are usually using data science principles, tools, and processes to build the the application.

Why is data science so important to us? Well, up until 2005, mankind had created approximately 130 exabytes of data (1 exabyte = 1,000 petabytes). But this number is growing quickly, and actually the amount of data created around the world is not growing in a linear fashion, but rather exponentially, with expectations that it will grow to 40 zettabytes in 2020. Such a large amount of data can hardly be processed by machines, or even data scientists, but a proper approach can increase the fraction of data that we'll be able to analyze.

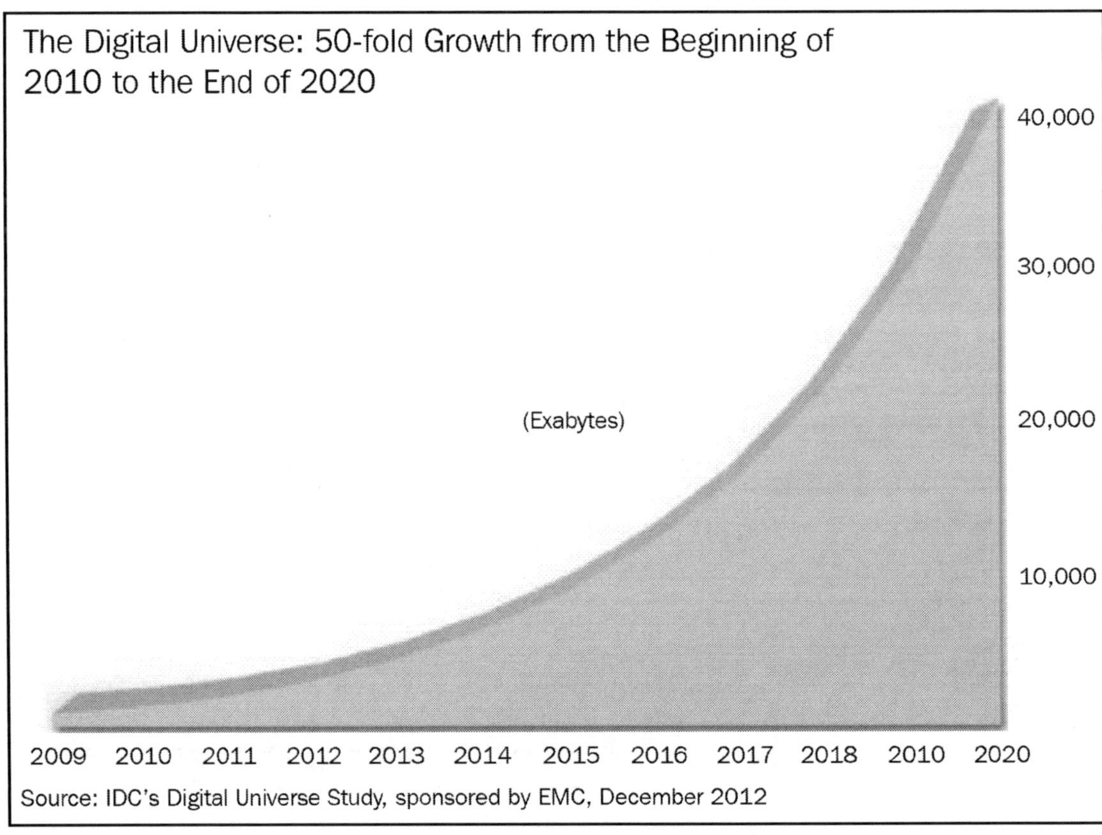

Data science project life cycle

There are different data science life cycles available, which can fit different projects. We'll focus most on the **Team Data Science Process** (**TDSP**) **life cycle**, which is defined by Microsoft and can be applied to data science with Microsoft SQL Server. The TDSP provides a recommended life cycle that you can use to structure your data science projects. The life cycle outlines the steps, from start to finish, that projects usually follow when they are executed.

Business understanding

When we work with a data science project, this project usually has several phases. Each data science project begins with the business problem, or identifying the question. There are key tasks addressed in this first stage of the project:

- **Define the goal or objective**: identify the required business variable that needs to be predicted by the analysis
- **Identify the data sources**: find the required data that you will use for the data science project

When you work with stakeholders to identify the key questions and project goals, you should use sharp questions that will help you identify the required data for your analysis.

If your question is, *What will my stock's sale price be next month?* then you'll need to analyze the data, which includes your stock's price history over months. Also, you will need to analyze the sales of your stock from those months. And, in a similar manner, you need to think about the business problem definition and ask specific questions that include the numbers, names, categories, and so on.

Based on the questions that you'll be trying to answer, you can also foresee the data science methods that you'll use to address such a question. Typical questions for data science projects would include the following:

- How much, or how many?
- Which category?
- Which group?
- Is this weird?
- Which option should be taken?

During the first phase of the project, you're also usually building the TDSP, which will consist of various personnel members, each specializing in a particular subject, which will be essential to the success of the project:

- **A data scientist**: A highly educated and skilled person who can solve complex data problems by employing deep expertise in scientific disciplines (mathematics, statistics, or computer science).
- **A data professional**: A skilled person who creates or maintains data systems, data solutions, or implements predictive modelling. These people will work in professions such as database administration, database development, or BI Development.
- **A software developer**: A person who designs and develops programming logic, and who can apply machine learning to integrate predictive functionality into applications.
- **A project leader**: A project leader manages the daily activities of individual data scientists and other project contributors on a specific data science project.

Getting data

The second phase of the project is related to data identification, acquisition, and understanding. Data comes from various data sources that provide data in a structured, a semi-structured, and an unstructured format. Data that we have on input may come with different quality and integrity, based on the data source that is used for storing the information. For the data analysis, we need to ingest the data into the target analytic environment, either an on-premise one, or in the cloud. These can include numerous services from Microsoft such as SQL Server (ideally with PolyBase to access external data) or cloud services such as Azure Storage Account, HDInsight, and Azure Data Lake.

Considering we'll load the data into Microsoft SQL Server, we need a good way to break down the dataset of the information into individual rows and columns. Each row in the table will present one event, instance, or item for our analysis. Each column on this table will represent an attribute of the row. Different projects will have data with a different level of detail collected, based on the available data sources and our ability to process such data.

When we talk about the initial loading of the data into SQL Server, this is usually referred to as a staging database. Since the data can be loaded from numerous different databases and repositories, dumping all the data from the source into a centralized repository is usually the first step before building the analytical storage. The next stage would be the data warehouse. **Data warehouse** is a common term for an enterprise system used for reporting and data analysis, which is usually a core of the enterprise business intelligence solution. While a data warehouse is an enterprise-wide repository of data, extracting insights from such a huge repository might be a challenging task. We can segregate the data according to the department or the category that the data belongs to, so that we have much smaller sections of the data to work with and extract information from. These smaller portions of the data warehouse are then referenced as data marts.

Data in the source systems may need a lot of work before and during loading it into a database or other analytical storage, where we can properly analyze the data. In general, one of the many steps in data science projects is **data wrangling**, a process of acquiring raw data and mapping and transforming the data into another format that is suitable for its end use, for us, the data analysts. Data wrangling basically has three steps:

- Getting and reading the data
- Cleaning the data
- Shaping and structuring the data

Reading the data sounds simple, but in the end, it's a complex task in the data science project, where one part of the project is a data flow and a pipeline definition on how to connect to the data, read the data with the proper tools, and move the data to the analytics store. This can end up with complex integration work as part of the data science project just to interconnect various data sources together and shape the data from various sources, so you can run powerful analytics on the data to get the insights. The Microsoft SQL Server includes very important services, such as SQL Server Integration Services, which, together with SQL Server Data Tools, can be used as one of the tools available for data wrangling with all three steps.

Once the data is loaded into the analytical store, we need to explore and visualize the available data with the toolset available to get the idea of the structure and develop initial understanding of the data. An initial understanding of the data can be achieved via numerous tools, but if we focus on Microsoft SQL Server, then the choices would include SQL Service Integration Services—Data Profiling Task and SQL Server Management Studio.

When you explore the data, you're looking for basic information such as this:

- Is the data organized?
- Are there any missing values?
- What does each row represent?
- What do columns represent?
- Is the data stored as a categorical or a numerical feature?
- Are there any transformations required?

Modelling and analysis

This part of the project might be the most creative one, since it includes numerous tasks, which have to be taken to deliver the final product. The list of tasks can be very long, and may include these:

- Data mining
- Text analytics
- Model building
- Feature engineering and extraction
- Model testing

Microsoft SQL Server has tools built in, which can provide a delivery platform for most of the tasks. When we talk about data mining, there are several different methodologies or frameworks to follow, where so far the **Cross Industry Standard Process for Data Mining (CRISP-DM)** is the most frequently used one, based on several different methods of research regarding the methodology usage. In 2015, IBM released a new methodology called **Analytics Solutions Unified Method for Data Mining/Predictive Analytics**, which refined and extended CRISP-DM. CRISP-DM is an open-standard process model that describes common approaches used by data-mining experts, and it's still the most widely used analytics model. CRISP-DM breaks the process of data mining into six major phases. The sequence of the phases is not strict and moves back and forth between different phases, as it is always required. The arrows in the process diagram indicate the most important and frequent dependencies between phases. The outer circle in the diagram symbolizes the cyclic nature of data mining itself. A data-mining process continues after a solution has been deployed. The lessons learned during the process can trigger new, often more focused business questions, and subsequent data-mining processes will benefit from the experiences of the previous ones:

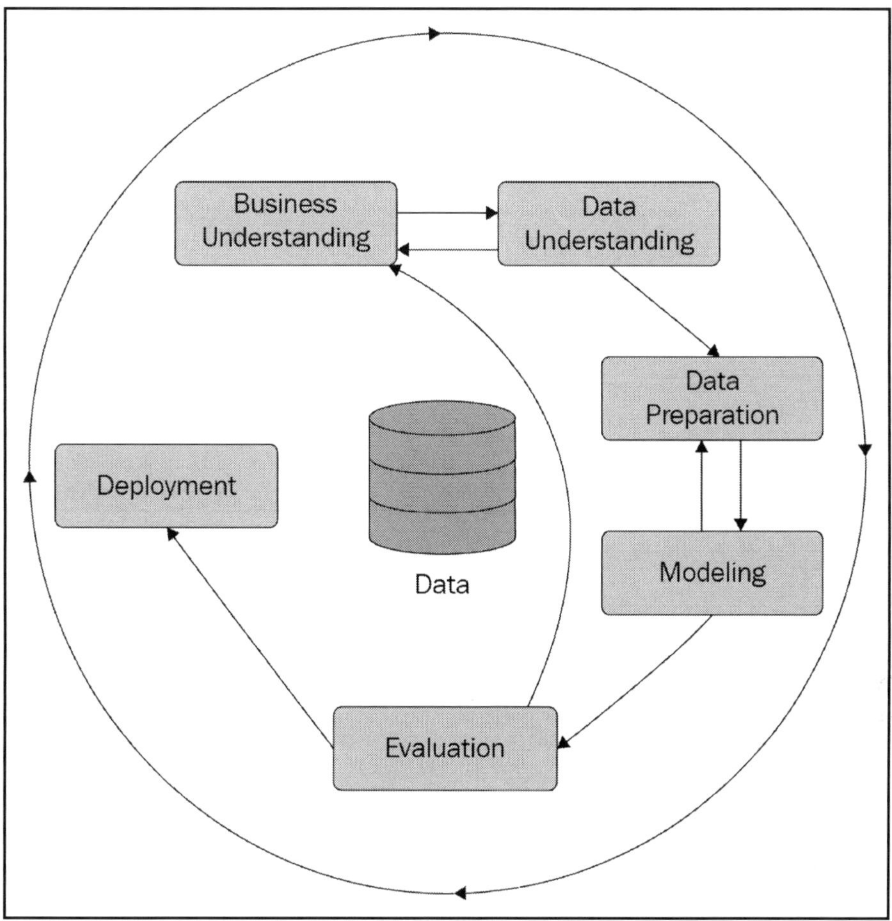

The purpose of data mining is to put structured and unstructured data in relation to each other so as to easily interface them and provide the workers in the sector with a system that is easy to use. The experts of each specified area of business will therefore have access to a complex data system that is able to process information at different levels. This has the advantage of bringing to light the relationships among data, predictive analysis, assessments for specific business decisions, and much more.

Data mining can be used for solving many business problems and to prepare the data for a more advanced approach, such as machine learning, which can be used for:

- Searching for anomalies
- Churn analysis
- Customer segmentation

- Forecasting
- Market basket analysis
- Network intrusion detection
- Targeted advertisement

Deployment and visualization

Once you have developed a functioning data science solution or some learning model, you're ready for deployment into production. Many of the systems have two primary modes of operations for a data science solution, either real-time operations or batch operation. In this part, we usually consider the data visualization and the proper toolset to deliver the results to our users. Tools such as Power BI or Tableau will help you bring interesting insights to your data in a visual way, which is usually best for the end users.

Final acceptance

The last step of the project is the final presentation and acceptance from the client or the customer. You'll present the insights and translate the findings into the language appropriate for your audience. In this part of the project, you'll work with the customer or the internal team, who will run and support the project once it gets into production, and you'll verify that the outcome meets the required needs.

Data science domains

Data science is linked to numerous other modern buzzwords such as big data and machine learning, but data science itself is built from numerous domains, where you can get your expertise. These domains include the following:

- Statistics
- Visualization
- Data mining
- Machine learning
- Pattern recognition
- Data platform operations
- Artificial intelligence
- Programming

Math and statistics

Statistics and other math skills are essential in several phases of the data science project. Even in the beginning of data exploration, you'll be dividing the features of your data observations into categories:

- Categorical
- Numeric:
    - Discrete
    - Continuous

Categorical values describe the item and represent an attribute of the item. Imagine you have a dataset about cars: car brand would be a typical categorical value, and color would be another.

On the other side, we have numerical values that can be split into two different categories—discrete and continuous. Discrete values describe the amount of observations, such as how many people purchased a product, and so on. Continuous values have an infinite number of possible values and use real numbers for the representation. In a nutshell, discrete variables are like points plotted on a chart, and a continuous variable can be plotted as a line.

Another classification of the data is the measurement-level point of view. We can split data into two primary categories:

- Qualitative:
    - Nominal
    - Ordinal
- Quantitative:
    - Interval
    - Ratio

Nominal variables can't be ordered and only describe an attribute. An example would be the color of a product; this describes how the product looks, but you can't put any ordering scheme on the color saying that red is bigger than green, and so on. **Ordinal variables** describe the feature with a categorical value and provide an ordering system; for example: Education—elementary, high school, university degree, and so on.

With quantitative values, it's a different story. The major difference is that ratio has a true zero. Imagine the attribute was a length. If the length is 0, you know there's no length. But this does not apply to temperature, since there's an interval of possible values for the temperature, where 0°C or 0°F does not mean the beginning of the scale for the temperature (as absolute zero, or beginning of the scale is 273.15° C or -459.67° F). With °K, it would actually be a ratio type of the quantitative value, since the scale really begins with 0°K. So, as you can see, any number can be an interval or a ratio value, but it depends on the context!

Visualizing the types of data

Visualizing and communicating data is incredibly important, especially with young companies that are making data-driven decisions for the first time, or companies where data scientists are viewed as people who help others make data-driven decisions. When it comes to communicating, this means describing your findings, or the way techniques work to audiences, both technical and non-technical. Different types of data have different ways of representation. When we talk about the categorical values, the ideal representation visuals would be these:

- Bar charts
- Pie charts
- Pareto diagrams
- Frequency distribution tables

A bar chart would visually represent the values stored in the frequency distribution tables. Each bar would represent one categorical value. A bar chart is also a base line for a pareto diagram, which includes the relative and cumulative frequency for the categorical values:

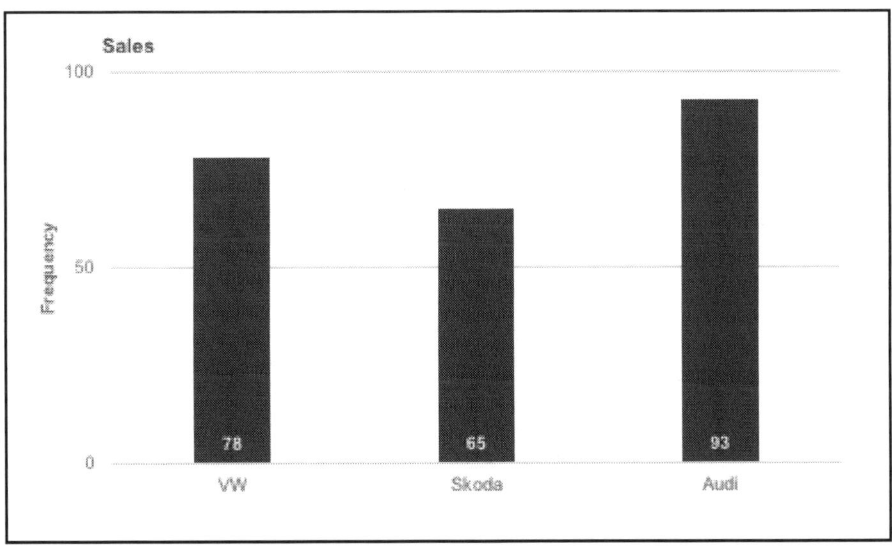

Bar chart representing the relative and cumulative frequency for the categorical values

If we'll add the cumulative frequency to the bar chart, we will have a pareto diagram of the same data:

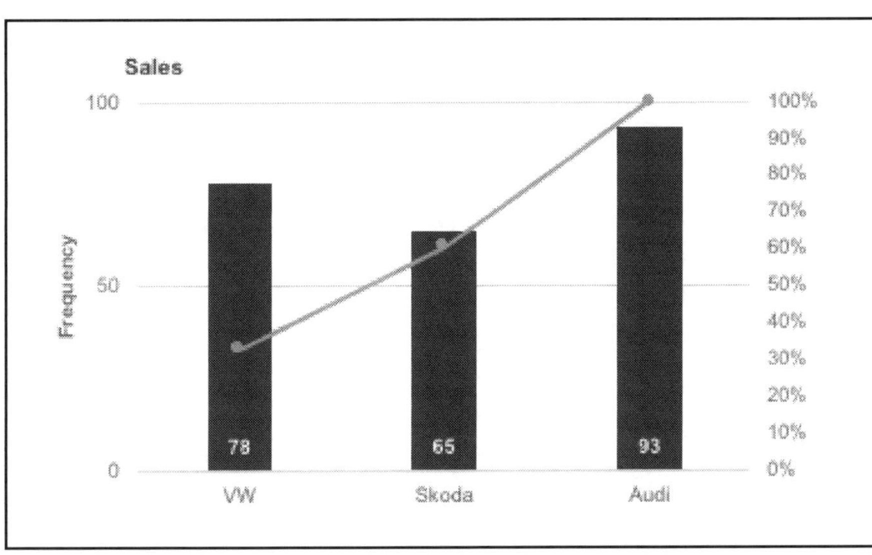

Pareto diagram representing the relative and cumulative frequency for the categorical values

Another very useful type of visualization for categorical data is the pie chart. Pie charts display the percentage of the total for each categorical value. In statistics, this is called the **relative frequency**. The relative frequency is the percentage of the total frequency of each category. This type of visual is commonly used for market-share representations:

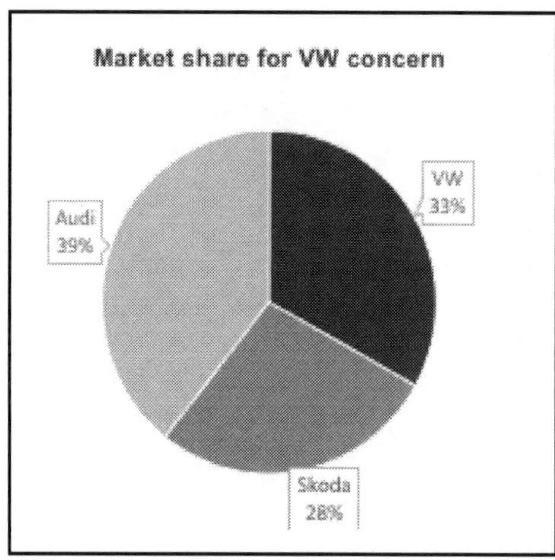

Pie chart representing the market share for Volkswagen

All the values are imaginary and are used just for demonstration purposes; these numbers don't represent a real market share by different brands in Volkswagen around the world, or in any city.

For numeric data, the ideal start would be a frequency distribution table, which will contain ordered or unordered values. Numeric data is very frequently displayed with histograms or scatter plots. When using intervals, the rule of thumb is to use 5 to 20 intervals, to have a meaningful representation of the data.

Let's create a table with 20 discrete data points, which we'll display visually. To create the table, we can use the following T-SQL script:

```
CREATE TABLE [dbo].[dataset](
 [datapoint] [int] NOT NULL
) ON [PRIMARY]
```

To insert new values into the table, let's use the script:

```
INSERT [dbo].[dataset] ([datapoint]) VALUES (7)
INSERT [dbo].[dataset] ([datapoint]) VALUES (28)
INSERT [dbo].[dataset] ([datapoint]) VALUES (50)
etc. with more values to have 20 values in total
```

The table will include numbers in the range of 0 to 300, and the content of the table can be retrieved with this:

```
SELECT * FROM [dbo].[dataset]
ORDER BY datapoint
```

To visualize a descrete values dataset, we'll need to build a histogram. The histogram will have six intervals, and the interval length can be calculated as a *(largest value – smallest value) / number of intervals*. When we build the frequency distribution table and the intervals for the histogram, we'll end up with the following results:

Frequency distribution table

Desired intervals	**6**
Interval width	**49**

Interval start	Interval end	Absolute frequency	Relative frequency
7	56	4	0,20
56	105	5	0,25
105	154	1	0,05
154	203	3	0,15
203	252	2	0,10
252	301	5	0,25
		20	1,00

A histogram based on the absolute frequency of the discrete values will look such as this one:

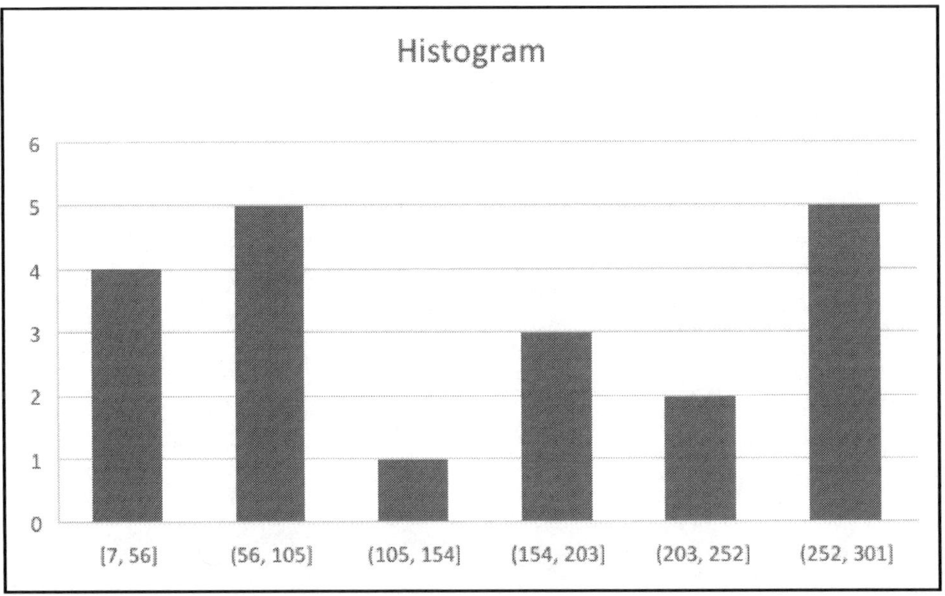

Statistics 101

A good understanding of statistics is vital for a data scientist. You should be familiar with statistical tests, distributions, maximum likelihood estimators, and so on. This will also be the case for machine learning, but one of the more important aspects of your statistics knowledge will be understanding when different techniques are (or aren't) a valid approach. Statistics is important for all types of companies, especially data-driven companies where stakeholders depend on your help to make decisions and design and evaluate experiments.

Central tendency

There are three descriptive measures of central tendency—the mean, the median, and the mode, but SQL Server does not have a way to calculate anything other than the mean directly. The arithmetic mean, or simply the mean (there are more types of mean in the central tendency), is the sum of all measurements divided by the number of observations in the dataset. The median is the middle value that separates the higher half from the lower half of the dataset. The median and the mode are the only measures of the central tendency that can be used for ordinal data, in which values are ranked relative to one another but are not measured absolutely. The mode is the most frequent value in the dataset. This is the only central tendency measure that can be used with nominal data, which has purely qualitative category assignments. For looking into such values with SQL Server, we will either need to define our own assembly with a custom aggregate or use complex T-SQL constructs to bypass the missing statistical functions. Another option would be to use the Python code or the R code; the code can be running inside the SQL Server, and you can pass the result set as the argument to the Python code or the R code to work on the descriptive statistics.

Skewness

Skewness indicates whether the data is spread symmetrically or is concentrated on one side of the graph. There are three different types of skewness:

- Positive skew
- Negative skew
- Zero skew

Correctly calculating the skew is quite complex, so we'll focus on understanding the skew, since Python and R have a way to calculate the skew for us correctly. As SQL Server is not a statistical tool, it does not have any built-in function for direct skewness calculation. But we can define the skewness based on the central tendency measures of mean and median:

- If the *mean* > *median*, then you'll observe the positive skew.
- If the *mean* < *median*, then you'll observe the negative skew.
- If the *mean* = *median*, you have zero skew:

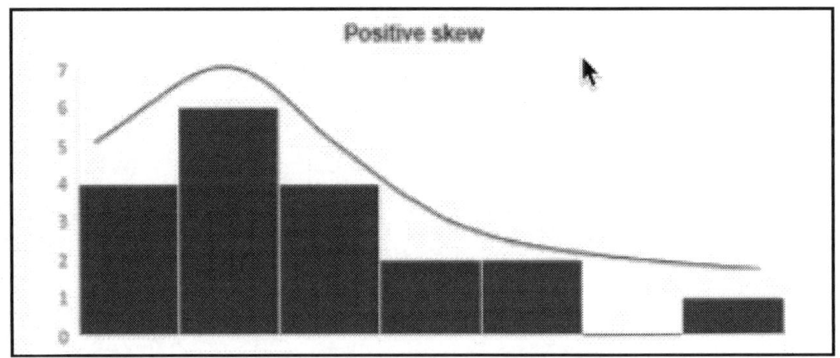

Skewness

Variability

If we would like to understand the variability of the data, there are three important measures that we can use to get a better understanding of our data set, and those include the following:

- Variance
- Standard deviation
- Coefficient of variation

Variance measures the distance of the data points around their mean value. Variance has a central role in statistics, where some ideas that use it include descriptive statistics, statistical inference, hypothesis testing, goodness of fit, and Monte Carlo sampling. Variance is an important tool in the sciences, where statistical analysis of data is common. The variance is the square of the standard deviation, the second central moment of a distribution, and the covariance of the random variable with itself.

Standard deviation is a measure of how spread-out numbers are, and based on the number describing the standard deviation, you can see the extent to which a set of numbers lies apart. In addition to expressing the variability of a population, the standard deviation is commonly used to measure confidence in statistical conclusions. Unlike variance, the standard deviation is expressed in the same units as the data, which is very useful.

The coefficient of variation is a measure of the dispersion of probability, or a frequency distribution. It's usually a percentage value, which is defined as a ratio of the standard deviation to the mean.

SQL Server has several built-in functions that can be used to calculate variance and standard deviation. To find out the variability measures from our table, we can run the following query:

```
SELECT AVG(datapoint),VARP(datapoint), STDEVP(datapoint) FROM dataset
```

Don't get confused with those function names, as for variance there are are two functions `VAR()` and `VARP()` and the same for the standard deviation, `STDEV()` and `STDEVP()`. This is very important from a statistics perspective, depending on whether we work with the whole population or just a sample of the population.

Variance for sample and population are not the same, as if you would check the formulas behind these functions have different denominators:

$$Popular\ variance\ \sigma^2 = \frac{\sum_{i=1}^{N}(x_i - \mu)^2}{N}$$

$$Sample\ variance\ \sigma^2 = \frac{\sum_{i=1}^{N}(x_i - \bar{x})^2}{n-1}$$

The full query to get the variability measures on our table, which would include both population and sample measures, would look such as this one:

```
SELECT AVG(datapoint) as Mean,
VAR(datapoint) as 'Sample variation',
VARP(datapoint) as 'Population variation',
STDEV(datapoint) as 'Sample standard deviation',
STDEVP(datapoint) as 'Population standard deviation'
FROM dataset
```

In such cases, the sample variability measures will be higher than the population measures, due to a lower denominator value. In the case of a sample, where you don't have the whole population data points, the concentrations of extremes and central tendencies can be different based on the whole range of values. When using such functions, you need to know whether you're working with just a sample of the data or the whole population of the data available, so the results are not skewed and you have the proper outcomes of these functions!

Machine learning

A very important part of data science is machine learning. Machine learning is the science of getting computers to act without being explicitly programmed. In the past decade, machine learning has given us self-driving cars, practical speech recognition, effective web search, and a vastly improved understanding of the human genome. Machine learning is so pervasive today that you probably use it dozens of times a day without knowing it.

SQL Server and machine learning

SQL Server has integrated machine learning with the version of 2016, when the first R services were introduced and with the 2017 version, when Python language support was added to SQL Server, and the feature was renamed machine-learning services. Machine-learning services can be used to solve complex problems and the tasks and algorithms are chosen based on the data and the expected prediction.

There are two main flavors of machine learning:

- Supervised
- Unsupervised

The main difference between the two is that supervised learning is performed by having a **ground truth** available. This means that the predictive model is building the capabilities based on the prior knowledge of what the output values for a sample should be. Unsupervised learning, on the other hand, does not have any sort of this outputs and the goal is to find natural structures present in the datasets. This can mean grouping datapoints into clusters or finding different ways of looking at complex data so that it appears simpler or more organized.

Each type of machine learning is using different algorithms to solve the problem. Typical supervised learning algorithms would include the following:

- Classification
- Regression

When the data is being used to predict a category, supervised learning is also called classification. This is the case when assigning an image as a picture of either a car or a boat, for example. When there are only two options, it's called **two-class classification**. When there are more categories, such as when predicting the winner of the World Cup, this problem is known as **multi-class classification**.

The major algorithms used here would include the following:

- Logistic regression
- Decision tree/forest/jungle
- Support vector machine
- Bayes point machine

Regression algorithms can be used for both types of variables, continuous and discrete, to predict a value, where for continuous values you'll apply **Linear Regression** and on discrete values, **Logistic Regression.** In linear regression, the relationship between the input variable (x) and output variable (y) is expressed as an equation of the form $y = a + bx$. Thus, the goal of linear regression is to find out the values of coefficients a and b and fit a line that is nearest to most of the points. Some good rules of thumb when using this technique are to remove variables that are very similar (correlated) and to remove noise from your data, if possible. It is a fast and simple technique and a good first algorithm to try.

Logistic regression is best suited for binary classification (datasets where $y = 0$ or *1*, where *1* denotes the default class. So, if you're predicting whether an event will occur, the instance of event occurring will be classified as *1*. It measures the relationship between the categorical dependent variable and one or more independent variables by estimating probabilities using a logistic function.

There are numerous kinds of regressions available, depending on the Python or R package that is used; for example, we could use any of the following:

- Bayesian linear regression
- Linear regression
- Poisson regression
- Decision forest regression
- Many others

We'll focus on implementing the machine-learning algorithms and models in the following chapters with SQL Server Machine Learning Services to train and predict the values from the dataset.

Choosing the right algorithm

When choosing the algorithm for machine learning, you have to consider numerous factors to properly choose the right algorithm for the task. It should not only based on the predicted output: category, value, cluster, and so on, but also on numerous other factors, such as these:

- Training time
- Size of data and number of features you're processing
- Accuracy
- Linearity
- Number of possible parameters

Training time can range from minutes to hours, depending not only on the algorithm, but also on the amount of features entering the model and the total amount of data that is being processed. However, a proper choice of algorithm can make the training time much shorter compared to the other. In general, regression models will reach the fastest training times, whereas neural network models will be on the other side of the training time length spectrum. Remember that developing a machine-learning model is iterative work. You will usually try several models and compare possible metrics. Based on the metric captured, you'll fine-tune the models and run comparison again on selected candidates and choose one model for operations. Even with more experience, you might not choose the right algorithm for your model at first, and you might be surprised that other algorithms can outperform the first chosen candidate, as shown:

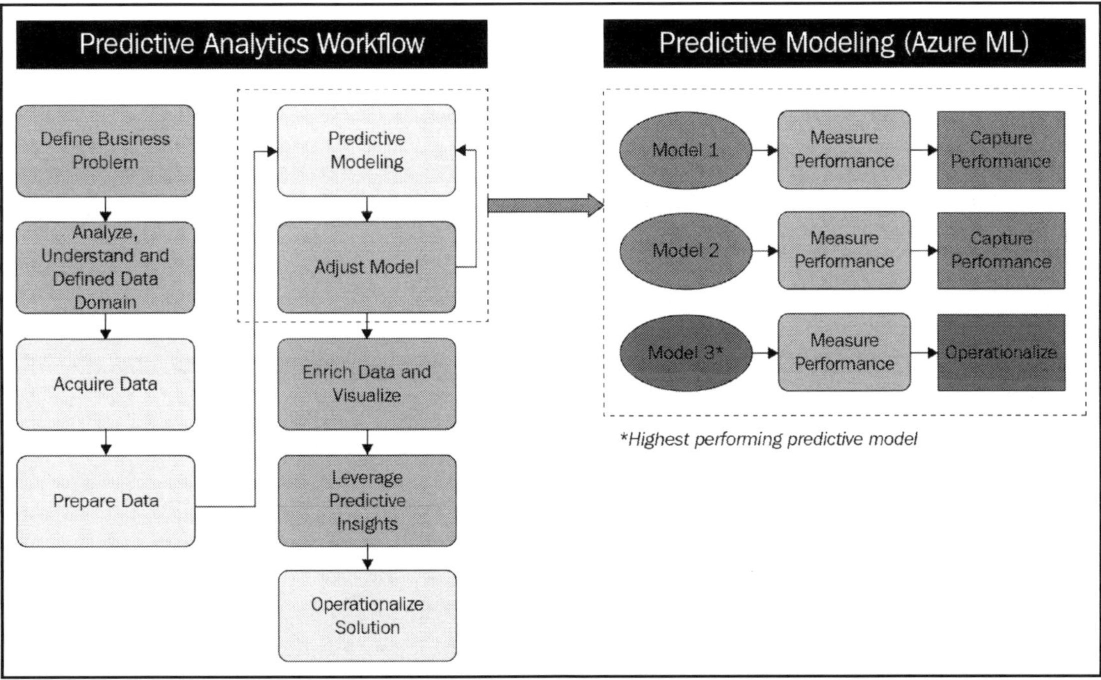

With accuracy, there are actually several different metrics, which we can consider when evaluating how a machine-learning model works and performs. Different types of algorithms have different metrics that can be used for comparing the performance, and you won't find the same metrics among those at all. The most common metrics for classification types of algorithms would include these:

- Confusion matrix
- Accuracy
- AUC
- Precision
- Recall
- F1 score

Confusion matrix is the primary one we'll usually use to evaluate the machine-learning model because it's very intuitive and easy to understand. The confusion matrix is actually a pivot table with actual and predicted dimensions displaying the amount of classes in those dimensions. This matrix is not used as a metric itself, but the numbers on the matrix are used for most of the other possible performance measures for the model:

True Positive	False Negative
8711	195
False Positive	**True Negative**
1496	4160

This matrix displays four values. **True Positive** is the amount of cases when the prediction was true and the actual data was also true. Consider again that we're in the supervised learning category, so this means that the model is training and scoring itself based on known data. So we know the current state—actual and check if the prediction can match the current state. **True Negative** is actually the opposite—the actual state was false and the prediction was right in predicting false. **False Positive** and false negative are cases where prediction and actual don't match. A **False Positive** is also known as a **Type I error**, and a **False Negative** as a **Type II error**, in statistics. The Type I error rate is also known as the significance level, and is usually set to 0.05 (5%). There will always be some errors with your model; otherwise, the model will be overfitted if there won't be any errors at all, and in real production after development, the model would not perform well with unknown data points. There's no rule on what type of error to minimize, this is solely dependent on the business case and the type of data science project and question that you're working on.

Accuracy can be another metric that is used to evaluate a model. Accuracy is represented by a number of correct predictions over all the predictions on the model:

$$Accuracy = \frac{TP + TN}{TP + FP + TN + FN}$$

Accuracy is a very good metric if the classes in the data are balanced, but it can be very misleading if one of the classes is extremely dominant compared to the other. As an example, consider a dataset with 100 emails, where only five emails are spam. If the model has a terrible performance and marks all emails as non-spam, it would classify 95 emails correctly and five emails incorrectly. Although the model was not able to classify any email as spam, it's accuracy would still be 95%. As you can see, this can be very misleading with the dataset, which is not balanced.

Very similar to accuracy is precision. Precision is a ratio between positive predictions and total predictions:

$$Precision = \frac{TP}{TP + FP}$$

Recall is very closely used with precision and the calculation is very similar, where another part of the confusion matrix is used in the denominator:

$$Recall = \frac{TP}{TP + FN}$$

Recall and precision give us information about the machine-learning model in regard of false negatives and false positives. Precision tells us how precise the model is, where recall is not about capturing the case correctly but more about capturing all cases with a given classification. If you would like to minimize false negatives, you would fine-tune the model to have high recall (nearly 100%) with reasonable precision, and the same if you would like to minimize Type II errors or false positives: you would focus on high precision in your model metrics.

As these two metrics are very close, they are also used to calculate F1 score, which is a combination of both expressed as Harmonic Mean:

$$F1\ Score = \frac{2 * Precision * Recall}{Precision + Recall}$$

When we see a machine-learning model being evaluated, you can usually find all these metrics, together with the confusion matrix, in one place:

True Positive	False Negative	Accuracy	Precision	Threshold	AUC
8711	195	0.884	0.853	0.5	0.864
False Positive	**True Negative**	**Recall**	**F1 Score**		
1496	4160	0.978	0.912		

The last missing piece of the basic performance metrics is the **Area under ROC Curve** (**AUC**) metric. AUC represents the model's ability to properly determine between positive and negative outcomes. When the *AUC = 0.5*, the model is actually randomly guessing the outcome, and when the AUC reaches 1.0, the model is 100% accurate. **Receiver Operating Characteristics** (**ROC**) can be broken down into two factors:

- **Sensitivity**: Defined as true positive rate, or actually the recall
- **Specificity**: Defined as false positive rate:

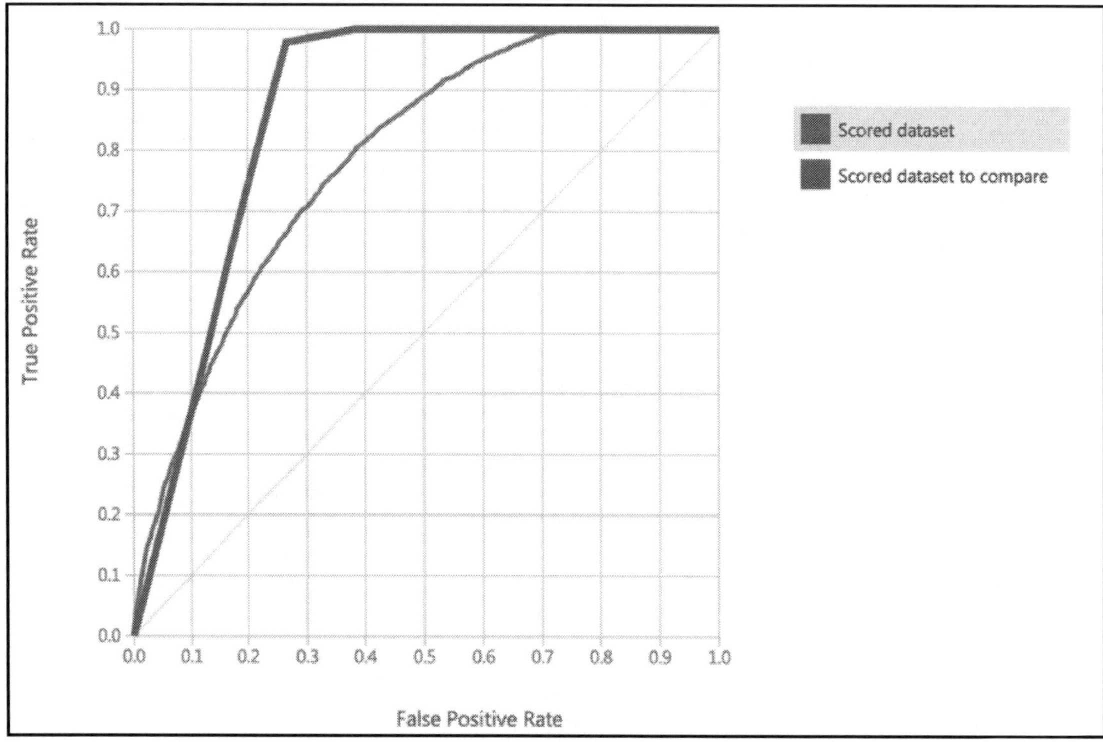

On the chart, you can see a comparison between two ROC curves for a machine-learning model, comparing the performance of two different algorithms used on the same dataset.

Big data

Big data is another modern buzzword that you can find around the data management and analytics platforms. The big really does not have to mean that the data volume is extremely large, although it usually is.

There are different imperatives linked to big data, which describe the theorem. These would include the following:

- **Volume**: Volume really describes the quantity of the data. There's a big potential to get value and insights from large-volume datasets. The main challenge is that the data sets are so big and complex that the traditional data-processing application software's are inadequate to deal with them.
- **Variety**: Data is not strictly a relational database anymore, and data can be stored in text files, images, and social feeds from a social network.
- **Velocity**: While we want to have the data available in real-time, the speed of the data generation is challenging for regular DMBS systems and requires specialized forms of deployment and software.
- **Veracity**: With a large amount of possible data sources, the quality of the data can vary, which can affect the data analysis and insights gained from the data.

Here are some big data statistics that are interesting:

- 100 terabytes of data are uploaded to Facebook every day
- Every hour, Walmart customers' transactions provide the company with about 2.5 petabytes of data
- Twitter generates 12 terabytes of data every day
- YouTube users upload eight years worth of new video content every day

SQL Server and big data

Let's face reality. SQL Server is not a big-data system. However, there's a feature on the SQL Server that allows us to interact with other big-data systems, which are deployed in the enterprise. This is huge!

This allows us to use the traditional relational data on the SQL Server and combine it with the results from the big-data systems directly or even run the queries towards the big-data systems from the SQL Server. The answer to this problem is a technology called **PolyBase**:

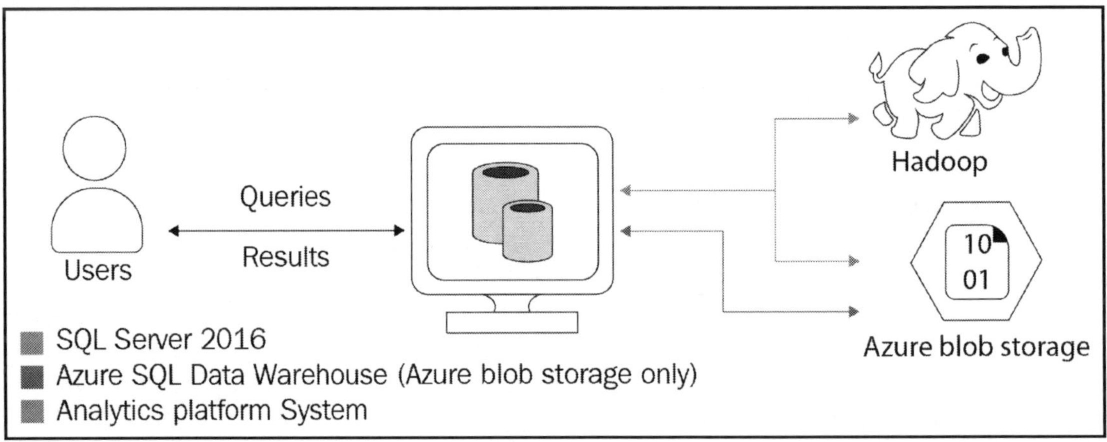

PolyBase is a bridge between SQL Server and big-data systems such as Hadoop, which can run in numerous different configurations. You can have your own Hadoop deployment, or utilize some Azure services such as HDInsight or Azure Data Lake, which are implementations of Hadoop and HDFS filesystem from the Hadoop framework. We'll get deeper into PolyBase in `Chapter 4`, *Data Sources for Analytics*. If you would like to test drive Hadoop with SQL Server, there are several appliances ready for testing and evaluation, such as Hortonworks Data Platform or Cloudera.

You can download prebuilt virtual machines, which you can connect to from SQL Server with the PolyBase feature to evaluate how the big-data Integration is working. For Hortonworks, you can check out `https://hortonworks.com/products/data-platforms/hdp/`
For Cloudera Quickstart VMs, you can check out `https://www.cloudera.com/downloads/quickstart_vms/5-13.html`

Hadoop itself is external to SQL Server and is described as a collection of software tools for distributed storage and the processing of big data. The base Apache Hadoop framework is composed of the following modules:

- **Hadoop Common**: Contains libraries and utilities needed by other Hadoop modules
- **Hadoop Distributed File System** (**HDFS**): A distributed filesystem that stores data on commodity machines, providing very high aggregate bandwidth across the cluster

- **Hadoop YARN**: Introduced in 2012 as a platform responsible for managing computing resources in clusters and using them for scheduling users' applications
- **Hadoop MapReduce**: An implementation of the MapReduce programming model for large-scale data processing:

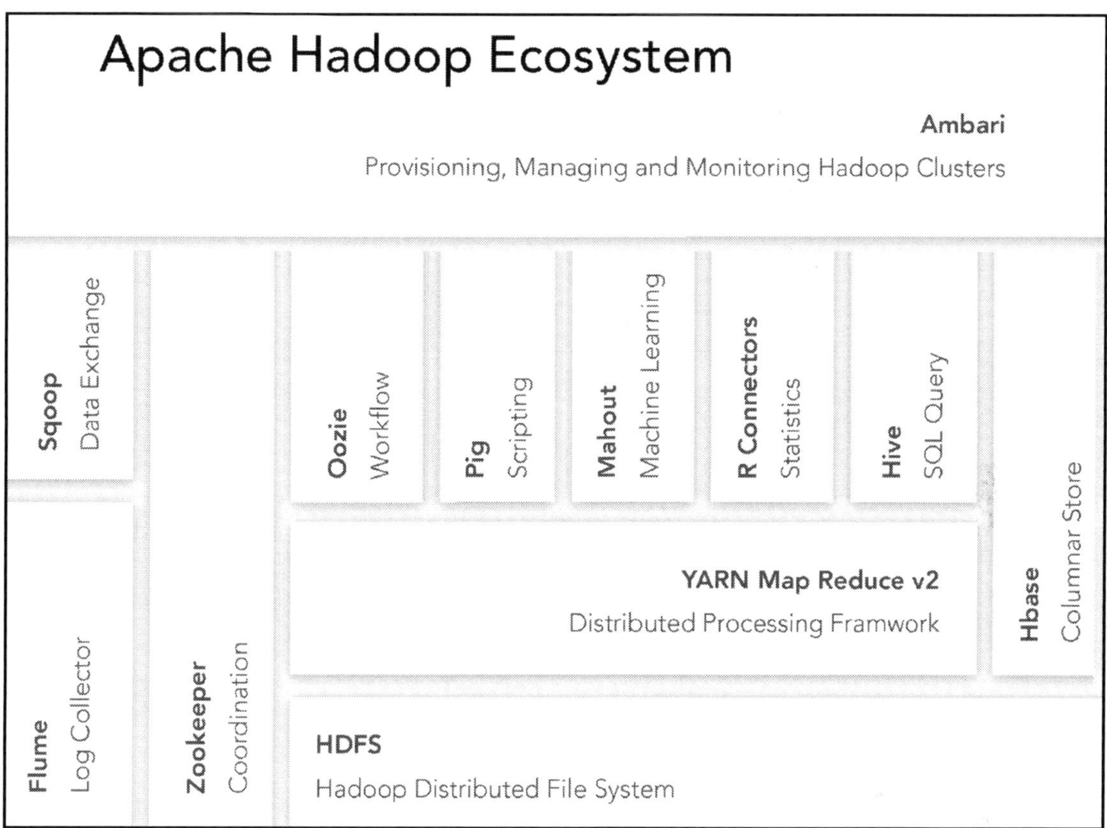

Summary

Data science is a very broad term that includes numerous tasks in regard to data management and processing. In this chapter, we have covered how these individual domains can be addressed with SQL Server and how SQL Server can be used as a data science platform in the enterprise. Although SQL Server is not primarily considered to be a data science tool, there are numerous data science tasks, where in SQL Server offers very mature services such as the importing and cleaning of data, integration with big-data systems, and rich visualizations, either with reporting services or with PowerBI Report Server.

In the next chapter, we'll go deeper into the SQL Server service overview and how all the services relate to individual data science domains and tasks and how you can fully utilize SQL Server in this new field.

2
SQL Server 2017 as a Data Science Platform

SQL Server is a relational database management system, but through the time it has evolved into much more. Right now, it's a very complex set of tools that work together to bring you superior experience while working with your data. Originally, SQL Server was not even written for the Windows operating system. The genesis of the SQL Server started with the OS/2 operating system in 1989 (it's a product that is nearly 30 years old). The first version of SQL Server available for Windows came in 1993. It was a version 4.21a.

Through various releases, SQL Server has introduced numerous features that can be utilized not only for regular database operations and production deployment of SQL Server, but also for the data science domain.

We will be covering the following topics in this chapter:

- SQL Server server evolution
- SQL Server Services and their use with data science

Technical requirements

SQL Server 2017 Evaluation Edition.
SQL Server Management Studio (version 17.7 was used at the time of writing the book as the latest edition).

SQL Server evolution

Let's get started with a brief overview of the features that are currently available with SQL and then skim over a brief history of SQL Server.

What's available in the pack?

The main core of the SQL Server is a DBMS (database management system), which is used to store the data in the databases. Through time and the various versions available, Microsoft has added other services as a part of the SQL Server that we can deploy and use for other data-related tasks. While these services are not necessary and required for database operations, they add value to your installation.

Without specifying any particular order for the services that expand the feature set of SQL Server beyond plain DBMS, the services include the following:

- SQL Server Integration Services
- SQL Server Reporting Services
- SQL Server Analysis Services
- Master Data Services
- Data Quality Services
- Polybase
- Machine Learning Services
- Power BI Report Server

History of SQL Server

SQL Server 1.0 was released as a 16-bit application for the OS/2 operating system, where Microsoft partnered with Sybase and entered the enterprise database world to compete with Oracle, IBM, and others. When the Windows NT 3.51 was released, there was a version 4.21 of SQL Server available. About that time, in 1993, Microsoft and Sybase parted ways and Microsoft pursued its own way with SQL Server for Windows NT. Sybase then renamed its product Adaptive Server Enterprise. In the following table you can see the version overview with release date for SQL Server.

Year of Release	SQL Version	SQL Release Name
1993	4.21	SQL Server 4.21a
1995	6.0	SQL Server 6.0
1996	6.5	SQL Server 6.5
1998	7.0	SQL Server 7.0
2000	8.0	SQL Server 2000
2005	9.0	SQL Server 2005
2008	10.0	SQL Server 2008
2010	10.50	SQL Server 2008 R2
2012	11.0	SQL Server 2012
2014	12.0	SQL Server 2014
2016	13.0	SQL Server 2016
2017	14.0	SQL Server 2017

Alongside of the major releases, there were other versions of SQL Server available. Some of the notables were:

- SQL Server 7.0 OLAP, released in 1999
- Azure SQL Database, released in 2010, initially built as version 10.25

SQL Server in the cloud

We will be covering the following aspects of SQL Server in the cloud:

- Azure SQL Database
- Azure SQL Data Warehouse

Azure SQL Database

When we're considering SQL Server deployment, we can use SQL Server either on-premises or in the cloud as a service. There are several different cloud offerings for SQL Server. We'll concentrate on the offerings in Microsoft Azure. Azure SQL Database is a managed cloud database, which went live around 2010. SQL Database is available as:

- A single instance
- A managed databases in elastic pool
- A managed instance

Azure SQL Database shares the code with the SQL Server Database engine, which allows for a code compatibility to some extent (some features or code are not available in the cloud service). While the on-premise SQL Server requires manual patching and upgrades to deliver new features, those are seamlessly delivered in the cloud first before they are available for the on-premise server at all, which is a great benefit, with those features being tested across millions of databases.

Performance of such a database is dependent on the pricing level, which you can choose when you're creating the Azure SQL Database or anytime afterwards. Scalability is one of the benefits of the Azure cloud, where you can change the performance tier as you go.

While selecting the performance tier, you can choose from three tiers:

- Basic
- Standard
- Premium

The basic tier allows you to create databases up to 5 GB of size and offers the performance of five DTUs. The standard tier allows you to create databases with a size up to 250 GB and has a variable DTU range available, ranging from 10 to 3,000. The premium tier, which is used for most IO-intensive operations, allows you to create databases with a size up to 1 TB and starts with 125 DTUs, which can be scaled up to 4,000. A DTU is a bundled measure of compute, storage, and IO resources that are available to the database. When your workload running in the database exceeds the the amount of any of the mentioned resources it get's automatically throttled.

You can find more about DTUs and how they link to a real database workload in this article about OLTP database Benchmark at `https://docs.microsoft.com/en-us/azure/sql-database/sql-database-benchmark-overview`

The differences between the tiers are not strictly only performance based, as you can see in the following table. There are also some disaster recovery and feature based-differences between the tiers, so the choice has to be made wisely. The DTUs scale linearly, so doubling the DTU will give you twice the performance on the SQL Server. As you may expect, the higher the DTU, the higher the cost of your Azure database deployment:

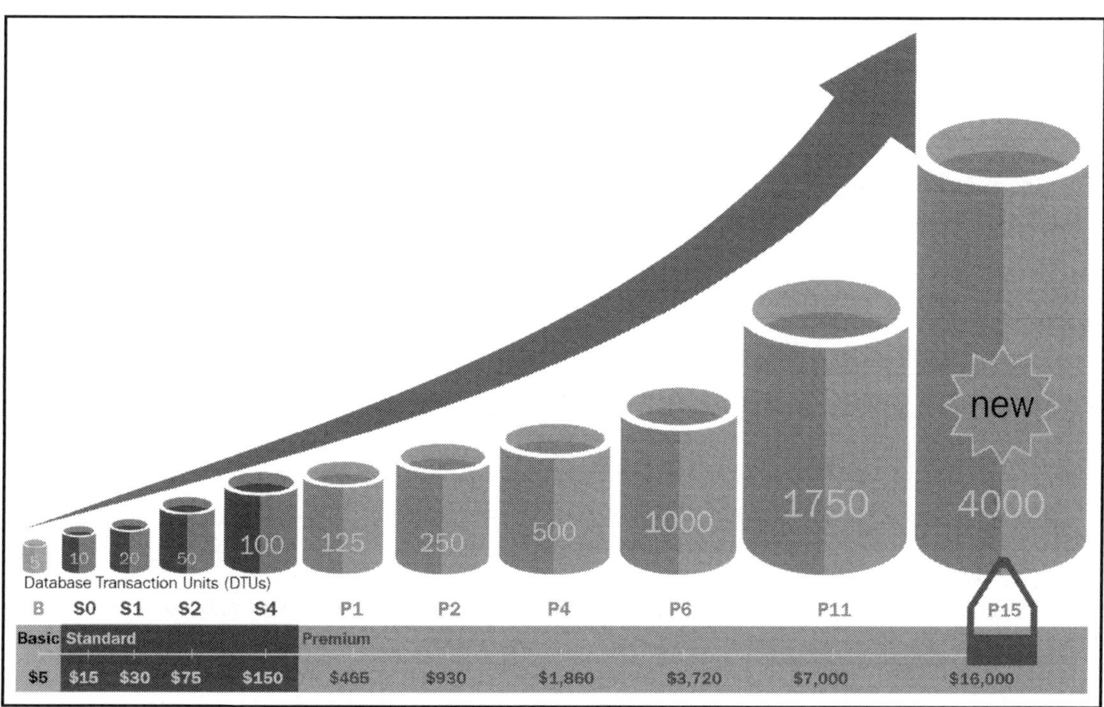

	Basic	Standard	Premium
Backup retention	7 days	35 days	35 days
CPU	Low	Low, medium, high	Medium, high
IO throughput	2.5 IOPS per DTU	2.5 IOPS per DTU	48 IOPS per DTU
IO latency	5 ms read, 10 ms write	5 ms read, 10 ms write	2 ms read / write
Column store indexing	No	S3 and higher	Supported
In-memory OLTP	No	No	Supported

When you're creating the Azure database, you can choose the performance tier and select the expected database size and expected performance demand:

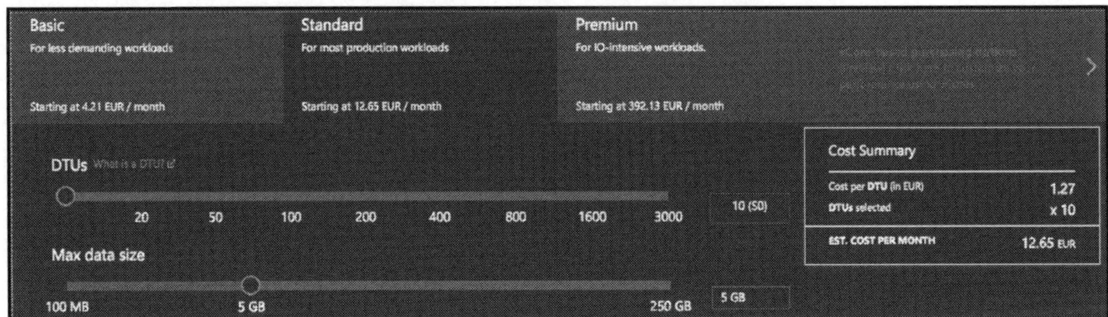

The very same dialog will be presented to you, when you would like to change the performance tier on an existing database, once it has been deployed. When the database has been successfully created, you can see the overview on the management portal, available at `https://portal.azure.com/`.

Another option, which is quite new to Azure SQL Database, is to use the vCore purchasing method for independent scaling of compute and storage resources. You can configure your Azure SQL Database to use up to 80 vCores and 4 TB of storage, allowing you to achieve superior IO performance with up to 200,000 IOPS.

As you can see from the following screenshot, Azure SQL Database does include numerous features, which are available also with on-premise SQL Server, and some of them were actually available first in the cloud offering, such as dynamic masking, allowing you to protect the data. Features such as advanced threat protection are not yet available with on-premise installation at all, and are still cloud-only offerings:

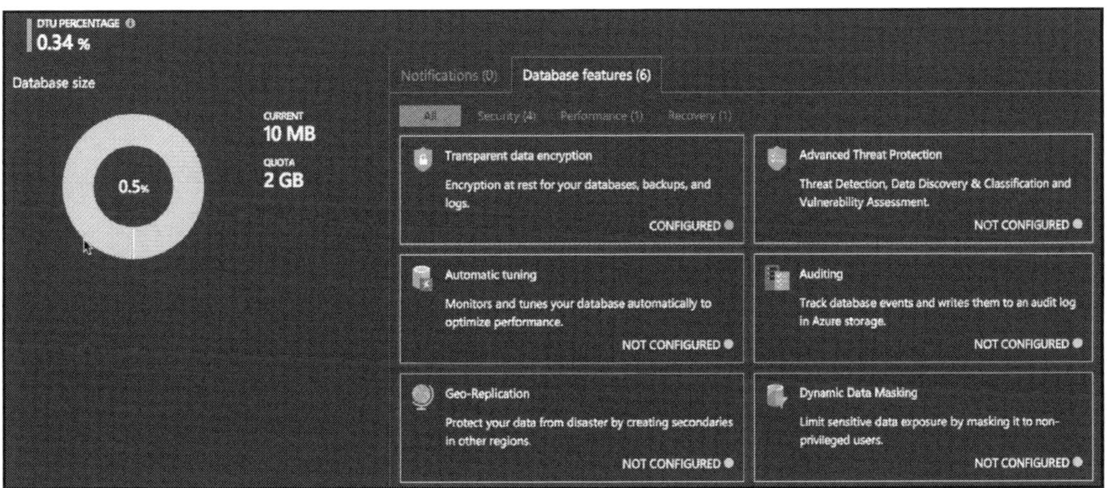

Once you have created your Azure SQL Database, you can log in to the SQL Server either with Management Studio, or SQL Operations Studio if you prefer the GUI interface, or any command-line tool that you would normally use with on-premise SQL Server. Bear in mind that, by default, the connection is controlled via a firewall, so you need to enter your IP address to the firewall list on the Azure portal, or add your IP address via the GUI tools, which may ask you to do so.

While having a cloud database available, you can use the data for analysis with other available services either in Microsoft Azure or other vendors who have online analytical services. Considering Microsoft Azure, another services used for data analysis in the Azure SQL Database could be the Power BI Service, Azure Analysis Services, and others.

While having a solitaire database in the cloud might be useful for some analysis, it will be much better to have the database synchronized with other data sources or on-premise databases. Azure allows you to configure Azure SQL Data Sync, which can keep your on-premise and cloud databases synchronized based on your selected schedule. While the data is primarily being stored on the on-premise server, you can perform data science tasks in the cloud with Azure services.

Configuring the synchronization requires an agent running on-premise, which can be downloaded at `https://www.microsoft.com/en-us/download/details.aspx?id=27693`

Azure SQL Data Warehouse

If the stored and analyzed data exceeds the options of the Azure SQL Database for both the storage and the compute capacity, we can consider Azure SQL Data Warehouse as another cloud-based solution for data analysis and data science with SQL Server. With on-premise and cloud, we have several options for the data store and data analysis. The advantage of Azure SQL Data Warehouse is the unlimited storage and massive scalability, which is available with two different configuration models. As you can see in the following diagram, there are several choices for running a database based on the scale needs and possibility to use cloud versus. on-premise solutions:

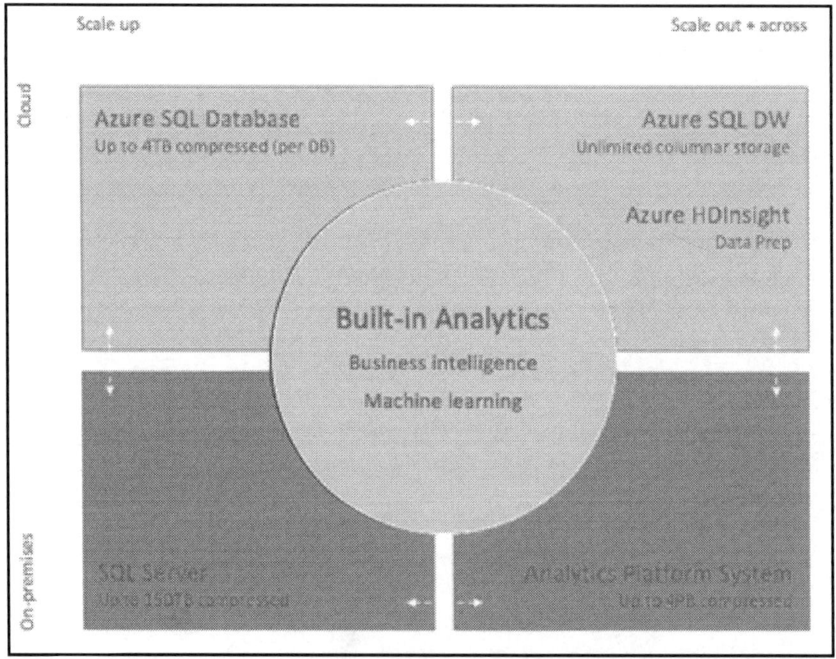

Choice for running a database

Azure SQL Data Warehouse uses a massive parallel processing with Azure storage, which offers great performance and scalability for your environment. As with Azure SQL Database, Azure SQL Data Warehouse uses an abstract performance unit named Data Warehouse Unit or DWU for short. DWU is based on three metrics:

- Search/aggregation operation, which is very IO intensive
- Read operation
- **Create table as select** (**CTAS**)

The architecture for the Azure Data Warehouse introduces two different layers of processing: control and compute nodes. These are used for work distribution and parallelism:

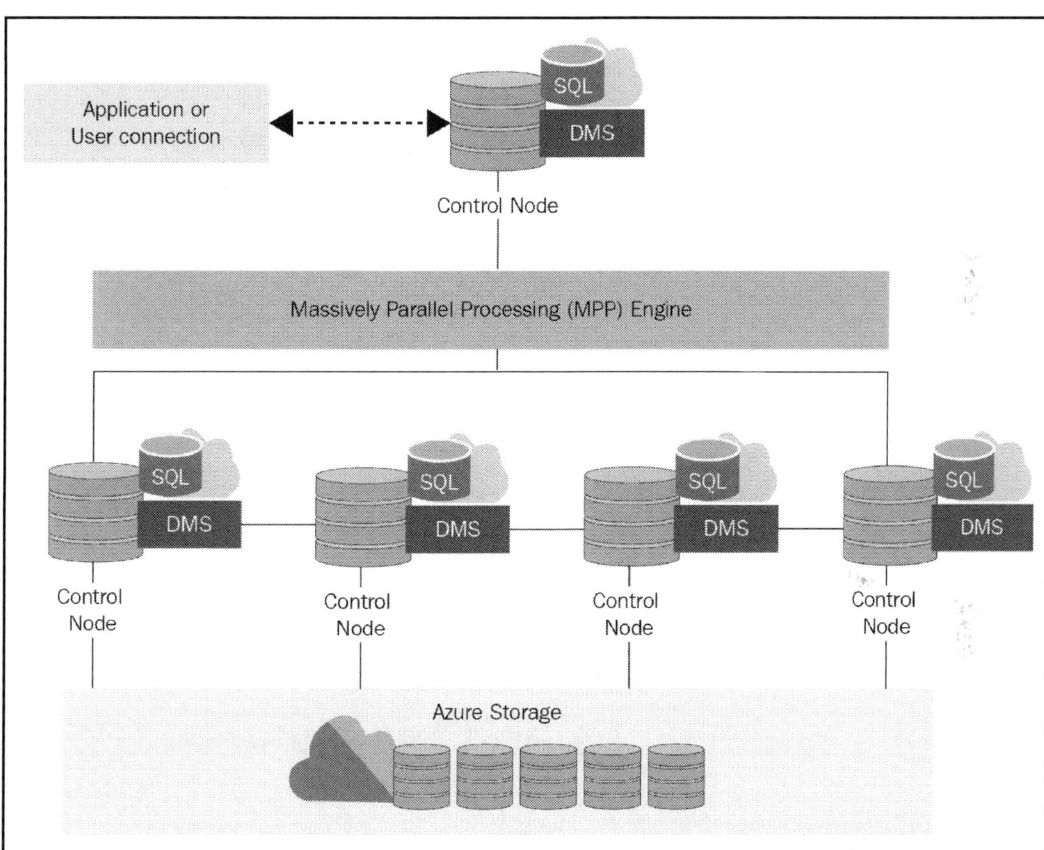

Applications connect to the control node, which is actually a SQL Server, and this control node splits and delivers the work requests to the compute nodes with massive parallelism.

For migration and data import, you can use several different approaches, one of them being Azure Data Warehouse Migration Utility, which can be used to transfer your on-premise databases or cloud databases to Azure Data Warehouse, including the check and report for any incompatibilities before moving forward:

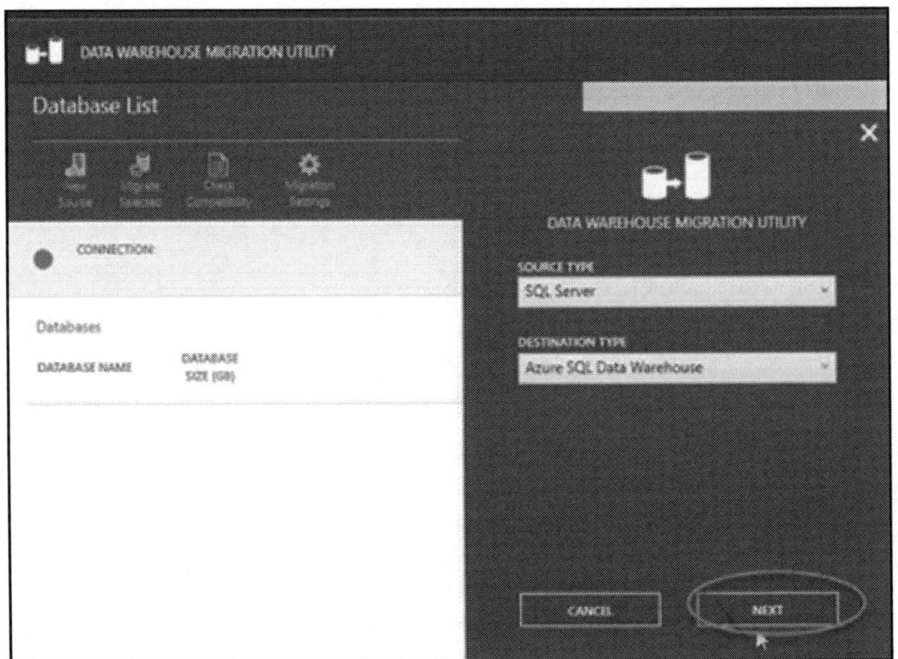

Azure Data Warehouse Migration Utility

Azure Data Warehouse Migration Utility can be downloaded for free from Microsoft's site at `https://www.microsoft.com/en-us/download/details.aspx?id=49100`

SQL Server Services and their use with data science

We will first start with SQL Server Integration Services. SQL Server analysis will be covered later. We will also be discussing Reporting Services, Power BI Report Server and machine learning services.

SQL Server Integration Services

SQL Server Integration Services (**SSIS**) was first introduced with SQL Server 2005, which was a major release, where Microsoft revised most of the Sybase code into Microsoft code. Numerous changes did happen in the background of the SQL Server and three main business intelligence services were introduced, SSIS being one of them. The concept of integration service used with SQL Server was, however, introduced with SQL Server 7.0, known as **Data Transformation Services** (or **DTS**). As a relic of this service, you can still find executables, such as `dtexec.exe`, which are used to start an integration services package from the command line on the server.

The main idea of SSIS is to allow the Extract Transform and Load process to be running on your SQL Server. ETL is crucial for the data science work on SQL Server, because on many occasions, we don't work only with the data that is stored and processed on the SQL Server, but we need to get the data into the SQL Server from other systems.

The extract part of the ETL solution is where we can connect to various source systems, such as other DBMS systems, flat files, and other possible data sources. SSIS provides default connectors, but can be also extended by installing proper ODBC drivers to your SQL Server to be able to connect to more data sources if needed.

Data may not be stored in the proper format on the source systems, so frequently the data has to be modified, cleaned, or changed to be stored on the SQL Server. This is where the transform part of the ETL comes into play. SSIS provides numerous tasks that can be used in a sequence to work with incoming data, and to change the data in a way that is optimized for follow-up work with the dataset on the SQL Server.

A major development tool for **Integration Services** is **SQL Server Data Tools** (often shortened as **SSDT**). There are different versions available, depending on your version of SQL Server and also on your environment, and whether you're already running your own version of Visual Studio or not. If you don't have Visual Studio up and running, SSDT will install a minimal shell for the SSDT, so that the tools will be working for you.

To install SSDT, you'll need to download the installation media, as since SQL Server 2014 onward, Data Tools is no longer included on the installation and is provided as a separate download.

You can find the installation files on the Microsoft site at `https://docs.microsoft.com/en-us/sql/ssdt/download-sql-server-data-tools-ssdt?view=sql-server-2017`, where you need to select proper installation media for your environment, depending on whether you already have or don't have Visual Studio running on your workstation.

While installing Data Tools, you can select what features should be included on your instance, depending on the business intelligence features you have on the SQL Server for which you're getting ready to develop:

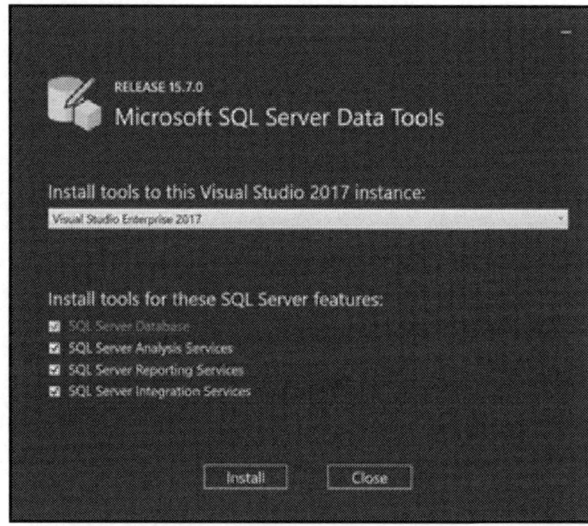

Installing the Data tools

Once the installation is over, you can create your **Integration Services** projects, which will include the control and data flow for the tasks inside of the packages:

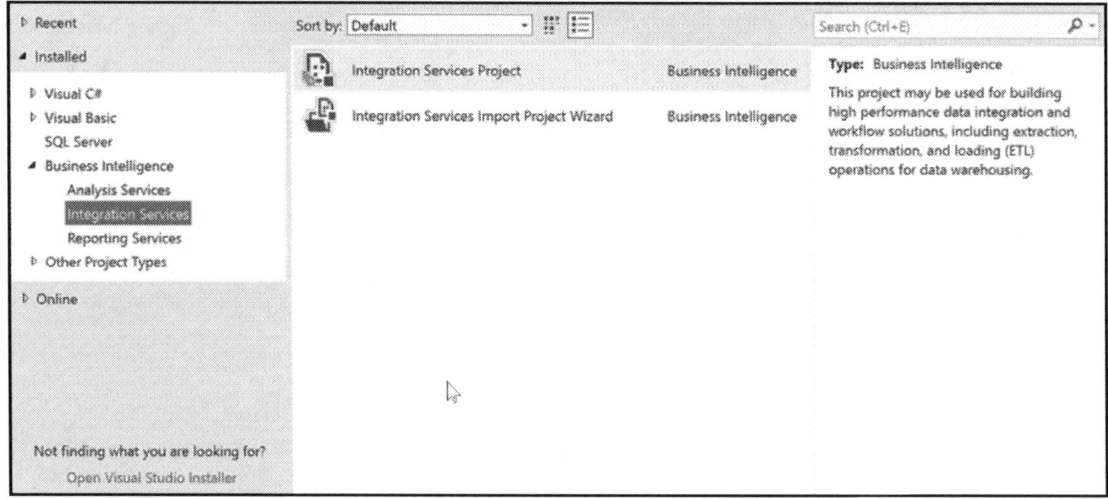

SQL Server Analysis Services

SQL Server Analysis Services, or **SSAS** for short, is an essential part of the business intelligence stack on the SQL Server used for **online analytical processing** (**OLAP**). Microsoft's first entrance to the OLAP world began in 1996 when Microsoft purchased a company called Panorama Software and implemented the solution into SQL Server 7.0, known as **SQL Server OLAP Services 7.0**, which was released 2 years after the purchase. Since SQL Server 2000, this component has been known as **SQL Server Analysis Services**. This was mainly due to the addition of data mining services into OLAP, which enhanced the feature set in a great way.

When we're working with Analysis Services these days, we can choose three types of installations. The oldest model was Multidimensional, then Microsoft added PowerPivot around the release of SQL Server 2008 R2, and the latest addition is the **Tabular Mode** introduced with SQL Server 2012:

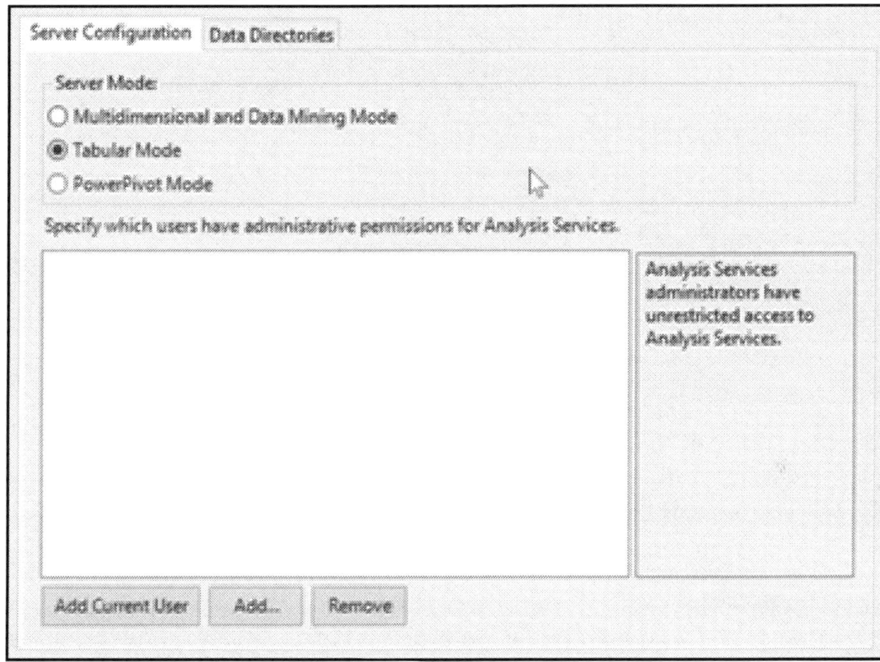

Tabular mode available in SQL Server Analysis Services

Tabular Mode

When you create a **Tabular Mode** database on the SSAS, you are using either in-memory or a **DirectQuery** mode, which accesses data from a relational database on a SQL Server. A great advantage of this mode is a superior compression and multi-threaded query processor for the analytical engine, which delivers fast access to the models from applications such as Excel or the Power BI Service, either running locally or as a cloud service running online.

Multidimensional mode

The Multidimensional mode uses the analytical multidimensional cubes for analyzing data across multiple dimensions. Once you create a new database in Analysis Services, you can see the different features displayed inside the database, in the same way as you can in Data Tools while developing the **Analysis Services** project:

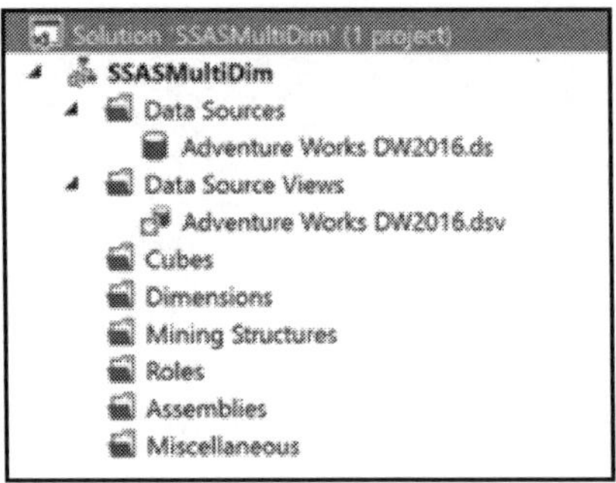

Features available in the database

The **Data Source** and **Data Source Views** will define what data you work with in the Analysis Services project. In most cases, this will be a database, or a data warehouse database, created by **Integration Services** to provide proper aggregations, denormalization of the data, and interconnection between various different information systems.

Once you have defined the **Data Source Views**, you can start building your multidimensional model by creating dimensions and cubes. Dimensions are objects used to get information about fact data in a cube or more cubes. Common attributes for date dimensions are year, quarter, week, month, and so on. For product dimensions, the common attributes might include name, category, size, price, and so on. When working with such attributes, you can usually build hierarchies based, so first you would see data aggregated by year, quarter, month, and then week if you drill down.

Once you have created all the objects which you need, you can deploy the project to your Analysis Services service and access the data via either Management Studio or other tools that can be used for data analysis:

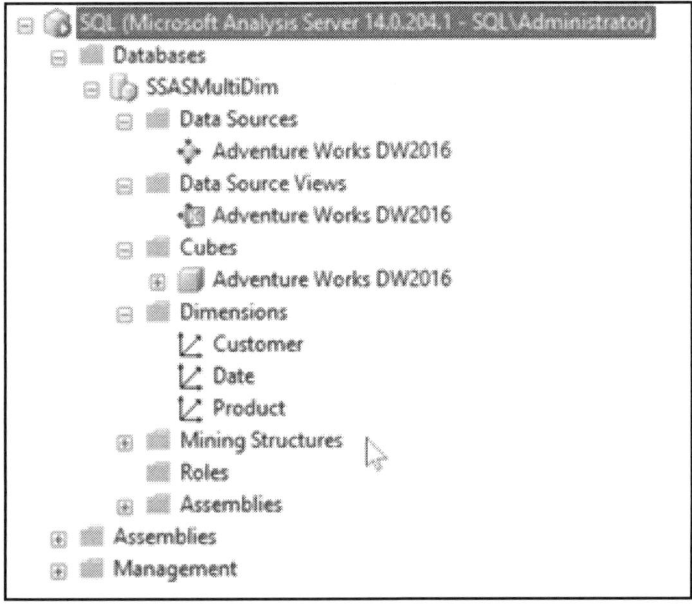

Features available in Analysis Services

Important features used for data science in Analysis Services are cubes, dimensions, and mining models. Once the cube and dimensions are created, you can create several mining models to get a larger insight into the data that is processed on SSAS. There are several mining models available, depending on the nature of the data and the task being accomplished. You can choose from the following:

- Association rules
- Clustering
- Decision trees
- Linear regression
- Logistic regression
- Naive Bayes
- Neural networks
- Sequence clustering
- Time series

Here is a screenshot of the available mining models:

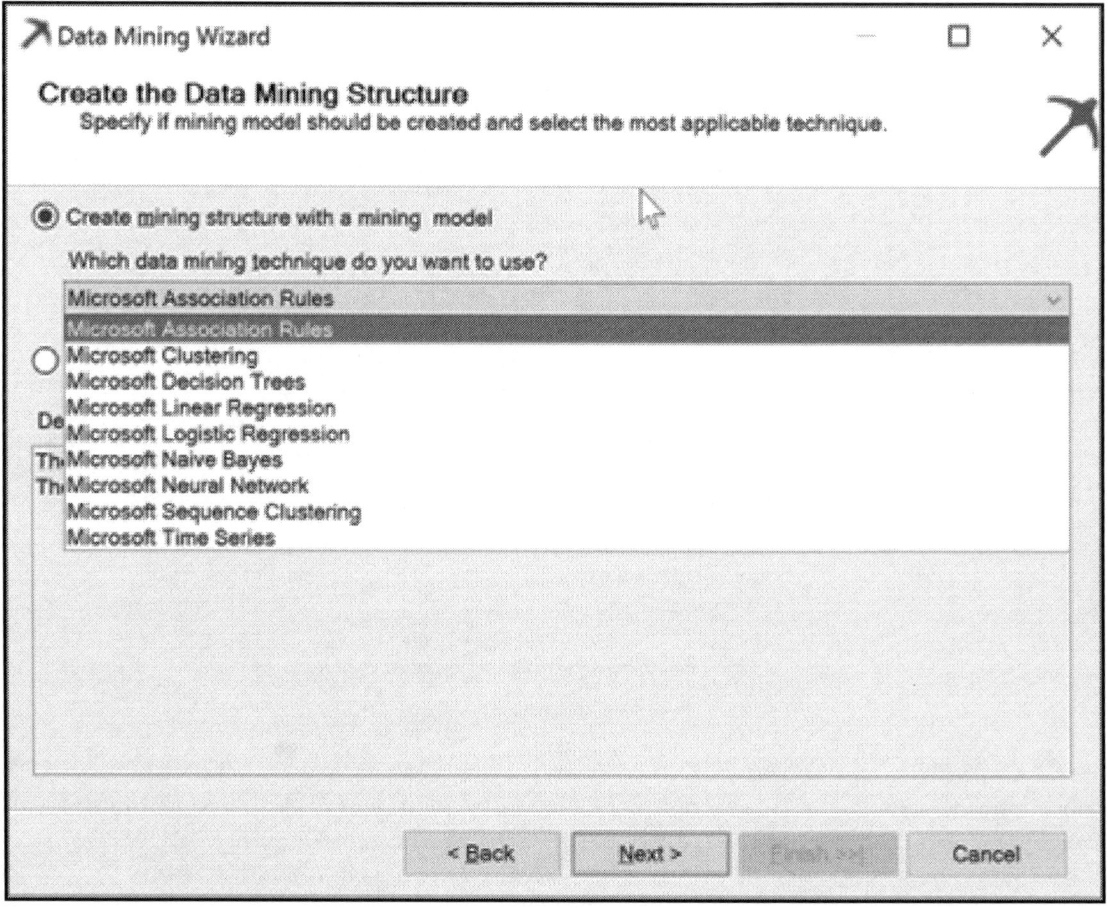

List of available mining models

These mining models get data from the mining structure and provide data analysis based on the specific algorithm. Until the structure has been processed and analyzed, the mining model will be empty. Once the model has been processed, you can see the results via Management Studio, or SQL Server Data Tools.

If we consider all the available algorithms, they can be split into the following categories:

- Regression algorithms predict numeric values, such as profit or loss
- Classification algorithms predict discrete variables
- Segmentation algorithms group data into clusters or find groups of items with similar properties
- Sequence analysis algorithms can be used for finding series, such as log events in the server log
- Association algorithms find correlation between attributes

PowerPivot Mode

The **PowerPivot Mode** is available with the Enterprise Edition of SQL Server. PowerPivot is still split into two different products: there's a PowerPivot add-on for Excel 2010 and 2013 and PowerPivot for the SharePoint SQL Server component. With Excel 2016, PowerPivot is natively a part of the application. PowerPivot allows Excel to work as a self-service business intelligence, where you can build analytical models with a local analytics engine and use specialized expression language to query data, create measures, and so on.

PowerPivot is also available as a mode for Analysis Services. This mode is used for the SharePoint data access mode on SharePoint 2016 and 2013 farms where you are running PowerPivot workbooks and you require the data access to the data sources.

Querying languages

There are several important languages that can be used with Analysis Services, including:

- DMX
- MDX
- DAX
- XMLA

Data Mining Expressions (**DMX**), as the name suggests, is a language used with Analysis Services to work with mining structures and mining models. You can use DMX to to create new models, train the models, and browse the data.

Multidimensional Expressions (**MDX**), is a querying language that you can use to work with Analysis Services for browsing and querying multidimensional data stored in the cubes. You can not only work with the cube, but also with dimensions, KPIs, and other features of the deployment.

MDX is based on XML for Analysis, which is a markup language used mostly for configuration of Analysis Services. You can use XMLA for backup, restore, or any movement of data.

Reporting Services

Reporting Services (or **SSRS** for short) is a visualization service from the business intelligence stack. From the three primary business intelligence services on the SQL Server, the SSRS is the newest one, being first released around 2004 as a part of the Service Pack for SQL Server 2000. Since then there have been several releases which kept the web user interface more or less the same and easy to navigate for the end users, until the release of SQL Server 2016, which was a major redesign of the user interface (and not only the UI) for Reporting Services to better align with cloud services and other modern tools being offered by Microsoft.

Development tools for Reporting Services

We have several tools available to build reports for Reporting Services. There are two major tools available:

- Report Builder
- SQL Server Data Tools

Report Builder is a native application available with Reporting Services, which you can have on the server where Reporting Services is running or locally on your developer workstation. With the latest version of SQL Server Reporting Services, the web portal offers you a download link that takes you to the Microsoft download site, where you can find the installation media for **Report Builder**:

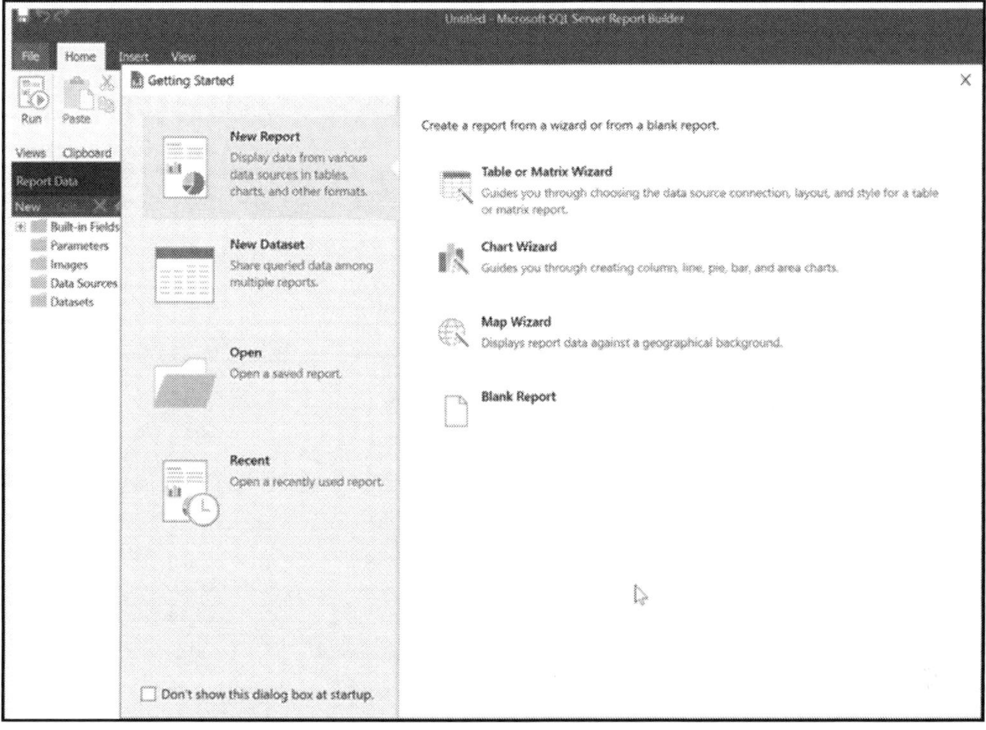

Getting started with installation of Report Builder

With SQL Server 2017, Reporting Services is no longer a part of the installation media and has to be downloaded separately. You'll see a link in the installation wizard, which will open up a website, where you can then download the installation file for Reporting Services:

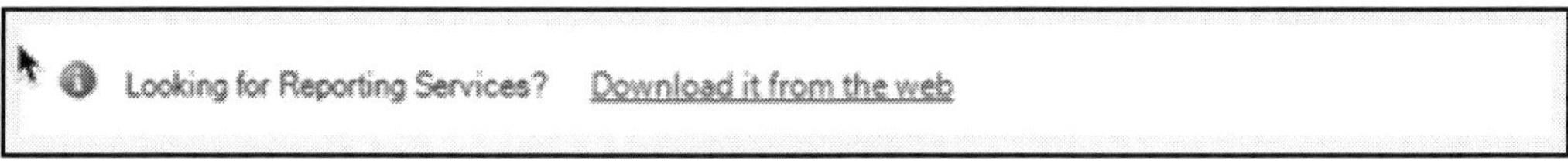

Link to download Report Services

You can find the installation media at `https://www.microsoft.com/en-us/download/details.aspx?id=55252`, where you can download a small installation file (around 100 MB). This file is used to deploy Reporting Services either to a standalone server or the same server running other SQL Server Services.

For the installation itself, you'll need a proper product key; otherwise, you'll be able to install one of the free versions only for evaluation. As the installation is separate from the SQL Server itself, the configuration of Reporting Services will require a running SQL Server, where Reporting Services will create a database:

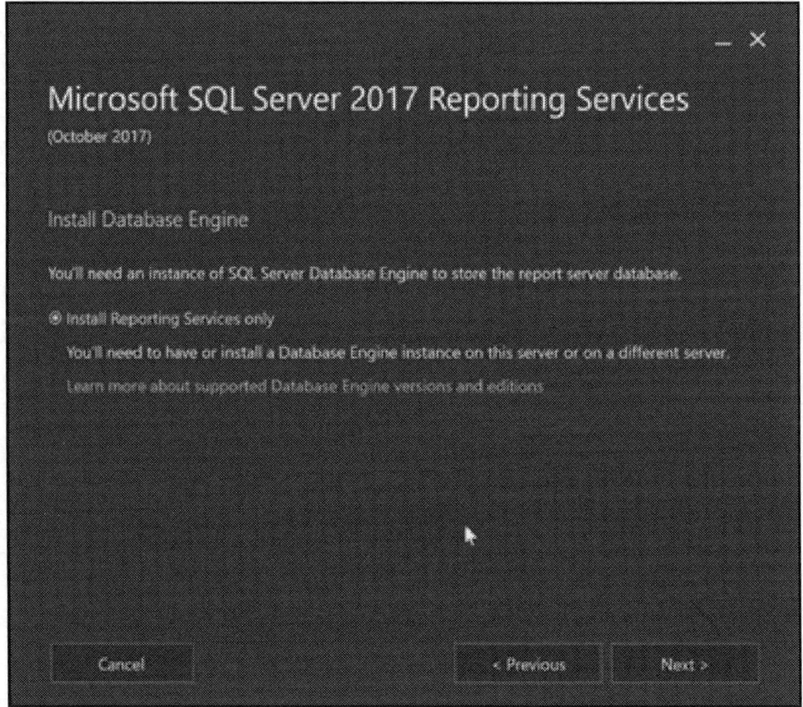

Installing Report Services

Power BI Report Server

As an addition to a cloud service `PowerBI.com`, Microsoft has released a server-based version of Power BI, called **Power BI Report Server**, which you can run locally on your system. From a licensing standpoint, this is not included with your regular SQL Server license, but actually it's a benefit from running either of the following:

- A SQL Server Enterprise with Software Assurance
- The `PowerBI.com` service with the Premium subscription type

However, when you download and install Power BI Report Server, you need to be careful about the configuration and available tools. Configuration is handled with a similar Configuration Manager to Reporting Services; you just need to connect to a proper instance running on your server:

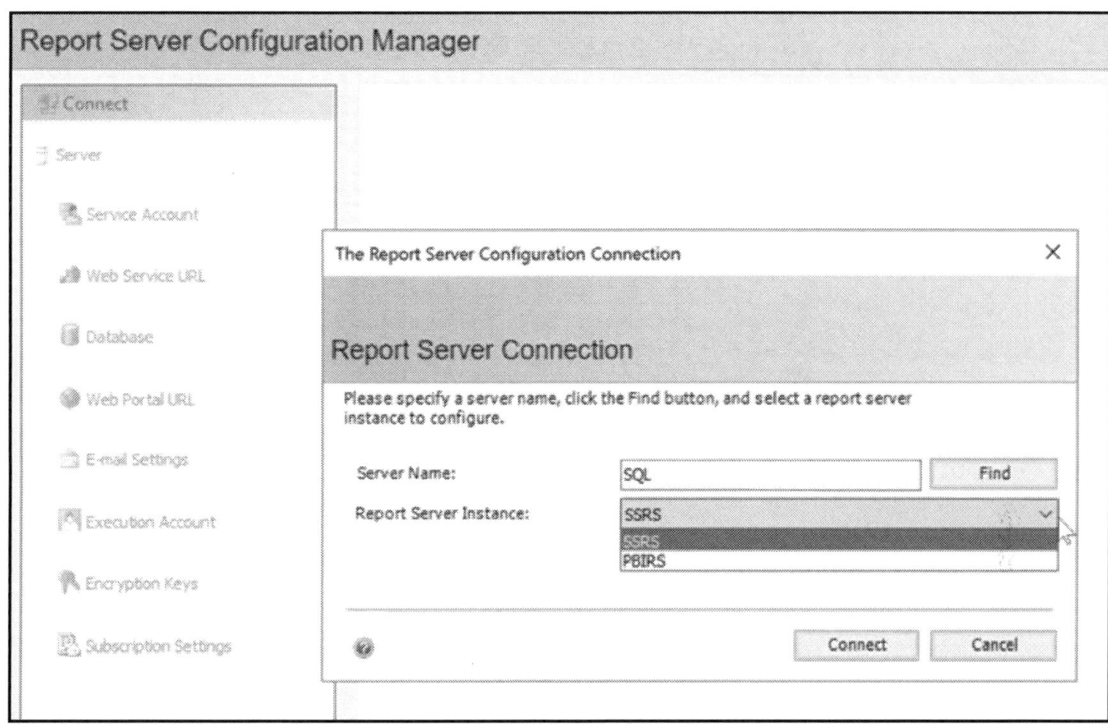

The development tool for Power BI Report Server is Power BI Desktop. With Power BI Desktop, there are two different flavors of the desktop client. One version of the client is used with the online service and the other version is used only for the local Report Server installation.

Power BI Report Server, such as Reporting Services, runs as a web application at your server. You can access Report Server with any browser of your choice at the URL, which is configured in the Configuration Manager. When you access the site, you'll see a blank site with no report by default:

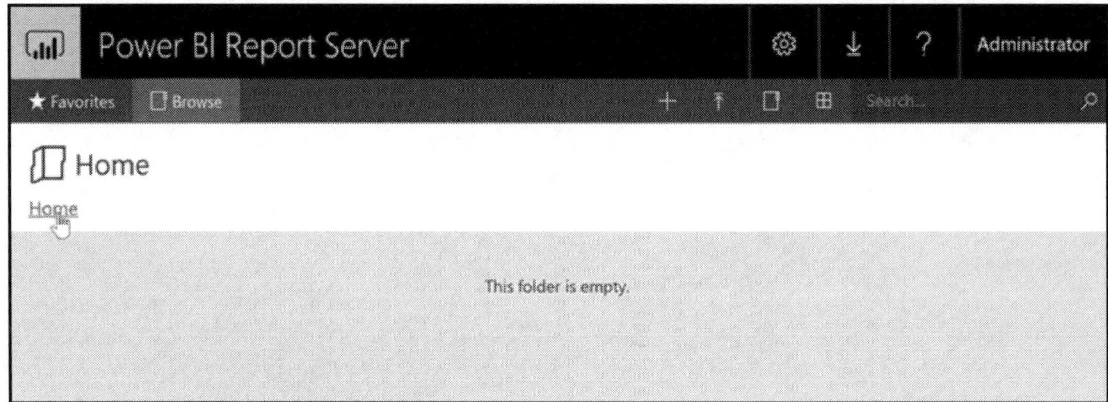

To create a report in Power BI Report Server, you can use a Power BI Desktop tool, which is available for download from the `www.PowerBI.com` website. If you navigate in the web interface of Report Server, there is a download link, which will take you to the **Download** page:

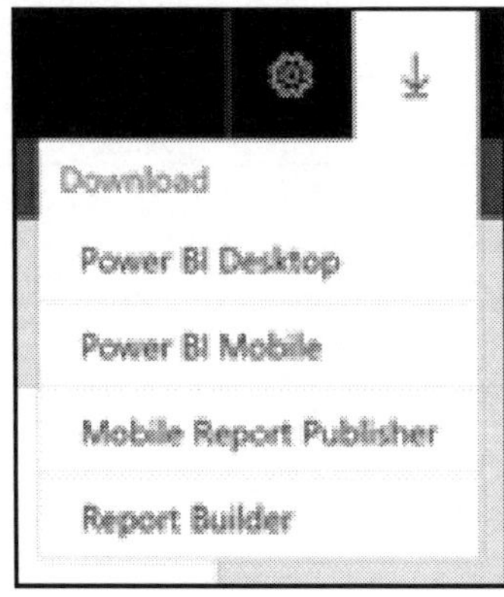

Downloading Power BI interface

Power BI Desktop is an application available for free download, which you can use to access your data, transform the data with Power Query (using M language in the background), and create reports with various visualizations:

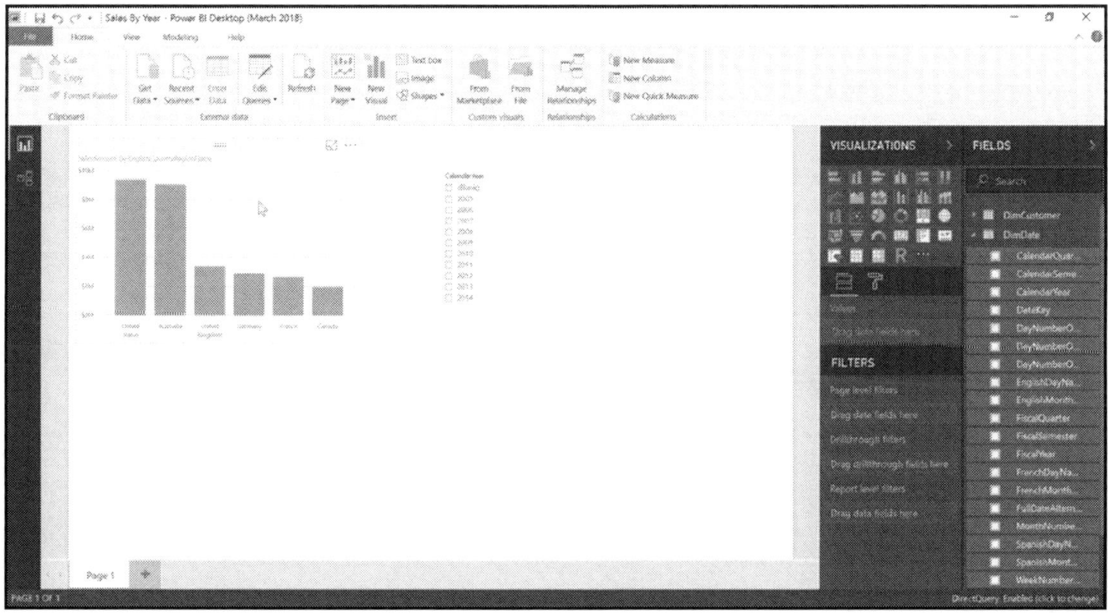

Power BI Desktop application

You can access a really wide range of data sources that can be linked together via their relationship. These relations are detected automatically based on the type of the data source, or you can configure these manually. There's a relationship designer available as the part of the application. On the left navigation bar, you can switch between the report design and relationship manager:

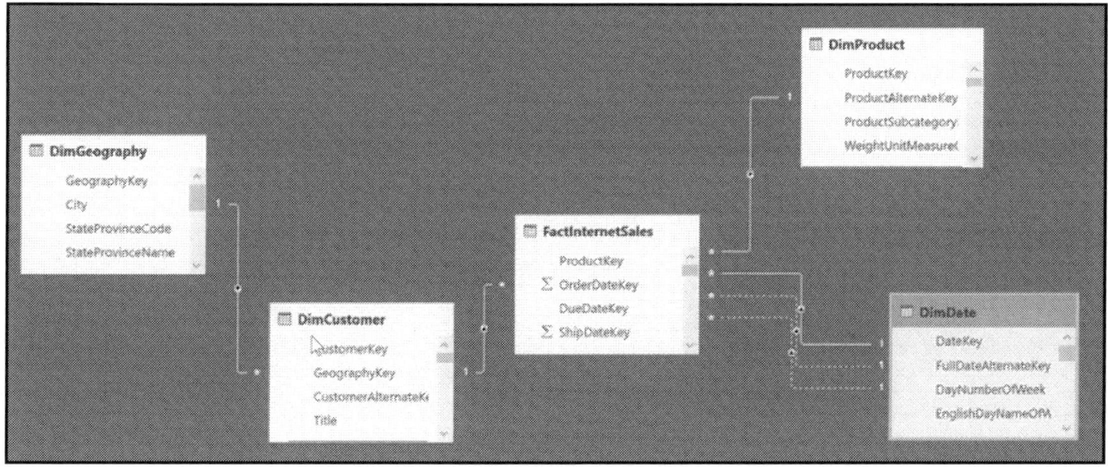

Machine Learning Services

SQL Server 2016 has introduced a very important service for data science with SQL Server and this was the integration of the R language and R scripts into the SQL Server. With the release of SQL Server 2016, this feature was still named R Services, as the R Server was also available as a standalone product or add-on to other programs or frameworks. With SQL Server 2017, Microsoft has added the support for the Python language too, so you can choose from both major languages used in data science.

Neither of the languages are installed by default, so you need to include any of them during the installation, where you can choose the proper environment as a part of **Machine Learning Services**, which is the new name used since the 2017 release:

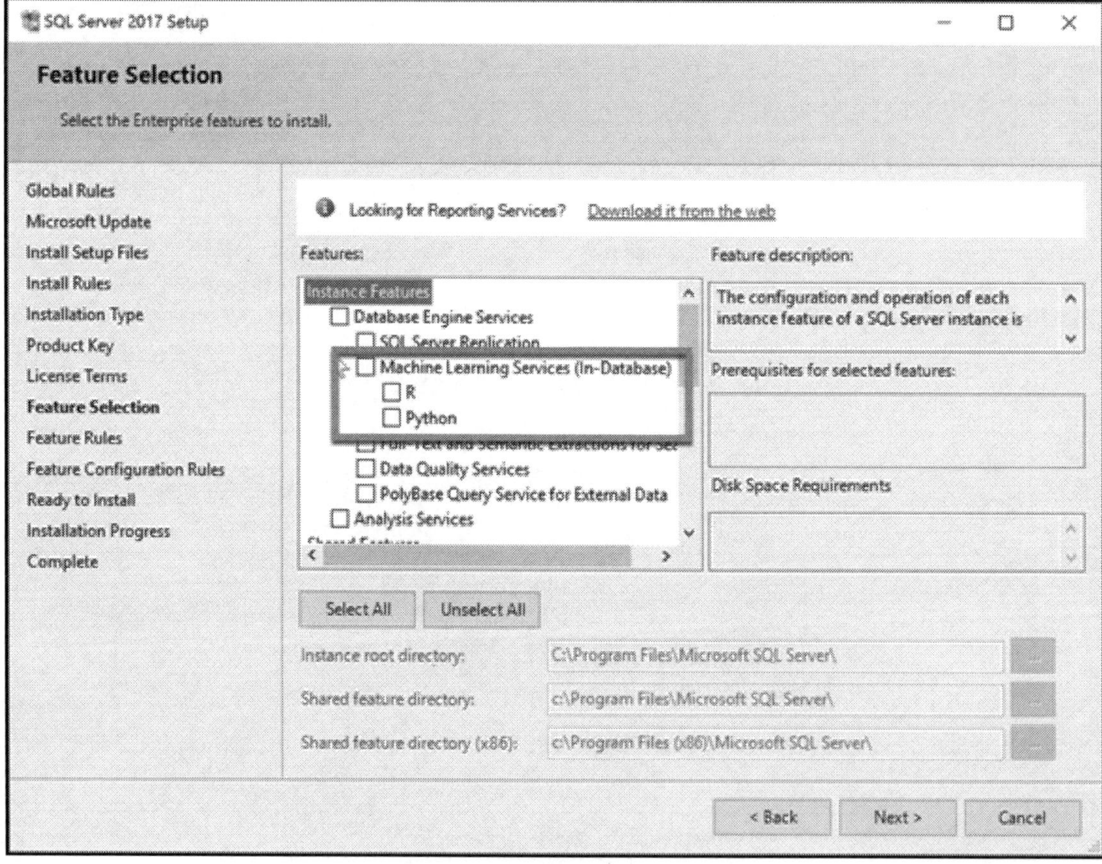

Installing languages R and Python

Machine Learning Services can be used to perform different work with the data stored or incoming to the database than we can regularly see on DBMS systems. As a common machine learning approach, with SQL Server, Machine Learning Services can be used to predict properties of new data by learning from a sample of data stored in the database. With Microsoft SQL Server 2016, the only way to run the R script inside of the database was to use a new stored procedure, `sp_execute_external_script`, which used, as one of the parameters, the R script that you would like to execute. With SQL Server 2017, you can also use a new function called **PREDICT**, which can be used for native scoring on the data, assuming that you have built and trained the models for machine learning before using that function.

Even if you install Machine Learning Services, running external scripts in R or Python is disabled by default. If you would like to enable the feature, you can use the following T-SQL code to make the configuration change on your instance:

```
sp_configure 'external scripts enabled',1
GO
RECONFIGURE
GO
```

When you use Python, you can use either Visual Studio, Visual Studio Code, Management Studio, or any other application used for Python development. However, you always need to consider which version of Python is being used with Machine Learning Services, as Python 2.x and 3.x differ a little. Microsoft is using Continuum Analytics Anaconda distribution of Python in Machine Learning Services; specifically, the version of Python 3.5.2 is being used at the time of writing this book.

To check which version of Python you are running, you can use following T-SQL code:

```
EXEC sp_execute_external_script @language = N'Python',
@script = N'import sys
print(sys.version)'
```

Important things to notice are the language parameter, which accepts two languages (either R or Python), marked with the `N` sign for unicode, and the script variable that contains the script itself, which is to be executed. If R is your language of choice, you can use a wide variety of tools available for development, if you keep in mind that version of R 3.3.3 is used with SQL Server. Using external tools for development can be more flexible and comfortable, compared with SQL Server Management Studio, but keep in mind that if you use any package that is not part of the SQL Server deployment, you'll need to do extra steps to install the package on the SQL Server, either for Python or for R.

As for Python, Microsoft has chosen the Anaconda distribution. The story with R language is different. R language was developed back in the 1980s, where it became a significant language used by data science and the academics community from the 1990s. When R become very popular and widely used, Microsoft joined the R consortium to help develop the R language and get better support for it. In 2015, Microsoft acquired a company named Revolution Analytics and rebranded many of Revolution Analytics's products. These included:

- Microsoft R Server
- Microsoft R Open
- Data Science VM (available in Azure)

As a part of the effort with R language, Microsoft has created its own package repository called **MRAN**, available at `https://mran.microsoft.com/download`

Microsoft Open R is based on the R language release, but includes numerous improvements for performance, platforms, and scalability, while keeping full compatibility with packages available on the CRAN repository, the official R package repository for the R project, which is available at `https://cran.r-project.org/`.

While Microsoft R Open is free and is available for download for numerous platforms, Microsoft has also rebranded Revolution R Enterprise into two different products. One stream went into the SQL Server as R Services or Machine Learning Services in 2017 release and the other is available as a standalone installation for different operating systems and frameworks, such as the following:

- Red Hat
- Suse
- Teradata
- Hadoop

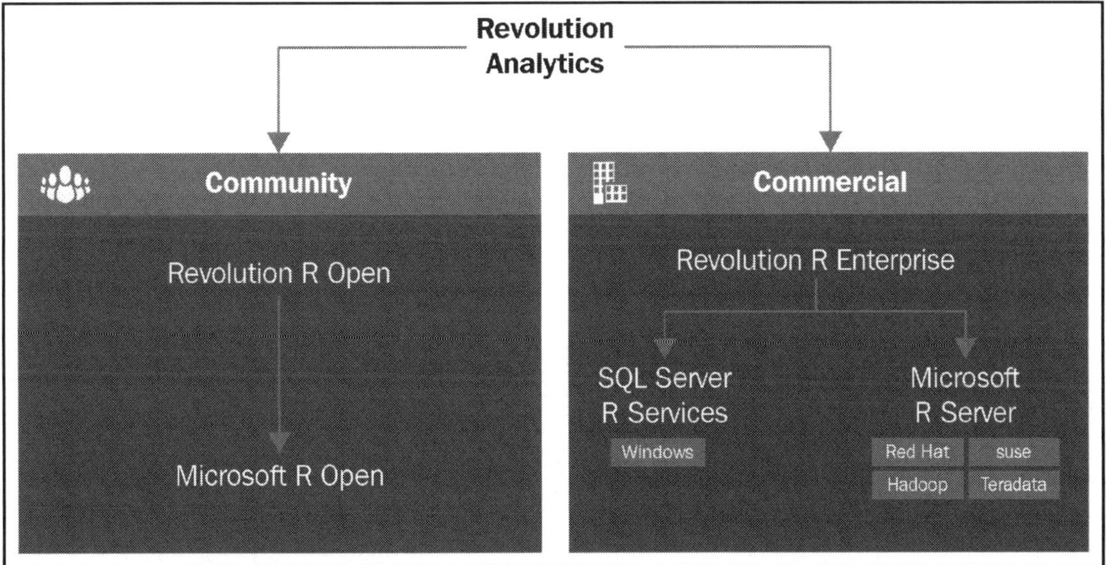

Summary

There are numerous services that make up the whole SQL Server environment, which you can run either on-premise or in the cloud. The core of the SQL Server is a database management system, which stores the data and provides us with the data operation engine, but the data also has to come in the SQL Server and it needs to be analyzed and represented. Therefore, we have companion services, such as Integration Services, which provide us the ETL solution for importing and cleaning the data before storing it on the SQL Server, Analysis Services, which is used for multidimensional modeling and data mining, and Reporting Services, which is a visualization part of the whole stack. No matter whether you choose the on-premise approach or the cloud services, there are always a number of offerings from the SQL Server that you can utilize for data science.

3
Data Sources for Analytics

In this chapter, we will review various sources of data that we can import and process in SQL Server for any analytical and data science techniques. This data can come from other database systems, flat files, application-specific files such as Excel, and web sources, among others. In regards to data structure, we can consider the data to be imported as structured, semi-structured, or unstructured. Based on the source and type of data, we have different tools in place that we can use to store the data in an SQL Server database.

We will cover the following topics in this chapter:

- Getting data from databases
- Importing flat files
- Working with XML data
- Working with JSON
- External data with PolyBase

Technical requirements

All the demonstrations will use SQL Server 2017, SQL Server Management Studio, and SQL Server Data Tools. With the current version of SQL Server 2017, both Management Studio and Data Tools are not provided directly upon installation, but have to be downloaded from the Microsoft site as separate installs. The source code for the chapter is located at `https://github.com/PacktPublishing/Hands-On-Data-Science-with-SQL-Server-2017`.

Getting data from databases

Before we can start analyzing the data in our SQL Server, we first need to acquire the data. One of the possible sources of the data can be another database. Regarding the import of data, the most easy-to-work-with source would be another SQL Server. We're using SQL Server 2017, so we should not face any issues with restoring or migrating the database into our environment. If we were to use an older version, we have to consider that you can't restore a backup from a newer version into an older version of SQL Server.

Importing data from SQL Server

When we're using SQL Server, we can use several different methods to transfer data into our SQL Server instance. Two very fast and straightforward options use backup, and the attach and detach option for SQL Server. If we're given a backup of a database, we can restore the backup to our SQL Server to get access to all tables and other objects that are stored in the database. Such a backup would usually be provided as one single file (the file extension really doesn't matter, but it's common to use `.bak`), which you can copy to your server and use either the SQL Server Management Studio or T-SQL code to restore the database in your environment:

```
USE [master]
GO

RESTORE DATABASE [DemoDB] FROM
DISK = 'c:\SQLData\DemoDB.bak'
```

Such simple code will grab the file located on our disk drive `C` in the folder `SQLData` and restore the backup as a `DemoDB` database. A `Data` file and `log` file will be placed to the default locations configured on your SQL Server installation, so it does not matter where and how the database was stored previously. There are numerous options that you can provide to the restore command, but for restoring the database from a backup, we don't need to go any deeper.

For full reference on the `restore` command, please visit `https://docs.microsoft.com/en-us/sql/t-sql/statements/restore-statements-transact-sql?view=sql-server-2017`, where you can find all the various options for restoring a database from a backup file.

If you would like to utilize Management Studio, you need to right-click **Databases** and select the **restore database** menu item. Navigate to the location on the disk where you have the backup file, select the backup file, and click **OK**. You'll then see the content of the backup file, and you can select the name for your new database where the data will be restored:

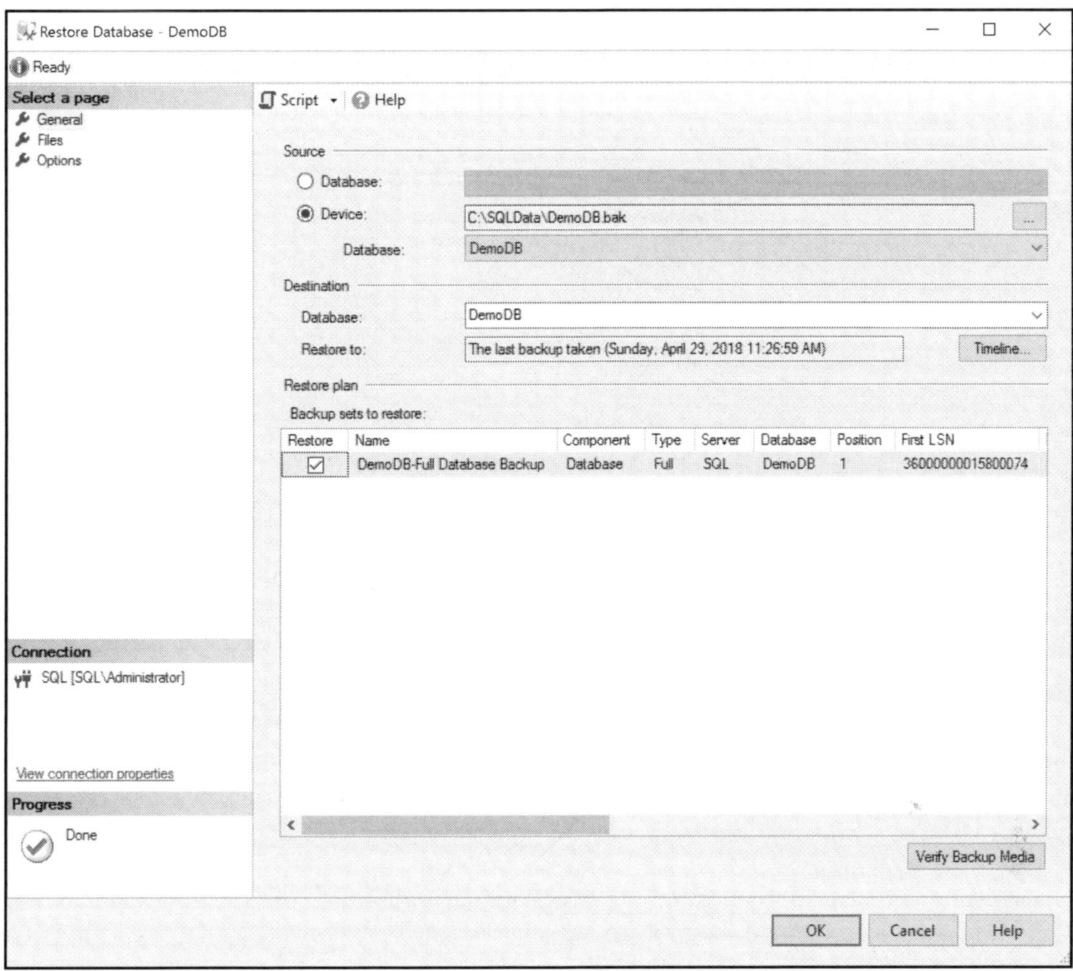

Depending on the size of the original database, the restore can take a few seconds, or up to a few hours, based on the size of the backup and the performance of your SQL Server environment.

Another option is to use **Data Tier Application** (**DAC** in SQL Server), which uses a special file type, `.bacpac`. This type of application can be created on SQL Server or deployed to SQL Server. It's a very interesting format for us, since this type of file is used frequently with Microsoft Azure SQL Database, which uses `.bacpac` files to import and export data. So if our primary source was a database running in the Azure public cloud, then the Data Tier application type of deployment would be used:

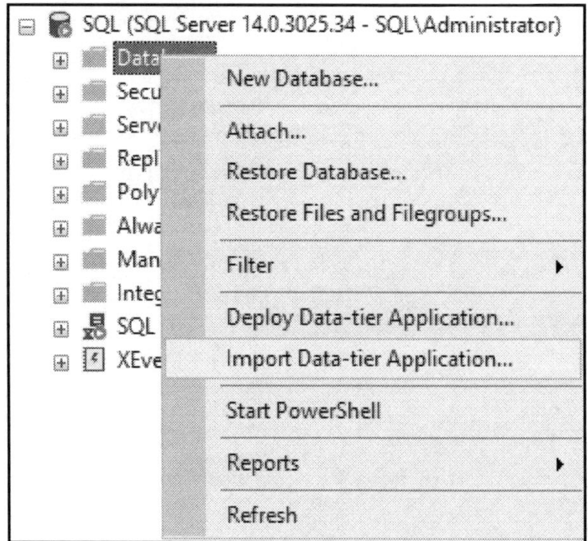

The Data Tier application is a logical unit that defines all of the SQL Server objects, such as tables and views, combined with instance level objects, such as logins, which are associated with the database. This offers great benefits for easy deployment, since the database users will be correctly mapped to SQL Server logins, which are part of the Data Tier application deployment. This approach allows developers and administrators to quickly exchange the `.bacpac` file for deployment, testing, and so on, without any need to exchange scripts or backup files that don't cover the entire configuration:

Once the import is finished, you can review all the steps that were part of the deployment plan:

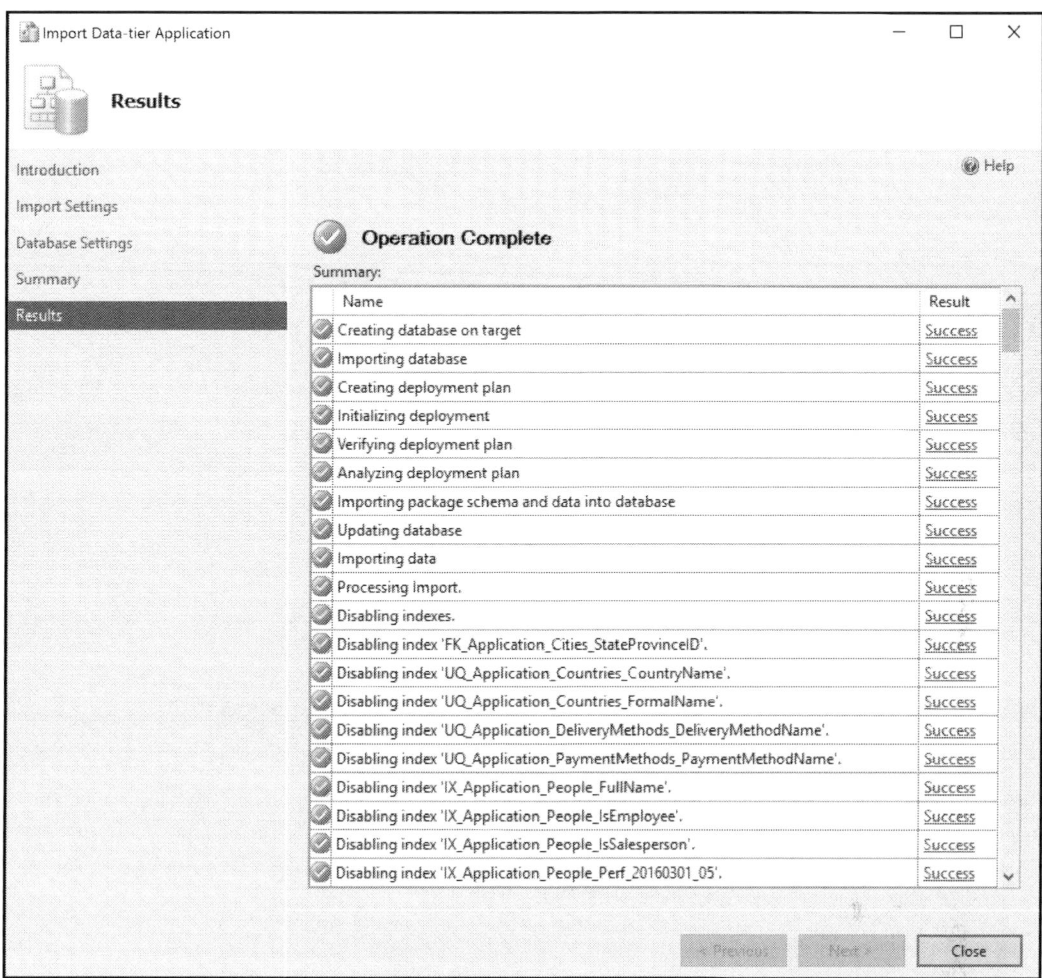

If we don't have access to files such as a backup or a DAC file, and we have access to the original SQL Server, we can use the Data Migration Assistant. This tool would be primarily used as a migration tool between various versions of SQL Server, and to assess the current state of SQL Server for migration to a newer version or to Microsoft Azure SQL Database. One of the useful features of this tool is the ability to migrate data directly from older versions of SQL Server, such as the 2005 and 2008 versions, where backups from 2005 in particular may cause problems when restoring new versions of SQL Server 2016 and 2017.

Importing data from other database systems

There are countless database management systems that are used in enterprise environments. SQL Server has built-in tools that can connect to some of those for data import. The availability of such a data source is usually dependent on the drivers, which have to be installed on the SQL Server. Microsoft provides a tool named the SQL Server Migration Assistant, which can help with such migration and data acquisition from several different types of databases. Those types include the following:

- MySQL
- DB2
- Microsoft Access
- SAP
- Oracle

Depending on the database type, the SQL Server Migration assistant may require more tools or binaries to be installed on your system. If we consider a simple scenario of importing a Microsoft Access database, we would need to install Microsoft Data Access Components, or Microsoft Access 2016 runtime to be able to connect to an Access database file:

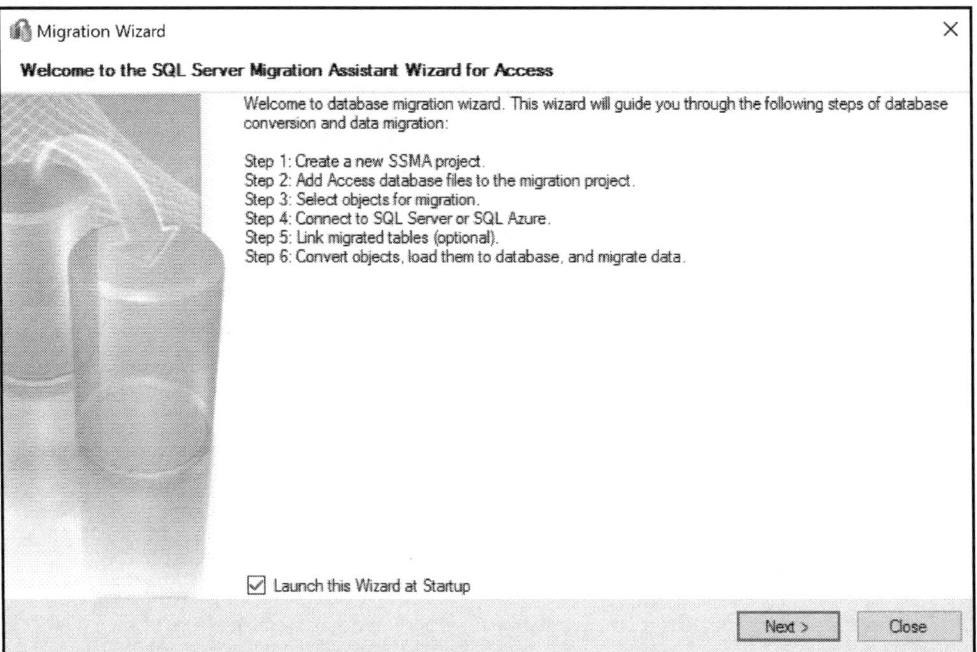

While importing data from Microsoft Access, you need to take care of several important transformations regarding the data types, indexes, keys, and other aspects of the data stored in the Microsoft Access format. This tool is very helpful for making many of the transformations on your behalf as demonstrated in the following screenshot:

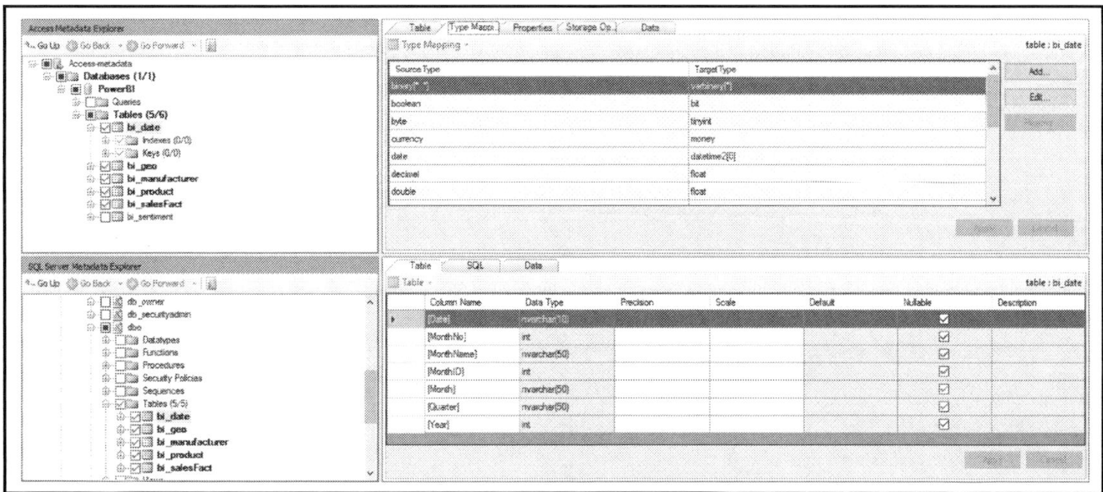

Overview of transformation window

Once you have reviewed the structure, you can synchronize the database into the selected tables:

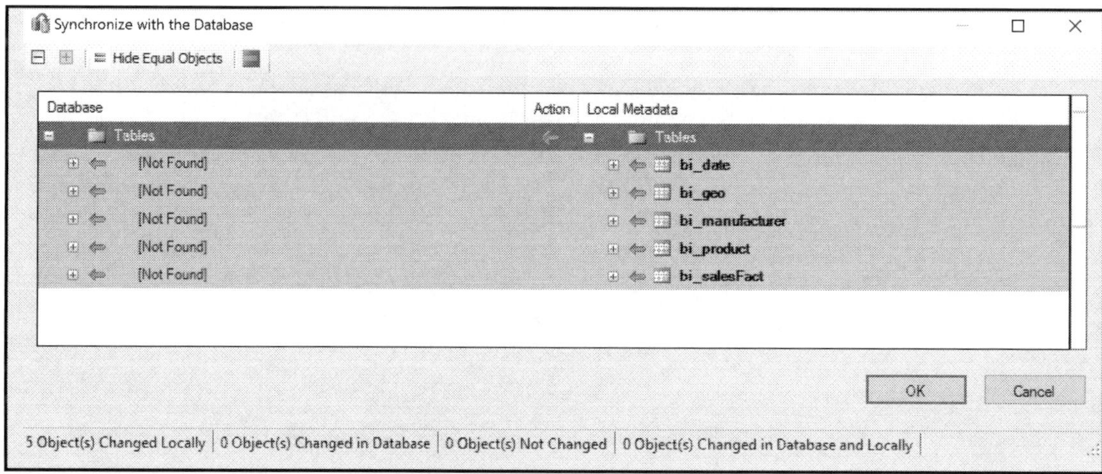

Importing data from other DMBS systems may be much more complex, and this tool is only a basic exploratory tool to see how the data is actually structured and how the migration project may appear.

Importing flat files

Many information systems can provide us with flat files as a sort of exported data. We can import those flat files directly into SQL Server via Management Studio, where you can select the **Import Flat File** option from the database tasks. Then, you can choose to import the `.csv` or `.txt` files, which will be imported into a new table. While you're choosing the table name, you can also select, via the drop-down list, a schema for the table.

Flat files are also generated by many systems as log files, which can then be further analyzed in SQL Server as one of the possible tools. In such cases, the import would be more complex, since you would not aim for one file, but more for a folder structure containing hundreds or thousands of files, where the required data is stored.

Importing the content of a single flat file can be achieved via SQL Server Management Studio, which has a specific task to work with flat files:

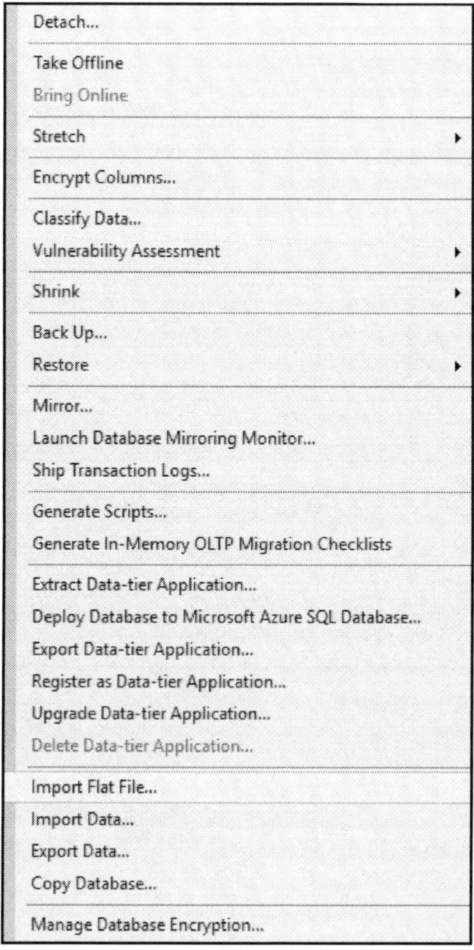

Once you open the dialog, you need to find the flat file on the disk and choose how the new table should be named in your database. This table will be created based on the structure of your flat file. In the next dialog window, you can configure the required data types for all columns from the imported file.

This wizard will automatically determine the field separator and will analyze the data for the suggested data type for you:

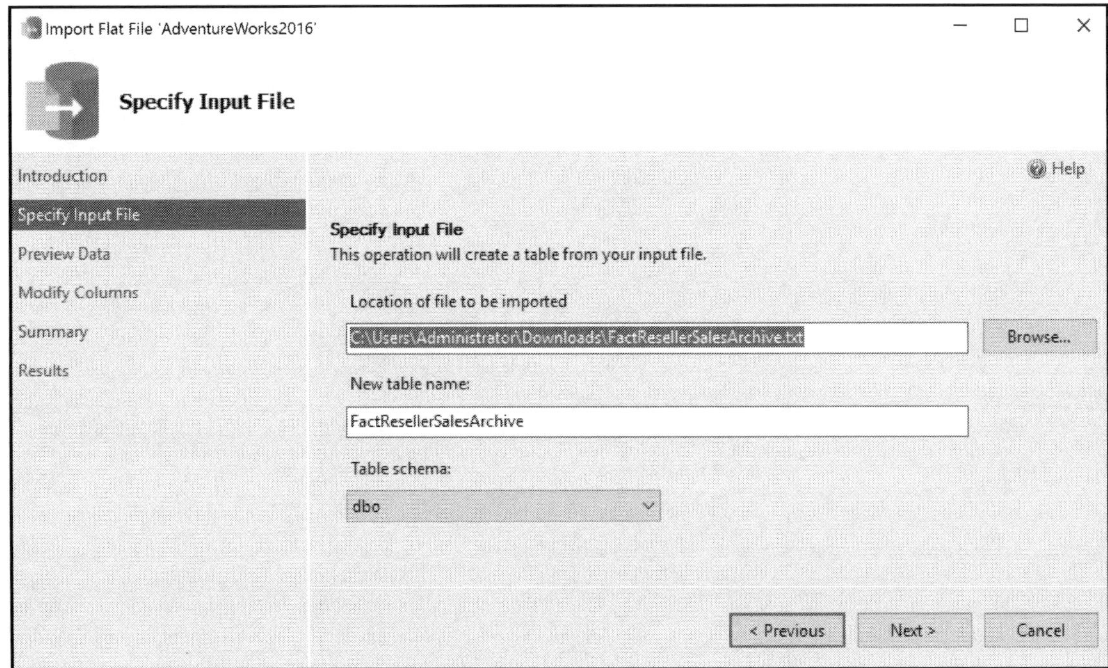

Working with XML data

SQL Server is more than capable of working with XML data. Since the 2005 version, it's actually one of the supported data types, which allows you to store up to 2 GB of XML content per record. When you type a query for SQL Server, the query returns data as a rowset—set of rows and columns. But you can retrieve all the data as an XML document too. You can add a special clause to the query, **FOR XML**, which will render the result as an XML document instead of the result set.

When you would like to create a `XML` document as a result of your query, you can use four different modes to render the `XML` file. These are as follows:

- Auto
- Path
- Explicit
- Raw

The raw mode will just generate an element representing a row from the result set. In this mode, each line will be used to build an element named <row>, with attributes representing the columns from the result.

Let's consider a query to find orders for a customer. This query will link two tables with a JOIN operator, and for each customer, it will list all the orders placed by that customer. If a customer has not placed an order, the customer will be skipped in the result set:

```
SELECT c.[CustomerID],soh.SalesOrderID FROM Sales.Customer c
JOIN [Sales].[SalesOrderHeader] soh ON c.customerID = soh.CustomerID
```

When we would like to format the output in the form of an XML file, we can add the FOR XML directive to the end of the query:

```
SELECT c.[CustomerID],soh.SalesOrderID FROM Sales.Customer c
JOIN [Sales].[SalesOrderHeader] soh ON c.customerID = soh.CustomerID
FOR XML RAW
```

Such a result will generate an XML document with the following fragment:

```
<row CustomerID="11000" SalesOrderID="43793" />
<row CustomerID="11000" SalesOrderID="51522" />
<row CustomerID="11000" SalesOrderID="57418" />
<row CustomerID="11001" SalesOrderID="43767" />
<row CustomerID="11001" SalesOrderID="51493" />
<row CustomerID="11001" SalesOrderID="72773" />
<row CustomerID="11002" SalesOrderID="43736" />
```

For one customer, we have several different XML elements, where each element represents a single order. The AUTO mode generates nesting for such XML elements. You have little to no control over the nesting in this mode, since that is done via heuristics and controlled by the SQL Server engine itself. However, if we were to use the query to grab the same data using AUTO mode, then the results would look more interesting:

```
SELECT c.[CustomerID],soh.SalesOrderID FROM Sales.Customer c
JOIN [Sales].[SalesOrderHeader] soh ON c.customerID = soh.CustomerID
FOR XML AUTO -- AUTO mode instead of the RAW mode
```

The results are now nested in a way that one customer element encloses more order elements if there are more orders for one customer:

```
<c CustomerID="11000">
  <soh SalesOrderID="43793" />
  <soh SalesOrderID="51522" />
  <soh SalesOrderID="57418" />
</c>
<c CustomerID="11001">
  <soh SalesOrderID="43767" />
  <soh SalesOrderID="51493" />
  <soh SalesOrderID="72773" />
</c>
```

This is particularly useful for many queries that include `JOIN` operations to link more tables together via their keys. The `XML` document on the output is not formatted well, so we can add a few more options to the query definition, such as naming the elements and adding a `root` document:

```
SELECT c.[CustomerID],soh.SalesOrderID FROM Sales.Customer c
JOIN [Sales].[SalesOrderHeader] soh ON c.customerID = soh.CustomerID
FOR XML RAW('customer'), ROOT('CustomerList')
```

This row tagging is, however, not allowed in `AUTO mode` and you would need to use a more advanced mode, `FOR PATH`.

Once we know how the XML output can look on the SQL Server, we can think of importing the data as XML into the SQL Server. There are two approaches we can take here. First option is to open the `XML` document and parse the information into columnar storage, to extract each value from the attribute, and store the values in proper columns. The second option would be taking the whole `XML` document and storing it in the column of an XML data type.

We will prepare a new table for importing XML documents via the following set of commands:

```
CREATE DATABASE ImportedData
GO
USE ImportedData
GO

CREATE TABLE XMLwithOpenXML
(
    Id INT IDENTITY PRIMARY KEY,
    XMLData XML,
    LoadedDateTime DATETIME
)
```

Once the storage for the documents is created, we can use a function named `OpenRowset`, which can open the XML document and store the document in the table:

```
INSERT INTO XMLwithOpenXML(XMLData, LoadedDateTime)
SELECT CONVERT(XML, BulkColumn) AS BulkColumn, GETDATE()
FROM OPENROWSET(BULK 'C:\SQLData\Import.xml', SINGLE_BLOB) AS importedXML;
```

XML documents stored in SQL Server have a limited size of 2 GB, and if you consider storing numerous XML documents in a table and then performing any query on such a large amount of data, this can get very slow in terms of processing time. SQL Server can help you speed up and optimize operations with the XML data type by implementing four different types of XML indexes that can be used. You can have a primary XML index and three different kinds of a secondary XML index for your XML data type.

The primary XML index provides a basic object tree representing the XML document structure. This is used to speed up access to the elements and attributes of the XML document without the need to read the whole XML document stored in the table. The secondary indexes are used for specific types of queries based on the XML type functions used to access the data; those indexes are for **PATH**, **PROPERTY**, and **VALUE**, and used with XQuery. Secondary indexes can only be created if the primary index is in place.

An XML index can be created either with T-SQL code or with SQL **Server Management Studio** (**SSMS**). If you use SSMS, then you'll need to navigate to your table where you want to create the index and right-click on the **Indexes** item:

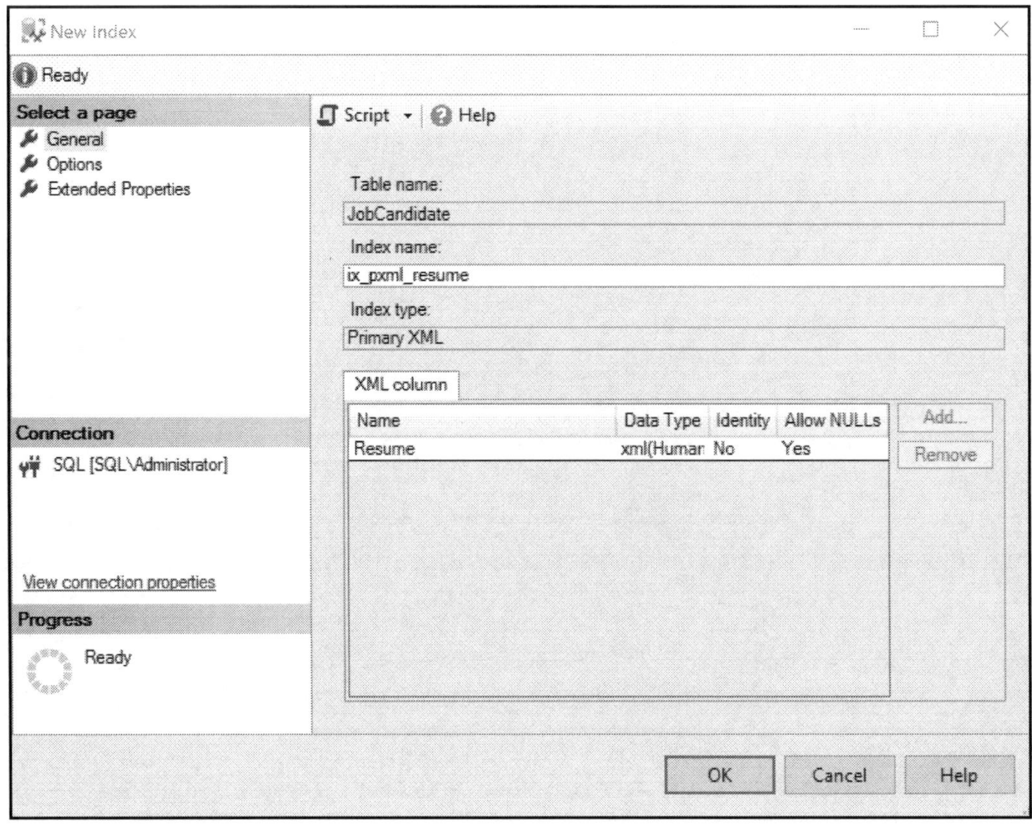

Once the primary index is available, you can create a secondary XML index for the proper XQuery functions, which you'll run on your XML data:

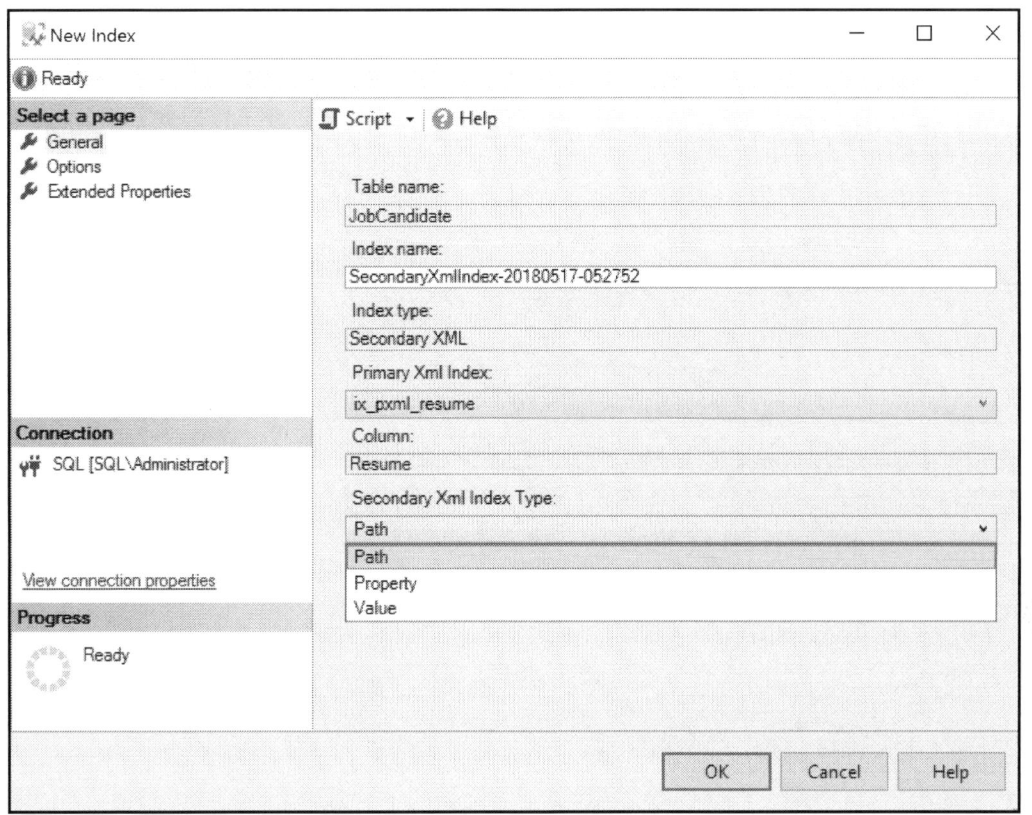

Working with JSON

JSON, or **JavaScript Object Notation**, is a popular format these days for exchanging data among various endpoints. The most common usage of JSON is on mobile and web services. JSON is also used to store data for NoSQL databases, such as the Azure Cosmos DB. While it might seem that, with NoSQL and JSON, we work with unstructured data, only it's actually not the case. The data has a structure, only it's schema agnostic and the storage schema is defined by JSON itself, based on the content.

SQL Server has supported working with JSON since SQL Server 2016. Unlike XML, however, JSON is not the native data type in SQL Server. You can, however, use many SQL Server functions and operators to work with JSON text and perform the following:

- Parse JSON text, and read or modify values
- Transform arrays of JSON objects into a table format
- Run any Transact-SQL query on the converted JSON objects
- Format the results of Transact-SQL queries in JSON format

Retrieve data as JSON

When we're working with our tables in the database, we might need to convert the results to JSON format. This works very similarly to the XML conversions. SQL Server has a directive for the `SELECT` command `FOR JSON`.

You can run the following query to get the `JSON` document:

```
SELECT
    [Title]
   ,[FirstName]
   ,[MiddleName]
   ,[LastName]
   ,[Suffix]
   ,[JobTitle]
   ,[PhoneNumber]
   ,[PhoneNumberType]
   ,[EmailAddress]
FROM [AdventureWorks2016].[HumanResources].[vEmployee]
FOR JSON AUTO
```

The result of such a query would be a JSON set of documents representing each employee record in the following format:

```
{"FirstName":"Ken","MiddleName":"J","LastName":"Sánchez","JobTitle":"Chief
Executive
Officer","PhoneNumber":"697-555-0142","PhoneNumberType":"Cell","EmailAddres
s":"ken0@adventure-works.com"}
```

Unlike with XML, with JSON, you have only two available modes, which can be used to process the query and transform the result set into JSON output. The modes are as follows:

- `FOR JSON PATH`
- `FOR JSON AUTO`

The first one offers you a way to modify the look of the results, which allows you to control how the wrapping and more complex outputs will be produced. With `JSON AUTO`, SQL Server will automatically format the JSON output based on the structure of the `SELECT` query you have executed.

Processing stored JSON data

More often than running queries to produce JSON, you'll be facing situations when you'll have data stored in the database as JSON and you'll need to query that data with JSON functions to link the values to other data stored in tables as regular columns. SQL Server has a set of functions that you can use to work with JSON data.

There are the five functions available to you:

- `ISJSON`
- `JSON_VALUE`
- `JSON_QUERY`
- `JSON_MODIFY`
- `OPENJSON`

The first function tests whether the input string is a valid JSON syntax for processing. SQL Server does not have a dedicated data type for JSON, so most of the time, the JSON record is stored as a `NVARCHAR(max)` data type, which allows you to store up to 2 GB of content to such a column. If we would like to test the validity of the string, we can query the output of the `ISJSON` function, as shown in the following example:

```
DECLARE @json NVARCHAR(4000) SET @json =
'{"name":"John","surname":"Doe","age":45,"skills":["SQL","C#","MVC"]}'

SELECT ISJSON(@json)
```

Such a `SELECT` statement should return a value of 1, if the input string is a valid JSON document. When we know that the string is valid, we can query the data from such a document using the `OPENJSON` function:

```
DECLARE @json NVARCHAR(4000) SET @json =
'{"name":"John","surname":"Doe","age":45,"skills":["SQL","C#","MVC"]}';

SELECT * FROM OPENJSON(@json)
WITH (
 name nvarchar(30),
 surname nvarchar(30),
```

```
 age int,
 skills nvarchar(max) as json
)
```

The result of such a query would be a result set comprising four columns; the first three with the respective data type, and the fourth one a string with JSON representing the skills of the user.

For extracting individual values, you can use a built-in function named `JSON_VALUE`, which extracts scalar values of the specified path in the `JSON` document:

```
DECLARE @json NVARCHAR(4000) SET @json =
'{"name":"John","surname":"Doe","age":45,"skills":["SQL","C#","MVC"]}';

SELECT
  JSON_VALUE(@json,'$.name') name,
  JSON_VALUE(@json,'$.surname') surname,
  JSON_VALUE(@json,'$.age') age,
  JSON_QUERY(@json,'$.skills') skills
```

As you can see, the last function called was different. This is because the last field is not a scalar value, but a nested JSON object, so a different function has to be used here to produce the proper output. If you would like to parse that nested object and return, for example, the first skill available, you can use this with the `JSON_VALUE` function, and you'll need to navigate the array of skills and return the desired one. Considering that C# is the second skill in the skills array, we can return the skill with the following notation:

```
DECLARE @json NVARCHAR(4000) SET @json =
'{"name":"John","surname":"Doe","age":45,"skills":["SQL","C#","MVC"]}';

SELECT
  JSON_VALUE(@json,'$.name') name,
  JSON_VALUE(@json,'$.surname') surname,
  JSON_VALUE(@json,'$.age') age,
  JSON_VALUE(@json,'$.skills[1]') csharp
```

The last function `JSON_MODIFY` allows you to change the data in the `JSON` document, where you'll use same path navigation as with `JSON_VALUE`. To change the name of the user in the sample record from `John` to `Mike`, we'll use the following code:

```
DECLARE @json NVARCHAR(4000) SET @json =
'{"name":"John","surname":"Doe","age":45,"skills":["SQL","C#","MVC"]}';

SELECT
  JSON_MODIFY(@json,'$.name','Mike'),
  JSON_VALUE(@json,'$.name') name
```

This `JSON_MODIFY` function does not change the value stored in the variable; it just modifies the output of the `SELECT` statement with proper modification of the `JSON` document for further processing. If you evaluate the result of the following call to the `JSON_VALUE` function, it still returns the original name of the user.

Since JSON is not available as a native data type, it does not have a native form of indexing, as the XML data type mentioned earlier. However, if you're working with large `JSON` documents, there's a way to optimize the operations with full-text indexes:

```
--create a full text catalog
CREATE FULLTEXT CATALOG jsonFullText
GO

--create a full text index on the column storing json data
CREATE FULLTEXT INDEX ON Person.Person_json(PhoneNumber)
KEY INDEX PK_Person_json_PersonID
ON jsonFullText
```

Once the full-text catalog and index are created, you can use the full-text functions available in SQL Server to search for the JSON data for particular strings. You have the following two functions available in SQL Server for the full-text operations:

- `FREETEXT`
- `CONTAINS`

While working with large datasets based on `JSON` documents, this can be very handy regarding the expected performance of the SQL Server.

You can find more details on the full-text functions at `https://docs.microsoft.com/en-us/sql/t-sql/queries/contains-transact-sql?view=sql-server-2017` and `https://docs.microsoft.com/en-us/sql/t-sql/queries/freetext-transact-sql?view=sql-server-2017`.

External data with PolyBase

With data acquisition, we frequently face situations when data is not available in the SQL Server, and for our analysis, we usually import or query data from various other database platforms or other systems. SQL Server 2016 has introduced a new feature called **PolyBase**, which can help us with accessing external data from the SQL Server. PolyBase is able to access Hadoop-type file systems to query external data and to push the computation to Hadoop so that the SQL Server does not get overloaded while accessing large amounts of data.

The great benefit of PolyBase is the unification of two very different worlds: structured data and unstructured data. Hadoop is a collection of open source utilities, which includes a distributed file system called **hdfs**. This data distribution is a challenge for data analysis, since the data is distributed and located in heterogeneous systems, which makes it very difficult to access and process from SQL Server. PolyBase allows you to interact between structured data, usually our tables in the SQL Server, and unstructured or semi-structured data, stored in the distributed file systems. PolyBase is not completely new to SQL Server; it was available as a component of the Parallel Data Warehouse from the Analytic Platform System tool, and it's just now been built into the SQL Server.

PolyBase is a feature that can be used to do the following:

- Query data stored in Hadoop
- Import data from Hadoop
- Query data stored in Azure blob storage
- Export data

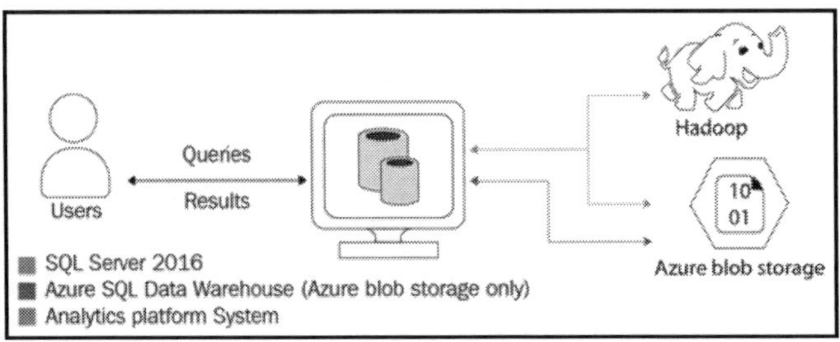

Installing and configuring

PolyBase can be installed as a part of SQL Server installation. You can choose whether PolyBase will be configured as a scale-out group. If you would like to use a scale-out group for maximum performance and throughput, you need to make sure that the following is correct:

- All nodes are in the same domain
- All nodes use the same account and password for the PolyBase service
- All nodes can communicate over the network
- All nodes are running the same SQL Server version

To install PolyBase, you will need a Java Runtime Environment available on your SQL Server, which is not part of the installation media, You'll be provided with a link to download the installation files for JRE.

You can confirm that PolyBase is installed on your server with the following:

```
SELECT SERVERPROPERTY ('IsPolybaseInstalled') AS IsPolybaseInstalled;
```

Also, when Polybase is installed, you'll see three used databases available on your SQL Server:

- DWConfiguration
- DWDiagnostics
- DWQueue

Once you have installed PolyBase, you actually need to enable the PolyBase feature in SQL Server by running a stored procedure, `sp_configure`, with proper parameters:

```
sp_configure @configname = 'hadoop connectivity', @configvalue = 1;
GO
RECONFIGURE
GO
```

The config value, as the parameter to this procedure, is used to determine the proper available data source. As of now, there are eight possible values, ranging from 0 to 7. All available config values used for various data sources are as follows:

- **Option 0**: Disable Hadoop connectivity
- **Option 1**: Hortonworks HDP 1.3 on Windows Server
- **Option 2**: Azure blob storage (WASB[S])
- **Option 3**: Hortonworks HDP 1.3 on Linux
- **Option 4**: Cloudera CDH 4.3 on Linux
- **Option 5**: Hortonworks HDP 2.0 on Windows Server
- **Option 6**: Azure blob storage (WASB[S])
- **Option 7**: Hortonworks HDP 2.0 on Linux
- **Option 8**: Cloudera 5.1, 5.2, 5.3, 5.4, 5.5, 5.9, 5.10, 5.11, 5.12, and 5.13 on Linux

- **Option 9**: Hortonworks 2.1, 2.2, 2.3, 2.4, 2.5, and 2.6 on Linux
- **Option 10**: Hortonworks 2.1, 2.2, and 2.3 on Windows Server
- **Option 11**: Azure blob storage (WASB[S])

Unlike many other configuration parameters, which you can change with the `sp_configure` procedure, after configuring Hadoop connectivity, you have to explicitly restart the SQL Server service; otherwise, the setting won't take effect. To update this configuration value, you have to be a member of sysadmin server fixed role or have the `ALTER SERVER` permission assigned to your login.

Once you have enabled Hadoop connectivity, you actually need to create several more objects inside your user database. When we're using PolyBase, we're connecting to a data source that usually stores numerous files containing the required information. When you want to access such files from SQL Server via the Polybase feature, you have to define the following:

- An external data source
- An external data file format
- An external table

The external data source defines the location of the the source defined with the access protocol, such as `hdfs` and `WASB`. The data source type can be of several different values where we will frequently work with `Hadoop` or `blob_storage` types. Other available types are `RDBMS` and `SHARD_MAP_MANAGER`, where the first is used with cross-database queries on Elastic Database Query on Azure SQL Database, and the second for sharing on the Azure SQL Database.

To create a data source for a `Hadoop` file system running on the internal network with a defined IP address, you can use the following query:

```
CREATE EXTERNAL DATA SOURCE Hadoop
WITH (
   TYPE = HADOOP,
    LOCATION = 'hdfs://192.168.1.100:8050'
)
```

This example presumes that you have a running `hdfs` storage on your IP address, 192.168.1.100, configured with default port 8050.

To get hands-on experience with `Hadoop` and `hdfs`, you can run a sandbox in your virtual machine, such as Hortonworks Data Platform or Cloudera CDH, which you can get as a quickstart virtual machines for numerous virtualization platforms.

Once we have defined the external data source, we need to define the format of the data stored in such a data source. This is handled via the definition of the `EXTERNAL FILE FORMAT`. This file format has several possible types:

- Delimited text: Simple text files with a predefined delimiter
- RCfile
- ORC: Optimized row columnar file, which is commonly used with Hadoop and offers reasonable performance and compression
- Parquet

For configuring the file format as a plain text file, where columns are delimited with the | character, we can use the following code:

```
CREATE EXTERNAL FILE FORMAT TextFile
WITH (
    FORMAT_TYPE = DelimitedText,
    FORMAT_OPTIONS (FIELD_TERMINATOR = '|')
);
```

Once the data source and the structure of the file are defined, we can create an external table in the database. This external table will define the columns for the data stored in the files and will work as a metadata wrapper for accessing the external data stored in the `hdfs` filesystem. We can either query that external data directly, or load the data into the SQL Server to new tables. We will work with a sample file containing sales records separated by the `|` character.

To create the table, we will use the following code:

```
CREATE EXTERNAL TABLE dbo.FactResellerSalesArchiveExternal (
    [ProductKey] [int] NOT NULL,
    [OrderDateKey] [int] NOT NULL,
    [DueDateKey] [int] NOT NULL,
    [ShipDateKey] [int] NOT NULL,
    [ResellerKey] [int] NOT NULL,
    [EmployeeKey] [int] NOT NULL,
    [PromotionKey] [int] NOT NULL,
    [CurrencyKey] [int] NOT NULL,
    [SalesTerritoryKey] [int] NOT NULL,
    [SalesOrderNumber] [nvarchar](20) NOT NULL,
    [SalesOrderLineNumber] [tinyint] NOT NULL,
```

```
    [RevisionNumber] [tinyint] NULL,
    [OrderQuantity] [smallint] NULL,
    [UnitPrice] [money] NULL,
    [ExtendedAmount] [money] NULL,
    [UnitPriceDiscountPct] [float] NULL,
    [DiscountAmount] [float] NULL,
    [ProductStandardCost] [money] NULL,
    [TotalProductCost] [money] NULL,
    [SalesAmount] [money] NULL,
    [TaxAmt] [money] NULL,
    [Freight] [money] NULL,
    [CarrierTrackingNumber] [nvarchar](25) NULL,
    [CustomerPONumber] [nvarchar](25) NULL,
    [OrderDate] [datetime] NULL,
    [DueDate] [datetime] NULL,
    [ShipDate] [datetime] NULL
)
WITH (
        LOCATION='/SalesData/',
        DATA_SOURCE=Hadoop,
        FILE_FORMAT=TextFile
);
```

Once the table is defined, we can query the table as this would be a regular table in our database, and the PolyBase service will access the external data and process the data movement for you automatically.

So, the query, which can access the data stored in the text files on the `Hadoop hdfs` storage, would look such as this:

```
SELECT * FROM dbo.FactResellerSalesArchiveExternal
```

If we're working in a small environment, we can use just one node to access the external data, and such a configuration would combine the compute and head node on a single server. In complex scenarios, we can use a feature of PolyBase to distribute the workload among the compute nodes and run the parallel query. Such a scale-out group requires a more complex configuration and enterprise edition on the head node.

The head node is a SQL Server instance that accepts the queries from the application or the user and distributes the work to the data movement service on the compute nodes for execution. Once processing is complete, all the results are sent back to the head node and returned to the client. In this manner, SQL Server can be used to process large datasets and access Big Data data sources for complex processing:

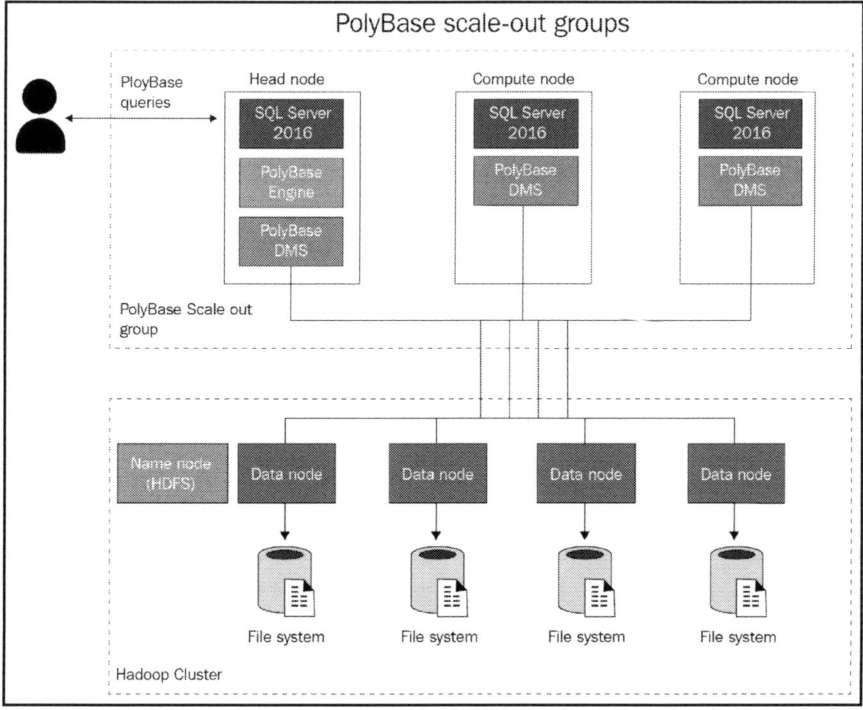

Summary

SQL Server is a relational database management system, but that does not mean we can rely only on data inside SQL Server for our analysis. There are several services and components in SQL Server that allow us to access data in structured, semi-structured, or even an unstructured form, and either query such data directly in its original storage (external to SQL Server) or import the data into SQL Server and transform the data into a relational form for further processing and wrangling with other existing datasets. Since the data coming into SQL Server may have different formats and can come from reliable and less reliable data sources, you need to carefully check the data during the cleaning phase so that you'll not import wrong, missing, or duplicate values to your database.

4
Data Transforming and Cleaning with T-SQL

`Data comes from a wide range of sources. It can be relational or non-relational, the connectivity can be unstable, and there are also many other issues when data has to be extracted from data sources. This is why developers, statisticians, and data scientists should never entirely believe in the quality of the source data. This chapter explains the techniques for data transformation and cleansing using Transact-SQL (**T-SQL**) language.

The following topics will be covered in this chapter:

- **The need for data transformation**: This section presents the main goal of data transformation for data science purposes and, using examples, also provides several cases of what could happen to incoming data.
- **Database architectures for data transformations**: Data transformations can vary from very simple to very complex. That's why it's necessary to find the right architecture to find the most reliable set of transform tasks.
- **Transforming data**: This includes accuracy checks, deduplication, high-watermark for incremental loads, and so on. There are also many other actions that could be seen as transformations.
- **Denormalizing data**: As a lot of data comes from relational databases, its format is strongly normalized. Denormalization is a part of data transformation, which is useful for fitting data better for analytical purposes.
- **Using views and stored procedures**: Views and stored procedures are very common database objects. This is the same when these objects are used for data transformations.
- **Performance considerations**: It would not be feasible to transform data longer than the analysis itself is executed. Another aspect of performance is the impact on source systems. That's why it's very important to be aware of data transformation performance.

Technical requirements

SQL Server 2017 is required to use all the scripts and projects in this chapter. If the SQL Server is the Express Edition only, then SSIS attempts will not be published into the **Integration Services Catalog**. SQL Server Data Tools should also be installed if you want to follow the SSIS example.

For all SQL scripts provided within this chapter, Management Studio Version 17.5 or higher is recommended.

All scripts and other files are provided here: `https://github.com/PacktPublishing/Hands-On-Data-Science-with-SQL-Server-2017/tree/master/CH5_Data_Transforming_and_Cleaning_with_T_SQL`. Scripts are ordered accordingly and are reported throughout the chapter.

In the `CSV` subfolder are files that contain sample customers and products used for samples.

The `CH05_11_complete_SSIS_solution_BookProjectSSIS.zip` file contains a working demo of the SSIS solution described in the *SQL Server integration services* section. Unzip this file locally if you want to play with it yourself. When you try to execute the package, please ensure that you review the server names and file paths first.

The need for data transformation

The crucial question is this: why do we need data to be transformed for data science? There are two principal reasons for this. The first of these reasons is to obtain datasets or small amounts of datasets because data science models are commonly based on the statistical population dataset. We can do JOINs in our data before they are analyzed or used for machine learning training, for example, but this often leads to unnecessary complications in the model, and it could also have a performance impact on the training time.

The second reason is a bit more complicated. The world is full of data, and the volume of it is always growing. The previous `Chapter 3`, *Data Sources for Analytics*, showed a lot of data sources and data creation methods. Let's summarize the increase of data from a different point of view. We can think about data from the perspective of the speed of data contention, as well as from the perspective of the data model used for its storage and manipulation.

First of all, a very traditional and also rather slow method of data creation is simply manually writing it. There are many systems such as accounting, stores, and so on, which are developed using a client-server model with many types of relational databases, such as Microsoft SQL Server, Oracle, Teradata, and others. Some of the systems are rather old, created, and used for maybe ten or more years. This leads to some inaccurate historical data because systems were often not designed to check data quality sufficiently, and so the genesis of development was not continuous.

Another type of data is produced either by machines or whole production lines. This type of data production is rapidly increasing, but the data could be a bit more simple than in the previous case. In this case, data is usually the same kind and describes the same measure or measures. The use of relational databases is also very common here.

Furthermore, a very modern way of generating data is through IoT or other similar applications. First of all, the main challenge is the speed of the data generation. This is because many simple devices create records at the same time. When it comes to applications such as this, the database should not be relational in most cases, because data processing on a database site is too slow. The speed of processing is the reason we are using the NoSQL concept rather than relational databases, including servers such as MongoDB or CosmosDB. NoSQL databases are intended to be used for very fast data processing in applications such as gaming or telemetry data, which acquired extremely quickly. The concept of NoSQL can be challenging , especially for T-SQL developers who are not familiar with data storage.

The speed of data contention and the data storage model are not only potential concerns for data scientists. Many organizations also use several systems that are not integrated with one another. This often leads to big problems, such as duplicated data describing the same entity as well as data stored in different formats with differing quality and accessibility.

Let's summarize the factors that have an impact on the need for data transformations, as described in the previous paragraphs:

- Speed of data creation
- Data models used for data manipulation and storage
- Data accuracy
- The combination of more data sources needed to get the eligible data for data science modeling

Let's now summarize some data science task requirements in accordance with the data source characteristics given in the preceding bullet list:

- Incoming data from data sources should be regularly used for machine-learning models training
- What constitutes an acceptable data delay is between the time that a new record is added to the source data and the time when a new record is analyzed using a trained machine-learning model

Previous paragraphs have given some examples of why we should not entirely believe in data sources as well as looking at which challenges could be met when data scientists want to tackle them. In the following chapters, we will explore the possibilities of technologies helping us to extract data from its source and transforming it to fit our needs.

The crucial question here is this: how do we use T-SQL to transform, clean, and deduplicate data correctly and efficiently? Unfortunately, this question does not have one simple answer because no one-size-fits-all solution exists. Consequently, in the next section, we will go through several architectures helping us to get data into a consolidated reliable schema for the next data science tasks.

Database architectures for data transformations

Database architectures that are needed for data transformations in data science can be similar to architectures used in data warehousing. In many applications, they can also be almost the same as the architectures used for **Extract-Transform-Load** (**ETL**) in common data warehouse applications. In this section, we will go through the scenarios used for data transformation from the perspective of cooperating databases.

Direct source for data analysis

The least complicated database architecture is uses source data directly as a data source for further analysis. The following screenshot shows this scenario:

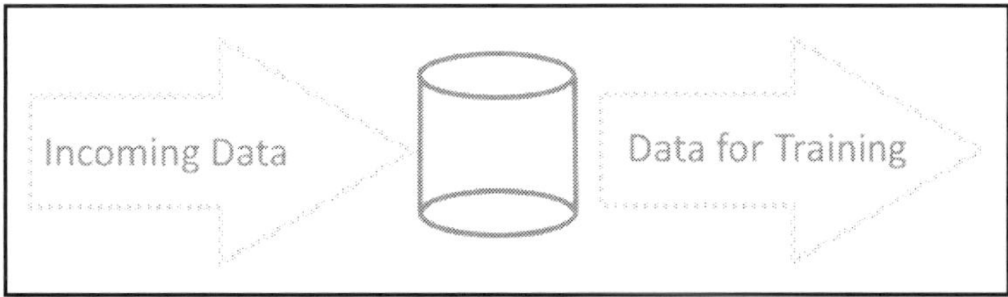

The only database in the preceding screenshot is used for both data manipulation from source applications as well as for reading data in machine-learning models. This architecture is generally suitable for limited scenarios only, and we have to consider its limitations. These include the following:

- First of all, we must not block incoming work by reading data into our data science model. Source databases are usually designed for DML operations or as a data warehouse. When the database is an **online transactional processing** (**OLTP**) database such as libraries, airlines or banks, we need to consider the fact that incoming transactions have priority over the range read operations generated by machine-learning training. When the source database is a data warehouse, the situations are not as complicated because data warehouses are designed for range reads.
- We have a very limited capability to adjust the database schema for our purposes (one or two datasets). In this case, almost the only way to transform data into a desired dataset is to create database views. The need for more complex transformations leads to the necessity to create new tables, and this is not a direct source.
- Furthermore, we have a very limited capability for checking data quality. We are used to believing in the data quality of original data. This limitation is quite similar to the previous two bullets; the only type of database object that is actually suitable is the database view.
- We also don't need other data sources to be combined with incoming data. It's very difficult and also inefficient to combine data from more data sources in this direct model because of the need for distributed queries with their probable impact on performance and accessibility.

Aside from the previously described limitations, this approach also has some of the following benefits:

- Data for making predictions is accessible as soon as it comes to the source database. Because of this, our machine-learning model can access incoming data directly without the extra effort that is required to transform data.
- Data for training is also always accessible. When the source system is running, our data is always accessible.

Staging–target scenario

The scenario described in the preceding section is good for very simple tasks, but it's more common that data comes from more sources. Let's imagine that the data is coming from an accounting system and a production-tracking system. In this case, data in the accounting system could somehow correlate with production data (for example, more downtimes in production has an impact on profit as well as inaccurate products). It's often desirable to have data from multiple sources to get a better picture of a certain subject. In this case, database architecture has to be more complex. The database architecture is shown in the following screenshot:

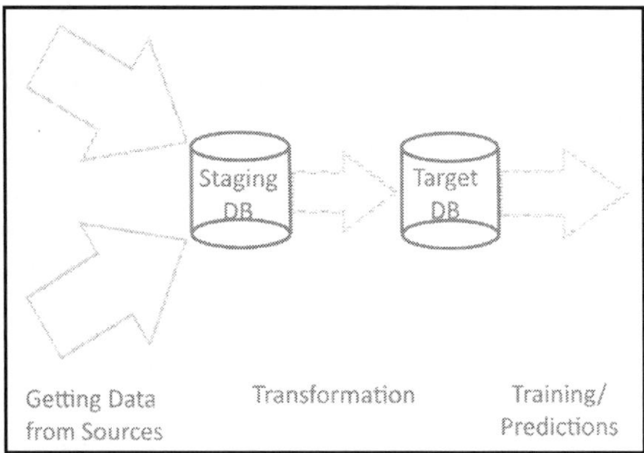

The preceding screenshot demonstrates the way in which data is obtained and transformed in two phases. In the first phase, data is taken from several data sources and saved into the **staging** database. In the staging database, almost all transformations are complete. In the second phase, prepared data is placed into the **target** database, which holds the final version of data that is eligible for machine-learning training and possibly also for making predictions.

Let's look into the staging database. In this database, the following tasks are done:

- Data is reliably copied from data sources
- If needed, the staging database holds high watermarks or mapping tables used for incremental data loads from sources
- Data is cleansed, deduplicated, and consolidated together
- Data is prepared (or almost prepared) for a simple movement into the target database

As seen in the preceding bullet list, a staging database is very diligent. So, what is the target database for? Basically, the target database holds clean and well-modelled schema and data, both strictly used to train predictive models, save trained models, and provide trained models for the purpose of making predictions. Aside from this base role that the target database plays, we can also use the database as a source of data for statistics computation or reporting purposes.

Using this architecture, we need to keep in mind several considerations:

- Data sources should provide rather reliable data from a data quality perspective.
- Data sources are of a similar type. In the best-case scenario, all data sources are relational databases.
- The data schema of data coming from data sources does not change, or it at least changes very infrequently.
- It's not easy to extract data continuously from data sources. Architecture with more cooperating databases is more prepared for batch data extraction. This could become a limitation later when predictions are made in real time.

In staging, the target model provides the following valuable benefits:

- Both databases (the staging database as well as the target database) have schemas designed by developers who know the requirements for later tasks in data science. Both databases will fully support final data science needs.
- Both databases are isolated from the workload coming to data sources. This reduces conflict between the incoming OLTP workload and analytical needs.

The described scenario presumes that reliable, rigidly designed data comes from accessible data sources. However, we also have a lot of schema-agnostic NoSQL data sources or data sources with unstable frequently changed schema, which are potentially not accessible every time. This is why we need to provide an example of more complicated scenario, which is covered in next section.

Landing–staging–target scenario

As mentioned in the preceding section, sometimes, actual data sources are not too reliable. This is why we need to add an extra layer to our architectures to defend against most uncertainties coming from data sources. This extra layer is called **landing**. The landing database is a zone used for only one thing: to catch data from data sources with no respect to their schema stability, accessibility, or data quality. The following screenshot shows a complete architecture containing the landing database:

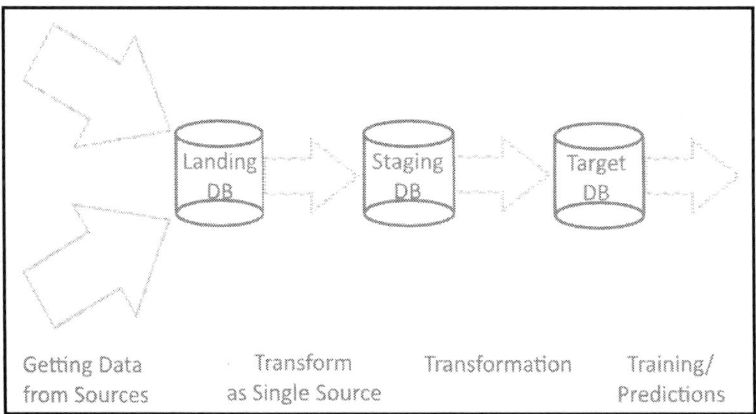

As seen in the preceding screenshot, the landing database is added to the staging/target database architecture. The landing database plays a vital role in scenarios in which data sources vary. As an example, let's take a set of CSV files stored on an FTP site or web services with XML or JSON responses. The schema of such data is not reliable enough, so the landing database could help us to recognize schema changes between two loads from data sources, and it can also help us to manipulate data from non-relational data sources.

Previous sections provided a description of typical database architectures for data transformations. Certain databases in staging-target and landing-staging-target scenarios could not be separated in isolated instances nor isolated databases; every part of data transformation could be created simply as a separated schema in a single database. This decision depends on several factors, such as owned resources, licences, or security requirements.

The question is how to develop data movements between certain data sources and databases. We have a wide set of options available for this.

Tools eligible for data movement

The database architectures described in the previous sections could be established from the only database containing several schemas, but more databases on more instances of the SQL Server could also be used. This difference determines how to develop data movement and transformations from one schema or database to another. We have a few options for this:

- If we have just one database divided into landing, staging, and target areas by database schemas, then the situation is quite simple because we mainly use T-SQL queries and transactions
- If we have more databases on just one instance of an SQL Server, then this leads to a very similar approach, because there are no complications involved in writing T-SQL queries between more databases hosted by a single instance
- However, if we have more instances of the SQL Server hosting certain databases, then we have more options than just T-SQL queries

The following few paragraphs will provide an overview of the certain data movement possibilities.

Distributed queries

A **distributed query** is a query typically involving more than one database server. The following screenshot shows how they work together:

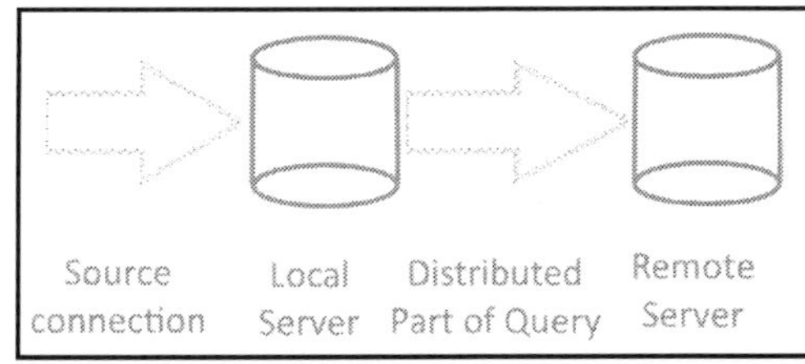

Let's take a look at the preceding screenshot. **Source connection** is the connection established from a user or application to the server known as the **Local Server**. The term local does not mean that the user must be logged locally to the server; it means that the server typically processes user queries locally. The **Remote Server** is then the one that hosts the database remotely from the **Local Server**. When a user issues a query to the **Local Server** using remote data, the **Local Server** divides the query into local and remote parts. Data hosted on a **Remote Server** is then processed in two possible modes: locally or remotely.

The execution of distributed queries requires existing reliable links between local and remote servers. The link can be established temporarily using the `OPENROWSET` function in the SQL Server. The second option is to create a server object called the **linked server** and use the `OPENQUERY` function or adhoc distributed queries. The linked server is named definition of the link between local and remote server. This definition contains several settings such as the remote database server engine type (SQL Server, Oracle, and so on), its name or IP address, and, most importantly, security settings. So, how do we decide which option to use: `OPENROWSET` or a linked server?

First, let's take the example of the `OPENROWSET` function. We have two SQL servers called `SQLLOCAL` and `SQLREMOTE`. `SQLLOCAL` is the server to which the user is connected, and `SQLREMOTE` holds some useful data, for example in the `Accounting` database table `dbo.Accounts`. The simplest query from `SQLLOCAL` to the `SQLREMOTE` server will look like this:

```
SELECT * FROM OPENROWSET('SQLOLEDB'
    , 'SQLREMOTE;user;password'
    , 'SELECT * FROM Accounting.dbo.Accounts');
```

However, this query results in an error. The full error message reads as follows:

```
Msg 15281, Level 16, State 1, Line 5
SQL Server blocked access to STATEMENT 'OpenRowset/OpenDatasource' of
component 'Ad Hoc Distributed Queries' because this component is turned off
as part of the security configuration for this server. A system
administrator can enable the use of 'Ad Hoc Distributed Queries' by using
sp_configure. For more information about enabling 'Ad Hoc Distributed
Queries', search for 'Ad Hoc Distributed Queries' in SQL Server Books
Online.
```

The reason for this error is very simple: security. If we take a look back to the original statement, we should see the following three parameters of the `OPENROWSET` function:

- The first parameter is the provider type (for MS SQL Server it's `SQLOLEDB`; for Oracle, it's `MSDAORA`).
- The second parameter consists of three parts such as server name, user, and password. However, the password being written in clear text is a security risk.
- The third parameter is a query written in the SQL dialect of the remote server.

If the `OPENROWSET` function is still desirable for any reason, the user with the administrator privileges must call the following configuration procedure to allow the `OPENROWSET` function:

```
use master
go

exec sp_configure 'show advanced options', 1
go
reconfigure
go

exec sp_configure 'ad hoc distributed queries', 1
go
reconfigure
go

exec sp_configure 'show advanced options', 0
go
reconfigure
go
```

If we read the preceding error message carefully, we will not see a word about the `show advanced options` configuration value, which needs to be configured. To resolve this, let's go through this piece of code slowly.

The first call of the `sp_configure` stored procedure with the `show advanced options` configuration parameter value reveals hidden configurations. The ad hoc distributed queries configuration option is normally hidden, and hidden options cannot be configured. This is why we need to reveal advanced options first, so then we can reconfigure the ad hoc distributed queries option itself. It is best practice to hide advanced options immediately. The `reconfigure` statement executed after each `sp_configure` execution turns the configured value immediately into operation without the need to restart the whole service.

When the ad hoc distributed queries option is on, we can use the `OPENROWSET` function. But the best practice is to avoid its usage for regular cases. When the `OPENROWSET` function was used and we don't need it anymore, it's important to switch the ad hoc distributed queries option off to hide potentially dangerous settings and to keep the SQL Server instance secured. The code for switching this code off is as follows:

```
use master
go

exec sp_configure 'show advanced options', 1
go
reconfigure
go

exec sp_configure 'ad hoc distributed queries', 0    -- only change is here
go
reconfigure
go

exec sp_configure 'show advanced options', 0
go
reconfigure
go
```

The `OPENROWSET` function can be used for querying files such as XMLs or JSONs directly from the disk in the form of `SELECT * FROM OPENROWSET(BULK 'path to file', SINGLE_CLOB) AS corrId`. For such cases, the reconfiguration of the *ad hoc distributed queries* option is not needed.

In the previous example code, we saw quite a dangerous function for querying remote relational data. Now let's find out more about reliable options for reading remote data. To be secure, we need to hide user context. The `Linked Server` object provides the option, so when we need to execute distributed queries, we need to configure the linked server first. Even though the `sp_addlinkedserver` system-stored procedure already exists, this is mainly used for scripting the linked server definition from GUI out to the T-SQL script.

A better option is to use GUI in the SQL Server Management Studio. The following screenshot demonstrates how to creates:

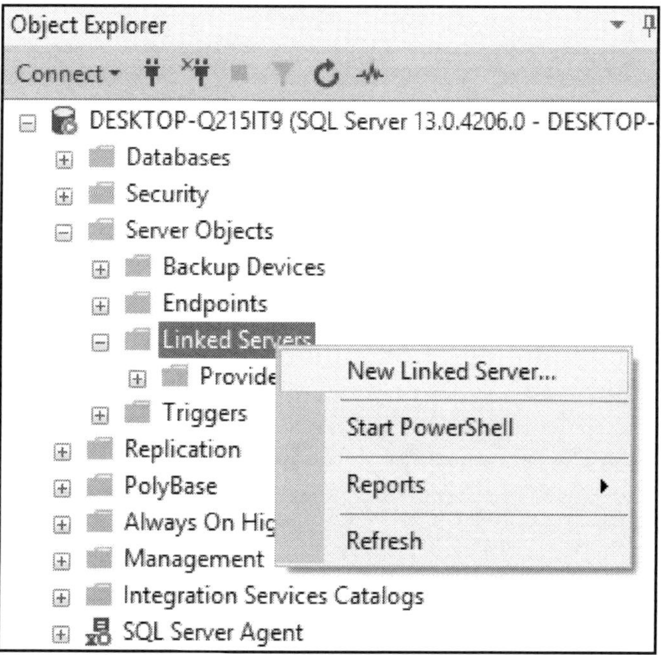

When the **New Linked Server...** option is clicked, a new window appears, as shown in the following screenshot:

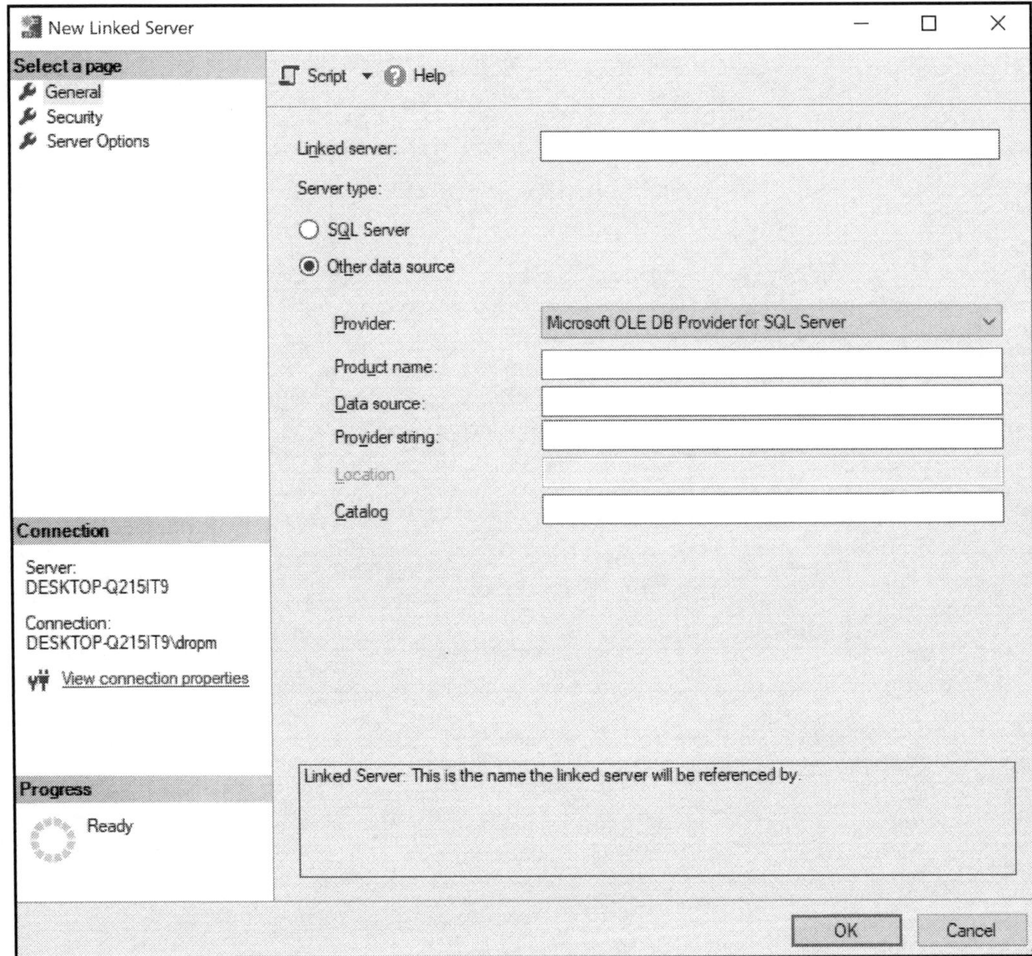

On the **General** page of the **New Linked Server** window, as shown in the preceding screenshot, we need to implement the appropriate combination of properties. The most simple way to do this is to create a link to another SQL Server. In this case, properties are filled like this:

- Under **Server type** select the **SQL Server** option
- The **Linked server** textbox must be filled with the complete name of the remote SQL Server (including the instance name in a form of `SERVERNAME\INSTANCENAME`, if the remote server is a named instance) or with the IP address (again, with an instance name if the remote server is named `instance`, the form is `192.168.1.1\INSTANCENAME`, for example)
- All other textboxes are disabled using the **SQL Server** option of the **Server type** radio button

The created linked server will have the same name as the actual remote SQL Server name. Sometimes, it is quite uncomfortable to write all the distributed queries with server names such as `IP_address\difficult_shortcut_for_named_instance_instance_name`, isn't it? This is why we can use different styles of linked server creation, even though it is still an SQL Server. We can fill the **General** page with the following elements:

- **Server type**: This radio button will remain switched to **Other data source**
- **Linked server**: This textbox can be filled with any descriptive names (for example, `ACCOUNTINGSQL` for a SQL server containing an accounting database)
- **Provider**: This dropdown should remain filled with the **Microsoft OLE DB Provider for SQL Server** value
- **Data source**: This will contain an actual server name or an IP address (including the instance name, if needed)
- **Catalog**: This will contain the name of the database on the remote server for which we want to access
- All other options will remain empty.

Both preceding instructions connect us to the SQL Server, but what if the remote server is a different type? In this case, we have the following two options:

- The first option is to install and configure the proper ODBC driver for another engine and then set the **Provider** dropdown to **Microsoft OLE DB Provider for ODBC Drivers** value.

- The second more-complicated-but-more-efficient option is to install and configure a client driver for a remote engine and register it as a new provider type on the SQL Server with the `master.dbo.sp_MSset_oledb_prop` system-stored procedure. We cannot go through all of the possible database engine types that could be met in infrastructures, so the best way is to Google the proper instructions for a certain database engine.

Once the **General** page is set up correctly, it's important to visit the second page, called **Security**. Let's explore this page in the following screenshot:

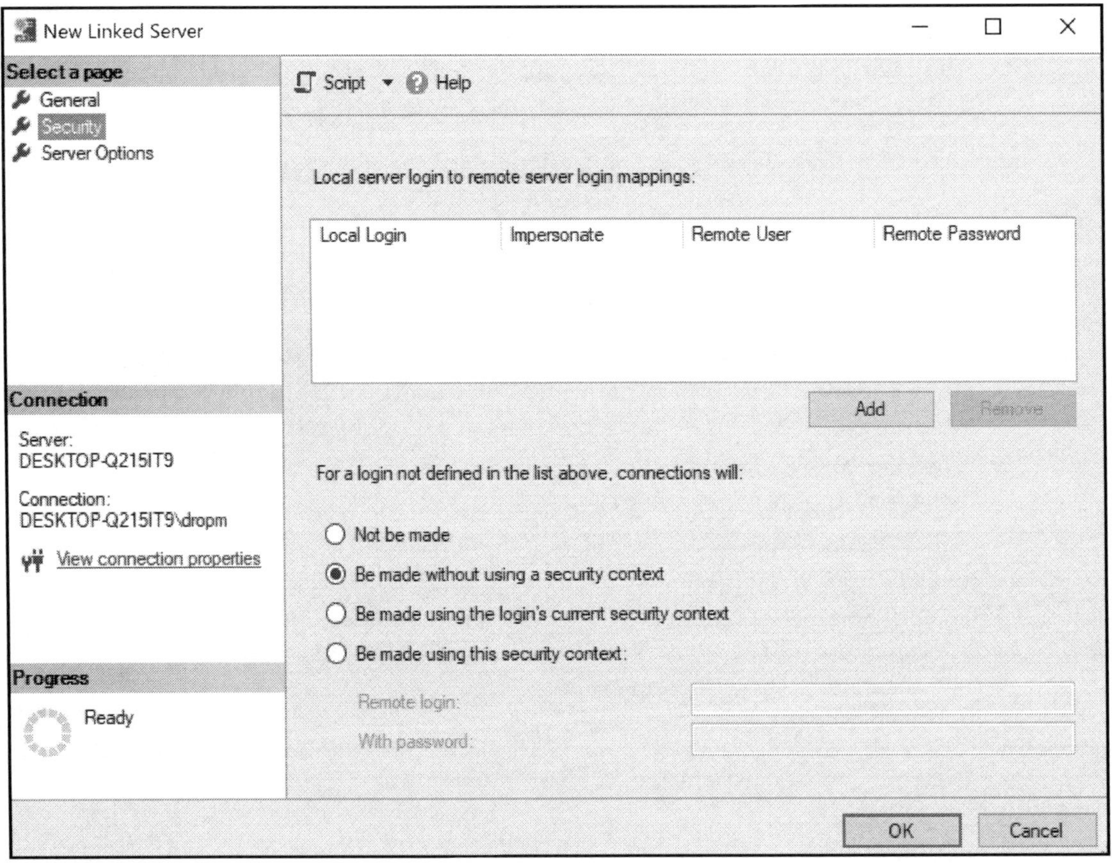

The **Security** page of the **New Linked Server** window is logically divided into two parts. The top part of the page is intended to map local logins to remote logins one by one. When the **Add** button is used, a new row appears in the preceding list, and we can add a local login here. The local login can be a standard SQL login or a Windows login added to SQL Server. Its correct name is added to the **Local Login** column. We then have two options: we can impersonate the local login to the same login added to the remote server, or we can map a local login to any existing remote login.

Impersonation means that our local SQL Server will use a local login's context to access the remote server. This approach has following several requirements:

- Both local and remote servers have to be members of the same domain and must have an **service principal name (SPN)** registered in Active Directory
- The local SQL Server must run under the context of a domain account that has **Delegation** properties in the Active Directory that are set to **Trust this user for delegation to any service**
- Domain logins for impersonated users must exist on both servers

The bottom part of the **Security** page contains settings that tell the SQL Server what to do with users not defined in the list on the top part of the page. Four options are possible here:

- **Not be made**: Whoever is not registered in the list will not be able to access the remote server.
- **Be made without using a security context**: This option establishes that the access to the remote server will be anonymous.
- **Be made using the login's current security context**: This option means that logins from the local server will be impersonated to the remote server.
- **Be made using this security context**: When this option is selected, both the **Remote login** and the **With password** textboxes are enabled. We can set the remote account used for accessing the remote server for all users who are not registered on the **Local server login to remote server login mappings** list.

After the linked server is created, we can check it using **Object Explorer** in **Management Studio**. The following screenshot shows what will happen when a newly linked server is created:

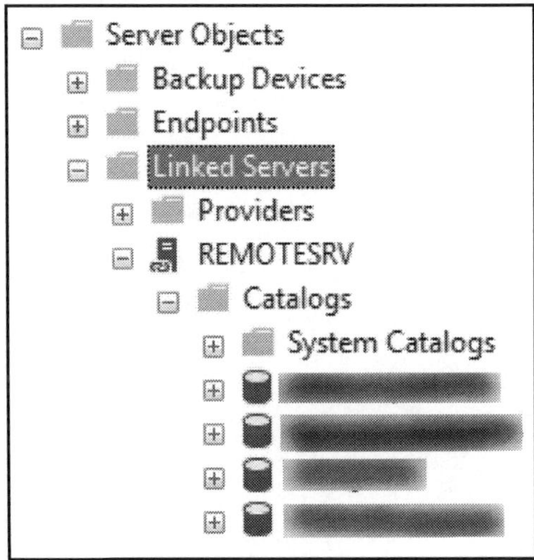

Under the `Server Objects` folder, the `Linked Servers` node of **Object Explorer**, a newly created linked server will appear (in the preceding screenshot, its name is `REMOTESRV`). Furthermore, all catalogs (databases in this case, because the linked server in the preceding screenshot is also SQL Server) to which a user has access are shown. We can continue to click down to tables and views of a certain catalog to see their structures as well as data.

When the definition of a linked server is successfully created, it's time to start querying objects managed by the linked server. We have two options of how to write queries.

The first option is to write ad hoc queries when objects from the remote server are directly referred to via their full names. The full name of every database object consists of the following four parts:

- Server
- Catalog
- Schema
- Object name

So, the most simple query used for the `Accounts` example table stored in the `Emuns` schema in the `Accounting` database on the linked server called `REMOTESRV` will be written in the following form:

```
SELECT * FROM REMOTESRV.Accounting.Enums.Accounts
```

The preceding simple statement is true for querying the remote SQL Server. But what about for the example of Oracle 11g? This (and older) versions of the Oracle database engine does not have a catalog equivalent. In a scenario in which part of object name is not supported by the database engine, we can omit this part of the name. However, despite the fact that the dots in between are non-existing parts of the name, we will not omit these. The same sample query against Oracle 11g will look like this:

```
SELECT * FROM REMOTESRV..Enums.Accounts
```

Using this ad hoc querying approach has one potential performance issue. SQL Server does not have access to statistics, so the distributed part of a query is not optimized. When a remote table is used—for example, in `WHERE` predicates or in `JOINs` —queries perform quite poorly. This is because SQL Server will wait for all data to be read from the remote server and then process all operations on the data locally. This is why it's necessary to be familiar with the `OPENQUERY` function. Against the previously mentioned `OPENROWSET`, the `OPENQUERY` function uses linked servers, which is why it does not lead to security issues and no additional settings on an instance's level are needed. Let's take the same example with the `Enums.Accounts` table stored on the `REMOTESRV` server in the `Accounting` database. The same sample query using the `OPENQUERY` function looks like this:

```
SELECT * FROM OPENQUERY('REMOTESRV', 'SELECT * FROM
Accounting.Enum.Accounts')
```

Even though this syntax may look a bit more complicated, it's often more efficient than previous ad hoc queries. The important difference is that SQL Server connects to the remote server referenced in the first parameter and issues the query set as the second parameter. So, the query is processed remotely and the local server only consumes its result set. The query set into the `OPENQUERY` function is written in the SQL dialect of the remote server, and if the remote server supports it, we can use all the SQL clauses and operators native to the remote server. Consequently, we can limit the result set from the remote query rapidly. A result from the `OPENQUERY` function can be consumed by the rest of the query like any other table or view. We can also join other tables or filter it in addition to any other table. Let's have one more example with the `Enum.Accounts` remote table as in previous examples, and let's have a local table called `dbo.AccountRecords`.

Let's assume that in both tables an integer column called `AccountID` exists. We need to join both tables together. The following query shows this solution:

```
SELECT *
FROM OPENQUERY('REMOTESRV', 'SELECT * FROM Accounting.Enum.Accounts') AS rq
    JOIN dbo.AccountRecords AS ar ON rq.AccountID = ar.AccountID
```

The preceding query shows very simple syntax of how to join tables together. The only important point here is that functions used in the `FROM` clause must have a so-called correlation ID (`rq` in the preceding example).

Distributed queries help us to reach data that is reliably accessible, typically in other relational databases. However, when data is provided from independent sites or in various formats such as CSVs or XML documents, distributed queries aren't robust enough to help us. This is why we need to discover a different technology to reach such data.

SQL Server Integration Services

SQL Server Integration Services (**SSIS**) is a part of SQL Server Enterprise and Standard Editions. SSIS basically serves as a rich ETL tool with many predefined transformations. There are many use cases such as loading data into data warehouse, migrate data from obsolete system to new system, and others. As part of SSIS, there are also delivered tasks that are not actually used for transformations themselves, but instead help us to execute a wide set of preparation or directing tasks. Plenty of books and materials can help you master SSIS (for example, the commonly known community web at `sqlis.com`). Consequently, this section is just an overview of SSIS with some highlights for developers.

Did you know that some SQL Server features such as **Database Maintenance Plans** or **Data Collection** are based on SSIS?

Let's ask ourselves the following questions:

- Why should we use SSIS?
- What is needed to develop an SSIS solution?
- Where should SSIS be used?
- Is there any alternative to SSIS solutions?

The following paragraphs will help to answer these questions.

Why should we use SSIS?

During data acquisition, or while transforming data, many challenges are encountered. This includes issues such as non-relational data sources, heterogeneous data sources, data sources that are accessible at only certain times, and so on. For instance, T-SQL syntax does not have resources to solve the data processing of many XML documents saved on a disk in one batch, because SQL Server does not have an eligible statement or function to iterate through a folder on the disk.

The internet is full of examples of how to use an extended system-stored procedure `xp_cmdshell` for accessing files in a folder. In combination with dynamic SQL, this is very dangerous because `xp_cmdshell` allows any operating system command, and dynamic SQL creates the opportunity for SQL injection. Please avoid constructs such as this!

When T-SQL resources are not sufficient for certain tasks, SSIS seems to be a very good option.

The second very important reason to use SSIS is that there are plenty of actions that can be written in any language, such as C# or Java, but the actions are very repetitive and almost still the same (for example, copying files from one folder to another). Due to the fact that SSIS provides a rich set of predefined tasks on the file system, FTP, web services, XML processing, and so on, any effort added to our own coding in common languages is useless. This is especially the case when we have additional requirements such as parametrization, logging, and diagnostics.

Finally, another reason to use SSIS is to be able to join non-relational data together. But how can we join data from CSV using a folder of pictures? Once again, SQL Server does not have any options in T-SQL for challenges such as this.

What is needed to develop an SSIS solution?

The only tool needed to create an SSIS solution is **SQL Server Data Tools** (**SSDT**). This tool is a part of Visual Studio and can also be downloaded separately from Microsoft Docs (`https://docs.microsoft.com/en-us/sql/ssdt/download-sql-server-data-tools-ssdt?view=sql-server-2017#ssdt-for-visual-studio-2017`) for free. Once SSDT is installed and opened, we'll start creating a new project. Every project is created from a template, and our desired template is **Integration Services Project**.

The following screenshot depicts how a dialog window looks when opened from the **File** | **New Project** menu:

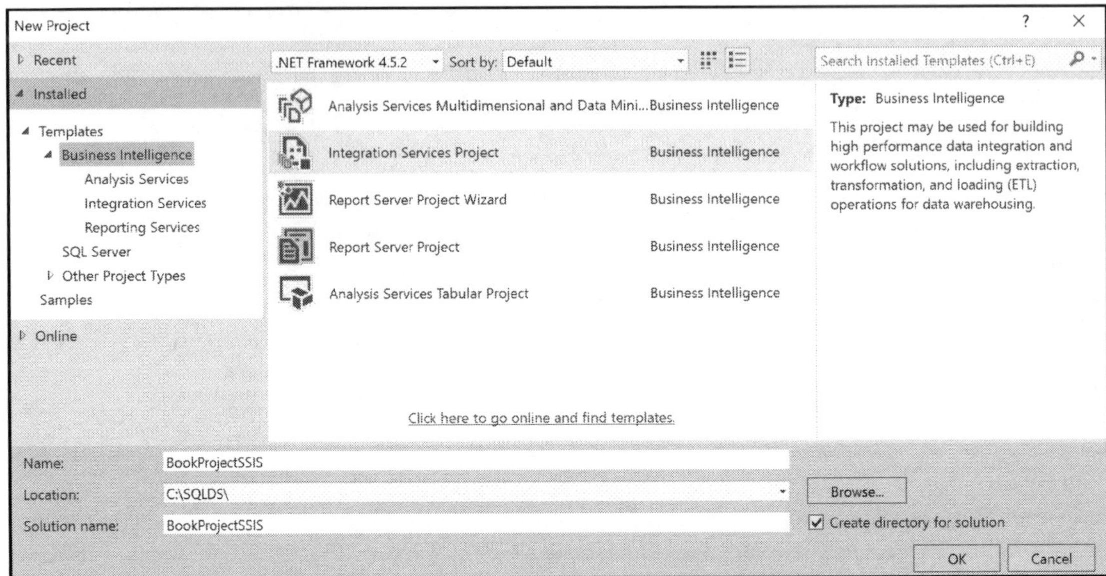

The preceding screenshot demonstrates how to find the **Integration Services Project** project type. It's important to choose the correct and descriptive name of the project (**BookProjectSSIS** is an example of this, as seen in the screenshot). Projects in Visual Studio (and SSDT is a part of Visual Studio, even though it's installed separately) are grouped into **Solution**. This is not too common for business intelligence projects such as SSIS projects, but it may happen. For this reason, there's also a **Solution name** textbox that defaults to the same value as the project name set in the **Name** textbox.

The newly created SSIS project creates **Solution Explorer** items such as **Project Parameters**, **Connection Managers,** and **Packages**. One empty package, simply called `Package.dtsx`, is created during project creation. This package is the cornerstone of every SSIS solution. We can imagine every package as an atomic unit of work, which is called independently from other packages. Every package consists of at least **control flow** and **data flow**. Control flow contains tasks that are not transformations itself. In other words, we can say that control flow is a programmatic logic of the package. Data flow is called from control flow with a control flow task called a data flow task.

It's beyond the scope of this book to explain everything that is accessible in SSIS projects; there are plenty of invaluable possibilities that we do not need to cover, but we will go through a simple step-by-step sample to get a better understanding of SSIS packages:

1. First, let's call a CSV such as `cust_en.csv`. This CSV contains a list of customers in the following format:
    - First name
    - Last name
    - Age
    - Yearly income

   The first row of the CSV is just a header.

2. We need to process the `.csv` file and save its content to a `DemoCust` database as well as a `dbo.Customers` table.
3. The first thing we need to do here is fulfill some prerequisites. To do this, we need to have a `DemoCust` database. The simplest code for creating a database using all properties with default values is as follows:

```
CREATE DATABASE DemoCust
```

4. When a database is created, we can start to work on data acquisition using an SSIS project. Let's create an empty SSIS project in SSDT with the same names as shown in the earlier screenshot. When a project is created, SSDT looks like the following screenshot:

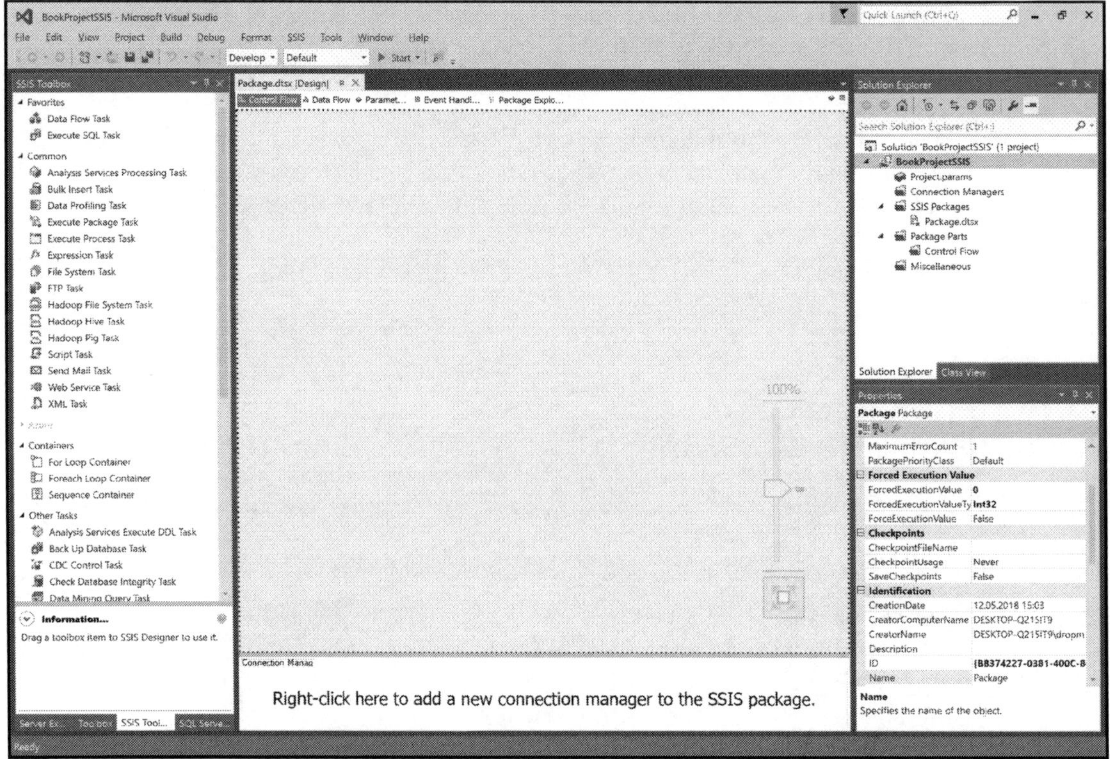

Creating a new project

As shown in the preceding screenshot, the surface of the SSIS project is divided into several parts. On the left side is a dockable window called an **SSIS Toolbox**. This window contains tools that are placed into the biggest central part, which contains package designers. The central part is the definition of the package itself. This is divided into tabs, which are placed at the top of screen. The package development always starts on an already-visible tab called **Control Flow**. The right part of screen is divided into two dockable windows: **Solution Explorer** and **Properties**. **Solution Explorer** is the window located at the top, and this serves as a navigation window showing all project content. Typically, under the **Solution Explorer** tab, there is a **Properties** window that shows the properties of an item currently selected on the package definition.

5. In our project, which consists of only one package, we will complete the following tasks:
    1. We will check whether a target table exists. If not, we will create it using **Execute SQL Task**
    2. We will truncate the table to be sure that no data from the previous load is still saved in it
    3. We will process the CSV using **Data Flow Task**
6. First of all, we need to create a connection manager within the previously created `DemoCust` database. Right-click on the **Connection Managers** node in the **Solution Explorer** tab and select the **New Connection Manager** option.

7. At this point, a dialog will appear asking you to select the proper connection manager type. Select the **OLEDB** connection manager type, as shown in the following screenshot:

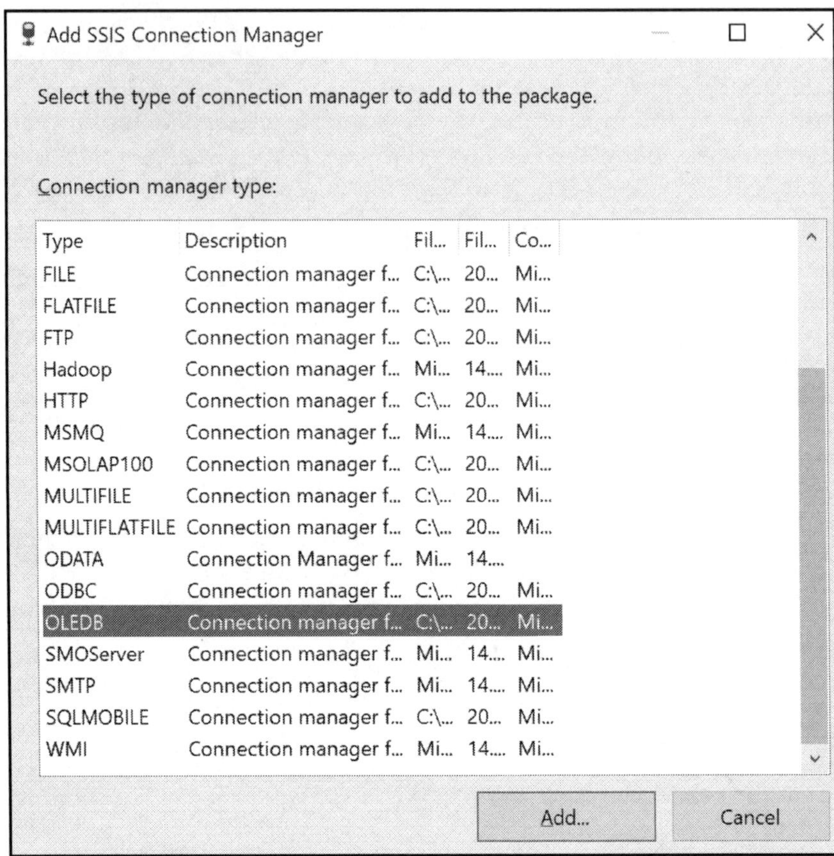

8. When selected, click the **Add** button, and a new dialog will appear. This is shown in the following screenshot:

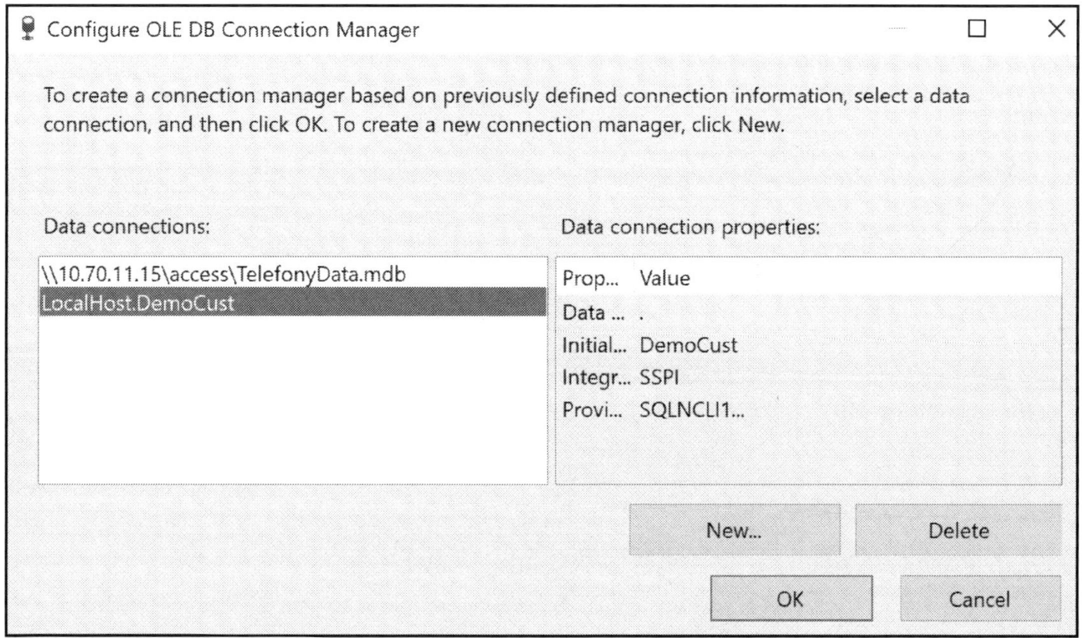

9. This dialog is almost empty, but clicking the **New...** button will open one more dialog used to define the connection string itself using the server name, security context, and database name. When properties in the dialog are set, we will have created a new project connection manager. We can then link to this from anywhere in the whole project.
10. Now that the connection manager is defined, let's create the first task. In the **SSIS Toolbox,** we will take **Execute SQL Task,** and, using drag and drop, we will place this into the **Control Flow** definition. When dropped in, it looks like the following screenshot:

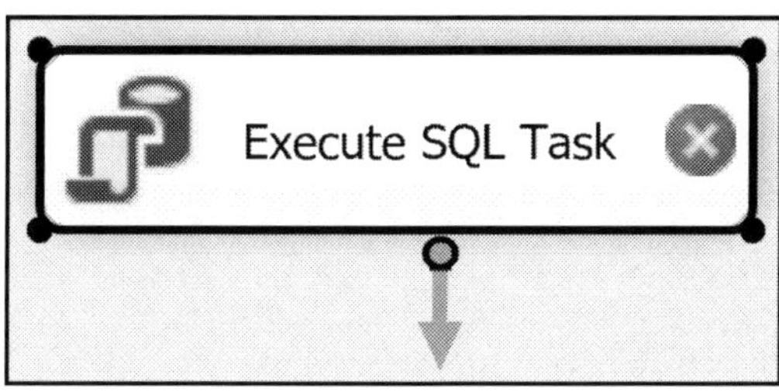

11. The red sign on the right side of the preceding screenshot indicates that the tasks need some more definitions or that some definitions are incorrect. Double-click on the task and populate the properties properly. The dialog is shown in the following screenshot:

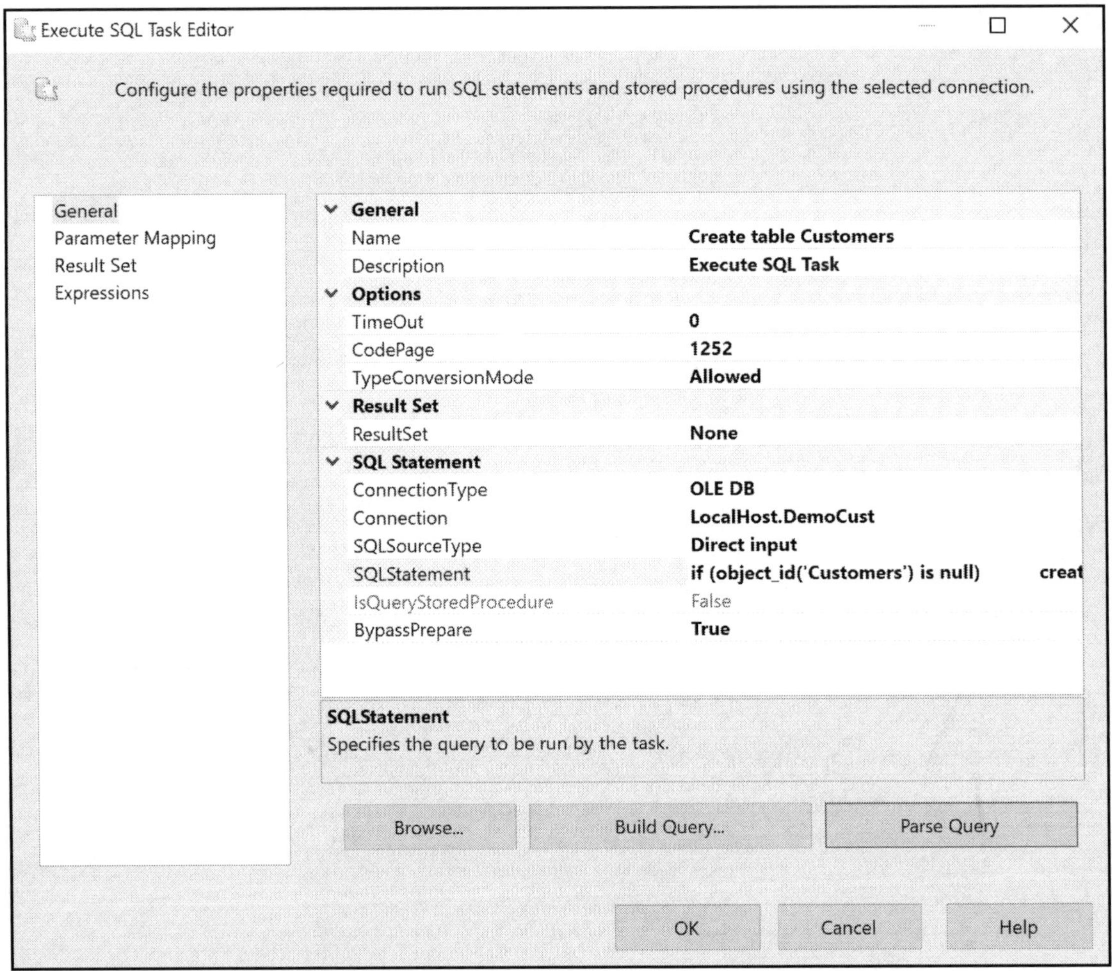

Here, we will only pay attention to some properties from the dialog shown in the preceding screenshot:

- **Name**: The default name of the task is **Execute SQL Task**, but when more tasks of the same type are added to the package with the same name, it becomes hard to differentiate between them, and this results in chaos. For this reason, it is a good idea to add some descriptive names to all tasks. In the case of the preceding example, the **Name** textbox was filled in as **Create table Customers**.
- **Connection**: This property contains a drop-down menu that lists available connection managers. Let's select the one created in the previous step (here, the name of the connection manager on the image is `LocalHost.DemoCust`, but names may vary).
- **SQLStatement**: If the table does not exist, then this property will contain an SQL statement for table creation. The statement is written in the following code block:

```
if (object_id('Customers') is null)
  create table Customers
  (
  Id int not null identity constraint pk_Customers primary key
  , FirstName nvarchar(30) not null
  , LastName nvarchar(30) not null
  , Age int null
  , YearlyIncome int null
  )
```

12. When everything is populated, we can click **OK**. The dialog is closed, and if everything was populated correctly, the red sign from the task should disappear.
13. We should keep in mind that the package will be called repeatedly. That's why the next step is to truncate the table if it already exists. Try to do this on your own using **Execute SQL Task**. The code for table truncation is as follows:

```
TRUNCATE TABLE Customer
```

When the second **Execute SQL Task** is defined, pull the green arrow from the first to the second task to connect them. The arrow leading from one task to another is called the **precedence constraint** and it is green, red, or blue. The green arrow says that the following task will be executed only when preceding tasks will finish successfully. The red arrow means that the follower will be executed if the preceding tasks fail, while the blue arrow means that the following task will be executed without evaluating the preceding task's result. Alright, now let's compare the current state of our development with the following screenshot:

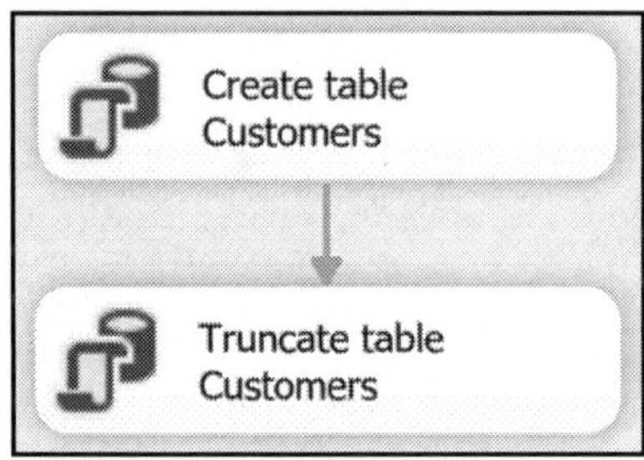

14. Maybe names vary, but generally we should have two Execute SQL Tasks connected by a green arrow. This screenshot looks fine, but is it working? We can test this, and we should also test our work during development. We can simply execute the package on which we are currently focused. On the main toolbox at the top of the image is a **Start** button. When we click on this, all tasks will be executed. If everything is correct, the control flow will look like the following screenshot:

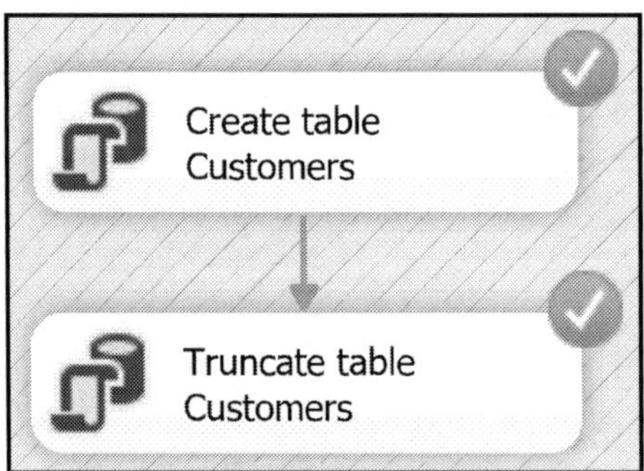

15. If both tasks are marked with the green icon in the upper-right corner, this means that tasks are working properly. Otherwise, a red icon will appear instead of the green one and an error message will also appear on the package designer's surface. In both cases, we must stop the package using the **Stop** button on the top menu.

The first two points of our assignment are successfully completed. Now let's use the simple data flow task to complete the sample. The data flow task itself is probably the most important task in SSIS. When this task is executed within a package execution, the execution context is switched from control flow to the data flow. Every data flow task is defined by a set of transformations, from extraction to load. In other words, every data flow task must start by extracting data from the defined source, then transformations may occur. The last step of the data flow task is to load data to the destination. In our sample, we will read data from CSV and load it into a database table as a destination.

To do this, drag **Data Flow Task** from the **SSIS Toolbox** on to the surface and connect it to **Truncate table Customers** using the green precedence constraint from **Execute SQL Task.** Now double-click the **Execute SQL Task** option. The surface will switch tabs from **Control Flow** to **Data Flow**, and the content of **SSIS Toolbox** will also change. The toolbox now contains **transformations** only. Every transformation has input, which is transformed to output. The only exceptions to this are sources and destinations. Sources are transformations that read data from a defined data source. The source then transforms data into first output to following transformations. Destination is doing almost the same thing, but in opposite way: it takes data on its input and then loads it into the destination data storage.

In the **SSIS Toolbox** tab in **Data Flow Task**, there are also two assistants: **Source Assistant** and **Destination Assistant**. Both assistants are actually very simple wizards that help us to define the source and destination connection for common data storages such as SQL Server and flat files.

When defining a data flow task, we must switch from source to destination. For this reason, the first thing to do is to double-click the **Source Assistant** option and follow its instructions (create new, select source file, review column, and row delimiters). We will then do the same for destination. When both source and destination are created, we will join them with an arrow leading from the source.

The result of these are shown in the following screenshot:

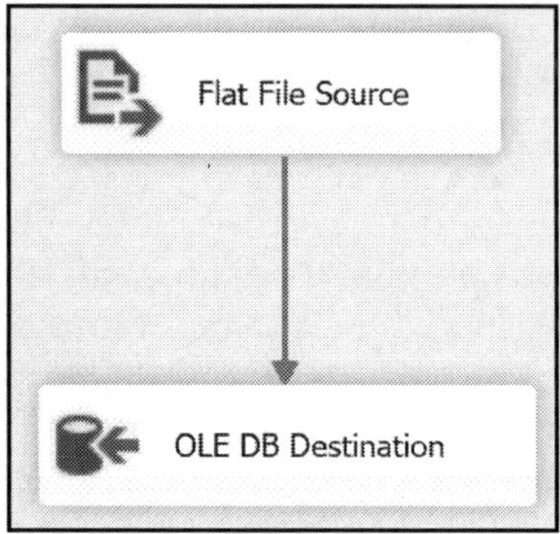

The preceding screenshot shows the simplest possible data flow with zero transformations. We can use all transformations provided by the toolbox, but explaining all of these is not the purpose of this book.

Now that the assignment is almost done, the final and most important thing to do is to test the package. We must not forget to execute the package one more time and then review the content of the destination table customers in Management Studio. If records from the CSV file are displayed, then we have succeeded!

Where should SSIS be used?

The most obvious answer to this question is that we need to transform data everywhere. However, it's not as simple as this. We can also ask ourselves where we should not use SSIS. Many transformations can be created using SSIS transformations as well as with T-SQL queries and transactions. When incoming data is relational, a T-SQL approach is often more readable and also more efficient than its SSIS equivalents. However, when data comes from non-relational sources, SSIS should be a better option.

The second most useful scenario is to not use SSIS as the main component when performing data transformations, but rather to use it to control the more complex data processing and transformations created by queries and stored procedures.

When an SSIS solution is created, it is deployed and managed by the Integration Services Catalog. The Integration Services Catalog is a database created in **Management Studio**. This database then holds all definitions created in SSIS solutions, and also provides great diagnostics and logging options through **Integration Services Dashboard**. It is also accessible in **Management Studio**.

SSIS supports two options for deployment. The older option is called **Package Deployment Model** (**PDM**). In this deployment model, SSIS solutions are deployed by isolated packages. This option does not provide centralized management, logging, diagnostics, and configuration. That's why only the **Project Deployment Model** (**PDM**) introduced with SQL Server 2012 is described in the book.

Let's go through the Integration Services Catalog configuration. The following screenshot demonstrates where to start creating **Integration Services Catalog** in **Object Explorer**:

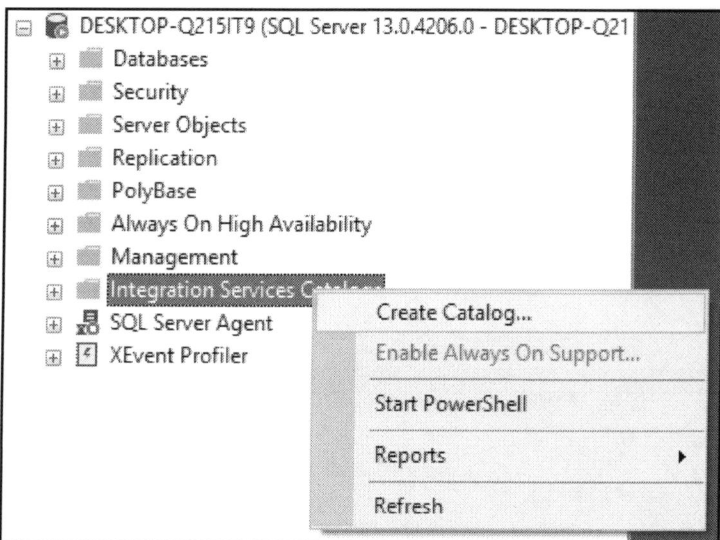

As shown in the preceding screenshot, **Object Explorer** contains node called **Integration Services Catalogs**. Right-clicking on this node brings up the popup menu. The first option, **Create Catalog...**, opens a window for creating an integration catalog. The following screenshot shows this window:

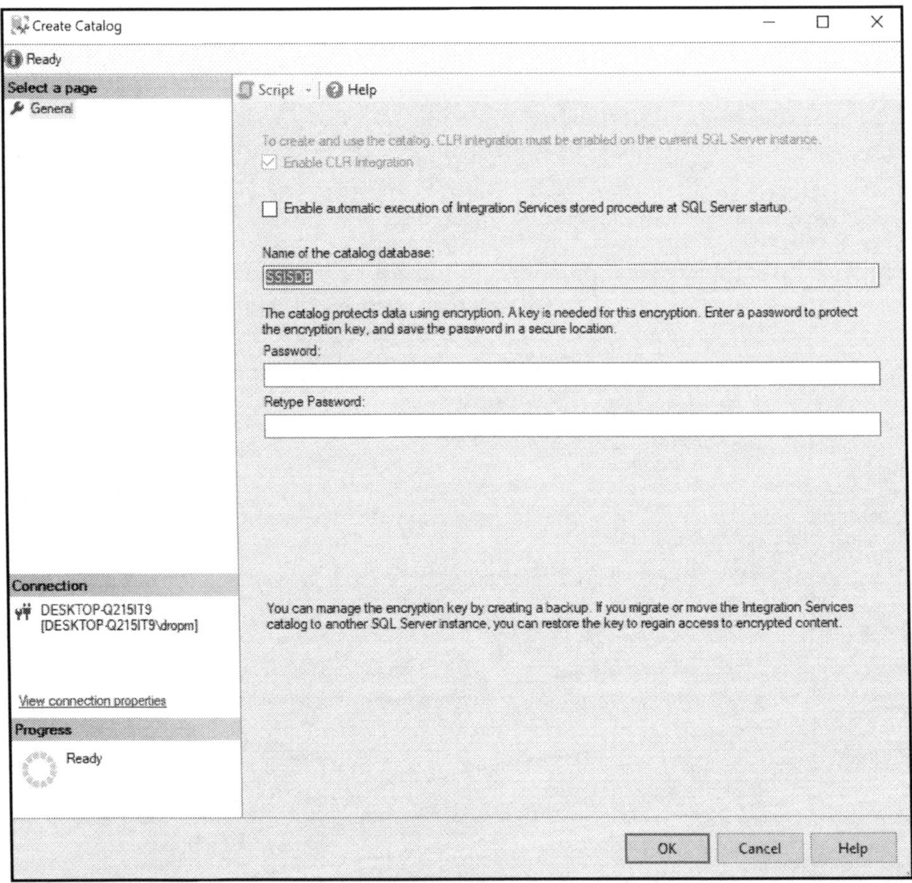

The only property that has to be set in the dialog shown in the preceding screenshot is **Password**. The password is used to encrypt sensitive data such as passwords or other sensitive values stored in the catalog. When you click **OK**, a new database called **SSISDB** will be created. This database appears in a list of all other user databases on the instance of SQL Server.

When the Integration Services Catalog is created, we should open the **Integration Services Catalog** node in **Object Explorer**. Here, we will only see the nested node, **SSISDB**. By right-clicking on the node, we should be able to create at least one folder for our projects. Under the **Reports** option in the same popup, we can find the **Integration Services Dashboard** report as well. Full pop-up content is shown in the following screenshot:

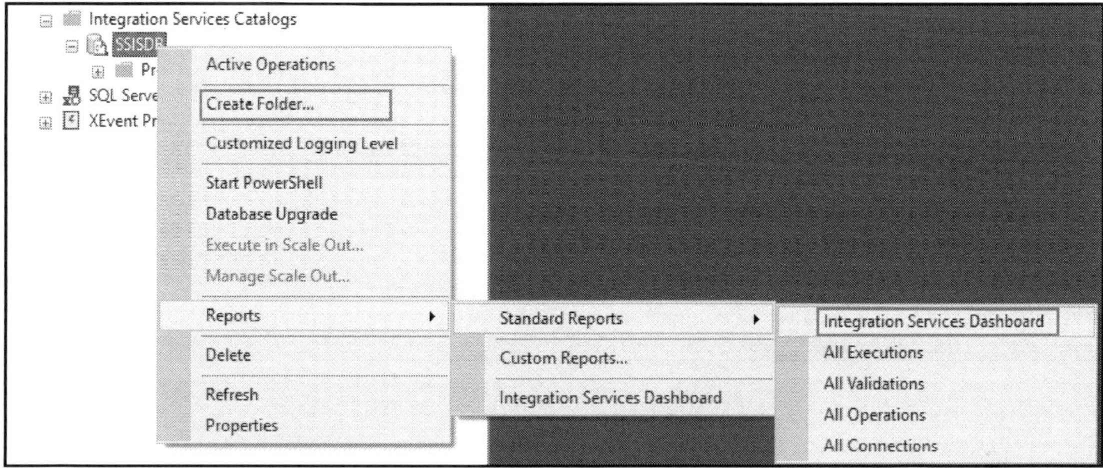

Both options described in the previous paragraph are marked with red rectangles on the preceding screenshot.

Is there an alternative to SSIS?

SSIS is not the only option when it comes to extracting data from sources, transforming it, and loading it to targets. As cloud environments such as Azure are used more and more over time, we face a challenge: how to work with data saved partially in cloud and partially on-premises. For this case, we have cloud services such as **Data Factory** or **Stream Analytics**, which are designed to get data from one cloud storage to another, or to move data between cloud and on-premises environments. However, using these services is beyond the scope of the book.

This section explained options and tools used for data movement, but data also needs to be transformed. In the next section, we will show that data can be transformed using T-SQL queries.

Transforming data

Data transformations refer to the infinite list of changes made on the data to reach its desired format. A lot of transformations can be done through simple expressions in queries, but there are also many challenges that are more complicated than these simple expressions. In this section, we will learn how to read data fully or incrementally, how to deduplicate data, and how to do data quality checks.

The first kind of transformation is often to recognize which data was loaded previously, if any. In the first section of this topic, we will learn how to load data fully or incrementally.

Full data load

Full data load means that every dataset extracted from the data source is fully loaded into the landing or staging table. The process of full load has two variants. The first variant consists of the following steps:

1. Content of landing or staging table is deleted or truncated
2. Full dataset is extracted using SSIS or distributed query
3. Extracted dataset is inserted into the table

Let's pay special attention to this list. In the first point, it is stated that the content of the table is deleted or truncated. Let's have a table simply named `Landing.Products`. This table contains the `ProductKey`, `ProductName`, and `ListPrice` columns. The table is placed in a database called `DemoCust`, created in an earlier example. Let's create this table first. We will create two identical tables called `Landing.Products` and `Landing.Products2`. This is because the following example code will compare the performance of two options used for data loading and data erasing. The code for the table creation is as follows:

```
USE DemoCust
go

CREATE SCHEMA Landing AUTHORIZATION dbo
go

CREATE TABLE Landing.Products
(
ProductKey int not null
, ProductName nvarchar(50) not null
, ListPrice dec(8, 2) not null
)
```

```
CREATE TABLE Landing.Products2
(
ProductKey int not null
, ProductName nvarchar(50) not null
, ListPrice dec(8,2) not null
)
go
```

In the previous code schema, `Landing` is created first and then the new `Products` tables are placed into it. Notice that the tables do not have any constraints. This is because the only purpose of landing tables is to store data in its original state without (almost) any checks. In our example, some basic data reliability is defined according to the exact data types and mandatory of columns (the `not null` property of each column). Sometimes, the content in incoming data is too weak, and then every column is designated as some `nvarchar` data type without mandatory, even though it might be described as a unique integer in the supplier's documentation, for example. When the tables are successfully created, we can add data to them. In our example, the simplest way to do this is to generate an estimate of 200,000 random records in a cycle.

Before the following code is executed, let's turn on **Client Statistics**, the Management Studio feature. This is a very nice feature in Management Studio, which can be used for comparing the performance of executed queries. Client statistics can be turned on using the *Shift* + *Alt* + *S* shortcut, or with an icon in the Management Studio toolbar.

The first execution of record generation is as follows:

```
declare @i int = 1
while @i <= 200000
 begin
  insert Landing.Products (ProductKey, ProductName, ListPrice)
  values (@i, 'Product ' + cast(@i as nvarchar), RAND() * 1000)
  set @i += 1
 end
```

The preceding code iterated 200,000 times to generate records to the `Landing.Products` table on a row-by-row basis. Now, in the same query window, let's populate the `Landing.Products2` table. This table will also be filled in with 200,000 records. However, the statement used for the population is `BULK INSERT` using a flat file as a data source for the same data. The full statement is as follows:

```
BULK INSERT Landing.Products2
FROM 'C:\SQLDS\CSVs\products.csv'
WITH
(
FIELDTERMINATOR =';',
```

```
ROWTERMINATOR = '\n',
FIRSTROW = 2
)
```

The `BULK INSERT` statement in the preceding code sample reads data from a file placed on the `C:\SQLDS\CSVs\products.csv` path. Other parameters added to the `WITH` clause describe field and row terminators. The last `FIRSTROW` parameter says that the data population should start from the second row in the file, because the first row is a header.

When both preceding statements are successfully executed, it's time to explore the client statistics. The following screenshot shows how client statistics are seen in Management Studio:

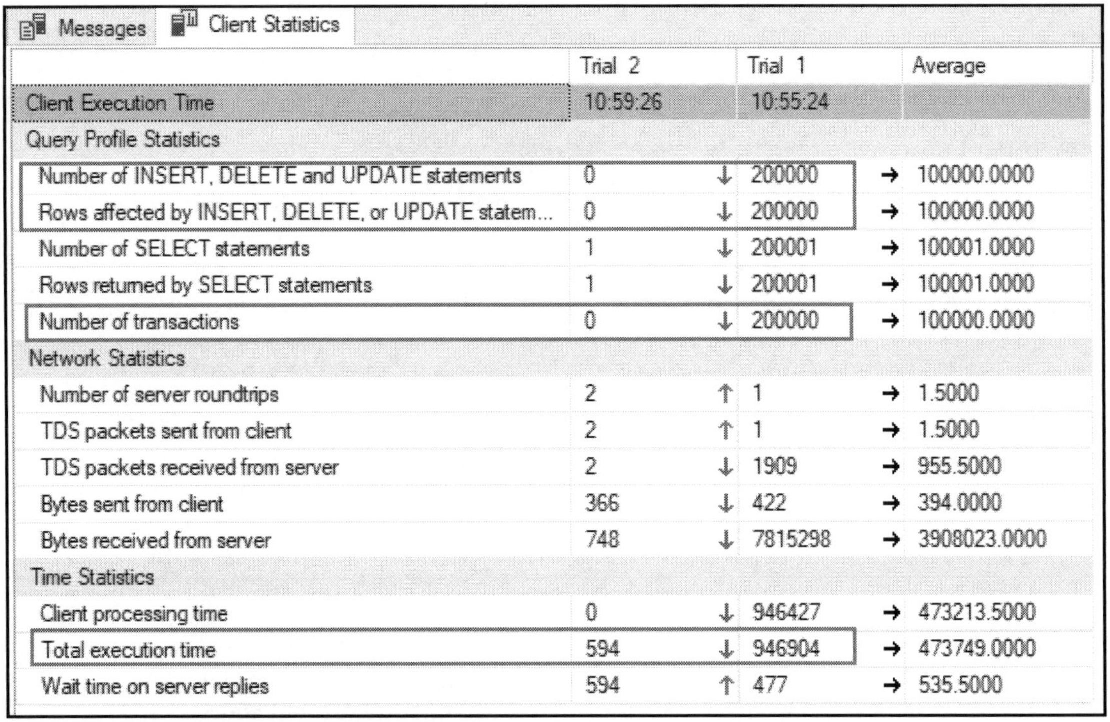

Messages | Client Statistics

	Trial 2		Trial 1		Average
Client Execution Time	10:59:26		10:55:24		
Query Profile Statistics					
Number of INSERT, DELETE and UPDATE statements	0	↓	200000	→	100000.0000
Rows affected by INSERT, DELETE, or UPDATE statem...	0	↓	200000	→	100000.0000
Number of SELECT statements	1	↓	200001	→	100001.0000
Rows returned by SELECT statements	1	↓	200001	→	100001.0000
Number of transactions	0	↓	200000	→	100000.0000
Network Statistics					
Number of server roundtrips	2	↑	1	→	1.5000
TDS packets sent from client	2	↑	1	→	1.5000
TDS packets received from server	2	↓	1909	→	955.5000
Bytes sent from client	366	↓	422	→	394.0000
Bytes received from server	748	↓	7815298	→	3908023.0000
Time Statistics					
Client processing time	0	↓	946427	→	473213.5000
Total execution time	594	↓	946904	→	473749.0000
Wait time on server replies	594	↑	477	→	535.5000

Client statistics show several measures that are useful for performance tuning. Every attempt to run a query is caught as a **Trial #.** Every column with the trial header is an executed statement or, in other words, a new attempt. Columns with statement metrics are ordered from right to left, so the preceding screenshot has statistics of the first `INSERT` attempt in the `Trial 1` column and the result of the `BULK INSERT` is in the `Trial 2` column.

Let's take a look at the highlighted rows in the screenshot. The last row shows the statement's execution time in milliseconds, and there is a big difference between `INSERT` and `BULK INSERT`, which performs much better. This is well known, but why exactly is `BULK INSERT` so efficient? The answer to this is shown in the rest of the highlighted rows in the screenshot. The number of `INSERT` statements is 200,000 in the `INSERT` case (column `Trial 1`), but 0 (zero) for the `BULK INSERT` case. The same is true for the number of transactions. This example shows that the `BULK INSERT` statements do not issue a transaction; they are logged very little and also do not work as the `INSERT` statements. However, when the `BULK INSERT` statement is running, SQL Server allocates new data pages directly populated with sections of records from the source file.

The preceding paragraphs show that we should not use the `INSERT .. VALUES` statements when they are not needed, and also that populating data using a `BULK INSERT` statement is a very efficient method to use when possible.

Up until this point, this section has shown ways to insert data into tables with different performance impacts. Now let's go through the following example code, which shows the same for data deletion before the data is inserted. We will delete data from the previously created and populated tables: `Landing.Products` and `Landing.Products2`.

Simple deletion is written in the following code. Before we execute this, let's turn on client statistics again as follows:

```
DELETE Landing.Products
```

In the same query window where the deletion was executed, let's execute a second statement using a duplicated table, but with the `TRUNCATE TABLE` statement. The code for truncation is as follows:

```
TRUNCATE TABLE Landing.Products2
```

It's now time to compare both executed statements using client statistics. In the result section of the query window, switch on the **Client Statistics** tab. It is possible that the total execution time in client statistics will be shown as having a 10 times better performance for the `TRUNCATE TABLE` statement. This is because the `TRUNCATE TABLE` statement is not a transaction; the SQL Server just misses allocated data pages when executing this statement. This way of working saves the resources needed to empty landing tables without the need to drop them completely arising. The `TRUNCATE TABLE` statement is eligible simply for full load scenarios because it does not support options such as the `WHERE` clause or the `JOIN` operator that delete records conditionally. Furthermore, existing foreign keys do not make it possible to use the `TRUNCATE TABLE` statement. These limitations must be considered when we are thinking about using the `TRUNCATE TABLE` statement.

The second variant of the full data load adds extra steps on the top of previous variants. This variant is typically used in cases when incoming data doesn't have a stable structure. This variant is described in the following list:

- The landing (not staging) table is dropped, if it exists
- The full data set is extracted using SSIS, distributed query, or proprietary application
- The landing table is created accordingly with the structure of the incoming extracted dataset
- The full dataset is inserted into the table

This is a better method to use when the incoming data has volatile structures that change rapidly. However, this approach usually needs extra programming efforts from T-SQL to create landing tables accordingly with the current schema of the incoming data.

The full data-load scenario is reliable because it eliminates the risk of duplication. However, for large, incoming data, it's almost impossible to keep a time frame dedicated to loads. This is why we need to find a more efficient way of data landing/staging. The following section will describe the incremental scenarios in a data load.

Incremental data load

The previous section was about how to fully load data. This approach is generally useful for landing part of our data transformation tasks. Once data is loaded into a landing database or a landing schema, we have our data in a homogeneous SQL Server environment. As it is a good approach to be able to detect changes and to work with changed data only, we profit from the homogeneous environment. This is why we are talking about **incremental loads**. In this section, we will discuss several of the techniques of incremental loads, namely the `MERGE` statement, using checksums, high-watermark, and temporal tables. There is no better or worse option; each scenario discussed here applies to different situations.

The MERGE statement

Let's show the `MERGE` statement in the following example. We will still use the `Landing.Products` table populated in the previous section. We also will create a new `Staging` schema and insert the schema into a new table, named `Staging.Products`.

If the table is empty as a result of the experiments truncating it, just populate it once again.

Let's start to create the staging table. This will be better normalized and it will also include one new column called `Discontinued`. The following code shows its creation:

```
USE DemoCust
go

CREATE SCHEMA Staging AUTHORIZATION dbo
go

CREATE TABLE Staging.Products
(
Id int not null IDENTITY
, ProductKey int not null
, ProductName nvarchar(50) not null
, ListPrice dec(8, 2) not null
, Discontinued bit not null CONSTRAINT df_Products_Discontinued DEFAULT(0)
, CONSTRAINT pk_Products PRIMARY KEY (Id)
, CONSTRAINT uq_Products_ProductKey UNIQUE (ProductKey)
)
go
```

Let's analyze the `Staging.Products` table briefly. The three columns such as `ProductKey`, `ProductName`, and `ListPrice` remain the same as in the `Landing.Products` table. This is because they keep the business values of each record. Some of the following new columns were also added:

- `Id`: This is an autogenerated primary key value. In this case, the question may arise, why is the `ProductKey` column not used as a primary key. There are several answers for this:
    - Because values in `ProductKey` may be `NULL`
    - Because values in `ProductKey` may not be unique
    - Because values in `ProductKey` may change from the source
    - Because previous situations were combined
- `Discontinued`: This column is set to `1` when a certain record from the source data disappears. We could delete such records in the staging table, but in some situations, it's better to use so-called **logical delete,** marking the record as inactive or `Discontinued`, as seen in the previous example.

As well as the new columns, the staging table is also more strict. This means that constraints are used to enforce basic data quality.

We are now handling the following three situations:

- Record exists in the source table (`Landing.Products`), but records of the same product do not exist in the target table (`Staging.Products`). Such records are inserted into the target table.
- Record exists in both tables, but something was changed in it. Such records will be updated with values from the source table.
- Records do not exist in the source table, but they already exist in target table. This record could be deleted in the target table, or it could be marked as `Discontinued`.

We can write three statements: one for insert, one for update, and one for logical or actual delete. However, we can do the same thing using the `MERGE` statement. The `MERGE` statement suggests what to do with every record. This operation is set-based, and every record is affected just once. This is why the `MERGE` statement often performs better than three isolated the `INSERT`, `UPDATE`, and `DELETE` statements. Let's use the `MERGE` statement in our example.

The following script shows how the statement looks:

```
MERGE Staging.Products AS sp
USING Landing.Products AS lp
  ON sp.ProductKey = lp.ProductKey
WHEN MATCHED THEN
  UPDATE SET
    ProductName = lp.ProductName
    , ListPrice = lp.ListPrice
    , Discontinued = 0
WHEN NOT MATCHED BY TARGET THEN
  INSERT (ProductKey, ProductName, ListPrice)
  VALUES (lp.ProductKey, lp.ProductName, lp.ListPrice)
WHEN NOT MATCHED BY SOURCE THEN
  UPDATE SET Discontinued = 1   -- this is a logical delete
                                -- when we want actual delete,
                                -- we'll just write DELETE
;
```

The preceding statement can be divided into two parts. The first part is a declaration of what will be modified and which data source will be used. What needs to be modified is set in the `MERGE` clause (the first row in the preceding code). The source set of data from which the modification is done is set in the `USING` clause (the second row in our example). Source and target data must have common values, because the `MERGE` statement needs to recognize which source record belongs to a certain target record. That's why the `ON` clause (which is very similar to `ON` part of `JOIN` operator) defines which columns source and target data are connected.

The second part of the `MERGE` statement defines what has to be done when:

- Record with the same join criteria exists in both source and target (the `WHEN MATCHED` part)
- Record exists in source, but not in target data (`WHEN NOT MATCHED BY TARGET` part)
- Record exists in target, but it no longer exists in the source (`WHEN NOT MATCHED BY SOURCE` part)

We can have more than three nodes of resolution if we need to. This is because every `WHEN` part is nothing more than a condition, and conditions can be combined. For example, let's only restrict access to records that have not yet been discontinued. If we need to, we can enhance a certain part of this `WHEN` condition: `WHEN MATCHED AND Discontinued = 0 THEN`. When working with more nodes in the `MERGE` statement, we must consider the fact that every target record must be met only once—otherwise, the statement is terminated.

Let's execute the MERGE statement for the first time. When it's executed, we can observe that 200,000 new records were inserted into the Staging.Products table. We can also see that the operation was fast. Now let's make some changes to the landing data. The following script does this for us:

```
delete Landing.Products where ProductKey between 20000 and 30000
update Landing.Products set ListPrice = 100000 where ProductKey between
50000 and 55000
insert Landing.Products (ProductKey, ProductName, ListPrice)
values (500000, 'Product half-of-million', 4.25)
```

The preceding code consists of three statements. The first statement deletes some records, the second one updates the price for some products, and the last one creates new record. We could execute the MERGE statement again, but before we do this, let's ask ourselves a question: can we track what was changed by the MERGE statement? The answer to this is yes; we have one special function called $.action, which is able to do this. The following code demonstrates the simple case of the $action function usage:

```
MERGE Staging.Products AS sp
USING Landing.Products AS lp
  ON sp.ProductKey = lp.ProductKey
WHEN MATCHED THEN
  UPDATE SET
    ProductName = lp.ProductName
    , ListPrice = lp.ListPrice
    , Discontinued = 0
WHEN NOT MATCHED BY TARGET THEN
  INSERT (ProductKey, ProductName, ListPrice)
  VALUES (lp.ProductKey, lp.ProductName, lp.ListPrice)
WHEN NOT MATCHED BY SOURCE THEN
  UPDATE SET Discontinued = 1 -- this is a logical delete
                              -- when we want actual delete,
                              -- we'll just write DELETE
OUTPUT inserted.Id, inserted.Discontinued, $action AS WhatHappens
;
```

When the preceding statement is executed, we will see a result set. This is because the last row with OUTPUT in the script was added. In the OUTPUT clause, we can work with inserted and deleted structures. These structures are usually known as **temporary tables**, and they are used in triggers. Both structures have the same schema as the target table. The inserted structure contains newly inserted records and new values of updated records, while the deleted structure contains deleted records as well as old values of updated records.

The result of the `OUTPUT` clause can be caught into a table by using the `INTO` clause. The following script shows how to use the `OUTPUT` clause:

```
CREATE TABLE #changes (Id int, Discontinued bit, WhatHappens nvarchar(10))
MERGE ...
OUTPUT inserted.Id, inserted.Discontinued, $action as WhatHappens INTO
#changes
;
```

The preceding piece of code was shortened because the rest of the `MERGE` statement remains the same.

When exploring the result set, we can see that every record existing in both tables is updated, even if it was not changed. This seems to be inefficient, which is why we would use another technique to decide which record was actually changed, and which remained the same. To do this, we can use `CHECKSUM`.

CHECKSUM

`CHECKSUM` is a integer-value computing function against its parameter. The result value is unique for incoming parameters. The following query shows how the `CHECKSUM` function reflects a parameter's value:

```
SELECT CHECKSUM('hello')        -- 533340124
   , CHECKSUM('Hello')          -- 533340124
   , CHECKSUM('olleh')          -- 1600790340
   , CHECKSUM('hloel')          -- 1606885152
```

This simple query shows that even if letters in a parameter of the function are the same, every change is reflected in the value produced by the function. Values are written as comments. We can also use the `CHECKSUM` function for computing the `CHECKSUM` value for one or more columns in a table. The following code demonstrates how to use more columns as parameters for a `CHECKSUM` function:

```
SELECT ProductKey, CHECKSUM(ProductKey, ProductName, ListPrice)
FROM Staging.Products
```

The preceding query uses the same `Staging.Products` table as in the previous section. Several columns from that table are passed as a list of parameters and the checksum value is computed as a single value for a row. Let's remember that in the previous section describing the `MERGE` statement, we established that all rows are still updated even though they were not changed. Using `CHECKSUM` could solve this issue.

In following example code, we will use the same pair of `Landing.Products` and `Staging.Products` tables. First of all, let's reset the data in both tables. The following script does this for us:

```
TRUNCATE TABLE Staging.Products
TRUNCATE TABLE Landing.Products
BULK INSERT Landing.Products
FROM 'C:\SQLDS\CSVs\products.csv'
WITH
(
FIELDTERMINATOR =';',
ROWTERMINATOR = '\n',
FIRSTROW = 2
)
```

After the preceding script is executed, the `Landing.Products` table contains 200,000 new records, but the `Staging.Products` table is empty, and we must simulate the first load of data. The next step is to enhance the `MERGE` statement rapidly. The following script shows several new parts of the `MERGE`:

```
DROP TABLE IF EXISTS #res -- temporary table used to catch what was done
CREATE TABLE #res (Id int, Discontinued bit, WhatHappens nvarchar(10))

-- common table expression is added to resolve a state of every record
;WITH cte AS
(
SELECT lp.*
  , IIF(sp.ProductKey is null, 'UPDATE', 'NONE') as DesiredAction
FROM Landing.Products AS lp
  LEFT JOIN Staging.Products as sp ON lp.ProductKey = sp.ProductKey
    AND CHECKSUM(lp.ProductKey, lp.ProductName, lp.ListPrice) =
      CHECKSUM(sp.ProductKey, sp.ProductName, sp.ListPrice)
)
MERGE Staging.Products AS sp
USING cte AS lp -- Landing.Products is used no more, instead the CTE is
used
  ON sp.ProductKey = lp.ProductKey
WHEN MATCHED and DesiredAction = 'UPDATE' THEN -- new condition added
  UPDATE SET
    ProductName = lp.ProductName
```

```
    , ListPrice = lp.ListPrice
    , Discontinued = 0
WHEN NOT MATCHED BY TARGET THEN -- this node remains without changes
  INSERT (ProductKey, ProductName, ListPrice)
  VALUES (lp.ProductKey, lp.ProductName, lp.ListPrice)
WHEN NOT MATCHED BY SOURCE and sp.Discontinued = 0 THEN -- new condition
added
  UPDATE SET Discontinued = 1 -- this is a logical delete
                              -- when we want actual delete,
                              -- we'll just write DELETE
OUTPUT inserted.Id, Inserted.Discontinued, $action AS WhatHappens into #res
;

SELECT * FROM #res -- inspecting results
```

The preceding script has been changed in many of the following ways:

1. A new temporary table is created as a first step. This table will help us to inspect all changed, inserted, or logically deleted records.
2. The second but biggest change is that **common table expression** (**CTE**) can be used instead of the source table here. CTE are named queries; they are used once in the query following the CTE declaration. Under the `;WITH cte AS` block, you can try to select and execute a query written in brackets. You will see 200,000 records as a result of this (the number of records will be seen if you have freshly populated the `Landing.Products` table and emptied the `Staging.Products` table). As you can see, the `Landing.Products` and `Staging.Products` tables are joined together using `ProductKey` in both tables as well as using the result of the `CHECKSUM` function over the same columns from both tables. The `LEFT JOIN` operator is used to establish that all records from the `Landing.Products` table are returned.
3. In the `USING` clause of the `MERGE` statement, the `Landing.Products` table reference was replaced by the result of the CTE using the name of the CTE (`cte` in our case).
4. Next, in the `WHEN MATCHED` node, the additional condition `AND DesiredAction = 'UPDATE'` was added. This new condition filters records to those that are already changed.
5. A similar additional condition was also added to the `WHEN NOT MATCHED BY TARGET` node. The `sp.Discontinued = 0` condition filters out already discontinued records so that our `MERGE` statement will not repeatedly update the `Discontinued` column to `1`.

6. The final change is that the `SELECT * FROM #res` statement was added as a last row in our script. This statement returns a set of records containing the `Id` of the record from the `Staging.Products` table and the value of the `Discontinued` column in the same table. In the last column, the result of the `$action` function is returned.

When we execute the whole preceding script the first time (when the `Landing.Products` table has 200,000 rows and `Staging.Products` is empty), inspecting query will return 200,000 records with new IDs and the result of the `$action` function will be `INSERT`.

Now let's make some changes to the `Landing.Products` table. The following script emulates some deleted records, some changed records, and some new records coming into the `Landing.Products` table:

```
delete Landing.Products where ProductKey between 20000 and 30000
update Landing.Products set ListPrice = 100000 where ProductKey between
50000 and 55000
insert Landing.Products (ProductKey, ProductName, ListPrice)
values (500000, 'Product half-of-million', 4.25)
```

Now, when the preceding script was executed, the whole `MERGE` statement was executed once again. When we do it, we can add one more simple inspecting query to see how many records were added (there should be one), how many records were updated and not discontinued (there should be 5,000), and how many records were logically deleted (there should be 10,001). This inspecting query is shown as follows:

```
select WhatHappens, Discontinued, count(*) as EventCount
from #res
group by WhatHappens, Discontinued
```

The preceding query will provide a very simple record set that shows exactly what was done during the `MERGE` statement.

Using `MERGE` is a very helpful technique for adjusting data from a source dataset to a target table. This section demonstrated how to use `MERGE` in conjunction with the `CHECKSUM` function. In the next section, we will explore another technique for recognizing the changes between two loads using temporal tables.

Temporal tables

Over the years, Microsoft has offered many features for tracking data changes. You may remember **Change Data Capture** or **Change Tracking**. Starting at SQL Server 2016, Microsoft provides a new powerful feature called **temporal tables**. Temporal tables are regular tables that are used for any desired data contention, but such tables are also supported by read-only tables that catch every change made in the source table. A big benefit of this is that creating temporal tables is transparent to applications.

The following example code shows how to create temporal tables. Let's use the `Src.Products` table. This table has the same structure as in previous samples, but it also works for end users of source business applications. Let's create the table using the following script:

```
USE DemoCust
GO

CREATE SCHEMA Src AUTHORIZATION dbo

CREATE TABLE Src.Products
(
ProductKey int not null identity
, ProductName nvarchar(50) not null
, ListPrice dec(8, 2) not null
, CONSTRAINT pk_Products PRIMARY KEY (ProductKey)
)
GO
```

The table created by the preceding script is not a temporal table. However, it is a regular table that may have been working in the same source database over the past few years. But how can we make it temporal? To do this, we need to perform two steps. The first step is to add two extra columns to the source table because SQL Server tracks the validity of the record, using two time values such as `valid from` and `valid to`. The following script alters the `Src.Products` table to enable its data versioning:

```
ALTER TABLE Src.Products ADD
ValidFrom datetime2 generated always as row start
, ValidTo datetime2 generated always as row end
, PERIOD FOR SYSTEM_TIME (ValidFrom, ValidTo)
```

The preceding script does not begin the versioning itself, it just adds two columns of whatever name and the `PERIOD FOR SYSTEM_TIME` clause says which two columns will be used for versioning. To start system versioning, we need to set options for the table in which we wish to capture changes. The following script sets the temporal table for `Src.Products`:

```
ALTER TABLE Src.Products
SET(SYSTEM_VERSIONING = ON (HISTORY_TABLE = Src.ProductsHistory))
```

The preceding script turns the system versioning on and also gives a name to the historical read-only table (`Src.ProductHistory` in our case).

Now let's see what is done when DML operations are issued against the table. The following script inserts one record every ten seconds, then the data from both tables are selected, to inspect what was done:

```
INSERT Src.Products (ProductName, ListPrice)
VALUES ('My first product', 100)
WAITFOR DELAY '00:00:10'
INSERT Src.Products (ProductName, ListPrice)
VALUES ('My second product', 110)
WAITFOR DELAY '00:00:10'
INSERT Src.Products (ProductName, ListPrice)
VALUES ('My third product', 10)

SELECT * FROM Src.Products
SELECT * FROM Src.ProductsHistory
```

As a result of the preceding query, we have three records in the `Src.Products` table and no records in the `Src.ProductsHistory` table. We can also see that the `ValidFrom` column is populated with time of record insertion, and the `ValidTo` column has a value of max date. Now let's update the second record. The following script executes a simple update as well as renaming a second product and its price:

```
UPDATE Src.Products
SET ProductName = 'Product 2A', ListPrice = 0.25
WHERE ProductKey = 2

SELECT * FROM Src.Products
SELECT * FROM Src.ProductsHistory
```

When the preceding script is executed, we will see two result sets. The first is from a current table and the second is from the historical table. As we can see, updated record is moved to the historical table before it is updated. In the historical `ValidTo` table, the value is the same as the `ValidFrom` value of the changed record in the current table. So, what about deletion? The following simple delete method removes one record from the current table and shows the state of the data in both tables:

```
DELETE Src.Products WHERE ProductKey = 3

SELECT * FROM Src.Products
SELECT * FROM Src.ProductsHistory
```

When the preceding script is executed, the record is deleted from the current table but its last version is added to the temporal table.

In a few previous examples, we explored the behavior and functionality of temporal tables. This feature could help us to seamlessly track data changes to client applications. Tracking data changes using temporal tables greatly helps in many business intelligence cases, but for data landing/staging purposes, we only need to use a quite simple technique called **high watermark**. High watermark is a procedure that works according to the following steps:

1. A configuration table is created to keep the date and time of last load.
2. When a data load is starting, the last saved date and time value is read from the configuration table:
    - If the date and the time are null, a full load is issued
    - If the date and the time are not null, only changes made from the date and the time are selected
3. The current date and time are caught and saved back to the configuration table.

Using the high watermark concept does not require temporal tables. Instead, it works against any suitable column such as `Last_Changed` in source tables, but temporal tables not only enable us to read the previous state of data, but to keep all changes within a certain time frame.

Let's look at a high watermark sample. First of all, we need to create a table that saves the date and time of last data load via the following script:

```
USE DemoCust
go

CREATE SCHEMA Config AUTHORIZATION dbo

CREATE TABLE Config.HighWatermark
(
```

```
TableName nvarchar(255) not null CONSTRAINT pk_HighWatermark PRIMARY KEY
, LastLoad datetime2 null
)
INSERT Config.HighWatermark (TableName) VALUES ('Src.Products')
```

The previous script creates schema `Config` for eventual future configuration tables. The script then creates a table called `Config.HighWatermark`. This table is designed for many tables which contains data that will be loaded depending on its changes. The first row is inserted for our `Src.Products` table. Now let's restart the `Landing.Products` and `Staging.Products` tables using the `TRUNCATE TABLE` statements. This is done in the following script:

```
TRUNCATE TABLE Landing.Products
TRUNCATE TABLE Staging.Products
```

Our landing and staging areas are clear, and now we can execute script using the first full load. The script for loading data is shown next:

```
TRUNCATE TABLE Landing.Products

DECLARE @start datetime2 =
  (SELECT LastLoad FROM Config.HighWatermark WHERE TableName =
'Src.Products')
DECLARE @end datetime2 = SYSUTCDATETIME()

INSERT Landing.Products (ProductKey, ProductName, ListPrice)
SELECT ProductKey, ProductName, ListPrice
FROM Src.Products
WHERE @start <= ValidFrom OR @start IS NULL

UPDATE Config.HighWatermark SET LastLoad = @end WHERE TableName =
'Src.Products'
```

The preceding script works in four parts. The first statement just clears the landing table's content, while the second part declares two variables. Furthermore, the `@start` variable is initiated by the time of the last previous load, and the `@end` variable is initiated by the current date and time in the `datetime2` data type. In the third part of the preceding script, records changed from the last load are inserted into the `Landing.Products` table. The last statement saves the `@end` time back to the configuration table.

When the script is completed and executed, we can execute the last `MERGE` statement from previous section and inspect the content of the `Staging.Products` table. By doing this, we should see two records.

As we are extracting only changed data to our `Landing.Products` table, we must consider not using the `WHEN NOT MATCHED BY SOURCE` node in our `MERGE` statement. This is due to the fact that pre-existing records are not inserted into the `Landing.Products` table.

When users make some more changes to our source table, the only changed data will be inserted into the landing table during each future execution of the previous example.

When we don't want to track the changes anymore, we'll just execute the following script:

```
ALTER TABLE Src.Products
SET(SYSTEM_VERSIONING = OFF)
```

Executing the preceding script does not remove the historical table; both tables are disconnected only, and they act as two independent read-write tables.

This section was a guide for data extraction and loads. Data that comes from different sources is often extracted without many changes, but for data scientific purposes, we need to transform data to the form of a dataset with meaningful values only. The next section provides an overview of transformation known as **selective denormalization**.

Denormalizing data

Data denormalization is the process of adjusting data from a structure that is better for transactional processing to a structure that is better for reporting or data science purposes. This section provides a brief overview of data normalization and looks at why we denormalize, what we denormalize, and how to denormalize.

Relational normalization

In relational databases, data should be saved in so-called normalized structures. The normalization of data structures is a process that discovers the best structure that is resistant against any uncertainties in data, user change requests, and so on. The normalization itself is controlled by a set of rules known as **normal forms**.

Every normal form describes how to adjust structure design to reach a degree of normalization. Furthermore, a higher degree can only be reached when all previous degrees of normal forms are reached already. Let's go through the first three most-used normal forms and show how every normal form works using examples.

First normal form

The first normal form (1NF) says that every attribute (column) in a relation (table record) is **atomic**. The atomicity of an attribute means that the value in the column is not divisible into simpler values. Let's take the example of a human name.

Names often consist of a first name, a last name and maybe a middle initial. If the name is saved in the form of Paul X White, it does not fulfill the 1NF. However, the division into three attributes makes it normalized in a 1NF.

Second normal form

The **second normal form** (**2NF**) says that the relation is in 1NF and every non-key attribute fully depends on every candidate key. This term needs some explanation. First of all, what is a **candidate key**? A candidate key is an attribute or combination of more attributes that uniquely identify the whole relation (record). Let's take a simple example of this.

We have a list of people attending an event. The list contains names, SIDs, and member numbers of every attendee. We have to ask the question of which attributes are suitable for uniquely identifying every single attendee. Two options are possible in our case: SID and member number. Theoretically, we can think about a combination of both columns, but the candidate key should be the smallest unique combination of attributes. We should also consider adding one more attribute, known as the surrogate key. This is an attribute that is meaningless to users. Usually, the attribute is auto generated and is often a whole number, which is very efficient for filtering or joining. If you are thinking about an `ID` column with the `IDENTITY` property now, then you are completely right!

Let's imagine that there are three candidates now: SID, member number, and surrogate ID. One of them will be a constraint called `primary key`. Primary key is a constraint enforcing the uniqueness of records added to a table. It's very uncommon to have tables without primary keys. The only reason to have such tables could be in landing databases, but it always needs additional checks.

Now we know what the 2NF is. Let's evaluate whether this is true for our example. Let's say we have an attendee with SID as `986532653734`, member number as 123, and his name is `John Doe`. Is the surname `Doe` a good attribute for unique identification? Actually, it's not, because Doe's whole family could attend our event using this as identification. So, is it his first name? Definitely not! This means that the unique identification is the SID. So, when we query the table, that is `SELECT * FROM myTable WHERE SID = 986532653734` or `SELECT * FROM myTable WHERE member number = 123`, it will return up to one record with no exceptions.

Attributes that are meaningful for users are often not the best candidates for primary keys. This is because when a user adds data manually, there's a risk of typos or other mistakes which lead to required value changes. This causes trouble for developers who must change the value everywhere it's used for foreign keys. That's why it's good practice to use surrogate keys that are meaningless to users.

Third normal form

The **third normal form** (**3NF**) states that non-key attributes fully depend on the primary key, but they are also independent of one another. Let's explore how this works.

Let's take an entity with purchase order details. The entity contains attributes that define the purchased product as well as attributes such as `Unit price`, `Quantity`, and `Total price`. We can say that the `Total price` attribute is just `Unit price` multiplied by `Quantity`. In other words, saving `Total price` is useless because we can compute it from other attributes, so `Total price` depends on other attributes.

Our previous example is very simple. If we will have real ordering database, we also need to take things such as sales tax or other fees into account. This leads to rounding of computation results. It's often better to compute and save values that contain rounding, because when it's used later (for example in reports), then the author of the report could round differently, and this could lead to inaccurate values.

To reach normal forms, an operation called **decomposition** is often required. Decomposition is just a division of one entity or more (usually two) new entities. Let's take an entity with a list of people and dogs. One person could have more than one dog, so we need to create two separate entities: one for people and a second for dogs. To ensure that we do not miss the information on which dog belongs to who, we need to maintain a relationship between the person and their dogs with a constraint called `foreign key`. Foreign key is a constraint that enforces the relationship between the master record and its slave records. It's created using the primary key value from the master table and the primary key's value inherited as a new attribute to a slave table.

When data structure is normalized correctly, we will never lose any information. We can use joins to establish who a dog belongs to, or to establish in which order records belong to certain customers. So, why do we need denormalization?

Need for denormalization

When we are creating a database, we should normalize its design every time to ensure that our data will be accurate in every circumstance. However, normalized data often needs many joins and other operations to project information to user. When the database is used for transactional processing, a higher degree of normalization is usually required. But when the database is used as a data storage for business intelligence applications or for analytical purposes, such database has many operations such as aggregates or long scans, and adding extra contention to an analytical database using many expressions or joins could lead to inefficient work. This is why we need to denormalize some sections of the database. The denormalization helps to achieve better efficiency of reports or data cube processing.

When we decide that denormalization is needed, we should carefully document all denormalized parts of the database. This is because when adding or updating data, we should also update denormalized data properly. Let's take the example of a purchase order record having unit price and quantity columns. Purchase orders are created in a transactional database where the quantity is often changed depending on customer requests or other factors. In an analytical database where we store the complete history of millions of purchase orders, changes are infrequent. However, in our analytical database, the total price is often aggregated. To compute a value for every row in every query, working with the total price column could be a resource-consuming task, so this is when we can think about saving the value in a new column. When an order changes its quantity or unit price, however, we need to recompute its saved value.

Ways of denormalization

The previous section looked at why denormalization may be necessary. Now let's go through several examples of how to do this.

Computed columns

Our first example shows probably the most common denormalization task: saving a computed value into a table. Let's look at the table with orders mentioned several times in previous sections and create this table. An example of this is shown in the following script:

```
CREATE TABLE Src.OrderLines
(
Id int not null identity
, ProductId int not null
, UnitPrice dec(8,2) not null
, Quantity int not null
```

```
, TotalPrice dec(8,2) not null
, CONSTRAINT pk_OrderLines PRIMARY KEY (Id)
)
```

The table created in the preceding script is very simple, but how do we insert a record into it? We must compute the `TotalPrice` value every time when we want to insert or update the record. Inserting a record looks like the following statement:

```
INSERT Src.OrderLines (ProductId, UnitPrice, Quantity, TotalPrice)
VALUES (1, 100.0, 2, 100. * 2)
```

When an update is executed, we need to remember that every change to `UnitPrice` or `Quantity` values makes it necessary to compute `TotalPrice`. The following script shows us how to do this:

```
UPDATE Src.OrderLines
SET Quantity = 3
  , TotalPrice = UnitPrice * 3
WHERE Id = 1
```

Missing the second updated column in the preceding statement leads to a situation in which the correct total for the record should be 300.00, but the saved value actually remains as 200.00. Even if this is not the usual issue in analytical databases, using **computed columns** is a good alternative to manual recalculation of column values.

Computed columns are columns that belong to a table structure, but are defined as an expression. The expression must depend only on other columns in the same record. U sub-queries, for example, is not allowed. Expressions can also contain scalar functions.

Computed column could be both **persisted** or non-persisted. The persisted computed column saves its values aside from the rest of a record. A non-persisted column computes the result of the expression during query execution, though not every column can be persisted. The main condition determining the ability of persistence is that the expression defining the computed column must not contain non deterministic functions such as `GETDATE()`. Let's change definition of our `Src.OrderLines` table using the following script:

```
ALTER TABLE Src.OrderLines
DROP COLUMN TotalPrice

ALTER TABLE Src.OrderLines
ADD TOtalPrice AS (UnitPrice * Quantity) PERSISTED
```

The preceding script demonstrates how to make the column computed and persisted. Since we already have a column with name `TotalPrice`, we must to drop it first, because `ALTER TABLE...ALTER COLUMN` cannot change the column definition from regular to computed. After doing this, the column is then created again with the same name, but previous `INSERT` and `UPDATE` statements will lead to an error. However, this is because the `TotalPrice` column is read-only. From now on, we don't need to think about the column. Let's try to modify data in `Src.OrderLines` table one more time. Execute the following script:

```
INSERT Src.OrderLines (ProductId, UnitPrice, Quantity)
VALUES (100, 10.52, 1)

SELECT * FROM Src.OrderLines

UPDATE Src.OrderLines SET Quantity = 4 WHERE ProductId = 100

SELECT * FROM Src.OrderLines
```

When we execute this script, we can see that inserting or updating data automatically leads to a computation or re-computation of the value in the `TotalPrice` column.

Computing values is not the only method of denormalization. Combining records from more tables together can also help data scientists to be more oriented on the analytical problem itself rather than writing many joins for creating useful datasets. So, the next denormalization technique is to save data together.

Denormalization using joins

In the previous section, we created a table named `Src.OrderLines`. When we select data from this, we can see product identifiers, which are already useless to a data consumer. Let's use the `Src.Products` and `Src.OrderLines` tables to identify which product was sold as follows:

```
SELECT *
FROM Src.OrderLines as ol
  JOIN Src.Products as p on ol.ProductId = p.ProductKey
```

Using the preceding script, we will get the full information on every order of a certain product. However, normalized structure is usually much more complicated. For example, do we want to write queries with complicated joins and do we want to spend system resources during their executions? Definitely not—this is why analytic databases tables are designed as denormalized to provide the simplest possible way of consuming data. Let's create a denormalized table using the following script:

```
CREATE SCHEMA Analytics AUTHORIZATION dbo

CREATE TABLE Analytics.Orders
(
OrderLineId int NOT NULL
, ProductKey int NOT NULL
, ProductName nvarchar(50) NOT NULL
, UnitPrice decimal(8, 2) NOT NULL
, Quantity int NOT NULL
, TotalPrice decimal(8, 2) NULL
, CONSTRAINT pk_Orders PRIMARY KEY (OrderLineId)
)
GO
```

The table created in the previous script is prepared namely for batch data loads using the `INSERT...SELECT` statement, which is shown in the following query:

```
INSERT Analytics.Orders
  (OrderLineId, ProductKey, ProductName, UnitPrice, Quantity, TotalPrice)
SELECT ol.Id as OrderLineId
  , ProductKey
  , ProductName
  , UnitPrice
  , Quantity
  , TotalPrice
FROM Src.OrderLines as ol
  JOIN Src.Products as p on ol.ProductId = p.ProductKey
```

It's almost impossible to describe all eventual examples and options of how to denormalize data, but it's important to know that whilst data denormalization could be damaging in transactional databases, it greatly helps in analytical databases. This is because it saves resources and also makes data more readable for analytics.

Resource saving and reliability of all data transformation with additional data checks could also be improved when statements are saved on a database side and called without a need to write complicated ad hoc queries. The next section will explain how to use views and stored procedures.

Using views and stored procedures

Physical data structures of relational databases become more complicated as the solved problem becomes more complex. Using physical data structures has only potentially negative impact on performance as well as the accuracy of repeatedly executed transactions or complicated queries. Aside from this effect, security is also something to consider. This is why it's a very good idea to cover physical data structures using objects dedicated to providing readable projection of data called **database views**. Also, data checks and transactions is good to encapsulate into dedicated objects called **stored procedures**. In this section, we will explain database applications. We will then play with views to add a layer of data transformation and denormalization, and in the last part of this section, we will provide several examples of stored procedures.

Database applications

The term **database application** could imply some client applications written in Java or C#. However, we will also use this term to give a name to the procedural objects defined, saved, and executed in a database. What is the procedural object? Procedural objects (also known as **modules**) are database objects defined using T-SQL or .NET languages. These objects do not hold data, but they work with data saved in declared structures such as tables.

We are usually working with several types of modules:

- **Views**: These are objects defined by the `SELECT` statement for data projection
- **Stored procedures**: These are complex objects mainly used for data manipulation, but also for data projection
- **Functions**: These are objects that must not change source data, but can be used to encapsulate expressions (scalar functions returning one value at a time), or to project data (table-valued functions)
- **Triggers**: This refers to a special type of stored procedure defined for a certain action (`INSERT`, `UPDATE`, or `DELETE`) on a certain object (table or view)

We will usually work with views and stored procedures, and we will also discover more about both module types later in this section.

Modular programming is used as a database aplication, and this provides several benefits:

- **Performance**: Data is processed where it's saved. SQL Server works more efficiently when it's optimizing stored batch as opposed to when it's working with ad hoc queries.
- **Schema readability**: It's much more comfortable for clients to execute simple `SELECT` statement when consuming data using view rather than to define all necessary joins, filters, expressions, or aggregations. This is much easier than writing every query themselves.
- **Schema stability**: From time to time, requests to change physical data structure occur. It is very probable that the changed physical schema can be adjusted in certain procedural objects in a way that is transparent to data consumers on the client side.
- **Security**: Physical data will contain many sensitive values that are not usually shown to clients. Modules can be the only way for clients to access data without the need to access base tables.

All reasons listed in this bullet list are very feasible for analytical purposes. This is why it's necessary to know how to work with modules.

Using views

A **view** (or **database view**) is the simplest procedural object. It's defined by whatever complicated but just one `SELECT` statement. The view gives a name to the statement and the whole definition is stored in a database's metadata. Let's define this simple view. In the previous section, we denormalized data from the `Staging.Products` and `Staging.OrderLines` tables and saved the result of the query to a new table called `Analytics.Orders`. However, as orders are still coming, we need to repeat the denormalization task often to omit the data delay. In some cases, it's better to not persist denormalized data, but to provide real-time view of it. The following script shows how to reach this using database view:

```
CREATE OR ALTER VIEW Analytics.viOrders
AS
SELECT ol.Id as OrderLineId
   , ProductKey
   , ProductName
   , UnitPrice
   , Quantity
   , TotalPrice
FROM Src.OrderLines as ol
  JOIN Src.Products as p on ol.ProductId = p.ProductKey
```

```
GO
```

The crucial part of the preceding script is the `SELECT` statement which was used in the previous section. However, the `SELECT` statement is not part of the `INSERT ... SELECT` statement; it's encapsulated using the simple header `CREATE OR ALTER VIEW`. Let's take a closer look at this header.

The basic syntax for creating modular objects is divided into two parts: header and body. The general syntax of this looks as follows:

```
CREATE ADJECTIVES OBJECT_TYPE schema_name.object_name
    parameter_list
WITH OPTIONS
AS
definition
GO
```

The `CREATE` keyword suggests that the object is going to be created. Due to the fact that it is not possible to create an object with the same name twice, SQL Server 2016 SP 1 introduced the `CREATE OR ALTER` keyword for procedural objects. The `CREATE OR ALTER` keyword is very useful when an object is created or altered, if it exists.

`ADJECTIVES` are optional, and they are not used in view definitions. As a short example of an adjective used in this `CREATE` statement; let's take a look at index creation:

```
CREATE NONCLUSTERED INDEX ix_Produts ON Staging.Products (ProductKey)
```

This simple statement creates a B-tree index on the `Staging.Products` table to speed up the process of searching through the `ProductKey` column. The `NONCLUSTERED` keyword is an example of an adjective used in the `CREATE` syntax.

Let's continue analyzing the `CREATE` general example. The `OBJECT_TYPE` keyword is replaced with the type of object we wish to create. For example, `CREATE VIEW`, `CREATE FUNCTION` (we also used `CREATE TABLE` many times), and so on.

If a certain object receives parameters (it's not possible in views, but we will use it in stored procedures), then they are declared within the header.

We can also define several options declaring additional behavior of created objects. For example, objects could be schema bound (such objects that control the data definition of underlying objects must not change), so in the `WITH` clause, the `SCHEMABINDING` keyword is used.

The heading of every object ends with an `AS` keyword, and the `definition` forms the body of a created object. When a procedural object is created or altered, it must be defined within its own batch. This is why it's recommended to end the whole object definition using the batch terminator `GO`.

It should now be clear how to create view. Our freshly created view is named `Analytics.viOrders`. So, how do we use the view? The answer is simple: just like any other table. View is used as a tabular object in the `FROM` clause of a `SELECT` statement. This could be joined together with other objects, and its columns could be filtered in the `WHERE` clause, and so on.

To provide an example of this, let's execute the following statement:

```
SELECT * FROM Analytics.viOrders
```

When the preceding statement is executed, we'll see the same result as when we did when selecting data from the previously created `Analytics.Orders` table.

We always consider whether it is better to use views or persisted data in the denormalized tables. In fact, views are a better option when data in underlying tables is created or modified continuously, but a table should perform better because almost no compute effort is needed when we read from it.

Views are great modules that are useful for organizing data into readable datasets. However, when we want to work with more complex data, view is not suitable. This is because, according to its definition, data must not be changed. We know that this can be done using updatable views, which are views used in the DML statements to modify data. However, this approach has many restrictions. Stored procedures are commonly used for data manipulation. Now let's explore the possibilities of stored procedures.

Using stored procedures

The previous section gave us an insight into how to create modules and show them on view. When compared to views that simply project data, stored procedures are very powerful modules that are also used for data projection. But the biggest strength of stored procedures arises when we either need to optimize difficult queries or when we want to manipulate data. Let's go straight into creating our first stored procedure now. We will still use the denormalization example from the previous sections, but we will encapsulate it into a stored procedure.

The following script demonstrates this:

```
CREATE OR ALTER PROC Staging.procLoadOrders
AS
DELETE Analytics.Orders
INSERT Analytics.Orders
  (OrderLineId, ProductKey, ProductName, UnitPrice, Quantity, TotalPrice)
SELECT ol.Id as OrderLineId
  , ProductKey
  , ProductName
  , UnitPrice
  , Quantity
  , TotalPrice
FROM Src.OrderLines as ol
  JOIN Src.Products as p on ol.ProductId = p.ProductKey
GO
```

The header in the preceding script has changed slightly. Instead of the keyword `VIEW`, which was used in the previous section, the keyword `PROC` (shortcut for `PROCEDURE`, which is also a usable keyword) is used. The previous script does not declare any parameters because none are required. As is also seen, we can use arbitrary statements in the body definition.

The previous sample is very simple and it simply encapsulates an ad hoc `INSERT .. SELECT` statement. However, the strength of stored procedures lies in the ability to handle whole batches including transaction controlling or data checks, for example. Let's enhance our example using the following two more actions:

1. First, we will check whether incoming data is correct. For example, we can test for non-existing product keys in the `Src.OrderLines` table, and so we can test if every `UnitPrice` and every `Quantity` columns has a meaningful value. When something goes wrong, we will control the batch using parameter.
2. Secondly, we will control the insertion using transaction.

We will write several ad hoc queries and then join everything together in the stored procedure definition.

The queries in the following script check for data quality:

```
DECLARE @missingProductsCount int
  , @incorrectProductsCount int
  , @missingErrMessage nvarchar(200) = N'Some products are unknown in Order
Lines'
  , @incorrectErrMessage nvarchar(200) = N'Some products have unknown
quantity or         unit price'
```

```
SELECT @missingProductsCount = COUNT(*)
FROM Src.OrderLines as ol
WHERE
    NOT EXISTS(SELECT * FROM Src.Products as p WHERE p.ProductKey =
ol.ProductId)

IF @missingProductsCount > 0
 BEGIN
  SET @missingErrMessage = REPLACE(@missingErrMessage, 'Some',
@missingProductsCount);
  THROW 60000, @missingErrMessage, 1;
 END

SELECT @incorrectProductsCount = COUNT(*)
FROM Src.OrderLines
WHERE UnitPrice IS NULL OR Quantity IS NULL

IF @incorrectProductsCount > 0
 BEGIN
  SET @incorrectErrMessage = REPLACE(@incorrectErrMessage, 'Some',
@incorrectProductsCount);
  THROW 60001, @incorrectErrMessage , 1;
 END
```

Checking queries in the preceding script just counts potentially incorrect records. The record count is then caught into declared variables. Every variable value is then evaluated using the `IF` condition. If the condition is true, an error is raised using the `THROW` statement.

The `THROW` statement has three parameters: custom error number, error message, and error state. The error number must be greater than 50,000, because numbers up to 50,000 are reserved for SQL Server's system purposes. If you want to design the user-friendly text of error message to provide complete information (not using sentences such as some products, but for example three products), then you must prepare a variable into which the message text is concatenated. The last parameter is error state. This is the integer state flag of the error. For example, if the same error could occur in several places within the batch, then the error state helps to identify the place in which the error occurred. Since the error state is required, when we don't need it, we can use any integer number. This number is usually `1`.

The `THROW` statement behaves like `RETURN`; when it occurs, whole batch is stopped. `RETURN` just finishes the batch without an error state, however.

We have now completed the first request to check for data quality. Now let's control data modification using transactions. Every transaction is starting using the `BEGIN TRAN` or `BEGIN TRANSACTION` statement. Once a transaction is started, we must finish it using either `COMMIT` or `ROLLBACK` statements. `COMMIT` commits data modified within a transaction, while `ROLLBACK` returns data to its original state. The following script shows how to control the `INSERT..SELECT` statement with a transaction:

```
BEGIN TRAN
DELETE Analytics.Orders
INSERT Analytics.Orders
  (OrderLineId, ProductKey, ProductName, UnitPrice, Quantity, TotalPrice)
SELECT ol.Id as OrderLineId
  , ProductKey
  , ProductName
  , UnitPrice
  , Quantity
  , TotalPrice
FROM Src.OrderLines as ol
  JOIN Src.Products as p on ol.ProductId = p.ProductKey
COMMIT
```

The previous code looks like `INSERT..SELECT`, which is covered by `BEGIN TRAN .. COMMIT` block. But what if something is going wrong here? Where should `ROLLBACK` be? Formerly, a special `@@ERROR` function was used after every statement to detect whether `ROLLBACK` is needed, but repeatedly using it was quite uncomfortable. However, we can use the `TRY..CATCH` block to control whole transaction. The following script shows how to use this:

```
BEGIN TRY
    BEGIN TRAN
    DELETE Analytics.Orders
    INSERT Analytics.Orders
      (OrderLineId, ProductKey, ProductName, UnitPrice, Quantity,
TotalPrice)
    SELECT ol.Id as OrderLineId
      , ProductKey
      , ProductName
      , UnitPrice
      , Quantity
      , TotalPrice
    FROM Src.OrderLines as ol
      JOIN Src.Products as p on ol.ProductId = p.ProductKey
    COMMIT
END TRY
BEGIN CATCH
    IF @@TRANCOUNT > 1
```

```
        ROLLBACK;
    THROW;
END CATCH
```

The TRY..CATCH construct is formed of two blocks which must be written side-by-side. The BEGIN TRY..END TRY block content describes so-called ideal scenario in which everything works and no errors are expected. However, when an error occurs in the BEGIN TRY..END TRY block, the batch flow immediately jumps into the BEGIN CATCH..END CATCH block.

If a transaction is controlled within a TRY block and the batch is routed to the CATCH block, the transaction is switched internally to **doomed state**. The doomed state means that we cannot write to the transaction, but we can still read data. The transaction is then not rolled back and commit cannot be issued.

So, in the CATCH block, we have the opportunity to inspect state of our data, diagnose the error, if needed, and then rollback our transaction. As it's shown in the preceding code, ROLLBACK is called conditionally. IF @@TRANCOUNT > 1 establishes whether or not transaction context still exists. But what does this mean? Our example is very simple, but in more difficult cases procedures are often nested so that the transaction nesting can occur. If nested transaction ends with ROLLBACK, everything is rolled back. It's very important to double-check whether the transaction context still exists!

The last statement in the preceding script is just an empty THROW; statement. If it's not written, the CATCH block hides the error state to a calling session. However, the client session should know that something does not work. The empty THROW statement sends a caught error state back to a client.

Now let's ensure that everything works together. Following script just declares stored procedure and in its body it checks data quality using exactly the same script as we explained earlier. After this occurs, the transaction begins to do its business:

```
CREATE OR ALTER PROC Staging.procLoadOrders
    @stopWhenIncorrect bit = 1
AS

DECLARE @missingProductsCount int
   , @incorrectProductsCount int
   , @missingErrMessage nvarchar(200) = N'Some products are unknown in Order
Lines'
   , @incorrectErrMessage nvarchar(200) = N'Some products have unknown
quantity or unit price'

SELECT @missingProductsCount = COUNT(*)
```

```
FROM Src.OrderLines as ol
WHERE
    NOT EXISTS(SELECT * FROM Src.Products as p WHERE p.ProductKey =
ol.ProductId)

IF @missingProductsCount > 0 AND @stopWhenIncorrect = 1
 BEGIN
  SET @missingErrMessage = REPLACE(@missingErrMessage, 'Some',
@missingProductsCount);
  THROW 60000, @missingErrMessage, 1;
 END

SELECT @incorrectProductsCount = COUNT(*)
FROM Src.OrderLines
WHERE UnitPrice IS NULL OR Quantity IS NULL

IF @incorrectProductsCount > 0 AND @stopWhenIncorrect = 1
 BEGIN
  SET @incorrectErrMessage = REPLACE(@incorrectErrMessage, 'Some',
@incorrectProductsCount);
  THROW 60001, @incorrectErrMessage , 1;
 END

BEGIN TRY
    BEGIN TRAN
    DELETE Analytisc.Orders    -- let old data is deleted
    INSERT Analytics.Orders
      (OrderLineId, ProductKey, ProductName, UnitPrice, Quantity,
TotalPrice)
    SELECT ol.Id as OrderLineId
      , ProductKey
      , ProductName
      , UnitPrice
      , Quantity
      , TotalPrice
    FROM Src.OrderLines as ol
      JOIN Src.Products as p on ol.ProductId = p.ProductKey
    COMMIT
END TRY
BEGIN CATCH
    IF @@TRANCOUNT > 1
        ROLLBACK;
    THROW;
END CATCH
GO
```

This script adds an additional promised feature: `parameter`. We can take a look at the second line in our script directly below the `CREATE OR ALTER` statement. There is also a `@stopWhenIncorrect bit = 1` row, and this is how parameters can be declared. The notation for name and data type is the same as for common variables. The assignment (`=1`) is optional and says that if the parameter will not be used by caller, the default value will be used.

We used the `@stopWhenIncorrect` parameter to control whether data checking leads to procedure interruption. Look at the `IF @missingProductsCount > 0 AND @stopWhenIncorrect = 1` row in the preceding script. If the `@stopWhenIncorrect` parameter is set to `0`, then data will be checked but the procedure will not be terminated.

There is only one way for stored procedures to be executed. The execution is very simple. The following script shows how to execute stored procedures:

```
EXEC Staging.procLoadOrders
-- or
EXEC Staging.procLoadOrders 1
-- or
EXEC Staging.procLoadOrders @stopWhenIncorrect = 1
```

The preceding script shows the same calling that is written in three variants. Every row executes the same procedure with the same parameter value. The first variant uses the default value of the parameter, the second variant calls the procedure with `by-position` explicitly setting the value of the parameter, and the last variant calls the procedure with `by-reference` explicitly setting the value of the parameter.

Because they are almost limitless objects, stored procedures can be used in an innumerable ways. Throughout the rest of this book, we will use stored procedures (and views) when finding new applications.

When code is written and works correctly, only part of our job is done. The second part is to ensure that the code will work efficiently. The following section gives a short overview of some performance tips for data transformation tasks.

Performance considerations

Previous sections covered the architecture of data transformations and we also learned how to transform data in many ways. When we work on data transformation tasks (and on all other tasks during data analysis life cycle), we also need to consider performance of our tasks. This is important because when we miss it, tasks become resource consuming and users also become disappointed due to delayed data. This section shows some techniques of how to reach desired performance.

Writing correct code

When the buzzword *performance* is mentioned, plenty of people start thinking about indexes. However, there are also many simple but feasible things to be considered. As well as correctly (de)normalized base tables, we also have to correctly manipulate data in tables. Let's summarize the following suggestions:

- Never use `*` (star) in your production queries. Overusing these results in the structure changing because every change in queried objects is propagated to the result. From a performance point of view, stars written into queries add unnecessary operations that SQL Server must complete.
- Avoid implicit conversions. This is an internally scalar function that casts the less-preferred data type to the more-preferred data type whenever two different data types are met. For example, when comparing columns with `int` and `bigint` data types, SQL Server casts the `bigint` to `int`. This conversion is done for every value in the dataset and could lead to performance problems.
- Make your database schema strict and use as many constraints as possible. SQL Server uses all accessible information for query optimization and constraints as well as correctly choosing data types. This greatly helps SQL Server to select an efficient query plan.
- Encapsulate your ad hoc queries into modules. When you do this, SQL Server knows that the text of your module is reliably saved into metadata and this is why it's possible to optimize it just once.
- Avoid loops in your procedures. Loops (mainly cursors) ensure that a process repeats many times. It's hard to predict how many times the loop will iterate, so try to rewrite cursors to set-based operations whenever possible.

- Prioritise the use of **common table expressions** (**CTE**) over temporary tables. CTE is part of a query, but a temporary table is created by its own query. This leads to more execution plans. Another issue is that SQL Server does not have statistics for temporary tables. When used in stored procedures, such a stored procedure is recompiled with every execution. The final reason is that a temporary table is written to a database `tempdb` on disk. When overused, this causes big performance troubles with the `tempdb` database.

When you follow all of the preceding recommendations but still need to enhance the performance, use indexes. These will be covered next.

Using indexes

Indexing is a very common way to tune up queries. We have several index types, and it's our responsibility to choose the right ones. We can think about B-tree indexes, but for data analysis, we also have column store indexes. Let's learn how certain index types help to improve queries.

B-tree indexes

A **B-tree index** is a kind of structure that is formed as a balanced tree with connected interleaved nodes. This tree contains a sorted copy of values and indexed columns or columns when the index is non-clustered. When an index is clustered, data rows are a leaf of index and these rows are sorted according to its index key. When SQL Server searches data, it traverses the B-tree index from its root to leaf to address rows filtered by a query.

Because a clustered B-tree index controls the order of records in a table, every record must be placed exactly to a position in accordance with the index. This is why the best practice is to design clustered indexes on small columns (for example, integer), which raise the ordering of new values. If you are thinking about a surrogate key here, then you are absolutely right!

B-tree indexes are generally used in two scenarios. The first scenario is to find one or a small amount of records. SQL Server uses an operation called **index search**. Either clustered or a non-clustered index can be used for this search.

The second scenario benefits from the fact that some columns in a table are queried or filtered more often than others. When all columns used in a query are included into a non-clustered index structure, then the index can either be searched or scanned. The **index scan** operation means that whole leaf pages of index are used to satisfy the query. The benefit is that a non-clustered index still saves less data than a base table.

Let's go through several examples. First of all, let's create an `Analytics.Orders` table. This table was used earlier in this chapter, so if you have one, the following script just drops a reminder to you:

```
CREATE SCHEMA Analytics AUTHORIZATION dbo

DROP TABLE IF EXISTS Analytics.Orders

CREATE TABLE Analytics.Orders
(
OrderLineId int NOT NULL
, ProductKey int NOT NULL
, ProductName nvarchar(50) NOT NULL
, UnitPrice decimal(8, 2) NOT NULL
, Quantity int NOT NULL
, TotalPrice decimal(8, 2) NULL
, CONSTRAINT pk_Orders PRIMARY KEY (OrderLineId)
)
GO
```

The preceding script shows a simple table with a primary key. Because the primary key is a constraint enforcing unique values in the column, it's internally implemented as a clustered B-tree index.

Let's use the following script to generate some data:

```
SET NOCOUNT ON
DECLARE @i int = 1
WHILE @i <= 100000
 BEGIN
  INSERT Analytics.Orders (ProductKey, ProductName, UnitPrice, Quantity)
  VALUES (ROUND(RAND() * 10 + 1, 0), N'Product ' + CAST(@i as nvarchar)
    , ROUND(RAND() * 1000 + 1, 2), ROUND(RAND() * 10 + 1, 0))
  set @i += 1
 end

UPDATE Analytics.Orders SET TotalPrice = UnitPrice * Quantity
```

The preceding script generates 100,000 records into the `Analytics.Orders` table. Now let's execute the following queries. The first finds out one record where an `OrderLineId` column equals `36001`, and the second finds all records where `ProductKey` equals `5`. Before we execute following script in toolbox or by using the *Ctrl + M* shortcut, turn on **Actual Execution Plan** in **Management Studio**.

```
SELECT * FROM Analytics.Orders WHERE OrderLineId = 36001
SELECT * FROM Analytics.Orders WHERE ProductKey = 5
```

When the preceding queries are executed, we can explore their execution plans. See the following screenshot:

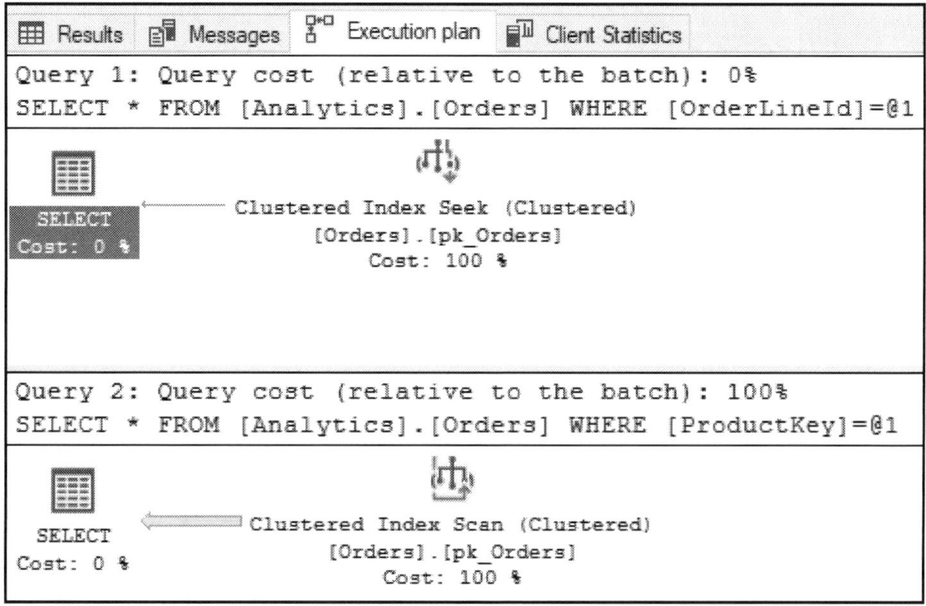

This screenshot shows two execution plans. The first of them has the right operator **Clustered Index Seek**. This means that the `WHERE` clause contains a column that is indexed. The second execution plan shows the **Clustered Index Scan** operator. This is because the second query uses a column, which is not indexed, so SQL Server needs to go over all data in the table to select all the desired records. The preceding example shows the difference between seek and scan operations.

If you want to explore both plans further, move your mouse over icons depicting operators and look at the number of rows that have been read.

From the previous sample, we can derive that the second (non-clustered) index on the `ProductKey` column should be created. The following script does this:

```
CREATE INDEX ix_Orders_ProductKey ON Analytics.Orders
(ProductKey)
```

Now let's try to execute both queries once more, especially the second one with condition on `ProductKey`. What happens here? Actually, nothing happens at all. The second query still scans whole tables. Maybe you can guess why, even though our index was created? The answer to this has two parts. The first is the `*` (star) symbol used in the `SELECT` clause. This conveys to SQL Server that we want whole records, but only `ProductKey` is in the index. So, SQL Server can search records with product key `5`, but then SQL Server must search for the rest of the records using a clustered index. This is useful when we need several records from whole table.

However, the data distribution of product keys is too dense. As data was generated with random product keys from `1` to `10`, we have approximately 1/10 of the data in the table in which the product key equals `5`. It's too much to be searched one by one. Let's try to rewrite the second query as in following script, and let's execute it with **Actual Execution Plan** still turned on:

```
SELECT OrderLineId, ProductKey FROM Analytics.Orders WHERE ProductKey = 5
```

The resulting execution plan is shown in the following screenshot:

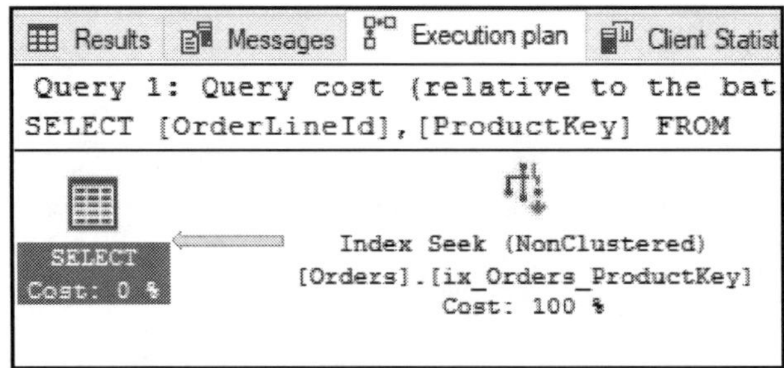

The final execution plan

In the preceding screenshot, we suddenly see the **Index Seek** operation. This is because only columns contained in index are used in the whole query. If you think about the index creation, you'll not find the `OrderLineId` column in its definition. However, all non-clustered indexes include the key value of the clustered index in its definition, and `OrderLineId` is a clustered index key column.

You can keep playing with the non-clustered index. Try to execute the last query again without the `WHERE` clause. Which operator will appear? Index scan is the right answer.

It's big mistake to think that indexes will heal every performance disease. We still have to keep in mind that index is helping storage, so every modification in data also affects index's content. This could lead to concurrency problems. From this point on, it's good to slow down when indexing, especially in tables with many data modifications.

B-tree indexes are generally a great help when we need to read a small subset of data from tables. However, in the data science domain, we need to execute many aggregation queries. SQL Server 2012 introduced a new storage type called **columnstore indexes**. In the next section, we will describe how this works.

COLUMNSTORE INDEX

`COLUMNSTORE INDEX` is a newer structure than B-tree indexes. The data from the row storage of a b-tree is divided into so-called row groups containing 1,048,576 records (if you're wondering what the number means, it's 2 powered on 20). Every row group is then divided into a column. So, in `COLUMNSTORE INDEX`, index data is saved in segments by columns with up to 1,048,576 values. Every segment is then compressed. This storage type is greatly prepared for big scans and aggregate queries. Nowadays, columnstore indexes can be either non-clustered or clustered. Against b-tree indexes, we always create one columnstore index.

Columnstore indexes don't support seek operation, so for big tables intended for both random seeks and wider scans, we can combine a clustered columnstore index with non-clustered B-tree indexes. Let's make an example of such a combination. First, let's copy the `Analytics.Orders` table into a new table called `Analytics.OrdersCS` and create a clustered columnstore index on the new table using the following script:

```
SELECT * INTO Analytics.OrdersCS FROM Analytics.Orders
CREATE CLUSTERED COLUMNSTORE INDEX cs_OrdersCS ON Analytics.Orders

ALTER TABLE Analytics.OrdersCS
ADD CONSTRAINT pk_OrdersCS PRIMARY KEY NONCLUSTERED (OrderLineId)
```

The previous script copies one table to another using a `SELECT .. INTO` statement. The clustered columnstore index is then created. The third statement in the script creates a primary key constraint on the new table. Note that the primary key is non-clustered. This is because one table cannot be stored in two storages at a time. When the preceding script is executed, let's make a simple comparison of data reservation for both tables. The following script uses a `sp_spaceused` stored procedure to show space consumption:

```
EXEC sp_spaceused 'Analytics.Orders'
EXEC sp_spaceused 'Analytics.OrdersCS'
```

Even though both tables are very small, we can see that the `Analytics.OrdersCS` table uses approximately one third of the space used by the `Analytics.Orders` table. Saving the storage is not the main goal of columnstore indexing. We can try to execute following statements to see what will happen in an execution plan:

```
SELECT ProductKey, AVG(TotalPrice) FROM Analytics.Orders GROUP BY
ProductKey
SELECT ProductKey, AVG(TotalPrice) FROM Analytics.OrdersCS GROUP BY
ProductKey
```

The result of the preceding statements is described by execution plans in the following screenshot:

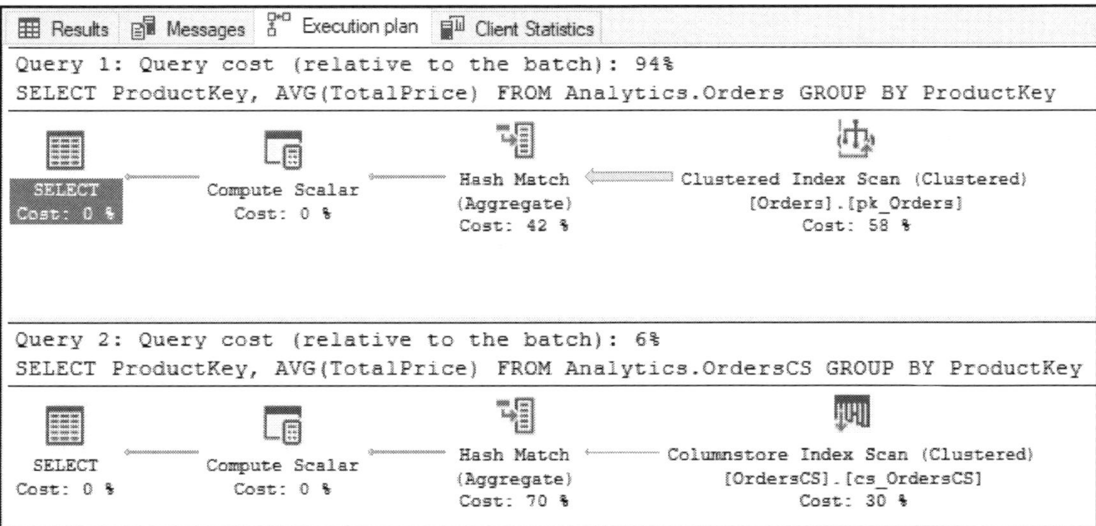

A simple comparison of **Query cost** of both plans shows that second plan using **Columnstore Index Scan** operator consumes only 6 % against the first execution plan using traditional **Clustered Index Scan**, which consumes 94 % of total resources.

If you move your mouse over both index scan operators, look at the **Actual Execution Mode**. In the **Clustered Index Scan** operator, the **Actual Execution Mode** is set to **Row** mode; rows are processed one by one. In the columnstore index scan, the execution mode is batch; SQL Server is able to process up to 900 rows at once.

The last part of our example combines clustered columnstore index with a non-clustered B-tree index. The following script creates the same non-clustered index on the `ProductKey` column:

```
CREATE INDEX ix_OrdersCS_ProductKey ON Analytics.OrdersCS (ProductKey)
```

When columnstore and B-tree indexes are combined as in the preceding script, this combination helps SQL Server to address the right segments for the `Columnstore Index Scan` operations using the `Index Seek` operation.

Summary

In this chapter, we learned why data is transformed. It is important to remember that we should not fully put our faith in incoming data from external sources. As well as this, we need to make many checks on incoming data, and we also need to adjust the data format to fit our expectations.

When the reason for data transformation was found, we went through several architectures suitable for data transformation in one or more steps. When the architecture was described, we learned how to transform data using tools such as SSIS or T-SQL.

Two sections of this chapter guided us through data transformation tasks with designing and implementing denormalization using ad hoc queries and procedural objects.

The last section was dedicated to recommended practices and indexing techniques for the best performance of our transformation jobs.

The following chapter will focus on discovering what is hidden in transformed data using T-SQL queries for descriptive and comparative statistics.

Questions

1. Why do we need to transform data?
   We need to make data consistent and prepared for our analytical purposes. Data can come from a range of data sources with very volatile quality.
2. Is it always good approach to consume source data directly?
   Sometimes, yes, but not always. One of the reasons why we should stage data aside is to avoid conflicts with common data contention coming to a source data.
3. Why is the `OPENQUERY` function preferred when writing distributed queries?
   The first reason is that security when using the `OPENROWSET` function is compromised. The second reason is to do with performance. Distributed queries written using the `OPENQUERY` function often perform better than those written using an ad hoc approach.
4. Can we modify data using views?
   No. The view definition is defined by the `SELECT` statement only. The modular object intended mainly for data manipulation is a stored procedure.

5. Which kinds of parameters can we use in stored procedures?
   We can use input and output parameters as well as mandatory and optional parameters. Our demo in the Stored Procedures section uses one input optional parameter.
6. Can the columnstore index help us with random seeks?
   The columnstore index never helps with random seeks on a small amount of records. It's used for queries with full or range scans. For random seeks, B-tree indexes are designed.
7. Can I have two clustered indexes in one table?
   No. This is not possible because the clustered index forms the physical storage of a table.

5
Data Exploration and Statistics with T-SQL

When creating our data science solutions, the data that we want to use in these tasks should be explored carefully. As we learned in `Chapter 5`, *Data Transformation and Cleansing with T-SQL,* when data is loaded into a desired format, we need to find the distributions and patterns within it. We should also use data exploration during the staging process to check and improve data quality.

In this chapter, we will learn how to use T-SQL language to get statistical results from our data. To do this, we will use the following techniques:

- **T-SQL aggregate queries**: This section explains what the aggregate query is and which statistical measures it can show.
- **Ranking, framing, and windowing with T-SQL**: Using framing and windowing helps to obtain results enriched by sorting or ranking. In this section, we will play with framing and windowing from the perspective of data exploration.
- **Running aggregates with T-SQL**: This section will join knowledge from the aggregation queries section and the framing and windowing section to help us to create running aggregates or comparisons of values between rows.

Technical requirements

To play with all the scripts and projects in this chapter, SQL Server 2017 is required.

For all SQL scripts provided within this chapter, Management Studio version 17.5 or higher is recommended.

All scripts and other files are provided at `https://github.com/PacktPublishing/Hands-On-Data-Science-with-SQL-Server-2017/tree/master/CH6_Data_Exploration_and_Statistics_with_T_SQL`. Scripts on GitHub are also ordered accordingly with scripts reported throughout the chapter.

T-SQL aggregate queries

Data exploration and descriptive or comparative statistics are very important tasks that have to be done repeatedly and iteratively during every data science project. This gives us better insight into the data that we want to process throughout all projects. T-SQL aggregate queries are an important part of data exploration.

A T-SQL **aggregate query** is a kind of query that basically summarizes groups of records from underlying datasets and typically provides aggregated numeric values for each group of records generated from the dataset. Groups of records are not needed for every case or every assignment. Such aggregation queries give an aggregation of summarized values over whole underlying datasets.

The simplest aggregation query does not require grouping. With or without grouping, aggregate queries use special kinds of functions, called aggregate functions. Almost every aggregate function takes a column of values as a parameter, and a result of the function is a number. The only exception to this is a function called `SUM(*)`, which simply counts records. SQL Server provides several aggregate functions, which will be covered in this chapter.

Common properties of aggregate functions

All aggregate functions have the same common behaviors:

- Every aggregate function has one parameter of a typically numeric column that computes one value over that column. Two exceptions are made through the following functions:
    - `COUNT(*)`: This function computes an amount of records.
    - `STRING_AGG`: This function concatenates strings from a column into one string so that it accepts the `varchar` or `nvarchar` columns as a parameter.
- Almost every aggregate function except `COUNT(*)` ignores records in which the aggregated column contains `NULL`. This is because the `COUNT(*)` function does not work with certain columns, but with whole records.
- Every aggregate function can be used in `SELECT` and `HAVING` clauses. In a `SELECT` clause, it provides scalar results. The `HAVING` clause serves as a conditional clause similar to the `WHERE` clause, but for the result of aggregations that are not yet known in a `WHERE` clause. We will cover more about the `HAVING` clause in the dedicated section later in this chapter.

Ignoring columns with `NULL` values by aggregate functions is a very important property of aggregate functions, and we must always consider this behavior. If we miss it, we can obtain inaccurate results from our queries.

Now it's time to introduce all aggregate functions using examples.

Aggregate functions

Now that we know the common properties of aggregate functions, let's start to describe and explore the aggregate functions one by one.

COUNT, COUNT(*), and COUNT_BIG

The simplest aggregate function is probably `COUNT(*)`. This function just computes an amount of records. The following script sample demonstrates how to use this:

```
SELECT COUNT(*) FROM Sales.SalesOrderDetail
```

The preceding statement goes over all records from the `Sales.SalesOrderDetail` table and counts how many rows there are. As seen in the sample, the aggregate function (or functions) can be written into a `SELECT` clause in the same way as any other expression. The rest of the query can be combined in the usual manner. For example, this may be the case if we want to compute the amount of records belonging only to product ID 710. The following sample statement shows this:

```
SELECT COUNT(*) FROM Sales.SalesOrderDetail WHERE ProductID = 710
```

The result of the preceding query is 44 rows. This is because the query-only filters records when `ProductID` is equal to `710`. In addition, the aggregation function only works with records for which the condition is true.

All aggregation functions work in the same way. Only records that meet whole `WHERE` predicates are processed using the aggregation function.

`COUNT(*)` is probably the simplest aggregate function provided by SQL Server. Sometimes it's changed with other aggregate functions, called `COUNT`. Even though both functions have the same name, the difference lies in the parameter. `COUNT(*)` uses the star (`*`) symbol to say that it just counts records, but the `COUNT` function uses certain columns to calculate a number of valid values. In other words, the `COUNT` function ignores all records where the aggregated column is `NULL`. Let's explore the behavior of both functions in the following query:

```
SELECT COUNT(*) AS RecordCount                          -- 19972
   , COUNT(MiddleName) AS PeopleUsingMiddleName         -- 11473
   , COUNT(DISTINCT MiddleName) AS MiddleNamesUsed --      70
FROM Person.Person
```

The preceding query uses `COUNT` or `COUNT(*)` in three variants. Comments in the script show the results. The first of these simply return a number of records (actually 19,972) in the `Person.Person` table, but `COUNT(MiddleName)` computes a number of people who use a middle initial. In other words, in 11,473 records, the `MiddleName` column is filled with any `NOT NULL` values.

The last column in the results from the preceding sample shows that aggregate functions can use the `DISTINCT` keyword to calculate how many distinct values are in a certain column (this is especially true for the `COUNT` function). As it's in the comment for the third column calculated in the preceding script sample, the column has 70 distinct values. Let's carry out a simple experiment using the following two queries:

```
-- the list of all MiddleName values
-- it has 71 rows and includes NULL
SELECT DISTINCT MiddleName FROM Person.Person
```

This statement is a very simple `SELECT DISTINCT` query that enumerates all possible values from the `MiddleName` column. In the result, you will see that one of the records will contain `NULL` because not every person uses a middle initial.

To be more scientific, let's prove the `NULL` value behavior of `MiddleName` in the following query using aggregate functions over a preceding result set:

```
-- computing aggregates over preceding query shows the difference
SELECT COUNT(*) AS RecordCount -- 71
  , COUNT(MiddleName) AS ValueCount -- the 71st value is ignored, it's NULL
FROM (SELECT DISTINCT MiddleName FROM Person.Person) AS x
```

The preceding query is composed of two queries. In the `FROM` clause, we are using an original query with a list of `MiddleName` values including `NULL`. The subquery in the `FROM` clause is the so-called derived table. Once a derived table is processed, SQL Server can use it to calculate the results of the `COUNT(*)` and `COUNT` aggregate functions, and when we execute the entire query, we will see the difference between both values.

The preceding example shows how important it is to keep in mind that `NULL` values could cause inaccuracies and mistakes in our data exploration.

The third function mentioned in the sub-heading of this section is `COUNT_BIG`. This function works in the same way as the `COUNT` or `COUNT(*)` functions, but its return type is always `bigint`. The `COUNT` function always returns `int`, and so we can use the `COUNT_BIG` function everywhere we expect to find a number of records bigger than 4,300,000,000.

`COUNT` aggregations are good for exploring how many records we are going to process. We can also use these to compute a number of records before or after processing our transformation. However, SQL Server provides more useful aggregate functions for our statistical needs. Let's explore these.

MIN and MAX

Some of the most important information is a range of values contained within a dataset. We can hardly offer statistics for the year 2016 in a situation in which our data contains records beginning in 2017. This is why we need to explore dates or numerical ranges. For such purposes, `MIN` and `MAX` functions are very useful, but both functions ignore `NULLs`. In other words, `NULL` is not the minimum or maximum value in datasets.

Let's take a look at the behavior of both functions. In the `AdventureWorks` database used in examples throughout this chapter is a table named `HumanResources.Employee`. In order to better imagine the `MIN` and `MAX` behavior, let's make a copy of the table and then we'll adjust a structure and data. To do this, execute the following script:

```
-- table is copied to new one
SELECT * INTO HumanResources.EmpCopy FROM HumanResources.Employee

-- some columns are modified to allow null
ALTER TABLE HumanResources.EmpCopy
ALTER COLUMN VacationHours smallint NULL

ALTER TABLE HumanResources.EmpCopy
ALTER COLUMN SickLeaveHours smallint NULL

-- every 7th record has VacationHours set to NULL
UPDATE HumanResources.EmpCopy
SET VacationHours = NULL WHERE BusinessEntityID % 7 = 0

-- every 9th record has SickLeaveHours set to NULL
UPDATE HumanResources.EmpCopy
SET SickLeaveHours = NULL WHERE BusinessEntityID % 9 = 0
```

However, the preceding script has nothing in common with the `MIN` and `MAX` functions; it only creates a copy of the `HumanResources.EmpCopy` table to keep the original table intact. It then makes the `VacationHours` and `SickLeaveHours` columns nullable, and the last part of the script sets `NULL` in both altered columns. Now we can fully understand how the `MIN` and `MAX` functions work.

As we can see in the following statement, the syntax for using the `MIN` and `MAX` aggregate functions is the same as for any other aggregate function:

```
SELECT
  MIN(VacationHours) as MinVacationHours
  , MAX(VacationHours) as MaxVacationHours
FROM HumanResources.EmpCopy
```

When the preceding query is executed, we should obtain `0` values for `MinVacationHours` and `99` for `MaxVacationHours`. Even though it was set for several records, `NULL` is not in the result. Now let's try to obtain the same numbers using the lowest and highest values from the sorted result set. The following statements are trying to find out the first lowest value and the highest value:

```
SELECT TOP (1) VacationHours AS MinVacationHours
FROM HumanResources.EmpCopy ORDER BY VacationHours

SELECT TOP (1) VacationHours AS MaxVacationHours
FROM HumanResources.EmpCopy ORDER BY VacationHours DESC
```

As we can see, when the preceding statements are executed, `MaxVacationHours` from the second query has the same result. However, `MinVacationHours` from the first query leads to `NULL`.

For sorting purposes, `NULLs` are placed as first rows (let's say *smallest* values), but statistically the correct result is from the `MIN` aggregate function, because `NULL` is not a value. `NULL` says that the value, if it exists, is unknown. This is why we cannot correctly decide whether the unknown value is minimal or maximal.

Using the `MIN` function on nullable columns forces us to think about `NULL`. This encourages to ask ourselves questions such as, Have records with `NULLs` been eliminated from aggregation, or have they actually been included? Or, How do I include records with `NULL` in a certain column? However, the answer to these questions is quite simple. We simply need to handle `NULL` occurrences using the `COALESCE` or `ISNULL` function. Both functions are almost the same, but the `COALESCE` function is more flexible than `ISNULL` in common situations. The `ISNULL` function has two parameters. If the first parameter is `NULL`, then the second parameter's value is returned; otherwise, the first parameter's value is returned. `COALESCE` works similarly to the `ISNULL` function, but the list of parameters can be more than two in this case. The `COALESCE` function then returns the first `NOT NULL` value reading parameter list from left to right. If all parameters in a list are `NULL`, then `NULL` is returned from `COALESCE`. The following example shows both functions using constants:

```
SELECT ISNULL(1, 2) -- returns 1
  , ISNULL(NULL, 5) -- returns 5
  , ISNULL(NULL, NULL)-- must return NULL

SELECT COALESCE(NULL, 1, 2, 3) -- returns 1
  , COALESCE(1, NULL, NULL) -- returns also 1

SELECT COALESCE(NULL, NULL, NULL) -- Leads to an error, all constants are
NULLs
```

```
DECLARE @a int, @b int, @c int
SELECT COALESCE(@a, @b, @c) -- Must return NULL

-- for to be sure that NOT NULL is returned
SELECT COALESCE(@a, @b, @c, 0) -- NOT NULL constant is added as extra
parameter
```

As we can see in the preceding script, the `ISNULL` function has exactly two parameters in the first `SELECT` statement, and its result depends on the combination of `NULL` values in the parameters. When using the `COALESCE` function, this is almost the same as using `ISNULL`, but possibly for more parameters. When we work with constants, not all can be `NULL`. For this reason, the third `SELECT` statement leads to an error. When we assign parameter list values into variables, such as in the last two `SELECT` statements, we can obtain `NULL` as a result of the `COALESCE` function when all variables are `NULL`. To be sure that something `NOT NULL` will be the result, we can add one extra concrete value (such as 0 in the preceding example) as a last parameter in the `COALESCE` parameter list.

When we know how to remove unwanted `NULLs`, we can adjust our example using `MIN` and `MAX` functions. The following statement is the same as the first in this section, but the parameters of the `MIN` and `MAX` functions are not raw column values; instead, they are `ISNULL` functions removing `NULL` from the original column values:

```
SELECT
  MIN(ISNULL(VacationHours, 0)) as MinVacationHours
  , MAX(ISNULL(VacationHours, 0)) as MaxVacationHours
FROM HumanResources.EmpCopy
```

As the preceding `SELECT` statement shows, we are now sure that `NULLs` don't have an impact on our results.

Using the `ISNULL` or `COALESCE` functions is also very common in combination with other aggregate functions. Now it's time to move to the next section, where we will describe the `SUM` aggregate.

SUM

A very common task is to simply add a column or numerical values. The `SUM` aggregate function is designed for this task. Using the `SUM` function is the same as using other aggregation functions, so let's explore this in the following example:

```
SELECT SUM(VacationHours) AS SumVacationHours    -- 12646 should be the
result
FROM HumanResources.EmpCopy
```

As shown in the preceding statement, the SUM function is used in exactly the same way as the MIN, MAX, or COUNT function. A result of the preceding query is the amount of hours an employee spends on vacation. In the preceding section, we started to learn about how NULL impact aggregation results. When we are using the SUM function, the impact is minimal. Let's execute the following statement to test how NULL is evaluated by the SUM function:

```
SELECT SUM(VacationHours) AS SumVacationHours                -- result: 12646
  , SUM(ISNULL(VacationHours, 0)) AS SumVacationHours     -- result: also
12646
FROM HumanResources.EmpCopy
```

When the preceding query is executed, the result for both columns is the same. This is because NULL is replaced with 0 (zero). When the NULL lasts in the column used as a parameter, SUM just ignores records with NULL. When NULL is replaced by 0, the 0 becomes what is known as a **neutral item** for additive operations. This is why, in common cases, the result will remain the same. In other words, we will only obtain different results in special cases when NULL has to be replaced by a number other than zero.

Although it's ignored by the SUM function, we can say that NULL does not often have a big impact on a result. However, the next AVG function can be strongly affected by NULL, as we will see in the next section.

AVG

The AVG aggregate function computes the mean of numerical values. This is useful when we want to explore a typical value in a set of values, for example. The mean is calculated as a summary of the values divided by the number of items (or records, in our case). So, theoretically, we can calculate the mean as an expression, such as SUM(column) / COUNT(*). Or can we think about the mean as more of an expression, such as SUM(column) / COUNT(column)? To figure out which of these is correct, let's make a comparison of both formulas and the AVG function in the following query:

```
SELECT SUM(VacationHours) / COUNT(*) AS Avg1                 -- result: 43
  , SUM(VacationHours) / COUNT(VacationHours) AS Avg2     -- result: 50
  , AVG(VacationHours) AS Avg3                              -- result: 50
FROM HumanResources.EmpCopy
```

As seen in the preceding query and its results, the `Avg2` column has the same result that the `AVG` function used to compute the `Avg3` column. We should have two questions about this:

- Why are all results integers?
- Why do the results of `Avg1` and other columns differ?

To answer the first of these questions, the `VacationHours` column has an `integer` data type. In addition, the result of `COUNT`, or `COUNT(*)`, has an `integer` return type. When any integer's calculation is done, this also results in an integer. This is commonly true, and we can try to execute the following simple expression to demonstrate this:

```
SELECT 1 / 2    -- result is NOT 0.5 but 0
```

As seen in the preceding expression, any calculation using integers leads to an integer result, even if it's very inaccurate.

However, we can adjust the preceding expression slightly. The following expression shows how to do this:

```
SELECT 1 * 1. / 2    -- result is 0.5 now
```

The only adjustment needed in order to obtain an accurate result is to convert one of the operands to a decimal data type. We can use regular `CAST` or `CONVERT` conversion functions here, or we can simply multiply one of the operands by `1`. The `1` value itself does not change the operand's value, but when it's written in a form of `1.0` (or `1.`, like in the preceding expression), it's a `decimal`, and the result of such expression (again, like in preceding expression) leads to a decimal value. When one of operands is of the `decimal` data type, the whole result will also be `decimal`.

We can make the same correction in our original query, and the first question regarding why all results are integers will be answered completely. See the following statement for more information:

```
SELECT SUM(VacationHours * 1.) / COUNT(*) AS Avg1              -- result:
43.607
   , SUM(VacationHours * 1.) / COUNT(VacationHours) AS Avg2    -- result:
50.787
   , AVG(VacationHours * 1.) AS Avg3                          -- result:
50.787
FROM HumanResources.EmpCopy
```

So, the first question is answered using the preceding statement, but what about different results between `Avg1` and `Avg2`? As mentioned in the previous section, `NULL` is the reason. In the following table, let's use a very short example without using a PC:

Record	**Number**
#1	1
#2	NULL
#3	2
#4	3
AVG	**(1+2+3)/3 = 2**

The preceding table shows a very simple set of records. There are 4 records here, but if record #2 isn't a number, then in the record is a `NULL` result. As mentioned in previous sections, whole records with `NULL` are ignored by aggregate functions, hence the resulting `AVG` computes the summary of numbers divided by the number of records that do not have `NULL` in an aggregated column. In the real world, sometimes we think about `NULL` as 0 (zero), so our calculation could be *6/4*, which leads to 1.5. This is the difference that we must consider every time we compute statistics with aggregate functions!

Mean has a big concern, because it can lead to a very inaccurate estimation of a typical value. When values in a set are scattered widely or lie away from the physical center of the set of values, the mean is not the best statistical measure. Instead, it has to be verified using other statistical functions, and these functions are `VAR` and `STDEV`, as described in the following sections.

VAR and VARP

Variance is a very important statistical measure that shows how much certain items are scattered on a numerical axis. Mathematically, it follows this formula:

$$\sigma^2 = \frac{1}{N}\sum_{i=1}^{N}(x_i - X)^2$$

The preceding formula is for the variance over the whole of a statistical population, and the following formula is for the variance over a sample of a statistical population:

$$\sigma^2 = \frac{1}{N-1}\sum_{i=1}^{N}(x_i - X)^2$$

What do the letters in the preceding formulas mean?

- *N* is the number of items in a dataset
- *i* is an item index
- x_i is the value of a certain item
- *X* is a mean

Both formulas are implemented in SQL Server. The variance for a full population (not subtracting 1 from the *N* number of items) is represented by the `VARP` aggregate function (the **P** at the end of this acronym stands for **population**). The variance of the sample is then represented by the `VAR` aggregate function. To make both formulas clear and to see how dedicated aggregates help us, let's go through the following sample. This sample will use the same `HumanResources.EmpCopy` table and the `VacationHours` column as used in the previous section. Let's calculate the variance without the `VAR`/`VARP` aggregate functions. Looking at the preceding formulas, we first need to calculate the X-mean of values in the `VacationHours` column. The following query does this for us:

```
SELECT
  SUM(VacationHours * 1.) / COUNT(VacationHours) AS Mean
FROM HumanResources.EmpCopy
```

This query generates the value of 50.787148, and this is X. The preceding query is used as a constant in the following query, computing the difference between X and every single amount of `VacationHours`. Let's now explore and execute the following query:

```
SELECT
  VacationHours -
  (
  SELECT
    SUM(VacationHours * 1.) / COUNT(VacationHours) AS Mean
  FROM HumanResources.EmpCopy
  ) AS Differences
FROM HumanResources.EmpCopy
WHERE VacationHours IS NOT NULL
```

The preceding query uses the original query by calculating the mean as a subquery. To eliminate all `NULL` from the query, the `WHERE` predicate is also used. As a result of the preceding query, we have a column of numbers. Let's try to add these together. To do this, execute the following query:

```
; WITH Diffs AS
(
SELECT
  VacationHours * 1. -
  (
```

```
    SELECT
      SUM(VacationHours * 1.) / COUNT(VacationHours) AS Mean
    FROM HumanResources.EmpCopy
    ) as Differences
  FROM HumanResources.EmpCopy
  WHERE VacationHours IS NOT NULL
  )
  SELECT SUM(Differences) FROM Diffs
```

The preceding query uses a **common table expression** (**CTE**). The CTE is a query encapsulated by a name (`Diffs`, in our case), what is then used by just one following statement. CTEs are very useful when we don't need to create too many subqueries or derived tables. The result of this is probably 0, or some number very close to this (the preceding sample query will actually return 0.000148, as it's given by little inaccuracy in rounding). In order to better understand why the result should be (and must be) zero, let's look at a very simple population, as shown in the following table:

Record	**Number**	**Mean**	**Difference from mean**	**Difference from mean^2**
#1	3	4	3-4 = -1	$-1^2 = 1$
#2	5	4	5 - 4 = 1	$1^2 = 1$
Summary			**-1 + 1 = 0**	**1+1 = 2**

As shown in this table, the summary of differences from the mean always leads to zero. This is why the power of two is added to formulas calculating variance. The power makes all the differences between the mean and certain items' value as positive numbers, and the result is not zero anymore. Let's do it in T-SQL in the following query:

```
SELECT
  POWER(VacationHours * 1. -
  (
  SELECT
    SUM(VacationHours * 1.) / COUNT(VacationHours) AS Mean
  FROM HumanResources.EmpCopy
  ), 2) as Differences
FROM HumanResources.EmpCopy
WHERE VacationHours IS NOT NULL
```

The only change made in the preceding query is that the `POWER` function is used. This function has two parameters. The first parameter is the expression that has to be powered by the second parameter. Now, when the preceding statement is executed, we have a result containing differences from the mean powered by two. The last step is to summarize the result of the preceding query and divide it by the number of records for `VARP`, or by the number of records minus one for `VAR`. To do this, let's take a look at the following query:

```
-- our sample
; WITH Diffs AS
(
SELECT
  POWER(VacationHours * 1. -
  (
  SELECT
    SUM(VacationHours * 1.) / COUNT(VacationHours) AS Mean
  FROM HumanResources.EmpCopy
  ), 2) as PoweredDiff
FROM HumanResources.EmpCopy
WHERE VacationHours IS NOT NULL
)
SELECT SUM(PoweredDiff) / COUNT(PoweredDiff) AS [VARP]
  , SUM(PoweredDiff) / (COUNT(PoweredDiff) - 1) AS [VAR]
FROM Diffs

-- built-in VAR/VARP aggregates for comparison
SELECT VARP(VacationHours) AS [VARP]
  , VAR(VacationHours) AS [VAR]
FROM HumanResources.EmpCopy
```

Calculating the complete variance requires more of a complicated query, as seen in the first of the preceding statements. We need to use the CTE called `Diffs` in order to encapsulate pre-calculation of powered differences, and then we can compute the variance of the population (the `[VARP]` alias output) and variance of the sample (the `[VAR]` alias output). The second of the preceding queries is the same task that was resolved using the `VAR` and `VARP` aggregate functions.

You may wonder why the example was written for you when we have dedicated aggregates. The answer to this is simple: T-SQL does not have aggregates for so-called **higher statistical moments** such as data skew or data sparkness. Even though they are seen visually in charts, sometimes we need to calculate them.

So, what does the statistical variance tell us? The bigger the number is, the more it is spread on a numerical axis. Let's compare variances as a result of the following simple queries:

```
SELECT VAR(c)
FROM (VALUES (2), (3), (2)) AS t(c)

SELECT VAR(c)
FROM (VALUES (2), (30), (100)) AS t(c)
```

As seen in the `FROM` clause in the first of the preceding queries, the numbers are close to each to other. However, in the second statement, they are not. The variance will be much greater for the second query. This is sometimes hard to interpret, which is why one more aggregate functions, called `STDEV` or `STDEVP`, are added. We will explore this in the next section.

STDEV and STDEVP

After reading the previous section on variance, this section will be very fast and easy to read. This is because **standard deviation**—what the `STDEV` aggregate function actually is—is just the square root of the variance. The standard deviation is the measure of variance for a numerical value. In other words, this measure is a number describing how data is scattered. The result of `STDEV` grows as data becomes more scattered. The only difference against variance is that standard deviation generates a more readable value.

Let's look at the following simple query:

```
SELECT VARP(VacationHours) AS [VARPVacation]          -- 822.874
   , VAR(VacationHours) AS [VARVacation]              -- 826.192
   , STDEVP(VacationHours) AS [STDEVPVacation]        --  28.686
   , STDEV(VacationHours) AS [STDEVVacation]          --  28.744
   , VARP(SickLeaveHours) AS [VARPSickHours]          -- 211.140
   , VAR(SickLeaveHours) AS [VARSickHours]            -- 211.962
   , STDEVP(SickLeaveHours) AS [STDEVPSickHours]      --  14.531
   , STDEV(SickLeaveHours) AS [STDEVSickHours]        --  14.559
FROM HumanResources.EmpCopy
```

The preceding query, and its rounded results shown in the comments, shows the difference between values. It's up to the reader to decide which option is more readable for them, but looking at results of `STDEV` or `STDEVP`, aggregates say that `VacationHours` spent by employees are twice as spread across the numerical axis than hours spent with illness.

For statistical and machine learning purposes, information provided by variance and standard deviation is very important. Simply put, as the variance grows, the parameter probably affects the resulting machine learning model more. Similarly, as the variance of a certain parameter becomes lower, the parameter will probably affect the prediction less.

All of the knowledge we learned in this section is true when the distribution of data is **normal**. This means that values are distributed evenly. To explore normal distribution (or Chi-square distribution), we should use higher statistical moments. But for higher statistical moments, T-SQL does not offer aggregate functions.

So far, we've worked with aggregate functions over whole datasets. This is useful in situations in which all records in our data set belong to the same kind of information. However, in common cases, we have datasets that contain data of the same type (for example, prices or expenses), but for several categories of information (for example, the price of a whole bike is even higher than the price of a bike tire only). This is why we need to use groups to divide sections or categories of data. The following section describes how grouping works and how to use it.

Using groups

Groups are what make aggregate queries even more useful and readable for users. This is why groups are used heavily in reporting. For statistical purposes, groups help to calculate aggregations across sections in data to divide the data in accordance with its meaning. Let's go straight to an example. We have a database called `AdventureWorks`. This database contains three tables in the `Production` schema: `ProductCategory`, `ProductSubcategory`, and `Product`. Products are assigned to subcategories, and subcategories are then assigned to categories, so the three tables form a simple hierarchy together. To explore the tables, execute the following query:

```
SELECT
  c.ProductCategoryID
  , c.Name AS CategoryName
  , psc.ProductSubcategoryID
  , psc.Name AS SubcategoryName
  , p.ProductID
  , p.Name AS ProductName
  , ISNULL(p.Color, 'N/A') AS Color
```

```
    , p.ListPrice
    , p.StandardCost
FROM Production.ProductCategory AS c
  JOIN Production.ProductSubcategory AS psc ON c.ProductCategoryID =
psc.ProductCategoryID
  JOIN Production.Product AS p on p.ProductSubcategoryID =
psc.ProductSubcategoryID
```

The preceding query groups nothing; it simply shows which data we have for our further experiments. At this point, we would calculate the count of products in each subcategory. Using `COUNT(*)`, for example, we almost know how to fulfill the task, but to reach the categorization we need to add an extra clause, called `GROUP BY`, to the query. To make the sample as simple as possible, the following query encapsulates the text of the preceding query into a common table expression called `Src`, and then the calculation itself is written on top of the common table expression:

```
; WITH Src AS
(
SELECT
  c.ProductCategoryID
  , c.Name AS CategoryName
  , psc.ProductSubcategoryID
  , psc.Name AS SubcategoryName
  , p.ProductID
  , p.Name AS ProductName
  , ISNULL(p.Color, 'N/A') AS Color
  , p.ListPrice
  , p.StandardCost
FROM Production.ProductCategory AS c
  JOIN Production.ProductSubcategory AS psc ON c.ProductCategoryID =
psc.ProductCategoryID
  JOIN Production.Product AS p on p.ProductSubcategoryID =
psc.ProductSubcategoryID
)
SELECT SubcategoryName
  , COUNT(*) AS ProductCount
FROM Src
GROUP BY SubcategoryName
```

The preceding query introduces the `GROUP BY` clause. This clause is used to declare a set of grouping criteria in the aggregate query. When aggregate query does not need to group by categories, the `GROUP BY` clause is not mandatory. But when we want to categorize our result, we must add the `GROUP BY` clause and declare all columns in the `SELECT` clause, which are not constants. We must also declare those which are not used as an aggregate function parameter. Let's have a go at doing this. To omit the part with the common table expression, let's persist the result of the source query into a temporary table called `#src` using the following statements:

```
DROP TABLE IF EXISTS #src

SELECT
  c.ProductCategoryID
  , c.Name AS CategoryName
  , psc.ProductSubcategoryID
  , psc.Name AS SubcategoryName
  , p.ProductID
  , p.Name AS ProductName
  , ISNULL(p.Color, 'N/A') AS Color
  , p.ListPrice
  , p.StandardCost
INTO #src
FROM Production.ProductCategory AS c
  JOIN Production.ProductSubcategory AS psc ON c.ProductCategoryID =
psc.ProductCategoryID
  JOIN Production.Product AS p on p.ProductSubcategoryID =
psc.ProductSubcategoryID
```

When the preceding query is executed, we should see a result message saying that 295 rows were affected. Now let's execute the following query:

```
SELECT
  COUNT(*) as RecordCount
FROM #src
GROUP BY SubcategoryName
```

The result of the preceding query is a column containing numbers that do not have any information with regards to which group (or `SubcategoryName`, in our case) `RecordCount` belongs. Not so meaningful, is it? However, this proves that we can use the `GROUP BY` clause, even though we don't need to see categories in a result.

We may sometimes use the preceding example to check whether some duplicate values exist. For example, an ID should be unique in extracted dataset, but is it actually?

Let's look at one more example. The following statement omits the GROUP BY clause, but some grouping criteria are declared in the SELECT clause:

```
SELECT SubcategoryName
  , COUNT(*) as RecordCount
FROM #src
```

The result of the preceding query is an error that states that the SubcategoryName column must be included in the GROUP BY clause. The error looks like the following example:

```
Msg 8120, Level 16, State 1, Line 24
Column '#src.SubcategoryName' is invalid in the select list because it is
not contained in either an aggregate function or the GROUP BY clause.
```

The final, following example shows that constants cannot be declared within the GROUP BY clause:

```
SELECT
 SubcategoryName
  , SYSDATETIME() as ResultTime
  , COUNT(*) as RecordCount
FROM #src
GROUP BY SubcategoryName
```

As you can see in the preceding query, the SYSDATETIME() function is not aggregated. However, even if the function is not added to the GROUP BY clause, the query still works.

So far, we have only used one grouping criteria in the GROUP BY clause, but we can also combine more criteria together. All that is needed is to write all of the grouping criteria we need to the GROUP BY clause separated by colons. Let's execute the following query:

```
SELECT
 CategoryName
  , SubcategoryName
  , COUNT(*) as RecordCount
FROM #src
GROUP BY CategoryName, SubcategoryName
```

The result of preceding query shows groups formed of Category names, and then of Subcategory names. Using the GROUP BY clause is relatively straightforward, but what if we want to add subtotals into our result? For this purpose, we have an additional syntax helper, called **grouping sets**.

Grouping sets are useful when we want to calculate not only raw groups, but also higher groups. In the previous example, we combined `CategoryName` and `SubcategoryName`. If you look carefully at this, you can see that the numbers in the `RecordCount` column are the same whether we have a `CategoryName` column added into our query or not. This is because subcategories are fully nested into categories without overlaps. The following sample query will not only calculate record counts for every group built from a combination of categories and subcategories, but it will also compute record count for categories only, and for whole datasets:

```
SELECT
  CategoryName
  , SubcategoryName
  , COUNT(*) as RecordCOunt
FROM #src
GROUP BY GROUPING SETS
(
  (CategoryName, SubcategoryName)
  , (CategoryName)
  , ()
)
```

The `GROUP BY` clause in the preceding query has changed. The `GROUPING SETS` keyword introduces brackets containing sets of grouping criteria also enclosed in brackets. Remember that both brackets are mandatory. In our example we have three grouping sets:

- `(CategoryName, SubcategoryName)`: This grouping set is the same as we have seen in earlier samples, combining both grouping criteria
- `(CategoryName)`: This grouping set ignores subcategories and calculates the result of aggregate functions for categories only
- `()`: Empty brackets, or empty sets of grouping criteria, calculate the aggregate for a whole dataset

When the preceding query is executed, we will see a result similar to the following table:

#	**CategoryName**	**SubcategoryName**	**RecordCount**
...	...	...	...
40	Components	Wheels	14
41	Components	NULL	134
42	NULL	NULL	295

The preceding table shows a part of the result from the preceding query. Here, we can see `NULL` in the `CategoryName` and `SubcategoryName` columns. When `NULL` is in the cell, the value of `COUNT(*)` was calculated without using the column. So in record #41, the record count for all Components is calculated, while for the last record, which has `NULL` in both columns (record #42), a value of 295 is just an amount of records in our #src table.

Using groups is a very important part of aggregate queries. This is because groups give meaning to our aggregations. Sometimes we also need to filter the result of aggregation before it's returned back to a user. In such cases, we use the `HAVING` clause, which we'll learn about in the next section.

Using the HAVING clause

After the aggregation is calculated, we often need to filter out some aggregated records. For example, we want to predict sales of some products, but products sold rarely are not significant for us. The problem is that a regular `WHERE` clause cannot use predicates on aggregated columns. This is why SQL languages have the special `HAVING` clause. Let's explore results from the previous section. Here, we had a result from the following query:

```
SELECT
  CategoryName
  , SubcategoryName
  , COUNT(*) as RecordCount
FROM #src
GROUP BY CategoryName, SubcategoryName
```

The result from the preceding query has 37 rows containing `RecordCount` values from 1 to 43. Let's say that subcategories with fewer than five products are not significant for us. We then have two options of how to filter out subcategories with a small amount of products. The first of these options is shown in the following query:

```
; WITH cte AS
(
SELECT
  CategoryName
  , SubcategoryName
  , COUNT(*) as RecordCount
FROM #src
GROUP BY CategoryName, SubcategoryName
)
SELECT * FROM cte WHERE RecordCount >= 5
```

This query uses CTE to calculate aggregations, and when the result of the CTE query is made, it is filtered using the `WHERE` clause of the query and the CTE. The preceding query works, but using the `HAVING` clause makes the task at least more readable. Let's look at the following query:

```
SELECT
  CategoryName
  , SubcategoryName
  , COUNT(*) as RecordCount
FROM #src
GROUP BY CategoryName, SubcategoryName
HAVING COUNT(*) >= 5
```

The preceding query does not use CTE, but it produces exactly the same result. From the preceding sample query we also see that the `HAVING` clause, if it's present, always follows the `GROUP BY` clause.

Now we have two clauses that are useful for data filtering, so let's explain what the difference is between both clauses. The `WHERE` clause filters data before it's aggregated; it impacts the amount of records coming into the aggregation. The `HAVING` clause filters data after it's aggregated. You may wonder whether we can add an aggregate function as part of a predicate into the `WHERE` clause. However, we must not do this because the result of the aggregate function is not known when the `WHERE` clause filters rows. Can we add a not aggregated column into the `HAVING` clause? Yes, we can, but it reduces the readability of our queries. Let's explore this in the following example. In this example, we don't want to aggregate data for the `Clothing` category; the following queries will do this for us:

```
-- confusing condition added to the HAVING clause
SELECT
  CategoryName
  , SubcategoryName
  , COUNT(*) as RecordCount
FROM #src
GROUP BY CategoryName, SubcategoryName
HAVING COUNT(*) >= 5 AND CategoryName != 'Clothing'

-- clearly written query filtering records on right places
SELECT
  CategoryName
  , SubcategoryName
  , COUNT(*) as RecordCount
FROM #src
WHERE CategoryName != 'Clothing'
GROUP BY CategoryName, SubcategoryName
HAVING COUNT(*) >= 5
```

Both queries in the preceding sample create the same result. However, the first query calculates all aggregations over all records and then filters out all categories with fewer than five records, including the `Clothing` category. The second query eliminates all records of the `Clothing` category first, and then calculates aggregations in the rest of the records. It then filters out all categories with fewer than five records.

When a developer is deeply immersed in development, sometimes things such as the first query in the preceding example may occur. SQL Server is intelligent enough to normalize the query in order to save resources (taking a look at estimated plans for both queries in the preceding example). However, it's always better to make things clear and readable, so ensure that you always refactor your queries to the most correct and readable script.

Using aggregate functions is a very common task, not only for data science/machine learning purposes, but also for many tasks in BI and reporting. Nowadays, T-SQL also contains a syntax that allows us to to rank the distribution of data in several ways. We will learn about these options in the next section.

Ranking, framing, and windowing

In the previous section, we went through almost all aggregate functions, from the most popular, the `SUM` or `AVG` aggregates, to slightly more complicated aggregates, such as `STDEV` and `VAR`. Aggregate functions give an overview of statistical measures that are useful for further analysis and machine learning parameters. However, we often also need to sort or somehow compare data in an incoming dataset. For such purposes, T-SQL provides a set of **ranking functions**. The ranking function is a function that gives a numerical evaluation to each record in a dataset. Rankings always work over whole datasets or on parts of the dataset in a similar way to the grouping feature of aggregate queries, but without creating groups of typical aggregates. This feature, which is tightly bound to ranking, is called **framing**. In this section, we will learn about framing concepts in conjunction with ranking functions.

Ranking functions

SQL Server offers four ranking functions, explained in this section. All ranking functions have similar behavior and common properties, including the following:

- The output of every ranking function is an integer.
- Using the integer value, every ranking function evaluates (or adds a sorting criterion to) every record in a dataset.
- Ranking functions always work over frames in incoming datasets. This is why ranking functions never stay alone without an `OVER` clause, which defines the frame.

In the next section, we will start with the first of the ranking functions, called `ROW_NUMBER`. Using this function, we will demonstrate how to declare frames.

ROW_NUMBER

The `ROW_NUMBER` ranking function gives numbers to every record in a dataset. So, when we need to sort records and add sorting numbers to the records, `ROW_NUMBER` does it for us. The `ROW_NUMBER` function, as with all other ranking functions, needs the `OVER` clause. The `OVER` clause declares sorted parts of records in a dataset called **frames**, and every ranking function works on every frame. The `OVER` clause has three parts:

- `PARTITION BY`
- `ORDER BY`
- `ROWS BETWEEN`

The best way to show what every part of the `OVER` clause is dedicated to is to go through several examples. The following example shows the basics of how to use the ranking function. We have a set of products in a table called `Production.Product` in the `AdventureWorks` database. Within this table, we need to add a serial number to each record. The syntax is as follows:

```
SELECT
  ProductID
  , Name
  , ListPrice
  , StandardCost
  , ROW_NUMBER() OVER() AS SerialNumber
FROM Production.Product
```

Did you try to execute the preceding query? If so, it didn't work. The goal of the preceding query is simply to show that the ranking function (`ROW_NUMBER`, in our case) must always be followed by the `OVER` clause. The brackets following the `OVER` clause then contain parts mentioned in the preceding bulleted list. When we carefully read the following error message generated by preceding query, we'll see that the error message exactly describes what's missing in the `OVER` clause. Take a look at the message in the following sample:

```
The function 'ROW_NUMBER' must have an OVER clause with ORDER BY.
```

When we add serial numbers to records using the `ROW_NUMBER` function, the `OVER` clause must at least contain the `ORDER BY` clause. This is because the numbering of records must be made in accordance with a sorting criteria. The `ORDER BY` clause itself has the same behavior as when used in the `SELECT` statement. So, let's get things working. The following sample shows the same query, but the `ORDER BY` clause is used within the `OVER` clause:

```
SELECT
  ProductID
  , Name
  , ListPrice
  , StandardCost
  , ROW_NUMBER() OVER(ORDER BY Name) AS SerialNumber
FROM Production.Product
```

Let's take a look at the result of the preceding query. We will see that every record has a number rising from 1 to the amount of records in the `SerialNumber` column; this is its intended behavior. However, let's explore the order of the records. In the result of the preceding query, the records are sorted according to the `SerialNumber` and `Name` columns, which is just a coincidence. The `ORDER BY` clause written within the `OVER` clause is used with the ranking function only; it is not used to sort a whole result set. We can prove how the sorting behaves using the `ORDER BY` clause as a clause of the `SELECT` statement. Let's execute the following query:

```
SELECT
  ProductID
  , Name
  , ListPrice
  , StandardCost
  , ROW_NUMBER() OVER(ORDER BY Name) AS SerialNumber
FROM Production.Product
ORDER BY ProductID
```

The result of the preceding query is sorted in accordance with the `ProductID` values, while `SerialNumber` is unsorted. The preceding sample shows that ranking functions do not force us to use sorting only dictated by the `ORDER BY` clause within the `OVER` clause of the ranking function.

The second clause that is often added to the `OVER` clause is `PARTITION BY`. This clause creates frames, which are groups of records for which the ranking function works. For example, we would repeat the number of records using `ROW_NUMBER` functions. We don't want to have one numbered list, but we want to start numbering from 1 for each category of products. The following statement shows how to use the `PARTITION BY` clause:

```
SELECT
  p.Name AS ProductName
  , pc.Name AS CategoryName
  , ROW_NUMBER() OVER
    (
      PARTITION BY pc.Name
      ORDER BY p.Name
    ) AS RecordNumber
FROM Production.Product AS p
  JOIN Production.ProductSubcategory AS psc
    ON p.ProductSubcategoryID = psc.ProductSubcategoryID
  JOIN Production.ProductCategory AS pc
    ON pc.ProductCategoryID = psc.ProductCategoryID
```

The preceding query joins the whole hierarchy of products, product subcategories, and categories to create a result set with category names and product names. We wanted to number records separately for each category, so it was necessary to add the `PARTITION BY` clause to the `OVER` clause. The following table represents a shortened result set:

ProductName	**CategoryName**	**RecordNumber**
All-Purpose Bike Stand	Accessories	1
Bike Wash – Dissolver	Accessories	2
...	...	...
Touring-Panniers, Large	Accessories	28
Water Bottle – 30 oz.	Accessories	29
Mountain-100 Black, 38	Bikes	1
Mountain-100 Black, 42	Bikes	2
...	...	...
Touring-3000 Yellow, 62	Bikes	97
AWC Logo Cap	Clothing	1
Classic Vest, L	Clothing	2
...	...	...

As depicted in the preceding table, the ROW_NUMBER function starts new numbers every time the CategoryName value is changed. This is what we declare using the PARTITION BY clause.

Using ROW_NUMBER is very common for tasks such as creating a report with a numbered list of people attending an event. However, the ROW_NUMBER function could also be used, for example, in the following situation:

Some source systems do not track changes in data, but we need to track changes in source data for further analysis. Let's assume that the source system is obsolete and does not support modern features such as the temporal tables mentioned in Chapter 5, *Data Transformation and Cleansing with T-SQL*. One of the ways to track data changes is to make a copy of data every day, and detect changed, new, or deleted records on our own. Let's prepare a source table first. This will be a table containing service tickets records with a column holding their status. Let's execute the following simple script to create a table, called ServiceTicket, and to add several sample records:

```
CREATE TABLE ServiceTicket
(
Id int not null IDENTITY CONSTRAINT pk_ServiceTicket PRIMARY KEY
, IssueDate date NOT NULL
, Description nvarchar(200) NOT NULL
, Status tinyint NOT NULL CONSTRAINT chk_Status CHECK(Status BETWEEN 1 AND
3)
)
GO

INSERT ServiceTicket VALUES
('20180511', 'New problem occured', 1)
, ('20180511', 'Second problem occured', 1)
, ('20180512', 'Network issue', 1)
GO
```

The preceding script simulates a source system. We are now starting to create structures for the archive table, which holds everyday copies of the source table. The following script prepares the table for us:

```
CREATE TABLE ServiceTicketHistory
(
Id int not null
, LoadDate date NOT NULL
, IssueDate date NOT NULL
, Description nvarchar(200) NOT NULL
, Status tinyint NOT NULL CONSTRAINT chk_StatusHistory CHECK(Status BETWEEN
1 AND 3)
```

```
, CONSTRAINT pk_ServiceTicketHistory PRIMARY KEY (Id, LoadDate)
)
GO
```

The preceding script creates a table called `ServiceTicketHistory`. Its structure is almost the same as the source `ServiceTicket` table, but the primary key constraint was changed as the `LoadDate` column was added into it, and the `Id` column no longer has the `IDENTITY` function.

Now we need a stored procedure in order to load data from the source to the destination table every day. The following sample shows the stored procedure:

```
CREATE OR ALTER PROC procLoadServiceTicketHistory
  @sampleLoadDate date = getdate
as
INSERT ServiceTicketHistory (Id, LoadDate, IssueDate, Description, Status)
SELECT Id
, @sampleLoadDate
, IssueDate
, Description, Status FROM ServiceTicket
GO
```

The preceding script creates a stored procedure called `procLoadServiceTicketHistory`, which simply takes data from the source table and inserts it into the history table. The `@sampleLoadDate` parameter is not needed, but we are going to simulate daily loads in a couple of minutes, so we will fake the load date using this parameter.

The initial load was executed on June 1 using the following statement:

```
EXEC procLoadServiceTicketHistory '20180601'
```

Starting on June 2, some changes occurred in the source table. Executed as shown here, the following script will simulate changes and history will load together:

```
-- some daily work is done
UPDATE ServiceTicket SET Status = 3 where Id = 2
INSERT ServiceTicket VALUES
('20180602', 'SQL Server stopped suddenly', 1)

-- new version of data is loaded
EXEC procLoadServiceTicketHistory '20180602'

-- some daily work is done
UPDATE ServiceTicket SET Status = 2 where Id = 4
-- new version of data is loaded
```

```
EXEC procLoadServiceTicketHistory '20180603'

-- and so on...
```

This script made some changes in the `ServiceTicket` table. These changes were caught daily by night load to the `ServiceTicketHistory` table. Loads were running daily from June 1 to June 3. Now we need to obtain the status of every ticket—let's take June 2 as an example. The following statement shows how to resolve this task:

```
; WITH cte AS
(
  SELECT *, ROW_NUMBER() OVER(PARTITION BY Id ORDER BY LoadDate DESC) AS rn
  FROM ServiceTicketHistory
  WHERE LoadDate = '20180602'
)
SELECT * FROM cte WHERE rn = 1
```

The preceding statement shows how to reconstruct some state from history snapshots loaded into a table. The problem is that ranking functions cannot be used in a `WHERE` clause of queries. This is why we need to resolve the problem in two steps. In the first step, we are going to calculate `ROW_NUMBER`. The result is then encapsulated into a common table expression. In the second step, we are going to filter the result of the `ROW_NUMBER` function from the common table expression in the same way as from a regular column. Common table expressions are very helpful in such cases.

This section probably used `ROW_NUMBER`, the most simple ranking function for explaining ranking and framing. The next few sections will describe the remaining ranking functions.

RANK

The `RANK` ranking function numbers records in a certain result set (or its partitions) from the perspective of sports results. Let's dive straight into an example of this. In the same way as in the previous section, we have a table of categorized products and we want to sort these products into categories according to their list price from most to least expensive. The following query is almost the same as one of the queries introduced in the previous section. The only change is that instead of the `ROW_NUMBER` function, we use the `RANK` function:

```
SELECT
  p.Name AS ProductName
  , pc.Name AS CategoryName
  , p.ListPrice
  , RANK() OVER
    (
```

```
        PARTITION BY pc.Name
        ORDER BY ListPrice DESC
    ) AS RecordRank
FROM Production.Product AS p
  JOIN Production.ProductSubcategory AS psc
    ON p.ProductSubcategoryID = psc.ProductSubcategoryID
  JOIN Production.ProductCategory AS pc
    ON pc.ProductCategoryID = psc.ProductCategoryID
```

The preceding query adds a serial number beginning with 1 into the `RecordRank` column. We already know that the numbering will start from 1 for every category of products. For this reason, the following table contains just part of the ranking results for products from the Accessories category:

ProductName	CategoryName	ListPrice	RecordRank
All-Purpose Bike Stand	Accessories	159.00	1
Touring-Panniers, Large	Accessories	125.00	2
Hitch Rack – 4-Bike	Accessories	120.00	3
Hydration Pack – 70 oz.	Accessories	54.99	4
Headlights - Weatherproof	Accessories	44.99	5
HL Mountain Tire	Accessories	35.00	6
Headlights – Dual-Beam	Accessories	34.99	7
Sport-100 Helmet, Red	Accessories	34.99	7
Sport-100 Helmet, Black	Accessories	34.99	7
Sport-100 Helmet, Blue	Accessories	34.99	7
HL Road Tire	Accessories	32.60	11
ML Mountain Tire	Accessories	29.99	12
...	...	...	...

Let's pay attention to the last two columns of this table. The `ORDER BY` clause contained in the `OVER` clause sorts list prices in descending order. When the price between two following rows is changed, then the new `RANK` value is added. This can be seen in the first six records in the table, for example.

When the price between two (or more) following rows is not changed (see the 7th to 10th record in the preceding table), the `RANK` value remains the same, but internally `RANK` still counts records. When the value of the price is changed between two following records, a value that is new but not increasing by one is substituted. This is seen between records containing Sport-100 Helmet, Blue, and ML Mountain Tire products.

Sports results operate in the same way as the `RANK` function. When two sprinters cross the finish line at exactly the same time, both will receive a gold medal, but the silver medal is not given to anybody. The next sprinter (crossing the finish line in the second best time) then gets the bronze medal.

When we don't want the option to skip numbers, we can use a very similar ranking function called `DENSE_RANK`, which we will learn about in the next section.

DENSE_RANK

The `DENSE_RANK` ranking function is very similar to the previously explained `RANK` function. The only difference here is that `DENSE_RANK` does not skip values when it ranks records. Let's simply repeat the previous sample query. The following statement adds one new column with the `DENSE_RANK` function. The comparison of results of both functions is then straightforward. The following statement also shows that we can use more ranking functions in one query:

```
SELECT
  p.Name AS ProductName
  , pc.Name AS CategoryName
  , p.ListPrice
  , RANK() OVER
    (
      PARTITION BY pc.Name
      ORDER BY ListPrice DESC
    ) AS RecordRank
  , DENSE_RANK() OVER
    (
      PARTITION BY pc.Name
      ORDER BY ListPrice DESC
    ) AS DenseRecordRank
FROM Production.Product AS p
  JOIN Production.ProductSubcategory AS psc
    ON p.ProductSubcategoryID = psc.ProductSubcategoryID
  JOIN Production.ProductCategory AS pc
    ON pc.ProductCategoryID = psc.ProductCategoryID
```

The preceding query generates the result set with two columns computed by the ranking functions. The `RecordRank` column uses the `RANK` function, and the `DenseRecordRank` uses the new `DENSE_RANK` function. The following table shows a part of the result with the differences between the `RANK` and `DENSE_RANK` functions:

ProductName	**CategoryName**	**ListPrice**	**RecordRank**	**DenseRecordRank**
...	...	...	...	...
HL Mountain Tire	Accessories	35.00	6	6
Headlights – Dual-Beam	Accessories	34.99	7	7
Sport-100 Helmet, Red	Accessories	34.99	7	7
Sport-100 Helmet, Black	Accessories	34.99	7	7
Sport-100 Helmet, Blue	Accessories	34.99	7	7
HL Road Tire	Accessories	32.60	11	8
...	...	...	...	...

The difference between the RANK and DENSE_RANK functions is best seen in the HL Road Tire record. The RANK function skipped the number of records with the same list price, but the DENSE_RANK did not. Consequently, when we want to have continuous numbering, the DENSE_RANK option is the right choice.

SQL Server has four ranking functions, and the next section will describe the last one, called NTILE.

NTILE

The NTILE ranking function is used to set integer values to records for even (or almost even) distribution. We can say that the NTILE function creates a numbered section of records. This function is also the only ranking function that consumes a parameter. The parameter's value sets the number of sections that we want to have. Let's explore how this works in the following statement. We still have the same list of products, but now we want to divide each partition into— let's say, three evenly-sized record parts:

```
SELECT
  p.Name AS ProductName
  , pc.Name AS CategoryName
  , p.ListPrice
  , NTILE(3) OVER
    (
      PARTITION BY pc.Name
      ORDER BY ListPrice DESC
    ) AS Section
FROM Production.Product AS p
  JOIN Production.ProductSubcategory AS psc
    ON p.ProductSubcategoryID = psc.ProductSubcategoryID
  JOIN Production.ProductCategory AS pc
    ON pc.ProductCategoryID = psc.ProductCategoryID
```

As has been seen in the preceding query, NTILE is used in exactly the same way as other ranking functions. The only mandatory clause for the OVER clause is ORDER BY, but we wanted to divide records within certain categories, which is why the PARTITION BY clause is also used. The following table shows a fragment of a result in the **Accessories** and **Bikes** category:

<table>
<tr><th>ProductName</th><th>CategoryName</th><th>ListPrice</th><th>Section</th><th>Comment</th></tr>
<tr><td>All-Purpose Bike Stand</td><td>Accessories</td><td>159.00</td><td>1</td><td rowspan="8">The Accessories category contains 29 rows.
29 is not divisible by 3.
This is why section #1 has 10 rows, section #2 has 10 rows, and section #3 has only 9 rows.</td></tr>
<tr><td>...</td><td>...</td><td>...</td><td>...</td></tr>
<tr><td>Sport-100 Helmet, Blue</td><td>Accessories</td><td>34.99</td><td>1</td></tr>
<tr><td>HL Road Tire</td><td>Accessories</td><td>32.60</td><td>2</td></tr>
<tr><td>...</td><td>...</td><td>...</td><td>...</td></tr>
<tr><td>Minipump</td><td>Accessories</td><td>19.99</td><td>2</td></tr>
<tr><td>Taillights – Battery-Powered</td><td>Accessories</td><td>13.99</td><td>3</td></tr>
<tr><td>...</td><td>...</td><td>...</td><td>...</td></tr>
<tr><td>Patch Kit/8 Patches</td><td>Accessories</td><td>2.29</td><td>3</td><td></td></tr>
<tr><td>Road-150 Red, 62</td><td>Bikes</td><td>3578.27</td><td>1</td><td rowspan="2">With each new category, sections are numbering from 1 again.</td></tr>
<tr><td>...</td><td>...</td><td>...</td><td>...</td></tr>
</table>

This table shows outer records of each section of the Accessories category, which is why the Comment column (which is not coming from the query) is added to the table to explain the amount of records in each section, and also to explain how the `NTILE` function works.

Ranking functions were introduced in SQL Server 2008, probably as a starting point for framing and windowing. In newer versions, SQL Server added new possibilities of how to use the `OVER` clause in conjunction with common aggregate functions, and also with new statistical percentile functions. In the next section, we will look at how this works.

Running aggregates

In the previous two sections, we learned about aggregate functions and then about ranking functions. With the help of ranking functions, we learned about framing. Beginning on SQL Server 2012, Microsoft introduced a feature using aggregate functions working over frames and windows. In this section, we will talk about this feature, which is called **running aggregates**. In the first part of the section, we will use common aggregate functions in combination with the OVER clause, and in the second part we will learn about percentile count.

Using aggregate functions in running aggregates

Aggregate queries are very common in tasks such as querying data for reporting purposes, processing data cubes in SQL Server Analysis Services, and checking (non) existing records during data transformations. But we also need to summarize values over dimensions.

As an example, we would mention the summary of expenses over time. This is exactly what the **running aggregate** term means. In earlier versions of SQL Server, when the need for running aggregates occurred, we basically had two options. The first of these was to calculate running values using cursors, while the second was to calculate running aggregates on the client side. For example, running aggregates were computed over collections in C#. Quite a good option for running value calculations is to use reports in SQL Server Reporting Services. Expressions in report definition have special functions called `RunningAggregate` for such tasks, but this does not solve the need to calculate running values efficiently on a database site.

Nowadays, it's very good to know that aggregate functions are not intended for common aggregate queries only, but we can also make them cooperate with the `OVER` clause. Let's explore aggregate functions now.

Using aggregate functions

In the previous section, we saw that the `OVER` clause does not aggregate records into grouped ones. This is the main benefit when it comes to giving raw values side by side with their aggregation. Running aggregates help to calculate what percentage is a certain raw value from a whole set of values, for example. Let's start with a very simple example of a running aggregate.

In the `AdventureWorks` database, we have a table called `Sales.SalesOrderHeader`. This table contains data about orders issued by customers. The table contains many columns, but for our games—which we are going to play with running aggregates—we just need a few of them:

- `OrderDate`: This column contains the date when the order was issued by the customer.
- `SalesPersonId`: This column contains the identifier of the person who processed the order.
- `SubTotal`: This is the gross price of the whole order.

Using this table makes it possible to see how much money is spent by customers over time. For the first time, we can make as small a result set as possible in order to transform data to year totals of purchase amounts. We will use a common table expression for this. The following query does the transformation and shows the raw result:

```
; WITH cte AS
(
SELECT YEAR(OrderDate) AS OrderYear
  , SUM(SubTotal) AS YearlySubtotal
FROM Sales.SalesOrderHeader
GROUP BY YEAR(OrderDate)
)
SELECT * FROM cte
```

When the preceding query is executed, we can see that data in the `Sales.SalesOrderHeader` table covers a period of four years from 2011 to 2014, so we have four rows with yearly `SubTotal` summaries. The preceding query does not calculate running values, but its result is small enough for the best readability of the following example. From now on, we will work with the query using `cte` only.

Now we need to add every `YearlySubtotal` to all `YearlySubtotals` from previous years. To resolve this task, we must combine the `SUM` aggregate (because we are going to add numbers) with the `OVER` clause (because we are not writing an actual aggregate query). The following query demonstrates how to do this:

```
; WITH cte AS
(
SELECT YEAR(OrderDate) AS OrderYear
  , SUM(SubTotal) AS YearlySubtotal
FROM Sales.SalesOrderHeader
GROUP BY YEAR(OrderDate)
)
SELECT *
  , SUM(YearlySubtotal) OVER
  (
    ORDER BY OrderYear
    ROWS BETWEEN UNBOUNDED PRECEDING AND CURRENT ROW
  ) AS RunningSubtotal
FROM cte
```

The preceding query uses the `SUM` aggregate function with a parameter of `YearlySubtotal`, but it also uses the `OVER` clause in almost the same way as in the previous section. However, there's one important novelty, and this is the `ROWS BETWEEN UNBOUNDED PRECEDING AND CURRENT ROW` element. Even though this part sounds tricky and hard to remember, it forms the **window**. So far, now we were talking about frames only because ranking functions does not work in windows, but for running values it's a necessity for making it work. Let's repeat existing knowledge about `OVER` clauses and make the new clause known:

- The `ORDER BY` part sorts data meaningfully. In our example, when we want to add subtotals year by year, the data must be sorted by years. Different or non-existent sorting would generate meaningless results.
- The `PARTITION BY` part is not used in our example. In such cases, a whole result set is the only section in which the calculation is done. However, when used, the `PARTITION BY` clause forms sections of records called **frames**.
- Many calculations, namely ranking functions, work over a whole frame. However, this is not completely true for running values. A running value runs over a window opened row by row until the end of a certain frame. This is the `ROWS BETWEEN` clause.

To summarize the `OVER` clause, we can explore the following table, which shows the results of the previous query:

OrderYear	YearlySubtotal	RunningSubtotal
2011	12,641,672.2129	12,641,672.2129
2012	33,524,301.326	46,165,973.5389
2013	43,622,479.0537	89,788,452.5926
2014	20,057,928.8113	109,846,381.4039

Let's check whether the running value in the RunningSubtotal column in the preceding table works. For the year 2011, the YearlySubtotal and RunningSubtotal values have to be the same. For the year 2012, YearlySubtotal's value is added to previous value of RunningSubtotal. In other words, *12,641,672.2129 + 33,524,301.326* is exactly *46,165,973.5389*. This means that we can continue to the end of the result set.

`ROWS BETWEEN` could not be written every time because its default behavior is `ROWS BETWEEN UNBOUNDED PRECEDING AND CURRENT ROW`. However, for better readability of our queries, it's good practice to write it every time. Try it yourself to execute the preceding query without `ROWS BETWEEN` and compare the results.

Let's play with the data a bit more. At this point, we may wonder whether we can calculate the running value from bottom to top. In answer to this, we can write it, but SQL Server will turn sorting criteria from ascending to descending only. We can try this using the following query:

```
; WITH cte AS
(
SELECT YEAR(OrderDate) AS OrderYear
  , SUM(SubTotal) AS YearlySubtotal
FROM Sales.SalesOrderHeader
GROUP BY YEAR(OrderDate)
)
SELECT *
  , SUM(YearlySubtotal) OVER
  (
    ORDER BY OrderYear
    ROWS BETWEEN UNBOUNDED FOLLOWING AND CURRENT ROW
  ) AS RunningSubtotal
FROM cte
```

In the preceding query, we changed `UNBOUNDED PRECEDING` to `UNBOUNDED FOLLOWING`. If you execute the preceding query, you will see that the results are incorrect because of an error. This is because SQL Server does not read data from bottom to top, meaning that `ROWS BETWEEN` makes an empty interval. If we want to calculate the running value, we must change the ROWS BETWEEN, sentence as shown in the following query:

```
; WITH cte AS
(
SELECT YEAR(OrderDate) AS OrderYear
  , SUM(SubTotal) AS YearlySubtotal
FROM Sales.SalesOrderHeader
GROUP BY YEAR(OrderDate)
)
SELECT *
  , SUM(YearlySubtotal) OVER
  (
    ORDER BY OrderYear
    ROWS BETWEEN CURRENT ROW AND UNBOUNDED FOLLOWING
  ) AS RunningSubtotal
FROM cte
```

The preceding query will return the result set where years will be sorted in a descending order so that running values will be calculated from the year 2014 to 2011. However, we can do the same thing without handling `ROWS BETWEEN`. We can leave the original default `ROWS BETWEEN UNBOUNDED PRECEDING AND CURRENT ROW`, or we can simply write nothing, and at the same time we can change sorting using the DESC keyword, as shown in the following query:

```
; WITH cte AS
(
SELECT YEAR(OrderDate) AS OrderYear
  , SUM(SubTotal) AS YearlySubtotal
FROM Sales.SalesOrderHeader
GROUP BY YEAR(OrderDate)
)
SELECT *
  , SUM(YearlySubtotal) OVER
  (
    ORDER BY OrderYear DESC
    ROWS BETWEEN UNBOUNDED PRECEDING AND CURRENT ROW
  ) AS RunningSubtotal
FROM cte
```

The result of both preceding options will be the same, but it's still useful to know that we can open the window from the preceding to the following rows. In many cases, we do not need to calculate the current running aggregate by adding a value row by row, but we would also need to calculate the aggregate over a whole section in the result set. We have two methods to achieve this. The following example contains two queries. Both queries calculate the summary of whole order subtotals. The first is written more traditionally and uses a subquery, while the second query uses running aggregates:

```
; WITH cte AS
(
SELECT YEAR(OrderDate) AS OrderYear
  , SUM(SubTotal) AS YearlySubtotal
FROM Sales.SalesOrderHeader
GROUP BY YEAR(OrderDate)
)
SELECT *
  , (SELECT SUM(YearlySubtotal) FROM cte) AS WholeSubtotal
FROM cte
ORDER BY OrderYear

; WITH cte AS
(
SELECT YEAR(OrderDate) AS OrderYear
  , SUM(SubTotal) AS YearlySubtotal
```

```
FROM Sales.SalesOrderHeader
GROUP BY YEAR(OrderDate)
)
SELECT *
  , SUM(YearlySubtotal) OVER
  (
    ORDER BY OrderYear
    ROWS BETWEEN UNBOUNDED PRECEDING AND UNBOUNDED FOLLOWING
  ) AS WholeSubtotal
FROM cte
ORDER BY OrderYear
```

Both queries in the preceding example use the same common table expression as input and they both generate exactly the same result. The result is shown in the following table:

OrderYear	YearlySubtotal	WholeSubtotal
2011	12,641,672.2129	109,846,381.4039
2012	33,524,301.326	109,846,381.4039
2013	43,622,479.0537	109,846,381.4039
2014	20,057,928.8113	109,846,381.4039

First of all, let's prove that the amount of 109,846,381.4039 in the WholeSubtotal column is actually the whole total. We can execute the subquery from the first query in the preceding example, and we will see that the result is the same number. We can also compare WholeSubtotal from the preceding table with the value of RunningSubtotal from two tables earlier. Both numbers are equal. So the aggregation works perfectly, and exactly as expected.

Another interesting point is the `ROWS BETWEEN UNBOUNDED PRECEDING AND UNBOUNDED FOLLOWING`. This says to SQL Server that even if we write the so-called running aggregate, we want to keep the same value for the whole frame in every record of it.

This may make us wonder why we need to learn new syntax if subqueries are well-known and traditional. This is because of performance. We are working with a very small amount of data, but the running aggregate is still twice as fast as the traditional subquery. It is useful to keep in mind that our only frame is whole datasets, meaning that we don't need to correlate the subquery with the main query. A correlated subquery might cause the main query to slow down even more.

Knowing running aggregates is useful for being able to resolve tasks asking for percent comparison, for example. Let's have one more example using running aggregates to compare what percentage of yearly subtotals is represented in the grand total. Let's explore the following query:

```
; WITH cte AS
(
SELECT YEAR(OrderDate) AS OrderYear
   , SUM(SubTotal) AS YearlySubtotal
FROM Sales.SalesOrderHeader
GROUP BY YEAR(OrderDate)
)
SELECT *
   , SUM(YearlySubtotal) OVER
   (
     ORDER BY OrderYear
     ROWS BETWEEN UNBOUNDED PRECEDING AND UNBOUNDED FOLLOWING
   ) AS WholeSubtotal
   , 100 * YearlySubtotal / SUM(YearlySubtotal) OVER
   (
     ORDER BY OrderYear
     ROWS BETWEEN UNBOUNDED PRECEDING AND UNBOUNDED FOLLOWING
   ) AS PercentOfWhole
FROM cte
ORDER BY OrderYear
```

The preceding query is just a copy of the already known query enlarged by the last expression. Because this expression is quite long, let's make it a bit simpler by reading it in the form of *100 * YearlySubtotal / Running aggregate*. As seen in this example, we can use running aggregates or even ranking functions within more complex expressions as and when they are needed. However, it's still true that we cannot use anything that has the `OVER` clause in the `WHERE` clause of the queries.

Let's take a look at the result of the preceding example in the following table:

OrderYear	YearlySubtotal	WholeSubtotal	PercentOfWhole
2011	12,641,672.2129	109,846,381.4039	11.5085
2012	33,524,301.326	109,846,381.4039	30.5192
2013	43,622,479.0537	109,846,381.4039	39.7122
2014	20,057,928.8113	109,846,381.4039	18.2599

This table shows the result with a percentage of yearly subtotals against the grand total. To show how useful it is to have information such as this, let's first think about why this is the case, taking into account the fact that the year 2014 has a dramatically smaller percentage. There could be many reasons for this—perhaps there was a crisis, or a factory strike. Let's go back to the beginning of this chapter and try to use one of the first aggregate functions before moving on to the following query:

```
SELECT MIN(OrderDate), MAX(OrderDate) FROM Sales.SalesOrderHeader
```

The result of this query suggests that the oldest record in the `Sales.SalesOrderHeader` table was inserted at the end of May 2011, and the newest record was inserted at the end of June 2014. In other words, the first and last years are not complete.

This is a great example of why data exploration and statistics are so important. We must always preview the data and continue to play with it, looking for any strange or abnormal values as well as ratios between values.

This section described how to work with running aggregates, but we also need to follow trends in our data. For these tasks, we have special functions, which we will read about in the next section.

Using the LEAD and LAG functions

The previous section was about running aggregates, which almost work in a cumulative approach. However, we also need to compare values, laying each value next to each other in order to monitor the progress of the value or its trend. For this kind of data exploration, SQL Server has the `LAG` and `LEAD` functions. Both functions use the `OVER` clause to sort data appropriately and to determine frames. The `LAG` function then searches backward for preceding values from the same column and sets it as its result, while the `LEAD` function searches for the next value in a dataset. Let's introduce a short example:

Our `Sales.SalesOrderHeader` table contains order dates (reduced using CTE to order years only to shorten the result sets), subtotals, and salespeople represented by their identifiers. We could join the appropriate table with the names of the people, but for now that is not important. We want to see how much of the subtotal every salesperson processes year by year, and we also want to know whether they process more or less than in the previous year.

First of all, we need to adjust the CTE used up so far. We'll add the `SalesPersonID` column into the `SELECT` and `GROUP BY` clause. Because not every order has a salesperson assigned, some records contain `NULL`. We should eliminate `NULL` in order to ensure that everything works fine. The complete CTE with the testing `SELECT` statement is as follows:

```
; WITH cte AS
(
SELECT YEAR(OrderDate) AS OrderYear
  , ISNULL(SalesPersonID, 0) as SalesPersonID
  , SUM(SubTotal) AS YearlySubtotal
FROM Sales.SalesOrderHeader
GROUP BY YEAR(OrderDate), ISNULL(SalesPersonID, 0)
)
SELECT * FROM cte
ORDER BY SalesPersonID, OrderYear
```

When exploring the preceding query, pay attention to the `SELECT` statement encapsulated within the CTE, simply called `cte`. The new expression, `ISNULL(SalesPersonID, 0) AS SalesPersonID`, was added to the `SELECT` clause, and it was also added into the `GROUP BY` clause (without the alias, as aliases are not permitted in `GROUP BY`) because it's mandatory. The `SELECT` statement under the CTE shows the results in the following table:

OrderYear	**SalesPersonID**	**YearlySubtotal**
...	...	...
2011	274	28,926.2465
2012	274	453,524.5233
...	...	...

Our data is prepared as shown in the preceding table, and now we can start to compare yearly subtotals for every salesperson over the years. So we need to use the `LAG` function over the `SalesPersonID` frame with sorted `OrderYears`. Are you brave enough to write a query on your own using the `LAG` function? If so, compare your query with the following one. If you are not, take a look at the following query right now:

```
; WITH cte AS
(
SELECT YEAR(OrderDate) AS OrderYear
  , ISNULL(SalesPersonID, 0) as SalesPersonID
  , SUM(SubTotal) AS YearlySubtotal
FROM Sales.SalesOrderHeader
GROUP BY YEAR(OrderDate), ISNULL(SalesPersonID, 0)
)
SELECT *
  , LAG(YearlySubtotal, 1, NULL) OVER
  (
```

```
    PARTITION BY SalesPersonID
    ORDER BY OrderYear
  ) AS PreviousYearlySubtotal
FROM cte
ORDER BY SalesPersonID, OrderYear
```

The preceding query uses the CTE described in the example with the running aggregate `SUM` function, so our attention should be on the `LAG` function only. As we have seen, the `LAG` (and also `LEAD`) function needs three parameters:

- The column or expression which has to be shown in the result (`YearlyIncome` in our example).
- The number of records to be skipped back when using `LAG`, or the number of records to be skipped forth when using `LEAD` (we want to see a value from previous record, which is why we set the parameter to 1).
- What to set as a result when a record is not found. In our case, we would set the value to `NULL`.

To be sure that the `LAG` function works, let's explore the following table with a part of the result set:

OrderYear	**SalesPersonID**	**YearlySubtotal**	**PreviousYearlySubtotal**
...	...	...	...
2011	274	28,926.2465	NULL
2012	274	453,524.5233	28,926.2465
2013	274	431,088.7238	453,524.5233
2014	274	178,584.3625	431,088.7238
...	...	...	...

This table shows that for the first record with a `SalesPersonID`, the previous value of `YearlySubtotal` does not exist, therefore `NULL` (or any other value for the third parameter of the `LAG` function) appears in the `PreviousYearlySubtotal` column. However, for the year 2012, the `PreviousYearlySubtotal` column contains values from the `YearlySubtotal` column in the previous record. Consequently, we can continue reading the preceding result set until the end of the frame. For the next salesperson (in an actual result set), everything repeats.

Using the `LEAD` function is syntactically the same as using the `LAG` function. We are using the same set of parameters with the same meanings, and we are working with the same `OVER` clause. However, the `LEAD` function looks forward instead of backward, unlike the `LAG` function. It would be beneficial to try to replace the `LAG` function name with `LEAD` and explore the result set on your own.

Using the results of the `LAG` and `LEAD` functions is very useful, especially when the result is visualized, as we will learn in `Chapter 7`, *Data Visualization*. This is because it helps us to see trending information.

When we are talking about framing, windowing, ranking, or running aggregates over the datasets, we must not forget to mention percentile counts. In the next section, we will look at what these are and how they work.

Calculating with percentiles

In the previous section, we sorted and ranked data in absolute numbers, but the **percentile count** has a slightly different meaning, as it compares data relatively. This means that values are sorted and then compared from a perspective of their position within a sorted set of numbers to which the value belongs. In this section, we will go through two pairs of functions. First we learn about `CUME_DIST` and `PERCENT_RANK`.

The PERCENT_RANK and CUME_DIST functions

Using these functions is not as common and obvious as using aggregate functions. The syntax for both functions uses the same `OVER` clause, as we learned earlier in this chapter.

The `PERCENT_RANK` function works in four steps:

1. The function calculates the number of records minus 1 (the evaluated value is omitted from the record count)—let's mark this as *X*
2. The function finds the position of the last occurrence of a certain value in the sorted dataset
3. The function counts the number of records under the evaluated value—let's mark this as *N*
4. The function computes the *N*/*X* fraction, which is the result of the computation

This process may look confusing, so the best way to make the `PERCENT_RANK` function clear is to provide an example. This example will be as simple as possible:

We have ten students writing a computer science test. The score of the test is inserted into a table called `TestResults`. Let's create such a table and fill it with data using the following statements:

```
CREATE TABLE TestResults
(
Id int NOT NULL IDENTITY CONSTRAINT pk_TestResults PRIMARY KEY
```

```
, StudentName nvarchar(10) NOT NULL
, Score tinyint NOT NULL
)

INSERT TestResults (StudentName, Score) VALUES
('Adam', 4), ('Bob', 4), ('Chris', 3), ('John', 8)
, ('Eve', 10), ('Adam II', 4), ('George', 5)
, ('Li', 8), ('Alexandro', 8), ('Jane', 5)
```

This batch creates a table for the test scores and inserts `10` rows. Now we want to compare students' scores using the `PERCENT_RANK` function. The following query demonstrates how to do this:

```
SELECT StudentName
    , Score
    , PERCENT_RANK() OVER (ORDER BY Score) as PercentRank
FROM TestResults
ORDER BY 3 DESC
```

This query uses the `PERCENT_RANK` function. As seen in the query, this function uses the same `OVER` as in other circumstances. However, there is one important difference here. Let's assume that as the value of the student's score grows, their results become better. When using all other functions in conjunction with the `OVER` clause, the `ORDER BY` declared in the preceding query will sort the score in an ascending manner (we will see the lowest value on top of the result). This is not the same case for `PERCENT_RANK`. The `PERCENT_RANK` function sorts data in accordance with the declared `ORDER BY`. However, we can imagine that the function works from bottom to top, which is why it looks as if the sort is descending in result sets.

To explain what the preceding query calculated, we need to explore the whole result set depicted in the following table:

StudentName	**Score**	**PercentRank**
Eve	10	1
Li	8	0.66
Alexandro	8	0.66
John	8	0.66
George	5	0.44
Jane	5	0.44
Adam	4	0.11
Bob	4	0.11
Adam II	4	0.11
Chris	3	0

The preceding table shows the results of the `PERCENT_RANK` function. To make it clear what the function calculates, let's go back to the description of its work and try to substitute concrete values into the calculation procedure. Let's start with the first record containing Eve's score:

- The result set contains 10 records. Excluding the evaluated record, we count 9 records.
- Eve is the only student who has a score of 10. This is why the last occurrence of the value 10 is found in the highest records; 9 records has a lower score than 10.
- 9/9 = 1 ,and this is the `PERCENT_RANK` value for Eve.

Let's try to substitute concrete values for the next record(s):

- The result set contains 10 records. Excluding the evaluated record, we count 9 records.
- Li, Alexandro, and John have the same score of 8. The last occurrence of score 8 is the 4th record, so there are six records under John's result (or under the result of all other boys with a score of 8).
- *6/9 = 0.66,* and this is the `PERCENT_RANK` value for all three boys with a score of 8.

When calculating percentages, we are thinking about the fraction of a whole. For example, John has a score of 8 and the maximum score is, let's say, 10. We can say that John has 80% of the maximum score *(8/10 * 100)*, but `PERCENT_RANK` says that John's score is better than *2/3 (0.66)* of other students. In other words, the percentile count compares or sorts records over the distance of a comparable measure.

The `CUME_DIST` function works in a similar way, but its procedure is a bit simpler. Let's summarize the steps for this:

1. Records in the result set or frame are counted—let's mark this as *X.*
2. A position of the first occurrence of a currently evaluated value is found—let's mark this as *N.*
3. All occurrences of the evaluated value are ranked using an *N/X* value.

To make it clear, the following example shows the `CUME_DIST` function and its result:

```
SELECT StudentName
  , Score
  , CUME_DIST() OVER (ORDER BY Score) as CumeDist
FROM TestResults
ORDER BY 3 DESC
```

This query shows us nothing special. The only syntactical difference here is that the `PERCENT_RANK` function name is replaced with `CUME_DIST`. To find out where the difference is, we must explore the result of the query in the following table:

StudentName	Score	CumeDist
Eve	10	1
Li	8	0.9
Alexandro	8	0.9
John	8	0.9
George	5	0.6
Jane	5	0.6
Adam	4	0.4
Bob	4	0.4
Adam II	4	0.4
Chris	3	0.1

Let's now explore how the `CUME_DIST` works and what values look like in the preceding table. Let's start with Eve's score again:

1. We have 10 records in the result set (or frame)
2. The first score is 10, and it is in the 10th position (counted from bottom to top).
3. *10/10* = <u>1</u>, and this is Eve's `CUME_DIST` value.

Let's calculate `CUME_DIST` for Li, Alexandro, and John:

1. We have 10 records in the result set (or frame).
2. All three boys have the score of 8. The first occurrence of value 8 is in the 9th position (counted from bottom to top).
3. 9/10 = <u>0.9</u>, and this is the `CUME_DIST` value for our three students—**Li**, Alexandro, and John.

Even though functions such as `PERCENT_RANK` and `CUME_DIST` are rarely used, they are very useful when we want to compare values in datasets in accordance with their relationship with other values in the same dataset. In our example, students had a score from 10 to 1. But let's imagine that the best of the students receives a score of 4. When computing this student's percentage of success, we will get 40%. This is a very small percentage. However, the student was the best of all other students, and this is what the percentile count shows.

We also have two more functions that show interesting values in data: `PERCENTILE_CONT` and `PERCENTILE_DISC`. In the following section, we will learn how to work with them and what to expect.

The PERCENTILE_CONT and PERCENTILE_DISC functions

Just like the `PERCENT_RANK` and `CUME_DIST` functions mentioned in the preceding section, the `PERCENTILE_CONT` and `PERCENTILE_DIST` functions are intended to find out range values for **quantiles**. The quantile is an even `n-th` section of distribution in data. Let's have normal distribution, then we can have quartiles, for instance. Quartiles are quarters of the distribution. In normal distribution, most values lie in the second and third quartile, while the first and fourth quartiles are the ends in a dataset. We would also find n-tiles with other *n* sometimes. For example, 10-tiles. This helps to decide which part of a distribution the data belongs to.

One of the values that divides a dataset into two of exactly the same parts is a **median**. The median is a value that is in the middle of the range of sorted values when the number of values in the range is odd. When the number of values is even, the median is calculated as a mean of two values in the middle. It is quite common to use `PERCENTILE_x` functions to find out what the median is. The following example will go through two simple datasets to show how both functions work:

```
-- preparing table for sample data
DROP TABLE IF EXISTS #test
CREATE TABLE #test
(
Number int
)

-- generating trivial data
DECLARE @i int = 1
WHILE @i <= 3 -- odd number of records
 BEGIN
  INSERT #test VALUES (@i)
  SET @i += 1
 END

-- observing results of PERCENTILE functions
-- and comparing it with AVG
SELECT *
   , PERCENTILE_CONT(0.5) WITHIN GROUP (ORDER BY Number) OVER() as PCont
   , PERCENTILE_DISC(0.5) WITHIN GROUP (ORDER BY Number) OVER() as PDisc
```

```
    , AVG(Number * 1.) OVER(
            ORDER BY Number
            ROWS BETWEEN UNBOUNDED PRECEDING AND UNBOUNDED FOLLOWING
      ) as Average
FROM #test

-- adding one more record to have even number of records
INSERT #test VALUES (8)

-- observing results of PERCENTILE functions again
-- and comparing it with AVG
SELECT *
    , PERCENTILE_CONT(0.5) WITHIN GROUP (ORDER BY Number) OVER() as PCont
    , PERCENTILE_DISC(0.5) WITHIN GROUP (ORDER BY Number) OVER() as PDisc
    , AVG(Number * 1.) OVER(
            ORDER BY Number
            ROWS BETWEEN UNBOUNDED PRECEDING AND UNBOUNDED FOLLOWING
      ) as Average
FROM #test
```

The preceding example consists of several commented parts. The first part with the `preparing table for sample data` comment simply creates a temporary table called `#test`. The table is then filled with values from 1 to 3. This is for scenarios in which we have an odd number of records.

The first query with the `observing results` comment shows both functions and their results first time. Let's focus on the syntax for a moment. Both percentile functions need a numeric parameter. The parameter works with the function to establish which n-tile we want to calculate. When computing the median, we want the value in the middle of the dataset (on 50 % of the range), which is why the parameters value is 0.5 for both functions.

Both percentile functions also have one extra clause in conjunction with the `OVER` clause. This is the `WITHIN GROUP` clause. This clause states on which range of numbers the computation has to occur. The `OVER` clause is then used to determine `PARTITION BY` when needed, otherwise the `PARTITION BY` clause is omitted, as in our example. However, it must still be written.

When the first query returns its result, one extra record is added to the #test table and the same query is executed once more. The second execution shows how percentile functions work over an even number of records. The following tables show results for both queries:

Number	**PCont**	**PDisc**	**Average**
1	2	2	2
2	2	2	2
3	2	2	2

The result of the first query is depicted in the preceding table. Because the result has three records, it's easy to find the value in the middle of the result set—this value is **2**. So, what is the difference between `PERCENTILE_CONT` and `PERCENTILE_DISC`? Let's take a look at the following table, which repeats the query over a set of four records:

Number	PCont	PDisc	Average
1	2.5	2	3.5
2	2.5	2	3.5
3	2.5	2	3.5
8	2.5	2	3.5

Looking at preceding table makes the difference between these components clearer to us. The `PERCENTILE_CONT` function calculates the mean of both middle values (*2+3 = 2.5*) and sets the result even if the value itself does not exist in the range of values. Against it, the `PERCENTILE_DISC` value searches for the lower of the two values in the middle and sets it as a result. So, in circumstances when we need the actual median, we should use the `PERCENTILE_CONT` function. If we need an existing value, even if it is not the actual median, the `PERCENTILE_DISC` function is the right choice.

But why is the mean in the `Average` column added to the result? A lot of statistics often work with the mean, but the mean may cause (sometimes big) inaccuracy issues. When we observe both results again, in the first of them, the median and the mean values are both equal to 2, and they're also equal to each other. This is because the line of numbers (1, 2, 3) is monotonous without outlying values.

Before we made the second attempt to calculate mean, a value of 8 was added as a new record. A new range of numbers (1, 2, 3, 8) is not monotonous and, in this very small data set, the value of 8 is a real outlier. It makes the mean higher, but the middle described by the median lasts the same. The greater the difference between the median and mean, the greater the number of outliers. These can be extremely small or extremely large numbers in the range. So for many cases, the median provides a more transparent value of data distribution as it eliminates the data affecting outlier values.

When working in the data science domain, never forget to compare both values—the median and mean. Doing this results in getting better insight into your data, rather than simply trusting the mean.

Percentile count is perhaps too scientific for many developers, but knowing how to use it makes our statistics even more accurate and efficient.

Summary

Data exploration is an important part of every data science project; without these insights into data, we will mostly make blind and inaccurate estimations that will not meet our intentions and needs. We learned about statistics made with T-SQL in three parts, going from the easiest to the most difficult.

In the first section of the chapter, we described almost all aggregate functions used for descriptive statistics. By using functions such as `COUNT` or `SUM`, we became familiar with their particular purposes and the roles they are playing in data science, and we also observed their common behavior. The `GROUP BY` and `GROUP BY GROUPING SETS` clauses of `SELECT` statements were also described in detail.

In the second section of the chapter, we introduced ranking functions and their functionality. With the help of ranking functions, we also learned about framing and windowing, helping us to work with ranges of data in one dataset.

Framing and windowing are commonly used for running aggregate calculations. In the third section of this chapter, we looked at many examples of how running values are obtained using a combination of aggregate functions and frames and windows in data. The last part of this section was dedicated to percentile count. The percentile count helps to describe the mutual relationship between records based on a numeric measure. It also helps to define n-tiles of data.

T-SQL language itself strongly helps to explore data, but to fulfill statistic needs, the set of built-in functions and features may be insufficient in some circumstances. The next chapter introduces the opportunity to our create own aggregate functions.

Questions

1. How do aggregate functions evaluate `NULL`?
   The `NULL` value is almost ignored in aggregate functions. `NULL` is not a minimal nor maximal value. The only exception to this rule is the `COUNT(*)` aggregate function, because it works with whole records.
2. When executing an aggregate query, the following error occurred: `Column '#src.SubcategoryName' is invalid in the select list because it is not contained in either an aggregate function or the GROUP BY clause`. What does this mean?
   This error means that we forgot to add a non-constant column to the `GROUP BY` clause from the `SELECT` clause.

3. What are `GROUPING SETS` used for?
   When writing aggregate queries, we sometimes need to have more combinations of grouping criteria. `GROUPING SETS` are used to define several combinations of grouping in aggregate queries.
4. How is the frame defined when the ranking function is used?
   When using ranking functions, the function name must always be followed by the `OVER` clause. The frame is then declared in the `OVER` clause using the `PARTITION BY` keyword.
5. Is the frame needed for every ranking or running aggregates?
   No, it is not. Base frame is whole dataset.
6. Is sorting needed for every ranking or running aggregates?
   Yes, this is often the case. This is because without sorting being declared in the `OVER` clause, the result of the ranking or running aggregates would be meaningless.
7. What is the difference between the `PERCENTILE_CONT` and `PERCENTILE_DISC` functions?
   In datasets with an even number of records, the `PERCENTILE_CONT` function calculates the real median. The `PERCENTILE_DISC` function searches fewer than two values in the middle of a sorted data range.
8. Can we calculate aggregation over a whole frame of data using the `OVER` clause?
   Yes, we can. This can be achieved when we use the `ROWS BETWEEN UNBOUNDED PRECEDING AND UNBOUNDED FOLLOWING` window definition. An added benefit here is that this approach performs better than a subquery calculating the same aggregation.

6
Custom Aggregations on SQL Server

The previous chapter demonstrated how to work with statistician summaries in data. However, T-SQL capabilities are sometimes quite limited to statistics and data science. This chapter is going to demonstrate how to create our own custom aggregates in order to enhance core T-SQL functionality.

The only way to create a custom aggregate is to use one of the .NET languages, as well as the result of development and deployment on the SQL Server. This chapter is not intended to fully describe how to use C# and learn it, but is intended to give an overview of SQL Server enhancement possibilities using .NET. This overview is especially targeted at custom aggregates.

The following topics will be covered in this chapter:

- **Overview of SQLCLR**: In the first section of this chapter, we will describe how .NET works on SQL Server, what the SQLCLR is, what can be developed, and how can it be helpful and feasible. This section also provides a basic overview of the development and deployment life cycle. We will also review what to set up when we want to customize SQL Server using CLR objects.
- **Creating CLR aggregation**: The second section of this chapter is dedicated to exploring an example of CLR aggregation creation. This example will cover the creation of our own aggregate function, because the .NET code for custom aggregates has several vital rules.
- **Limitations and performance considerations**: The last section of this chapter will describe considerations that we have to keep in mind from architectural, security, and performance points of view.

Technical requirements

SQL Server 2017 is recommended so that you can play with all of the scripts and projects in this chapter. It's also recommended that you restore the `AdventureWorks` database on an installed instance of SQL Server.

Visual Studio 2015 or higher should also be installed if you want to follow the C# examples. The community edition is sufficient for all examples here.

For all SQL scripts provided within this chapter, Management Studio version 17.5 or higher is recommended.

All scripts and other files are provided at `https://github.com/PacktPublishing/Hands-On-Data-Science-with-SQL-Server-2017/tree/master/CH7_Custom_Aggregations_on_SQL_Server`. Scripts are ordered accordingly and are reported throughout the chapter.

The `CH07_BookProjectCLR.zip` file contains a working demo of all custom CLR objects described throughout this chapter.

Overview of SQLCLR

Starting in a new millennium, Microsoft introduced **.NET Framework**. The .NET Framework is a runtime environment that serves all aspects of code running into it, and it is also a rich object model, encapsulating almost any common interfaces between an application and the operating system's APIs. This may include working with disk folders and files, memory, or other peripherals such as a network or a mouse. As well as these features, the runtime itself has more competencies, such as type-safety checking, type casting, and exception management.

The .NET Framework soon became a very popular environment. This is partly because it is rich, but it is also because Microsoft provided several languages that can be used to develop applications, websites, or even Windows services. Nowadays, the most expanded and commonly used language is **C#**, the language built on top of C syntactic habits. As the language is fully object-oriented and also very clear in its syntax, it's no wonder that it's so popular.

Beginning with SQL Server 2005, Microsoft introduced an integration of a .NET Framework and a data engine. This integration introduced new ways to enrich built-in T-SQL features with .NET code. .NET integration also means that .NET Framework 4.6 is a prerequisite of the SQL Server 2016/2017 installation.

As .NET runtime is often denoted as **Common Language Runtime** (**CLR**), the integration of .NET runtime on SQL Server is shortened to **SQLCLR**.

SQLCLR is not an optional feature of SQL Server's installation—it's mandatory. Every SQL Server has CLR integrated into it.

In the following sections, we will learn where to use SQLCLR capabilities as well as look at what is needed to successfully execute CLR modules written in .NET languages.

Use cases of using SQLCLR

SQL Server is mainly intended for data manipulation, and the best approach for working with data is through the T-SQL language. However, in some instances, T-SQL does not have efficient, or even sufficient, tools for manipulating data as required. Let's introduce two examples where T-SQL is not enough.

The first example is that T-SQL does not have an option to save a result set of a query to a file. When this task is needed on the server side, developers often use the command-line application, `bcp.exe`. However, this command line must be called as a **separate program,** and it's impossible to do this using T-SQL statements. In other words, we cannot securely call applications from within SQL Server, so all tasks that are needed when saving data to a file are developed on the client side.

T-SQL has a bunch of functions that can be used to manipulate character strings. However, when we need to process many strings (for instance, hundreds or thousands of strings), it quickly becomes a very slow and fan-out operation. .NET provides classes dedicated to string processing, such as `StringBuilder` and `Regex`. Using .NET in this case makes it possible to write efficient CLR functions for string processing.

We could find many more examples of SQLCLR feasibility, but the previous two examples illustrate two main reasons to use SQLCLR:

- When T-SQL does not have the resources to fulfill a certain task
- When T-SQL does have the resources to fulfill a certain task, but they do not work efficiently enough

Using SQLCLR is a very attractive option, especially for application developers, but we must consider that SQL Server is just a database server. Overusing SQLCLR leads to the confusion of roles of SQL Server and application servers.

How to work with SQLCLR

SQL Server supports several types of objects that can be developed using .NET. The following table shows all of the object types that could be created using C# or other .NET languages:

Object Type	**Created using T-SQL**	**Created using .NET**
Stored procedure	Usually created, typical object for any data manipulation	Rarely created, that is, when results have to be saved into files
Trigger	Usually created, and a supporting object, that is, for data denormalization	Rarely created
Function	Usually created when it's data-bound	Rarely created, typically when string manipulation or complicated calculations that are less data-bound are required
Data Type	Alias data types only	Our own complex data types
Aggregates	Not supported in T-SQL	Only option when our own aggregate function is required

As seen in the preceding table, our decision depends on the ability of T-SQL to fulfill our needs. Only when a task is less data-bound (for instance, math formulas) can we choose to use the CLR object as a good option.

Objects are not written directly on SQL Server; they are encapsulated in compiled assemblies: `dll` files containing our source code that's been compiled into so-called **Microsoft Intermmediate Language** (**MSIL**). From a .NET perspective, it does not matter whether the compiled assembly has `EXE` or `DLL` extensions. However, SQL Server only consumes `DLLs`.

Our whole development of CLR projects is done using Microsoft Visual Studio. We can develop common Class Library projects to create an assembly that will be finally hosted on SQL Server, but for testing purposes and for a simpler deployment of our assemblies, the best approach of development is to use **SQL Server Database Project**. The following screenshot shows where we can find a new project:

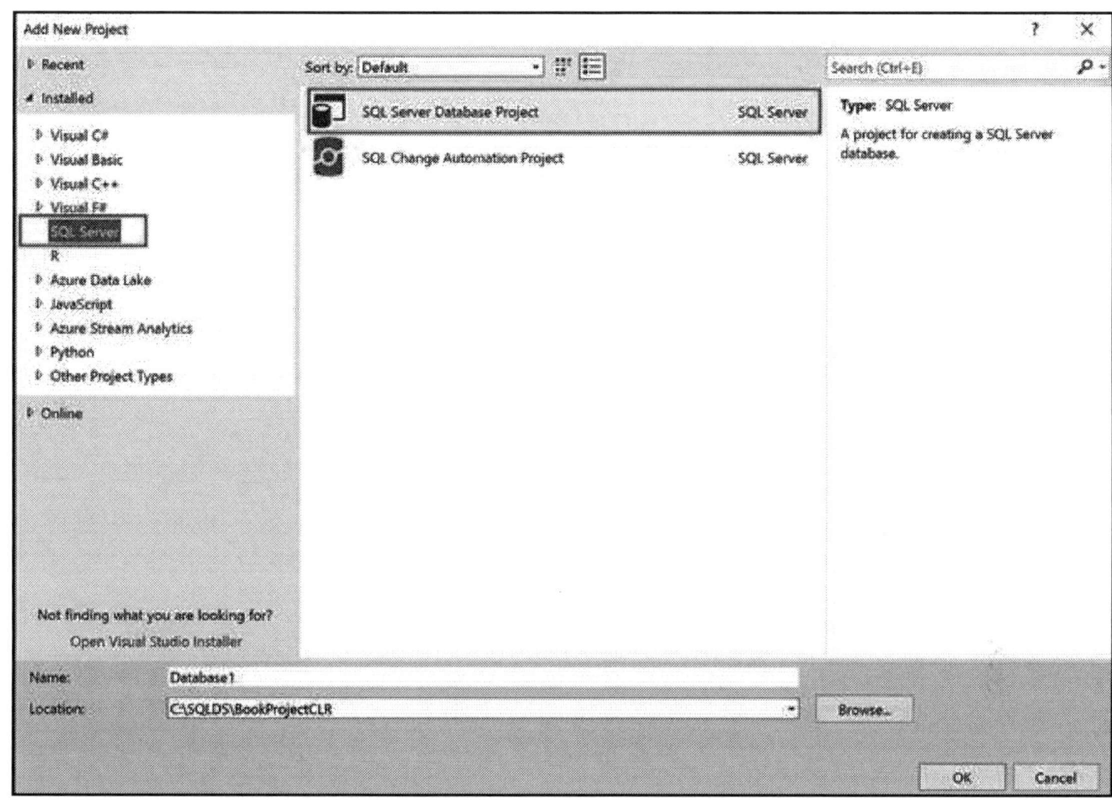

Creating a new SQL Server Database Project

The red rectangle on the far left of the preceding screenshot marks the **SQL Server** node. Clicking on the node filters a list of project types in a main area in the central part of the dialog,which is depicted in the preceding screenshot. The **SQL Server Database Project,** which is marked with the other central red rectangle, is the project type designed for creating the whole database schema, and it also contains tools for SQLCLR object creation. Once the correct project type is selected, we should give the project a meaningful name, such as `BookProjectCLR`. When the dialog has been filled in, we will click the **OK** button to create an empty **SQL Server Database Project**.

When a new project is created, many tasks are done using Visual Studio's **Solution Explorer** window. **Solution Explorer** serves as a navigation window that's usually placed on the right-hand side of Visual Studio. This provides features such as copying or pasting files, opening files, and it also contains context menus for manipulating project items or configuration.

A new object is usually added to the project using **Solution Explorer**. The following screenshot shows the context menu for adding new objects:

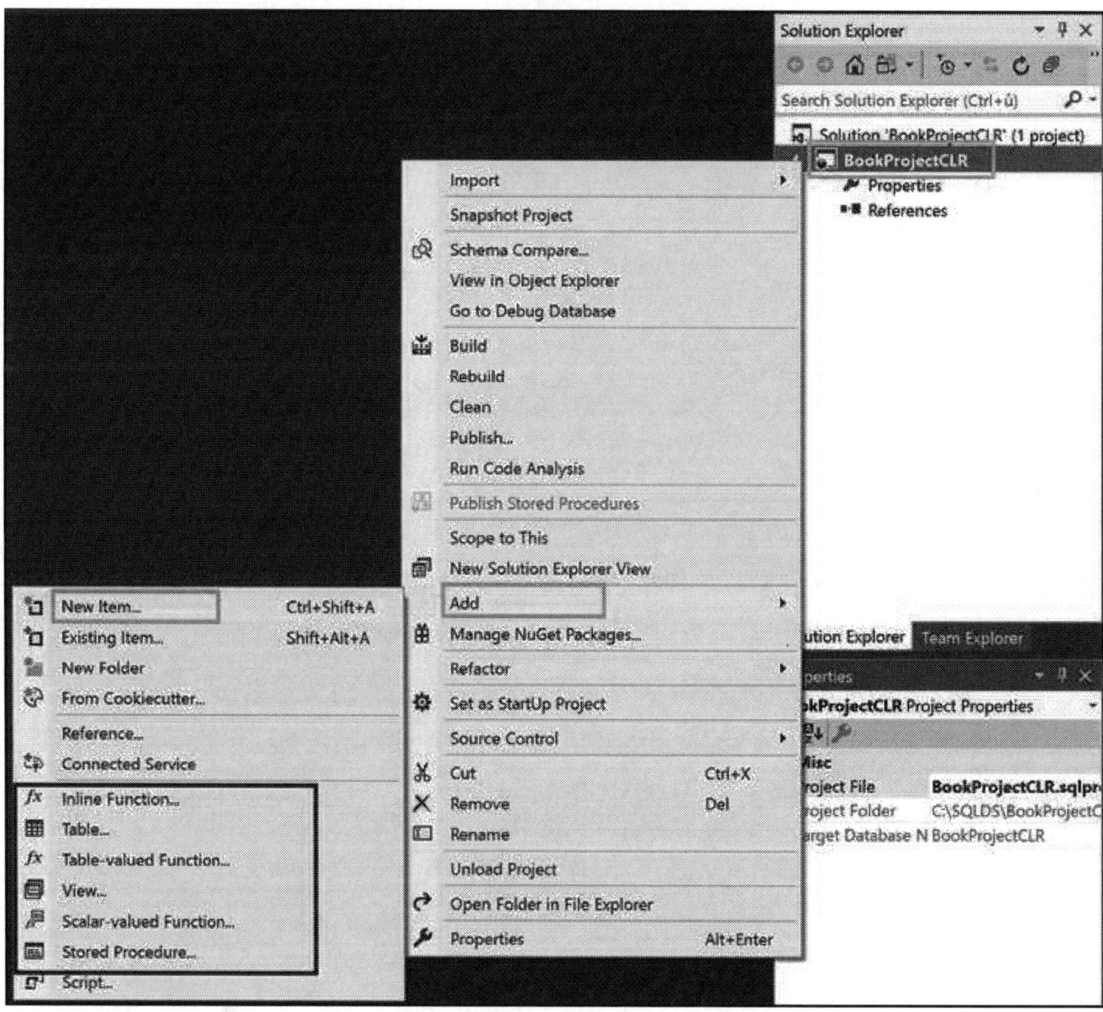

Context menu for adding new objects

Let's pay attention to the orange rectangles in the preceding screenshot. The procedure of adding a SQLCLR object into a project flows from right to left:

1. Right-click on the project node in **Solution Explorer.**
2. Select the **Add** option in the context menu.
3. Click on the **New Item...** option to open a dialog window with database item types.

As mentioned earlier in this section, **SQL Server Database Projects** are used for complete database schema development. Options marked with a dark red rectangle in the preceding screenshot are used to create common T-SQL objects. These options are not intended for SQLCLR object creation.

When the **New Item...** menu option is selected, a new dialog window appears. This is depicted in the following screenshot:

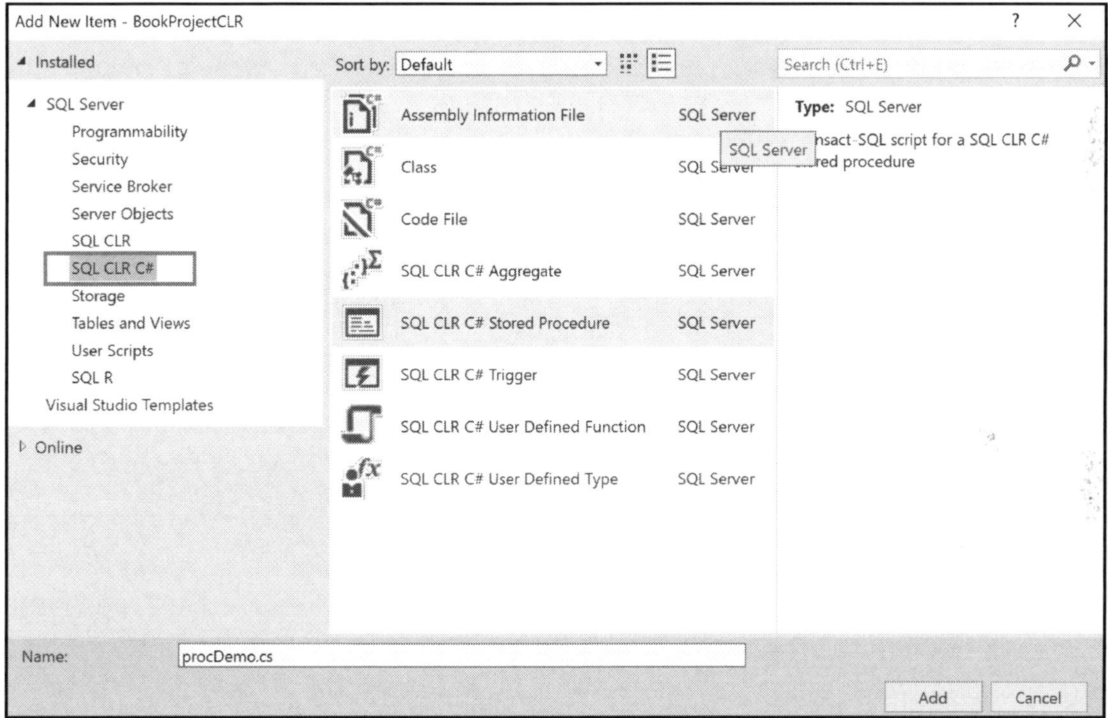

The red rectangle in the preceding screenshot highlights the right option for item type selection. In our example, we can choose the **SQL CLR C# Stored Procedure** option, give a name to it in the **Name** textbox (`procDemo.cs`, in our example), and click on the **Add** button at the bottom of the dialog.

When a SQLCLR object is added to the project, its code appears in Visual Studio and a new item is added to the **Solution Explorer**. The newly created stored procedure in our example will do nothing, but we will use it for the exploration of the following source code:

```
public partial class StoredProcedures
{
    [Microsoft.SqlServer.Server.SqlProcedure]
    public static void procDemo ()
    {
        // Put your code here
    }
}
```

The preceding code sample shows that C# code is organized into blocks. Here, the main block is called **class**. Class is a set of class members, methods, and properties. For our purposes, we only need to know that class is a container for methods. In C#, a method must not stand alone and it must always belong to class. When the new CLR stored procedure is created in Visual Studio, a class called `StoredProcedures` is created.

The `partial` keyword says to the C# compiler that the class definition is divided into more files. It is important to try to create the second CLR stored procedure in the same project. A new file with a newly stored procedure name will be created, but the class declaration in the first row of code will be the same.

CLR objects, such as stored procedures, triggers, and functions, are always implemented as static methods. This is why the `procDemo` name that we used to give a name to the newly created stored procedure is also declared as the method name.

When applications, such as websites or desktop apps, are written in C#, the vast majority of class members are so-called **instance members**, not static members. This is because class is instantiated as an object (or many objects of the same type) during runtime. We can think of classes as technical documentation. When a program is running, new products are created in accordance with the technical documentation—this is how instantiation works. For stored procedures, triggers and function methods are never running in an instance of class, which is why the static keyword is always needed.

Last but not least, part of the preceding code sample is the row with a so-called decorator. C# uses attributes—classes not used during runtime, but during compile-time—to insert additional information about a class or class member to a compiled assembly. Attributes are used directly above a declared class or class member. In our code sample, the `[System.SqlServer.Server.SqlProcedure]` attribute is used to better identify methods by SQL Server when new CLR objects are created in certain databases.

In the next section, we will look at an example of a stored procedure that is more focused on real work. But for the sake of simplicity, let's leave the body of the stored procedure empty for now and summarize the most important information:

- CLR stored procedures, CLR functions, and CLR triggers are always declared as static methods
- Methods always belong to classes and never stay alone
- Every static method should be decorated with one of the following attributes:
    - `System.SqlServer.Server.SqlProcedure` for a stored procedure's method
    - `System.SqlServer.Server.SqlFunction` for a function's method
    - `System.SqlServer.Server.SqlTrigger` for a trigger's method

The preceding bulleted list is useful when we decide to create a common `Class Library` project, which will be used for CLR objects on SQL Server.

Visual Studio provides an option to directly deploy projects on servers. When our project is ready, we can deploy it directly from Visual Studio:

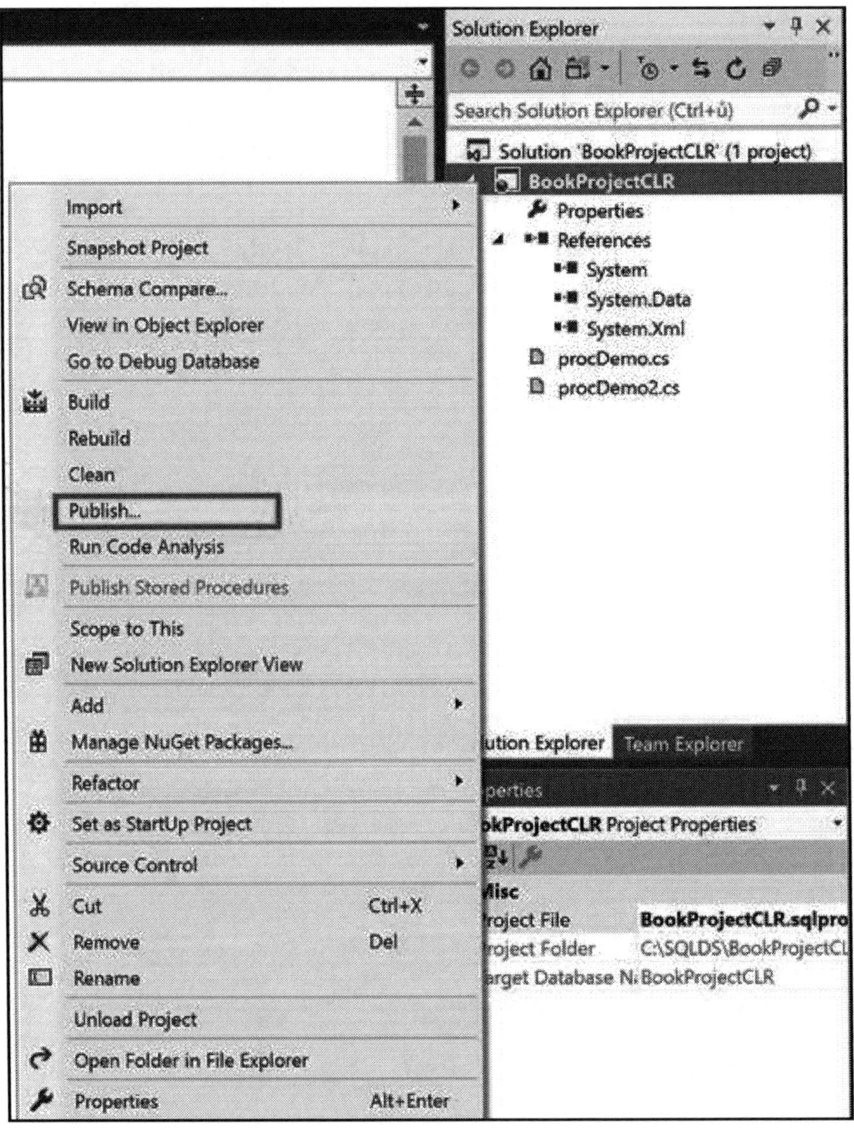

Deploying a project from Visual Studio

The preceding screenshot highlights the **Publish...** option, which opens a new dialog window where the user can set publish settings and start the publishing process. The following screenshot shows the **Publish Database** dialog:

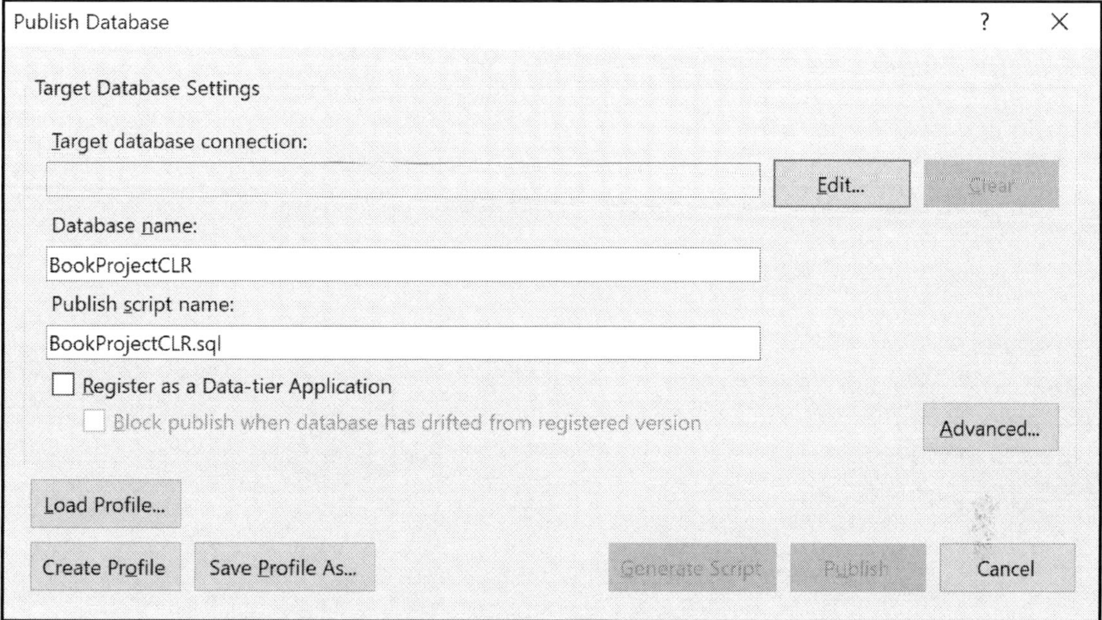

The first setting we have to fill in is the **Target database connection** field. This field is not directly editable, so we are going to use the **Edit...** button to make changes. This button opens one more dialog, which is depicted in the following screenshot:

The Connect dialog box

This screenshot shows a **Connect** dialog, which is used to set a connection to a SQL Server instance and a database on it where we want to publish our solution. This dialog also remembers earlier connections, so we can create new connections at the bottom half of the dialog or select from previously created connections in a list of connections in the top half of the **Connect** dialog.

Once the connection is defined and the **OK** button is selected, we can use the **Publish** button on the **Publish Database** dialog, at which point the publishing process will start. When publishing is finished, we have to check whether everything was published successfully. This check is made in **Management Studio**. The following screenshot shows part of the **Object Explorer** window in **Management Studio** with all objects published from Visual Studio:

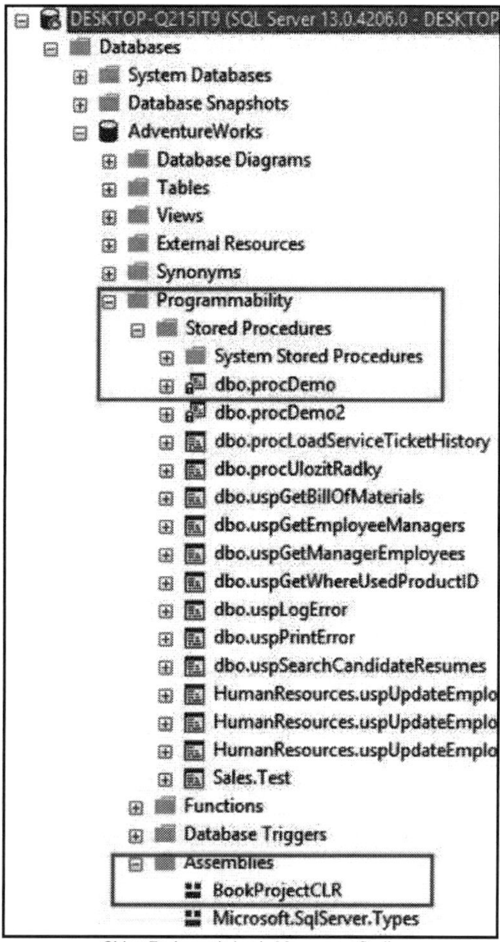

Object Explorer window in Management Studio

The preceding screenshot contains two highlighted places. The red rectangle at the bottom of the screenshot shows that a new assembly was loaded into the database, whereas the red rectangle at the top of the screenshot shows a newly stored procedure.

Let's briefly explore the source code of our newly created objects.The `BookProjectCLR` assembly is a database object that was created using the following statement:

```
CREATE ASSEMBLY [BookProjectCLR]
FROM 0x4D...00     -- this binary string is hugely shortened
GO
```

This statement was extracted from a pre-existing `BookProjectCLR` assembly. This is useful when we need to copy an assembly from one database to another. However, we would also have an assembly created for us by someone else in a typical `dll` file format (for instance, the `<some assembly>.dll` file containing all code needed for further stored procedures and other CLR objects). The `CREATE ASSEMBLY` statement could be also used to create a new assembly from a file. The following code sample shows the syntax:

```
CREATE ASSEMBLY DummyAssembly
FROM 'C:\MyAssemblies\<the name of the assembly>.dll'
GO
```

The preceding statement shows that it's also possible to create assemblies from files. When a new assembly is created, the file used for its creation is no longer needed. This is because all of the file's content is loaded into metadata of the database hosting the assembly.

When the assembly is created in a database, we can start to create CLR objects. The following statement demonstrates the creation of the `procDemo` CLR stored procedure, which was created during this section:

```
CREATE PROC [dbo].[procDemo]
AS
EXTERNAL NAME [BookProjectCLR].[StoredProcedures].[procDemo]
GO
```

The `CREATE PROC` statement starts as the usual `CREATE PROC` statement for common T-SQL stored procedures. The main difference is in the body of the stored procedure definition. The stored procedure does not have its own body, but it points to a fully-qualified name of the static method written in the assembly.

Objects created in a database can be common T-SQL objects that have been defined using Transact-SQL, or they can be CLR objects pointing to a certain member of the assembly. SQL Server does not support objects with hybrid definitions.

In the case of CLR stored procedures, CLR triggers or CLR functions consist of three parts:

- Assembly name (`BookProjectCLR` in our example)
- Class name (`StoredProcedures` in our example—to remind yourself where the class name is defined, go back to the source code generated for us in Visual Studio)
- Method name (`procDemo` in our example)

Never forget to use the `[]` symbols to enclose name parts. This is very important because every part of a fully-qualified name is divided using the dot (`.`) symbol, but classes, for instance, often also have names containing dots.

Let's do a final check to confirm that everything works as expected. The following statement calls the `procDemo` stored procedure:

```
EXEC procDemo
```

As our first CLR stored procedure has an empty body and also has no parameters, our test from the preceding line of code should succeed with no result, or it could lead to the following error:

```
Msg 6263, Level 16, State 1, Line 5
Execution of user code in the .NET Framework is disabled. Enable "clr
enabled" configuration option.
```

If this error occurs, it means that we forgot to configure the SQL Server instance properly. The following section describes configurations on which executing CLR objects is dependent.

Instance and database configurations to use with SQLCLR

We can develop and publish our own CLR objects without any special configuration of the SQL Server instance, but when we want to call them, the CLR execution must be enabled. Otherwise, error 6263, which was mentioned at the end of the previous section will occur. The configuration enabling CLR code is quite simple and is shown in the following code sample:

```
EXEC sp_configure 'clr enabled', 1
RECONFIGURE
```

The configuration option that has to be enabled is `clr enabled`. The `sp_configure` system-stored procedure is used to reconfigure this option. The `RECONFIGURE` statement executed after the `sp_configure` execution changes the reconfigured instance property into a running value without having to restart the whole SQL Server service. Configuring instance properties, such as `clr enabled`, is allowed for SQL Server logins with `ALTER SERVER STATE` or `CONTROL SERVER` permissions.

We can now repeat our attempt from the previous section and call the `procDemo` stored procedure once again. This is done as follows:

```
EXEC procDemo
```

When the preceding statement is executed now, we should obtain the `Commands completed successfully` result.

The stored procedure in the preceding script does nothing, but we often need to develop CLR objects for accessing file systems, calling web services, or even calling unmanaged code. When we want to complete these assignments, we must properly set the assembly's property, called **permission set**. The permission set property determines how the code in the assembly can access surroundings of the SQL Server instance. The permission set property has three levels:

- `SAFE`: This assembly cannot access anything outside of SQL Server
- `EXTERNAL_ACCESS`: This assembly can access computer's subsystems, such as network or filesystem
- `UNSAFE`: This assembly can access anything outside of SQL Server, including unmanaged code

The `SAFE` permission set level is the default level for every published assembly until we explicitly set it to a different level. Setting the permission is possible during assembly creation or any time during the assembly's lifetime. The following statement shows how to set the permission set for an assembly:

```
ALTER ASSEMBLY BookProjectCLR
WITH
PERMISSION_SET = EXTERNAL_ACCESS
```

This statement could fail with the following error:

```
Msg 10327, Level 14, State 1, Line 15
ALTER ASSEMBLY for assembly 'BookProjectCLR' failed because assembly
'BookProjectCLR' is not authorized for PERMISSION_SET = EXTERNAL_ACCESS.
The assembly is authorized when either of the following is true: the
database owner (DBO) has EXTERNAL ACCESS ASSEMBLY permission and the
```

```
database has the TRUSTWORTHY database property on; or the assembly is
signed with a certificate or an asymmetric key that has a corresponding
login with EXTERNAL ACCESS ASSEMBLY permission.
```

When a higher (less secure) permission set is desired, we must set the database hosting the assembly as `TRUSTWORTHY`. The following statement demonstrates how to set the database properly:

```
ALTER DATABASE AdventureWorks SET TRUSTWORTHY ON
```

The preceding statement sets the `AdventureWorks` database as a trustworthy database. We can then repeat the attempt to set a higher permission set once again, as follows:

```
ALTER ASSEMBLY BookProjectCLR
WITH
PERMISSION_SET = EXTERNAL_ACCESS
```

This statement should now succeed.

It is not recommended to set the permission set to an unnecessary level. This is because setting a database as trustworthy is considered a minor security issue.

Within this section, we learned what SQLCLR is and how the development process flows. In the next section, we will use this knowledge to develop our first custom CLR aggregation.

Creating CLR aggregations

As `Chapter 5`, *Data Exploration and Statistics with T-SQL* described, SQL Server provides a rich set of very feasible built-in aggregate functions to fulfill our statistical needs. However, for deeper insight into our data, the list of built-in functions could be insufficient. This section is a walkthrough example of how to create our own custom aggregation using C# and the CLR aggregate SQL Server object.

Example goal and assignment

In `Chapter 5`, *Data Exploration and Statistics with T-SQL*, we learned about variance as well as the rate of parameter scattering. Let's revisit the following formula:

$$\sigma^2 = \frac{1}{N}\sum_{i=1}^{N}(x_i - X)^2$$

We can generalize the preceding formula. If we replace the power of *2* with (almost) any number, *k, the* adjusted formula will look at the following:

$$m_k = \frac{1}{N}\sum_{i=1}^{N}(x_i - X)^k$$

This formula is a definition of a **statistical moment of the k-th degree**. Many data science tasks and solutions assume that data in datasets are in a normal (Gaussian) layout, but this is not always true. Using the statistical moment of the third degree helps to determine a coefficient of **data skewness**, while a statistical moment of the fourth degree helps to determine a coefficient of **data spikes**.

Let's introduce data skewness graphically. The following diagram shows what is meant by this term:

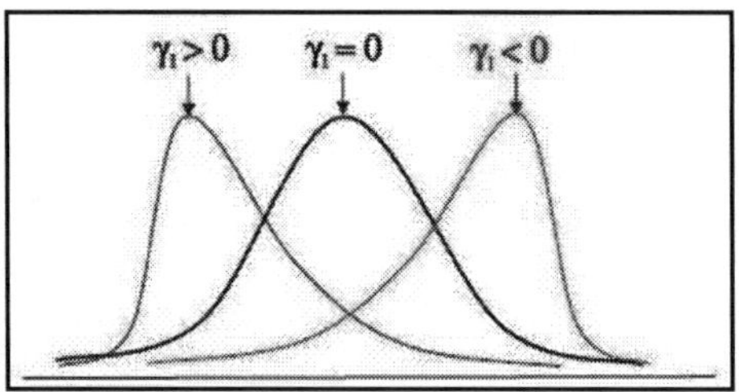

Graphical representation of data skewness

In preceding diagram, the black curve depicts the normal layout of the data. When the data is scattered with more large values, we can say that the data is skewed left. In the preceding diagram, left-skewed data is the blue line and the gamma is therefore a positive number. And vice versa—when a population of data contains more small values, then the data is skewed right, as shown by the red curve. In this case, gamma is a negative number.

The complete formula for computing data skewness is as follows:

$$\gamma_1 = \frac{m_3}{m_2^{\frac{3}{2}}}$$

As seen in the preceding formula, the second (m_2) and third (m_3) statistical moments are used in fractions. This is because the third power of the m negative number can be a result of the formula.

Let's explore data spikes in a similar way to data skewness. First let's take a look at following diagram:

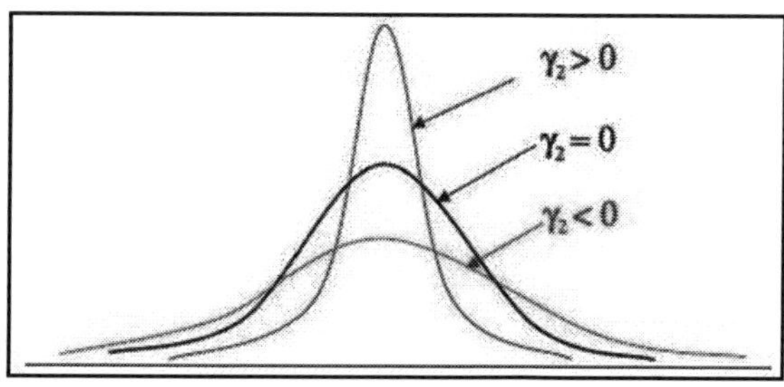

Data spikes

The black curve in the preceding diagram shows a normal layout of the data. When more data from an explored dataset is concentrated close to the middle of the population, the curve becomes steeper. In this case, we say that the data is spikier. Spiky data is depicted by the blue curve in the preceding diagram. In contrast, when the data is more scattered, it is less spiky, as shown by the red curve. The complete formula for the coefficient of the data spike is as follows:

$$\gamma_2 = \frac{m_4}{m_2^2} - 3$$

In our example of custom aggregation, we will not compute whole data spikes and data skewness, but for illustration purposes, we will develop a function calculating a certain statistical moment, m_k. Such a function could be feasible in future for both data skewness and data spike calculations.

Now, let's stop discussing theory and move onto the next section, where we will develop something real.

Skeleton of CLR aggregation

All CLR aggregations have the same skeleton. Every CLR aggregation is a class or a structure that contains four methods:

- `Init`
- `Accumulate`
- `Merge`
- `Terminate`

These methods are found and used by SQL Server for the calculation of aggregation.

There is a substantial difference between class and structure in object-oriented programming, but this is beyond the scope of this book. For us, it is simply important to know that structures probably have a smaller memory footprint than objects instantiated from classes.

When an empty CLR aggregation is created in Visual Studio, the source code looks such as the following script:

```
[Serializable]
[SqlUserDefinedAggregate(Format.Native)]
public struct StatMoment
{
    public void Init()
    {
        // Put your code here
    }

    public void Accumulate(SqlString Value)
    {
        // Put your code here
    }

    public void Merge (StatMoment Group)
    {
        // Put your code here
    }

    public SqlString Terminate ()
    {
        // Put your code here
        return new SqlString (string.Empty);
    }

    // This is a place-holder member field
```

```
        public int _var1;
    }
```

The preceding script shows empty declarations generated by Visual Studio when a new SQL Aggregation is added into a project. When SQL Server executes a custom aggregation, it works in a cycle. The `Init` method is an entry point for an aggregation, which is often used for the initiation of variables needed for our calculations. The `Accumulate` method runs in a cycle and takes the next value from a dataset. The `Accumulate` method also often adds the value into a calculation. The `Merge` method also runs in a cycle and takes the previously-calculated result. The `Terminate` method terminates CLR aggregation, which returns the complete result back to a SQL Server. The structure of custom aggregation is decorated as `[Serializable]` (see the first line of the preceding code sample). This means that after initiation, the instance of the structure is saved as a byte array after every `Accumulate` call, and then reconstructed from the byte array with every `Merge` call.

We can change data types of parameters and returned value, but we should not change the names of these four methods.

We should keep in mind that SQL Server simply sees the current occurrence of the CLR aggregation structure. This means that the intermediate result set has to be stored in a class variable. This is quite simple when we implement our custom `SUM` aggregate function—for instance, because the function simply takes the next number and adds it into the previous intermediate result. However, when we implement more complicated aggregation, such as statistical moments, a simple class variable is not sufficient. This is because we must first read all values from a certain dataset and then make the calculation based on this. In the following section, we will implement all methods and write two helper methods to reach the requirements for storing whole sets of values.

Implementing methods

First of all, we should consider what needs to be done when we want to calculate statistical moments:

1. We must develop our own method of serialization. This is because we will not work with simple class variables, but with a more complicated list of values. Consequently, the first step will be to implement the `IBinarySerialize` interface.
2. We have to arrange reading all values from a dataset into a list.
3. We calculate the mean and count of values.
4. We calculate the difference between each value and mean.

5. We calculate the nth power of the difference from the previous point.
6. We calculate the sum of differences.
7. We return summarized differences from #4 divided by the number of values calculated in #3.

The first two steps will be implemented as interface implementation and development of the interface's `Read` and `Write` methods. The rest of the steps will then be implemented in the `Terminate` method.

Implementing custom serialization

Our example must read all values from a dataset and then calculate the statistical moment over all values. This is why we must store the list of values in .NET lists. At the moment, native serialization used internally in CLR aggregates fail. This is because .NET lists are too complicated for the simple method of serialization. Consequently, the first adjustment in our source code is to implement the `IBinarySerializable` interface. Furthermore, the decoration of the `SqlUserDefinedAggregate` attribute also has to be changed. The following section of the code shows what to do here:

```
//original code generated by Visual Studio
[Serializable]
[SqlUserDefinedAggregate(Format.Native)]
public struct StatMoment

//adjustments
[Serializable]
[SqlUserDefinedAggregate(Format.UserDefined)]     //different way of
serialization
public struct StatMoment: IBinarySerialize         //declaration of the
interface
```

The preceding code example displays the header of the source code before and after the customization. When the `IBinarySerializable` interface implementation is declared, we must add two methods declared by the interface:

- `Read()`: This reads serialized data from a byte array and deserializes it back to class variables
- `Write()`: This takes data from class variables and stores their state into a byte array

For now, we can leave both methods empty. However, we must recognize which two class variables we need:

- A list of values from a dataset. This will be implemented as `List<double>`.
- `n` to determine the degree of statistical moment. This will be implemented as `double`.

Visual Studio creates one default integer class variable, called `_var1`. This is often placed at the end of the source code. We can erase a whole line with the default variable and replace it with our own variables. The following part of code shows a comparison before and after the change:

```
//before change
public int _var1;

//after change
private List<double> values; //list of values to be aggregated
private double n; //n-th power determining statistical moment
```

When the default variable, `_var1`, is erased and two new class variables are declared (as shown in the preceding script), we know what to serialize. Let's start to implement the `Write` method first. Here is the code for the `Write` method:

```
//how to write data to serialized byte array
public void Write(BinaryWriter w)
{
    using (var stream = new MemoryStream())
    {
        var binaryWriter = new BinaryWriter(stream);
        binaryWriter.Write(this.values.Count + 1);

        foreach (var tempDec in this.values)
        {
            binaryWriter.Write(tempDec);
        }
        binaryWriter.Write(this.n);
        w.Write(stream.ToArray());
    }
}
```

When we want to serialize any object, we are going to write an object called **stream**. File streams, networks streams, and memory streams are commonly used for this. In our case, we need to use `MemoryStream`. Writing a stream is done using a proper writer object. As we want to save a byte array of all class variables, we are using the `BinaryWriter` object here. In the preceding code, the local `BinaryWriter` object is created in the `var binaryStream = new BinaryWriter(stream);` row. The `Write` method of the `BinaryWriter` object writes a number of values in the list of values, followed by all of the values one by one, and the final written value is the value of the `n` class variable. This code is then used when a state of current instance of the `StatMoment` structure is written to a memory.

The role played by the `Read` method is the opposite of the `Write` method. This method reads a byte array from memory and reconstructs all values from it back to a class variable. The code of the `Read` method is as follows:

```
public void Read(BinaryReader r)
{
    using (MemoryStream stream = new
MemoryStream((byte[])r.ReadBytes(Convert.ToInt32(r.BaseStream.Length))))
    {
        BinaryReader binaryReader = new BinaryReader(stream);
        binaryReader.BaseStream.Position = 0;

        int count = binaryReader.ReadInt32();

        if (count > -1)
        {
            this.values = new List<double>(count);
            for (int i = 0; i < count; i++)
            {
                this.values.Add(binaryReader.ReadDouble());
            }
        }

        this.n = binaryReader.ReadDouble();
    }
}
```

The preceding code is intended to be read from the memory stream, so instead of BinaryWriter, the BinaryReader object is created, and then it reads stored values from the serialized stream. This process of deserialization reconstructs the state of an object from its serialized version.

Serialization and deserialization are very commonly-used concepts in object-oriented programming. On the other hand, this is commonly unknown for database developers. For statistician purposes, we can use the code of the preceding Read and Write methods as it is without making any changes.

The methods described in this section do nothing for the calculation of statistical moments, but they are necessary as helper methods for transferring data from one Merge and Accumulate call to another. Without these methods, our example will never work. The next short section describes how to use the Init method.

Implementing the Init method

Structures of custom aggregation do not support the direct initialization of class variables. This is why the Init method is the only place for the initialization. In our example, we must initialize the list of values declared as private List<double> values; in the first step. The code of the Init method is very simple as it creates new instances of the List<double> object. Here is the code for the Init method:

```
public void Init()
{
    values = new List<double>();
}
```

At this point, we may wonder why double n is not initialized in the same way. This is because .NET distinguishes between value types and reference types. double n is a value type that has its own default initial value of 0. However, List<double> is a reference type that does not have an initial value, and hence it must be initialized explicitly. Every time we have class variables of the reference type, we must initialize them within the Init method.

The next section is going to explain what the Accumulate method does and how it can be implemented.

Implementing the Accumulate method

Built-in aggregates, such as `SUM` or `AVG`, usually have one parameter. For this reason, the generated declaration of the `Accumulate` method contains one parameter of the `SqlString` type. However, there are two problems with using these. First of all, we don't want to work with strings. Second of all, we need two parameters. The first parameter is designed for incoming values from the dataset, while the second is intended for n determining the nth degree of the statistical moment. Consequently, the first adjustment to be made is in the declaration of the method. The following code shows the difference before and after our adjustment:

```
//before - generated by Visual Studio
public void Accumulate(SqlString value)
//after
public void Accumulate(SqlDouble value, SqlInt32 n)
```

The preceding script shows that the type of the `value` parameter is changed to `SqlDouble`, and one more parameter, `SqlInt32 n`, is added. These changes in the declaration will lead to the usage of the custom aggregation with two parameters.

Now let's explore the whole implementation of the `Accumulate` method. The following code sample shows the complete body of the method:

```
public void Accumulate(SqlDouble value, SqlInt32 n)
{
    this.n = (double)n;

    if (value.IsNull)
        return;
    values.Add(value.Value);
}
```

The first line of the method's body from the preceding code converts the incoming integer parameter, `n`, into a double and stores it in the `n` class variable declared in the first step of this walk-through example. At this point, we may ask ourselves why the `n` parameter is not directly declared as `SqlDouble`. This is because statistical moments are always of the integer degree, and so we want to offer users the correct parameter type. However, when we are calculating the statistical moment, `double` is used as a generalized data type of the nth power.

The `if (value.IsNull)` condition is used to eliminate `NULL` values from an incoming dataset, as this is usual for any other built-in aggregate.

The `Accumulate` method is used internally for taking incoming parameters, while the `Merge` method resets values with every internal iteration of custom aggregation. The next short section will show its implementation.

Implementing the Merge method

We can think about `Merge` method as a method working repeatedly for every record in the incoming dataset. This method takes results from previous processed records and merges them onto current iterations. The following code sample shows what the Merge method does:

```
public void Merge (StatMoment group)
{
    this.values.AddRange(group.values);
    this.n = group.n;
}
```

As seen in the preceding code sample, the `Merge` method has one parameter of the `StatMoment` type. The `StatMoment` type is the structure of custom aggregation that we are currently implementing. This is why code is only written to set values of the current instance of the `StatMoment` group from the parameter.

`Merge` is reset internally with every new group defined in the `GROUP BY` clause of `SELECT` statements where custom aggregation is used.

The last—but very important—method we must implement is the `Terminate` method. We will explain this method in the following section.

Implementing the terminate method

The Terminate method returns the result of aggregation calculated over every group. Let's dive right into its definition, shown in the following code sample:

```
//declaration generated by Visual Studio
public SqlString Terminate ()
//complete code with changed declaration of the method
public SqlDouble Terminate ()
{
    double valueCount = (double)values.Count;
    //calculating mean
```

```
        double sum = 0;
        foreach (var item in values) //sum of values in the list
        {
            sum += item;
        }
        double mean = sum / valueCount; //mean of values in the list

        //powered differences
        double poweredDiffsFromMean = 0;
        foreach (var item in values) //the difference between value and the
    mean
        {
            poweredDiffsFromMean += Math.Pow((item - mean), this.n);
        }

        //complete moment
        return poweredDiffsFromMean / valueCount; //result ready and returned
    }
```

The preceding code sample is divided into two parts. The first part shows a declaration of the method generated by Visual Studio. We don't want to use a string result here, hence the return type of the method has to be changed to `SqlDouble`.

The body of the Terminate method processes all of the values that have been added to the list of values and calculates the moment. Let's remember the formula from the introduction of this chapter:

$$m_k = \frac{1}{N}\sum_{i=1}^{N}(x_i - X)^k$$

Using this formula, we will describe how certain symbols are calculated in the preceding code:

- **x_i**: Every value from the `values` list
- **k**: The degree of the statistical moment, set as a parameter in the `Accumulate` method and stored as a `double n` class variable
- **N**: `double valueCount = (double)values.Count;`—the number of values in the aggregation
- **X**: This is a mean of values in the aggregation, calculated by a part of code commented as `calculating mean`

- **The sum of the kth powered differences of values from the mean**: Calculated in the section of code commented as `powered differences`
- **m_k**: The result of aggregation. This is calculated in a return statement

The code is now complete. We can revise all of our work in the following code sample:

```
[Serializable]
[Microsoft.SqlServer.Server.SqlUserDefinedAggregate(Format.UserDefined,
MaxByteSize = -1, Name = "STAT_MOMENT", IsNullIfEmpty = true)]
public struct StatMoment: IBinarySerialize
{
    public void Init()
    {
        values = new List<double>();
    }

    //takes next value from a list of numbers to a list of values
    public void Accumulate(SqlDouble value, SqlInt32 n)
    {
        this.n = (double)n;

        if (value.IsNull)
            return;
        values.Add(value.Value);
    }

    //merges current instance of aggregation with previous instance
    public void Merge (StatMoment group)
    {
        this.values.AddRange(group.values);
        this.n = group.n;
    }

    //calculates n-th moment and returns result back to a client
    public SqlDouble Terminate ()
    {
        double valueCount = (double)values.Count;

        double sum = 0;
        foreach (var item in values) //sum of values in the list
        {
            sum += item;
        }

        double mean = sum / valueCount;

        double poweredDiffsFromMean = 0;
```

```
        foreach (var item in values)
        {
            poweredDiffsFromMean += Math.Pow((item - mean), this.n);
        }

        return poweredDiffsFromMean / valueCount;
    }

    //how to read data from serialized byte array
    public void Read(BinaryReader r)
    {
        using (MemoryStream stream = new
MemoryStream((byte[])r.ReadBytes(Convert.ToInt32(r.BaseStream.Length))))
        {
            BinaryReader binaryReader = new BinaryReader(stream);
            binaryReader.BaseStream.Position = 0;

            int count = binaryReader.ReadInt32();

            if (count > -1)
            {
                this.values = new List<double>(count);
                for (int i = 0; i < count; i++)
                {
                    this.values.Add(binaryReader.ReadDouble());
                }
            }

            this.n = binaryReader.ReadDouble();
        }
    }

    //how to write data to serialized byte array
    public void Write(BinaryWriter w)
    {
        using (var stream = new MemoryStream())
        {
            var binaryWriter = new BinaryWriter(stream);
            binaryWriter.Write(this.values.Count);

            foreach (var tempDec in this.values)
            {
                binaryWriter.Write(tempDec);
            }
            binaryWriter.Write(this.n);
            w.Write(stream.ToArray());
        }
    }
```

```
        private List<double> values; //list of values to be aggregated
        private double n; //n-th power determining statistical moment
    }
```

The preceding code sample contains the complete code for our first custom aggregation. Here, we explained every method implemented in the `StatMoment` structure. Now it's time to publish the code as a new aggregate function on SQL Server and test its results. Let's skip this in the next section.

Deployment and testing

Once the aggregation is complete, we will publish it from Visual Studio, as described in the *How to work with SQLCRL* section. There's one difference between built-in T-SQL aggregates and custom aggregations: T-SQL aggregate functions are server-wide, but custom aggregations are database-wide. So, if we want to have our custom aggregations in more databases, we must publish them to every database where we need it.

When the custom aggregation is published, we can see this in Management Studio's **Object Explorer**:

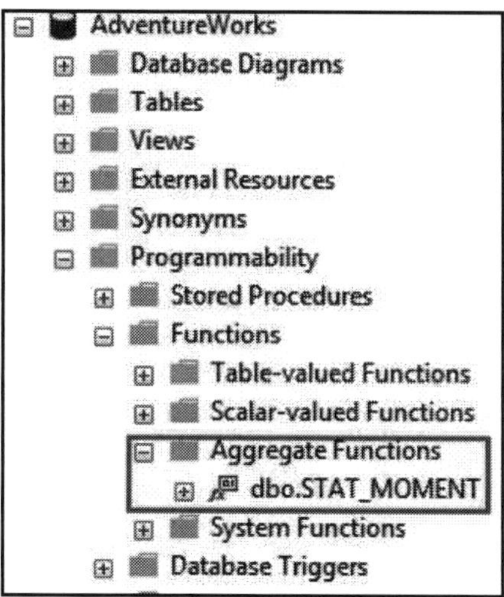

Custom aggregation function in Object Explorer

The preceding screenshot shows that our custom aggregation, `STAT_MOMENT`, is enlisted in the database schema, `dbo` in our case. Having the schema name as a part of the custom aggregation's name is required in every call of the custom aggregation.

Now that our custom aggregate function is successfully published, we can start testing. We will test the values of the third statistical moment in the following example. To have as simple a dataset as possible, we will create a dummy dataset that contains three simple values. The following script shows the dataset:

```
;with cte as
(
select * from (values (1.), (2.), (3.)) as vals(c)
)
select * from cte
```

The result of the preceding script is a list of values: 1, 2, and 3. Let's try to see the result of the `dbo.STAT_MOMENT` aggregation in the following script:

```
declare @nThMoment int = 3
;with cte as
(
select * from (values (1.), (2.), (3.)) as vals(c)
)
select dbo.STAT_MOMENT(c, @nThMoment) from cte
```

The result of this script should be zero and the mean of the values of 1, 2, and 3 is 2. Let's try to add a smaller value than the mean into the list of values and then repeat the attempt. The following script shows how to do this:

```
declare @nThMoment int = 3
;with cte as
(
select * from (values (1.), (.5), (2.), (3.)) as vals(c)
)
select dbo.STAT_MOMENT(c, @nThMoment) from cte
```

In the list of values in the common table expression from the preceding script, the value of 0.5 was added. This shows that the data set has more values smaller than the mean. The result has now changed to 0.24609375. We can now see that the `dbo.STAT_MOMENT` calculates a number, but is this number correct? We can find the answer when we try to write an alternative of our custom aggregation in T-SQL, if possible. The following script shows both alternatives, using T-SQL to calculate the third statistical moment, and also using our custom aggregation:

```
declare @nThMoment int = 3
-- calculation using T-SQL
;with cte as
(
select * from (values (1.), (.5), (2.), (3.)) as vals(c)
) , cte2
```

```
as
(
select
  power(c - (select AVG(c) from cte), @nThMoment) as pwr
from cte
)
select sum(pwr) / (select count(*) from cte2)
from cte2

-- calculation using dbo.STAT_MOMENT custom aggregation
;with cte as
(
select * from (values (1.), (.5), (2.), (3.)) as vals(c)
)
select dbo.STAT_MOMENT(c, @nThMoment) from cte
```

The preceding script returns two results and the first is calculated using T-SQL. As we can see, we must use the `cte2` common table expression to pre-calculate the power of differences between every item and the mean, at which point we can calculate the statistical moment itself. In the second option, we are just using custom aggregation. So, what about results? The T-SQL alternative returns **0.246093**, while the second alternative returns **0.24609375**. We can say that both results are almost equal to each other. The `dbo.STAT_MOMENT` result has greater precision, and this is the only difference between them.

We explained how to create our own aggregations if needed, but using CLR objects has its limits. We will summarize these limits in the next section.

Limitations and performance considerations

The previous section explained the concept of creating custom aggregations. The custom aggregation was then compared to T-SQL script, calculating the same value as the statistical moment. It is not straightforward to decide which is a better way of working. When custom aggregation is developed, it's very simple to use this in the same way as built-in aggregate functions. However, the development of the custom aggregation becomes tricky very quickly, especially when a database developer is not familiar with .NET concepts and languages such as C#. Consequently, the first limitation that we face is in the development itself.

Development issues and risks

As mentioned in the introduction of this section, many database developers are highly experienced in T-SQL, but not every developer knows how to develop object-oriented applications. Database development has its own rules—for instance, it is designed for set-based operations. However, object-oriented development is supposed to work with objects, classes, and structures, which is a completely different approach when compared to database development.

Even though object-oriented programming is familiar to certain developers, it's not easy to develop objects and methods for CLR objects, because debugging the code is not possible during development-time. For example, CLR objects, such as CLR stored procedures or CLR functions, often use a special kind of connection through a hosting database, called **context connection**. Context connection, when compared to common client's connection to a database, works only in the context of a certain database. Consequently, using it from within the source code of developed CLR objects is impossible.

Another problem is debugging applications. CLR objects are developed in Visual Studio, which is a client tool. Only the SQL Server gives the context of execution to the developed code. However, the code is never executed alone, it's always encapsulated by a declared CLR object. This is why breakpoints are useless during development-time.

Previous paragraphs summarize some difficult places which developers must overcome. Administrators also have their own issues when the maintenance of CLR objects is needed. The next section will show some examples of this.

The final issue that may occur during deployment time is as follows: Let's assume that we need to develop a CLR stored procedure that will call a web service. Developing such a CLR stored procedure forces a developer to create an almost complete web client, which has to be secure enough. This requirement makes it necessary to publish many system assemblies to an SQL Server on which our own assembly is dependent.

Maintenance issues and risks

When it comes to custom assemblies, issues that arise include knowing what is actually in them. From an administrator's point of view, every assembly is a black box. This leads to a limited knowledge about the accuracy of the code, limited performance diagnostics, and potential security risks. In this case, it's very hard to be responsible for what happens on the SQL Server's instance.

Possibly the biggest concern here is security. Until the assembly requires data from a hosting database, its PERMISSION_SET should remain SAFE. However, when some of the objects contained in the assembly need access to SQL Server's neighborhood, the permission set must be configured to EXTERNAL_ACCESS or even to UNSAFE. These two configuration options are available only when the database is set as TRUSTWORTHY. Trustworthy databases are a point from which an attacker could take the entire SQL Server and put it under their control using a dbo database user account.

Performance issues and risks

A custom aggregation developed during the walk through example in the *Creating CLR aggregations* section read all values from a dataset or group and then made the calculation of an aggregated value. When this was tested, it worked well. However, the test was intended to check the accuracy of the calculation, not the performance. Let's go back to the section and replace a set of testing values with something more real.

The following script replaces dummy values from the testing made at the end of the *Creating CLR aggregations* section with values from the Sales.SalesOrderHeader table that have been placed in the AdventureWorks database:

```
declare @nThMoment int = 3
-- calculation using T-SQL
;with cte as
(
-- select * from (values (1.), (.5), (2.), (3.)) as vals(c)
select year(OrderDate) as OrderYear
  , cast(SubTotal as dec(10, 4)) as c
from sales.SalesOrderHeader
) , cte2
as
(
select OrderYear,
 power(c - (select AVG(c) from cte x where cte.OrderYear = cte.OrderYear),
@nThMoment) as pwr
from cte
)
select OrderYear, sum(pwr) / (select count(*) from cte2)
from cte2
group by OrderYear

-- calculation using dbo.STAT_MOMENT custom aggregation
;with cte as
(
select year(OrderDate) as OrderYear
```

```
    , cast(SubTotal as dec(10, 4)) as c
  from sales.SalesOrderHeader
  )
  select OrderYear, dbo.STAT_MOMENT(c, @nThMoment) from cte
  group by OrderYear
```

This script uses a `SELECT YEAR(OrderDate) as OrderYear, CAST(SubTotal as dec(10, 4)) FROM Sales.SalesOrderHeader` query in the `cte` common table expression. The `OrderYear` column is then used for grouping. The conversion of the `SubTotal` column is necessary here because money is originally the data type used in the `SubTotal` column, and its scale is insufficient. It's not important to see the results of both queries, but let's ask Management Studio for Estimated Execution Plan. Which variant of the preceding script will perform better: the T-SQL variant or our custom CLR aggregation? The following screenshot shows both plans together:

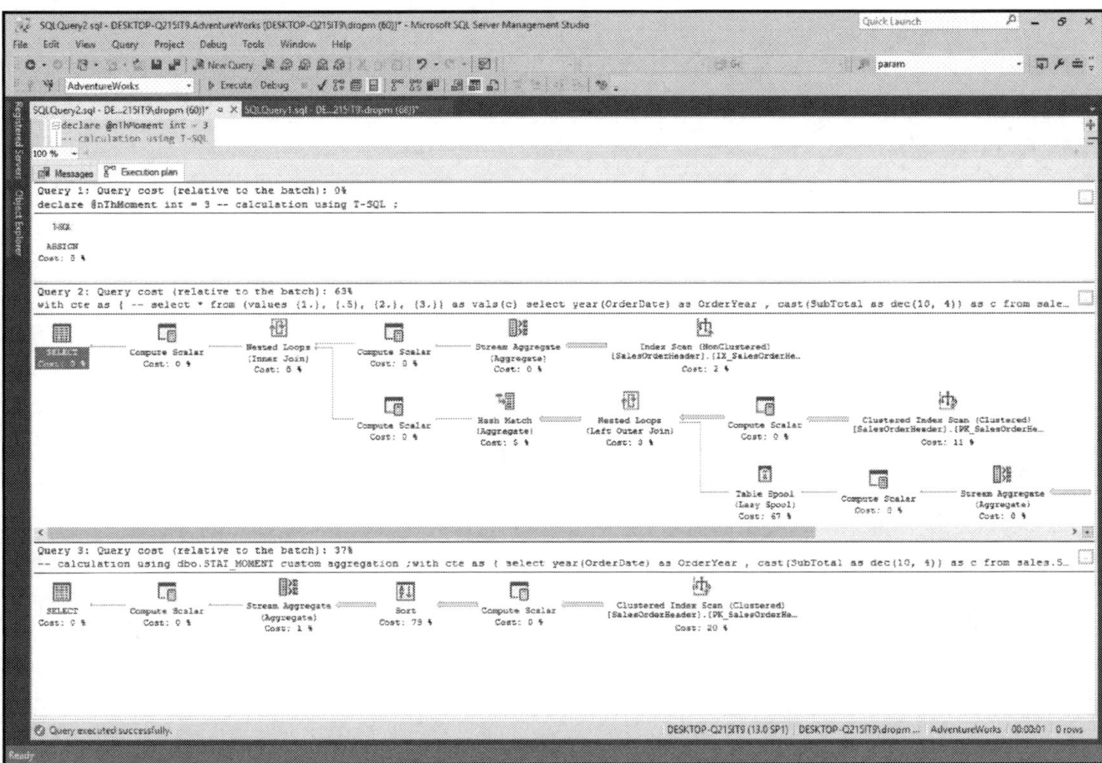

The preceding screenshot shows three estimated execution plans. From top to bottom, the first plan is just a variable assignment, which is not important to us. The second plan shows the T-SQL variant of the statistical moment calculation. This second plan is more complicated than the third execution plan, showing how SQL Server works with data when the `dbo.STAT_MOMENT` custom aggregation is used. Both execution plans have their query costs displayed as a percentage in their headers. We can see that the T-SQL variant of calculation is slightly more expensive than the CLR variant.

However, when both queries are executed, the results seem to be different. The following screenshot shows client statistics for both queries:

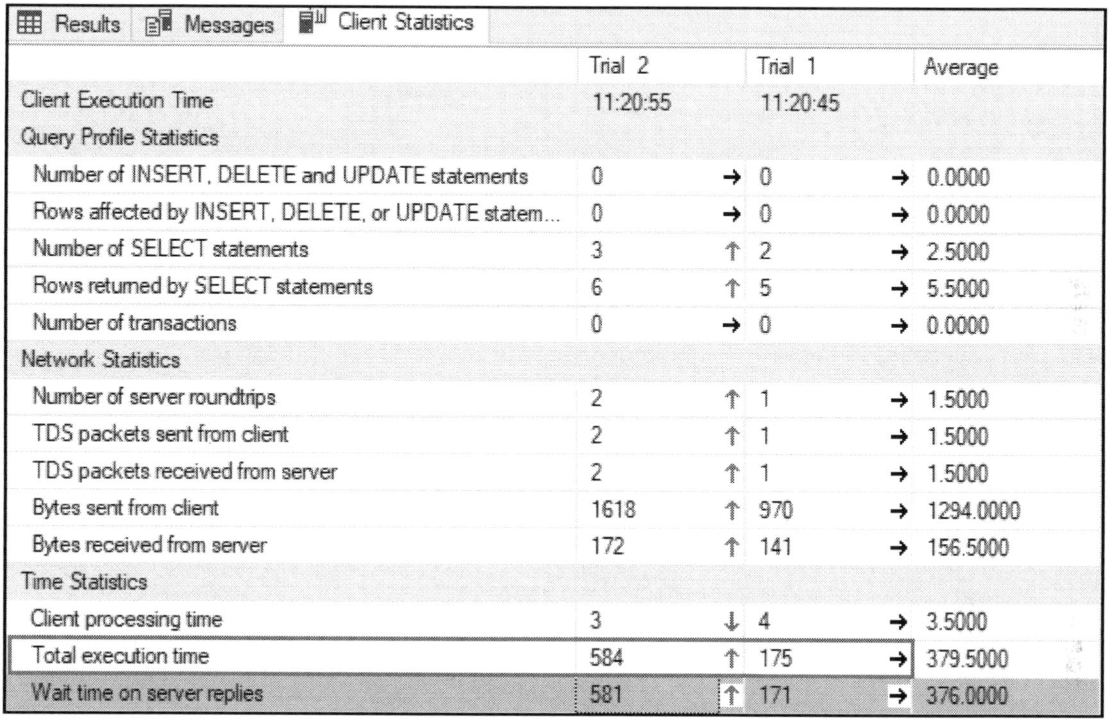

Results | Messages | Client Statistics

	Trial 2	Trial 1	Average
Client Execution Time	11:20:55	11:20:45	
Query Profile Statistics			
Number of INSERT, DELETE and UPDATE statements	0 →	0 →	0.0000
Rows affected by INSERT, DELETE, or UPDATE statem...	0 →	0 →	0.0000
Number of SELECT statements	3 ↑	2 →	2.5000
Rows returned by SELECT statements	6 ↑	5 →	5.5000
Number of transactions	0 →	0 →	0.0000
Network Statistics			
Number of server roundtrips	2 ↑	1 →	1.5000
TDS packets sent from client	2 ↑	1 →	1.5000
TDS packets received from server	2 ↑	1 →	1.5000
Bytes sent from client	1618 ↑	970 →	1294.0000
Bytes received from server	172 ↑	141 →	156.5000
Time Statistics			
Client processing time	3 ↓	4 →	3.5000
Total execution time	584 ↑	175 →	379.5000
Wait time on server replies	581 ↑	171 →	376.0000

The preceding screenshot shows client statistics. Trial 1 is the statistic for the T-SQL variant of the query and Trial 2 is the CLR variant of the same query. As can be seen in the highlighted row of the client statistics, the Total execution time is longer when CLR aggregation is used, even though the estimated execution plan using CLR custom aggregation seems to be more simple and straightforward than the execution plan using T-SQL resources only. This difference is given by the fact that CLR objects must be initialized internally and they are doing their job in a separate part of the SQL Server engine.

The preceding performance example shows how usual performance diagnostics, such as execution plans, can fail in accuracy when custom CLR code is incorporated into queries and batches.

Summary

In this chapter, we covered an overview of .NET development on SQL Server. Using .NET, custom objects help us to enhance SQL Server's capabilities in many ways. This is especially true when we need to create our own aggregation functions, as .NET programming is the only way to do it. However, overusing CLR objects may also lead to many issues and disappointed users.

The first part of this chapter was dedicated to providing an overview of SQLCLR. Here, we looked at how this works and when it is beneficial to use it. We then started to create an empty end-to-end **SQL Server Database Project** to demonstrate the development life cycle.

After the introductory section, we explored development in more detail. During this section, we developed and published our own CLR aggregation calculating statistical moments. The additional knowledge taken from this section describes what the statistical moment term means and for what purpose it is intended.

Nothing has only positives, and this is the same case for the CLR customization of SQL Server. In the final section, we summarized some considerable risks and issues that should be addressed when we are thinking about CLR development.

With all of its formulas and source code, this chapter was a tough one. It's important to know how things work, but we also need to have a good imagination when it comes to the results of the internal work. The visualization of results is invaluable for the deep insight into what the data means. In the next chapter, we will explore how to visualize information.

Questions

1. Which version of SQL Server was the first version with SQLCLR?
   The first version was SQL Server 2005.
2. Can I decide which version of .NET Framework I will use?
   No—as SQLCLR is a mandatory part of SQL Server, the version of .NET Framework is bound to a version of SQL Server.
3. Which types of objects can I create as CLR objects?
   Five types of CLR objects are supported. These are stored procedures, triggers, functions, data types, and custom aggregations.
4. Where is the assembly stored when it is published?
   It's stored in a database's metadata and nothing remains on the filesystem.
5. Can I use any .NET Framework types in my CLR objects?
   Yes, but consider the possible security issues as well as the potential difficulty of publishing many dependent assemblies.
6. Why does my successfully-published assembly and created CLR object not work?
   The most probable cause of this is that the CLR code is not enabled on the instance level. Check the configuration using the `sp_configure` system-stored procedure.
7. Which methods must CLR aggregation contain?
   Every CLR aggregation has four required methods: `Init`, `Accumulate`, `Merge`, and `Terminate`.
8. Is the execution of the CLR object faster than the execution of common T-SQL queries?
   It depends. Some tasks, such as massive string processing a CLR function, should be faster, but in many cases CLR objects do not enhance performance.

7
Data Visualization

A picture is worth a thousand words is an old phrase that is also true in the data science domain. Having a large amount of numbers will not be as useful as representing them with a graph or other graphics element. SQL Server does provide two major services used for data visualization or representation: SQL Server Reporting Services and Power BI Report Server. Both run locally on your SQL Server and offer you a variety of development options for data visualization projects. Another option would be the machine learning services and the available packages for Python and R. Both languages have their own set of visualization packages with different options.

Developing a visualization solution requires numerous roles, proper planning, and design for a successful rollout in the enterprise environment. Usually these visualization projects are handled by the business intelligence team, which understands the nature of the data and understands business user requirements for report content, layout, and functionality. There are numerous roles which together build a team of professionals who can make this happen.

These roles include the following:

- Project or program manager, who's role includes
    - Determining requirements with stakeholders
    - Budgeting
    - Impact analysis on the project rollout
    - Building teams
- Business intelligence developer, who's role includes
    - Building **ETL** (**Extract**, **Transform**, **Load**) packages
    - Developing cubes and data warehouses
    - Design and development of the reports

- Database architect, who's role includes:
    - Developing a data architecture for the enterprise
    - Performing logical modeling
    - Planning and operating the databases
- Technical architect, who's role includes:
    - Evaluating development technologies
    - Evaluating the business intelligence platforms
    - Deciding on appropriate directions for development and choice of a platform

Technical requirements

- SQL Server 2017 Evaluation Edition
- SQL Server Management Studio
- SQL Server Reporting Services
- Power BI Report Server
- Power BI Desktop for Report Server
- Report Builder
- SQL Server Data Tools

Data visualization – preparation phase

We can't just start directly with data visualization, unless we understand our environment and its needs. To understand our environment, we have to realize who are our users, what they need to do to access the report, and how they will use the data for appropriate business decisions.

If we want to make a good looking report, we need to have our data. And all the technologies that we'll see in the chapter will work on a similar concept. At first, we need to define a data source or a query for accessing our data, on which we'll make the visualizations to represent the data in a more understandable format.

Power BI Report Server

One of the available services that we can utilize on the SQL Server is a local version of Power BI, which was originally a cloud service running at www.PowerBI.com. Power BI has also a local variant, which is called **Power BI Report Server**, which offers a visually close interface to SQL Server Reporting Services, but in the background works little bit differently and has different development tools. Power BI Report Server has one primary client: Power BI Desktop for Report Server.

At the time of the writing, the latest available version of Power BI Report Server and Desktop optimized for Report Server was the March 2018 update, available at https://www.microsoft.com/en-us/download/details.aspx?id=56722. Power BI Report Server and the Desktop client have different release frequencies compared to the desktop client available for the online https://powerbi.microsoft.com/en-us/ service.

Starting with Power BI Desktop

Once you have installed the **Power BI Desktop**, you can open the application. If you haven't turned off the initial popup, you'll see the welcome screen with some initial available tasks:

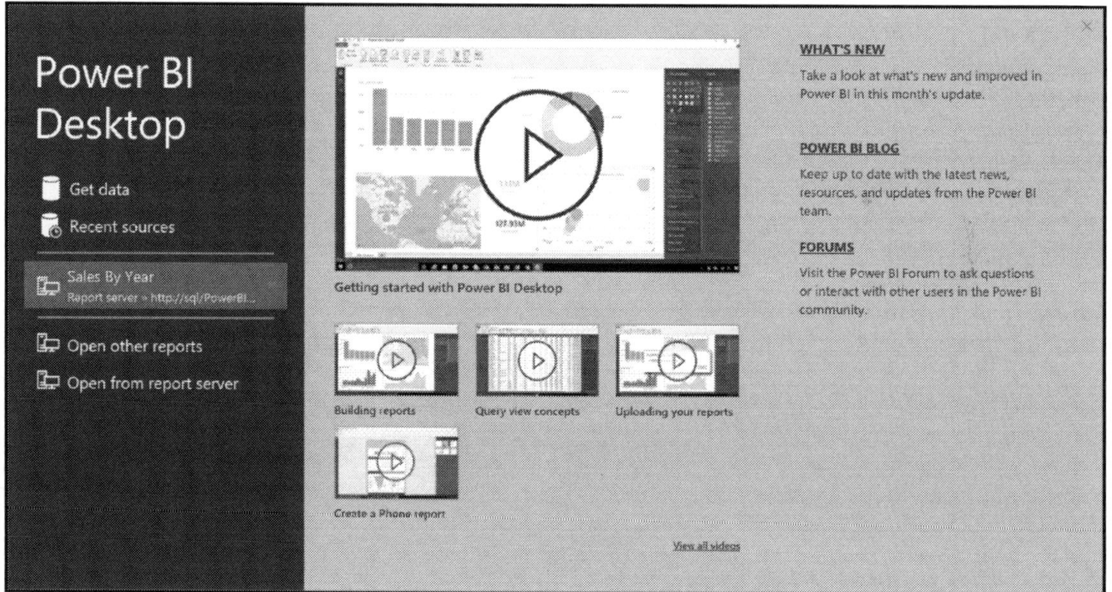

On the welcome screen, you can also see your latest projects on which you have worked and you have several links to the forums, documentation, and Power BI blog, where you can find new and interesting information about the service development, mixing both local, and cloud versions.

Defining the data source

For a fresh start, our journey will begin with the **Get Data** link on the upper-left part of the welcome screen. You'll be presented with a dialog window with a large variety of available data sources, which you can add to your Power BI model. Based on the available data, we can then create the Power BI Report, which is a set of visual components and their interactions.

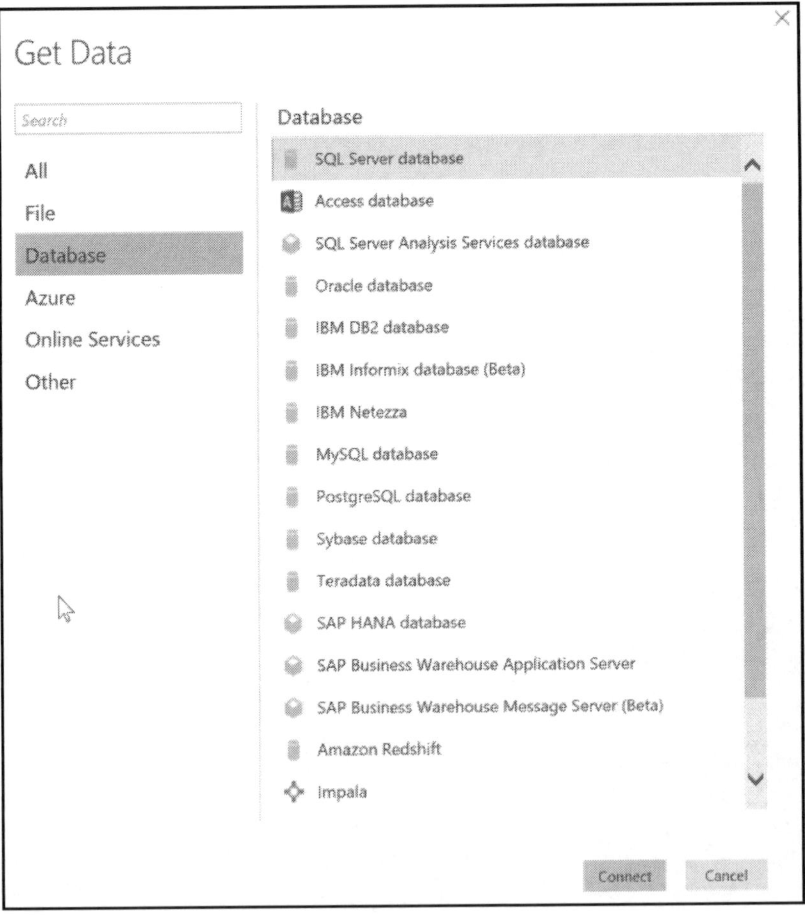

As you can see on the dialog, even if you filter out just the Database type of data sources, there's still a plenty of choices for you. The first one listed is the SQL Server database. This one expects a SQL Server to be running locally. If you have your data in the cloud in any Azure data service, which does not have to be SQL Server, there's a whole new category of data sources residing in Azure. With SQL Server, we have three major data sources in Azure:

- Azure SQL Database
- Azure SQL Data Warehouse
- Azure Analysis Services

If we will select the SQL Server as our primary data source, you are then presented with two very different options for the Data Connectivity mode in the Power BI model to work with. And those are as follows:

- **Import**
- **DirectQuery**

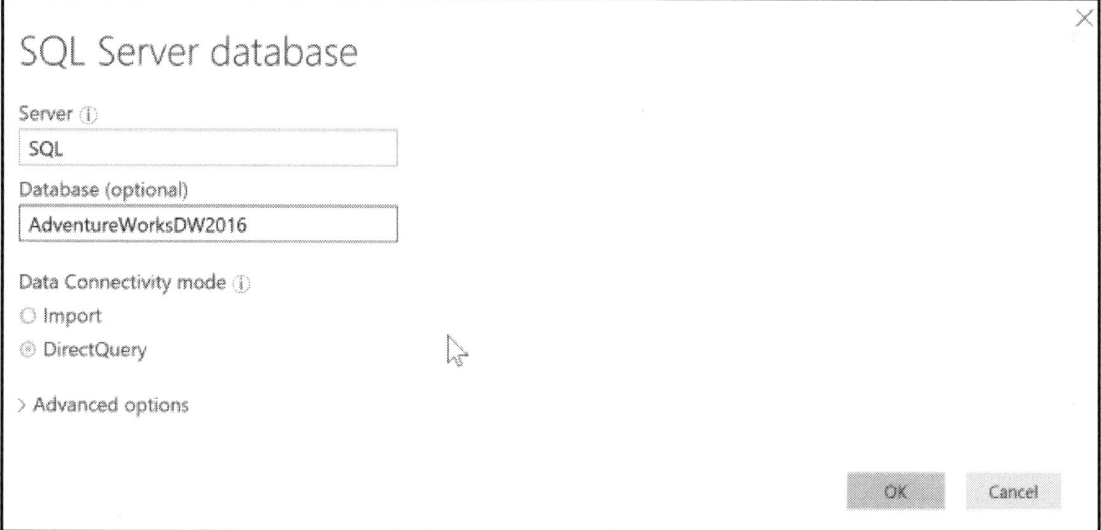

As the names of the modes suggest, with the **Import** mode, you will import the data into Power BI. In this mode, all the selected tables from the database will generate a query, which can be edited for filters, aggregates, or join operations to other tables and views and will load all the data into the Power BI cache. Once you add any visual elements to the Power BI report, the imported data will be queried. Since the storage is very fast, all changes to the visual elements will be implemented quickly with immediately applied changes. However, a drawback is that any change to underlying data in the original data source is not reflected on the report, until the data is imported again. Once the report from **Power BI Desktop** is published to the service, a dataset will be created. This dataset will include the imported data. You can then schedule a task to refresh the imported data from the original data source on a periodic basis.

The second mode, **DirectQuery**, works in a different way. No data will be imported to Power BI during the load and when you add any visual element to the report, a query will be executed against a live data source. Each interaction with the visuals will then initiate a connection to the data source and the performance and user experience of the report will be dependent on the performance and current load of the underlying data source. There are several scenarios where the **DirectQuery** mode will be a good choice:

- Frequent data changes on the data source
- Real-time reporting
- Very large datasets
- Multidimensional data sources, such as SQL Server Analysis Services or SAP BW

When you select the mode and define the data source as the connection to the local SQL Server, you can then view the tables from your database. Selecting the proper views and tables that you want to import is handled via a checkbox next to each item from the database. If the database tables and views have properly defined relations, then you can also import related tables.

On the wizard, there is a button named **Select Related Tables**, which will add all tables that are linked with table relations to the selected table or tables. On the right side of the wizard, you can see a preview of the data from the table in a truncated version, so only a small subset is visible:

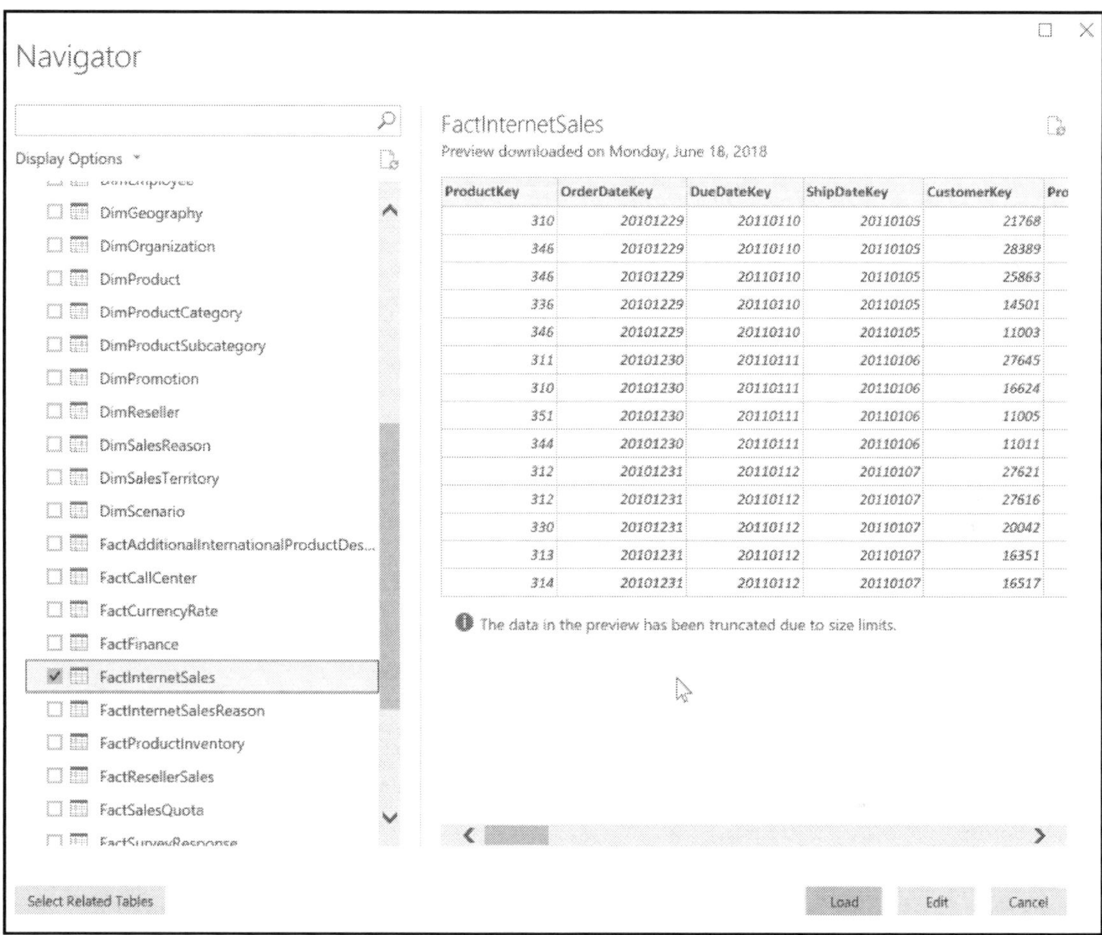

If you don't want to edit the data, you can directly load the data into Power BI and start working on the visual elements for the data. All data from selected and related tables will be loaded to Power BI and you will see all the tables in the **Power BI Desktop** data model:

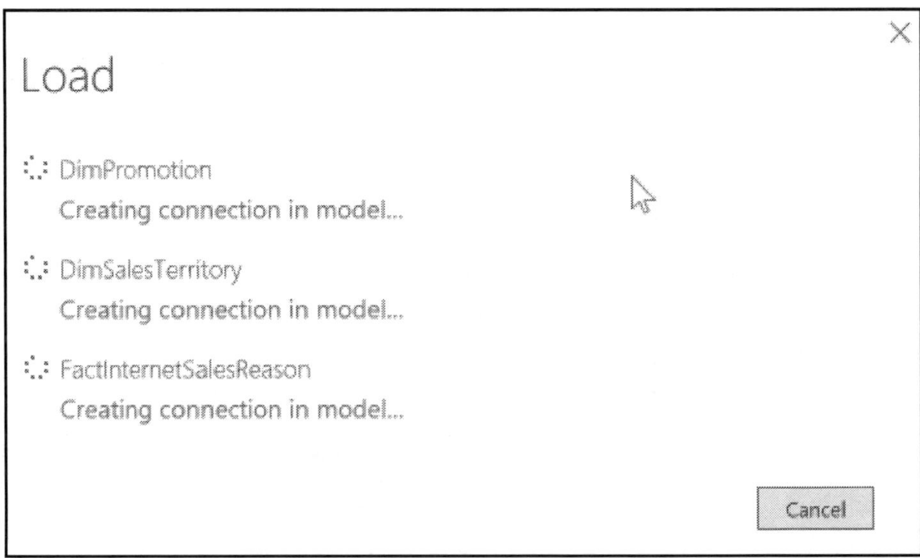

Adding visualizations to the Report

Once the data is loaded on the right side of the **Power BI Desktop**, you can perform the following steps:

1. You will see all the tables and views that you have imported to Power BI with all their selected columns. You can expand each table to see the columns, hierarchies, and measures that are available:

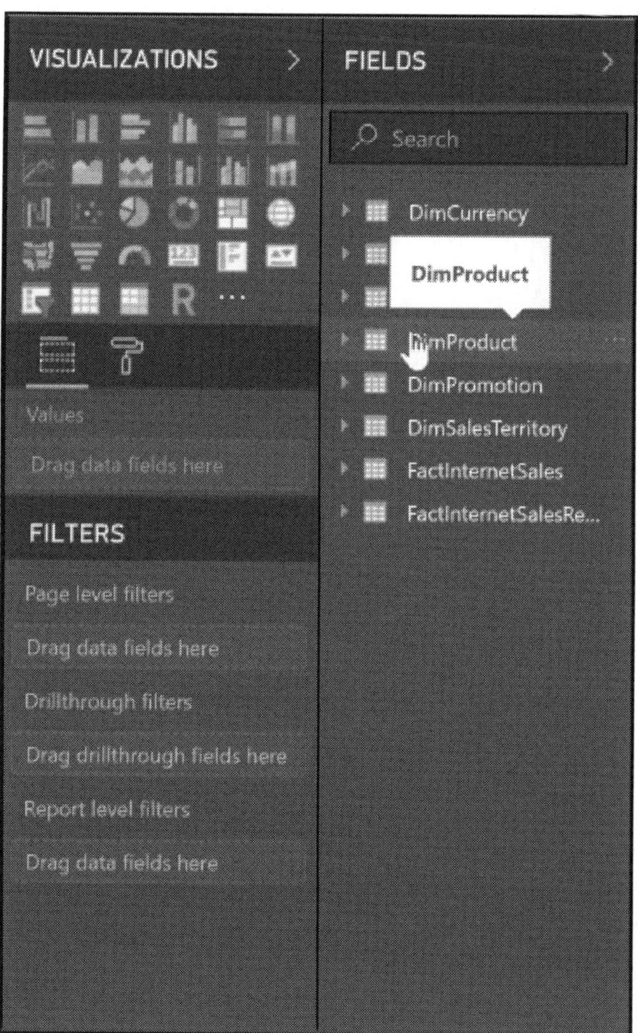

2. Next to the imported data you can see the built-in set of visual elements that are available for your report. You can use the visuals in two different ways. Either choose the column from your dataset and drag that column on the report pane, or select a visual and drag that visual on the report pane. Based on the data type of the column, **Power BI Desktop** will automatically suggest a visual type for the data and add a visual to the report.
3. When the **SalesAmount** column is selected and dragged to the report, Power BI selects a **Clustered Column Chart** as the default visual for this type of data. You can, however, change the visual type by clicking on the existing visuals to change the appearance of the presented data:

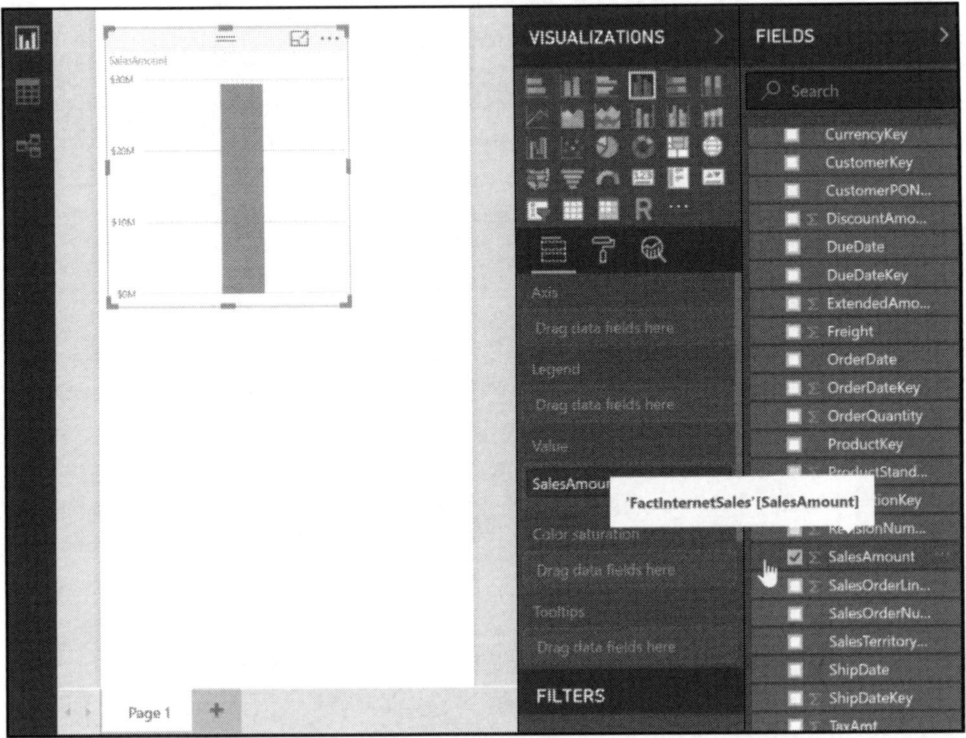

Selecting the SalesAmount option

4. In this way, only one axis of the chart is defined and we need to add more data to have a visual correctly representing the data. You can drag and drop another column to the **Axis** property of the visual to add another dimension of the data to display. Once the column **EnglishDayofTheWeek** column from **DimDate** table is added to the visual, it immediately changes and displays the correct sales amount by the week day:

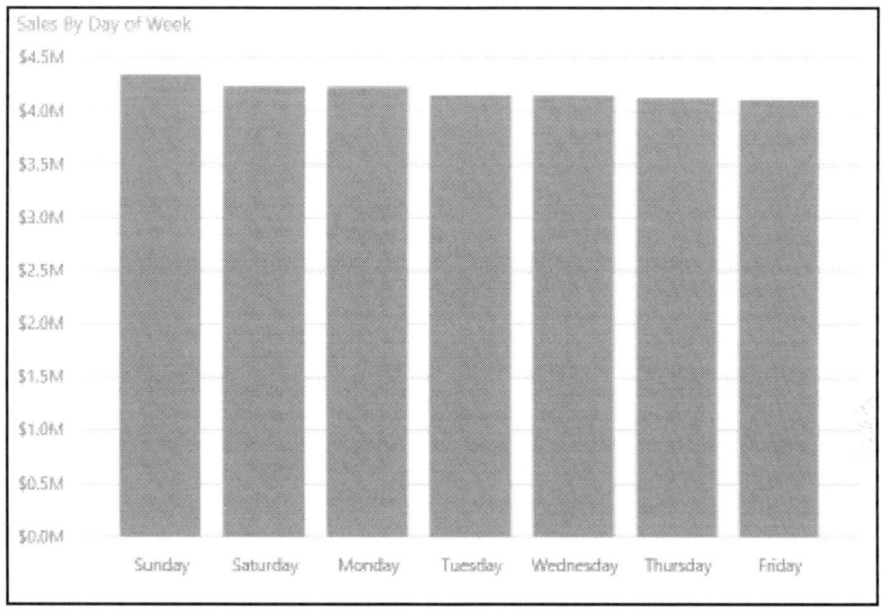

Visualizing the report of Sales

5. By adding more data, you can enrich the report with more visuals showing different perspectives on the available data. The report structure allows you to have more pages of the visuals, depending on the nature of the presented data, so you can logically group the visuals on the report pages to display perspectives on the data based on the user demands:

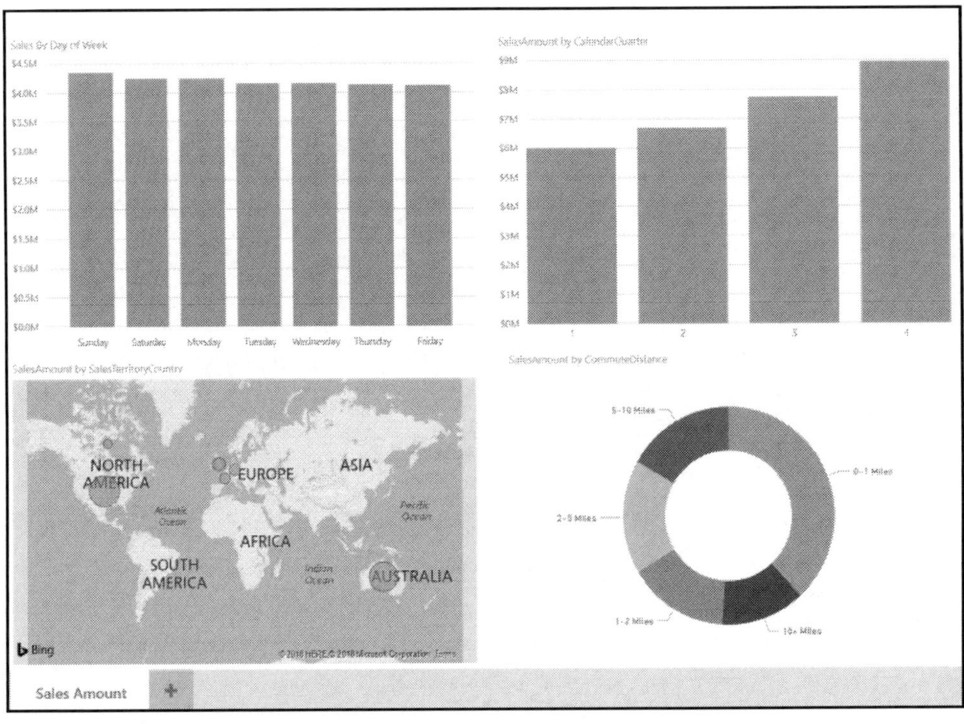

Visuals showing different perspectives on the available data

6. When working with visuals, you have a default choice of visuals that are available in the client, but you can add more visuals to your project if needed. You can search the Power BI Market Place, where you can find numerous visuals online available for you to use, most of them for free, actually:

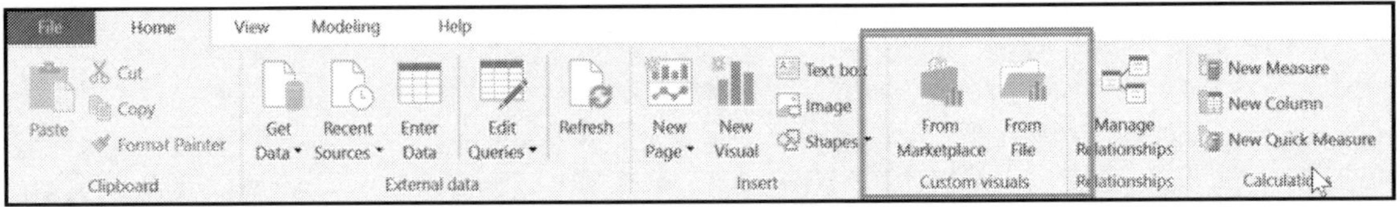

7. Or you can add a visual from a file, either downloaded from the web, or created by your development team for you to use.

Creating custom visuals is a development effort which is way out of the scope of this book, but if you feel comfortable with developing your own visuals you can start here `https://docs.microsoft.com/en-us/power-bi/service-custom-visuals-getting-started-with-developer-tools`

Visual interactions

A great wow effect with Power BI comes from Visuals interaction. If you click into any visual, depending on the selection, other visual elements will adjust their values and displayed data. Each visual can act as a filter for other visuals on the report. This, of course, is configurable for each visual element on the report. If you select any visual, you can edit the interactions on the **Format** menu:

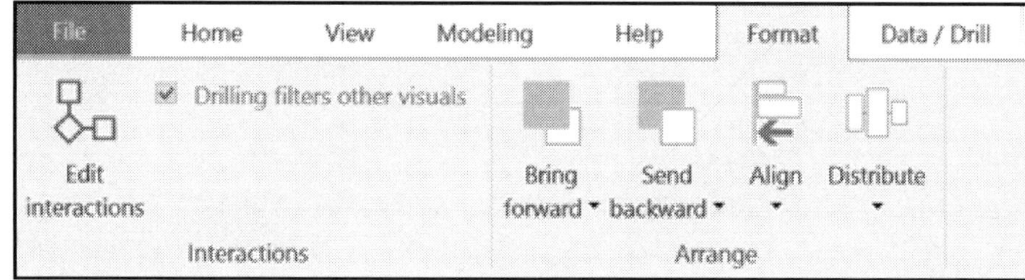

Format menu

Once you go into **Edit interactions**, three new icons will be visible on other visuals allowing you to set up the behavior for the interaction.

Those options are as follows:

- Filter
- Highlight
- None

When you select none, the last icon, the visual will not interact with the others. Highlight will just visually depict the portion on the graph that belongs to the selected range from the other visual and the filter will adjust the values based on the selected value:

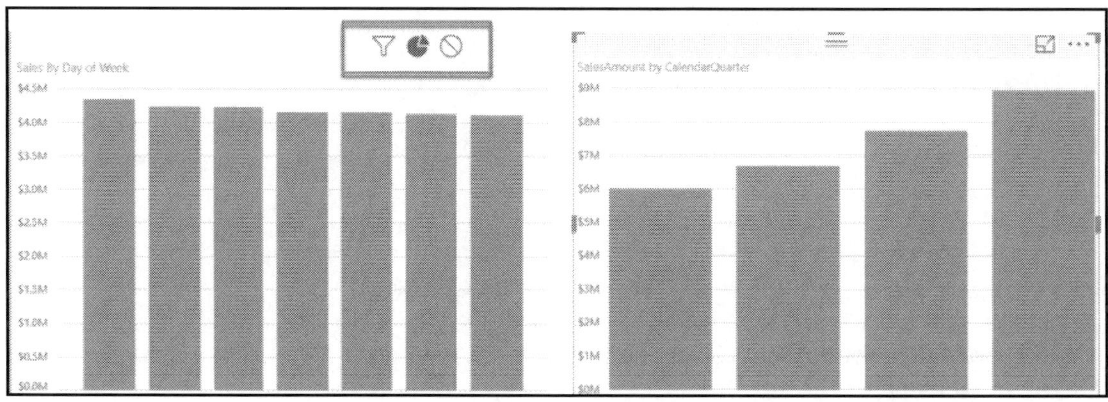

Visual depicting Sales by day of week and SalesAmount by CalendarQuarter

With data hierarchies that you can define, you can also drill through the report into lower level of the hierarchy. A typical example would be a date dimension, where the visuals will first display the years, then quarters, and each month of the quarter as the filter level:

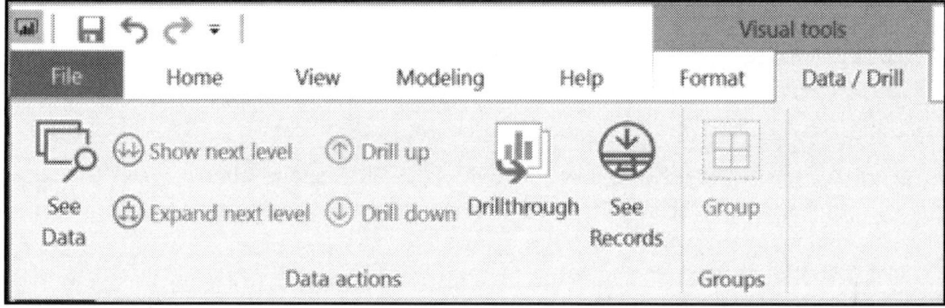

Publishing reports

Once you have finished your report, you can save the report locally for your later use, or upload the report to the Power BI Report Server, which is running in your local environment.

1. In the menu, you can use **File** | **Save As** | **Power BI Report Server** and navigate to the URL used by the Report Server:

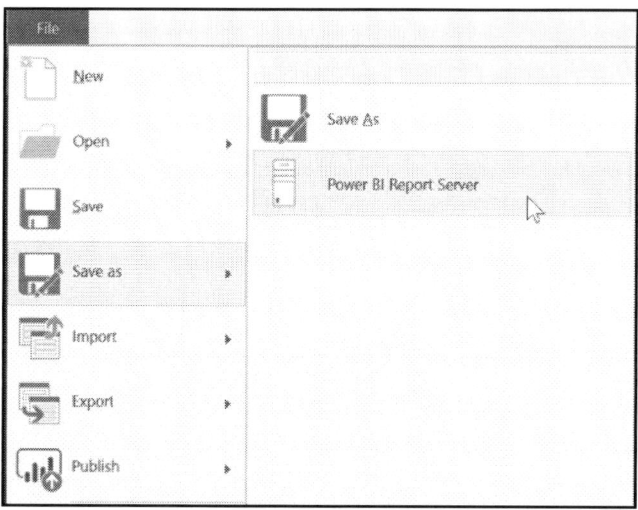

2. Once you have selected the URL, you have to also define the report name. On this URL, you can later on find all the reports that you have published to the local website:

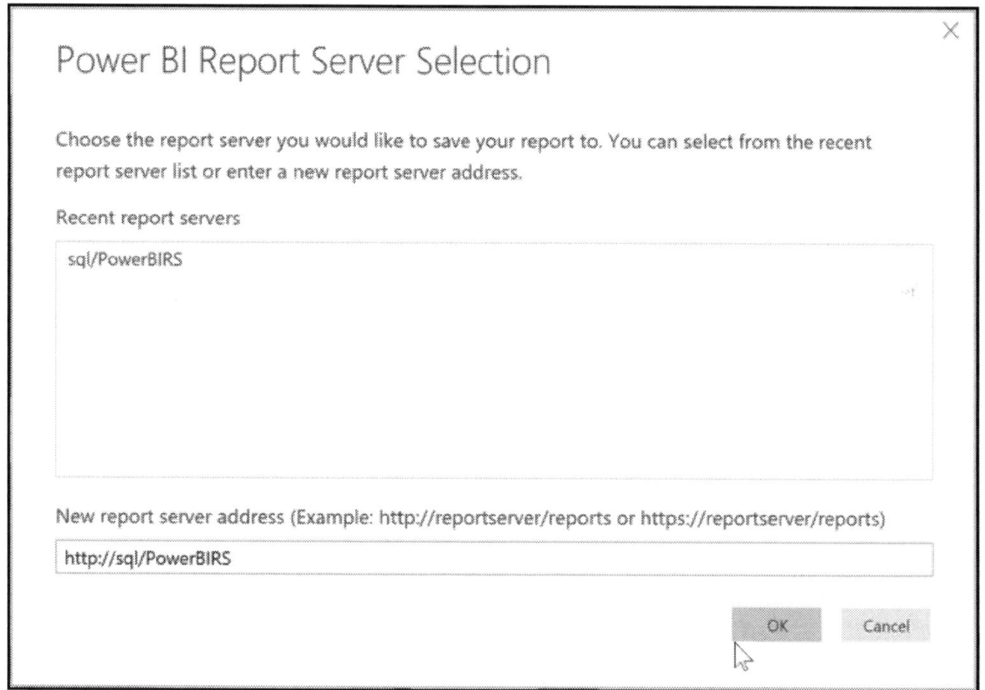

3. Once the report is deployed, you can see that report on your Power BI Report Server. Each report can be individually managed, edited, and so on. via the breadcrumb menu on the right side of each report:

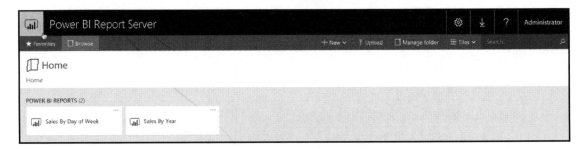

One of the important tasks after uploading the report to the Report Server is to manage the schedule for the data refresh and security of the report. As we have seen in previous part of the report creation, while defining the data source, you can choose to import or **DirectQuery** the data. If the data is imported, it does not reflect any change on the data source in the report. In order to keep the report current, you can add a refresh schedule for the data source:

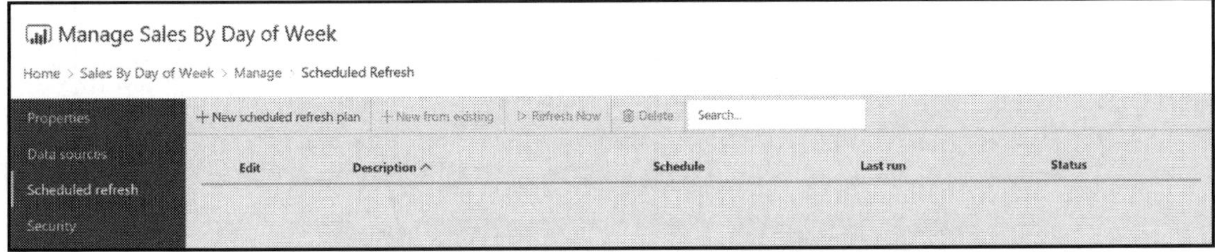

This plan will define how frequently the data will be refreshed for the report. In order to configure a refresh plan, you have to first define the username and password for the connection to the data source on the **Data Sources** page of the report management. You can also trigger a manual refresh, but only after you have created the scheduled refresh plan.

While configuring the security of the report, if we'll stick to the basics, you can configure several different roles for each user or group from your Windows Active Directory domain, and add those to the report security with proper role assignment. You can choose one or more roles to assign to the same principal:

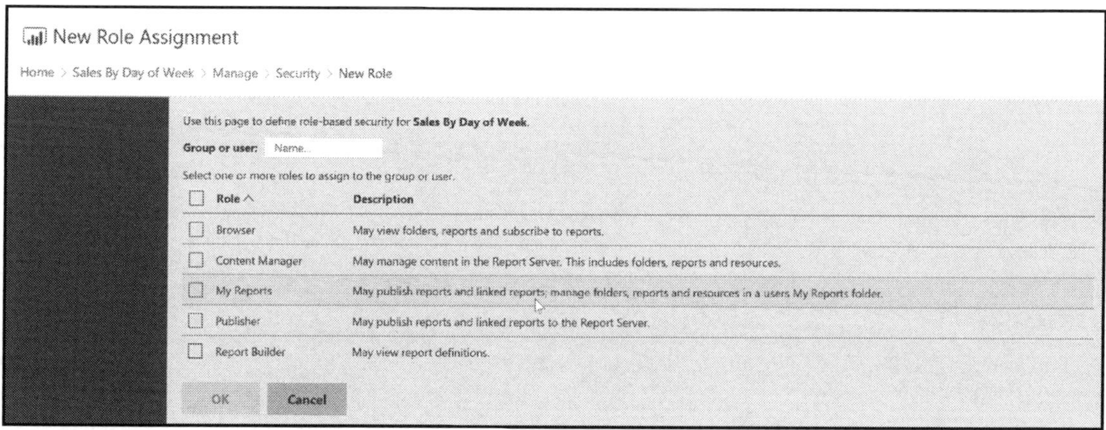

SQL Server Reporting Services

SQL Server Reporting Services, or **SSRS** for short, has been with us for quite some time. SSRS was introduced back in the days of SQL Server 2000. Since then SSRS has made its journey to become a very important visualization platform among Microsoft software stack. Not only is SSRS a major service in SQL Server, which we use for the whole business intelligence deployment and workflow (importing, analyzing, and displaying the data), but SSRS is also an essential part of other pieces of software from Microsoft, which we use in the modern environment. You can find SSRS working together with the following:

- SharePoint Server
- Skype for Business (or previously Lync Server)
- System Center products, such as Configuration or Operations Manager, and more

SSRS is used as a reporting platform, where numerous tools have their own set of reports, and SSRS is just a delivery tool to display all the required information.

There are two primary tools for designing reports for SSRS: Report Builder and SQL Server Data Tools. Report Builder is available for download from Microsoft's site as a free application, which you can install either to the server, or preferably to your developer workstation. Report Builder has a similar concept, but is a little bit different to UI/UX, such as the Power BI Desktop. You can choose to create a blank report or use a wizard for one of the typical charts or visuals to display data:

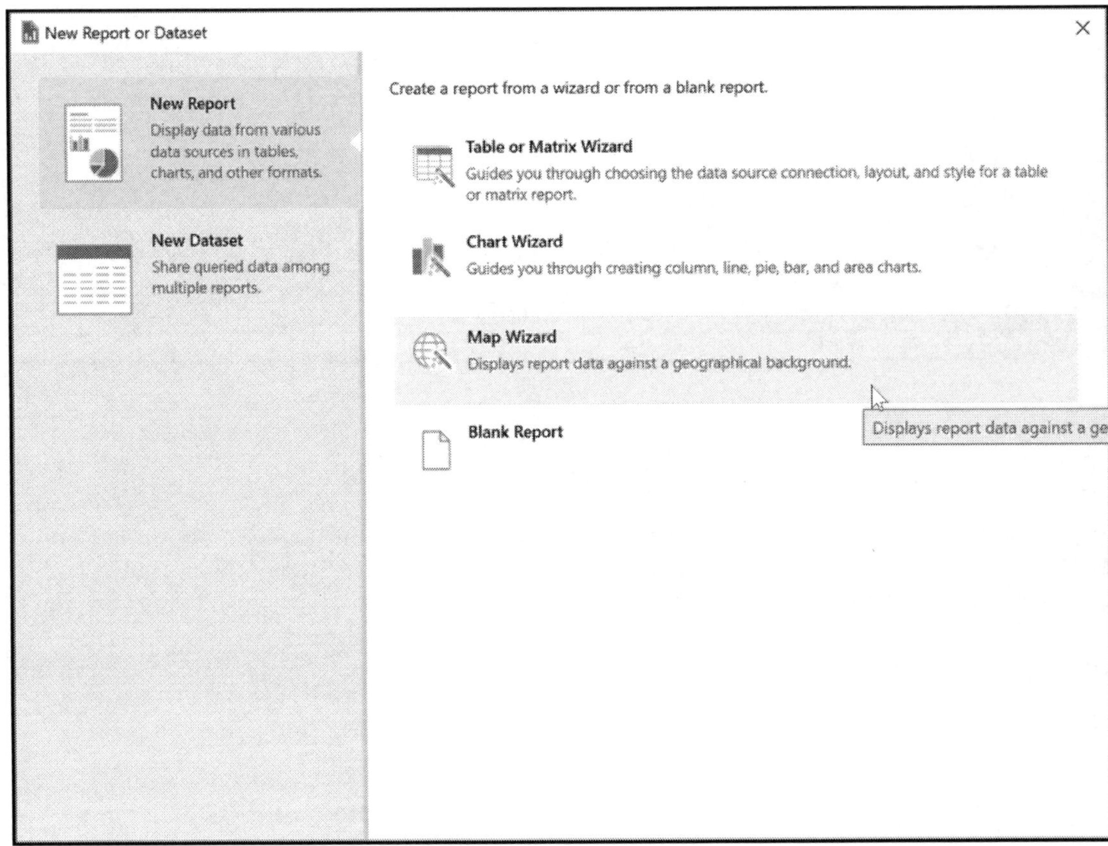

If you create a blank report, you will see a menu on the left with several items.

1. First create a `Data Set` and `Data Source`, which define the access to your database and a query to run, which will prepare the data for you to display.
2. When you're creating a data source, there are two different options for the report. Either the data source will be embedded to the report, or the data source will be created directly on the Report Server and shared for multiple reports:

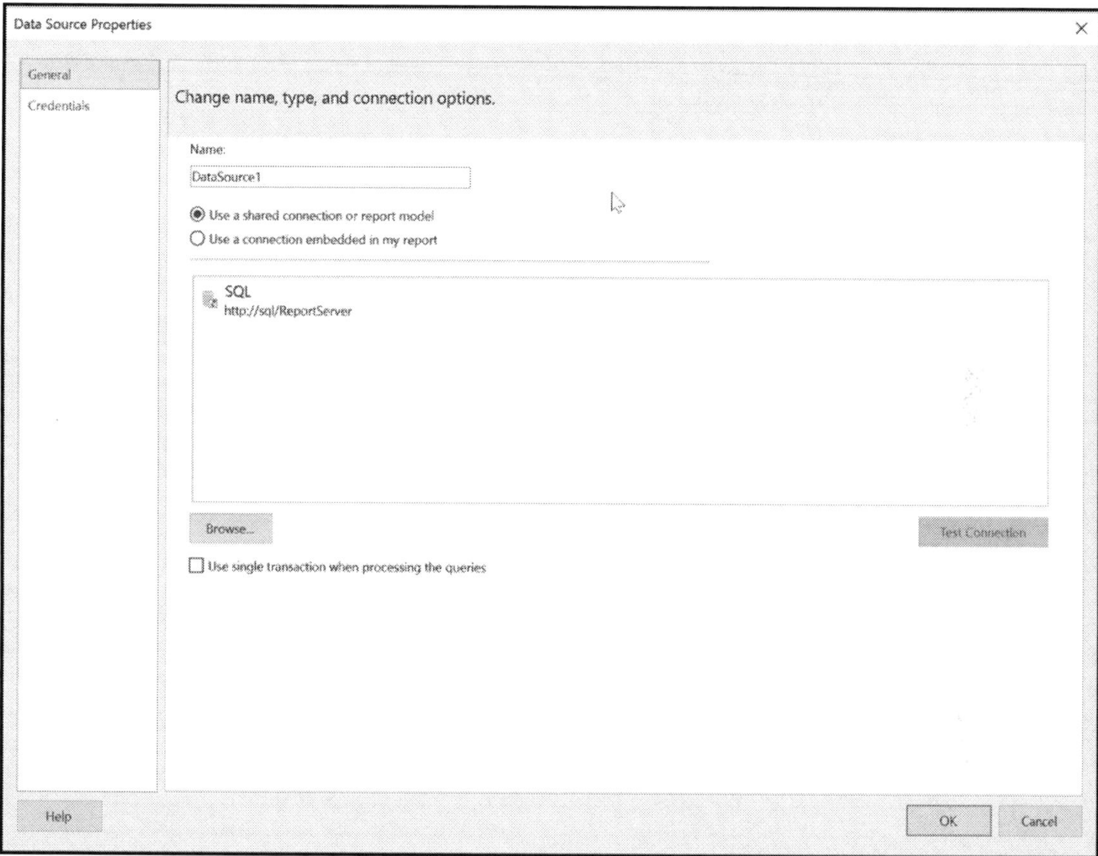

3. A shared data source may require additional settings on the infrastructure, especially if you would like the Report Server to impersonate each user and connect to the data source with the credentials of the user viewing the report.
4. A dataset is built on top of the data source and presents a query or stored procedure that should be executed to return a result set and formatted based on the visual:

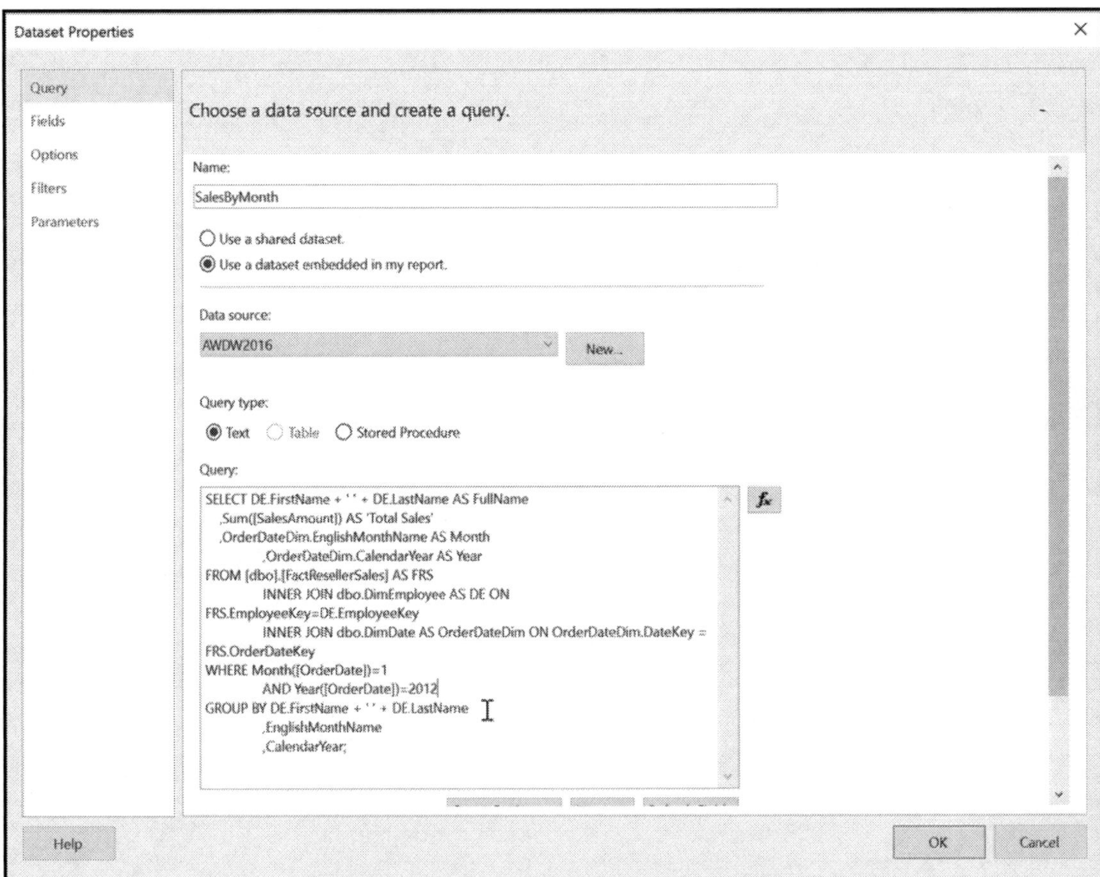

5. Once we have defined the dataset, we can start bringing visuals to the report to display our data. As you can see, there is a large variety of the visuals that can be used on the report, ranging from displaying the raw values in the table or matrix to the graphic elements, such as charts, gauges, and so on:

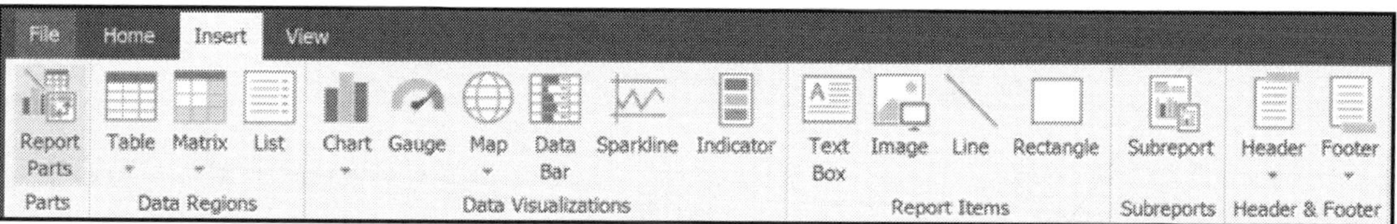

6. If you would like to test the look and feel of your report, you can run the report via the **Run Report** button on the Home menu. The report will connect to the data source and render and display all the elements so that you can see the progress of you work:

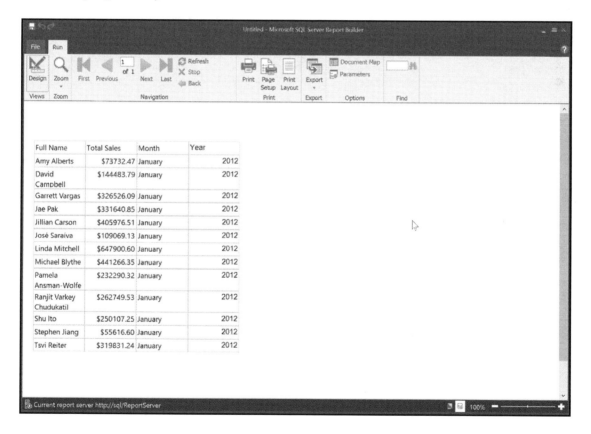

Untitled - Microsoft SQL Server Report Builder

File Run

Design Zoom First Previous 1 of 1 Next Last Refresh Stop Back Print Page Setup Print Layout Export Document Map Parameters

Views Zoom Navigation Print Export Options Find

Full Name	Total Sales	Month	Year
Amy Alberts	$73732.47	January	2012
David Campbell	$144483.79	January	2012
Garrett Vargas	$326526.09	January	2012
Jae Pak	$331640.85	January	2012
Jillian Carson	$405976.51	January	2012
José Saraiva	$109069.13	January	2012
Linda Mitchell	$647900.60	January	2012
Michael Blythe	$441266.35	January	2012
Pamela Ansman-Wolfe	$232290.32	January	2012
Ranjit Varkey Chudukatil	$262749.53	January	2012
Shu Ito	$250107.25	January	2012
Stephen Jiang	$55616.60	January	2012
Tsvi Reiter	$319831.24	January	2012

Current report server http://sql/ReportServer 100%

Adding charts to Reports

You can add more types of visuals to your report. To enhance the report with some charts, we can add a chart with the chart wizard:

1. For the chart, we will use the same dataset that was displayed to the table:

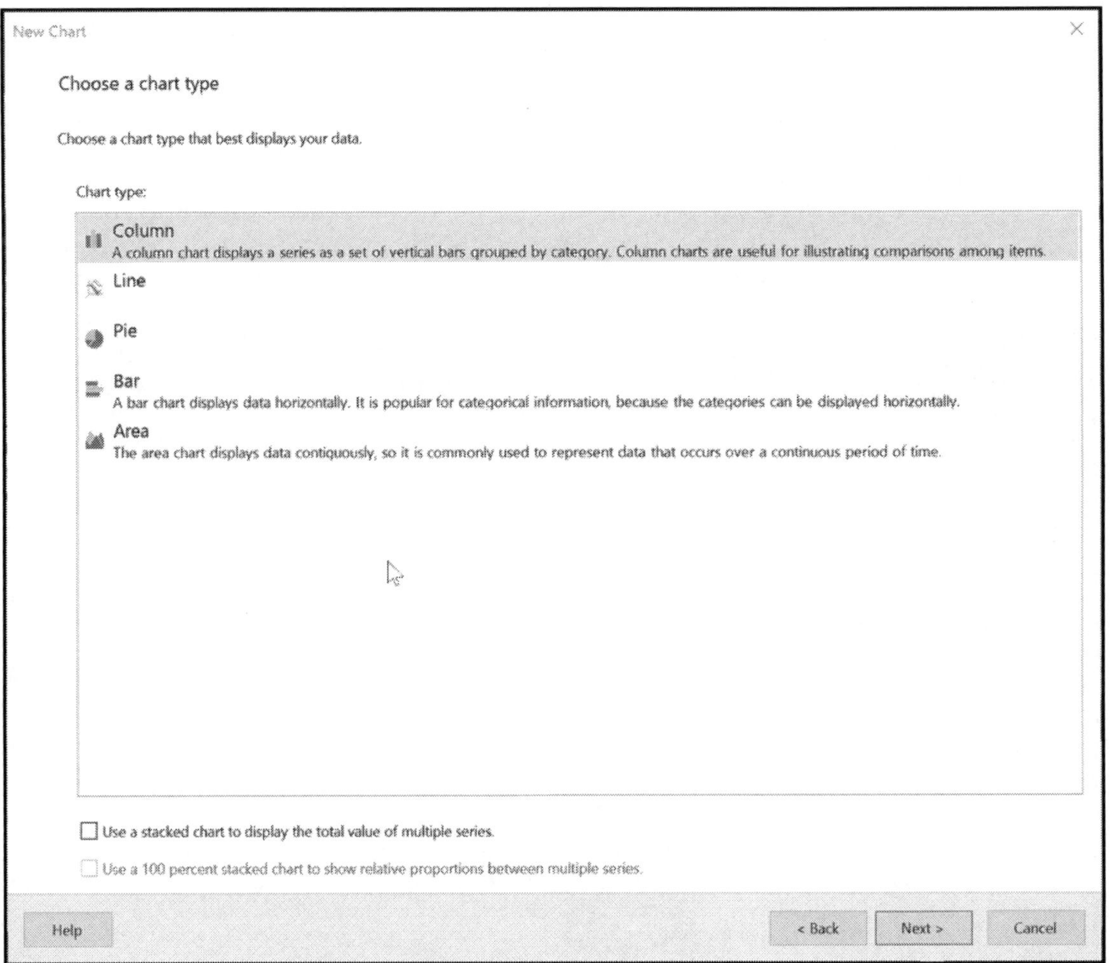

2. Once the chart type is selected, you can place the chart on the report and position it as needed.
3. If you run the report, it will render the correct data, although in the designer only sample values are used to display values in the chart:

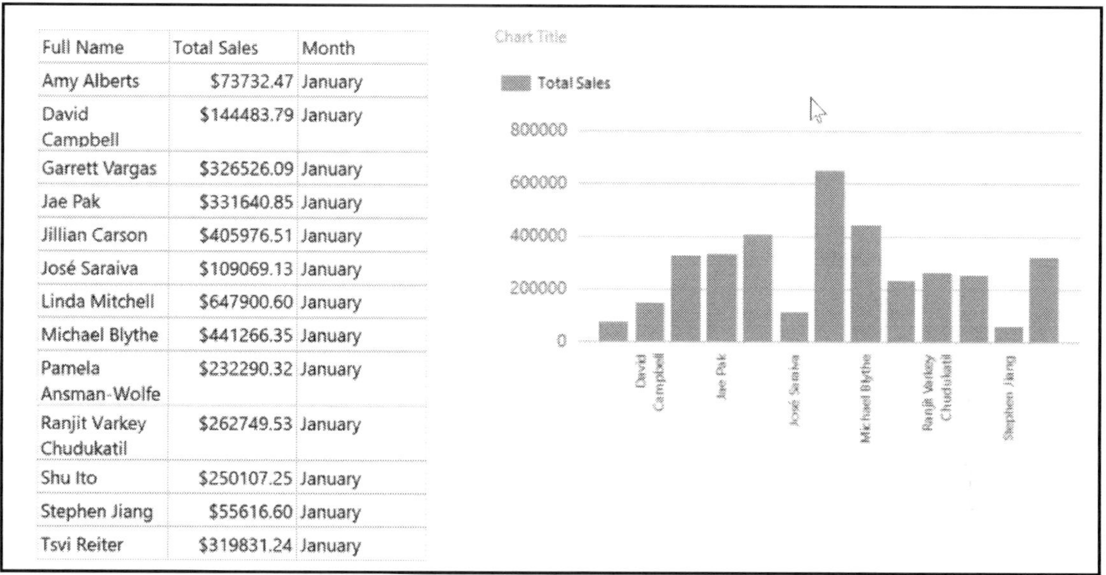

Full Name	Total Sales	Month
Amy Alberts	$73732.47	January
David Campbell	$144483.79	January
Garrett Vargas	$326526.09	January
Jae Pak	$331640.85	January
Jillian Carson	$405976.51	January
José Saraiva	$109069.13	January
Linda Mitchell	$647900.60	January
Michael Blythe	$441266.35	January
Pamela Ansman-Wolfe	$232290.32	January
Ranjit Varkey Chudukatil	$262749.53	January
Shu Ito	$250107.25	January
Stephen Jiang	$55616.60	January
Tsvi Reiter	$319831.24	January

Chart depicting the total sales of the month

4. Once the report is finished, you can save the report to the SSRS web service, and navigate yourself to the website of SSRS. On the website, you'll see your report (displayed as a paginated report) and the dataset, which can be shared among multiple reports. We haven't chosen to embed the dataset into the report itself:

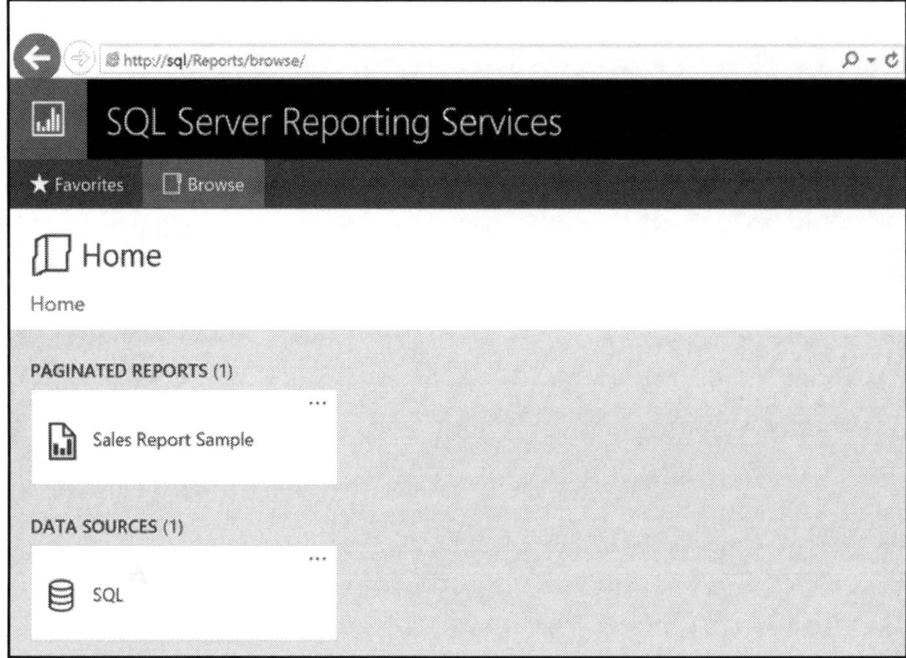

5. On the site, you can manage your report via the report menu and edit report security, subscriptions, and so on. If the report is created and the dataset is saved with the credentials to log in, you can create subscriptions for your report. Based on the configuration of the SSRS service, there will be two primary options for the subscriptions: either send an email with an attachment or save the report to a file share. The report can have many formats, including Office documents, **PDF**, and so on:

Delivery options (E-Mail)

To: Administrator
Cc:
Bcc:
(Use (;) to separate multiple e-mail addresses.)
Reply-To:
Subject: @ReportName was executed at @Exe
Include Report Render Format: PDF
Include Link
Priority: Normal
Comment:

Word
Excel
PowerPoint
PDF
TIFF file
MHTML (web archive)
CSV (comma delimited)
XML file with report data
Data Feed

Using SQL Server Data Tools

Another development environment you can utilize for your reports is SQL Server Data Tools. This tool is no longer part of the installation media for SQL Server and has to be downloaded separately. Data Tools can work independently or together with the installation of Visual Studio. If you don't run Visual Studio, there will be a small Visual Studio shell installed on your development machine and you can start working on your business intelligence projects. Data Tools is an integrated development tool that is used not only for Reporting Services, but also for other business intelligence tools for Microsoft SQL Server.

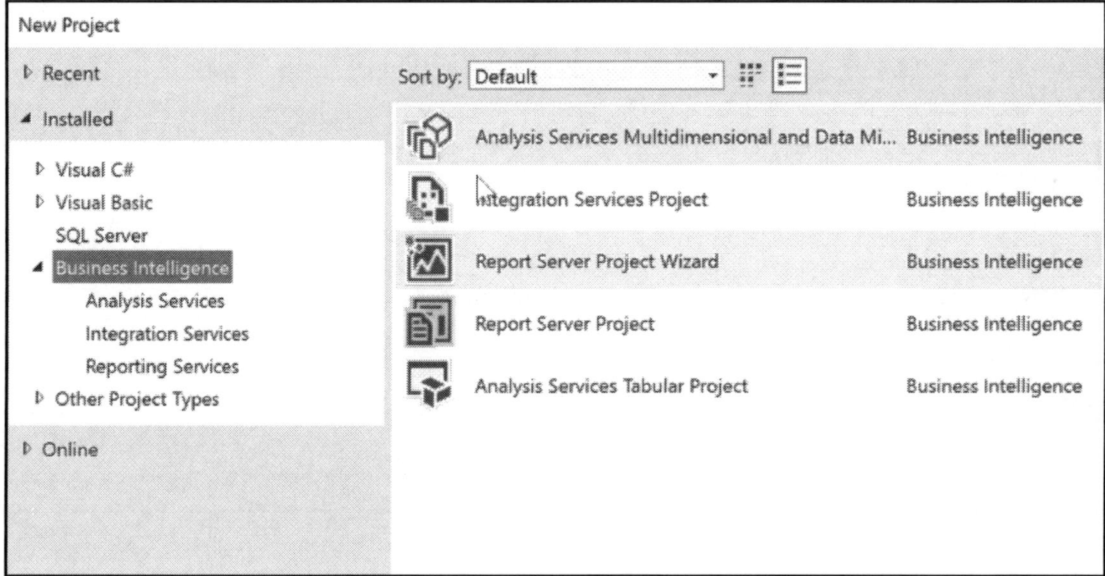

For **Reporting Services**, we'll use the **Report Server Project Wizard** or **Report Server Project** templates. We will define the very same data source to the SQL Server, connecting to `AdventureWorks2016DW`. The query for getting the data for the report can be embedded or we can use a shared data source, such as Report Builder.

The content of the report can be visible in the left menu of Data Tools and you can find the dataset and data source settings, static images used for logos, and other graphics, parameters, and built-in fields:

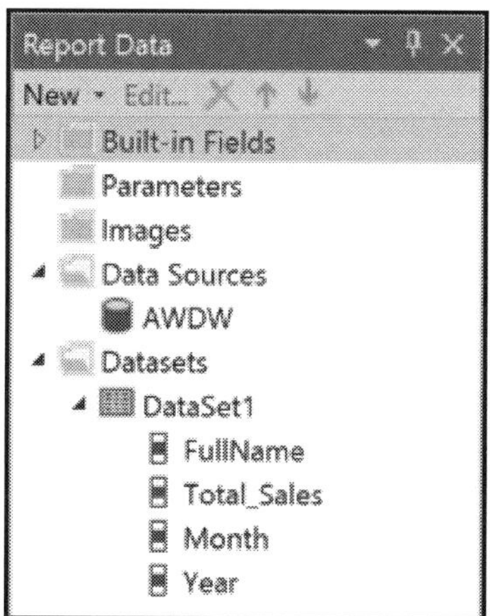

When you have defined the `Data Source` and `Datasets` via wizard, you can start adding elements to the report from the Toolbox:

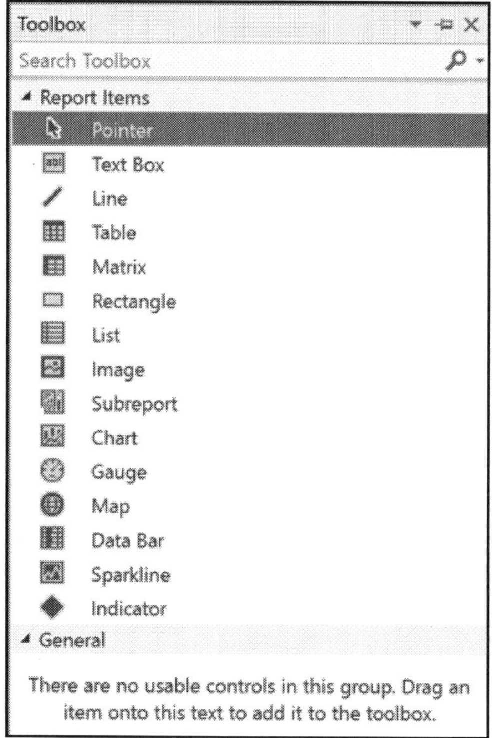

If you would like to add a chart visual, for example, double-click on the **Chart** item and a new wizard will show up offering you a large variety of different charts. Based on the displayed data, you can select a proper chart and configure the axis values:

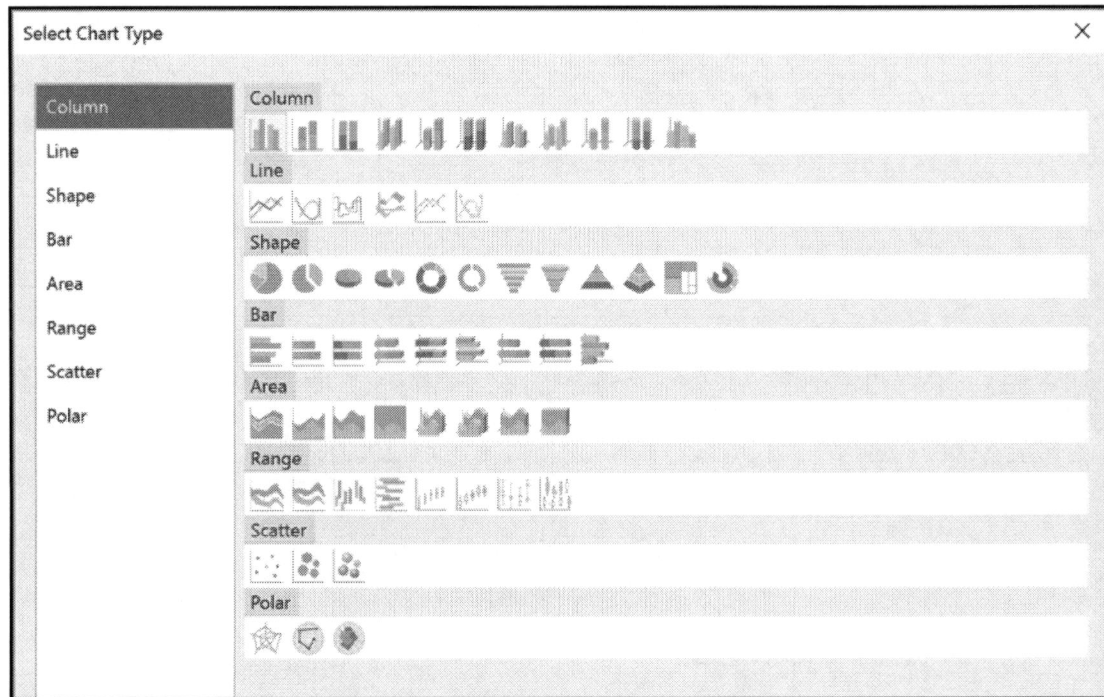

For the chart, you have to configure values, groups, and series, so that the data is correctly displayed on the axis:

For the deployment of the report, you can use the **Deployment Wizard** from your project. If you right-click the solution in **Solution Explorer** in Data Tools, you can deploy the report and the data source with the dataset to your server and then configure the security, subscription settings, and so on, like with reports created with Report Builder. Both tools create the same type of paginated report, which will be available on the **Reporting Services** website:

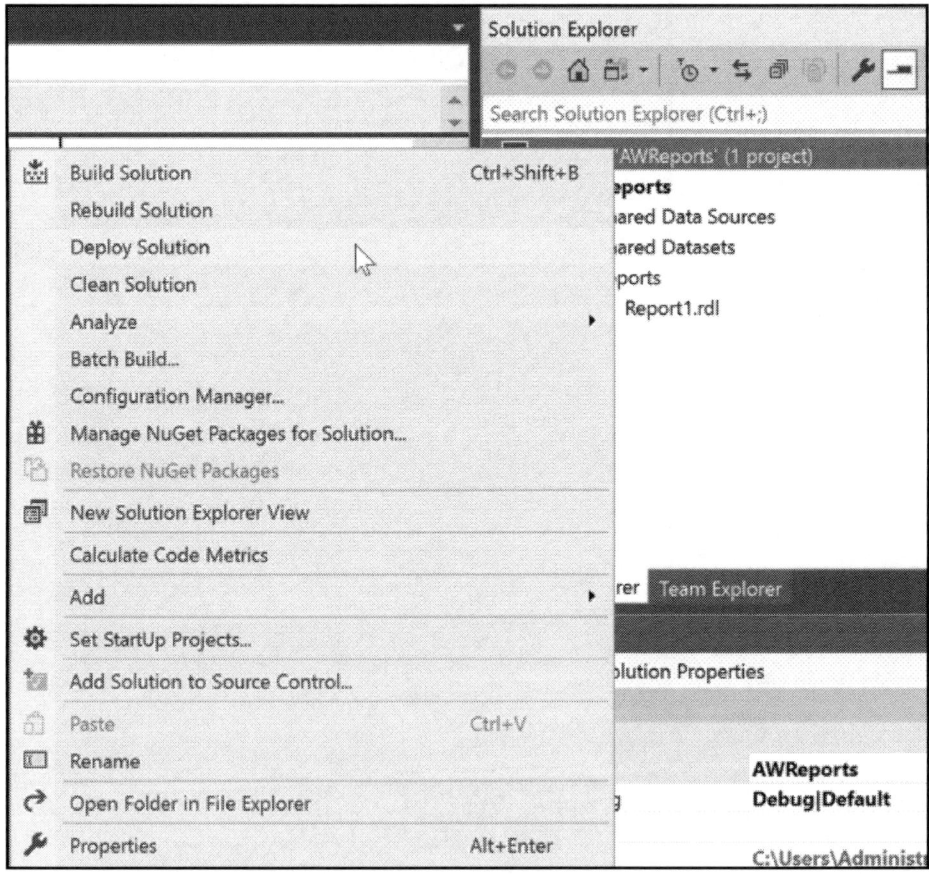

These reports can be consumed by your enterprise users with various web browser types. There are more integration options for report, if your environment has SharePoint Server available.

Summary

In this chapter, we learned that SQL Server provides two major services used for data visualization or representation: SQL Server Reporting Services and Power BI Report Server. We saw how to add visualizations and charts to these services to produce reports based on your data available in heterogeneous data sources.

In the next chapter, we will summarize the main points in all the previous chapters and conclude with some outcomes. The chapter will also provide ideas of how to continue working with data science, trends that are likely in the future, and other technologies that will play a strong role in data science.

8
Data Transformations with Other Tools

In `Chapter 5`, *Data Transformation and Cleaning with T-SQL*, we explored the need for data transformation for the purpose of data consolidation, accuracy checking, and cleansing. From there, we went on to learn how to explore data from a statistical point of view in `Chapter 6`, *Data Exploration and Statistics with T-SQL*. In `Chapter 7`, *Data Visualization*, we used some very helpful techniques for data visualization. Using techniques from all three of these chapters leads to the need to transform data once again.

This chapter is intended to explain how to replace missing values, normalize data, or standardize data used as an input into further machine learning models. For many of these tasks, T-SQL is an inadequate language, so we will use other tools and languages to meet our requirements.

In this chapter, we will learn the following topics:

- **Categorization, missing values, and normalization**: The first section of the chapter introduces several statistical terms. This is important as it tells us the importance of normalizing and standardizing our data. It's also important not to delete records with empty values.
- **Using integration services for data transformations**: **SQL Server Integration Services** (**SSIS**) was already mentioned in earlier chapters, but in this section we will use SSIS to do some of the transformations that we learned about in the first section of this chapter.

- **Using R for data transformations**: R is a statistically and analytically-oriented language. Starting with SQL Server 2016, we can use the R language as an enhancement to T-SQL. R provides wider possibilities of data transformation than T-SQL. In this section, we will explore the basics of R and some of its functions that are useful for data transformation.
- **Using Data Factory for data transformations**: Data Factory is an Azure service that is used for data transformations in cloud and hybrid scenarios. This section is going to be an overview of Data Azure Factory features.

Technical requirements

For readers who want to experiment with the examples provided throughout this chapter, the following tools are needed:

- SQL Server 2016/2017 in at least Express edition (downloadable for free from `microsoft.com`)
- SQL Server Management Studio (downloadable for free from `microsoft.com`)
- SQL Server Data Tools for Visual Studio 2015 (downloadable for free from `microsoft.com`)
- The R environment (downloadable for free at `https://cran.r-project.org/bin/windows/base/`)
- Optionally RStudio (downloadable for free at `https://www.rstudio.com/products/rstudio/download/`)
- An Azure subscription (this subscription can be created for free)
    - The Azure SQL Server database: `AdventureWorksLT`
    - An Azure storage account

Categorization, missing values, and normalization

For correct and accurate predictions calculated with machine learning models, the incoming data should be presented in the ideal format. The ideal format means that all values are present in a dataset, numerical data is used in numerical features and not categories or labels, or the distribution of features is even (Gaussian). However, many presumptions are not always true in the real world. For this reason, after basic transformations, such as joining or merging data, are done, we should undertake statistical research that shows the real format of data. Based on statistical research, we will know the difference between the ideal and real format of incoming data. This section will describe techniques used to transform data from its real format to its ideal, comparable, and meaningful format.

Categorization

Business applications often speak in the form of codes or abbreviations. Let's take the very simple example of sales order statuses. Every sales order goes through several statuses. For instance, when it's new, the order is approved, payment is received, the item is supplied to a customer, and the order is closed. A dataset extracted from an application such as this will often describe the sales order status using numerical codes stored in an integer column. For instance, code 1 means that the sales order is new, while code 2 means that the sales order is approved, and so forth.

Let's have an assignment to analyze sales orders according to their status. For such an analysis, machine learning models will recognize the sales order status column as a numerical feature useful, for example, as a regressor. However, we know that the sales order status should be a **category** of sales order states. The category serves as a grouping column, not a numerical feature. This is the main reason why we need to categorize some columns.

Categorization is quite a simple task that can be fulfilled using several techniques. The technique used for certain columns depends on our preferences as well as the amount of distinct code values in the column. Basically, category values can be one of the following:

- **Converted into a character string**: This is very simple and straightforward. We can use the T-SQL `CAST` or `CONVERT` functions as well as SSIS **Derived Column** transformation. This categorization approach has one disadvantage: the resulting model will still show numerical values that are not readable to end users.
- **Hard-coded using the `CHOOSE` T-SQL function**: This is also a very simple method of categorization, but it's meaningful for a small amount of values in a categorized column.
- **Joined from a table enumerating numerical codes and their values**: This approach to categorization requires creating a simple table with a key-value structure, and then joining the table with a basic dataset. We can often load the contents of the enumerating table from source systems, or we can maintain the content of the table manually.

In addition to simply replacing a numerical value with a string, we often want to categorize data according to another value. Let's take the example of a data set containing a list of people and their yearly income. The income can be anything from 0 to 1,000,000 yearly (substitute the figures with the currency of your preferences). Here, we want to say who has a low, rather low, intermediate, rather high, or high income. In other words, we want to categorize data into five distinct categories. For this, we have the following two options:

- Set hardcoded ranges for every category. For example, the low income category will consist of a range from 0 to 200,000; the rather low income category will consist of a range from 200,001 to 400,000, and so on. This option of categorization assumes a normal distribution of data. However, when we explore the income in a population, we must consider outliers (highly-educated experts or politicians often have exceptionally high income). So, let's always keep in mind that data skewness will deform outgoing categorized data. On the other hand, using hardcoded categories is quite simple and we can still use T-SQL for this.
- Categorize data based on its percentile. The percentile sorts data more evenly, even if the data is not distributed evenly itself. This option of categorization is a bit more complicated. Even if we use T-SQL to calculate `PERCENTILE_DIST` of the dataset over the yearly income and then categorize the percentile value, using built-in functions of analytical languages, such as R or Python, will probably be more comfortable for us.

Missing values

In many statistical or data science projects, questionnaires are used. However, questionnaires are often left incomplete because some questions are annoying to attendees or these attendees simply do not know what to answer (for example, some people do not like to answer questions about their religion). Because of this, some values from questionnaires are missing, making the results less reliable.

One way to overcome this issue could be to completely eliminate whole rows with missing values. However, this could lead to a significant loss of information, especially when the dataset is rather small (up to several thousand records), and the null ratio of the value (fraction of missing values against all records in a dataset) is rather high. Another method for handling missing values is to omit whole columns of values where many of them are missing. However, this could also cause us to miss valuable information. For this reason, we often try to find a method that allows us to substitute a missing value with meaningful values that will not lead to a deformation of data.

Simple and commonly used methods for finding a replacement value are as follows:

- **Mean**: Substitution of missing values by mean. This method assumes a normal distribution of data.
- **Modus**: Substitution of missing values by the value with the highest amount of occurrences in a dataset.
- **Median**: Substitution of missing values by the value in the middle of an ordered list of values.
- **Custom value**: Substitution of missing values by a value that a data scientist selects upon their past experience or from other similar data science tasks. The special case of custom value is to use zero (0), but it is commonly used for less important features only.

More sophisticated methods also exist for replacing missing values. For example, these may include the following:

- **Previous value**: This method uses the non-missing value preceding the missing value. This is useful in situations in which values in the column have a trend.
- **Linear regression**: Here, concrete values in a column are calculated as points on a bisector of a linear regression in the column containing the missing value.
- **Weights of complete cases**: We can add a column that stores the weight of each record. The more complete the record is, the greater the weight that is set to it. This option can be useful when we don't have any other method of finding an accurate value instead of the missing value.

When working with missing values, no universal solution exists. This is why we should evaluate the result of the substitution. The best way to evaluate this is to visually compare the distribution of data before and after the substitution using histograms.

Normalization

Normalization is a commonly-used statistical term that has several meanings. We can think of normalization as a formula that rescales data to have values between 0 and 1. It helps to calculate this with features that have different scales and units.

Normalization is often used interchangeably with **standardization**. However, standardization actually means that data is rescaled to have a mean of zero and a standard deviation of one.

Methods of normalization (or standardization) that are often used are Z-score and feature-scaling. Let's take a closer look at both of these terms.

Z-score

Z-score is often used as a definition of normalization, even if standardizing data is an option. This is defined by the following formula:

$$z_i = \frac{x_i - \overline{x}}{s}$$

The variables in the preceding formula are defined as follows:

- z_i: Normalized value
- x_i: Member value of sample population
- $\overline{x}$: Mean of sample population
- s: Standard deviation of sample population

This formula adjusts features to the same mean value of zero. This is a substantial condition for the training of successful machine learning models.

Let's try to calculate the standardized value in the following T-SQL example. Here, we have a table called `Production.Product` in the `AdventureWorks` database. The table contains a column called `ListPrice`. Not every product has its list price set; some products have a list price of 0. First of all, we will eliminate products without list prices, and then we will compute input into the preceding formula. The following statement adjusts the dataset:

```
SELECT ProductID
  , ListPrice
  , (SELECT AVG(ListPrice) FROM Production.Product WHERE ListPrice != 0) AS
AvgListPrice
  , (SELECT STDEV(ListPrice) FROM Production.Product WHERE ListPrice != 0)
AS StDevListPrice
FROM Production.Product
WHERE ListPrice != 0
```

The preceding statement returns 304 rows with product IDs, list prices, the mean of all list prices, and the standard deviation of list prices. We will use the preceding statement as a CTE definition in the following statement, which implements the formula of Z-score:

```
;WITH cte AS
(
SELECT ProductID, ListPrice
  , (SELECT AVG(ListPrice) FROM Production.Product WHERE ListPrice != 0) AS
AvgListPrice
  , (SELECT STDEV(ListPrice) FROM Production.Product WHERE ListPrice != 0)
AS StDevListPrice
FROM Production.Product
WHERE ListPrice != 0
)
SELECT ProductID, ListPrice
  , (ListPrice - AvgListPrice) / StDevListPrice AS StandardizedListPrice
FROM cte
```

The core part of the preceding statement is in the `(ListPrice - AvgListPrice) / StDevListPrice` expression, which is contained in a query using the CTE. This expression is the Z-score formula. When we explore a result of the preceding query, we will see new values that are completely different to the original list prices. Let's take a look at the following table, which shows some of the records generated by the preceding statement:

ProductID	ListPrice	StandardizedListPrice
514	133.34	-0.671234834854629
515	147.14	-0.655638452699328
516	196.92	-0.599378459678247
...	...	...

The preceding table shows the first 3 of 304 rows generated by the preceding query. The standardization says that the mean of the transformed value should be 0, and the standard deviation of the transformed value should be 1. We are now going to provide some proof that this is true. The following statement encapsulates the Z-score calculation from the preceding statement into a second CTE (called `ctest`) and calculates the mean and standard deviation over the standardized column:

```
;WITH cte AS
(
SELECT ProductID, ListPrice
  , (SELECT AVG(ListPrice) FROM Production.Product WHERE ListPrice != 0) AS
AvgListPrice
  , (SELECT STDEV(ListPrice) FROM Production.Product WHERE ListPrice != 0)
AS StDevListPrice
FROM Production.Product WHERE ListPrice != 0
), ctest AS
(
SELECT ProductID, ListPrice
  , (ListPrice - AvgListPrice) / StDevListPrice AS StandardizedListPrice
FROM cte
)
SELECT AVG(StandardizedListPrice) AS NormalizedMean
  , STDEV(StandardizedListPrice) AS NormalizedStDev
FROM ctest
```

The preceding statement returns a result set with one row and two columns: `NormalizedMean` and `NormalizedStDev`. The values of both columns are shown in the following table:

NormalizedMean	NormalizedStDev
7.58405314211113E-08	1

As seen in the preceding table, the normalized mean is not a pure 0, but the number is very small and is very close to 0. The normalized standard deviation is then 1, exactly as it is in the Z-score definition.

Feature-scaling

Feature-scaling is an option of data normalization that is made using the following formula:

$$x_{i_{new}} = \frac{x_i - x_{min}}{x_{max} - x_{min}}$$

The preceding formula uses min and max values of a variable to calculate a ratio of each value in the range of values. This formula rescales all variable values into a range from 0 to 1.

Let's repeat our example from the preceding paragraph to calculate a scaled feature. In this case, we have the same `Production.Product` table with the `ListPrice` column, and we want to rescale it. First of all, we must calculate minimum and maximum values in the `ListPrice` column. The following query is used for this calculation:

```
SELECT ProductID, ListPrice
  , (SELECT MIN(ListPrice) FROM Production.Product WHERE ListPrice != 0) AS
MinListPrice
  , (SELECT MAX(ListPrice) FROM Production.Product WHERE ListPrice != 0) AS
MaxListPrice
FROM Production.Product
WHERE ListPrice != 0
```

The preceding query shows the `ProductID` and `ListPrice` columns and uses subqueries to calculate aggregations over a whole dataset. Now we will enclose the preceding query into a CTE and calculate the feature-scaling itself. The following query does the calculation:

```
;WITH cte AS
(
SELECT ProductID, ListPrice
  , (SELECT MIN(ListPrice) FROM Production.Product WHERE ListPrice != 0) AS
MinListPrice
  , (SELECT MAX(ListPrice) FROM Production.Product WHERE ListPrice != 0) AS
MaxListPrice
FROM Production.Product
WHERE ListPrice != 0
)
SELECT ProductID, ListPrice
  , (ListPrice - MinListPrice) / (MaxListPrice - MinListPrice) as
NormalizedListPrice
FROM cte
```

The core expression using the feature scaling formula is `(ListPrice - MinListPrice) / (MaxListPrice - MinListPrice)`. As a result of the preceding query, we will see a new column called `NormalizedListPrice`. A sample of the result is shown in following table:

ProductID	ListPrice	NormalizedListPrice
514	133.34	0.0366
515	147.14	0.0405
...	...	...

The preceding table shows that the value of `NormalizedListPrice` is completely different to the original value of `ListPrice`. As a last step, let's prove that normalized values are truly in the range of 0 to 1. The following query encapsulates the feature-scaling query from the preceding query into the second CTE, called `ctest`, and calculates minimum and maximum values in the `NormalizedListPrice` column:

```
;WITH cte AS
(
SELECT ProductID, ListPrice
  , (SELECT MIN(ListPrice) FROM Production.Product WHERE ListPrice != 0) AS
MinListPrice
  , (SELECT MAX(ListPrice) FROM Production.Product WHERE ListPrice != 0) AS
MaxListPrice
FROM Production.Product
WHERE ListPrice != 0
), ctest AS
(
SELECT ProductID, ListPrice
  , (ListPrice - MinListPrice) / (MaxListPrice - MinListPrice) as
NormalizedListPrice
FROM cte
)
SELECT MIN(NormalizedListPrice)
  , MAX(NormalizedListPrice)
FROM ctest
```

When the preceding query is executed, it returns just two values: 0 for the minimum and 1 for the maximum of the `NormalizedListPrice` column, so we can say that our example of normalization is successful.

Normalization and standardization have many other implementations. However, this book is not intended to be a scientific publication, so other options to normalize and standardize data are beyond the scope of this book. You can learn more at `http://www.statisticshowto.com`, for example.

Now, let's work with data transformations more practically. The following section will describe how to create some transformations with SQL Server Integration Services.

Using Integration Services for data transformation

SSIS have been part of the SQL Server since version 2005. A brief introduction to SSIS was written in `Chapter 5`, *Data Transformation and Cleaning with T-SQL*. Now we will jump deeper into one of the control-flow tasks, called **Data Flow Task**. The previous section showed us some of the data transformations used in data science. In this section, we will create a simple categorization of source data.

Setting up a SSIS project

First of all, we need to know which data we have as input. Here, we have two `CSV` files. One of them is named `Products.csv`, while the second is named `Categories.csv`. The `Products.csv` file contains a list of products with their names, list prices, and a `CategoryID` column, which is a reference to a certain category placed in the `Categories.csv` file. From the previous section, we know that machine learning models tend to recognize numerical values as features, but we also know that the `CategoryID` column is just a reference and it makes no sense for this to be a feature. This is why we need to join data from both files to create a dataset with records containing the name of the category.

Let's start to create a new project in Visual Studio:

1. A new project is created from the menu at the following location: **File | New | Project**
2. When this menu is used, the **New Project** dialog window is opened
3. In this dialog window, the **Integration Services Project** template is selected and a name and path to the disk is then chosen

A detailed description of a new project creation is described in the `Chapter 5`, *Data Transformation and Cleaning with T-SQL*.

The **New Project** dialog is depicted in the following screenshot:

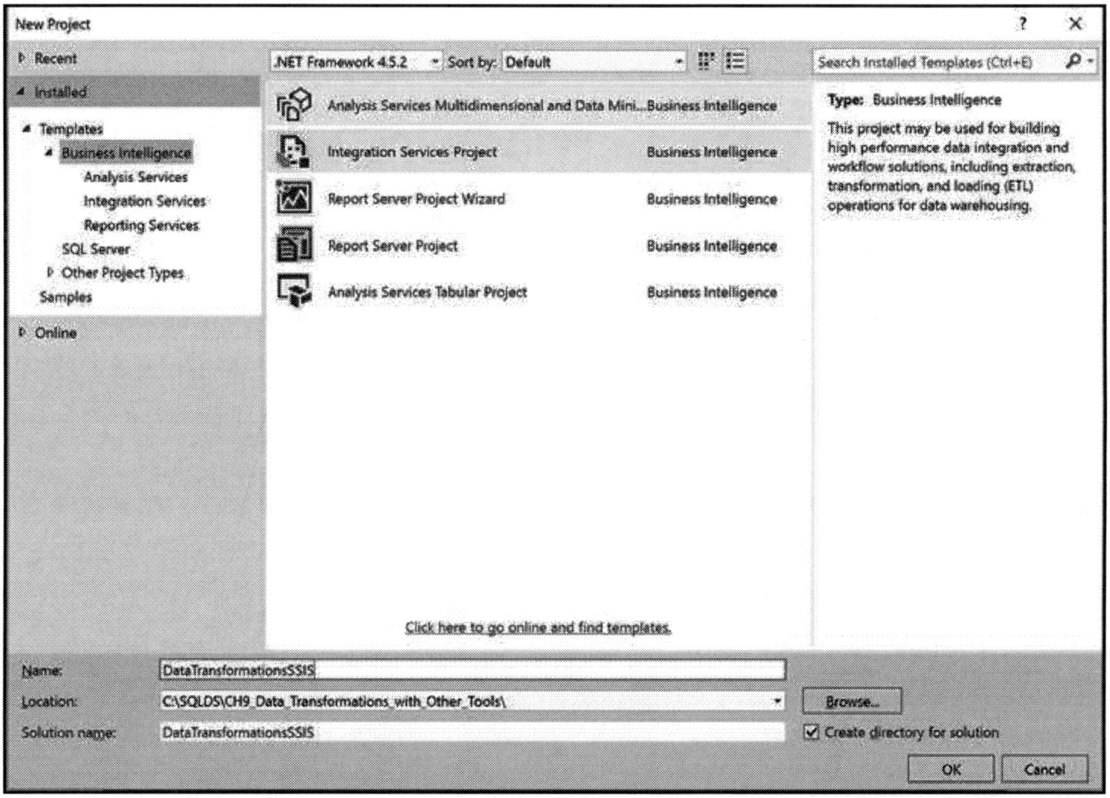

New Project dialog box

The **Business Intelligence** and **Integration Services Project** options in the preceding screenshot lead to the creation of a proper project type. The **Name** (`DataTransformationsSSIS`), **Location**, and **Solution name** textboxes are used to give a name and path to the project.

Once the project is created, it contains one SSIS package simply named `Package.dtsx`. Renaming—and also copying, moving, or deleting packages is done in **Solution Explorer**, often via the context menu that is opened using a right-click. The following screenshot shows part of Visual Studio's interface with the context menu:

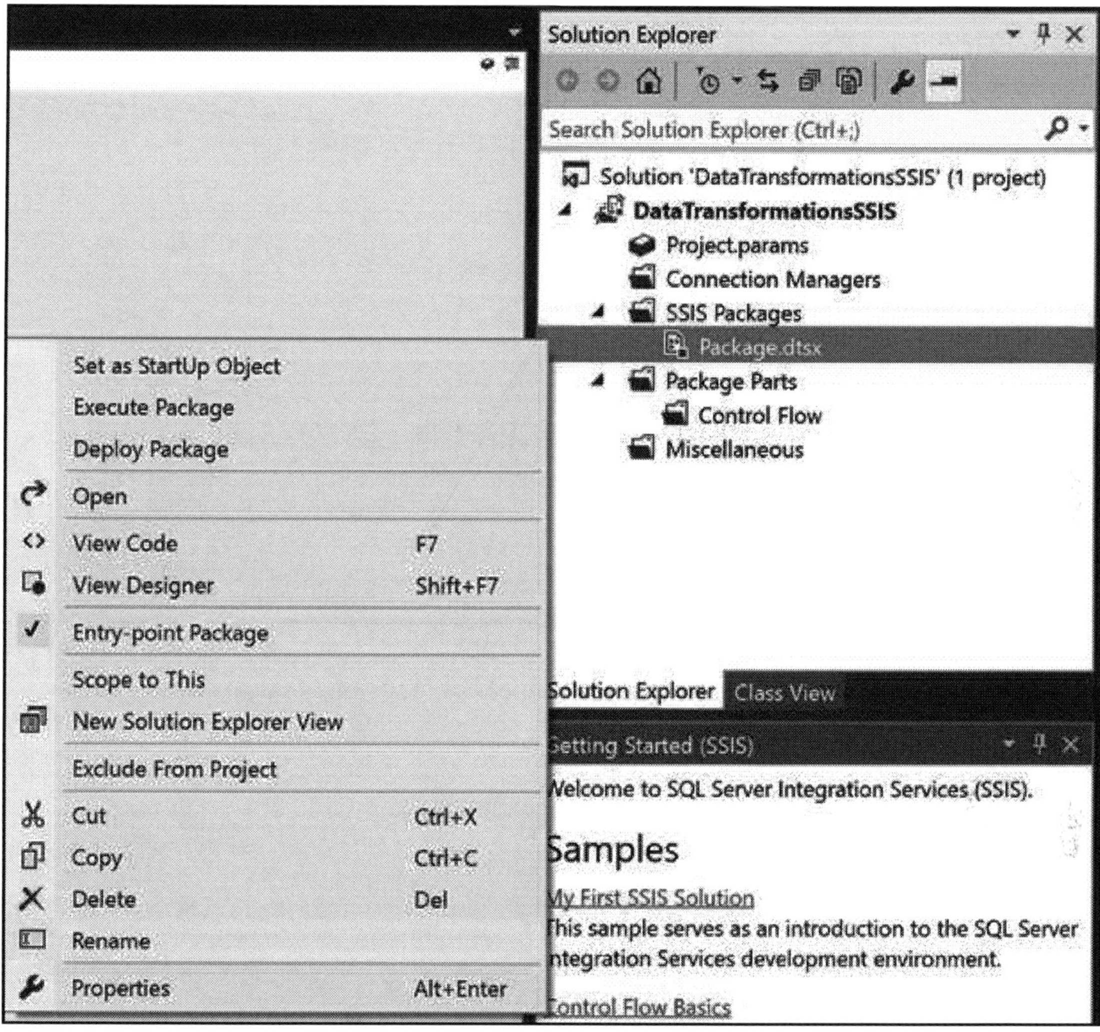

Visual Studio interface displaying the context menu

When the **Rename** option shown on the preceding screenshot is used, we are able to rewrite a package's name—our package's new name is `ProductTransformations.dtsx`. We are now prepared to start the transformation development.

Every SSIS package consists of three main parts:

- **Control-flow**: Contains task controlling actions, such as FTP files downloads, and XML tasks.
- **Data flow**: Does not contain tasks, but it contains transformations going from a data source to a data destination. The data flow part of a package is executed from control-flow using **Data Flow Task**.
- **Event-handlers**: Event-handlers are eventually called control-flows defined upon an event. For instance, when an error occurs in control-flow, the event-handler is raised. We will not use event-handlers in our project.

All three parts of a package are viewed in the Visual Studio as package designer tabs. The following screenshot shows these tabs:

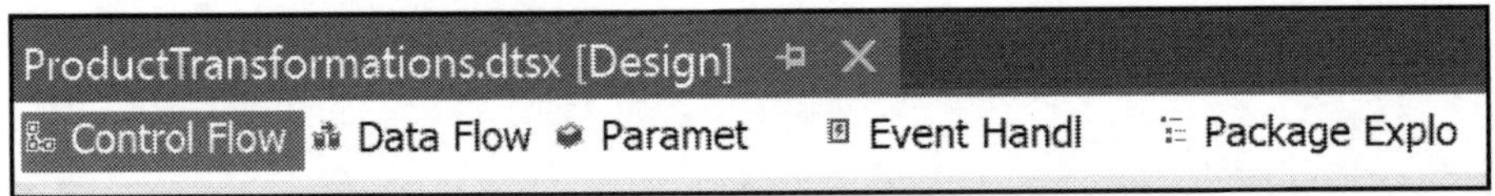

In our example, we want to transform data, so we are going to define the data flow. Surprisingly, the data flow definition starts from the **Control Flow** part of a package. We will select **Data Flow Task** from the left toolbox, called **SSIS Toolbox**, and drag and drop it anywhere into the **Control Flow**'s surface. It is then useful to add a meaningful name to each task (or later to every transformation) to keep the package's definition readable. The following screenshot shows the state of our package when **Data Flow Task** is added there and named properly:

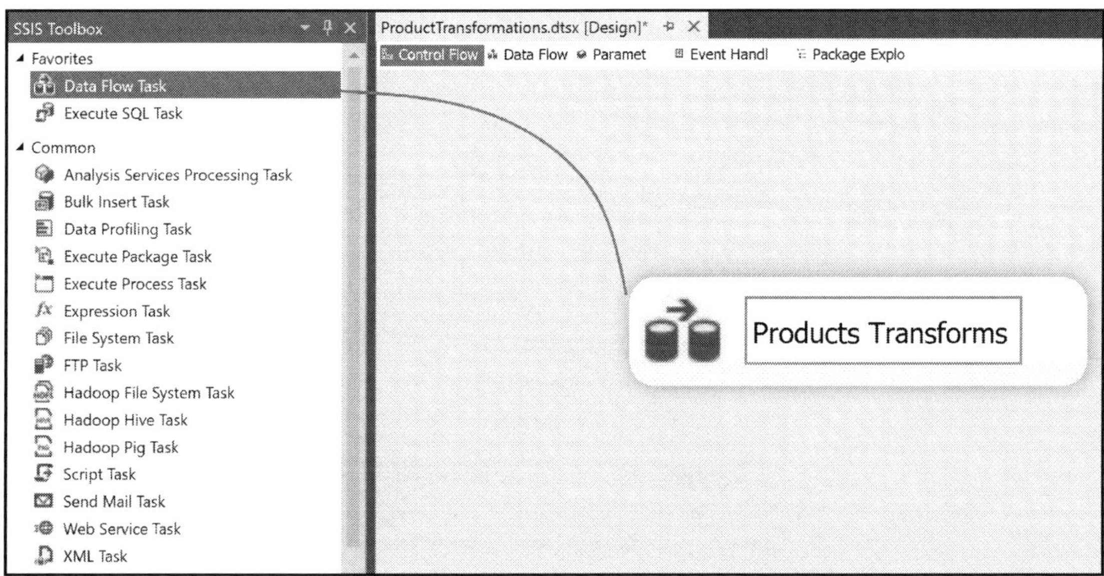

The red curve on the preceding screenshot shows from where the **Data Flow Task** appears on the **Control Flow**'s surface. The newly-created **Data Flow Task** is simply named *Data Flow Task*. Clicking on this name enables us to rename it; the blue rectangle on the preceding screenshot demonstrates where the renaming is done.

Sometimes SSIS Toolbox is not visible in Visual Studio. If this occurs, simply right-click on the empty Control Flow's surface and select the **SSIS Toolbox** option from the context menu.

Now we have an empty **Data Flow Task** called **Product Transforms** prepared for the transformation definition. In the next section, we will make the first of our transformations.

Categorizing the products

The first of our intended transformations has to take a list of products and add a category name to each product in the list. The following recipe goes through the step-by-step procedure involved in the transformation definition:

1. Every Data Flow Task's definition is defined in the **Data Flow** tab of a package. We can visit the tab by double-clicking on certain **Data Flow Tasks** in the **Control Flow** tab, or we can get direct access to a **Data Flow** tab.

   More **Data Flow Tasks** are often defined within a package, so we should check which **Data Flow Task** definition we are creating. The following screenshot shows a drop-down list of **Data Flow Task** in the **Data Flow** tab:

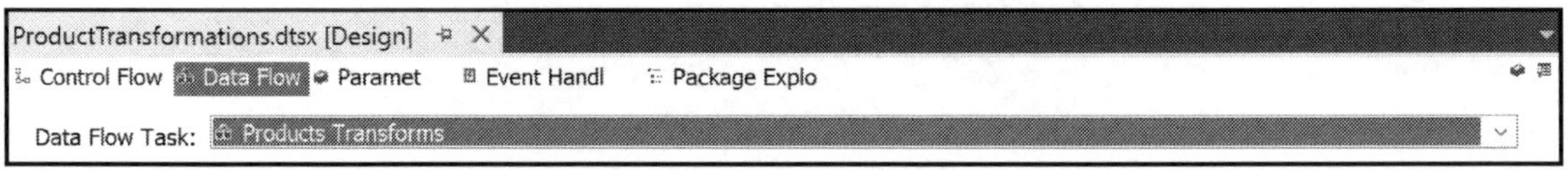

2. As we have only one **Data Flow Task** with the name **Product Transforms** defined, the drop-down list will contain one value only.

Each **Data Flow Task** represents one ETL action. **ETL** means **Extract**, **Transform**, **Load**. ETL is a journey of data from its source to a destination. In other words, every Data Flow Task starts with special kind of transformation: data source. Even if data sources (and later data destinations) do not transform data, for example, it does not add new computed columns, we can think about data sources as a transformation of data taken from outside into the buffer of date eligible for processing with further transformations. For flat files, we can use **Source Assistant**, which is a simple wizard that helps us to define **Connection Manager**. Connection Manager is named connection string to a data source. **Source Assistant** is not available for all data sources added to SSIS, but for basic data sources, such as **SQL Server** database or **Flat File**, the **Source Assistant** is feasible.

Source Assistant is reachable from SSIS Toolbox. This is dragged and dropped into a **Data Flow** surface, at which point it starts. The following screenshot shows the beginning of a data source definition using **Source Assistant**:

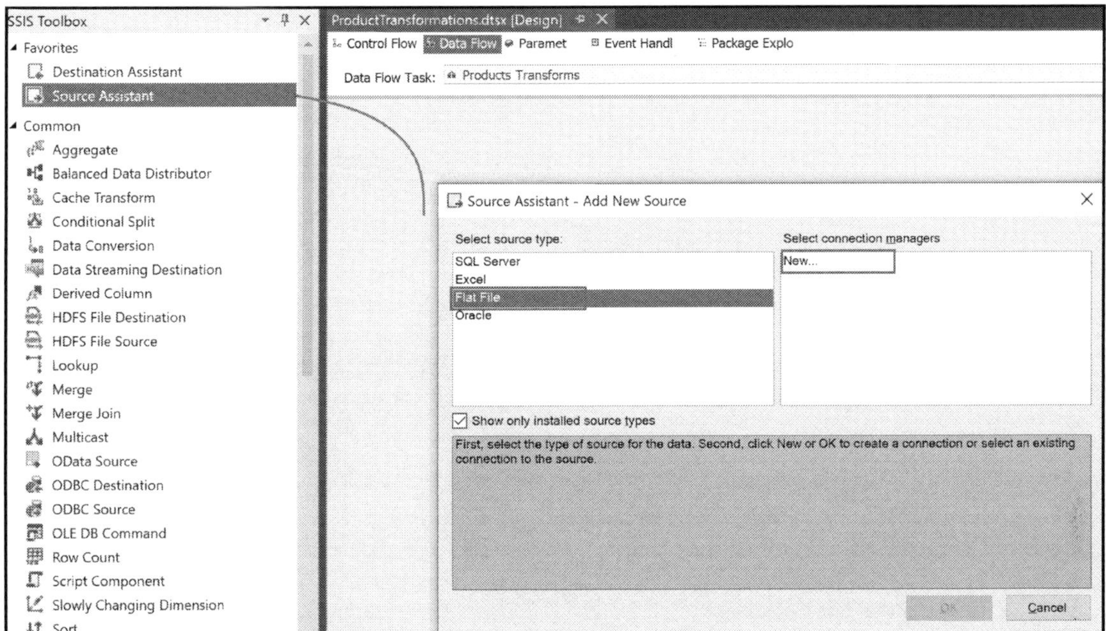

The preceding screenshot shows how to start **Source Assistant**. Follow the red curve to drop the **Source Assistant** to a **Data Flow** surface, select **Flat File** as a source type (left green rectangle), and then click **New...** (right green rectangle). One more dialog will be opened to define which file the data source is for following the transformations. The following screenshot shows the **Flat File Connection Manager Editor** window with all fields filled in:

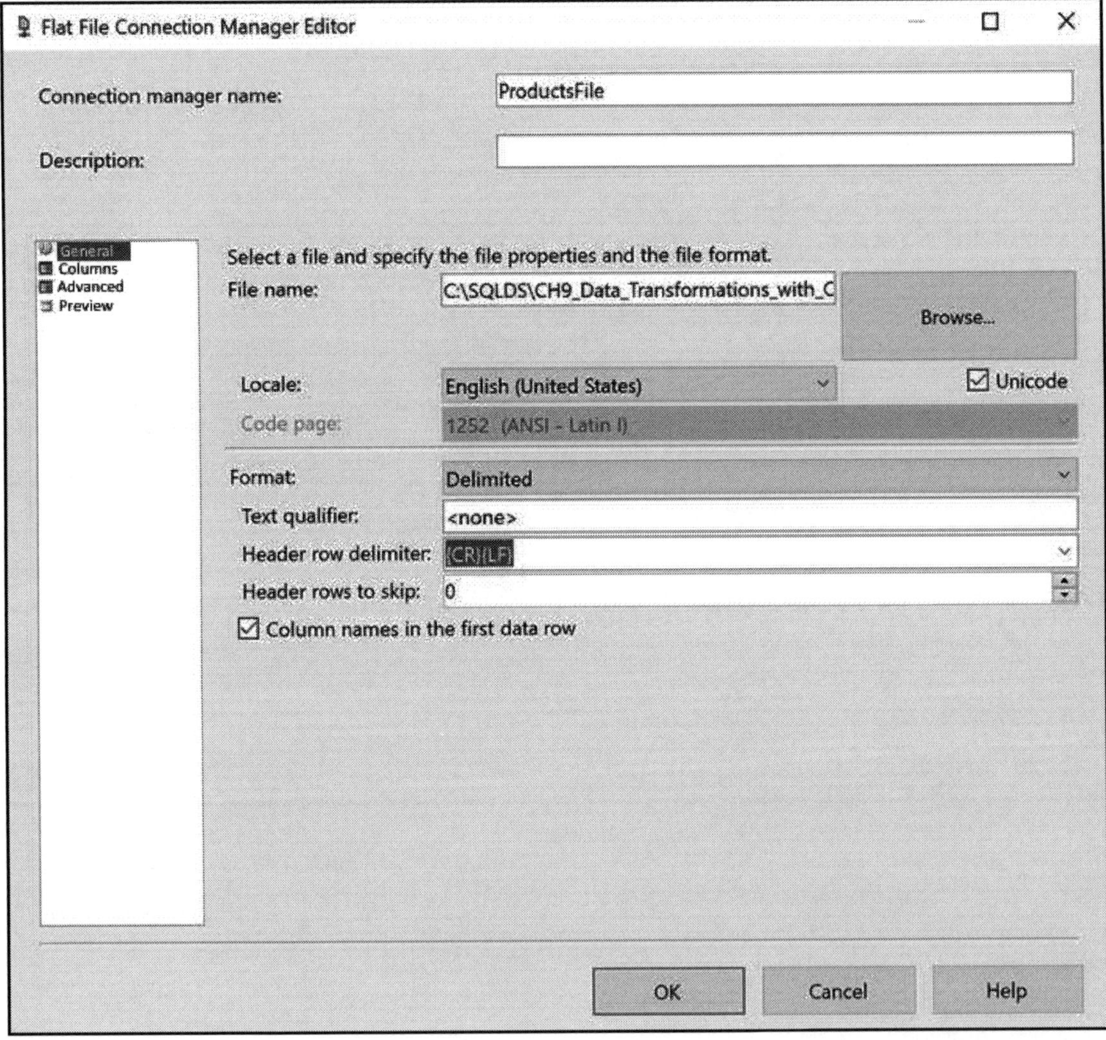

Flat File Connection Manager Editor window

The preceding screenshot shows how to define the connection to a `Products.csv` file, which has to be transformed. The **Connection manager name** field could be left with a default value, but for better orientation it's good to add some meaningful value to it. **File name** must point to an existing file. In our example, we are pointing to the `Products.csv` file. Here, we should know that the file uses Unicode encoding.

The preceding screenshot shows the Flat File Connection Manager window with some deformations. This is a minor bug in **SQL Server Data Tools** (**SSDT**) 2015 when it is installed on Windows 10 Pro on Microsoft Surface Pro 4. Several dialog windows in SSDT are rather old so they suffer from a display that has a resolution that is too high.

The **Flat File Connection Manager Editor** window has four pages:

- General
- Columns
- Advanced
- Preview

Never forget to visit the **Columns** page of the editor. There's no action needed from the developer's side, but when we click on the **Columns** page, the Connection Manager recognizes the column delimiter and maps existing columns in accordance with the defined column delimiter.

The **Advanced** page is shown in the following screenshot:

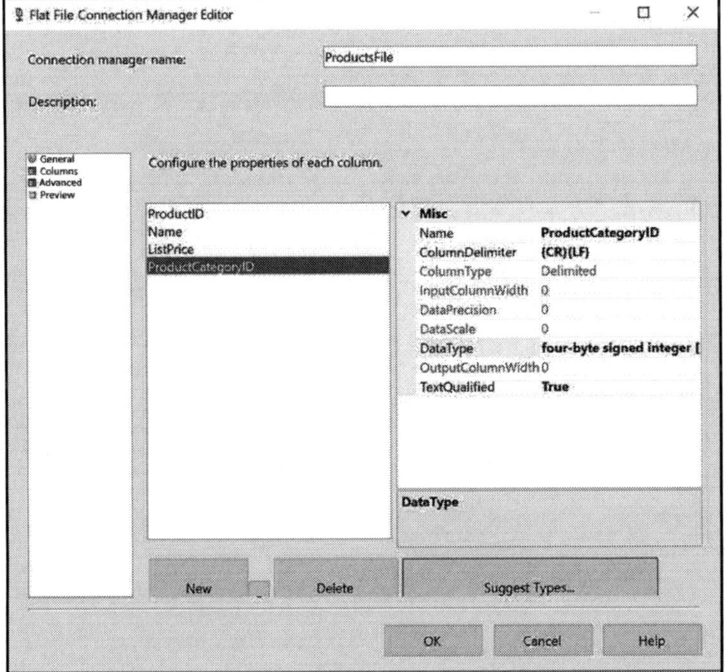

Advanced page

The **Advanced** page is used to revise and correct data types of incoming columns. The Flat File Connection Manager Editor does not manage data types correctly, because everything in `CSV` or `TXT` files is simply saved as a string. For this reason, it's up to a developer to adjust data types. Every column in the left list is selected, and its properties are set in the right part of the **Advanced** tab. Our `Products.csv` file contains four columns, and the following bulleted list assigns a proper data type to every column:

- `ProductID`: Four-byte signed integer
- `Name`: Unicode string
- `ListPrice`: Currency
- `ProductCategoryID`: Four-byte signed integer

The last **Preview** page is used to see a sample of the first 200 records of data.

When the definition is created, two objects are created in the package. The data source itself is an icon on the data flow surface as well as a connection manager. The following screenshot shows how the **Data Flow Task** looks after data source creation:

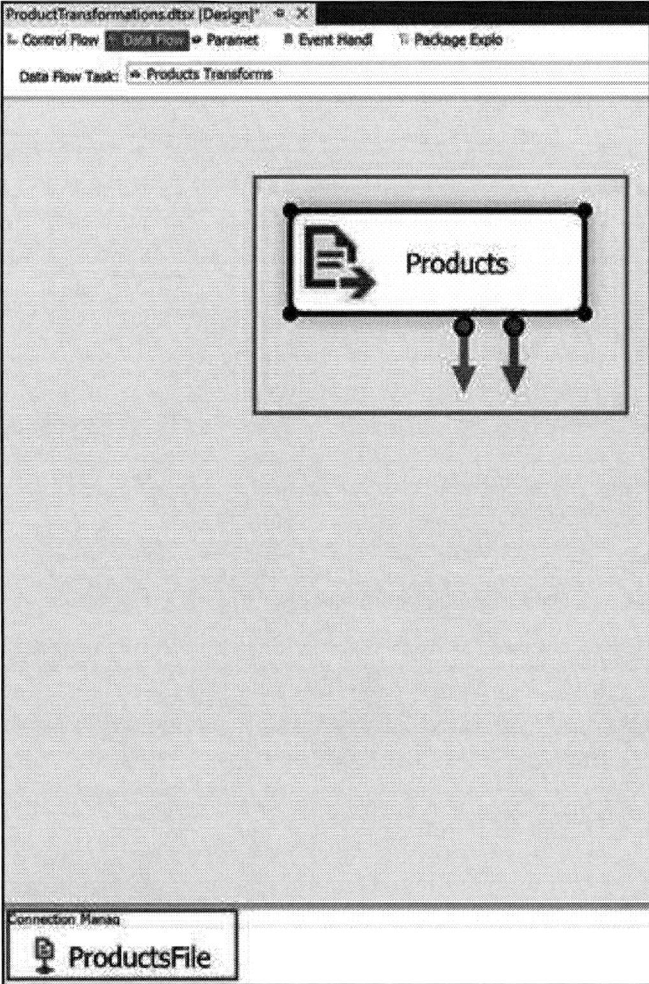

Data Flow task after data source creation

The red rectangle in the screenshot marks a new object called **data source**. A data source can be thought of as a special type of transformation with input from the outside (from the `CSV` file, in our example), and with output to the following transformations. The data source uses a definition called **connection manager**. The connection manager stores the definition of the address of a source data (for instance, the path to a file or a connection string to a database), security context of the source data, if needed, and also the format of the source data. The connection manager defined in the preceding step with **Source Assistant** is saved in the bottom part of a package and this is highlighted in a blue rectangle in the preceding screenshot.

As seen in the preceding screenshot, the data source, called **Products**, has two arrows. The blue arrow is the path of output to a later transformation that doesn't yet exist, whereas the red arrow can be used for error output. Error output is a very feasible diagnostic tool in the cases that some records from incoming data are incorrect. The error output distinguishes between two types of errors: a truncation error (when a value, typically a character string, is longer than declared), and other errors (for instance, conversion errors). In our example, we will avoid using error output for the sake of simplicity, but in real projects, keep in mind that the error output saves many annoying moments when something goes wrong with the transformation.

Let's revisit categorization. In our example, we have to join data from two CSVs to add meaningful category names to products:

1. The transformation used to join data from two sources is **Merge Join**. The Merge Join transformation needs two sorted inputs of data.
2. The first input is our **Products** data source, which has already been created.
3. The second input will be from the `Categories.csv` file.
4. The definition of this source is created in the same way as the data source for `Products.csv`. The only difference here is in the path to the source file.

5. When a second data source is created, the **Data Flow Task** definition should look such as the following screenshot:

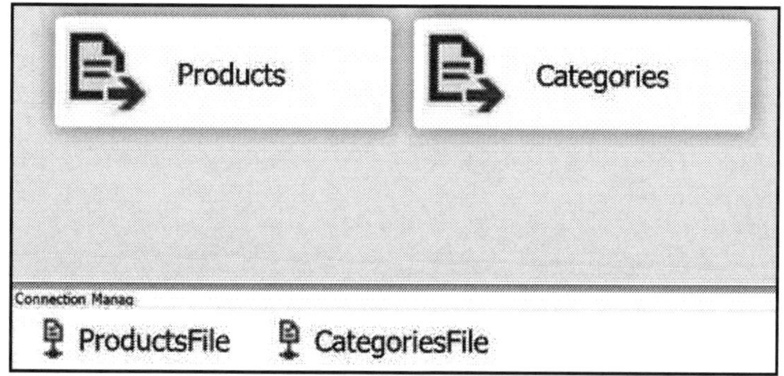

Data Flow Task after the second data source is created

Both data sources from the preceding screenshot are flat file data sources. The **Products** data source points to a connection manager called **ProductsFile,** while the second data source, called **Categories**, points to a connection manager called **CategoriesFile**. The **CategoriesFile** connection manager defines two columns:

- `ProductCategoryID`: Four-byte signed integer
- `Name`: Unicode string

Joining both data sources together is possible using the **Merge Join** transformation. The Merge Join transformation works similarly to a `JOIN` operator used in T-SQL. For successful usage of the Merge Join transformation, we must meet one prerequisite: both input to the Merge Join must be sorted by columns used as joining criteria. Sorting algorithms are quite expensive, so if we are sure that data coming as an input to a Merge Join transformation has already been sorted already, we can set an **IsSorted** property for the output.

- The **IsSorted** property is accessible in the **Advanced Editor** of any transformation
- The **Advanced Editor** dialog window is opened when the **Show Advanced Editor...** option is used in the context menu of certain transformations
- The **Advanced Editor** is a tabbed window

The following screenshot shows the **Input and Output Properties** tab:

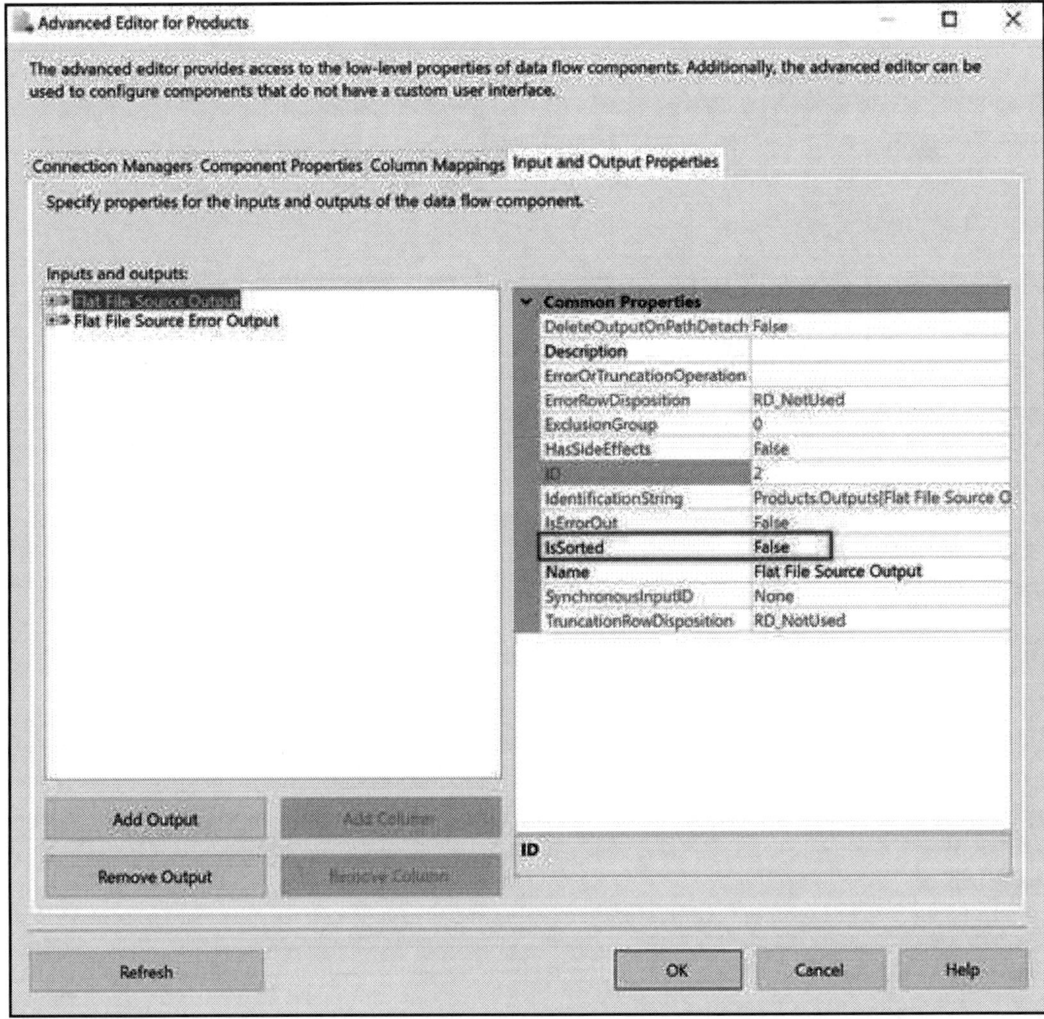

Input and Output Properties tab

The preceding screenshot shows where to find the **IsSorted** property. The default value for the **IsSorted** property is `false`, and we should reset this to `true` only when we are absolutely sure that the sorting is useful for following the Merge Join transformation.

Our example has no records sorted by the `ProductCategoryID` column, so we need to add **Sort** as a transformation following each data source. The following screenshot shows how the **Data Flow Task** looks when both **Sort** transformations are added:

Data Flow Task when Sort transformations are added

The preceding screenshot shows two **Sort** transformations added to the Data Flow task using the drag-and-drop tool from the SSIS toolbox. Each **Sort** transformation is joined to the preceding data source with a blue arrow. Both Sort transformations are also renamed for better orientation. The red sign on the transformations tells the developer that the transformation is not correctly configured. In our case, we need to configure the sorting criteria. In both Sort transformations, the sorting column is `ProductCategoryID`. The **Sort Transformation Editor** dialog window is accessible by double-clicking a certain **Sort** transformation.

The following screenshot shows the editor dialog window for the **SortProducts** transformation:

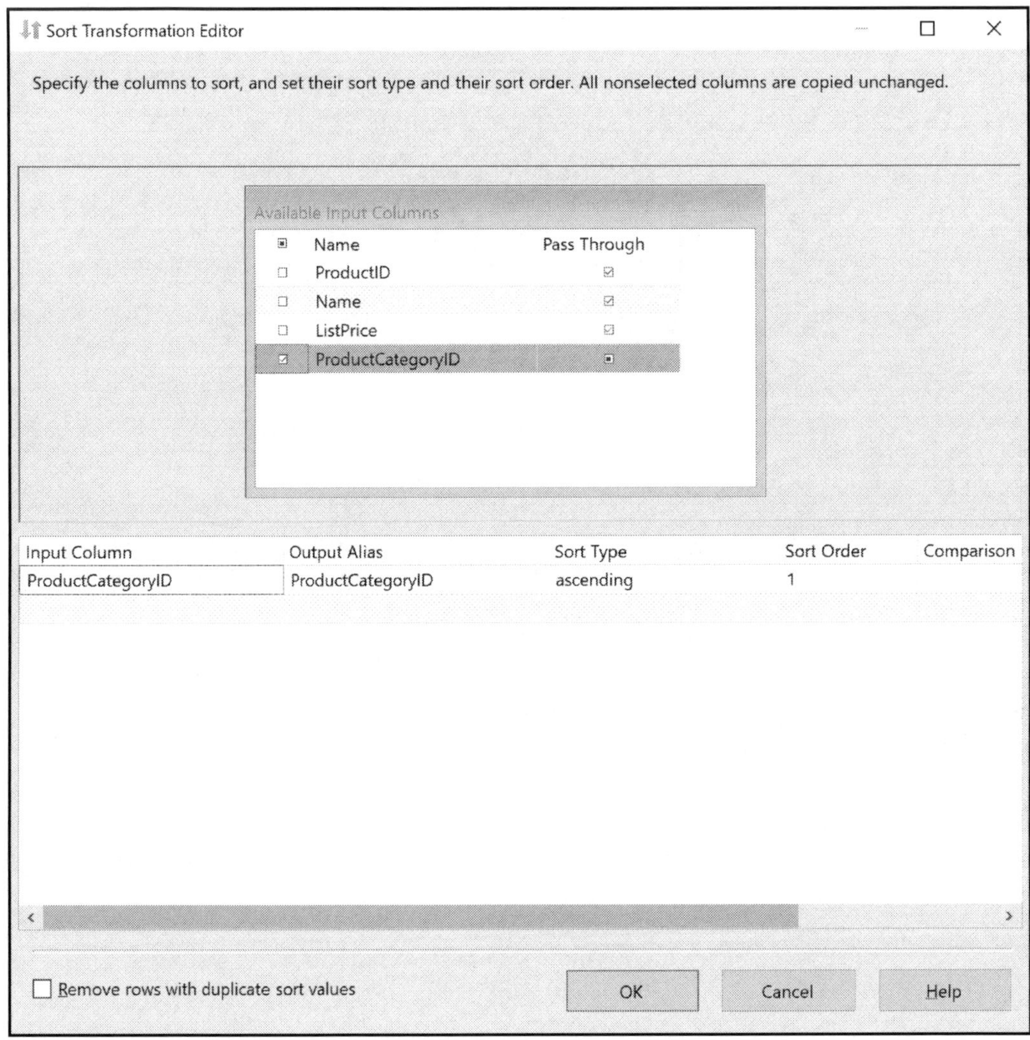

Sort Transformation Editor

The only action needed on the preceding dialog window is to select a column from **Available Input Columns** placed on the top part of the dialog window. The preceding screenshot shows the dialog on which `ProductCategoryID` is already selected. After clicking on the **OK** button, the dialog is closed and the red mark on the **Sort** transformation icon should disappear.

When both data sources are sorted, the data is ready to be joined together. Let's take the Merge Join transformation from the SSIS toolbox and place it under all previously-defined transformations. Because the transformation merges two input, we'll start to join blue arrows between sort transformations to the Merge Join transformation. Let's begin with **SortProducts**. When the arrow is placed over the Merge Join icon, the dialog shown in the following screenshot appears:

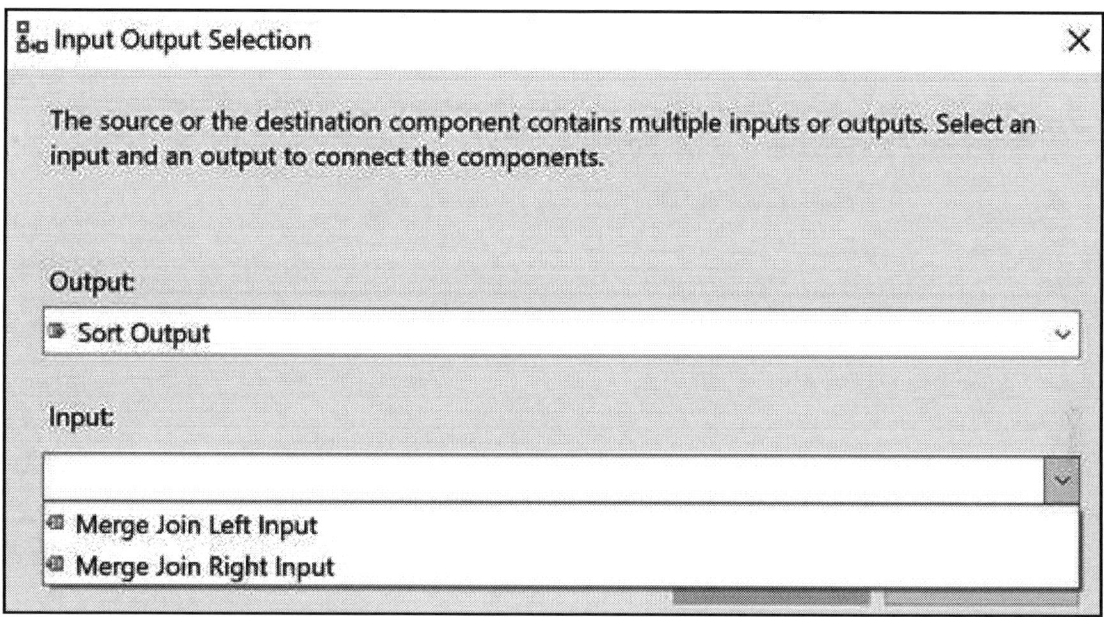

Selection of input and output roles

The dialog shown on the preceding screenshot is used to define which role the input will play in joining the transformations. We can think of the input roles as the left and right sides of a JOIN operator. We must consider this in cases when we expect that data from one of the input will not have a counterpart from the second input. In our example, we can expect that every product will be in a certain category. So, let's use the first of these options in the **Input** drop-down list from the preceding screenshot.

Once we have joined the output from the Sort transformations with the Merge Join transformation, we have to configure the remaining Merge Join transformation properties in the **Merge Join Transformation Editor** dialog window. The dialog is accessible by double-clicking on the Merge Join icon. The following screenshot shows this dialog:

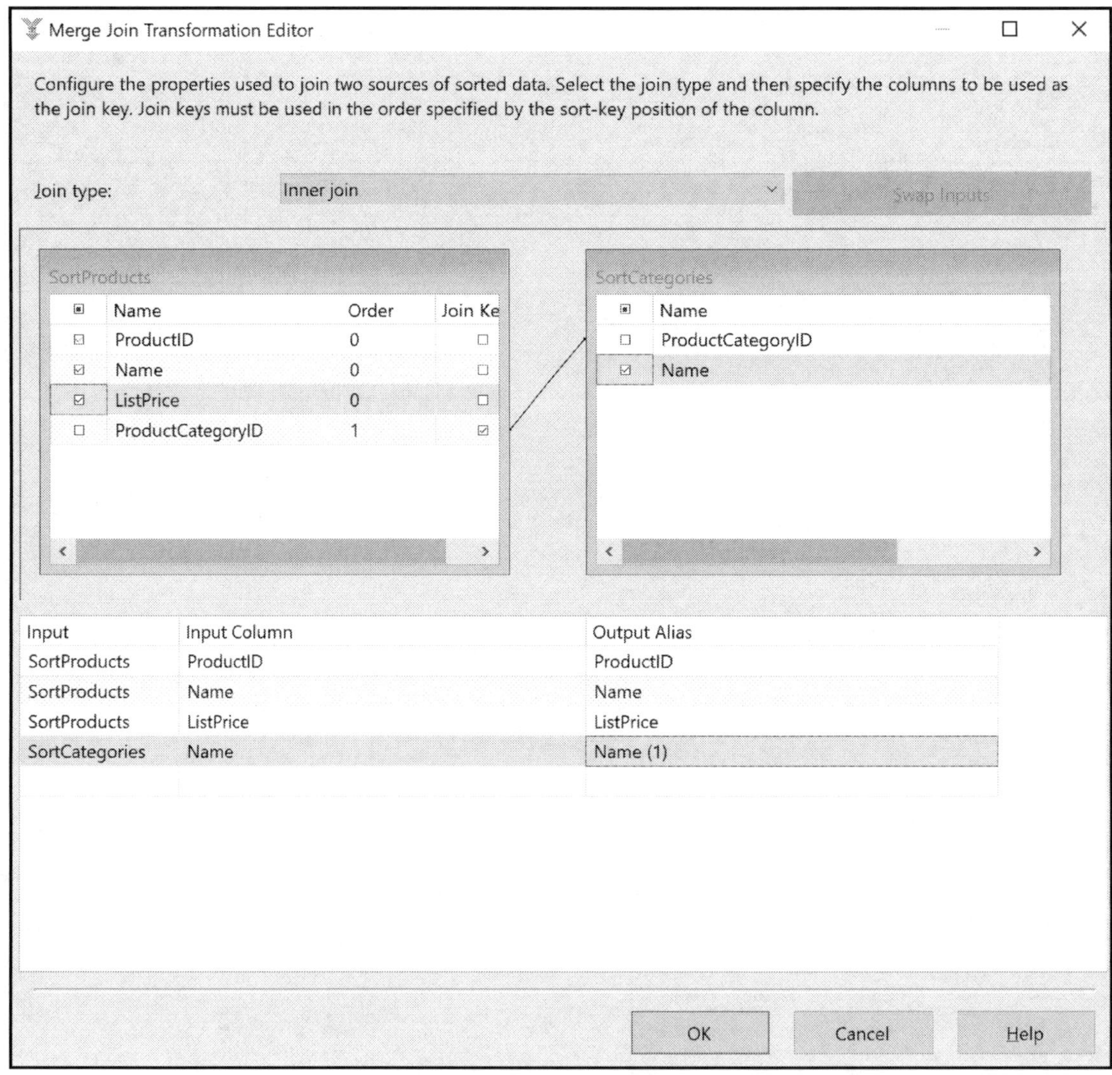

Merge Join Transformation Editor dialog window

The preceding screenshot shows the **Merge Join Transformation Editor** dialog window. In this window, three configurations are defined:

- The type of join is selected in **Join type** drop-down list. In our example, when the dialog is opened, the configuration option is set as INNER JOIN by default. We will not change the value.
- **Joining criteria**: If columns from input have the same name, the editor suggests it as a joining criteria. Otherwise, we'll drag our mouse between columns from one table placed on the top half of the dialog to the other.
- **Output columns**: We are creating output columns by selecting checkboxes in the tables placed on the top half of the dialog.

Sometimes column names are the same in both input. In our example, products as well as categories have a column named `Name`. When this situation occurs, the editor adds an index to the second column with the same name. You can see this in the fourth row of the preceding screenshot—here, the output column's default name is **Name (1)**. It's useful to rename this for better readability; let's set the name to **CategoryName**.

Now we have two sources extracted from flat files. Both sources are sorted by the `ProductCategoryID` column and joined together. Every ETL task is a journey starting from a data source or data sources, and ending in a data destination. We must never leave the **Data Flow Task** without a destination. The last action is to decide where to save transformed data. For our example, it's good enough to save the data back to a flat file.

For a destination of the transformation, the Destination Assistant also exists. However, this does not work for flat file destination definition. For this reason, we have to take a **Flat File Destination** destination from SSIS toolbox (the **Flat File Destination** option is hidden under the **Other Destinations** section in the SSIS toolbox).

When the destination is added to the **Data Flow Task** definition, we'll connect it with the **Merge Join** transformation using also the blue arrow leading from the **Merge Join** transformation. The following screenshot shows how to do this:

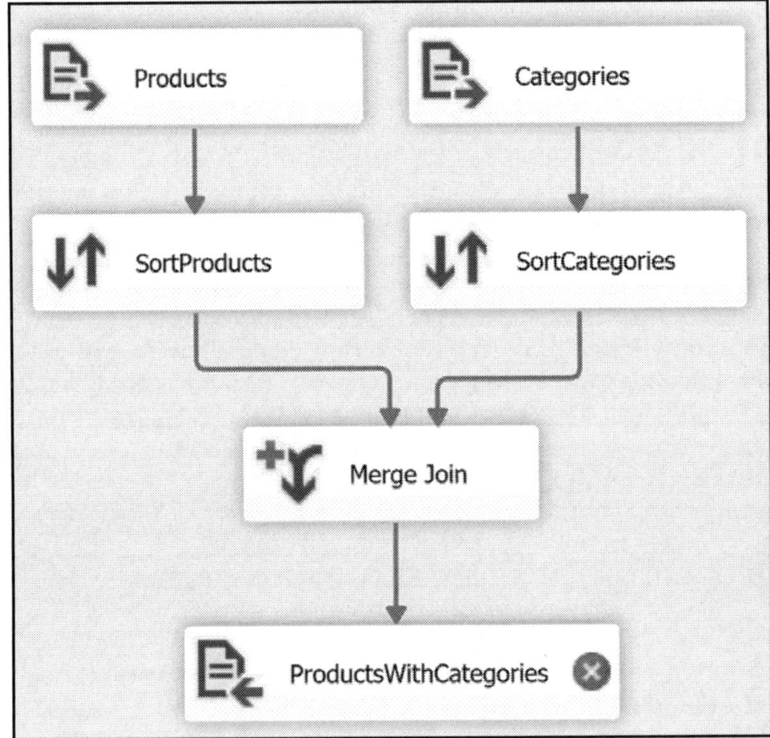

Data Flow Task after connecting the Merge Join transformation

The preceding screenshot almost shows an almost complete definition of the Data Flow Task. The red mark on the **ProductWithCategories** destination says that we have not yet defied the path to the destination yet. Consequently, we'll double-click on the **ProductWithCategories** destination to define the rest of the configurations.

The following screenshot shows the empty **Flat File Destination Connection Editor** dialog window:

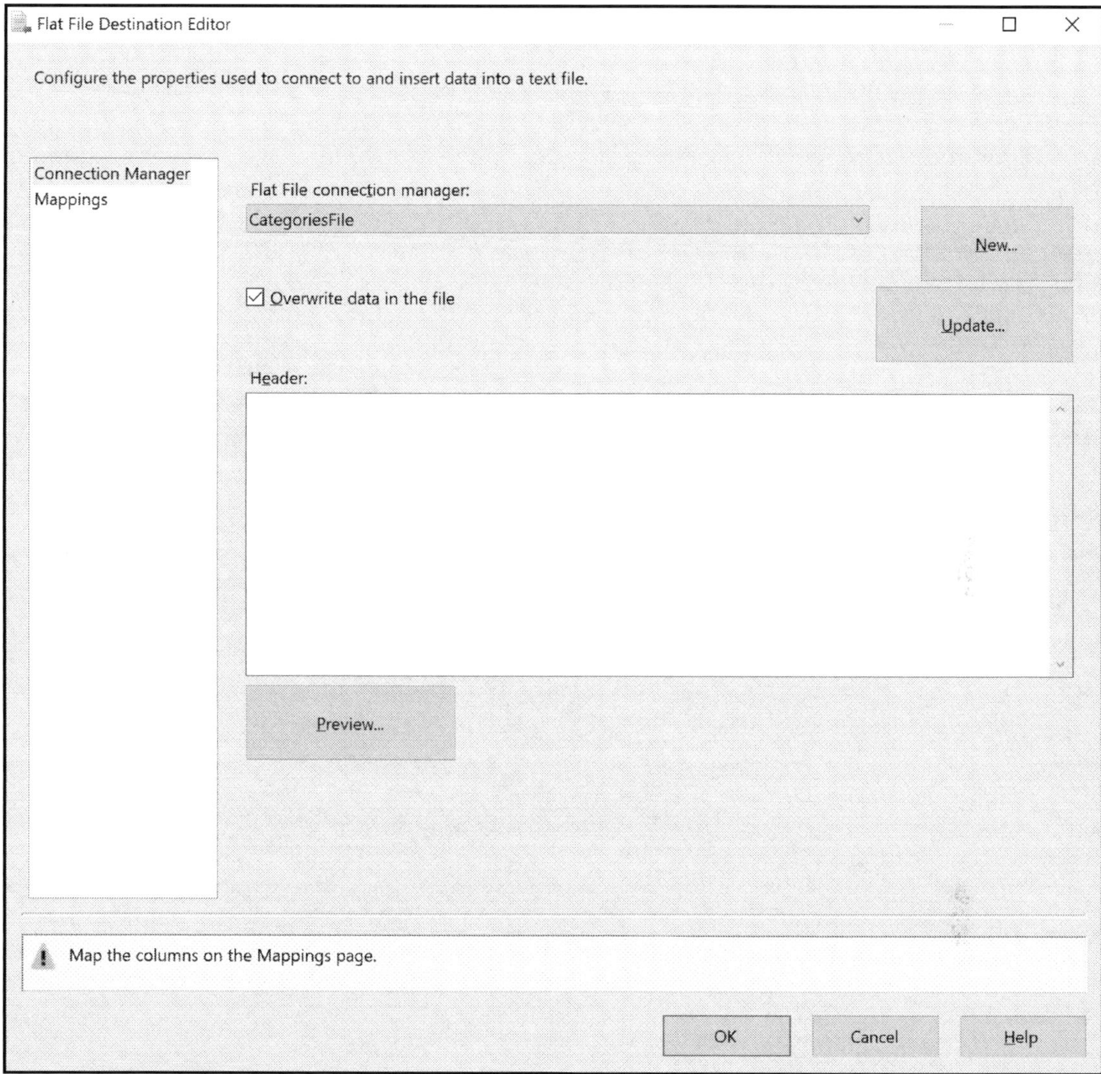

Flat File Destination Connection Editor dialog window

We have to take care when working with all connection editors. This is because if any connection manager that has already been used exists, then the connection editor offers the connection manager as a default value. In the preceding screenshot, the offered connection manager is seen in the drop-down list labeled **Flat File connection manager**. We don't want to save transformed data back to source files, which is why it's necessary to click the **New...** button and define the destination file as a new connection manager. When the connection manager is defined (its definition is done in the same way as the definition of source connection managers), we must not forget to access the **Mappings** page of the preceding dialog window. On the **Mappings** page, no action is needed from the developer's side, but the dialog must map input columns to further output columns.

The last action of the development is to execute the package, review its progress, and review the result. On the top toolbox of Visual Studio is the **Start** button, which starts an execution of a currently-opened package. Let's click on it.

When we do this, the package is executed and is not finished in Visual Studio, but it is still in a running state. It also makes it possible to explore the state of every task in control-flow as well as the state of every transformation in data flow. The following screenshot shows a successfully executed package's data flow task:

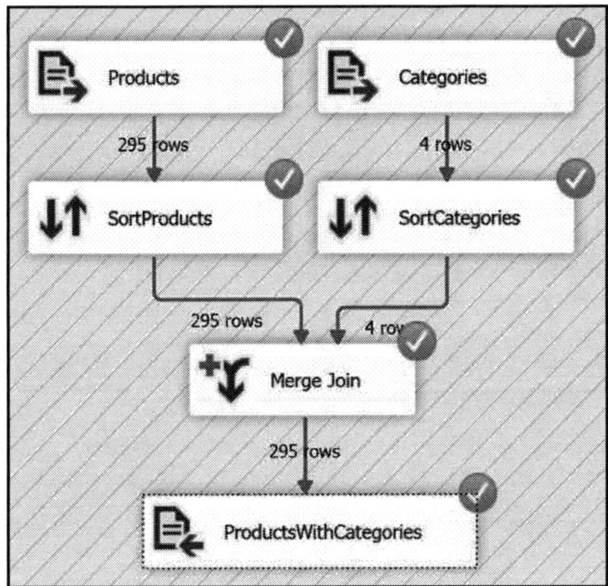

The preceding screenshot shows that all transformations were successful. The amount of processed rows is also shown here. We can see that the **Products** data source extracted 295 rows and the **Categories** data source extracted four rows. Both extracted datasets were sorted and then joined together. Output from the **Merge Join** transformation also has 295 rows, so every product is successfully joined to its category. Joined rows were saved to the **ProductsWithCategories** destination.

When the review is done, we can stop the package execution using the **Stop** button on Visual Studio's toolbox.

This simple example shows how SSIS can be used for data transformations. We can also calculate our values using the **Derived Column** transformation, combining built-in transformations with custom transformations written in C#, or with **Execute SQL Task** in control-flow to combine SSIS transformations with T-SQL queries. However, for deeper data science purposes, such as normalization or standardization, SSIS may lead to a big development overhead. For this reason, we would use other tools. One of the most popular tools (or environments) is the R language. We will play with R in the next section.

Using R for data transformation

R is a programming language oriented on statistical and data science computations. Although R is quite old, its popularity has been growing in recent years together with more projects oriented on statistics and predictions. Starting in 2016, Microsoft introduced *R Services* as a part of SQL Server. SQL server 2017 then renamed R Services to *Machine Learning Services* because Python support was added to SQL Server 2017.

While R is very popular, many data scientists warn against using languages such as R or Python. The main argument is that both languages are too syntax-oriented, hence the developer handles the source code and forgets to solve the assigned statistical or data science problem. The same data scientists prefer more drag-and-drop-oriented technologies. For developers who mainly want to work with Microsoft technologies but are not familiar with the data science domain, a good starting point would be Azure Machine Learning and its Machine Learning Studio (for further exploration of this topic, see `https://studio.azureml.net/`).

This book is intended to work with the T-SQL language primarily, but since R can be used within SQL Server, this section provides a brief overview of R to inspire readers in the future.

Preparing client R environment

The whole R project is maintained by **R foundation**, which is a non-profit organization. The website of the R foundation is `https://www.r-project.org/`. On this website is a link to **Comprehensive R Archive Network** (**CRAN**). This is a set of mirror sites for downloading the R environment for macOS X, Linux, or Windows.

Preparing for experiments with R consists of two steps. The first step is to install R itself, the second optional step is to install a developer tool for writing in R.

As a first step, we need to download the R environment from a selected CRAN mirror and install it on our PC. The downloaded setup file for Windows is relatively small (62 MB) and contains both 32-bit and 64-bit distributions. The setup process itself is very straightforward because it's done using a setup wizard. Within the installation of R, a simple GUI is also installed. This is called **RGui** and after installation it's placed onto the Windows **Start** menu. This GUI is very simple but it is only good enough to use with R for the very first few steps. For this reason, it's often better to use other development tools.

We can choose from many tools provided by third parties. For developers who use Visual Studio on a daily basis, Microsoft offers R Tools for Visual Studio. R Tools for Visual Studio is a free add-in that can be installed into existing Visual Studio 2015 or Visual Studio 2017 at any time. Another very popular tool is **RStudio** (`https://www.rstudio.com/`). **RStudio** exists in two versions: RStudio Desktop for single-client usage, and RStudio Server, which is accessible using the web browser. Both versions can be obtained under an open source (free) or commercial license. The commercial license offers email support in up to eight hours, or in the case of RStudio Server, it also offers enhanced security features and performance monitoring. For our purposes, RStudio Desktop Open Source Edition is enough. RStudio is also distributed for more platforms. The downloaded file is an `exe` file that starts as a very simple setup wizard. When the wizard is completed, we are prepared to start our R experiments. Because the R syntax is peculiar, the next section shows some of the basics of this.

R Syntax first steps

Even though R is not Microsoft's product, how sad would this book be without at least one Hello world! example? The following example is the simplest one used just for using RStudio for the first time, and the following screenshot shows its main window:

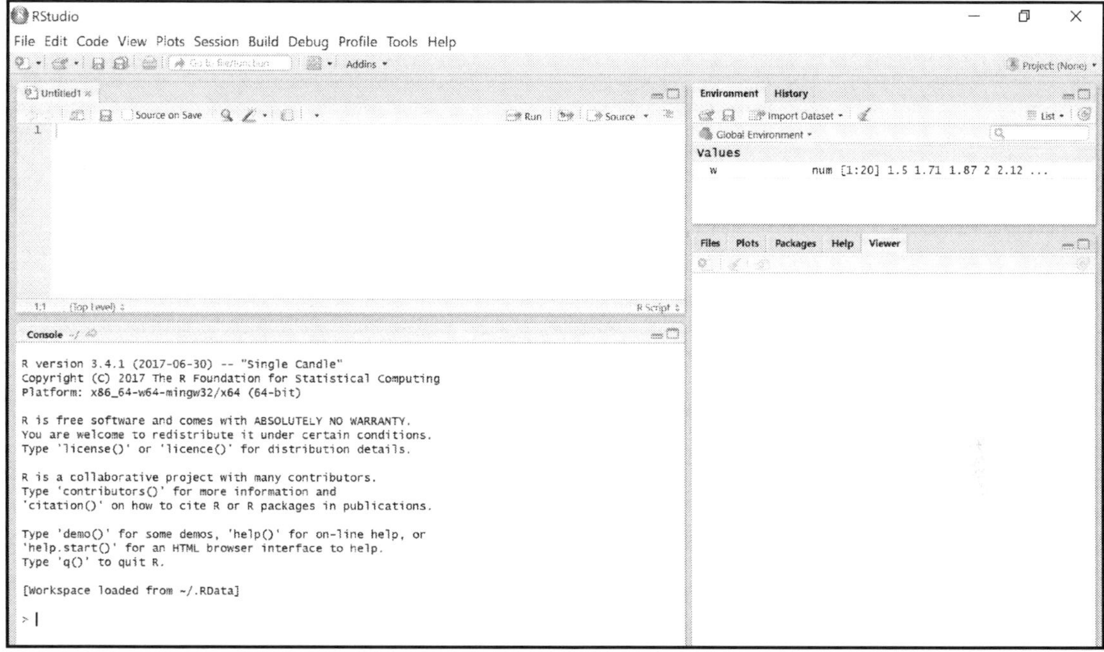

RStudio homescreen

RStudio is divided into four sections by default. The bottom-left quarter of the screen contains the console. Everything written to the console is executed directly. The top-left quarter of the screen contains files with the `.R` suffix. Code blocks written to files are executed in the console. The main difference between files and the console is that content written in the console cannot be saved.

The top-right quarter of RStudio's main screen contains tabs with variables and a history of executed statements. The bottom-right part of RStudio contains several tabs for graphics created using proper R functions, R packages imported into RStudio workspace, and also a help tab, which links to help topics on the web.

Now let's write the `"Hello world!";` text directly into the console and press *Enter*. The result written into the console will be `[1] "Hello world!"`. Writing anything into a console leads to a result with one item vector. This is why the result is numbered (`[1]`). The same is true for any scalar expression. For instance, let's write an expression, `1 + 1;`, into the console. We will then obtain the new result: `[1] 2`.

The preceding two very simple examples give us a very important piece of knowledge about the R language: everything is a vector.

Every language uses variables. The following example shows how to compute several values and how to compare them. Let's still use the console and follow up this process as follows:

1. Write the `a <- 1+1;` statement into the console and press *Enter*.
2. Write the `b <- 2+3;` statement into the console and press *Enter* again.
3. Review the top-right quarter of RStudio in the Environment tab. Here, you will see the `a` and `b` variables and their values (`2` and `5`).
4. Compare the a and b variables using the `a > b;` statement.
5. Press *Enter*. We should see the `[1] FALSE` result in the console.

Variables are declared when they are first used in statements. If we want to check which is a data type of a variable, R provides the `typeof()` function. For instance, the `typeof(a);` statement prints `[1] "double"` as the name of data type of the `a` variable.

The `<-` symbol used in the preceding example is an assignment. In newer versions of R, the `=` symbol for assignment to a variable could also be used.

This simple example taught us one important property of R: unlike many other development tools, the R console remembers variables until it is closed.

As R is intended to work with vectors, the following example shows several actions upon vectors. A vector is created using the `c();` function, where **c** is short for **combine**. Let's write the following statement:

```
c(1, 2, 3)
```

The preceding statement prints the following result into the console:

```
[1] 1 2 3
```

Another way to create a vector is through the `seq();` function. Using this function, we can create vectors of numbers, as shown in the following code example:

```
c(5:9);          #creates vector [1] 5 6 7 8 9
seq(5, 9);       #creates the same vector [1] 5 6 7 8 9
seq(5, 9, 2)     # creates vector [1] 5 7 9
```

The preceding example shows several ways to create vectors. We can also do calculations upon vectors. Possibly the most simple set of calculations is to combine a vector and scalar value. Let's execute the following code example:

```
v <- c(1, 2, 3);
v+1
```

This simple example creates the `v` vector with items 1, 2, and 3, adding 1 to every vector item. The result of this example is `[1] 2 3 4`. The preceding example showed an addition, but this works for all other arithmetic operators.

The preceding examples provide a very short introduction to the R syntax. The syntax itself is not difficult, but R Foundation and various third parties provide many R packages which make a developer's life easier. The only concern could be that thousands of packages are provided nowadays and it's a long experience to select the right package for certain tasks. The following section will be a guide to processing data from the `CSV` file to standardize values, and several functions will be used to reach the result.

Working example of Z-score computed in R

The previous section briefly introduced the R syntax. We worked with scalar variables and simple vectors. A set of vectors is called a `data.frame`. `data.frame` is an important base for every further calculation over datasets. Let's make this calculation.

We calculated a standardized value called **Z-score** in the *Introduction* section. Now we will calculate the Z-score one more time, but with R. For the following example, we will use the `ProductsWithCategories.csv` file created in the *Using Integraton Services for data transformation* section. To calculate Z-score, perform the following steps:

1. Read the `ProductsWithCategories.csv` file from disk to a `data.frame`
2. Check for the data type of the `ListPrice` column, convert it into a double if needed

3. Calculate the mean and standard deviation of the `ListPrice` column
4. Calculate Z-score of all values in the column
5. Add the calculated Z-score back to the `data.frame` as a new column

R likes to work with text files encoded with UTF-8. To be successful without any concerns, we must be sure that the `ProductsWithCategories.csv` file is encoded with **UTF-8.** Open the file in any text editor, such as Notepad++ or PSPad, and check the encoding.

Let's ensure that step #1 worked. For reading files from a filesystem, R has a couple of functions, such as `read.csv`, `read.csv2`, and `read.delim`. These functions are very similar to each other. The main difference is in the default values of parameters defined within these functions. For instance, the `read.csv` function defaults a `sep` (separator between column values) parameter's value as a comma (`,`) symbol. The `read.csv2` function defaults a `sep` parameter's value to a semicolon (`;`).

R functions often have many parameters, but do not pay too much attention to differences such as those between `read.csv` and `read.csv2` functions. Using built-in help for functions is the simplest way to work with R.

The `read.csv2` function fits our needs. The first parameter of the function is a `file` parameter. In this case, we can use a full path to a file, or we can set a working directory to have a shorter and more readable syntax. The following statement written to RStudio's console will set a working directory for our example:

```
#adjust the path according with your environment
setwd("C:\\SQLDS\\CH9_Data_Transformations_with_Other_Tools\\CSVs\\")
```

The preceding code uses the `setwd` R function to set the path from which we can read files. This function has no output value. Notice that we are using double backslash symbols here (`\\`). These are required because a single backslash introduces special characters (for instance, `\n` for line breaks).

We can also check which path is set as the working directory through the simple `getwd();` function.

When the working directory is set properly, we are going to use the `read.csv2` function to extract the `ProductsWithCategories.csv` file into a `data.frame`. The following line of code will do this:

```
df <- read.csv2("ProductsWithCategories.csv", dec=".")
```

The preceding statement creates a `df` variable and assigns a result of the `read.csv2` file to it. The first parameter is the filename. If the working directory is not set previously, we can use the full path. The first parameter is set by position. This means that the parameter's name is not used. The second `dec` parameter in preceding statement is not actually second in an order of parameters defined within the `read.csv2` function. This is because several parameters are skipped, and so we have to use the assignment of the parameter by reference. For this reason, the parameter's value is set in the form of `dec="."`. The `dec` parameter says to the function that the period (`.`) symbol is used as a decimal place separator in decimal values.

When the `data.frame` called `df` is obtained, we can do some inspecting actions on it. For example, we can just see its content. We can simply write the `df;` statement into a console. This statement writes a beginning of the `data.frame` into a console. The second way to see the content of the `df` variable is to use the RStudio GUI. The following screenshot shows where to find this:

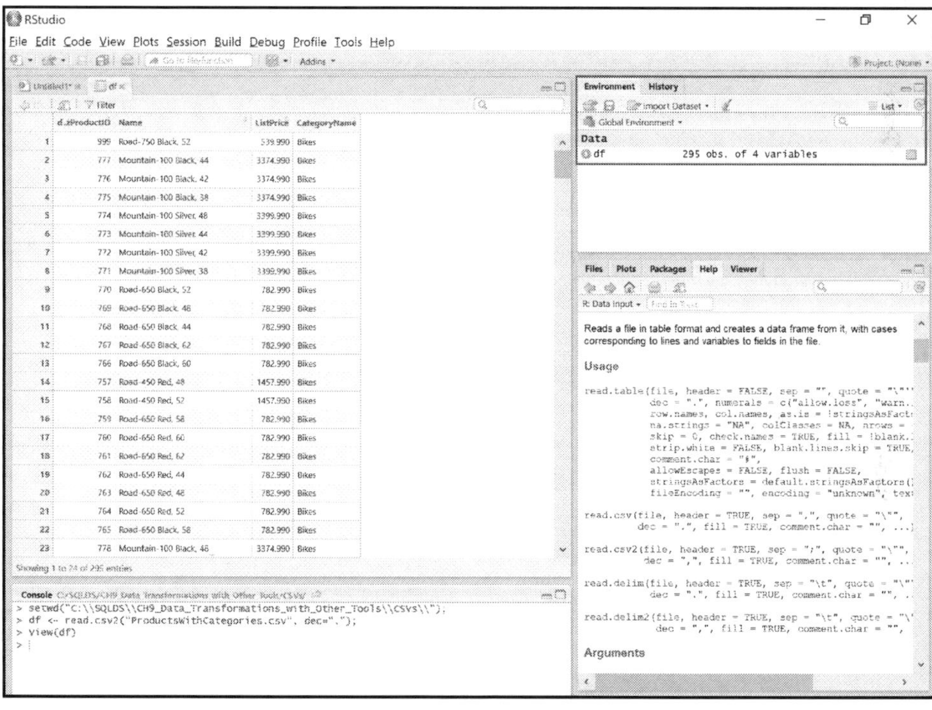

Setting up the environment variable

The preceding screenshot highlights the top-right corner of the RStudio's surface with a blue rectangle. Once a statement that creates a new variable is executed, the variable (and later, all variables within a session) is seen in the highlighted part. Every variable contains a small button. Clicking on the button opens a grid with the content of the `data.frame`. This grid is seen in the preceding screenshot as a tab called `df`.

When the `CSV` file is successfully extracted into a `df` variable, we can continue to step #2 to check a data type from the `ListPrice` column. We can do this by using the `typeof()` function. Write the following statement into a console:

```
typeof(df$ListPrice)
```

The result of preceding statement is a `"double"` text. The `df$ListPrice` syntax used in the preceding code line is just a reference to a `ListPrice` variable of `data.frame`, called `df`. If the result of preceding statement is not the `"double"` value, we must add one more statement for the conversion of `ListPrice` to a double data type. The following statement uses the `sapply` function for conversion to a new variable called `price`:

```
price <- sapply(df$ListPrice, as.double)
```

We can also inspect a result of preceding statement's result using both syntax (`price;`) or GUI, as shown previously.

Now, when we are sure of the correct data type of the list price, we can fulfill step #3, which consists of calculating the mean and standard deviation of the price. The following code sample shows how to do this:

```
meanPrice <- mean(price);
sdPrice <- sd(price);
c(meanPrice, sdPrice)
```

The preceding code defines two new variables for a mean of the `price` variable (`meanPrice`) and for a standard deviation of the `price` variable (`sdPrice`). R provides functions for descriptive statistics, the `mean()` function calculates the mean, and the `sd()` function calculates the standard deviation. The third line of code creates a vector of both values and writes the vector to a console.

The core step is step #4. Now we are going to calculate the Z-score itself and save the result in a new variable. The following statement shows how to do this:

```
zOfAllPrices <- (price - meanPrice) / sdPrice
```

The preceding statement creates new variable, called `zOfAllPrices`, and calculates the standardized value of `ListPrice` (converted to the `price` variable in preceding code sample). This is achieved using the formula introduced in the *Introduction* section.

Now let's revisit the *Introduction* section, focusing on the statement that the mean of a normalized variable is 0 and the standard deviation is 1. Use the following code to check whether this statement is true:

```
result <- c(mean(zOfAllPrices), sd(zOfAllPrices));
nms <- c("Mean of...", "St. dev. of...");
names(result) <- nms;
result
```

The preceding code creates a variable called `result`, which holds a vector of the mean and standard deviation of the `zOfAllPrices` calculated before. The second `nms` variable holds a vector of names of both values for better readability of the result. The `names()` function assigns headers to a vector's values. Try to omit the third line of the preceding code. Once this is done, your result will look as follows:

```
[1] 2.382929e-17 1.000000e+00
```

Using the third line of the preceding code will generate a more readable result:

```
    Mean of... St. dev. of...
  2.382929e-17   1.000000e+00
```

Independent of the form of the result, can we say that the mean of the standardized value is 0 and its standard deviation is 1? Yes, we definitely can!

The last step of our assignment is step #5. The aim here is to add the normalized value for the `data.frame` source called `df`. This is very simple and the following statement does it:

```
df$zScorePrice <- zOfAllPrices
```

The preceding statement adds a new column called `zScorePrice` to the `df data.frame` and assigns its values from the `zOfAllPrices` variable. We can check the result using the GUI again.

The example is complete. The full code, including checks, is as follows:

```
#setting working directory
getwd();
setwd("C:\\SQLDS\\CH9_Data_Transformations_with_Other_Tools\\CSVs\\");
getwd();
```

```
#reading CSV
df <- read.csv2("ProductsWithCategories.csv", dec=".");

#checking and converting ListPrice's column data
df$ListPrice;
typeof(df$ListPrice);
price <- sapply(df$ListPrice, as.double);

#calculating mean and st. dev.
meanPrice <- mean(price);
sdPrice <- sd(price)
c(meanPrice, sdPrice);

#calculating Z-score
zOfAllPrices <- (price - meanPrice) / sdPrice;

#checking Z-score properties
result <- c(mean(zOfAllPrices), sd(zOfAllPrices));
nms <- c("Mean of...", "St. dev. of...");
names(result) <- nms;
result;

#adding the new column back to a data.frame df
df$zScorePrice <- zOfAllPrices;

#showing result
df
```

This section is intended to show a very small part of the R language's possibilities. R is very powerful language for data science computing, and using it for data transformations is only a part of its abilities. We will use R more when we train our predictive models in the coming chapters.

The next section introduces one more technology intended for data transformation, which is cloud-based. Let's take a look at Azure Data Factory.

Using Data Factory for data transformation

So far, we have used on-premise technologies, such as SSIS or R. This short section steps out of an on-premises environment. As a growing amount of data is stored in the cloud, Microsoft introduced a cloud-based technology, **Azure Data Factory** (**ADF**), which is a technology intended for the following tasks:

- Data acquisition from a wide set of data sources, including on-premise data sources (E phase of ETL processes)

- Data transformations using several languages (T phase of ETL processes)
- Publishing data for further usage (L phase of ETL processes)

Reviewing the preceding bullet list, we can say that ADF is a cloud-based SSIS. Here, we also define sources of data, data manipulation, and the data storage destination. However, the technology background is completely different and terminology also differs from SSIS.

ADF is provided in two versions: v1 and v2. The current v2 version provides an Integration Runtime, which makes it possible to use the native SSIS packages hosted in the Azure environment as part of activities.

ADF uses the following core terms:

- **Linked service**: This is a data storage definition, such as SQL Server database (including on-premises instances), and Hadoop TBD.
- **Dataset**: This is a matrix of values obtained from Linked Services.
- **Activity**: Here, one task works on a dataset. An activity takes a dataset and produces a new, transformed dataset that can be processed by another activity or stored back to a Linked service.
- **Pipeline**: This is a unit of ETL management. Pipeline is used, for instance, for scheduling repeated data transformation tasks or monitoring and diagnosing tasks.

In the following sections, we will create ADF and a simple job to show how to work with ADF.

Creating Azure Data Factory

This section will introduce us to the Azure Data Factory. In this section, we will go through the most simple definition created using a Data Copy wizard. A goal of our example is to copy data from some SQL Server database tables into a `CSV` file stored in an Azure storage account.

As a prerequisite, we need an Azure subscription. A free subscription is enough. In the subscription, create an SQL Server database from a sample. This will create a database named `AdventureWorksLT`. After doing this, create an Azure storage account containing one blob storage in a folder named `files`. These preparation tasks are quite simple and we will not spend too much time describing how to do them. When our environment is prepared, we can start to create our first ADF pipeline.

First of all, we need to have an empty Data Factory as a resource in Azure under our Azure subscription. The ADF could be defined using PowerShell modules for Azure and .NET Azure SDK, but for our example, we can use Azure Portal. First of all, sign in to the Azure Portal on `https://portal.azure.com`. After successful login, find the resource of the Data Factory type. The following screenshot shows the main page of the Azure Portal with the **Create a resource** panel opened:

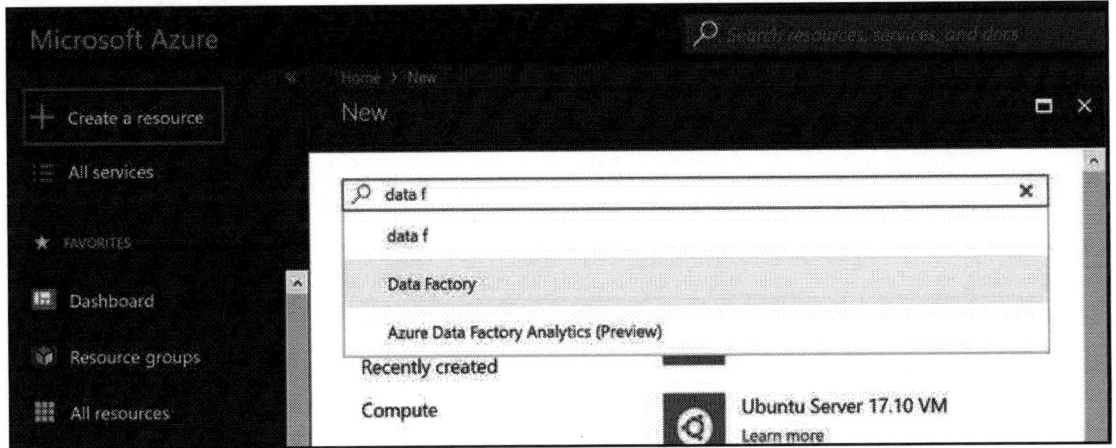

Azure Portal with the Create a resource panel

The preceding screenshot has the **Create a resource** link highlighted in a red rectangle. Using the link opens a panel labeled **New**. The **New** panel contains a search textbox, and in here we will write **Data Factory**. The search textbox finds the best matches of searched text. We'll click the **Data Factory** offer and the ADF creation will begin.

The first panel of ADF creation is shown in the following screenshot:

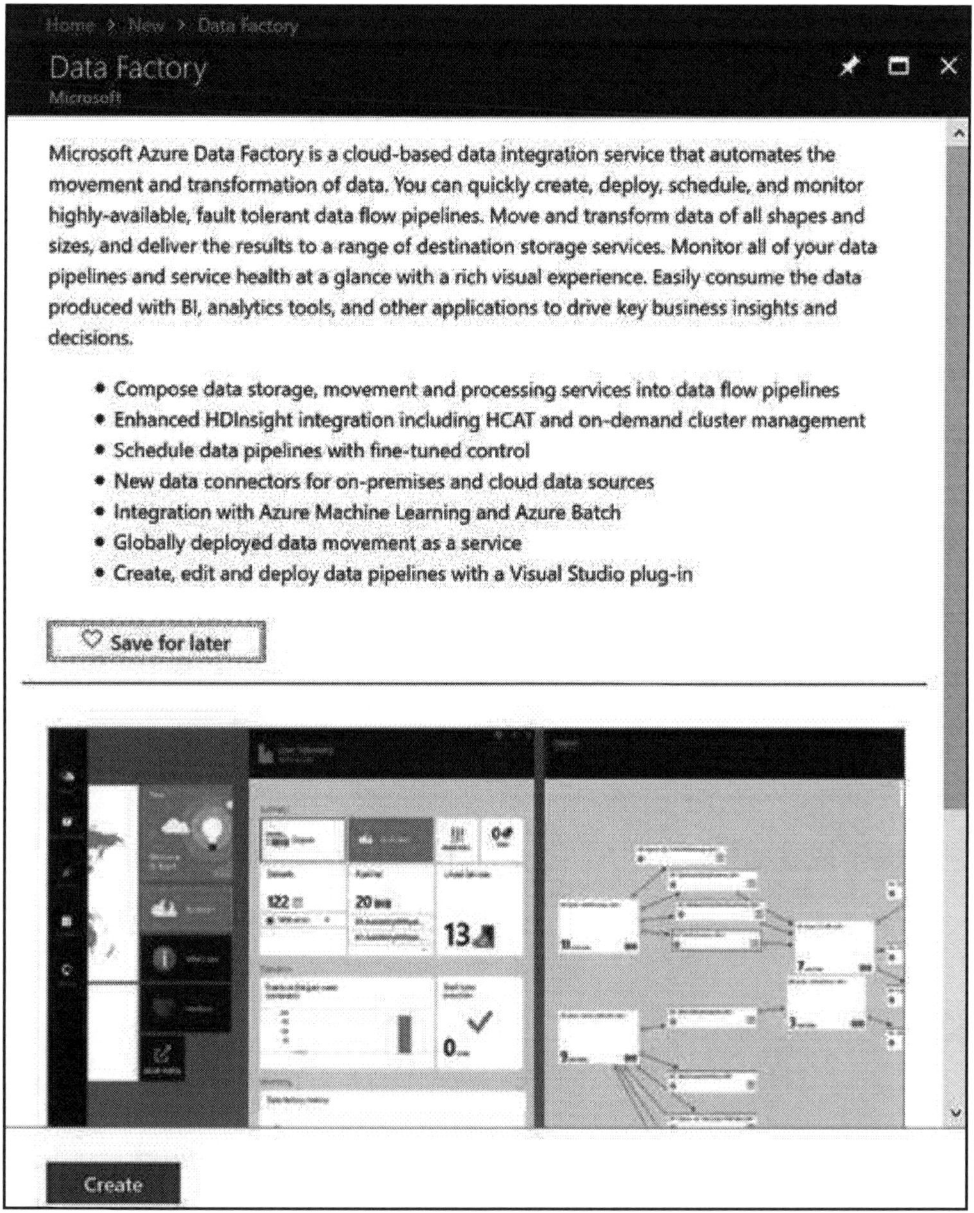

Creating ADF

The most important element of the panel shown on the preceding screenshot is the **Create** button, however. When we click on it, the next step appears. The following screenshot shows all values that are needed to create the new ADF:

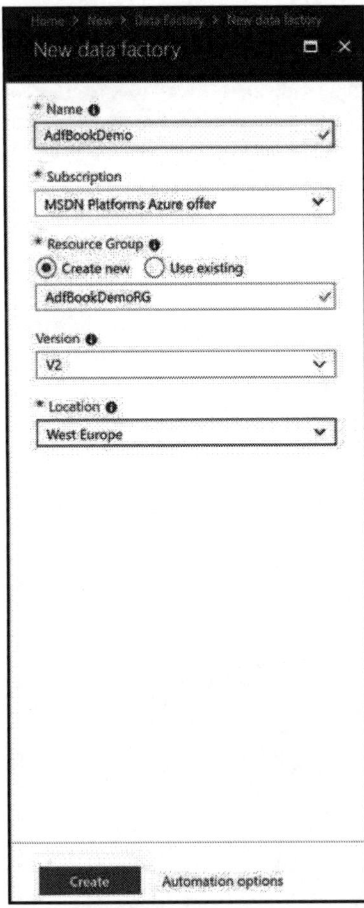

Displaying the field values for creation of ADF

Let's take a look at all fields from the panel shown in the preceding screenshot:

- **Name**: This field is mandatory and contains the unique name of our newly-created ADF. In the preceding picture, the `AdfBookDemo` value was set.
- **Subscription**: This is the existing subscription to which we are logged in. The ADF's expenses will be charged from the selected subscription.
- **Resource Group**: These are used to group depending parts of our Azure solutions together. We can use an existing resource group or create a new resource group. In the preceding screenshot, a new resource group with the name `AdfBookDemoRG` is created.
- **Version**: Microsoft provides two versions. V1 version is deprecated, so let's use the current version, V2.
- **Location**: This is the location of the Azure server room. Select the server room closest to your actual location.

When all fields are filled in with the correct values, the **Create** button is used and the deployment of a new ADF starts. This is a very fast process. When the ADF is created, we are informed via a notification. It's useful to pin the ADF to the dashboard in Azure Portal for fast and simple access. The following screenshot shows the notification:

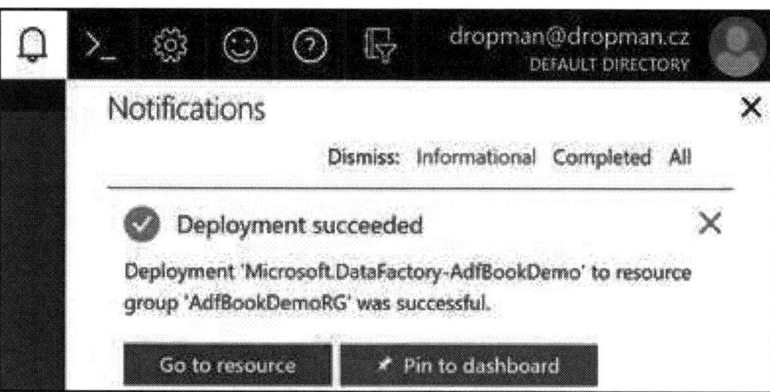

Deploying ADF

Using the **Pin to dashboard** button from within the notification shown in the preceding screenshot adds the freshly-created ADF on the dashboard. Now we can access the ADF and start to work on our data-transformation solution. The starting point for creating a new pipeline is the Home panel, as shown in the following screenshot:

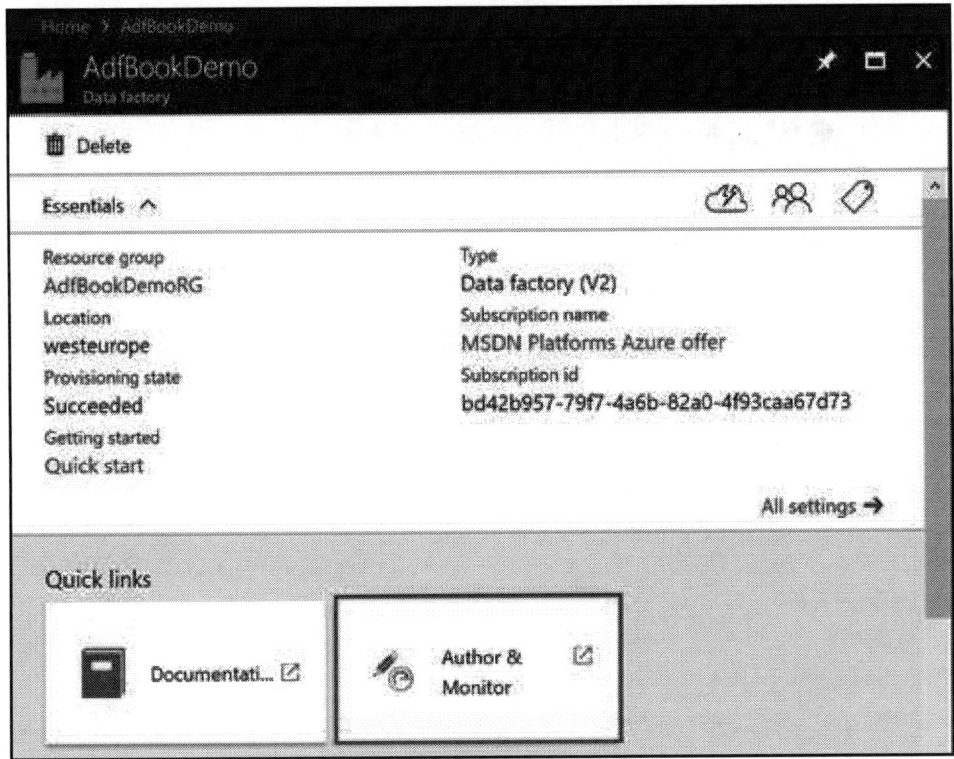

Home panel of ADF

The preceding screenshot shows the home panel of the created ADF. The red rectangle highlights a link to the **Author & Monitor** section, which opens a new browser window containing the environment for creating a pipeline definition.

Creating simple copy data with ADF

The ADF web tool starts with the **Let's get started** page, which provides several links to a quick start. To see how ADF works, the simplest way is to use the **Copy Data** link on the **Let's get started** page. The **Copy Data** link provides a set of steps for the definition of a simple data-movement pipeline. The following screenshot shows the starting point of the **Copy Data** wizard:

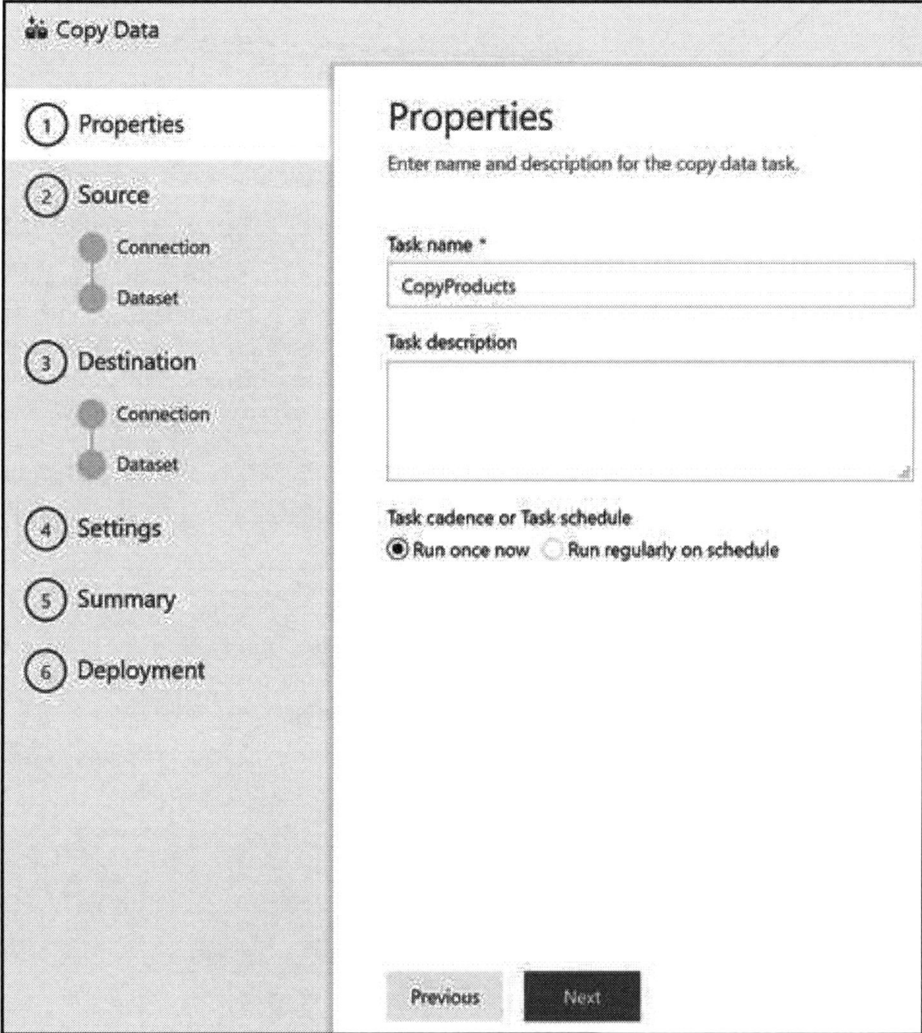

Copy Data wizard window

The **Copy Data** wizard starts with a **Properties** step, for which we'll set a name for the job (`CopyProducts`, in our example). We'll also decide whether to execute the job once or based on a schedule. When the **Next** button is clicked, we are going to configure a source connection and a dataset that has to be extracted. The following screenshot shows the **Source** step of the **Copy Data** wizard:

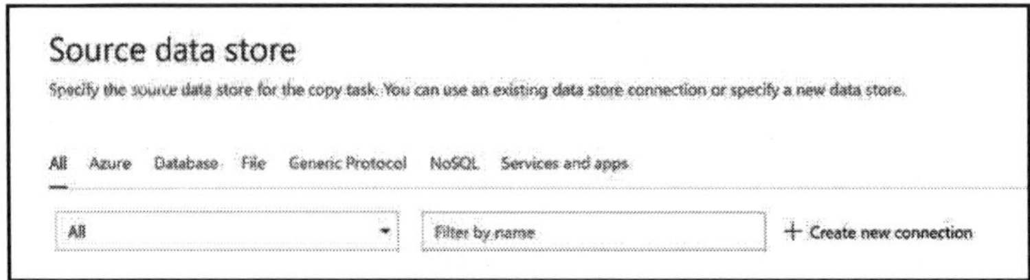

Source data store of the Copy Data wizard

The **Source data store** page of the **Copy Data** wizard shown in the preceding screenshot shows a list of already-defined connections. Our list of connections is empty, so we need to use the **Create new connection** link, which opens one more page with all the services or data storage types to which we can connect. We will select SQL Server as a data source for our task. The following screenshot shows the **New Linked Service** page with **SQL Server** selected as a data source:

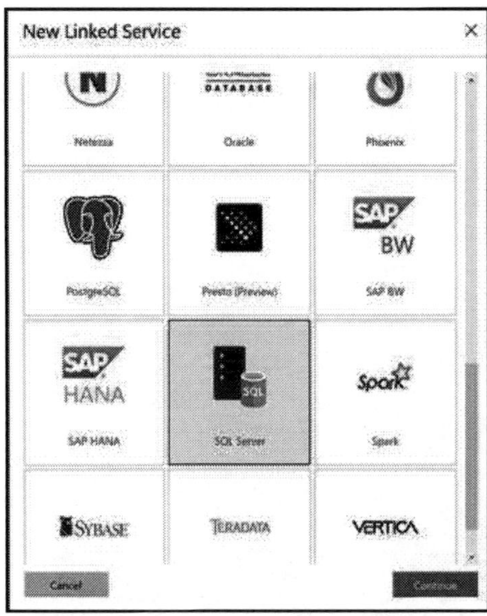

New Linked Service page with SQL Server

The preceding screenshot shows how to select **SQL Server** as a data source. Then the **Continue** button is used and the **New Linked Service** page continues with a next step for the SQL Server instance's definition. The following screenshot shows the definition page with the settings filled in:

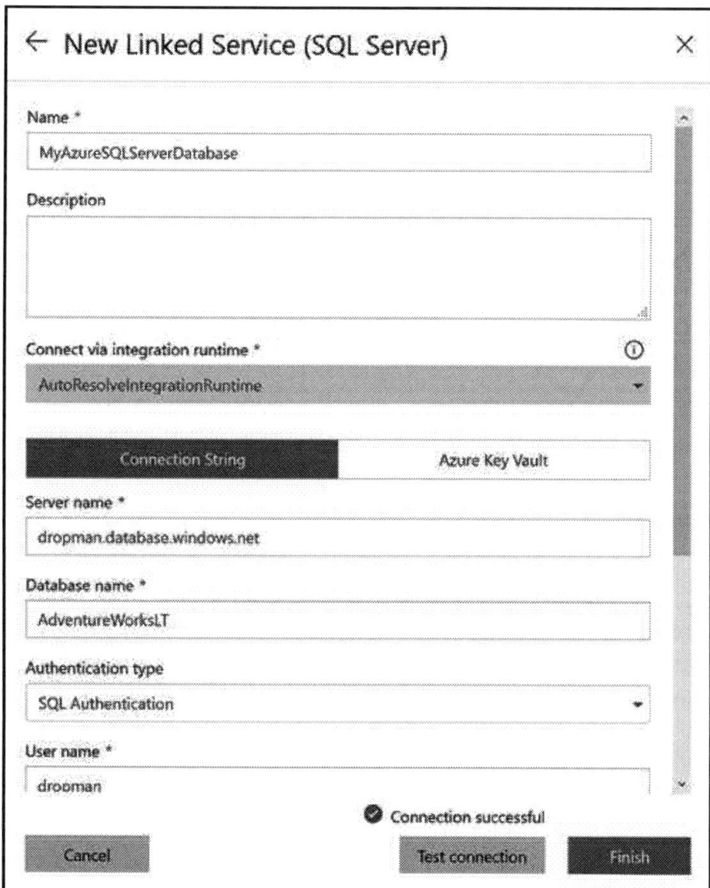

Field values for New linked Service page

As shown in the preceding screenshot, we must fill several connection settings:

- **Name**: This is the descriptive name of our linked service
- **Server name**: This is the name of the address of SQL Server on which our database is hosted
- **Database name**: This is the name of the database containing the table we want to extract
- **Authentication type**: In our case, the SQL Authentication using login name and password is used

We can test our settings using the **Test connection** button. If the test succeeds, we can click **Finish** and save the settings. The new connection then appears on the screen and we can use the **Next** button to move on. The **Data Copy** wizard connects a defined server and database and shows a list of tables. The following screenshots show the steps of the **Data Copy** wizard:

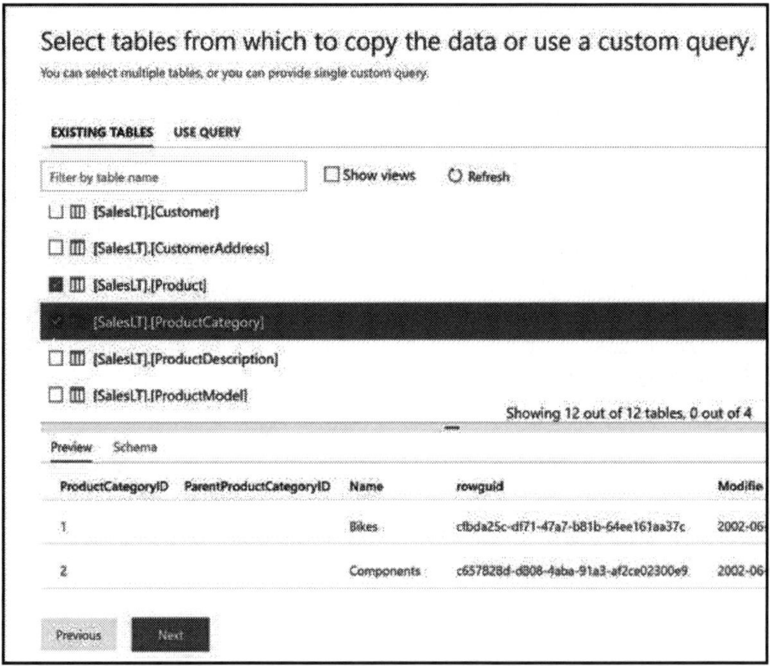

Steps of the Copy Data Wizard

The preceding screenshot shows a list of tables from which we can select tables to copy. We can select one or more tables, or we can write a query to create our own dataset. After the selection of the source dataset is done and we have clicked on the **Next** button, the destination-connected service-definition page appears. The page for destination-connected service is the same as for the source-connected service. As a destination, we will define **Azure Storage** account with blobs. The following screenshot shows how to configure the storage account as a destination:

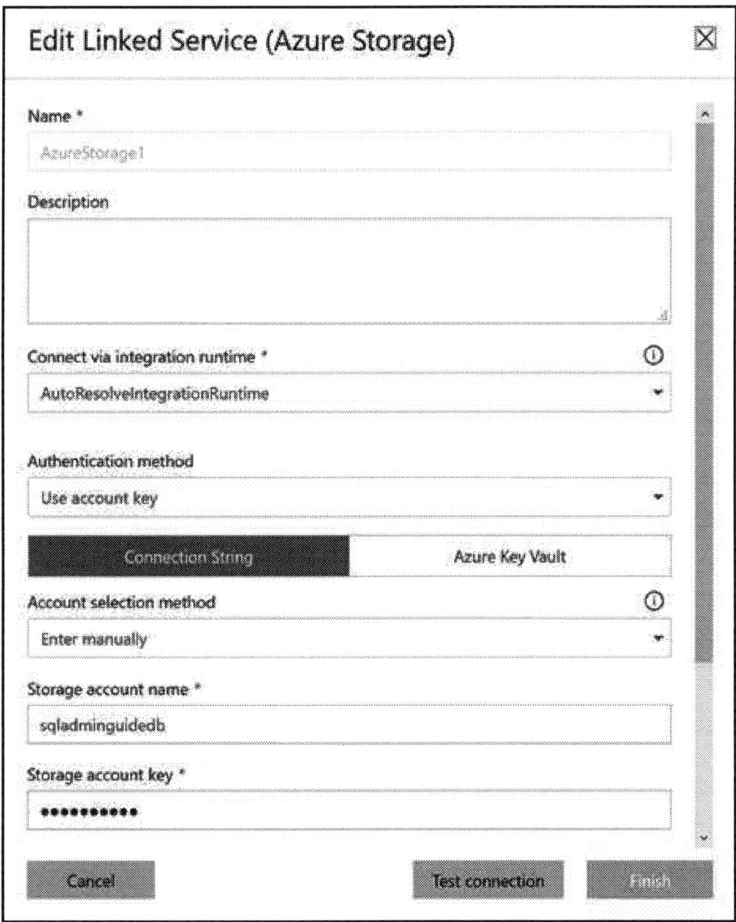

Configuring the storage account as a destination

The preceding screenshot shows the dialog window for connecting to an **Azure Storage** account. We need to configure the following:

- **Name**: The descriptive name of the connected service
- **Storage account name**: The name of the previously-created storage account
- **Storage account key**: This key is accessible on Azure Portal in the **Keys** section in the storage account configuration in the **Keys** section

When connection is successfully tested using the **Test connection** button, we'll save it with the **Finish** button. The configuration page is closed and we are back in the **Copy Data** wizard. After clicking **Next** in the **Copy Data** wizard, we have to select the Azure storage service type. This should be set to **Azure Blob Storage**. The next step in the wizard is shown in the following screenshot:

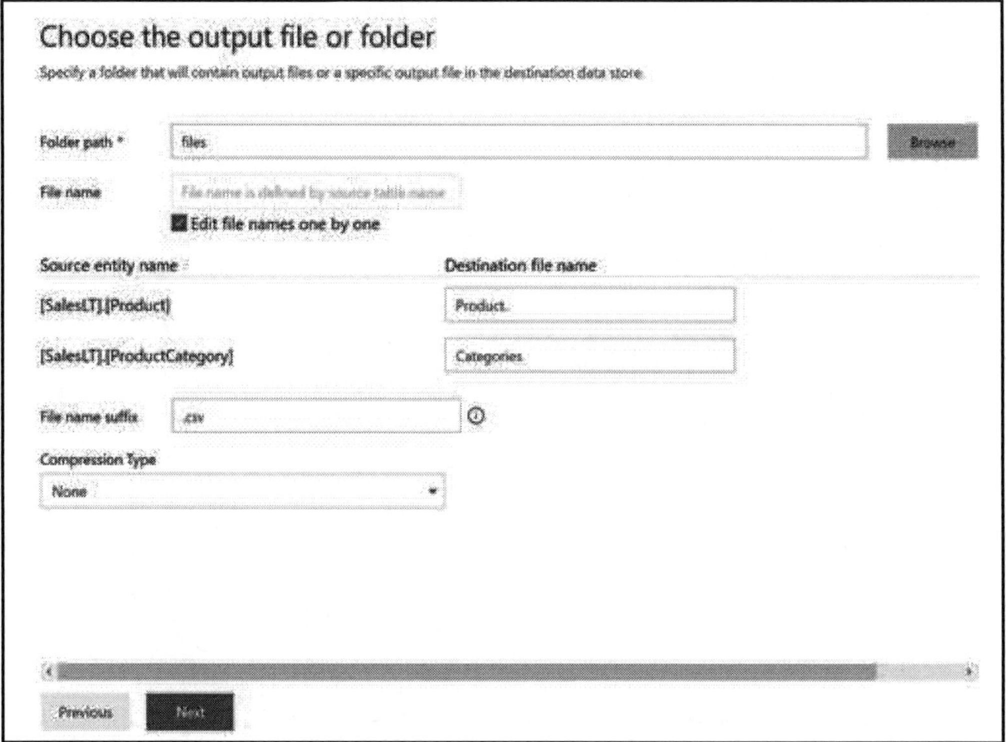

Choosing the output file

The preceding screenshot shows the step of the Copy Data wizard, where following fields has to be set:

- **Folder path**: Using the **Browse** button will offer a directory structure previously defined in the storage account.
- **File name**: Because we are copying more tables, we should switch on the **Edit file names one by one** to edit the name of every output file. The table with source entity names and destination filenames then appear. Using the filenames of your choice (the **Product** and **Categories** names are used in the preceding screenshot), write the filenames without suffixes.
- **File name suffix**: The `.txt` suffix is set by default. Change this to `.csv`.

After configuring the destination file, names, and formats, we have to decide on the format of the files. The following screenshot shows the next page of the **Copy Data** wizard with the configuration of the destination file:

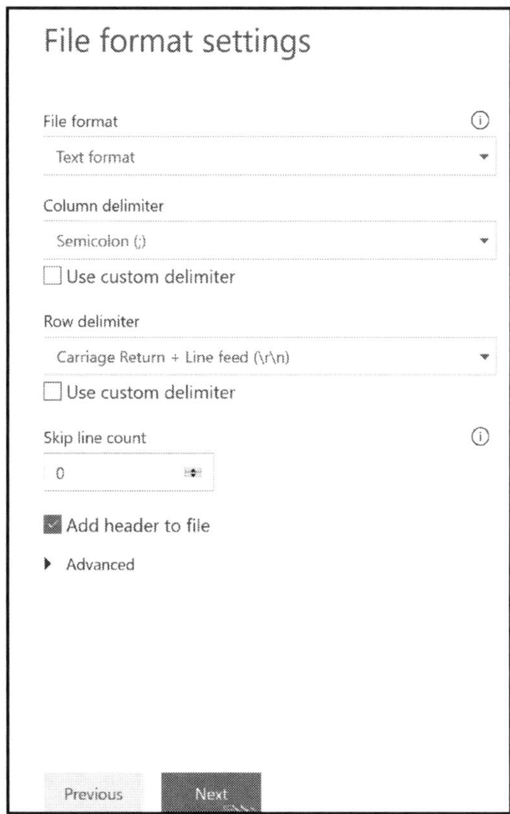

Configuration of the destination file

The File format settings page shown in the preceding screenshot is used to configure column and row delimiters. We can set a semicolon as a **Column delimiter** and we can leave **Row delimiter** with the default value.

The next page of the **Copy Data** wizard is used to set fault-tolerance. We can set the following options:

- Abort activity on first incompatible row (default)
- Skip incompatible rows
- Skip and log incompatible rows

Due to the fact that in our example we believe in data quality from the source database, we can leave the default option configured.

The next page of this quite-long **Data Copy** wizard is **Summary**. This is shown in the following screenshot:

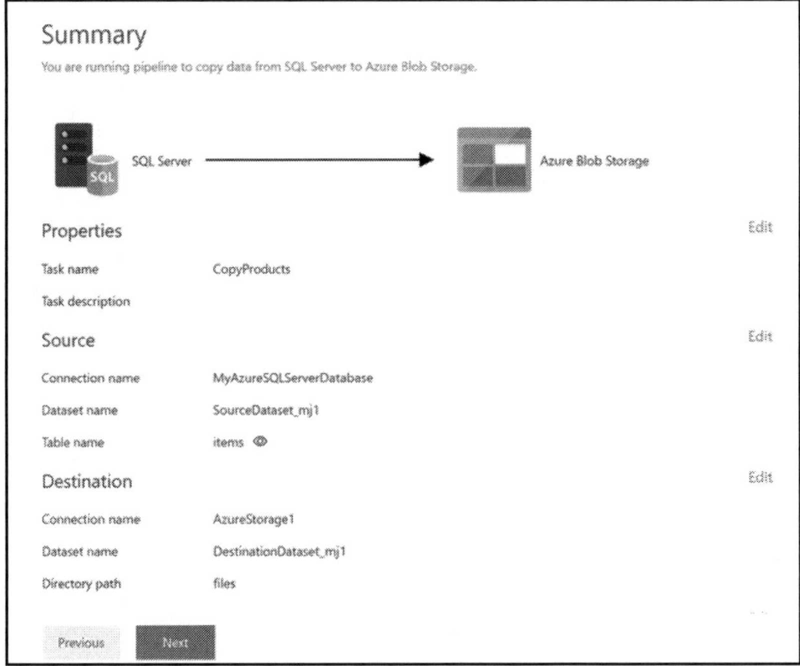

Summary page of Data Copy wizard

The **Summary** page shown in the preceding screenshot is the last point at which we can adjust our settings if needed. When **Next** is clicked, the **Copy Data** wizard deploys our work, creating datasets and new pipelines. Because we selected the run once option at the beginning of the wizard, the pipeline is executed immediately. The following screenshot shows the result page:

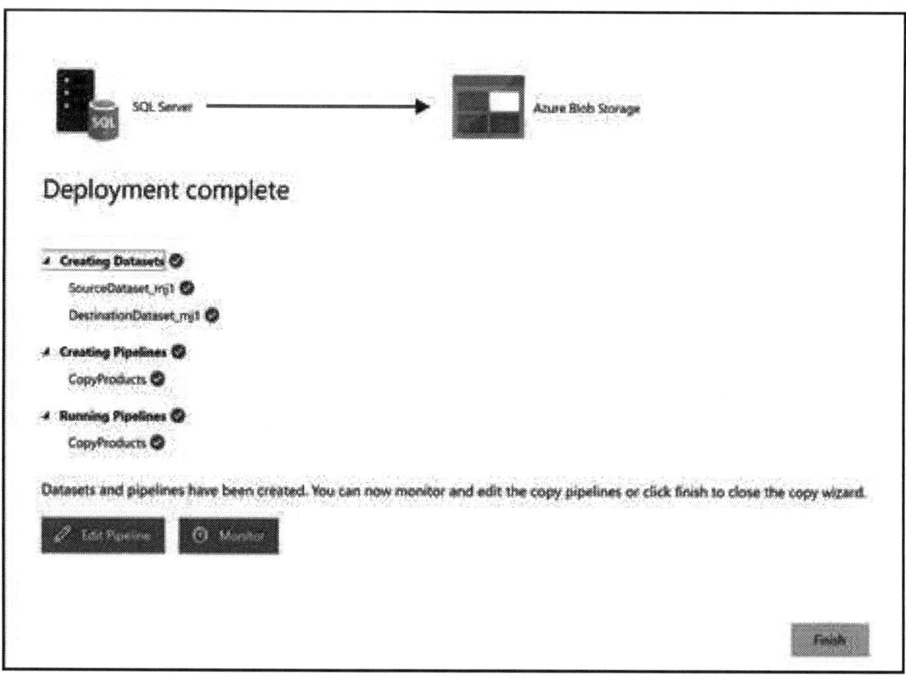

Deployment of Copy Data wizard

The Deployment complete page of the **Copy Data** wizard shows the result of all actions executed by the wizard. We can also edit the pipeline or just finish the wizard.

Summary

This chapter showed that T-SQL is not the only language or environment used in data science for data transformation. All of the technology shown in this chapter deserves—and has—its own publications. The goal of this chapter was to show technologies beyond T-SQL and to offer inspiration for further studies.

The first section of this chapter was an introduction to several types of transformations often needed in the data science domain. We also learned about categorization, standardization, and missing-value imputations in the form of terms and formulas.

The knowledge obtained in the first section was used to introduce SQL Server Integration Services in the second section. Here, we created a simple package to show how the development is done. During the development of the Data Flow task, we learned about some transformations and their usage.

The section on SSIS was slightly more graphical. This is why we changed the scope of data-transformation development to a strictly coding environment called R. R is a very rich language that has thousands of packages. Even if we used pure R without any additional packages, we would still be able to standardize data.

In the last section, we moved from an on-premises environment to a cloud environment. Here, we explored ADF, which is a rich technology used for data-handling and transformations from a wide set of sources, not only in the cloud.

Once our data is prepared, we can start predictive modeling. The next chapter will cover how to prepare a SQL Server instance for predictive modeling, how to create a database schema for predictive models, and how to create and evaluate a predictive model.

Questions

1. What is the best way to handle missing values?
   In this case, the best thing is to remove a whole column or row. However, this can lead to a significant loss of information. For this reason, other methods are used, such as replacing missing value with the mean, mode, or median. We can also use custom values and more sophisticated methods for missing-value imputation, including the mean of closest neighbors or linear regression.
2. Why do we normalize data?
   We do this because we need to rescale data to be more comparable.
3. Which editions of SQL Server contain SSIS?
   SQL Server from 2005 until now, Enterprise, and Standard Editions.

4. Which components of the SSIS package execute the data transformation?
   The data transformation starts in a control-flow task called Data Flow Task. Internally, the Data Flow Task causes the data-flow engine to start and execute the data transformation itself. Then the control is brought back to a control-flow engine.
5. How do we declare new variable in R?
   R uses implicit declaration. The variable is declared when it is first used.
6. Which form of data comes into a calculation in R?
   `data.frame`.
7. Can Azure Data Factory access data stored on-premises?
   Yes. Azure uses so-called gateways for this. A gateway is an application installed on-premises.

9
Predictive Model Training and Evaluation

So far, all the chapters of this book have been dedicated to showing how to gather, transform, and statistically summarize data from a wide range of sources using different technologies. In this chapter, we are going to learn how to prepare SQL Server as an environment for predictive modeling. We're also going to look at how to create database structures and modules that are useful for efficient predictive model training. We will go through the following topics:

- **Preparing SQL Server**: The first section of this chapter will show you how to configure the machine learning services of SQL Server and how to prepare them for custom packages
- **Creating data structures**: The second section of this chapter will demonstrate how to create database objects that are used to create, train, and maintain machine learning models
- **Creating and evaluating a predictive model**: The last section of this chapter will go through a simple example that demonstrates how to create and evaluate a predictive model

Technical requirements

For all the examples in this chapter, we will need SQL Server, either the 2016 or 2017 edition. We will also need the specific script files that are mentioned throughout this chapter. The reader has the option of trying to play with the R language using R Studio.

Preparing SQL Server

Microsoft SQL Server is very powerful engine for carrying out data science tasks. The server contains ML services that can be used for advanced R or Python analysis. Every feature offered within SQL Server, such as .NET integration or mail-sending, needs to be enabled in order for developers to be able to use them later. Machine learning also has to be enabled and configured correctly. This section shows which options to configure on the SQL Server, how to configure them, and also how to check whether the configuration is correct.

Setting up and configuring ML services

SQL Server's **ML Services** is based on a feature called satellite queries. The purpose of ML Services is to allow us to use languages other than the common T-SQL language so that we can have access to further data-processing options, primarily in data science tasks. From an architectural perspective, ML Services contain R and Python runtimes, which are reachable via a helper service called **SQL Server Launchpad**. This service is installed alongside the SQL Server when the Machine Learning feature is selected during the setup process.

First of all, we have to check which runtimes are installed. We also should check whether the SQL Server Launchpad service is running. The installation folders of both R Services and Python Services can be found in the basic installation path of the SQL Server, which is typically `C:\Program Files\Microsoft SQL Server\MSSQL14.MSSQLSERVER`. In this path, we should see the `R_SERVICES` folder, the `PYTHON_SERVICES` folder, or both folders, depending on which feature selection was chosen during installation. As an example, let's try to run a command-line application for R Services. The command-line application is contained within the `R_SERVICES\bin` directory and its name is simply `R.exe`. We can find this application using File Explorer, or we can execute it directly in the Command Prompt. When the application is running, it should look as follows:

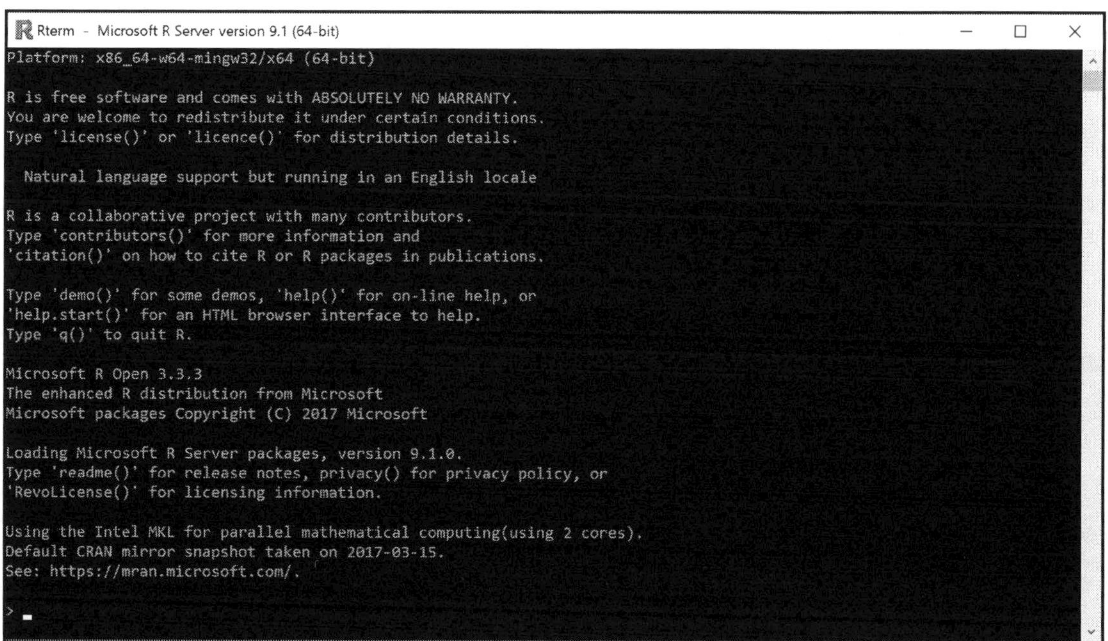

The preceding screenshot shows the `R.exe` application upon startup. The > symbol is a starting point where we can begin writing our code. Let's try entering a very simple piece of code, `1+1`, followed by the **Enter** key. The result of this expression, `[1] 2`, should appear on the next line in the console. The R language works with vectors, so the result is a vector with one `[1]` coordinate and a value of `2`. Once we have carried out this test successfully, we can continue setting up R Services.

SQL Server Launchpad, which is required for communication between SQL Server and its particular satellite, can be found in **SQL Server 2017 Configuration Manager**. Its startup mode should be set to **Automatic**. The following screenshot shows the **SQL Server 2017 Configuration Manager** with the **SQL Server Launchpad** successfully started:

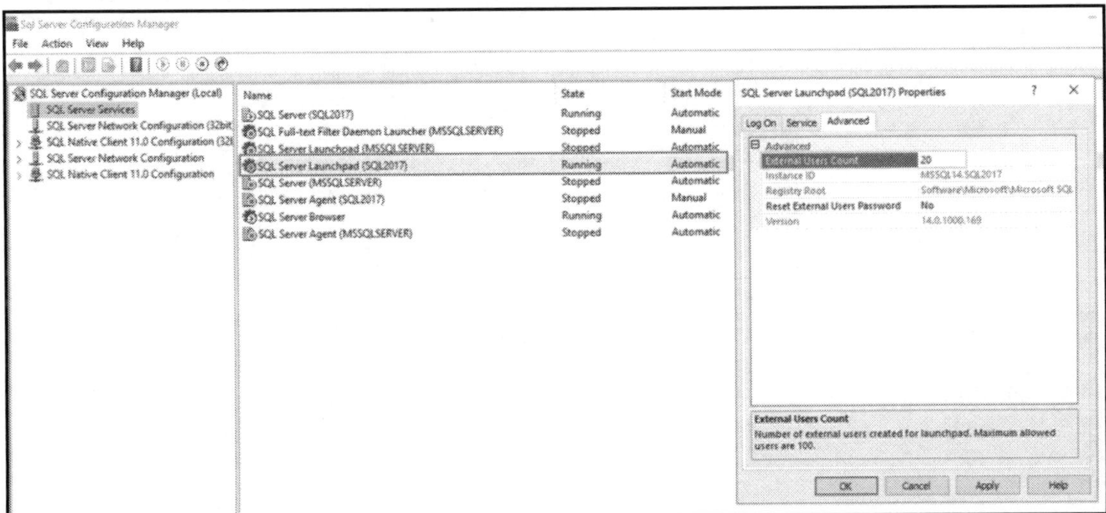

The red rectangle in the preceding screenshot marks the **SQL Server Launchpad** service in the list of all other services that are installed within the **SQL Server**. The dialog window on the right-hand side of the preceding screenshot shows the advanced properties of **SQL Server Launchpad**. The most important setting is highlighted by the yellow rectangle. This is the number of local Windows users that will be used to process the satellite code in parallel. We can adjust this amount of users to control the maximum amount of parallel threads that are created while processing the R or Python code.

When both of the preceding checks are done, we have to enable the execution of external scripts on the instance of the SQL Server. To do this, we will use the common system procedure, `sp_configure`. This can be executed as follows:

```
EXEC sp_configure 'external scripts enabled', 1
RECONFIGURE -- does not work at this point
```

The first line here executes the `sp_configure` system procedure with the `external scripts enabled` property set to `1`, which means that it is enabled. Usually, when the stored procedure is executed, the `RECONFIGURE` statement follows the execution. This allows us to use the property without having to restart the whole SQL Server service. However, in this case, because we want to enable the execution of the external script, the configuration must also be provisioned to the **SQL Server Launchpad**, so we do have to restart the SQL Server.

After the restart, we can carry out a final test to see whether everything works as expected. Let's execute the following code in Management Studio:

```
exec sp_execute_external_script
    @language = N'R'
  , @script = N''
```

The preceding code calls the `sp_execute_external_script` stored procedure with an empty R script. The result of the preceding execution is just a message that the command was executed successfully. If any errors occur, revise all your configurations one more time.

Let's take a closer look at the preceding script. The `sp_execute_external_script` procedure requires at least two input parameters: `@language` and `@script`. Both parameters are of the `nvarchar` data type, so we must not omit the leading capital `N` on the parameter values to indicate this.

`sp_execute_external_script` also returns one or more result sets. The following example shows very simple code that calculates a value from an expression, converts it into a `data.frame`, and returns it back to the caller:

```
exec sp_execute_external_script
    @language = N'R'
  , @script = N'OutputDataSet <- as.data.frame(1+1);'
```

In the preceding execution, we used the R language for the first time. The statement provided as the value of the `@script` parameter works in the following order:

1. The `1+1` expression is evaluated.
2. The result is encapsulated into a `data.frame` object with a function called `as.data.frame(...)`.
3. The `data.frame` is assigned with the `<-` assignment operator to a variable called `OutputDataSet`.
4. The `OutputDataSet` content is propagated as a result set back to a client.

Variables in R are implicitly declared. This means that any variable is created when it is used for the first time. When we use the `OutputDataSet` variable, it serves as a point of data exchange from the R script back to the SQL Server. `OutputDataSet` is case-sensitive and must contain a value that is strictly of a `data.frame` data type. SQL Server is then able to show the content of the variable back to the user as a regular dataset in the same form as a result set obtained from the commonly-used SQL `SELECT` statement.

The dataset that comes from the preceding example will not have column names or well-defined data types. We need to define its structure. The following example is almost the same as the previous one, but it adds one more line to the `sp_execute_external_script` stored procedure:

```
exec sp_execute_external_script
    @language = N'R'
    , @script = N'OutputDataSet <- as.data.frame(1+1);'
with result sets undefined
```

Both of the preceding scripts will generate the same result, which is shown in the following screenshot. The second execution, however, explicitly declares that we do not want to define the structure of the dataset:

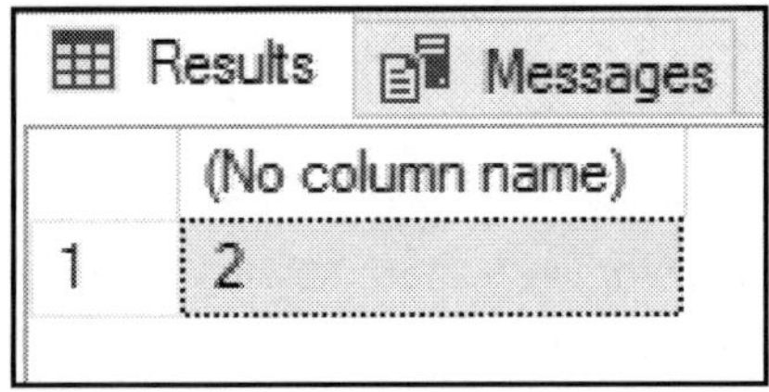

The preceding screenshot shows the correct result of the `1+1` expression, but the result set itself contains unnamed columns. We can correct this by changing the preceding statement as follows:

```
exec sp_execute_external_script
    @language = N'R'
    , @script = N'OutputDataSet <- as.data.frame(1+1);'
with result sets (
    (Result int)
)
```

The `WITH RESULT SETS` option used in the preceding code enables us to define one or more result sets. The list of result sets is enclosed in brackets and each result set is then further enclosed in brackets within this. Our result set contains just one column of data type int. When the preceding statement is executed, the result set should look as follows:

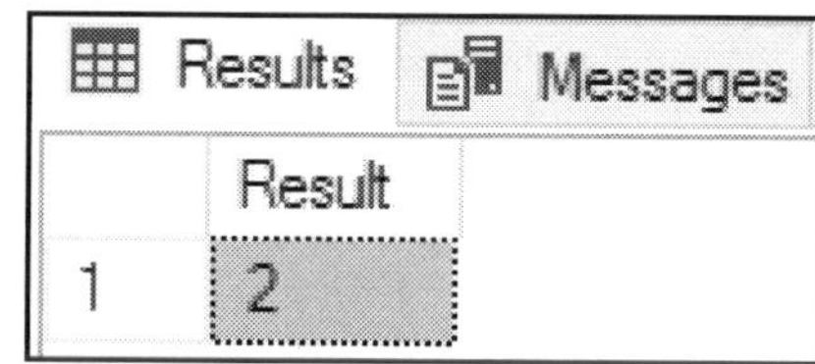

The result set from the preceding screenshot has column names, which is important to be able to process the data set in other SQL queries or in client applications.

This basic configuration enables us to start writing and executing scripts written in R or Python. In the data science domain, however, it is very common to use custom packages. In the following section, we will look at how to install custom packages on SQL Server.

Preparing to install our own R packages

Machine learning models are usually developed using dedicated tools, such as R Studio or Canopy. Both environments are supported by big communities, so we can find many packages that can help us to build typical machine learning models. These packages are usually accessible for free from the internet. The R language allows us to install the necessary packages locally and use them for our own development. However, it is important to bear in mind that the installed packages are only accessible in the environment in which they are installed. Even though SQL Server provides a huge list of packages, we will probably need to install our own package that covers the specific needs of our machine learning project.

First of all, let's take a look at all the installed packages. The following SQL code shows a simple R script, which describes all the packages that are visible and accessible from the SQL Server:

```
exec sp_execute_external_script
    @language = N'R'
    , @script = N'OutputDataSet <- as.data.frame(installed.packages());'
with result sets undefined
```

The core of the preceding script is an R function, `installed.packages()`. This function can be used in every R environment to look at which packages are installed within the environment. The rest of the R script works in a similar way to previous examples. The result of the `installed.packages()` function is encapsulated into the `data.frame` object, which is then assigned to the `OutputDataSet` variable.

If we want to see whether a certain package is installed, we can use the following script:

```
exec sp_execute_external_script
    @language = N'R'
    , @script = N'
        OutputDataSet <-
        as.data.frame("recommenderlab" %in%
rownames(installed.packages()));'
with result sets ((PackageExists bit))
```

From a T-SQL perspective, the code is still the same, it simply executes the `sp_execute_external_script` stored procedure. The content of the R parameter, however, has grown. Let's take a close look at the R script. The `installed.packages()` function returns a set of all the R packages that are installed on the instance of the SQL Server. The first column from the result set contains the package names. The `rownames()` function ensures that the first column from the `installed.packages()` result set will be used for row-naming. Row-naming is very common in R; it aids orientation in statistical populations. The whole `"recommenderlab" %in% rownames(installed.packages())` expression is a condition, returning `1` if the searched package, called `recommenderlab` in our example, is already installed, or `0` if the package does not exist.

The `recommenderlab` package is a very useful package, used to produce recommendations of movies or to indicate products that are commonly bought together, and so on. We will use this package as an example of an external package imported on SQL Server.

If the package does not exist in a certain environment, the R language provides the `install.packages()` function. This function downloads the package, along with all the other packages on which that package depends, and installs them into the environment. We can use this function as follows:

```
exec sp_execute_external_script
    @language = N'R'
    , @script = N'install.packages("recommenderlab");'
```

The preceding script calls the `install.packages()` function with the name of the desired package as a parameter. However, it is likely that the script will fail, because SQL Server does not enable custom package installation by default. Because we are only going to install the package once, the simplest way to do this is to use the command line, `RTerm.exe`, which works with the R environment that is installed within SQL Server's context. The command line can be found in the installation path of R services, which is typically `C:\Program Files\Microsoft SQL Server\MSSQL14.MSSQLSERVER\R_SERVICES\bin\x64`. `RTerm.exe` is very similar to the `R.exe` command line. When it has started, we can just put the `install.packages()` function in the command line and wait until it finishes downloading and installing. We can then check whether the installed package is visible to the SQL Server with the `sp_execute_external_script` stored procedure.

Everything that we needed to set up is now ready. In the following sections, we will use this configured environment to create a machine learning model that can be accessed using common T-SQL.

Creating data structures

The concept of machine learning on SQL Server is based on the idea that relational data is mostly suitable for being processed in machine learning models directly, without the need for data transfers back and forth between SQL Server and any external environment. In this section, we will create a relational model to use and maintain a machine learning model.

The concept of machine learning in databases

When we start to create databases that contain machine learning models, there are several things that we need to be aware of. First of all, the machine learning model itself is a structure of information that has to be stored directly in a database and restored every time someone needs to make a prediction. Each different kind of machine learning model has its own structure. In other words, it's very difficult to create a strict relational model for every type of machine learning model that we want to create. The easiest way to store machine learning models is to serialize them into a bytestream and store them as BLOBs.

The second consideration is that data always changes over time, so we need to retrain our models periodically and compare the efficiency between versions. There are two possible ways to carry out the versioning of machine learning models. The one we choose depends on our preferences and also on the technical limitations of SQL Server.

As mentioned previously, we can store our model as BLOBs natively on SQL Server in row-based data structures. For bigger BLOBs, however, this method might not work very well. For this reason, SQL Server offers **filestream** storage. A filestream is a folder in which SQL Server inserts BLOBs sequentially, without having to shred and organize them into 8-kB database pages. Filestream as storage is a better option for bigger BLOBs. When we use filestreams for our machine learning models, we should develop our own versioning system.

The second versioning option is very simple and uses a modern way of tracking changes in relational tables. In version 2016, SQL Server introduced a new feature called **temporal tables,** which are common relational tables. For every table designed as temporal, a second table with the same structure is created and SQL Server catches every change that is made on the data in the original table and saves the changed records to the second table. This is a very simple and native way of model versioning, but temporal tables cannot handle filestream data, because this is physically stored outside the data files.

The last consideration is that we will use the models in two ways: to execute training and to make predictions. For this reason, we will develop a pair of batches. One will be executed periodically for training, while the second will be used to make predictions on demand.

To summarize the previous paragraphs, we can say that the core of the database model for machine learning models is some kind of BLOB storage with versioning. It is also important to think about the other details of the database structure, including, for example, whether we want to store all the models of different types in a common database schema. The following section will guide us through the relational model, which was created as a universal solution for multiple types of models. We will also create both alternatives for machine learning model versioning.

Creating physical data structures

The preceding section described some important concepts to do with the design of our database. In this section, we're going to walk through how to create a database model. We will create two physical designs. The first will use a filestream file group, while the second will use temporal tables.

Creating common objects

In this section, we will create a new database, a schema, and several tables that we will use for both of the aforementioned scenarios. The following statement creates a new database that has default values for all the properties:

```
CREATE DATABASE DemoModel;
```

After the preceding statement is executed, a new database is created.

It's useful to create a database schema that is dedicated to objects that belong to the management of machine learning models. The following statement creates a new schema in the `DemoModel` database:

```
USE DemoModel
go
CREATE SCHEMA Models AUTHORIZATION dbo;
```

All objects that participate in the training and storage of the model will be placed in the schema, called `Models`, that is created by the preceding statement.

Let's assume that we will save all our machine learning models in the same table. We have to create a table that will contain a list of machine learning models. This can be done as follows:

```
USE DemoModel
go
CREATE TABLE Models.ModelTypes
(
Id int not null identity
, ModelName nvarchar(50) not null
, Description nvarchar(250) not null
, CONSTRAINT pk_ModelTypes PRIMARY KEY (Id)
);
```

The `Models.ModelTypes` table will contain a list of machine learning models. The sample records that are inserted into the table with the following `INSERT` statements will explain the purpose of the table:

```
INSERT Models.ModelTypes (ModelName, Description)
VALUES ('Movie Recommender', 'Sample ML model for movie recommendation
based on user ratings')
, ('Price estimation (logistic regression)', 'An price estimation of new
movies based on genre, director and stars of similar movies')
```

The preceding table will serve as a parent table for a table that is created in two different ways in the following sections.

Creating objects using filestreams

The filestream alternative is useful when the volume of the stored machine learning models is large. Filestreams help us to read and save our machine learning model efficiently. Remember that when we use filestreams, we have to manage version-tracking manually because the SQL Server cannot provide an efficient versioning feature.

Using filestreams needs additional configuration at the instance level of the SQL Server instance. The configuration is outside the scope of this book, because this is a DBA responsibility.

First, we have to configure the `DemoModel` database to allow filestreams to be used. The following statement adds a new `filestream` file group to the database and also creates a file (or folder in this case) where the data will be physically stored:

```
use master
go
alter database DemoModel add filegroup FS contains filestream;
alter database DemoModel add file
(
name = 'FSData'
, filename = 'C:\temp\fs'    -- change the path to yours existing one
) to filegroup FS;
```

The preceding code example contains two `ALTER DATABASE` statements. The first adds a new `filestream` file group to the database, while the second creates a new folder called `fs` on the existing path, `c:\temp`.

The table itself will contain both trained and serialized machine learning model versions. Its structure should contain the following attributes:

- A primary key
- A foreign key identifying the model type
- A `rowguidcol` column, which is needed by the SQL Server to identify which byte stream saved in the `filestream` belongs to which record
- The date and time of the creation of the machine learning model, which will provide the versioning
- The stream of the machine learning model itself

This table can be created as follows:

```
use DemoModel
go

create table Models.ModelVersions
(
Id int not null identity
, ModelTypesId int not null
, StreamId uniqueidentifier rowguidcol not null
    constraint df_ModelVersions_StreamId default(newid())
, CreationDate datetime2 not null
    constraint df_ModelVersions__CreationDate default(sysdatetime())
, ModelStream varbinary(max) filestream
, constraint pk_ModelVersions primary key (Id)
, constraint fk_ModelVersions_ModelTypes foreign key (ModelTypesId)
    references Models.ModelTypes (Id)
, constraint uq_ModelVersions_StreamId unique (StreamId)
);
```

`filestream` file groups are suitable for `varbinary(max)` columns only. The `ModelStream` column in the `Models.ModelVersions` table is the column for serialized machine learning models. A table that uses `filestream` must also contain a mandatory column of the `uniqueidentifier` data type, marked as `rowguidcol`. In the preceding example, this is the `StreamId` column.

Using this approach, we never need to update our existing records. Every retrained model will be inserted as a new record into the `Model.ModelVersions` table. All records have the date of creation supplied with the default constraint on the `CreationDate` column. Later, when selecting the desired version of the machine learning model, the user can choose the exact date and time of its creation.

The following section will describe an alternative way to provide versioning natively, using temporal tables.

Creating objects using temporal tables

Temporal tables were introduced for the first time with SQL Server 2016. This feature is intended for transparent data-change tracking and it has the ability to reconstruct a state of data at a point in time. We can use temporal tables to carry out machine learning model versioning.

Creating a temporal table is not difficult. You do not require any additional settings at the database or instance level. The following statement creates a new table, called `Model.ModelVersionsTemporal`, with system versioning:

```
create table Models.ModelVersionsTemporal
(
Id int not null identity
, ModelTypesId int not null
, ModelStream varbinary(max)
, RecordStart datetime2 generated always as row start
, RecordEnd datetime2 generated always as row end
, period for system_time (RecordStart, RecordEnd)
, constraint pk_ModelVersionsTemporal primary key (Id)
, constraint fk_ModelVersionsTemporal_ModelTypes foreign key (ModelTypesId)
    references Models.ModelTypes (Id)
)
with
(system_versioning = on (history_table =
Models.ModelVersionsTemporalHistory))
```

Let's briefly explore the preceding script. The `ModelStream` column is still of the `varbinary(max)` type, but its values are not placed into a `filestream`, because this wouldn't work with temporal tables. The `StreamId uniqueidentifier` column disappears because it is no longer needed. The table schema does contain two new columns, however, which are `RecordStart` and `RecordEnd`. Both columns have the `datetime2` data type and their values are used by the SQL Server to mark the validity of the version. Both values are generated automatically every time a record is created, updated, or deleted.

The `PERIOD FOR SYSTEM_TIME` clause in the script tells the SQL Server which columns should be used for versioning. The last option that has to be set is `SYSTEM_VERSIONING = ON` in the `WITH` clause. The `(HISTORY_TABLE = Models.ModelVersionsTemporalHistory)` option is optional, but when it is not used, SQL Server automatically gives the historical table a name that is not very readable, so it's better to set an explicit name. The result of the preceding script is the creation of a new table in the **Object Explorer**. The following screenshot shows the relationship between the current and historical tables:

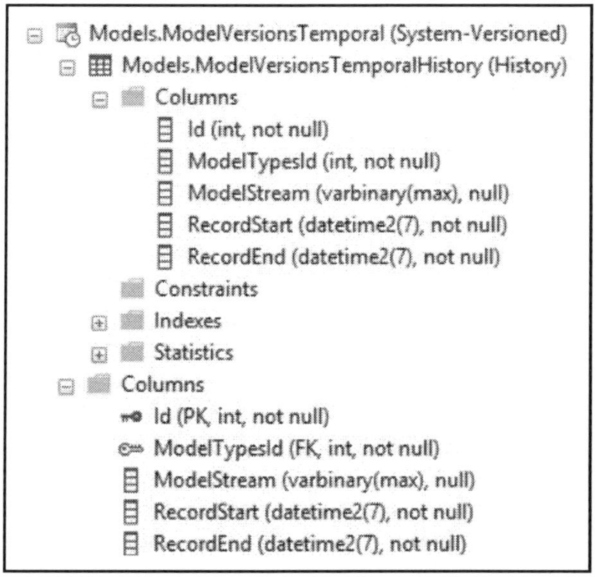

Models.ModelVersionsTemporal (System-Versioned)
Models.ModelVersionsTemporalHistory (History)
Columns
Id (int, not null)
ModelTypesId (int, not null)
ModelStream (varbinary(max), null)
RecordStart (datetime2(7), not null)
RecordEnd (datetime2(7), not null)
Constraints
Indexes
Statistics
Columns
Id (PK, int, not null)
ModelTypesId (FK, int, not null)
ModelStream (varbinary(max), null)
RecordStart (datetime2(7), not null)
RecordEnd (datetime2(7), not null)

The preceding screenshot shows part of **Object Explorer** with a newly-created temporal table. Temporal tables are placed in a list of all the tables in a specific database, but we can recognize them easily because temporal tables carry an icon with a small clock. When the temporal table node is expanded, we will see common nodes, such as `Columns` and `Indexes`, but we'll also see a second table nested directly after the temporal table. When we expand the `Column` nodes of both tables, we can see that they have identical structures. Both tables are also seen as regular tables by users, so a user can query the current table as well as its historical version. The only difference between both tables from a user's perspective is that the historical table is read-only.

The advantage of using temporal tables in the management of our machine learning models is that we can create a model just once and then we can simply update it, and its versions will be maintained automatically by SQL Server. Even if the historical table later contains many versions of each machine learning model, the historical table is page-compressed.

Let's compare both types of structures. Using `filestream` file groups leads to better performance when SQL Server handles BLOBs, but machine learning versioning has to be developed manually. Temporal tables allow us to carry out machine learning model versioning very simply, but we cannot use filestreams. Which option we choose depends on our own preference.

When database structures are designed for machine learning models, we can also consider adding more columns, such as a table for user comments and recommendations, or whatever else we need. In this section, however, we have created data structures that definitely work, so it is now time to deploy and train our first machine learning model.

Deploying, training, and evaluating a predictive model

In this section, we will write code based on a physical data schema that we created in the previous section. In this section, we're going to use R scripting to create a `recommender` machine learning model. We're not going to explain all aspects of the R language but we will go through the elements that are important to build a fully-functioning machine learning model maintained by SQL Server.

In the previous sections, we configured ML Services on SQL Server and we also imported an external package called `recommenderlab`. The `recommenderlab` package, as its name suggests, is used for recommendations. The input for the `recommender` that is provided by this package is a matrix in the form of items in columns, users in rows, and ratings in the matrix itself.

First, we need to gather some data and create a matrix in this format. It is easy to download data from the IMDB movie database in CSV format, load it to a database, and then pivot it, but in this case we are just going to use a small subset of the data to learn how to work with it. The code to create a table and load data can be found in the `16_RatingMatrixSampleTable.sql` file, which is located on the GitHub repository for this book. The table contains the 20 most-rated movies, which were rated more than 12,000 times by different users. Even if we could create a rating matrix that contains all the ratings on the IMDB movie database using R, the matrix occupies more than 1.5 GB of memory, so it is too big for our experiments. The script creates a table, `dbo.RatingMatrix`, which is shown in the following screenshot:

Results | Messages

	UserId	i1454468	i770828	i816711	i1300854	i993846	i1670345	i1408101	i1535109	i1483013	i1343092	i1951264	i1392214	i16636
1	u4032	8	0	0	0	9	0	0	10	0	0	0	0	0
2	u7945	0	7	7	8	0	7	8	8	7	0	7	0	7
3	u8277	0	0	0	0	0	0	0	0	0	0	0	0	0
4	u12522	0	0	0	0	7	0	0	0	0	0	0	0	0
5	u13186	0	0	0	0	0	0	0	0	0	0	0	0	0
6	u17431	0	5	0	6	0	9	0	0	0	0	0	0	0
7	u16435	0	0	0	0	9	7	0	0	0	0	0	0	0
8	u19684	0	0	0	0	0	0	0	0	0	0	10	0	0
9	u22008	0	0	0	0	0	0	0	0	0	10	0	0	0
10	u25921	0	0	0	0	0	0	9	0	0	0	0	0	0
11	u26253	0	0	0	0	7	9	0	0	0	0	0	7	0
12	u6926	0	0	0	0	0	0	9	0	0	0	0	0	0
13	u4719	9	0	0	0	0	0	0	0	0	0	0	0	0
14	u8254	0	0	0	0	0	0	0	0	0	10	0	0	10
15	u5715	0	0	4	0	0	0	0	0	0	0	0	0	0
16	u12213	0	7	0	0	0	0	0	0	0	0	0	0	7
17	u13209	0	0	0	0	0	9	8	0	0	0	0	0	0
18	u25566	0	7	7	0	0	8	9	0	6	0	0	0	5
19	u14205	0	0	0	0	0	0	0	0	0	0	0	0	0
20	u17076	0	6	6	0	0	0	0	0	0	7	0	0	0
21	u15748	0	0	0	0	9	0	0	0	0	0	0	0	0
22	u20703	10	0	0	5	0	0	0	0	0	0	0	0	0

In the first column of the `RatingMatrix` table, we have the user IDs. All the other columns are named according to the movie ID, and the content of all the movie columns is the ratings set by users for the movies.

We now need to read the data from the `RatingMatrix` table to an R script, transform it, and train the model. First, we have to learn how to read data into a script from SQL Server with the `sp_execute_external_script` stored procedure. This can be done as follows:

```
exec sp_execute_external_script
    @language = N'R'
    , @script = N'
        OutputDataSet <- InputDataSet
    '
    , @input_data_1 = N'select * from RatingMatrix'
```

This task will return an undefined result set, but the result set will contain data from the `RatingMatrix` table. As can be seen in the code sample, we have set another parameter, called `@input_data_1`. This parameter accepts an arbitrary string containing a query that will return a result set. The result set is then placed into an `R` variable, which is called `InputDataSet`. The preceding example just assigns the `InputDataSet` variable to the `OutputDataSet` variable, which sends its value back to a SQL Server user.

We will use the `InputDataSet` variable as a source of data for our `recommender` model. The following code sample shows the whole R script written as a `@script` parameter of the `sp_execute_external_script` stored procedure:

```
exec sp_execute_external_script
    @language = N'R'
    , @script = N'
        #import needed library
        library("recommenderlab");
        #make the first column as a row names in further matrix
        rownames(InputDataSet) <- InputDataSet[,1];
        InputDataSet[,1] <- NULL;
        #create object realRating Matrix
        matrix <- as(InputDataSet, "realRatingMatrix");
        #create the model
        model <- Recommender(matrix, method="UBCF");
        #serialize the model and return it back to a caller
        OutputDataSet <- as.data.frame(serialize(model, NULL));
    '
    , @input_data_1 = N'select * from RatingMatrix'
```

The script provided as a `@script` parameter in the preceding code sample has a few more lines than in previous examples. In a real development environment, the R script is actually developed in **R Studio**, which is a free tool for R scripting that is widely used by R developers. It can be downloaded for free from the internet.

Let's now turn our attention to the R part of the preceding script. Because we are creating a `recommender` model using the `recommenderlab` package, we must first import this package, which is the first line of the R code.

The second step is to adjust the data to fit in the form of a matrix. The first column of the incoming data set contains user identifiers. We will set these as the names of rows using the `rownames()` function. When the line of code that calls the `rownames()` function is executed, we have to remove the column with user IDs, because it is no longer part of the matrix. To do this, we call `InputDataSet[,1] <- NULL;`. `NULL` denotes an empty object and must be written in uppercase, otherwise we'll obtain an R error. The `[,1]` notation refers to the first column of every row. The R language indexes lists starting from 1, not from 0, unlike many other languages.

The `recommender` engine from `recommenderlab` uses matrices in its own particular format. According to the `recommenderlab` documentation, this format is `realRatingMatrix`. The `as` function is a conversion function in R.

After all the preparation tasks are done, we can create the model and then return it to the caller. The last line of the preceding code serializes the processed model using the `serialize()` function, which consumes two parameters. The first parameter is the object to be serialized (the `model` variable in our case) and the second parameter is a provider that takes the serialized model (for example, a file). In this case, however, we just want to serialize the model to a variable and return it as a result set, so the second parameter will be `NULL`. The serialized value must be converted into a `data.frame` to fit into the `OutputDataSet` variable. In this form, we will see the result shown in the following screenshot:

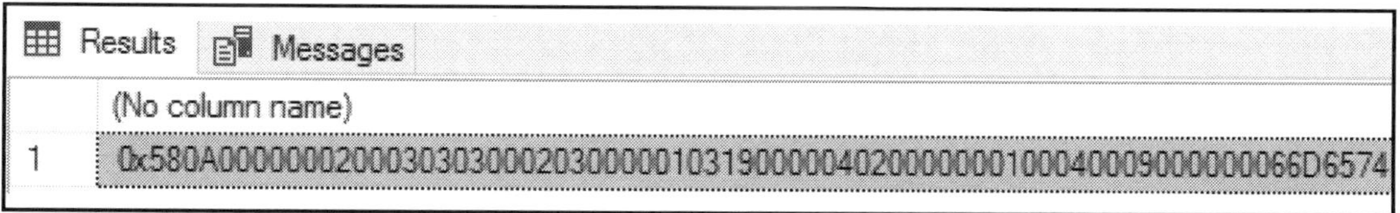

The result of the machine learning model training is serialized as a binary string and returned to the caller as a result set with one row and one column, as we can see in the preceding screenshot. This is the result that we are going to save. The simplest way we can do this is to prepare a temporary table and use the `INSERT..EXEC` statement to save the value of the trained machine learning model to the temporary table. The following script sample adds the preceding sample result to the `#result` temporary table and uses the table for the result of the `sp_execute_external_script` procedure:

```
create table #result (result varbinary(max))

insert #result
exec sp_execute_external_script
    @language = N'R'
    , @script = N'
        #import needed library
        library("recommenderlab");
        #make the first column as a row names in further matrix
        rownames(InputDataSet) <- InputDataSet[,1];
        InputDataSet[,1] <- NULL;
        #create object realRating Matrix
        matrix <- as(InputDataSet, "realRatingMatrix");
        #create the model
        model <- Recommender(matrix, method="UBCF");
        #serialize the model and return it back to a caller
        OutputDataSet <- as.data.frame(serialize(model, NULL));
    '
    , @input_data_1 = N'select * from RatingMatrix'
```

```
select * from #result
```

The last line of the preceding script sample is just used to show that the `#result` table was filled with data.

All that's left now is to complete the preceding batch with the rest of information that is needed to save the new machine learning model version successfully in the database. Two alternatives will be shown in the following sections, corresponding to the two versioning systems that we designed in the previous section.

Saving our machine learning model to filestreams

Saving our machine learning model to the `Models.ModelVersions` table is straightforward. Every new version of the machine learning model is just inserted into the table as a new row. We just need to fill all columns correctly. Let's recall the table's structure:

- `Id`: This column is filled automatically, because it is `IDENTITY`.
- `ModelTypesId`: We must provide the correct value for this column from the list of machine model types that is stored in the `Models.ModelTypes` table.
- `StreamId`: This column will be filled automatically, because we declared a default value.
- `CreationDate`: A default value of the current date and time is declared in this column, so this will also be filled automatically.
- `ModelStream`: This column will be filled with a value from the temporary `#result` table.

As shown in the preceding list, we actually don't need to add any values except for the `ModelTypesId` and `ModelStream` columns. The `ModelTypesId` column must be filled with a parameter value that is obtained from the user, while the `ModelStream` column will be filled from the `#result` temporary table. The complete solution is shown in the following script:

```
create or alter proc Models.procTrainModel
    @modelTypeId int
as
create table #result (result varbinary(max))

insert #result
exec sp_execute_external_script
    @language = N'R'
    , @script = N'
```

```
        #import needed library
        library("recommenderlab");
        #make the first column as a row names in further matrix
        rownames(InputDataSet) <- InputDataSet[,1];
        InputDataSet[,1] <- NULL;
        #create object realRating Matrix
        matrix <- as(InputDataSet, "realRatingMatrix");
        #create the model
        model <- Recommender(matrix, method="UBCF");
        #serialize the model and return it back to a caller
        OutputDataSet <- as.data.frame(serialize(model, NULL));
    '
    , @input_data_1 = N'select * from RatingMatrix'

insert Models.ModelVersions (ModelTypesId, ModelStream)
select @modelTypeId, result from #result
go
```

The preceding sample shows the creation of a stored procedure, `Models.procTrainModel`, with a parameter, `@modelTypeId`. A significant part of the body of the stored procedure is the `sp_execute_external_script` execution, but we are more interested in the edges of the stored procedure. The `@modelTypeId` parameter is used to set which type of machine learning model is being trained. At the beginning of the body, we create the `#results` temporary table. This is followed by the `INSERT..EXEC` construct. The last statement of the stored procedure inserts a new row into the `Models.ModelVersions` table. It's now time to test our work. This can be done as follows:

```
select * from Models.ModelTypes
exec Models.procTrainModel @modelTypeId = 1
select * From Models.ModelVersions
```

The preceding script contains three statements:

- The first `SELECT` statement simply reads all the data from the `Models.ModelTypes` enumeration table. We need to find out the `Id` value of the proper model type as a parameter value in order to execute the stored procedure.
- The value in the `ID` column for the `recommender` model is 1, so the second line of the preceding code sets the `@modelTypeId` parameter's value to 1 as well. When the `Models.procTrainModel` stored procedure is executed, we must check whether a new model version has been added to the `Models.ModelVersions` table.

- The last line of the code in the preceding script should return a row from the `Models.ModelVersions` table. With every repeated execution of the `Models.procTrainModel` stored procedure, another row will appear.

In the following section, we'll look at how to do this using temporal tables.

Saving a machine learning model to temporal tables

The preceding section showed how to store machine learning models in a common table. When we are using temporal tables to provide native versioning of records in a table, we need to be able to control when to add a new row and when to update an existing row. The `INSERT` statement should occur only when no machine learning model exists for a certain `ModelTypesId`. The following code shows a stored procedure that is very similar to the previous one, but with one change at the end of the body:

```
create or alter proc Models.procTrainModelTemporal
    @modelTypeId int
as
create table #result (result varbinary(max))

insert #result
exec sp_execute_external_script
    @language = N'R'
    , @script = N'
        #import needed library
        library("recommenderlab");
        #make the first column as a row names in further matrix
        rownames(InputDataSet) <- InputDataSet[,1];
        InputDataSet[,1] <- NULL;
        #create object realRating Matrix
        matrix <- as(InputDataSet, "realRatingMatrix");
        #create the model
        model <- Recommender(matrix, method="UBCF");
        #serialize the model and return it back to a caller
        OutputDataSet <- as.data.frame(serialize(model, NULL));
    '
    , @input_data_1 = N'select * from RatingMatrix'

if exists(select * from Models.ModelVersionsTemporal where ModelTypesId =
@modelTypeId)
 begin
    update Models.ModelVersionsTemporal
```

```
      set ModelStream = (select top 1 result from #result)
      where ModelTypesId = @modelTypeId
   end
  else
   begin
      insert Models.ModelVersionsTemporal (ModelTypesId, ModelStream)
      select @modelTypeId, result from #result
   end
  go
```

As we can see in the preceding example, the first part of the stored procedure is exactly the same for both cases. When the machine learning model is trained, however, we have to choose whether to insert a new row or to update the existing row. The `if` statement uses the `exists` operator to detect whether a row with a particular machine learning model type already exists. If it does, this is updated, otherwise a new row is inserted. Let's test this solution with the following script:

```
select * from Models.ModelTypes
exec Models.procTrainModelTemporal @modelTypeId = 1
select * From Models.ModelVersionsTemporal
select * From Models.ModelVersionsTemporalHistory
```

The test executed by the preceding script starts by obtaining a value of the `@modelTypeId` parameter from the `Models.ModelTypes` table. Then, the newly-created `Models.procTrainModelTemporal` stored procedure is executed. When the stored procedure is executed for the first time, the result from the `Model.ModelVersionsTemporal` table should have one row, and the result from the historical `Models.ModelVersionsTemporalHistory` table should be empty.

Let's repeat the same test for a second time. How do the results from the `Models.ModelVersionsTemporal` and `Models.ModelVersionsTemporalHistory` tables differ? Take a look at the following screenshot, which shows both results:

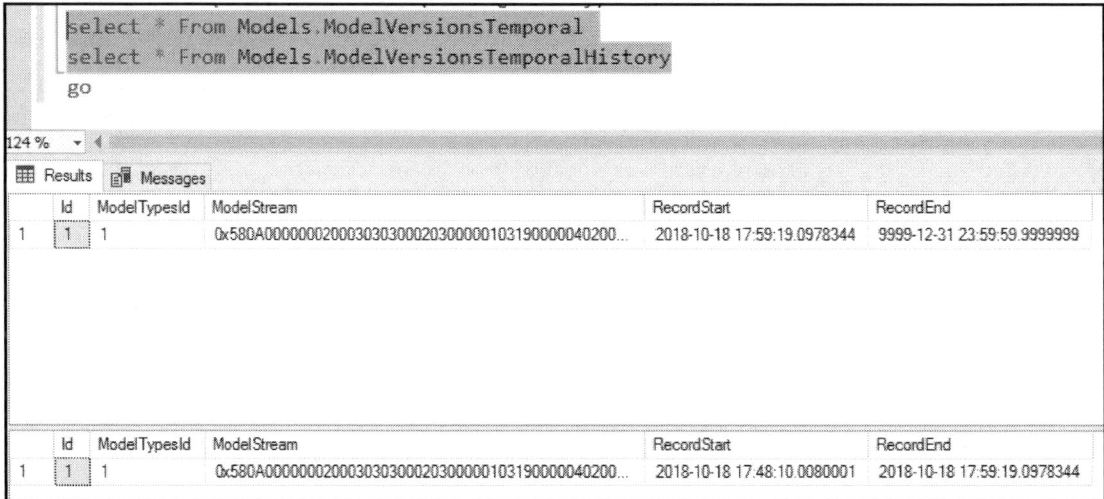

In the current table, `Models.ModelVersionsTemporal` still has just one record, but the history table is no longer empty; it contains a record with the same model of the version before we trained the model for the second time. We can see this by comparing the value of the `RecordStart` column of the current record, which is the upper result, with the value of the `RecordEnd` column of the historical record, which is the lower result. These two values are equal.

Later, when we use trained machine learning models to make predictions, we have two choices regarding how to read the desired version. If we want to use the current version, we just select the record from the current table. If we want to go back to a historical version, we also have to query the current table, but we need to use a new operator to indicate the point in time for which we want to reconstruct the data. This can be done as follows:

```
select *
from Models.ModelVersionsTemporal for system_time as of '2018-10-18 17:50'
```

The preceding query still uses the current table, but the record obtained in the result will be a previous version of the machine learning model stored in the table.

Summary

SQL Server advanced significantly when ML Services was introduced. In this chapter, we used ML Services to train a simple predictive model. Because of the relational nature of SQL Server, we used the R language, which is suitable for predictive modeling.

In the first section, we started by learning how to check whether ML Services is installed and which languages are supported. Having an installation of ML Services is not enough; it must be properly configured in conjunction with a SQL Server instance. We learned how to configure the whole environment for external languages.

In the second section, we created a physical database schema that can be used to maintain trained predictive models. Different versions of predictive models are usually kept for comparison, so we looked at two approaches to carry out machine learning model versioning.

In the third section, we created, trained, and saved a really simple predictive model for movie recommendations. We learned that the trained model has to be serialized and saved into a database as a binary string.

In the next chapter, we will use the machine learning model from this chapter and make predictions on the model.

Questions

1. Which external languages are supported by SQL Server?
   Python and R.
2. Which service must be running for the successful execution of external code?
   SQL Server Launchpad.
3. Can we combine filestreams with temporal tables?
   No, temporal tables do not support the versioning of filestream data.
4. We are calling the following code: `exec sp_execute_external_script @language = 'R', @script = '';`. The script does not work and returns an error. Why?
   Every parameter of the procedure is of the nvarchar data type. All parameter values must start with a leading capital N: `N'text in the parameter'`.
5. We are calling the `sp_execute_external_script` stored procedure. Inside the R script, we have the following line: `Outputdataset <- as.data.frame(1+1);`. The code does not return a result. Why?
   This is because the R language is case-sensitive. The correct casing is `OutputDataSet`.

10
Making Predictions

In the previous `Chapter 9`, *Predictive Model Training and Evaluation,* we created an example of a machine learning model that could provide a movie recommendation based on the movies watched and rated by a user. Predictive models created and stored on SQL Server are used to predict future values or events. This chapter goes through the different options of how to consume prepared predictive models.

This chapter consists of the following sections:

- **Reading models from a database**: In this section, we will learn how to read different versions of predictive models from temporal tables and from common tables. We will then look at how to send the model to an external script.
- **Submitting parameters to an external script**: The prediction itself works with known parameters of the estimated item. This section will show how to correctly declare the parameters for the execution of the external script. We will also look at how to submit parameter values from a database to an external script.
- **Using the `PREDICT` keyword**: This section will demonstrate a new feature of SQL Server 2017: the `PREDICT` keyword. This keyword makes estimations easier when compared to using external scripts.
- **Making the model self-train**: In this section, we will learn how to establish the whole architecture in order to make the model learn with new incoming predictions automatically.

Technical requirements

In order to complete the examples in this chapter, you'll need any edition of the SQL Server 2017. You should also have already completed all the examples from the preceding `Chapter 9`, *Predictive Model Training and Evaluation*, because we will continue using the objects that we created previously here.

Reading models from a database

Predictive models are stored in a database as binary strings. This is the best and the simplest option for a relational database, but the binary string cannot be used in R or Python script directly. When the model has to be used for predictions, it must be queried from a database table in which it is saved and the the model must be transformed back to a format that is suitable for the external script.

In `Chapter 9`, *Predictive Model Training and Evaluation*, we created two alternative database schemas that can be used for the storage and versioning of predictive models. First, we used common tables without any kind of built-in record versioning. These tables the filestreams to store the binary string of the models. Secondly, we used temporal tables, which provide a very native method of record versioning. In this section, we will read the desired versions of the models from both database schemas back to the external script.

The following diagram shows a physical database schema of the objects that are involved in the maintenance of a predictive model:

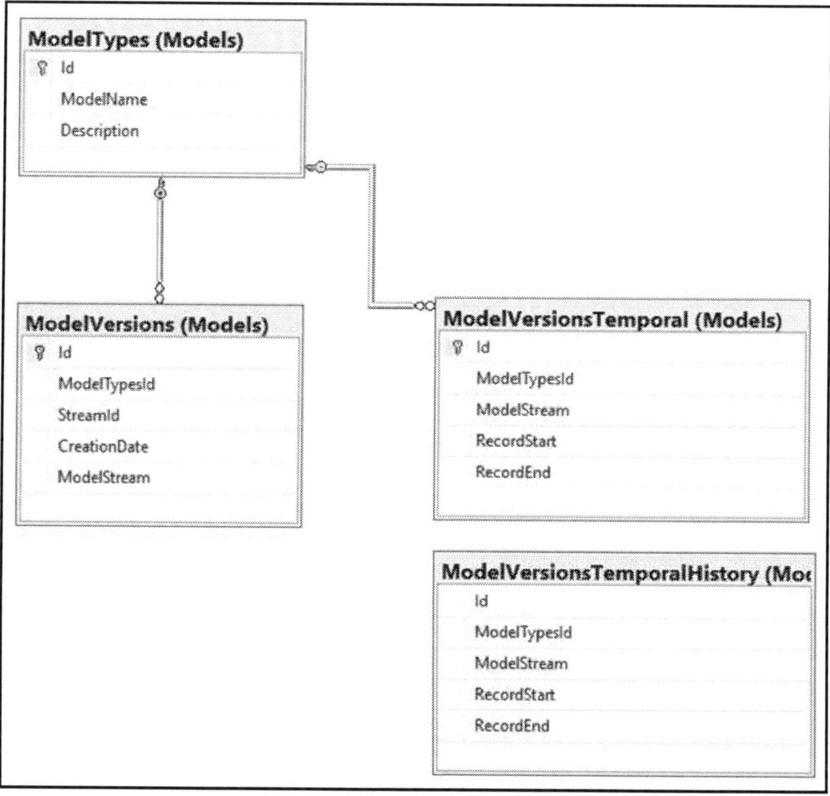

Physical database schema of the objects required for the maintenance of a predictive model

The tables in the physical schema shown in the preceding diagram were created in the previous `Chapter 9`, *Predictive Model Training and Evaluation*. The following list provides us with a reminder of the purpose of each table:

- `Models.ModelTypes`: The preceding physical database schema can be used as a unified solution for many predictive models. This table is a list of all the predictive models that are stored in the database. When a prediction is made, this table is used to choose the right predictive model.

- `Models.ModelVersions`: This table stores all the versions of the trained predictive models. Every record stored in this table is a version of a certain predictive model.
- `Models.ModelVersionsTemporal`: This table also stores all the trained predictive models, but only the latest version of each. When a user wants to use the last version of a trained predictive model, they just query that model type in this table.
- `Models.ModelVersionsTemporalHistory`: This table is used mostly by the SQL Server in a conjunction with the `Models.ModelVersionsTemporal` table. When a predictive model is created, its record in the `Models.ModelVersionsTemporal` table is updated. The SQL Server automatically keeps the track of changes and stores them in this `Models.ModelVersionsTemporalHistory` table.

The `Models.ModelVersions` and the `Models.ModelVersionsTemporal` tables are the same as each other. The following two sections describe how to query for the right version of a certain predictive model using both version management alternatives.

Reading the model from a common table

In this short section, we will use a common table to query for certain predictive model versions. In our example, the `Models.ModelVersions` table will be used. We need to have two parameters: the type of predictive model, and the desired version of the model.

The model type is simply taken from the `Models.ModelTypes` table. Let's execute the following query to review what is in the table:

```
select * from Models.ModelTypes
```

The result of preceding query shows a list of all the predictive models. This will look as follows:

Results | Messages

	Id	ModelName	Description
1	1	Movie Recommender	Sample ML model for movie recommendation based ...
2	2	Price estimation (logistic regression)	An price estimation of new movies based on genre, d...

The preceding screenshot shows two records with different predictive models. In the previous chapter, we looked at how to create the first of these models, the **Movie Recommender**. In real applications, we can offer the result of the preceding query to a user through the GUI of a client application. For our experiments, however, we just need to remember the value of the `Id` column, which, in our case, is the number `1`.

Now, we will select a list of predictive model versions. The `Models.ModelVersions` table contains three columns that are needed for this task: the `ModelTypesId` column, which we will use as a filter, the `CreationDate` column, which holds the time the version was created, and the `Id` column, to identify the predictive model that we want to use later. The following query shows how to obtain a list of model versions:

```
select Id, CreationDate from Models.ModelVersions
where ModelTypesId = 1
order by CreationDate desc
```

The result of the preceding query is shown in the following screenshot:

Results | Messages

	Id	CreationDate
1	3	2018-10-18 10:47:44.7910825
2	2	2018-10-18 10:47:10.5237016
3	1	2018-10-18 10:32:39.1080974

The preceding screenshot shows a list of the `Id` numbers and the creation dates of the model versions sorted in descending order. The list is filtered by the `ModelTypesId` column to obtain a set of predictive models that are trained for certain purposes. The user is likely to opt for the latest version of the model, which is why the list is sorted in descending order.

In the real world, both the preceding queries (the query for model types and the query for the model versions) would probably be covered within a client application. In our case, however, we are working on the database level. When both the preceding queries are executed, we can see that the `Id` of the correct predictive model version is `3`.

We can now read the predictive model definition itself. This is the value of the `ModelStream` column from the `Models.ModelVersions` table. The following simple query returns the stream of the predictive model in a form that is suitable to later be used to make predictions that are calculated with R script:

```
declare @stream varbinary(max) =
    (select ModelStream from Models.ModelVersions where Id = 3)
select @stream as ModelStream
```

The core of preceding script is in the `SELECT` statement used for the initialization of the `@stream` variable. The `SELECT` statement itself returns a result set, but we need to provide the model stream into the R script as a scalar variable, which is why the `@stream` variable was used. The `SELECT @stream as ModelStream` statement in the third line of the preceding script is used just to see what was placed into the variable.

Now, let's leave the result for a moment before using it to make a prediction. First, let's look at a second alternative of how to select the predictive model from a database table. The following section will look at how to use a temporal table for this task.

Reading the model from a temporal table

In the preceding section, we used common database tables that hold predictive model versions to select the desired predictive model stream. In this section, we will do the same task, but using system versioned temporal tables.

The beginning of the task is the same for both alternatives. We will execute the `SELECT * FROM Models.ModelTypes` query to show a list of all the predictive models stored in the database. As in the preceding section, we decide that we want to use the type of model that has an `Id` of 1.

We need to know the times that the model was trained and versioned in order to be able to choose which version of the predictive model will be used. Let's execute the following two queries in order to understand how versions of records are stored and maintained in temporal tables:

```
select Id, RecordStart from Models.ModelVersionsTemporal
where ModelTypesId = 1

select Id, RecordStart from Models.ModelVersionsTemporalHistory
where ModeltypesId = 1
```

The result of the preceding two queries is shown in the following screenshot:

	Id	RecordStart
1	1	2018-10-27 09:36:24.9345244

	Id	RecordStart
1	1	2018-10-18 17:48:10.0080001
2	1	2018-10-18 17:59:19.0978344

The preceding screenshot actually shows two results. The upper result is from the current table, `Models.ModelVersionsTemporal`, and shows only the most recent version of the predictive model. The lower result set is from the `Models.ModelVersionsTemporalHistory` and shows all versions that were caught when the current record was updated. The `RecordStart` column in both results shows the time from which the record was current. Bear in mind that the `Id` column has the same value, even if it is the primary key of the table. This is why it seems like we need to identify the desired version of the predictive model with two parameters from a union of two results sets. The temporal tables provide a special predicate used for a selection of the desired record version. If we want to see all versions of a particular record stored in a temporal table, we can use this predicate, as shown in the following query:

```
select Id, RecordStart
from Models.ModelVersionsTemporal for system_time all
where ModeTypesId = 1
```

The result of the preceding query is shown in the following screenshot:

	Id	RecordStart
1	1	2018-10-27 09:36:24.9345244
2	1	2018-10-18 17:48:10.0080001
3	1	2018-10-18 17:59:19.0978344

If we review the two preceding screenshots, we can see that the records shown are exactly the same. The difference is that in the first of the two preceding examples, we queried two tables, whereas in the second of the two preceding examples, we queried just the current table, `Models.ModelVersionsTemporal`, with the new predicate `FOR SYSTEM_TIME ALL`. The predicate is written into the `FROM` clause directly after the name of the table in the following form: `Models.ModelVersionsTemporal FOR SYSTEM_TIME ALL`.

Let's summarize how to work with the temporal table. If we want to use the recent version of the predictive model, we will query the `Models.ModelVersionsTemporal` table and use a filter of the model type, as shown in the following statement:

```
select ModelStream from Models.ModelVersionsTemporal where ModelTypesId = 1
```

If we do not want the recent version of the predictive model, we will focus on the time when the desired version became valid. This is done as follows:

```
select ModelStream
from Models.ModelVersionsTemporal
   for system_time as of '2018-10-18 17:48:10.0080001'
where ModelTypesId = 1
```

The preceding query will return the second version of the predictive model. Both of the preceding queries will return the desired version of the model stream, which will be later used for prediction. All we need to do is store the stream of the model version to a variable as we did in the preceding section. The following example shows the complete code for this task:

```
declare @stream varbinary(max) =
(select ModelStream
from Models.ModelVersionsTemporal
    for system_time as of '2018-10-18 17:48:10.0080001'
where ModelTypesId = 1)

select @stream as ModelStream
```

We now have the serialized stream of the trained predictive model. We will pass it as a parameter to the R script to make the prediction. The stream is a variable that must be submitted to a `sp_execute_external_script` procedure. The following section will demonstrate how to do this.

Submitting values to an external script

Every time we used the `sp_execute_external_script` stored procedure previously, we used just one dataset as an input. However, we will always need more values to be passed back and forth between the T-SQL and external scripts and we also need to provide variable values as inputs for new predictions. This section will explain how to pass values and records between the SQL Server and external scripts and how to work with them inside the external script.

Submitting values into the external script

The stored procedure, `sp_execute_external_script`, can interact with the rest of the T-SQL batches using parameters. The procedure contains an input parameter called `@params`, which is used to declare parameters and enhances the list of parameters of this stored procedure itself. The declared parameters can then be seen inside an external script. Let's begin with following statement, which shows how to pass a simple parameter into the stored procedure, `sp_execute_external_script`:

```
declare @x int = 1, @y int = 1
exec sp_execute_external_script
    @language = N'R'
    , @script = N'
       print(a + b)
    '
    , @params = N'@a int, @b int'
    , @a = @x
    , @b = @y
```

The preceding script shows how to send parameters from the outer T-SQL batch into the R script. The first line of the preceding script declares two integer variables, called `@x` and `@y`. The value of both variables is set to `1`.

The `@params` parameter of the `sp_execute_external_script` stored procedure contains a string written as a common declaration of T-SQL variables. These variables are then visible as new parameters of the same instance of the `sp_execute_external_script` stored procedure. We can enhance the list of the parameters of the `sp_execute_external_scripts` stored procedure with the `@a` and `@b` parameters that are passed to the `@params` parameter.

Inside the R script, we will use both variables as R variables with the same name, but without the leading `@` symbol. The preceding script will have the following text result:

```
STDOUT message(s) from external script:
[1] 2
```

The preceding example used the `print()` R function, so we get the result of the `1 + 1` expression as a one-member vector, calculated within the R script.

The described technique is used to pass the predictive model in the form of a `varbinary` value, as well as all the other variables that are needed in the R script for the prediction calculation. However, the predictive model in binary form must be deserialized before it is used in the prediction. The following short section will demonstrate how to carry out this deserialization.

Deserializing a predictive model

In the two preceding sections, we left the `varbinary` value of the correctly selected version of the predictive model stored in a database table. It's now time to use the value and pass it into the R script, which will make a prediction on it. Let's remind ourselves of the query we wrote to take the binary stream of the predictive model:

```
declare @stream varbinary(max) =
    (select ModelStream from Models.ModelVersions where Id = 3)
```

We will now combine the preceding query with the execution of the `sp_execute_external_script` stored procedure:

```
declare @tStream varbinary(max) =
    (select ModelStream from Models.ModelVersions where Id = 3)
exec sp_execute_external_script
    @language = N'R'
    , @script = N'
        #code will be written here
    '
    , @params = N'@stream varbinary(max)'
    , @stream = @tStream
```

The preceding script simply sent the obtained stream of the predictive model to the R script. The deserialization of the stream itself is then executed in the R script. The R function for the deserialization is as follows:

```
newModel <- unserialize(as.raw(stream));
```

The preceding R statement is used inside the R script and prepares the model for the prediction. We will reveal how to predict results from the model in the following section.

Making the prediction

In the preceding sections of this chapter, we went through all the steps that are needed to take a predictive model saved into a database table and pass it to an external script. In this section, we will finalize our work and predict recommended movies for a particular user.

The previous section ended with the following script, which queried for a model from the database table, passed it into the R script, and deserialized it:

```
declare @tStream varbinary(max) =
    (select ModelStream from Models.ModelVersions where Id = 3)
exec sp_execute_external_script
    @language = N'R'
    , @script = N'
        newModel <- unserialize(as.raw(stream));
    '
    , @params = N'@stream varbinary(max)'
    , @stream = @tStream
```

The preceding script does not yet have any output. We have to add several lines of code in the script to pass the user ID, calculate the prediction, and return back an output dataset with results.

The recommender model uses an affinity matrix, where the user IDs are row headers and the movie IDs are column headers. Cells in the matrix are filled with ratings from 1 to 10. If a certain user did not rate a particular movie, the cell has a rating of 0.

Throughout this section, we are using the R library, `recommenderlab`. This R library works with matrices and with indexes of matrix cells. For this reason, we need to send not the user ID itself, but its index as a row number. The following script is an enhancement of the preceding script and shows how to query for the user index and how to send it to the R script:

```
declare @tStream varbinary(max) =
    (select ModelStream from Models.ModelVersions where Id = 3)
declare @userId nvarchar(10) = 'u10011'
    , @userIndex int

-- this CTE will create numbered list of user ids, the row number will be
used as -- an user index
;with cte as
(
select userId, row_number() over(order by userId) as rn from RatingMatrix
)
select @userIndex = rn from cte where UserId = @userId
```

```
exec sp_execute_external_script
    @language = N'R'
    , @script = N'
        newModel <- unserialize(as.raw(stream));
    '
    , @params = N'@stream varbinary(max), @userIndex int'
    , @stream = @tStream
    , @userIndex = @userIndex
```

The preceding script has two new variables: `@userId` and `@userIndex`. The value of the `@userId` is known as the **user identifier**. The common table expression `cte` creates a result set with user IDs and row numbers. The row number without any adjustment is the user index. This is because the R language indexes items in lists and matrices starting from 1, not from 0, such as many other languages.

The rest of the prediction is made in the R script. The following example is a full version of the script, which will carry out the following steps:

1. Reconstruct the predictive model
2. Reconstruct the source data
3. Take the user's index and transform it
4. Make the prediction
5. Transform the predicted movie indexes to movie IDs
6. Return the result

```
declare @tStream varbinary(max) =
    (select ModelStream from Models.ModelVersions where Id = 3)
declare @userId nvarchar(10) = 'u10011'
    , @userIndex int

;with cte as
(
select userId, row_number() over(order by userId) as rn from RatingMatrix
)
select @userIndex = rn from cte where UserId = @userId

exec sp_execute_external_script
    @language = N'R'
    , @script = N'
        library(recommenderlab);

        #adjusts the data for the model one more time
        rownames(InputDataSet) <- InputDataSet[,1];
        InputDataSet[,1] <- NULL;
        matrix <- as(InputDataSet, "realRatingMatrix");
```

```
        #takes trained predictive model
        newModel <- unserialize(as.raw(stream));
        #create an matrix of user indexes
        newData <- matrix[userIndex,];

        #PREDICTION
        user <- predict(newModel, newData, n=movieCount, type="topNList");

        #list of predicted movies (their indexes)
        result <- c(as(user, "list"));
        #transforms indexes to movie IDs
        movieIndexes <- as.integer(unlist(result, use.names=FALSE));

        #movie IDs back to an user -> result of the script
        OutputDataSet <-
as.data.frame(colnames(InputDataSet)[movieIndexes]);
    '
    , @input_data_1 = N'select * from RatingMatrix'
    , @params = N'@stream varbinary(max), @userIndex int, @movieCount int'
    , @stream = @tStream
    , @userIndex = @userIndex
    , @movieCount = 5
```

The preceding script prepares data that is then processed in R script. This book will not go into too much detail on R script, but we can see how the dataset and variables are accessed within the R script in this example.

The preceding example is quite complex because we used the external library, `recommenderlab`. We also used the new keyword `PREDICT`, which we will examine in the following section.

Using the PREDICT keyword

SQL Server 2017 introduces the new `PREDICT` function. This function makes prediction computations much simpler than those that are calculated using R or Python languages, which we looked at in the preceding section. However, the `PREDICT` function doesn't work with every model that is trained in the arbitrary R (or Python) library.

When the SQL Server started providing machine learning services, new libraries called `RevoScaleR` for R and `RevoScalePy` for Python were introduced. These libraries contain their own implementation of several predictive algorithms and also offer the ability to process data in parallel.

Using one of these libraries is a prerequisite when we want to use the `PREDICT` function. We must also fulfill the following prerequisites:

- We should use one of following algorithms:
  - `rxLinMod`
  - `rxLogit`
  - `rxBTrees`
  - `rxDtree`
  - `rxForest`
  - `rxFastTrees`
  - `rxFastForest`
  - `rxLogisticRegression`
  - `rxOneClassSvm`
  - `rxNeuralNet`
  - `rxFastLinear`
- We should serialize the generated model using the `rxSerializeModel` function.

For a complete list of prerequisites and other details, consult the following link: `https://docs.microsoft.com/en-us/sql/advanced-analytics/real-time-scoring?view=sql-server-2017`.

Let's make a very simple linear regression model to learn how the `PREDICT` function works. Our example will go through the following steps:

1. Data and structure preparation
2. Model training and saving
3. Using the `PREDICT` function

The first step is used to prepare data. We will use the same data structures for model versioning and maintenance:

1. We will insert a new model type to the `Models.ModelTypes` table. This can be done as follows:

```
insert Models.ModelTypes values ('Sample linear regression', 'Model
used for a demo of PREDICT function')
select scope_identity() as NewModelTypeId    -- should be 3
```

The preceding `INSERT` statement will add a record to the list of model types and then return the new primary key value of the new record. We then need to prepare a table with sample data.

2. The table that we are going to use is called `dbo.DemoData` and it consists of the columns `MaritalStatus`, `Gender`, `TotalChildren`, and `YearlyIncome`. The script file `ADD URL` for creating the table with the data can be found at the GitHub repository for this book. When the table is created, it will look as follows:

	MaritalStatus	Gender	TotalChildren	YearlyIncome
1	M	M	2	90000.00
2	S	M	3	60000.00
3	M	M	3	60000.00
4	S	F	0	70000.00
5	S	F	5	80000.00
6	S	M	0	70000.00

The table `DemoData`, several records of which are depicted in the preceding screenshot, contains roughly 12,000 records. We want to estimate someone's yearly income, depending on their marital status, their gender, and the number of children they have.

3. When the data is prepared, we can train, serialize, and save the model. This is done as follows:

```
declare @model table (model varbinary(max))
insert @model
exec sp_execute_external_script
    @language = N'R'
    , @script = N'
        formula <- YearlyIncome ~ MaritalStatus + Gender +
TotalChildren;
        model <- rxLinMod(formula, data = InputDataSet);
        #summary(model);
        OutputDataSet <- as.data.frame(rxSerializeModel(model,
realtimeScoringOnly = TRUE));
    '
    , @input_data_1 = N'select * from DemoData'

insert Models.ModelVersions (ModelTypesId, ModelStream)
select 3, model from @model
```

The preceding script defines a table variable, `@model` and takes the results of the `sp_execute_external_script` stored procedure. The result of this stored procedure is a trained predictive model, which is serialized as a binary string and then inserted to the `Models.ModelVersions` table created in a previous chapter. The `3` constant used in this insertion is actually the `ModelTypesId` that was generated during the preparation of the data in the previous step.

Remember that the predictive model and the serialization function that we use are from the `RevoScaleR` library. As a reminder, we can use the following simple naming rule: when a function starts with the `rx` prefix, this means it is from the `RevoScaleR` library.

4. We are now going to carry out the final step, in which we are going to make a prediction from the model. This can be done as follows:

```
DECLARE @model varbinary(max) =
    (SELECT ModelStream from Models.ModelVersions where
ModelTypesId = 3);

WITH newData as (
    SELECT * FROM (values('S', 'F', 1), ('S', 'F', 0))
    as t(MaritalStatus, Gender, TotalChildren)
)
SELECT d.*, p.*
FROM PREDICT(MODEL = @model, DATA = newData) WITH(YearlyIncome_Pred
float) as p
```

The preceding script starts with an `@model` variable declaration. This variable is populated with the binary string of the predictive model. The common table expression, `newData`, defines a result set that is made up of the row constructors for two people. The row constructor is the `VALUES` part of the common table expression. Even though the set of data is created from row constructors or by another query from base tables, it is fundamental to keep the column names or aliases the same as the column names that were used for the model training.

We are making a prediction based on a linear regression model, so we are trying to estimate how much yearly income a person has depending on their marital status, gender, and number of children. For this reason, all of the incoming parameters (`MaritalStatus`, `Gender`, and `TotalChildren`) must be present in the dataset. The result of the `newData` common table expression is then passed as a `DATA` parameter to the `PREDICT` function. The second `MODEL` parameter is populated with the predictive model stored in the `@model` variable. The `WITH` clause at the end of the statement defines the columns for predicted value.

Linear regression models predict the value of dependent variables. The dependent variable in this case is `YearlyIncome`, so the output column will have the name `YearlyIncome_Pred`. The result of the preceding query will look as follows:

Results | Messages

	MaritalStatus	Gender	TotalChildren	YearlyIncome_Pred
1	S	F	1	51477.862764408
2	S	F	0	47382.0030340915

The preceding screenshot shows the results of the `SELECT` statement using the `PREDICT` function. The first three columns contain data that is used as input, while the last column, `YearlyIncome_Pred`, contains the predicted values. The numbers may not be very accurate in this example, as this linear model was just used to show how the `PREDICT` function works.

Using the `PREDICT` function, we can easily make real-time predictions. There are many situations in which an incoming data member has to be scored on-the-fly. However, it is important to bear in mind that not every predictive model can be calculated using the `RevoScaleR` library.

Every predictive model should be trained repeatedly because new data points are valuable inputs in order to make our model more precise. In the next section, we will learn how to make the predictive model self-training.

Making the predictive model self-training

One of the common myths about machine learning and predictive models is that they are naturally self-learning, which means that they can re-calculate themselves automatically based on every prediction made. This is not actually true; re-training a predictive model can be very time-consuming. In this section, we'll go through two tips about how to execute regular re-calculation of a predictive model.

Re-calculating a predictive model regularly

In the previous `chapter 9`, *Predictive Model Training and Evaluation*, we created a stored procedure called `Models.procTrainModel`. Let's briefly remind ourselves about what the stored procedure does. It is used to train a movie recommendation model based on user ratings of movies. The stored procedure takes source data and executes the calculation of the recommender machine learning model. The trained model is then saved by this stored procedure into a base table and, for the moment, the model is not refreshed. The calculation should be made by the stored procedure regularly because new records with user ratings are added to the database constantly and users continually change their preferences. If the predictive model is not recalculated, it becomes inaccurate. When data comes to a database regularly, with roughly the same amount of records every day, for example, the simplest way to recalculate the model is to execute the training of the stored procedure regularly, such as once a week.

Every instance of the SQL Server, except for the SQL Server Express edition, contains a service called the **SQL Server Agent**. The SQL Server Agent service is supposed to be used for planning, execution, and monitoring of a wide range of routine tasks, such as database backups, index maintenance, or database consistency checks. Every planned task is called a **job**. A job is a named container that is usually defined in the Management Studio. It can consist of **job steps** and might also contain **schedules**. A job step is a unit of work that might be an SQL script, the execution of an SSIS package, or a PowerShell script. When a job contains job steps, these form a sequence of actions to be executed. Schedules, on the other hand, define the times at which jobs have to be executed. The following step-by-step example shows how to define a job for the regular re-calculation of our recommender model.

A new job can be created from the **Object Explorer**. The pop-up menu is depicted in the following screenshot. When we want to create a new job, we'll just right-click on the **Jobs** node and we'll select the first **New Job...** option:

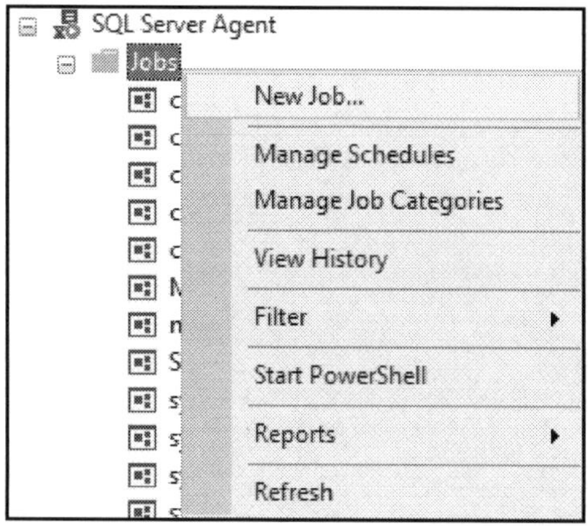

When we click on **New Job...**, a new dialog window opens, in which we can define a job. The **New Job** window is shown in the following screenshot:

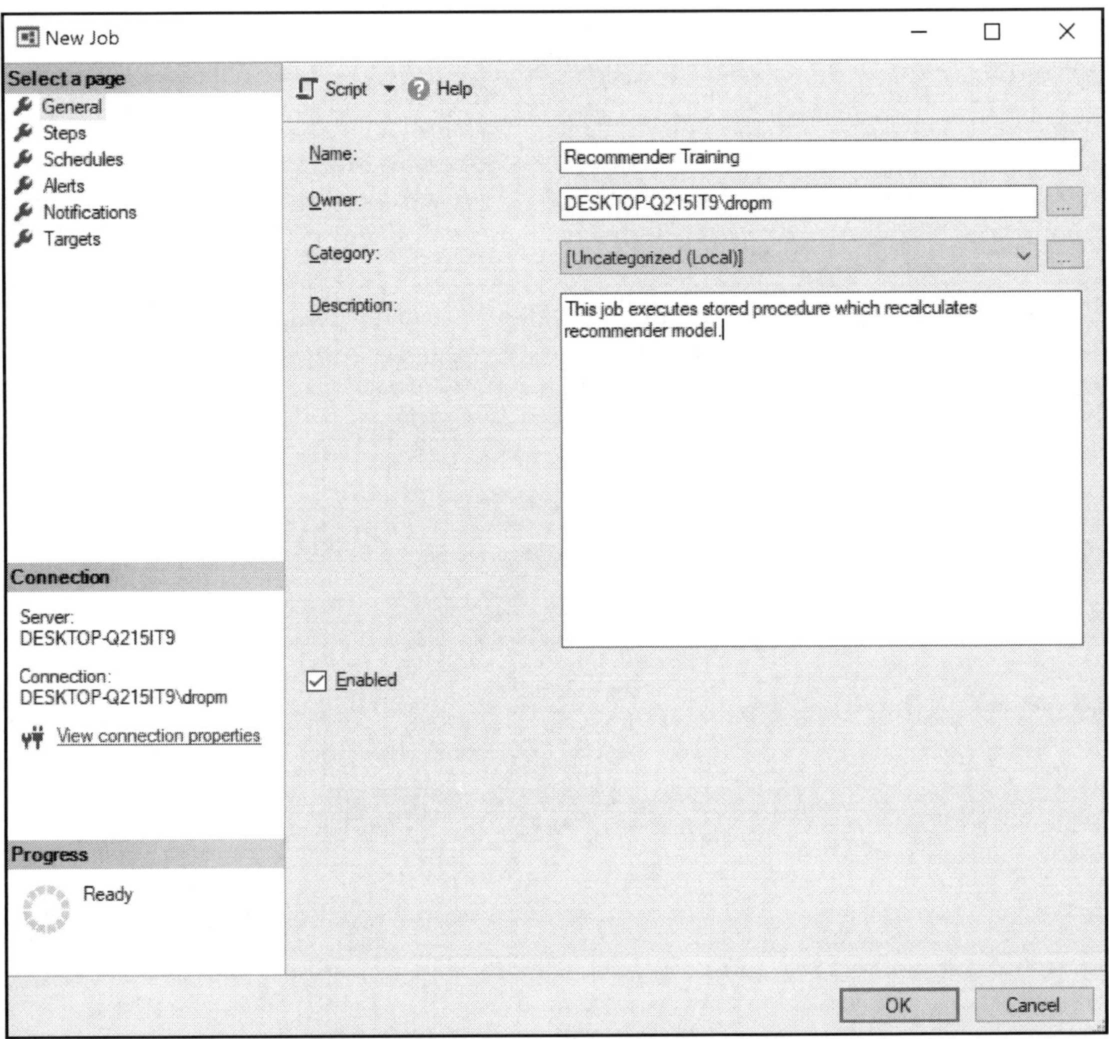

The **General** page of the **New Job** window contains several basic fields. For our purposes, the only mandatory field is the **Name**. In our case, we have named our job `Recommender Training`. We can also choose to categorize jobs using the **Category** drop-down list or fill the **Description** field, but neither of these two controls has an impact on the function of the job.

Once we have finished with the **General** page, we can move on to a page called **Steps**. This page contains a list of defined steps. We can start a new job step using the **New...** button at the bottom of the **Job step list**. The **Steps** page looks as follows:

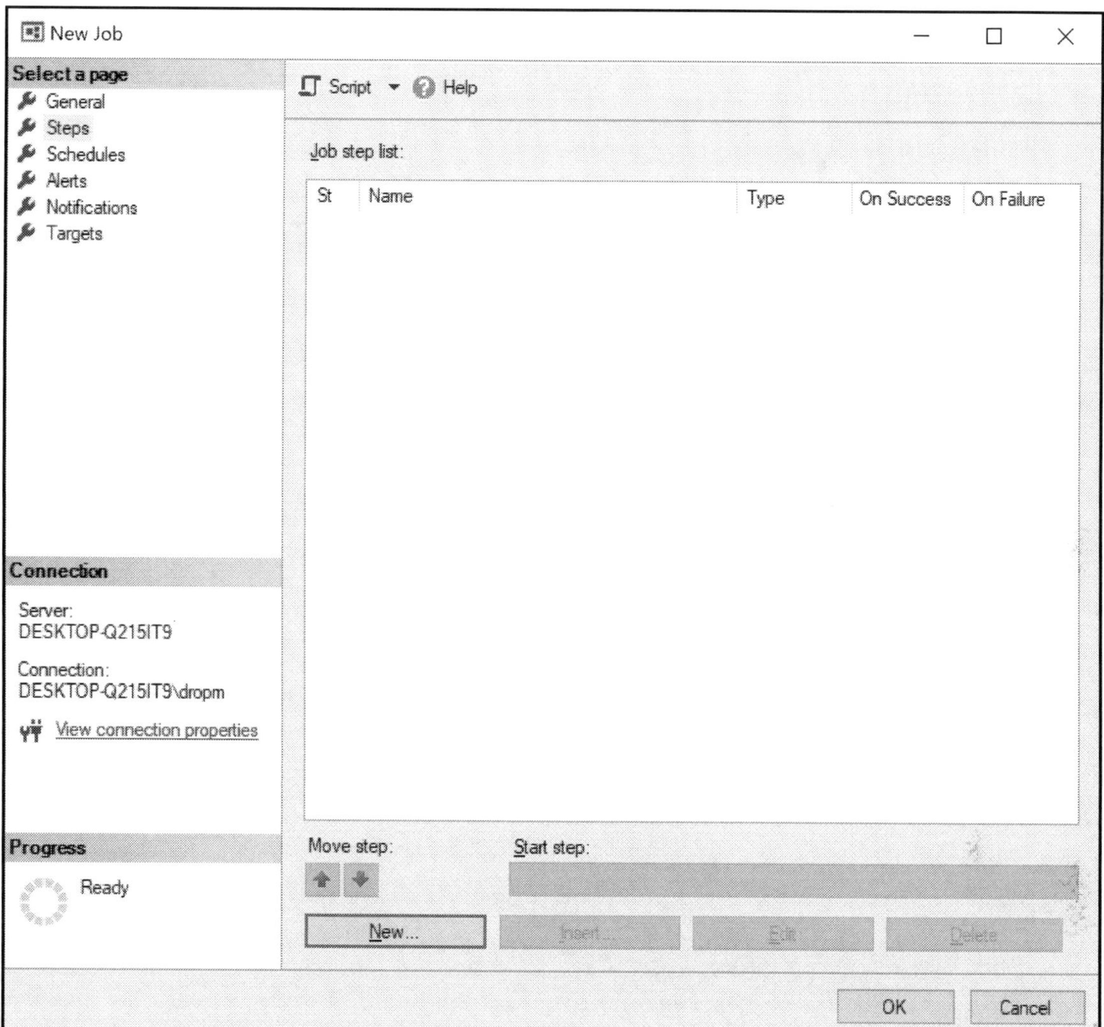

The preceding screenshot shows an empty job step list. When the **New...** button is clicked, a second dialog box opens. This looks as follows:

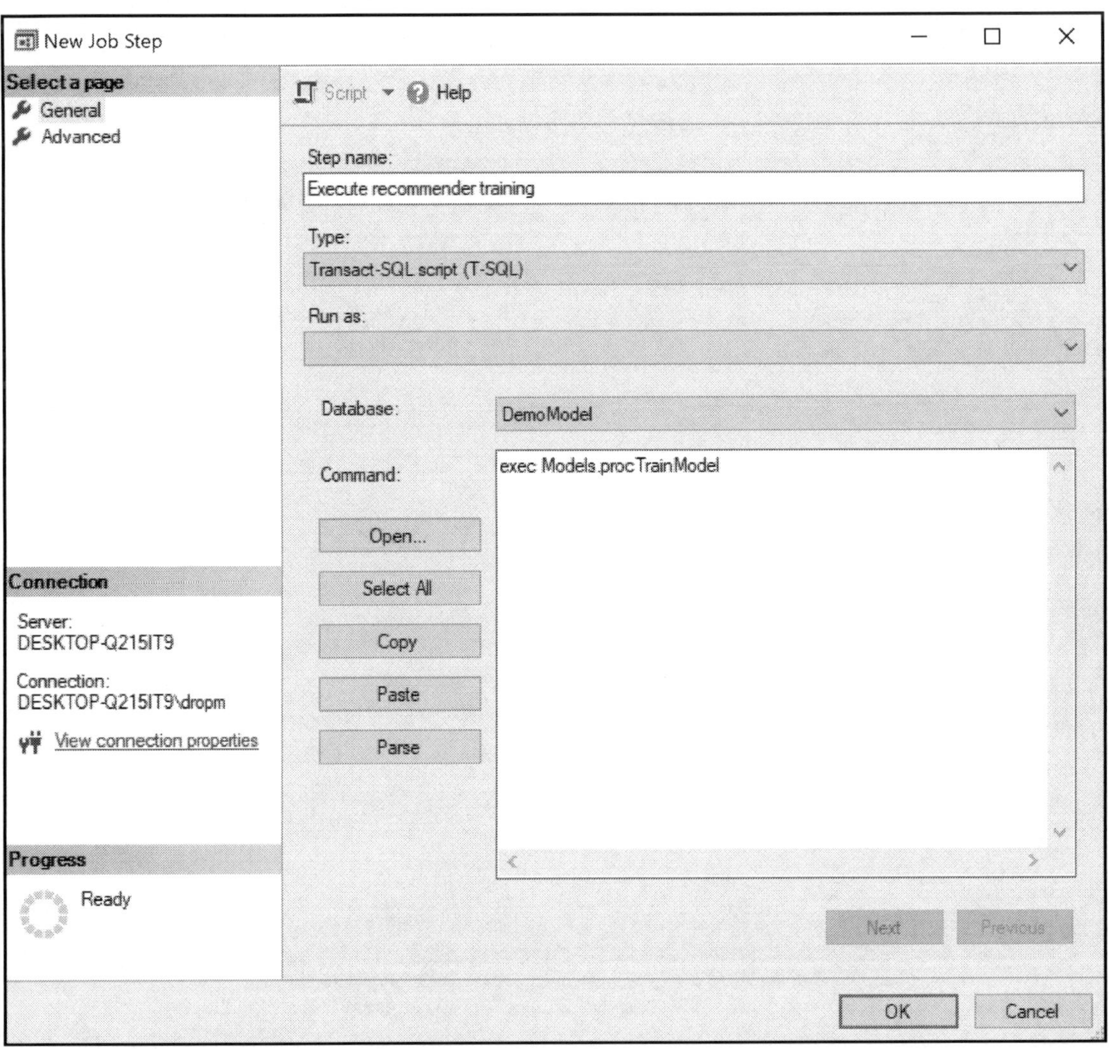

The preceding screenshot shows the **New Job Step** dialog box with the **Step name**, **Type**, **Database,** and **Command** fields already filled. The **Step name** field is mandatory and contains a descriptive name of the job step. This name is used in the diagnostic window **Job History**. The **Type** drop-down list is used to select the type of the job step, which, in our case, is **Transact SQL Script (T-SQL)**.

The **Database** drop-down list shows a list of all the databases on the instance of SQL Server; here, we have selected the **DemoModel** database. Last, but not least, however, is the **Command** field. This field is used to define a script to be executed. In the preceding screenshot, you can see that we have entered the `exec Models.procTrainModel` statement.

When at least one job step is defined, we can continue on to the **Schedules** page of the **New Job** dialog. The **Schedules** page contains a list of created schedules and looks very similar to the **Steps** page. The **Schedules** page also has a **New...** button, which is used to define a new schedule. When the **New...** button is pushed, the **New Job Schedule** dialog box is opened. This looks as follows:

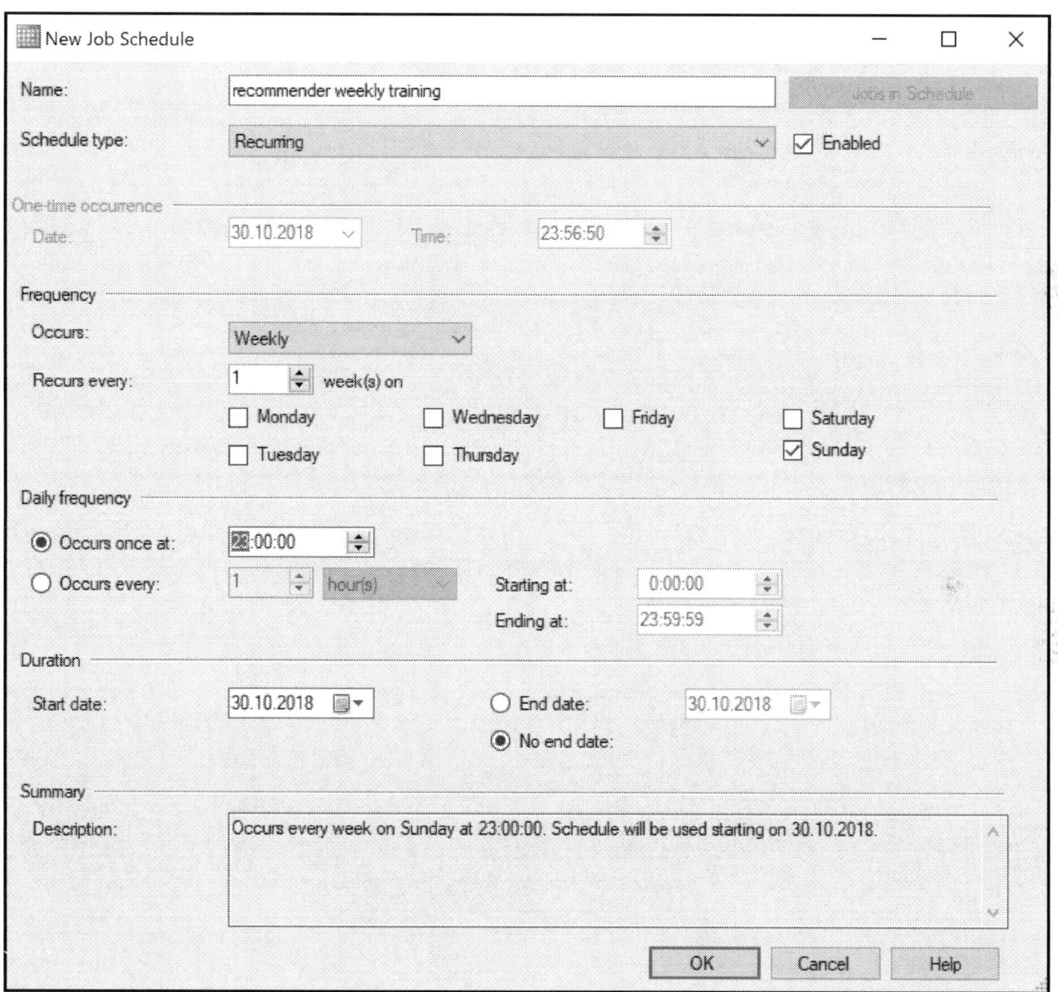

As the preceding screenshot shows, the **New Job Schedule** dialog box can be used to define a typically recurring schedule for a particular repeating pattern. If a more complicated job execution plan is required (for example, if we plan to execute a particular job every day at 8 a.m. apart from Sunday, when we want to execute it every 3 hours), we need to define two schedules. In our case, however, we just need to calculate the new model version once a week. As you can see in the preceding screenshot, we have filled the **Name** field and the **Schedule type** field in the header. We have also selected an option from the **Occurs** drop-down list in the **Frequency** section and from the **Occurs once at** field in the **Daily frequency** section.

We need to fill in the preceding three pages of the **New Job** dialog box to create a job, to define its steps, and to schedule it to execute on a recurring basis. We can also define a type of notification in case the job fails, but job notifications are mainly used by database administrators, so this isn't necessary for our purposes.

When the job is successfully created, we can see it in a list of all the jobs in the Object Explorer. This is shown in the following screenshot:

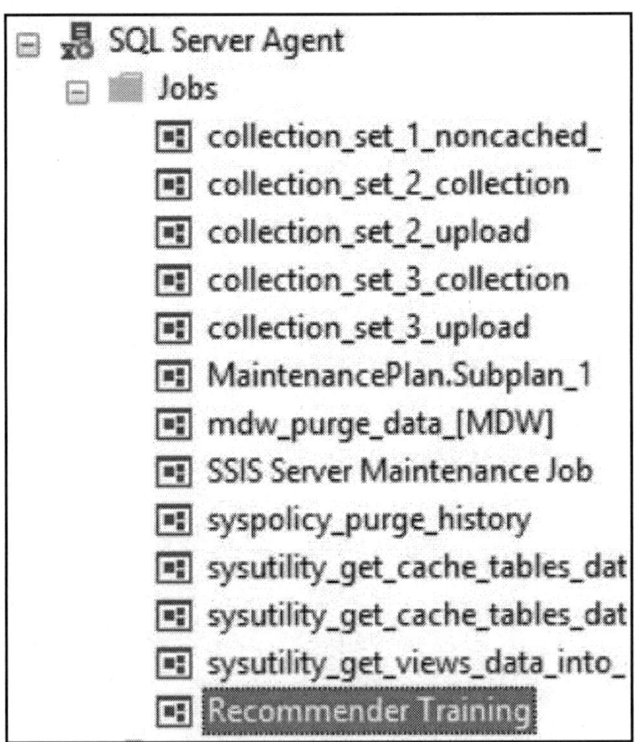

From here, we can right-click on the name of the job, and either start the job manually, edit it, or view its history. The job history is a diagnostic window showing all the executions of a particular job, including the results of the execution. If a job fails, we can look for error messages or other information in the **Log File Viewer** window, which is shown in the following screenshot:

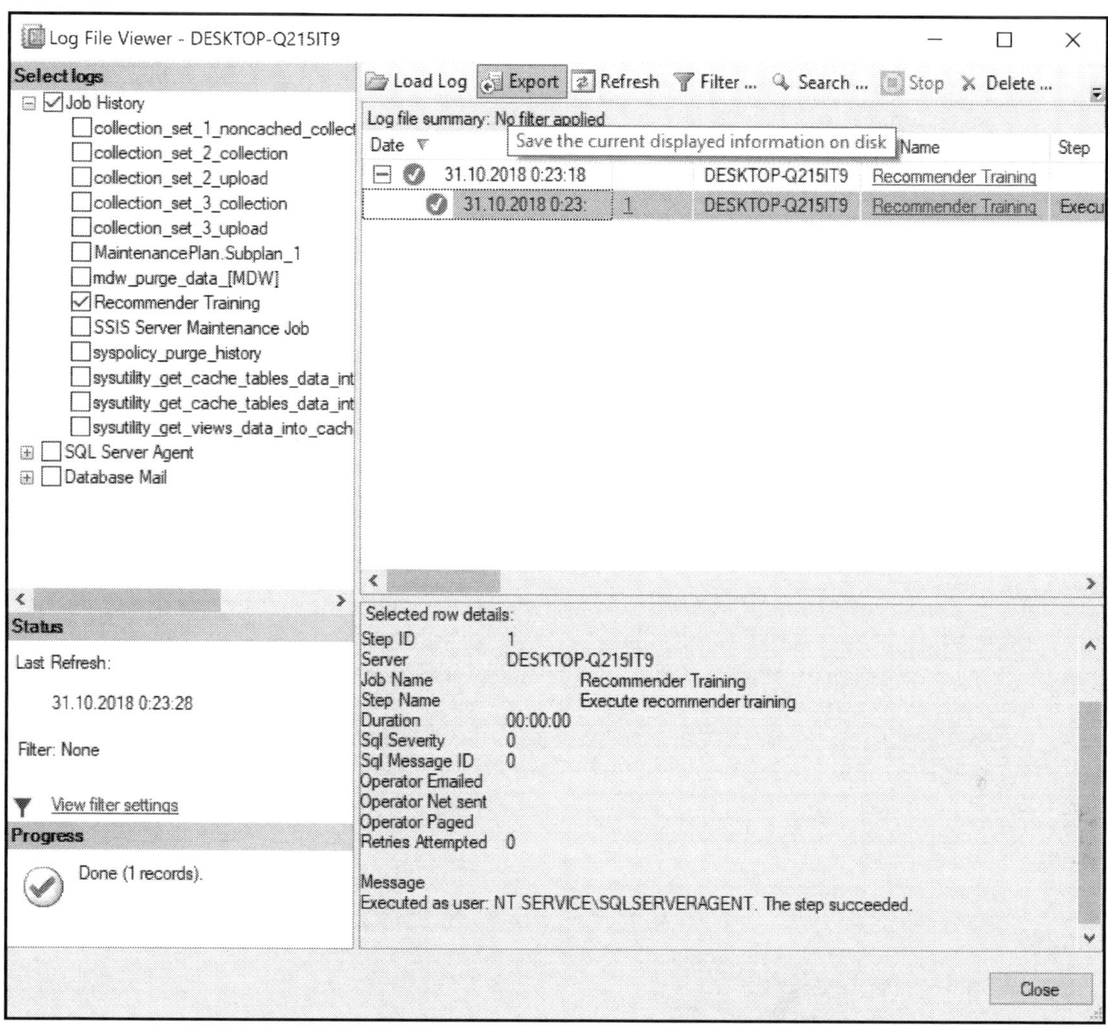

Checking for errors in in the Log File Viewer window

The preceding screenshot shows the **Log File Viewer** window with the details of the successful `Recommender Training` job execution. In the first row of the upper list, we can see an overview of the whole execution, while the second row of the upper list contains detailed information about the results of the job steps. The bottom part of the window shows information related to the selected row. In the preceding screenshot, we can see a final message that states that the step succeeded.

Using SQL Server Agent jobs is very straightforward, but we can also plan to recalculate the model based on data growth. In the following section, we will show how to develop a conditioned re-calculation based on a change in the record count.

Re-calculating a predictive model asynchronously

Sometimes, it's not beneficial to carry out model re-calculation at regular time intervals because data comes in at random times and quantities. Instead, we can recompute the model every time the amount of data changes significantly. In other words, we can track the record count at the moment when the model was trained last time and compare this to the record count at the moment when the new row arrives. When the difference between last record and the current record count becomes, for example, 10 %, we can execute the model training.

The model training is often quite a long-running task, so we cannot allow the prediction to wait until the training has completed. The SQL Server offers a feature called a **service broker**. This feature is completely built-in to a database, so we are not required to install or configure additional software. It can be used in many different asynchronous scenarios. In our case, the execution of the training of the recommender model will be started from the stored procedure to make a prediction, but the prediction itself will return its result immediately without the waiting for the new version of the recommender model.

To use the Service broker, we need to develop the following objects:

- **Message type**: This defines the format of a message sent from one service to the other. This might be any valid XML, an XML of a certain XML schema, or an empty message.
- **Contract**: This defines the type of messages that can be sent from an initiator service to a target service and vice-versa.

- **Queue**: This is an object in which sent messages are queued to later be processed by a service program.
- **Service**: This is a definition that states which contract has to be placed with which queue.
- **Service program**: This is typically a stored procedure that takes and processes messages sent to a queue.

In the following sections, we are going to create all of these objects.

Creating a message type

The message type is a simple definition of the format of the messages sent between the initiator and target services. The message type is often an XML definition. The message type is used to start the training calculations and can contain any valid information. The following script shows how to create a new message type:

```
create message type AsyncTrainingRequest validation = well_formed_xml
```

The preceding code creates new message type that can be any valid XML. Our message type is used for one purpose only. Using this message type, we will send a message asking for the recommender model to be trained again.

In more complex service broker applications, we often need more message types, but the stored procedure that will be created later in this example does not require the results of the training. This is why only one message type is required to send the training request later on. Message types are grouped into contracts, which we will explore in the following section.

Creating a contract

Contracts are used to define which message types can be sent by a source service broker service, which message types can be sent back from a target service broker service, and which message types can be sent by both service broker services. The following short script shows how to define a contract:

```
create contract AsyncTrainingContract
(
AsyncTrainingRequest sent by initiator
)
```

The preceding code shows the definition of a contract with only one message type, `AsyncTrainingRequest`, which can be sent by the **initiator**—the source service broker service. In our example, we only need to send one message and the initiator will be the procedure that calculates the predictions. Even if we need to send only one message, we still need to define the contract.

When message types are defined and ordered in the contract, we can continue to create queues and services.

Creating queues and services

The service broker service is a definition that waits for messages of the proper message type. Incoming messages are placed into a queue. In all service broker applications, the communication flows between two services, so we need two services and also two queues, even if we are just sending a request for the training of the recommender model without expecting any response.

The following script creates two queues and two services:

```
-- the queue and the service to which requests for training come
create queue TrainingResponseQueue

create service TrainingResponseService
on queue TrainingResponseQueue (AsyncTrainingContract)

-- the queue and the service from which requests for training depart
create queue TrainingRequestQueue

create service TrainingRequestService
on queue TrainingRequestQueue
```

The preceding script shows how to create queues and services. The first queue, called `TrainingResponseQueue`, will be used as a target queue for the requests of the recalculation of the recommender model. The service, `TrainingResponseService`, is built on `TrainingResponseQueue`. This service is an endpoint for incoming requests. In the preceding script, we can see that the `TrainingResponseService` service allows that only messages defined within `AsyncTrainingContract` can enter the queue. If a message of a different type is received, an error will occur.

The `TrainingRequestService` and `TrainingRequestQueue` objects created with the preceding script are used as a starting point of the training requests.

We have now created all the request objects. The following section shows how to initiate a conversation between services, and how to send a message in the conversation.

Sending a request to train a new model

All objects created in the preceding sections are used together to establish and maintain asynchronous dialogs. To start the dialog, we have to execute the `BEGIN DIALOG` statement. We can then send a message using the `SEND` statement. The whole script for starting a conversation and sending a message is as follows:

```
-- unique identifier of the conversation
declare @conversation_handle uniqueidentifier;

-- dialog is started between two services
begin dialog conversation @conversation_handle
from service TrainingRequestService
to service 'TrainingResponseService'
on contract AsyncTrainingContract
with encryption = off;

-- message is sent to the new conversation
send on conversation @conversation_handle
message type AsyncTrainingRequest('<TrainingRequest/>');
```

The preceding script consists of three parts:

1. The first part is just a declaration of an `uniqueidentifier` variable, `@conversation_handle`. This variable is used to catch the conversation identifier. This identifier is used in bigger service broker solutions, where we might have more parallel conversations running between two services.
2. The second part of the script is the dialog invocation itself. The syntax of the `BEGIN DIALOG` statement needs two services (which are the options `FROM SERVICE` and `TO SERVICE`) and also a contract defined between these services.

3. The third part of the preceding script, beginning with the `SEND` keyword, is used to create and send the message from one service to the other. The conversation in the `SEND` statement is identified by the `@conversation_handle` variable. The message itself is any valid XML encapsulated into the previously created message type, `AsynctTrainingRequest`. Once the message is sent from the initiator service (`TrainingRequestService`) to its target service (`TrainingResponseService`), the message is placed into an outgoing queue and the SQL Server tries to send the message to the target queue defined by the target service. In other words, the SQL Server takes all the responsibility of delivering the message delivery. This is a very useful feature.

In the following section, we will look at how target services can process incoming messages.

Consuming requests and sending responses

Messages placed into a queue have to be processed. In order to process a message, we can use the following script:

```
DECLARE
    @conversation_handle uniqueidentifier
    , @msgBody xml
    , @msgType sysname;

receive top (1)
@conversation_handle = conversation_handle,
@msgBody = CAST(message_body AS XML),
@msgType= message_type_name
from TrainingResponseQueue

if @msgType = N'AsyncTrainingRequest'
begin
    end conversation @conversation_handle;
    exec Models.procTrainModel
end
```

The preceding script shows how to take an incoming message from the queue and how to process it. In our example, the `RECEIVE` statement takes the next message and saves its attributes into the prepared variables. The conditional `IF` statement tests if the message is of the expected type. If it is, the body of the `IF` block starts to process the request. Usually, the information from the `@msgBody` parameter is used to read the data of the request and process it as needed. In our sample, however, because we are using automated training, the only statement executed within the `IF` statement is the `END CONVERSATION` statement. This indicates that the dialog has finished correctly. The training of the recommender model is placed in the `IF` statement. The content of the `IF` block is actually the execution of the stored procedure, `Models.procTrainModel`, that we created in the previous chapter.

The request processing is not automated by default. If we want that the incoming message to be processed immediately, we must encapsulate the preceding script into a stored procedure and then configure the service activation on the queue. The following script creates a stored procedure, `Models.procTrainModelAsync`, which contains the script from the preceding sample:

```
create proc Models.procTrainModelAsync
as
DECLARE
    @conversation_handle uniqueidentifier
    , @msgBody xml
    , @msgType sysname;

receive top (1)
@conversation_handle = conversation_handle,
@msgBody = CAST(message_body AS XML),
@msgType= message_type_name
from TrainingResponseQueue

if @msgType = N'AsyncTrainingRequest'
begin
    end conversation @conversation_handle;
    exec Models.procTrainModel
end
go
```

The preceding script simply surrounds the processing of the service broker request in a stored procedure. This is because the following script, which shows how to automate the processing of the incoming request processing, needs just the name of the stored procedure:

```
alter queue TrainingResponseQueue
    with activation
    (
      status = on,
```

```
        procedure_name = Models.procTrainModelAsync,
        max_queue_readers = 1,
        execute as self
    )
go
```

The preceding statement adds the automatic activation of the processing to the queue to which requests are sent. The ACTIVATION block stipulates that the automatic activation calls the Models.procTrainingModelAsync stored procedure, and that the stored procedure will be executed just once at a time (this is the MAX_QUEUE_READERS option). Automatic activation can be disabled by setting the STATUS option to OFF.

We are now almost finished with our example. The following section will test the whole solution.

Testing the asynchronous solution

The preceding sections created the objects needed for the service broker. These objects were then used for sending and processing the training request. In the previous section, we automated the processing. Now, let's test if everything works as expected. First of all, we need to enhance the script that is used to make predictions:

```
declare @tStream varbinary(max) =
 (select ModelStream from Models.ModelVersions where Id = 3)
declare @userId nvarchar(10) = 'u10011'
 , @userIndex int

;with cte as
(
select userId, row_number() over(order by userId) as rn from RatingMatrix
)
select @userIndex = rn from cte where UserId = @userId

exec sp_execute_external_script
 @language = N'R'
 , @script = N'
 library(recommenderlab);

 #adjusts the data for the model one more time
 rownames(InputDataSet) <- InputDataSet[,1];
 InputDataSet[,1] <- NULL;
 matrix <- as(InputDataSet, "realRatingMatrix");

 #takes trained predictive model
 newModel <- unserialize(as.raw(stream));
```

```
    #create an matrix of user indexes
    newData <- matrix[userIndex,];

    #PREDICTION
    user <- predict(newModel, newData, n=movieCount, type="topNList");

    #list of predicted movies (their indexes)
    result <- c(as(user, "list"));
    #transforms indexes to movie IDs
    movieIndexes <- as.integer(unlist(result, use.names=FALSE));

    #movie IDs back to an user -> result of the script
    OutputDataSet <- as.data.frame(colnames(InputDataSet)[movieIndexes]);
    '
    , @input_data_1 = N'select * from RatingMatrix'
    , @params = N'@stream varbinary(max), @userIndex int, @movieCount int'
    , @stream = @tStream
    , @userIndex = @userIndex
    , @movieCount = 5

-- request for the retraining
declare @conversation_handle uniqueidentifier;

-- dialog is started between two services
begin dialog conversation @conversation_handle
from service TrainingRequestService
to service 'TrainingResponseService'
on contract AsyncTrainingContract
with encryption = off;

-- message is sent to the new conversation
send on conversation @conversation_handle
message type AsyncTrainingRequest('<TrainingRequest/>')
```

The preceding script looks quite long, but don't be afraid! It is just a script for providing a recommendation of movies. The last part, starting with the comment `request for the retraining`, is the message that is sent as a request between the service broker services.

When the preceding script is executed, the prediction will work as usual, so the user will receive the result immediately. However, behind the scenes, the `TrainingResponseService` has been activated and the training of the recommender model has started. After a while, we can query the `Models.ModelVersion` table created in the preceding chapter and we will see a new version of the recommender model.

Summary

Our goal in this chapter was to make predictions using trained predictive or machine learning models. In the first section of this chapter, we learned how to select the right version of the predictive model. We used the two models of versioning described in `Chapter 9`, *Predictive Model Training and Evaluation*. In the second section, we learned that we need to provide data and parameters from the T-SQL part of the SQL Server to external scripts. We looked at how to pass parameters to the external script executed by the `sp_execute_external_script` stored procedure. We also explored how to consume results from the stored procedure.

In the third section, we discussed the use of the `PREDICT` keyword as an alternative to the predictions calculated by external scripts. In this section, we also considered the limits of the `PREDICT` keyword. In the final section, we joined our work on training and making predictions together. Many people believe that machine learning models are self-learning, but this is not actually the case. For this reason, we created two alternatives of automated predictive model training using SQL Server Agent jobs and using the lesser-known service broker service.

In the next `Chapter 11`, *Getting It All Together – A Real-World Example*, we will offer an overview of the many techniques learned throughout this book. We will also look at how to make different elements cooperate with each other.

Questions

1. Which predicate can be used when we are looking for the proper version of record in a temporal table?
   We can use the `FOR SYSTEM_TIME` predicate written directly after the temporal table name used in a `FROM` clause of the query.
2. Which parameter of the `sp_execute_external_script` is used to define the parameters passed into the external script?
   This is the `nvarchar` parameter, which is called `@params`.
3. What do we need to do with a model stream sent to the `sp_execute_external_script` stored procedure?
   We need to deserialize it.

4. Does the `PREDICT` function work on any predictive model?
   No, this function works only with models that are calculated using predictive functions that start with the `rx` prefix.
5. Which service is needed for regular model retraining?
   The SQL Server Agent. This service is present with any commercial instance of the SQL Server. We should ensure that the service is automatically started and that it is running correctly.
6. Which type of SQL Server Agent object is used to define the regular retraining of a model ?
   A job.

11
Getting It All Together - A Real-World Example

The previous chapters in this book taught us how to use particular technologies or features within or outside of SQL Server, but this chapter is going to be different. We will use some of the technologies and features described earlier, and we will also build an entire predictive solution. This chapter will guide us through the following sections:

- **Assignment and preparation**: First of all, we need to know the topic of our real-world example. We also need to prepare the environment for further work. This section is all about the assignment of the project and its preparation tasks.
- **Data exploration**: Our projects already have data saved into a relational database. In this section, we will explore what the data contains, how reliable the data quality is, and we'll develop a statistical summary of the data
- **Data transformation**: Based on the Data exploration section, we will probably see a need for some transformations. We will develop set of transformations to reach the best possible quality of data.
- **Training and using predictive models**: During all of the sections of this chapter, we will get to know our data even better. During this section, we will build the final predictive model and use it for predictions.

Technical requirements

To work on examples provided in this chapter, we'll need the following tools:

- SQL Server of any edition with machine learning services installed
- SQL Server Data Tools for SQL Server Integration Services examples
- R Studio for R scripts

You can find, and download, all the solutions, scripts, and projects used in this chapter on GitHub at `https://github.com/PacktPublishing/Hands-On-Data-Science-with-SQL-Server-2017/tree/master/CH12_Real_World_Example`.

Assignment and preparation

Our real-time example will be used to show some simple predictions made as regression models built at the top of a data gathered by a very small virtual cellphone service provider. We want to estimate how many text messages and voice calls a new customer will make. This will help us to recommend a proper prepaid service plan to the new customer.

Our prediction will be based on the knowledge that we will put into our predictive model. The results of the prediction will be very approximate because the amount of data is rather small and the model will also have a very limited set of input parameters.

Before we start to develop anything, we will need to set up a basic environment. The following section will briefly suggest the necessary configurations for the success of our project.

SQL Server

Before beginning development, we need to configure, or even review, our existing environment. First of all, we will need an instance of SQL Server with machine learning services installed and configured. We will not install external packages into the machine learning services instance, so the only configuration property that needs our attention is the `external scripts enabled` property. For its configuration, use the following script:

```
exec sp_configure 'external scripts enabled', 1
go
reconfigure
go
```

The preceding script executes the `sp_configure` stored procedure to set the configuration option to the enabled state, and the `RECONFIGURE` statement sets the option's value without a need to restart the whole service. In this particular case, the `RECONFIGURE` statement is not sufficient because the SQL Server Launchpad service also needs to restart, so we must restart the whole SQL Server.

The `sp_configure` stored procedure can be called even if the `external scripts enabled` configuration option is already enabled.

After the SQL Server configuration, we can check whether everything is working as expected. The following call executes an empty R script:

```
exec sp_execute_external_script
    @language = N'R'
    , @script = N''
```

The preceding script, when executed in Management Studio, should end with a `Commands completed successfully` message. If not, we have to troubleshoot the whole installation of machine learning services using Microsoft's documentation.

When the environment is configured correctly, we can start to describe the data we have at our disposal.

Data description

The structure of the source data in our project is very simple. The following screenshot shows the physical schema of tables contained within the `Phones` database:

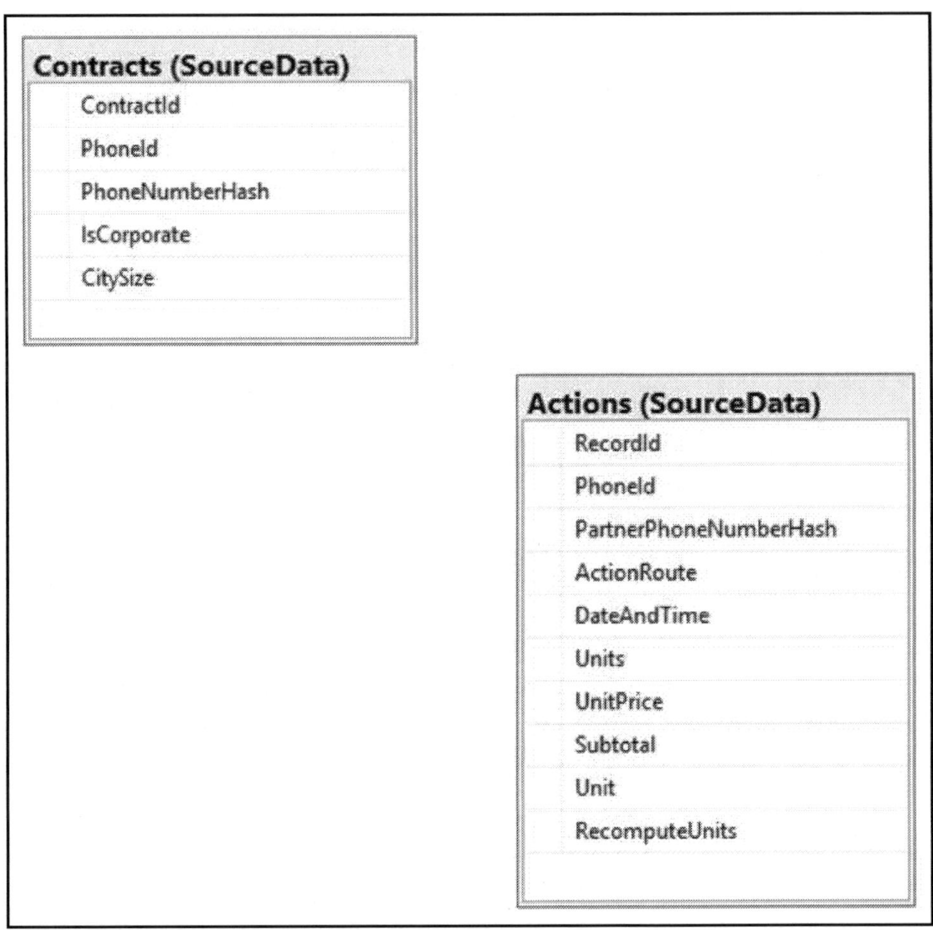

Tables present within the Phones database

The whole physical schema of the source data is placed into a database called `Phones`. It is then placed within a database schema called `SourceData`. The `SourceData` schema contains just two tables:

- `SourceData.Contracts`: This table stores records about customers of the virtual cellphone service provider. The table consists of the following columns:
    - `ContractId`: This column should be an identifier of a record in a table, but no uniqueness is declared on the column
    - `PhoneId`: This column should be an identifier of every phone that belongs to a certain contract
    - `PhoneNumberHash`: This column originally contained phone numbers, but these values are hashed to mask real values to maintain the privacy of phone users
    - `IsCorporate`: This column is a bit flag that determines whether the phone number is used as a work phone or a private phone
    - `CitySize`: This column contains a number of citizens living in the city where the phone is registered
- `SourceData.Actions`: This table stores records describing every single action made by a phone user. Actions can be voice calls or text messages. The table has the following columns:
    - `RecordId`: This column is the identifier of each record, but no primary key or other unique constraint is declared upon this column.
    - `PhoneId`: This column should be a reference to a `PhoneId` column in the `SourceData.Contracts` table, but a foreign key is not declared to enforce the reference.
    - `PartnerPhoneNumberHash`: This column contains masked (hashed) phone numbers that receive the text message or the voice call.
    - `ActionRoute`: We must explore the meaning of values in this column.
    - `DateAndTime`: This describes the timestamp of the text message or the voice call.
    - `Units`: This is the amount of measured units spent by the action (for instance, seconds of a phone call).
    - `UnitPrice`: This is the price of one unit.
    - `Subtotal`: This column contains a result of the `Units * UnitPrice` expression.

- `Unit`: This is the unit of the number stored in the `Units` column.
- `RecomputeUnits`: This column contains a bit flag that states whether the unit should be recomputed. For instance, voice calls are stored in the `Units` column in seconds, but the length of the voice call is later shown on receipt in hours and minutes.

As can be seen in the preceding screenshot, both tables miss primary keys, and the reference between these tables is also missing. We don't know the quality of the data, so although we think that the `ContractId` column in `SourceData.Contracts` is unique, we are not sure. In addition to this, we don't know the statistics and data distribution of columns in the `SourceData.Actions` table. Consequently, our next step is to explore data, ensure its quality, and normalize the data. The following section will demonstrate several data-exploration techniques.

Data exploration

Data exploration is an extremely important task in every data science or machine learning project. Without good knowledge of the data, we'll never succeed with our further predictive models. In this section, we will show you how to explore data using T-SQL queries, the SSIS Data Profiling Task, and a simple R function.

Exploring data using T-SQL

For simple data exploration, we can use T-SQL queries. Here, we will explore the uniqueness of values in columns where we estimate the uniqueness, a quality of reference between the `SourceData.Contracts` and `SourceData.Actions` tables, and also a rate of NULLs in several columns.

First of all, let's query both tables to obtain a sample of data and the structures of the tables. The following queries will achieve this:

```
select top 10 * from SourceData.Contracts
select top 10 * from SourceData.Actions
```

The results of the preceding queries show the first 10 rows of each table. The result is shown in the following screenshot:

	ContractId	PhoneId	PhoneNumberHash	IsCorporate	CitySize
1	1	1	1328503222	1	1294513
2	1	2	1248926897	1	1294513
3	23	3	681368751	1	290450
4	1	4	1445844406	1	1294513
5	1	5	1595609291	1	1294513
6	1	6	1595609337	1	1294513
7	1	7	1595609327	1	1294513
8	1	10	-637527709	1	1294513

	RecordId	PhoneId	PartnerPhoneNumberHash	ActionRoute	DateAndTime	Units	UnitPrice	Subtotal	Unit	RecomputeUnits
2	1003391	99	-1976227780	O	2015-10-22 18:22:03.000	558	1.00	9.30	min	1
2	1003392	99	-998728767	O	2015-10-22 19:36:35.000	1	1.00	1.00	pc	0
2	1003393	99	617461899	O	2015-10-23 08:39:42.000	60	1.00	1.00	min	1
2	1003394	99	-445253439	O	2015-10-23 08:45:02.000	211	1.00	3.52	min	1
2	1003395	99	-1977016082	O	2015-10-23 10:03:04.000	259	1.00	4.32	min	1
2	1003396	99	878980539	O	2015-10-23 11:17:58.000	123	1.00	2.05	min	1
2	1003397	99	1473068696	O	2015-10-23 14:11:58.000	159	1.00	2.65	min	1
2	1003398	99	-1251071485	O	2015-10-23 16:27:03.000	60	-1.00	0.00	min	1

Queries presenting the first 10 rows of each table

The preceding screenshot shows the sample results of both queries. The first result contains records from the `SourceData.Cotracts` table. We can see that the `ContractId` column is not unique, but the `PhoneId` column probably could be unique. Other interesting information could be hidden in the values of the `CitySize` column. So, what is the distribution of data in this column? We will answer this question shortly.

The second part of the preceding results shows a sample of records from the `SourceData.Actions` table. This table offers units of text messages and time units of voice calls. We should interpret values in the `Units` column correctly. When the value in the `Units` column is 1 and the `Unit` column has a **piece** (**pc**) value, it is a text message. When the `Units` column contains a bigger value, for instance 211, and the `Unit` column contains the *min* value, it looks like some kind of timespan of a voice call. 211 minutes of a voice call probably doesn't make sense, but in conjunction with the `RecomputeUnits` column containing a bit flag marking some need of recalculation of the value in the `Units` column, the 211 value seems like the time spent by the voice call in seconds. Let's try to divide 211 by 60. The result of this is roughly 3.52. As indirect proof of the meaning of the relationships between values, we can take a look at the `UnitPrice` and `Subtotal` columns. The `UnitPrice` for the record with the 211 value of `Units` is just 1.00.

The Subtotal price is 3.52, and this is the price of the whole call. This is exactly the same value as the value calculated using the 2111/60 expression. Consequently, it is very probable that the `Units` column contains the length of a call measured in seconds.

Let's summarize the knowledge that we have obtained so far:

- Text messages are always 1 pc with a definite price
- Voice calls are measured in seconds, but the price of each call is calculated in minutes
- The `RecomputeUnits` column could be used as an indicator of voice calls
- `PhoneId` and `RecordId` should be identifiers of records in tables used in the model

We've got a very useful, but not sufficient, overview of our source data. Now we have to perform more detailed observations. We are going to test both tables for the uniqueness of the `PhoneId` and `RecordId` columns. The following queries are will prove the uniqueness:

```
select PhoneId
from SourceData.Contracts
group by PhoneId
having count(*) > 1

select RecordId
from SourceData.Actions
group by RecordId
having count(*) > 1
```

When the results of the preceding queries are empty, the uniqueness of `PhoneId`, or `RecordId` respectively, is proven. Now we can ask whether it is feasible to declare primary keys upon these columns. Unfortunately, a straightforward answer does not exist here, but we can determine a rule for it. If source data tends to be static with no further changes and uploads of new records, we can modify source-data structures directly. But when we expect that the source data will grow or change over time, or its structure could change in the future, we should keep the source-data structure intact and create a staging copy of the source data. For the task that we are resolving in this chapter, we can expect changes in data and also in structure, so we could create new tables that are very similar in structure to our `SourceData.xxx` tables, but with primary keys and foreign key between them. However, for the sake of simplicity, we will use the `SourceData` schema objects as a final object with the data of our interest.

Before we create primary keys and other constraints, we should check for NULL occurrences in the candidate key and also in other columns. The test for nullability is very simple. We'll just write queries that should return zeros as a result. The following query shows an example of the nullability test:

```
select count(*)
from SourceData.Contracts
where PhoneId is null

select count(*)
from SourceData.Actions
where RecordId is null

select count(*)
from SourceData.Actions
where Units is null
```

The preceding code block shows three queries testing how many records contain `NULL` in the `PhoneId` (the `SourceData.Contracts` table), `RecordId`, and Units (both in `SourceData.Actions`) columns. All testing queries are very simple; they count the amount of records in which a certain column used in the `WHERE` clause contains `NULL`. In our project, every column is filled correctly because the source system is very accurate.

The last of the tests that will be made using T-SQL queries is a query that is looking for records that are not paired between both tables. The following code sample shows the query:

```
select a.RecordId
    , c.PhoneId
from SourceData.Actions as a
    full join SourceData.Contracts as c on c.PhoneId = a.PhoneId
where a.RecordId is null
    or c.PhoneId is null
```

The preceding query will return roughly 2,800 records. Many of the records will contain the `RecordId` value while `PhoneId` is `NULL`, but some of the records at the end of the result will contain `PhoneId` without a value in the `RecordId` column. Records with a non-empty `PhoneId` column value represent phones for which no action is recorded. In contrast, records with `ActionId` without `PhoneId` are bad records where we don't know for which phone the action was recorded. We can lose both types of odd records we can lose because the amount of records is quite small, and we also do not have a method for replacing missing records with meaningful substitutions. However, this test showed that a foreign key cannot be created between both tables because of records in the `SourceData.Actions` table, which don't belong to a certain phone number in the `SourceData.Contracts` table.

With the tests we made so far, we can make first adjustments in the database schema. We will create primary keys to ensure that we can always uniquely identify records in both tables. At the same time, we will not create foreign key constraints because the relationship between tables is not fully correct. For the creation of primary keys, we will use the following script:

```
alter table SourceData.Actions
add constraint pk_Actions primary key (RecordId)

alter table SourceData.Contracts
add constraint pk_Contracts primary key (PhoneId)
```

For better exploration of data, we want a more statistical overview. We can still use T-SQL queries, however, but for a fast and efficient overview, we can also use SSIS and its Data Profiling Task. We will explain how to use this in the following section.

Exploring data using the SSIS Data Profiling Task

In this section, we'll define a very simple SSIS package with two Data Profiling Tasks: one for the `SourceData.Contracts` table, and a one for the `SourceData.Actions` table. The results of both Data Profiling Tasks will show a distribution of data, missing values in data, and so on. For this part of data exploration, we need to create a new SSIS project in Visual Studio. We are going to create a new project with the following steps:

1. Open Visual Studio.
2. Go to the **File - New...** menu and select the **Project** option.
3. The **New Project** dialog appears. Select the project template named **Integration Services Project**.
4. Give the name **Phones** to the project, select a location for the project, and then click the **OK** button.

When the preceding steps are complete, the new SSIS project is created with one empty package, called `Package.dtsx`. We'll rename this package to `DataProfiling.dtsx` in `Solution Explorer`. When the project is prepared, we'll drag **Data Profiling Task** from **SSIS Toolbox** and place it in the `DataProfiling.dtsx` designer. The task is renamed to **Contracts Profile**. The following screenshot shows the state of the created project with an empty task:

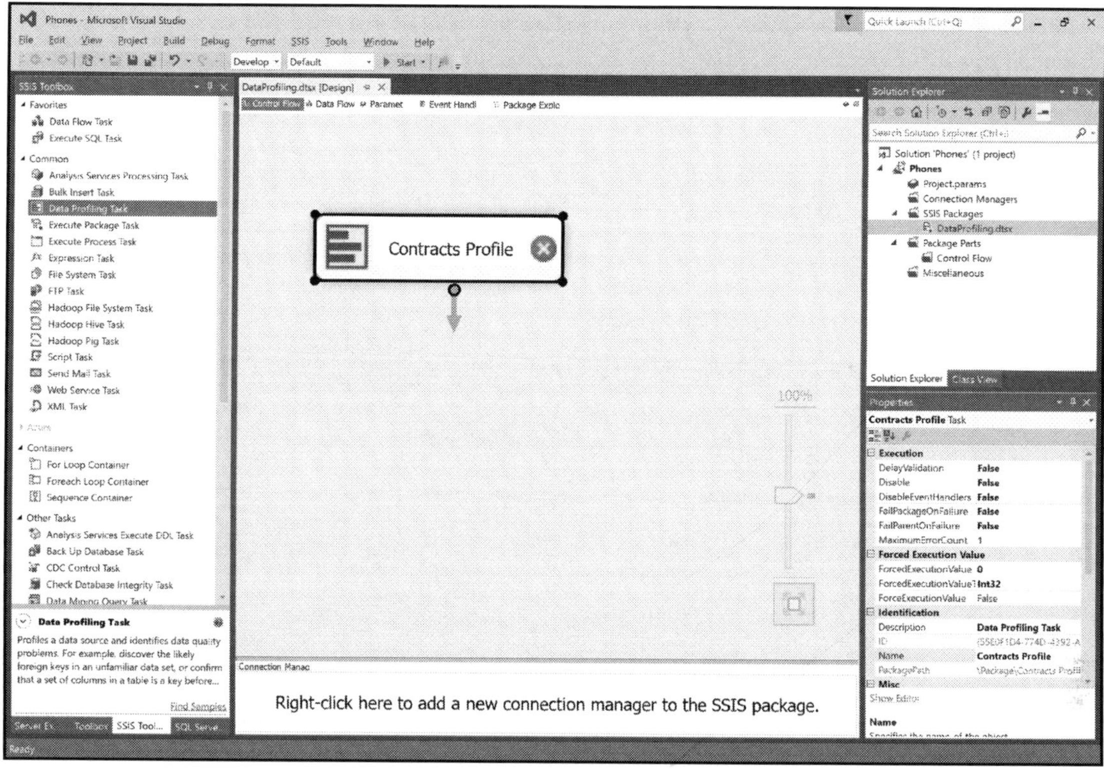

Screenshot depicting the state of the created project with an empty task

The preceding screenshot shows Visual Studio with the **SSIS Toolbox** on the left side and the not-yet-configured Data Profiling Task renamed to **Contacts Profile**. We can also review the result of all the steps from the procedure that describe how to create and prepare a new SSIS project.

The Contracts Profile task contains the red mark, which means that the task needs to be configured. The configuration of the task consists of two parts:

- **A destination for the data profile results**: This an XML file and we have to set its location on disk
- **Profile requests**: A set of data-profile definitions

When the task is double-clicked, a dialog, which is shown in the following screenshot is opened:

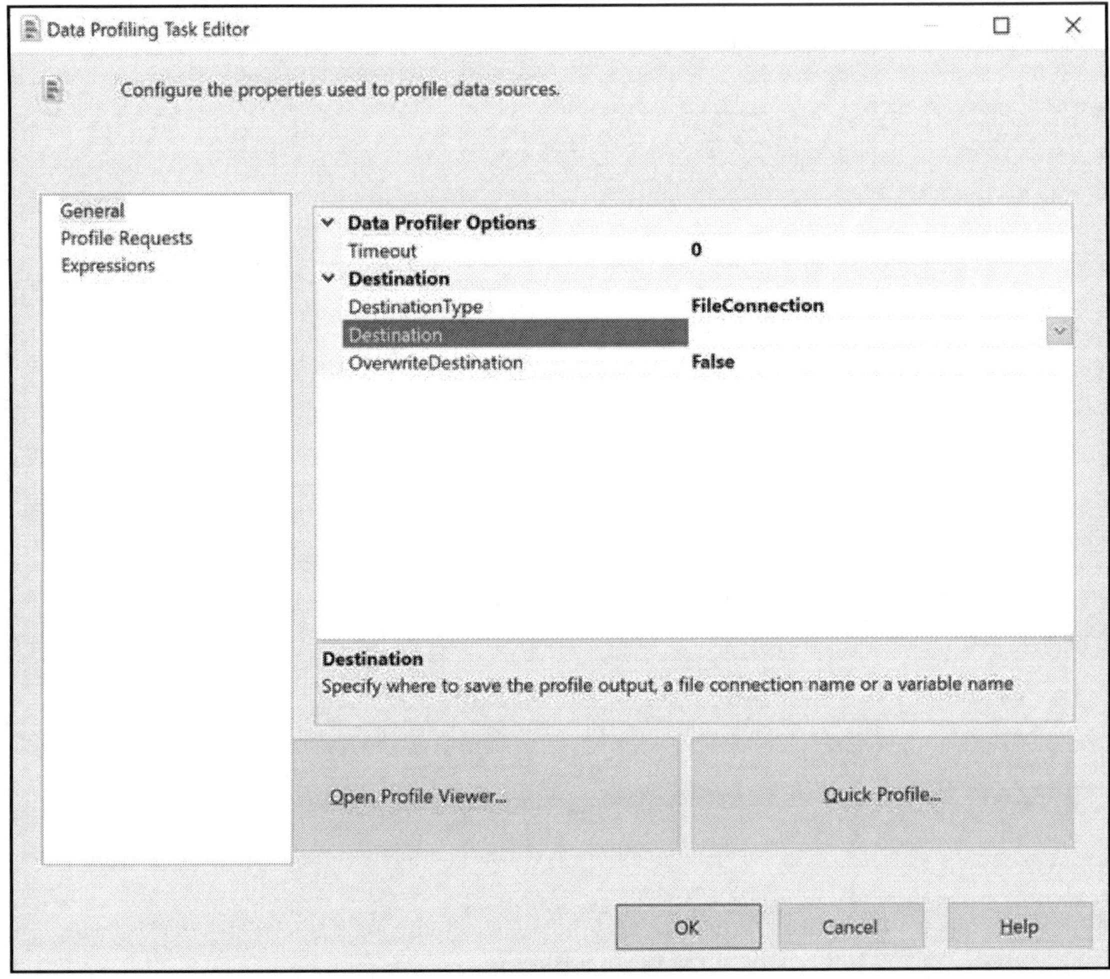

Data Profiling Task editor

The **Data Profiling Task Editor** in the preceding screenshot consists of three pages. The **General** page is used to configure the **Destination**. This is a file location with profiling results. The **Destination** property is selected in the preceding screenshot. When the drop-down button is clicked, an empty list with the **<New file connection...>** option is collapsed. We will use this option to define an arbitrary path to a filesystem.

Then we will define profile requests. The following screenshot shows the **Profile Requests** page of the **Data Profiling Task Editor** with the first profile request defined:

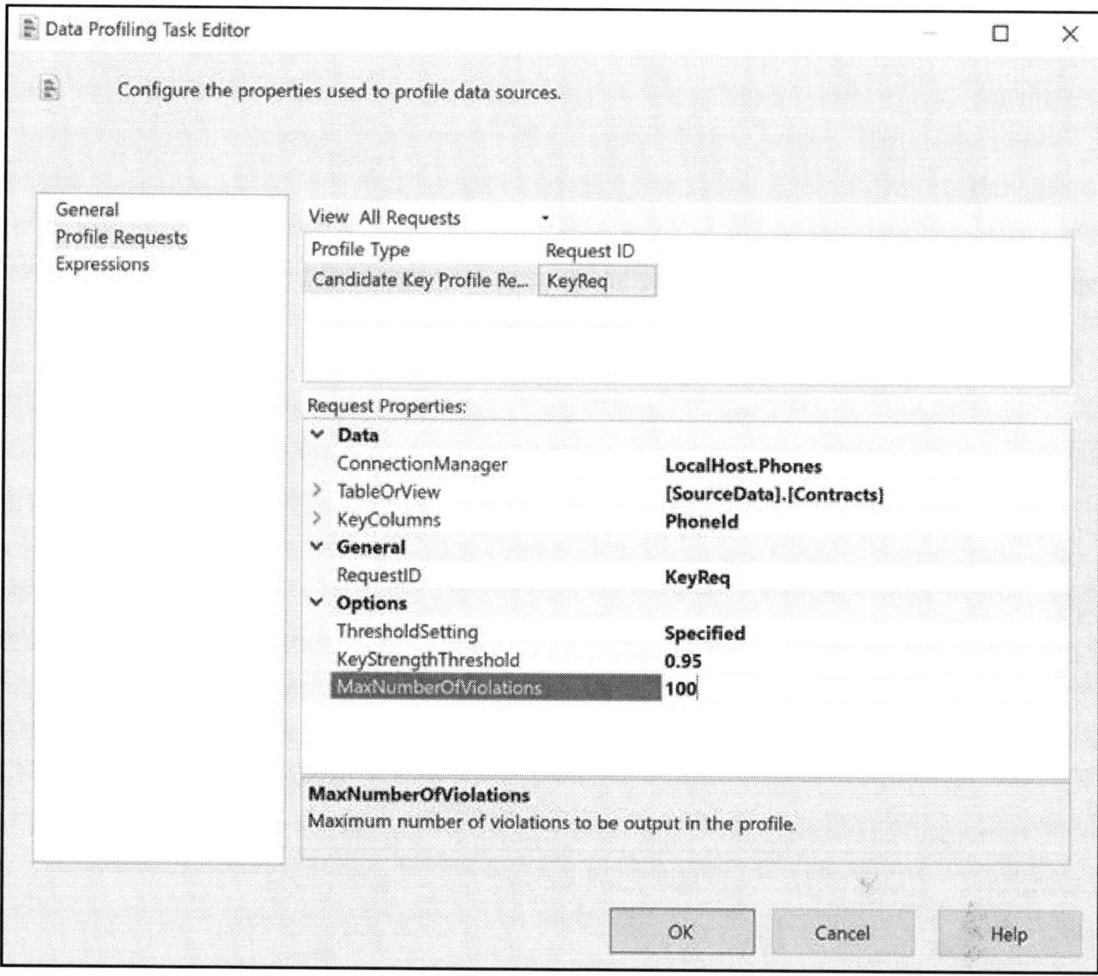

Profile Requests page of the Data Profiling Task Editor

The **Profile Requests** page of the newly-created data-profiling task is actually empty, but on the preceding screenshot, one new profile request was already defined to illustrate the whole look of the page. A new profile request is created by clicking on the **Profile Type** cell in an empty row of the list placed in the upper part of the dialog. The **Profile Type** column contains a drop-down list with all possible profile types. Once a certain profile type is selected from the drop-down list, the lower part of the dialog contains detailed properties of the profile request type. We always need to configure the connection manager for the server and database connection, table or view, and we need to select columns that we want to explore. The rest of the detailed properties depend on the profile request type selected.

We will create the following profile requests:

- **Candidate key profile request of the** `PhoneId` **column**: Already created on the preceding screenshot, this profile request tests the uniqueness of the `PhoneId` column.
- **Column null ratio profile request of the** `PhoneNumberHash` **column**: We should have every phone number known. If not, the data is not correct and we should request new, corrected data.
- **Column value distribution profile request of the** `IsCorporate` **column**: This profile request will show a ratio between private and corporate phones.
- **Column statistics profile request of the** `CitySize` **column**: The size of cities in which customers live is a continuous variable and it could be interesting in further models, so its statistical description is interesting.
- **Column value distribution of the** `CitySize` **column**: The distribution of the `CitySize` column value is also important and interesting from the perspective of further predictive models.

When all profile requests are defined, the Profile Requests page will look such as the following screenshot:

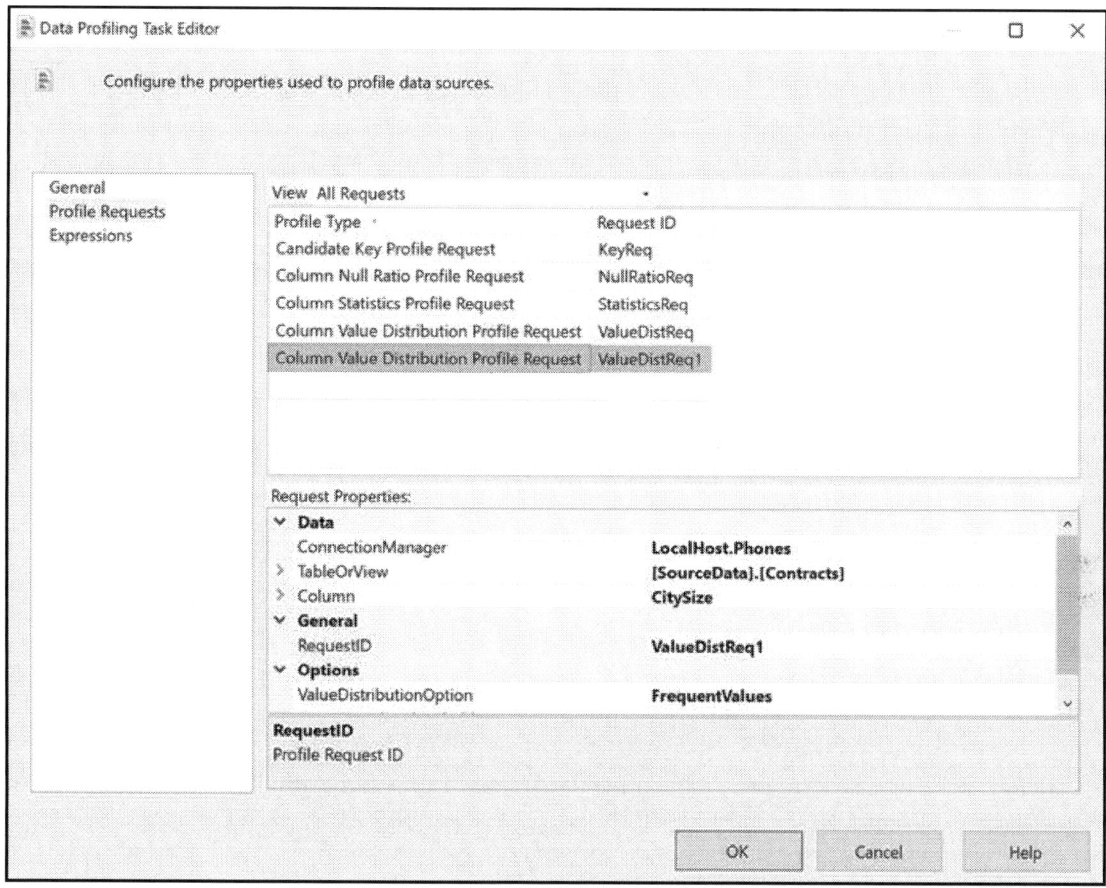

Profile Requests page when all profile requests are defined

This shows how the **Profile Requests** page of the **Data Profiling Task Editor** looks when all profile requests are defined. All changes are saved using the **OK** button of the **Data Profiling Task Editor**. When this data-profiling task is created, we can execute it and review results. Let's use the following procedure for the execution of the task:

1. Right-click on the **Contracts Profile** task on the package's **Control Flow** pane.
2. Click on the **Execute Task** option on the pop-up menu that appeared.

3. Wait until the task is executed, then stop the package on the Visual Studio's main toolbox using the **Stop Debugging** button.
4. Double-click the **Contracts Profile** task to open the **Data Profiling Task Editor** window again.
5. Click on the **Open Profile Viewer...** button on the **General** page of the editor.

When all of the preceding steps are complete, we will see graphical results of the profile in the newly-opened window. The following screenshot shows the **Data Profile Viewer** window with the result of the Column statistics profile request of the `CitySize` column:

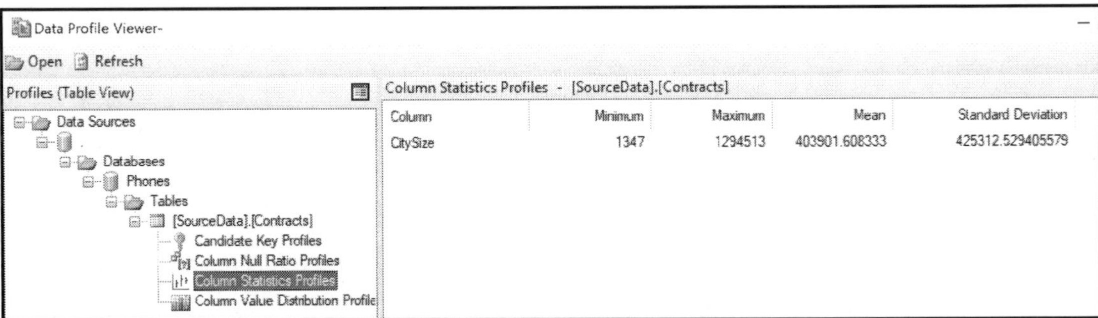

The preceding screenshot shows a significant part of the **Data Profile Viewer** window. The tree view **Profiles** are used to select the desired profile request result, while the right pane shows the result itself. In the screenshot, we are looking at the statistics of the `CitySize` column. We can see interesting information here, including the fact that the average number of citizens in cities where customers live is roughly 40,000, but the standard deviation of values is more than 425,000. Such a large value suggests that the distribution of data is very wide and so we should explore the distribution of values in the `CitySize` column. The following screenshot shows the results of the Column Value Distribution Profile Request of the `CitySize` column:

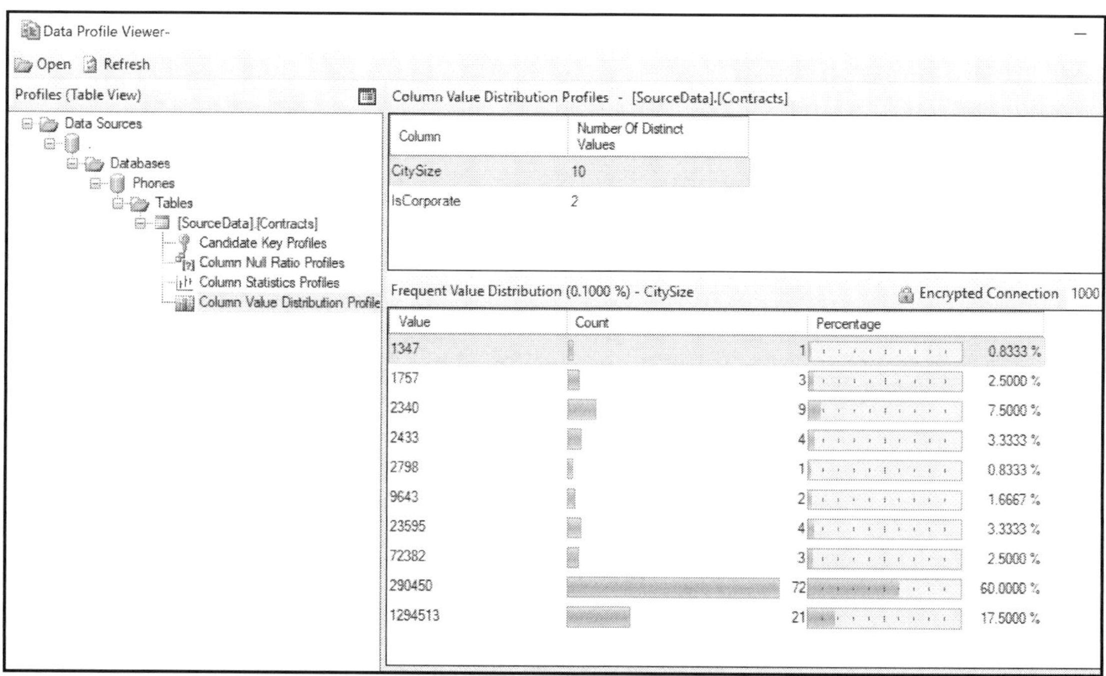

As you can see in the preceding screenshot, in the `SourceData.Contracts` table are customers from several very small villages that have fewer than 10,000 citizens, customers from two small cities of between 20,000 and 100,000 citizens, customers from a city with up to 300,000 people, and customers from a big city of more than 1,000,000 citizens. The distribution is not regular, so the column is not too feasible as a variable in further predictive models. However, we could transform it later as a factor, which will categorize customers to small, mid-sized, and big cities. We can see that the amount of customers from cities with up to 100,000 citizens is 27 (the 27 is a summary of numbers from **Count** column for all records with a **Value** lower than 100,000), which is a similar value to 21 customers from a big city. A mid-sized city has 72 customers. This transformation adds up the number of customers from small villages, creating a normal distribution.

Explore all other profiling request results on your own. You will see that corporate and private customers are divided half in half. You will also see that data does not have NULLs, and that columns estimated as unique actually have unique values.

Exploring the SourceData.Actions table

We will also explore the `SourceData.Actions` table in the same way. Let's add a second Data Profiling Task from SSIS toolbox to the package's Control Flow pane, rename it to **Action Profile,** and configure the destination for the profile results file on the **General** page of the **Data Profiling Task Editor** window of the newly-added task. We will define the following profiling requests:

- **Candidate key profile request of the `RecordId` column**: This profile request tests for the uniqueness of the `RecordId` column.
- **Column null ratio profile request of the `PhoneId` column**: This profile request is going to test whether all records have an identifier of the phone that made the action.
- **Value inclusion profile request of the `PhoneId` column**: This profile request tests to determine whether for every `PhoneId` value in the `SourceData.Actions` table, a corresponding `PhoneId` value exists in the `SourceData.Contracts` table.

When profile requests are defined, we will execute the task and see results in the **Data Profile Viewer** window. The Candidate key profile request and Column null ratio profile request will show that the `PhoneId` column always has a value, and that the `RecordId` column is completely unique. The following screenshot shows the results of the Value-inclusion profile request, which tests how values coming from two tables are related to each other:

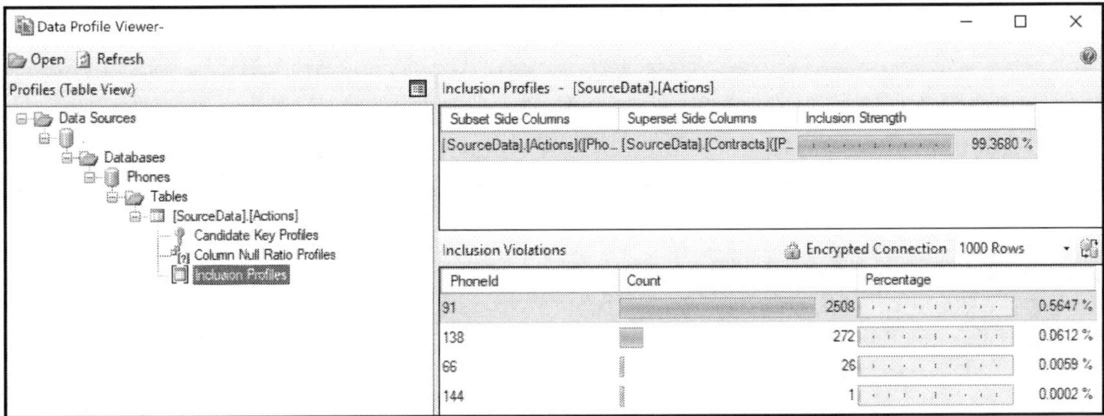

This screenshot shows that the relationship between the `SourceData.Contracts` and `SourceData.Actions` tables is quite strong, but not ideal. We can see four phone IDs that do not have a contract. Phone IDs **66** and **144** are probably mistakes, but phone IDs **138** and **91** show that the `SourceData.Contracts` table very probably misses some contract. Basically, we have two options of how to handle these phone IDs.

The first option is to attempt to create one fake contract for each lost phone ID. Both contracts will be placed in a mid-sized city; the contract for phone 91 with ID 91 (with more actions) will be marked as corporate, while the second contract will be marked as private. The second option is to ignore the records of all phone IDs. In our real-world example, let's miss all records, because this is less than 1% of all records in the `SourceData.Actions` table.

Using the SSIS Data Profiling Task is a very fast and comfortable option regarding data exploration, and this section showed that we are able to obtain very readable results quickly. However, for more sophisticated exploration, we have another option: the R language and its functions. The next section looks at data exploration using R.

Exploring data using R

In the previous section, we found several patterns in the data, such as the behavior of the `CitySize` column. Now we are going to look at a better picture of the columns in the `SourceData.Actions` table using R. For this data exploration, we will use R Studio with additional libraries `RODBC` for access to SQL Server and `ggplot2` for visualization of data.

When R Studio is started, let's write the following lines of code in R:

```
install.packages('RODBC');
install.packages('ggplot2');
```

The `install.packages()` function installs both libraries. For the preceding code to succeed, we need access to the internet from the computer running R Studio. The `install.packages()` function downloads the package with all its prerequisites and installs it into the environment.

When both packages are installed, the next step is to load both packages into the R session. We'll use the following simple code for this:

```
library('RODBC');
library('ggplot2');
```

From the moment both libraries are loaded into the session, we can read data from SQL Server and manipulate it using the very popular `ggplot2` library. Data is taken from SQL Server using the following script:

```
connString <- "Driver={SQL
Server};Server=(local);Database=Phones;Trusted_Connection=yes";
conn <- odbcDriverConnect(connString);
actions <- sqlQuery(conn, "select * from SourceData.Actions");
```

The first line of the preceding script creates a variable called `connString` and sets a connection string to it. The connection is configured for local instances of SQL Server and the `Phones` database, using a trusted (Windows) security context.

In the second line of the script, the `odbcDriverConnect()` function is used. This function creates a connection to the database and stores it in a `conn` variable. The last line of preceding script uses the `sqlQuery()` function for the query of the `SourceData.Actions` table. The result is placed into an `actions` variable.

The first actual data-exploration action is to summarize data in the `actions` dataset. The following line of code uses the `summary()` function for this:

```
summary(actions);
```

The result of the preceding simple line of code is as follows:

```
    RecordId            PhoneId        PartnerPhoneNumberHash ActionRoute  DateAndTime                        Units                UnitPrice
 Min.   : 893910   Min.   :  1.00   Min.   :-2.145e+09     I: 19902    Min.   :2015-06-30 07:39:20   Min.   :       1   Min.   : -1.0000
 1st Qu.:1122136   1st Qu.: 54.00   1st Qu.:-1.209e+09     O:424245    1st Qu.:2016-05-27 19:47:52   1st Qu.:       1   1st Qu.: -1.0000
 Median :1279947   Median : 97.00   Median :-4.395e+07                 Median :2017-03-16 07:45:57   Median :       1   Median : -1.0000
 Mean   :1304957   Mean   : 85.23   Mean   :-6.484e+07                 Mean   :2017-03-04 02:43:00   Mean   :    1942   Mean   :  0.1089
 3rd Qu.:1520836   3rd Qu.:122.00   3rd Qu.: 1.115e+09                 3rd Qu.:2017-12-07 16:20:00   3rd Qu.:       1   3rd Qu.:  1.0000
 Max.   :1645156   Max.   :148.00   Max.   : 2.147e+09                 Max.   :2018-09-30 23:47:09   Max.   :96342016   Max.   :449.0000
    Subtotal            Unit         RecomputeUnits
 Min.   :   0.000   min :235863   Min.   :0.000
 1st Qu.:   0.000   pc  :208138   1st Qu.:0.000
 Median :   0.000   NA's:   146   Median :1.000
 Mean   :   1.051                 Mean   :0.531
 3rd Qu.:   1.000                 3rd Qu.:1.000
 Max.   :1057.940                 Max.   :1.000
```

The `summary()` function calculates basic statistical measures of each column in the `actions` dataset. Statistics for the `RecordId`, `PhoneId`, and `PartnerPhoneNumberHash` columns are not important now, but we can see several interesting things highlighted in preceding screenshot with the following results:

- `ActionRoute`: This column shows actions (text messages or calls) going out (O) from a certain phone number or incoming (I) to the phone number. The summary for the `ActionRoute` column shows that the majority of actions are heading outwards, but some incoming actions are also paid.

- `DateAndTime`: Our dataset covers data from the middle of 2015 up to the end of the third quarter of 2018. This is more than three years of data.
- `Units`: This column contains pieces of text messages (always a value of 1) and seconds of voice calls. However, according to the summary, this column contains outliers, which are abnormally big values. Units will be used to handle these outliers.
- `UnitPrice`: The summary of this column shows that many unit prices were set to -1. When the provider was asked why unit prices are negative numbers, they said that calls and text messages operated within their network are not paid, and the -1 value means that the total price for any certain action is 0. This is crucial information because we will be limited to an estimation of prices for a new customer. Furthermore, the maximum value of unit price (449) is too high to be correct. Such high unit price values could also signify the presence of outliers in the data.
- `Subtotal`: The summary of the Subtotal column is derived from the summary of the `UnitPrice` column.
- `Unit`: This summary shows that the dataset contains a few more records about voice calls measured in minutes (min) than pieces of text messages (pc). We can also see that the column contains 146 records with an empty (NA) value of the `Unit` column.

The simplest way of observing values that are too big and missing values in the dataset is to go back to Management Studio and write the following queries:

```
select * from SourceData.Actions where Units = 96342016
select count(*) from SourceData.Actions
where Units > 1
    and unit = 'pc'
    and UnitPrice = -1
    and Subtotal != 0
```

First off, the `SELECT` statements in the preceding script query for the records with exactly the same value as the biggest of the observed values in the `summary()` function. One record only is found here. The values of the record are as follows:

- `Units`: 96342016
- `UnitPrice`: -1
- `Subtotal`: 503.43
- `Unit`: pc
- `RecomputeUnits`: 0

In accordance with the fact that records with the -1 `UnitPrice` are free, the non-zero `Subtotal` seems strange. Another question could be, *What strange kind of action has so many units?* The answer is simple: this record describes data consumption. The *pc* value of the `Unit` should be B-bytes. In other words, bigger amount of units with unit price -1 and Unit pc means an action describing consumption of mobile data in bytes. Because we are going to predict how many text messages and voice calls an incoming customer will need, we can ignore all records with units higher than 1 and the *pc* unit value. For the test of an amount of records, we can execute a second query from the preceding script and we will take 292 records only here.

At this moment, we need to slightly transform data. We will just add conditions eliminating records with data consumption to the query used in the `sqlQuery()` function, and we will repeat the query and `summary()` function. The following code sample shows the whole action:

```
#query
actions <- sqlQuery(conn, "select * from SourceData.Actions
  where not (Units > 1
      and unit = 'pc'
    and UnitPrice = -1
    and Subtotal != 0)
    and Unit is not null");

#exploration
summary(actions);
```

Let's summarize the `WHERE` clause of the `SELECT` statement used in the preceding R script. The `WHERE` clause contains all conditions a eliminating records with data consumption. Notice the `NOT` operator before the condition enclosed in brackets. The last predicate, `Unit IS NOT NULL`, also eliminates records without the value of `Unit` provided. The `summary()` function then gives the following results:

```
    RecordId            PhoneId        PartnerPhoneNumberHash ActionRoute  DateAndTime                          Units               UnitPrice
 Min.   : 893910   Min.   :  1.00   Min.   :-2.145e+09     I: 19902    Min.   :2015-06-30 07:39:20   Min.   :    1.00   Min.   : -1.0000
 1st Qu.:1122362   1st Qu.: 54.00   1st Qu.:-1.209e+09     O:423807    1st Qu.:2016-05-28 19:23:00   1st Qu.:    1.00   1st Qu.: -1.0000
 Median :1280135   Median : 97.00   Median :-4.395e+07                 Median :2017-03-16 14:47:00   Median :    1.00   Median : -1.0000
 Mean   :1305212   Mean   : 85.22   Mean   :-6.490e+07                 Mean   :2017-03-04 12:32:13   Mean   :   16.46   Mean   :  0.0934
 3rd Qu.:1520947   3rd Qu.:122.00   3rd Qu.: 1.115e+09                 3rd Qu.:2017-12-07 20:36:00   3rd Qu.:    1.00   3rd Qu.:  1.0000
 Max.   :1645156   Max.   :148.00   Max.   : 2.147e+09                 Max.   :2018-09-30 23:47:09   Max.   :10873.00   Max.   :449.0000
    Subtotal            Unit       RecomputeUnits
 Min.   :   0.000   min:235863   Min.   :0.0000
 1st Qu.:   0.000   pc :207846   1st Qu.:0.0000
 Median :   0.000                Median :1.0000
 Mean   :   1.022                Mean   :0.5316
 3rd Qu.:   1.000                3rd Qu.:1.0000
 Max.   :1057.940                Max.   :1.0000
```

The preceding screenshot shows the adjusted results of the `summary()` function. The `ActionRoute` column does not have NA values, and the maximum amount of units spent in one action is 10,873. This was probably a very long voice call (a little bit more than three hours; unusual, but possible). The biggest `UnitPrice` and `Subtotal` values are still large, but it could be, for example, an SMS payment.

The last few paragraphs showed a very important thing: data exploration and data transformation go together, and affect each other. It also shows that we work very iteratively. Finding patterns in data leads to the need to make adjustments, which leads to the need for new exploration, and so on.

The next step in data exploration is to visualize the data to gain better insights. For the visualization, we will use functions of the `ggplot2` library. The following R statement will visualize a consumption of actions by phone ID:

```
#ggplot
ggplot(actions, aes(x=PhoneId, y=Units)) + geom_point(aes(col=Unit),
size=3);
```

The preceding R statement initializes the `ggplot` object. The parameters of the `ggplot` function are the dataset on which the visualization will be made (the `actions` dataset as a first parameter) with the coordinates as the second parameter. Coordinates are set using the `aes()` function. The `geom_point()` function sets the form of the graph to the `ggplot` object (scatter plot in this case). In the preceding statement, the `geom_point()` function uses the `Unit` column as a category. The `size` parameter sets the size of points in graph.

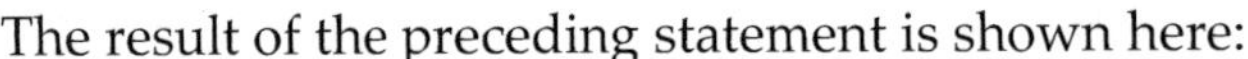

The result of the preceding statement is shown here:

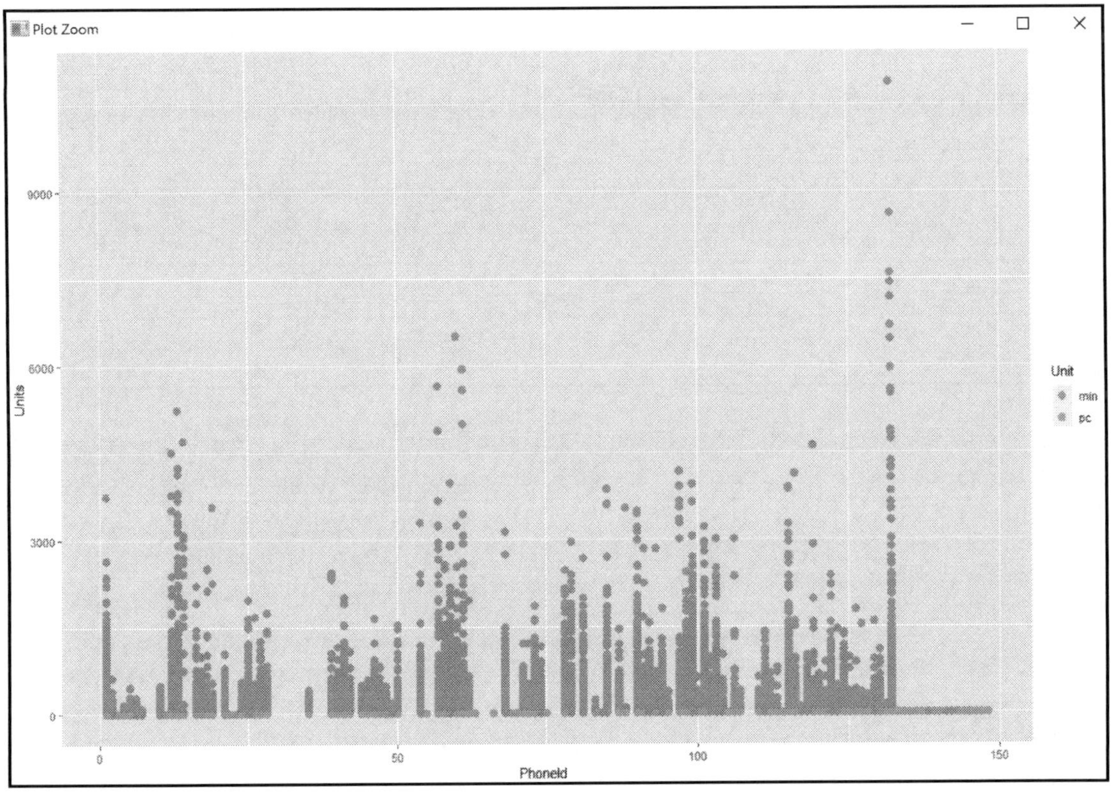

This graph shows that all text messages are always saved in data as just one piece, and that most voice calls are up to one hour in length. Some calls are longer, and some are exceptionally long.

For a better understanding of the data, we will probably need more information, such as a progress of action consumption over time or in certain regions, but without more transformations, the data is not eligible to provide such information. This is because, for instance, every action is documented in exact time, but we want aggregated data in months and years.

However, we have still obtained some very useful knowledge about our data. Let's summarize what we know now:

- We need to transform `CitySize` values to small/mid-sized/big categories
- We need to eliminate records with data consumption
- We need to join data from both tables together, even if we lose some records
- We need to aggregate data over time
- We must go back and explore transformed data again

The following section is going to transform data coming to the predictive model.

Data transformation

The last section explained several very useful techniques of data exploration. In our real-world example, we explored the data and decided that we need to transform it before we continue working with it. In this section, we will make all desired transformations. The most comfortable way of making transformations is to use T-SQL, because all transformations that we need are rather straightforward.

The first of the transformations is just a join of both source tables. This will eliminate records from the `SourceData.Actions` table that do not have contracts, and it will also create a base for further analytical datasets. The following statement joins both tables together:

```
select
    contracts.PhoneId
    , contracts.IsCorporate
    , contracts.CitySize
    , actions.ActionRoute
    , actions.DateAndTime
    , actions.Units
    , actions.Unit
    , actions.RecomputeUnits
from SourceData.Contracts as contracts
    join SourceData.Actions as actions on contracts.PhoneId =
actions.PhoneId
where not (actions.Units > 1
    and actions.Unit = 'pc'
    and actions.UnitPrice = -1
    and actions.Subtotal != 0)
    and actions.Unit is not null
```

The preceding statement produces a result set that joins both tables together. In the statement is also the `WHERE` clause, with all conditions found during the R data exploration. The `WHERE` clause eliminates data consumption records and also eliminates records without the unit provided. The preceding query will return 441,048 records.

The second aggregation is about to make the `CitySize` and `IsCorporate` columns as factors. This transformation is needed because both columns are numerical, but we don't want the further predictive model to use these columns as numbers. For this aggregation, we must prepare a table with ranges of citizen amounts to determine the level of the city size. The following script shows the preparation for this:

```
create schema Helpers
authorization dbo
go

create table Helpers.CitySizes
(
Id int not null identity
, MinAmount int not null
, MaxAmount int not null
, Size nvarchar(10)
, constraint pk_CitySizes primary key (Id)
)

insert Helpers.CitySizes (MinAmount, MaxAmount, Size)
values (0, 100000, 'Small')
, (100001, 1000000, 'Middle')
, (1000001, 2000000000, 'Big')
```

Since we'll probably need more tables helping to determine levels of factors or other tasks, the preceding script creates a new schema, called `Helpers`. The new table, called `Helpers.CitySizes`, is then created and three records are added into the table. Every record sets a range of citizens for small, medium-sized, and big cities. These ranges were found during data exploration using the SSIS Data Profiling Task.

When the preparation task is done, we can enhance the query-joining tables to make factors from the `CitySize` and `IsCorporate` columns. The following query shows all the changes:

```
select
    contracts.PhoneId
    , iif(contracts.IsCorporate = 0, 'Private', 'Corporate') as IsCorporate
    , contracts.CitySize
    , sizes.Size
    , actions.ActionRoute
    , actions.DateAndTime
```

```
    , actions.Units
    , actions.Unit
    , actions.RecomputeUnits
from SourceData.Contracts as contracts
    join SourceData.Actions as actions on contracts.PhoneId =
actions.PhoneId
    join Helpers.CitySizes as sizes on contracts.CitySize
        between sizes.MinAmount and sizes.MaxAmount
where not (actions.Units > 1
    and actions.Unit = 'pc'
    and actions.UnitPrice = -1
    and actions.Subtotal != 0)
    and actions.Unit is not null
```

Let's highlight news in the preceding query. The `IsCorporate` column contains just two values: 0 and 1. This is why we simply used the `IIF()` T-SQL function to decide whether to return the `Private` or `Corporate` value.

The transformation of the `CitySize` column is a little bit more complicated. We joined the `Helpers.CitySizes` table with `SourceData.Actions`. The `JOIN` predicate places the current value of the `CitySize` column between the minimum and maximum amount of citizens determined in the `Helpers.CitySizes` table. This way of joining tables is usually slow and unwanted, but the `Helpers.CitySizes` table has three rows only. This is why we cannot be afraid of the performance.

The last transformation we will make is an aggregation of actions by years and months. To write the aggregate query, we need to transform values in the `DateAndTime` column from current times to one time in every month. A very simple way to do this is to use the `EOMONTH` function, which finds the date of the last day in a month. Using this function, we will replace the `DateAndTime` value with only date in a month, and then we can aggregate data using the `SUM` function. The following query shows the solution:

```
select
    contracts.PhoneId
    , iif(contracts.IsCorporate = 0, 'Private', 'Corporate') as IsCorporate
    , contracts.CitySize
    , sizes.Size
    , actions.ActionRoute
    , EOMONTH(actions.DateAndTime) as MonthAndYear
    , SUM(actions.Units) as Units
    , SUM(actions.Subtotal) as TotalPrice
    , actions.Unit
    , actions.RecomputeUnits
from SourceData.Contracts as contracts
    join SourceData.Actions as actions on contracts.PhoneId =
```

```
actions.PhoneId
    join Helpers.CitySizes as sizes on contracts.CitySize
        between sizes.MinAmount and sizes.MaxAmount
where not (actions.Units > 1
    and actions.Unit = 'pc'
    and actions.UnitPrice = -1
    and actions.Subtotal != 0)
    and actions.Unit is not null
group by contracts.PhoneId
    , iif(contracts.IsCorporate = 0, 'Private', 'Corporate')
    , contracts.CitySize
    , sizes.Size
    , actions.ActionRoute
    , EOMONTH(actions.DateAndTime)
    , actions.Unit
    , actions.RecomputeUnits
```

This query returns an amount of units (pieces of text messages or seconds of voice calls) consumed by a certain phone number every month.

Now we should answer the following question: do we need to persist the result of preceding query or will it be used ad hoc? The answer to this question depends on several factors. How much data is in the source? Is the source frequently changed and do we need to train the predictive model often and on live data? In our case, data is not too big and the only changes in the source data are made on a monthly basis when a new monthly report is uploaded. Consequently, we can use both methods, we can use a database view or we can persist data into a table and refresh the table every month after new data arrives. In our example, we'll encapsulate the query into a view. The following shortened script shows the solution:

```
create view SourceData.viInputCalls
as
select
    ...
from SourceData.Contracts as contracts
    join SourceData.Actions as actions on contracts.PhoneId =
actions.PhoneId
    join Helpers.CitySizes as sizes on contracts.CitySize
        between sizes.MinAmount and sizes.MaxAmount
where not (actions.Units > 1
    and actions.Unit = 'pc'
    and actions.UnitPrice = -1
    and actions.Subtotal != 0)
    and actions.Unit is not null
group by
    ...
go
```

The most important lines in the preceding script are just the first two lines. These lines of code are just a header of newly-created view, and this is the only change made to the query that we are looking at in this section.

Cleansing and transforming data leads to a need to explore the data once more. The following R script makes several more transformations of the data and summarizes the output as follows:

```
#import libraries
library('RODBC');

#reading data from database
connString <- "Driver={SQL
Server};Server=(local);Database=Phones;Trusted_Connection=yes";
conn <- odbcDriverConnect(connString);
actions <- sqlQuery(conn, "select IsCorporate, Size, ActionRoute,
MonthAndYear, Units, TotalPrice, Unit, RecomputeUnits from
SourceData.viInputCalls");

#factorization
actions$MonthAndYear <- as.Date.factor(actions$MonthAndYear);
actions$RecomputeUnits <- as.factor(actions$RecomputeUnits);

#exploration
summary(actions);
```

This script imports the `RODBC` library, making it possible to read data from SQL Server. It then establishes a connection to a SQL Server and reads important columns from the prepared `SourceData.viInputCalls` view. When data is obtained, the section of the script commented as `#factorization` makes values in `MonthAndYear` and `RecomputeUnits` as factors. This action is made because `MonthAndYear` is taken by R as a string, but we want to have it as a time category, and the `RecomputeUnits` values are as numbers in R, but we also want them also as categories—factors.

The last function in the preceding R script returns a statistical summary of the dataset. Its result is shown here:

```
  IsCorporate        Size       ActionRoute  MonthAndYear              Units              TotalPrice          Unit       RecomputeUnits
Corporate:4520   Big    : 885   I:1775       Min.    :2015-06-30   Min.    :     1.0   Min.    :   0.00   min:4153   0:4581
Private  :4214   Middle:5818    O:6959       1st Qu.:2016-06-30   1st Qu.:     7.0   1st Qu.:   1.00   pc :4581   1:4153
                 Small  :2031                Median :2017-04-30   Median :    30.0   Median :  13.66
                                             Mean   :2017-03-28   Mean   :   829.9   Mean   :  50.79
                                             3rd Qu.:2017-12-31   3rd Qu.:    82.0   3rd Qu.:  55.63
                                             Max.   :2018-09-30   Max.   :123854.0   Max.   :4289.00
```

The preceding screenshot is a snapshot of the statistical summary of our data after all transformations. Even if we can still see some extremely large values in the `Units` and `TotalPrice` columns, data is now transformed enough to start making predictions. The following section will explain how to train predictive models.

Training and using predictive models for estimations

Before now, we have worked hard to know our data and we have made it eligible for predictions. This section is going to create a regression predictive model, where we will be training it and using it for prediction.

Preparing the schema for the model

In `chapter 9`, *Predictive Model Training and Evaluation*, we discussed two options for the predictive model storage and versioning. We will use this knowledge to create a simplified physical schema that will be used for a versioned stream of the predictive model.

We'll create a database schema, called `Models`, in the `Phones` database, and we will place all objects attending to the predictive modeling into this schema. First off, the objects placed into the `Models` schema will be a table called `Models.ModelVersions`. The following SQL script creates the database schema and the table:

```
create schema Models authorization dbo
go

create table Models.ModelVersions
(
Id int not null identity
, CreationDate datetime2 not null constraint df_ModelVersions_CreationDate
default (sysdatetime())
, ModelStream varbinary(max) not null
, PredictedUnits nvarchar(10) not null
, constraint pk_ModelVersions primary key (Id)
)
go
```

The preceding script creates the database schema and the `Models.ModelVersions` table. This table contains an identifier of record as a `primary key`, the date and time of the model training, model stream and the flag column `PredictedUnits`. The last column will be used to mark which measure is predicted, including minutes of the voice calls or an amount of text messages. Once the data structures are prepared, we are going to work on the model training. The next section will explain all the training steps in detail.

Training the model

In this section, we will switch our R scripts into a SQL Server and we will execute the R script within the `sp_execute_external_script` stored procedure.

The training of any predictive model works according to the following steps:

1. The training model takes the data
2. The data is adjusted, if needed
3. The data is divided into training and testing datasets
4. The training model is executed using the training dataset
5. The trained model is evaluated against testing dataset
6. The results are compared
7. If the results are not accurate enough, the cause of the inaccuracy should be found, corrected, and the process of the training and test is repeated

The seventh step of the preceding procedure can lead to a very long way back to the data gathering and exploration and to the application of more transformations.

The first three tasks in the predictive model deployment are to take data, adjust it, if needed, and divide it into two subsets. The following script shows how to make it:

```
exec sp_execute_external_script
    @language = N'R'
    , @script = N'
        actions <- InputDataSet;

        #factorization of the date
        actions$MonthAndYear <- as.Date.factor(actions$MonthAndYear);

        #divide data for training and scoring
        sample.size = 0.85 * nrow(actions);
        sample.count <- sample(seq_len(nrow(actions)), size = sample.size);
        actions.training <- actions[sample.count, ];
        actions.test <- actions[-sample.count, ];
```

```
'
, @input_data_1 = N'select PhoneId, IsCorporate, Size, ActionRoute
      , MonthAndYear, Units, Unit, RecomputeUnits
   from SourceData.viInputCalls'
```

The preceding T-SQL script uses the `sp_execute_external_script` stored procedure with an input of data from the `SourceData.viInputCalls` view. Data is seen in the R script as a variable called `InputDataSet`. Before now, we worked with the input data in a variable called `actions`. The first line of the R script just assigns `InputDataSet` into a new variable `actions`. All data except for the `MonthAndYear` column in the dataset is well-transformed. The second action in the R script converts the `MonthAndYear` values to a date, and then turns these values into factors.

The last part of the R script, commented as `#divide data...`, calculates an amount of records in the dataset, calculates 85 % of the amount, and calculates a random amount of the records in the actions dataset. Then the dataset is divided into `actions.training` and `actions.test` datasets.

The preceding R script does not have an output yet, but steps 1, 2, and 3 from the preceding procedure are made and we can continue with steps 4, 5, and 6: the model training and evaluation. The following R code snippet just shows a part of the R script that computes the model. The following lines of code will be added to the end of the R script, and will be added as an `@script` parameter in the preceding code sample:

```
...
        #formula for linear regression
        formula <- Units ~ IsCorporate + Size + ActionRoute + MonthAndYear;

        #model from training data
        model <- rxLinMod(formula, actions.training);
        #prediction from test data
        prediction <- rxPredict(modelObject = model, data = actions.test);

        #result of prediction back to the test data
        actions.test$PredictedValue <- prediction$Units_Pred
        #results of the training
        OutputDataSet <- data.frame(actions.test);
...
```

This part of the R script defines the formula of the linear regression. The formula simply says that from the `IsCorporate`, `Size`, `ActionRoute`, and `MonthAndYear` variables, the amount of Units will be predicted.

Looking at the set of depended variables, we can discuss a sufficiency of incoming data at this moment. Let's cut off the discussion. We have too little data to be accurate in our predictions. More variables, such as the marital status and age the customer, would be nice to have for better predictions, but unfortunately other possibly-feasible variables are not at our disposal.

Using the rxLinMod function and finishing the model

Let's explore the R script more. The model is calculated with the `rxLinMod` function, which has at least two parameters: the predictive formula and the training dataset. The result of the function will be saved into the `Models.ModelVersions` table later. We also want to see the quality of the model. The preceding R script uses a very simple method. It calculates a set of predictions using the `rxPredict` function with parameters of trained models and the testing dataset, and then it adds predicted values back to a testing dataset as a new column. The last line of preceding code returns the testing dataset with the predicted values, and we can compare the accuracy of the estimations. The following screenshot shows part of the results from the previously-developed script:

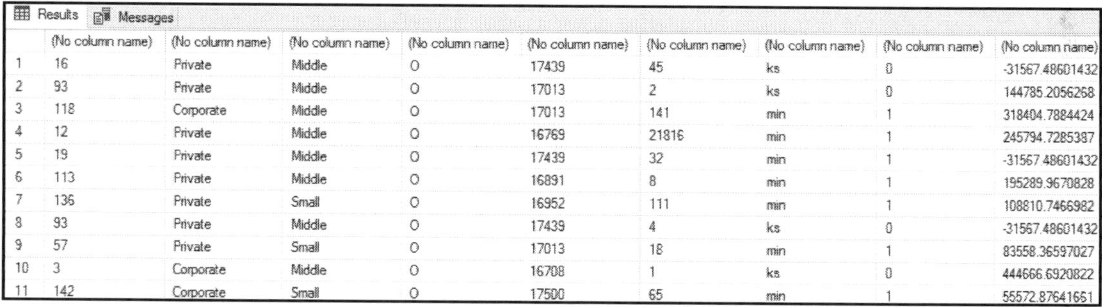

Results | Messages

	(No column name)	(No column name)	(No column name)	(No column name)	(No column name)	(No column name)	(No column name)	(No column name)	(No column name)
1	16	Private	Middle	O	17439	45	ks	0	-31567.48601432
2	93	Private	Middle	O	17013	2	ks	0	144785.2056268
3	118	Corporate	Middle	O	17013	141	min	1	318404.7884424
4	12	Private	Middle	O	16769	21816	min	1	245794.7285387
5	19	Private	Middle	O	17439	32	min	1	-31567.48601432
6	113	Private	Middle	O	16891	8	min	1	195289.9670828
7	136	Private	Small	O	16952	111	min	1	108810.7466982
8	93	Private	Middle	O	17439	4	ks	0	-31567.48601432
9	57	Private	Small	O	17013	18	min	1	83558.36597027
10	3	Corporate	Middle	O	16708	1	ks	0	444666.6920822
11	142	Corporate	Small	O	17500	65	min	1	55572.87641651

This screenshot shows the result set, which has content that is not very nice, because columns in the result do not have names, so the orientation in the data is almost impossible. However, we can still estimate that in the sixth column are actual values, and in the last column are predicted values. For instance, in the first record, we can see the actual value of 45 pieces of text messages, but the predicted value is negative. In the second record, the situation is similar. Here, the customer used 2 text messages, but the estimation is more than 144,000 text messages. This shows that this model does not work.

Now it's time to find out the reason for this inaccuracy. We should go to the data exploration and transformations, but for the sake of simplicity the answers are here:

- The first year in the source data has too many actions when it's compared to all of the later years. This is because a crucial corporate customer finished a contract at the end of 2016.
- Text messages and voice calls must not be mixed together.

Having this new information, we have to adjust the source query with a proper `WHERE` clause. The following query is used in the `@input_data_1` parameter of the `sp_execute_external_script` stored procedure:

```
select PhoneId, IsCorporate, Size, ActionRoute
    , MonthAndYear, Units, Unit, RecomputeUnits
from SourceData.viInputCalls
where MonthAndYear > '2017-01-01' and Unit = 'min'
```

This query adds a condition that filters out all records from the first year. The condition also filters out records with text messages.

The second issue found with the result set of the first prediction attempt was the lack of column names. The column names of results returned from the `sp_execute_external_script` stored procedure are named as an optional clause after the stored procedure's execution. The following script shows the whole solution of the training and evaluation together:

```
exec sp_execute_external_script
    @language = N'R'
    , @script = N'
        #formula for linear regression
        formula <- Units ~ IsCorporate + Size + ActionRoute + MonthAndYear;
        actions <- InputDataSet;

        #factorization of the date
        actions$MonthAndYear <- as.Date.factor(actions$MonthAndYear);

        #divide data for training and scoring
        sample.size = 0.85 * nrow(actions);
        sample.count <- sample(seq_len(nrow(actions)), size = sample.size);
        actions.training <- actions[sample.count, ];
        actions.test <- actions[-sample.count, ];

        #model from training data
        model <- rxLinMod(formula, actions.training);
        #prediction from test data
        prediction <- rxPredict(modelObject = model, data = actions.test);
```

```
        #result of prediction back to the test data
        actions.test$PredictedValue <- prediction$Units_Pred

        #how to obtain column names from the prediction data set
        #OutputDataSet <- data.frame(colnames(prediction));

        #results of the training
        OutputDataSet <- data.frame(actions.test);

    '
    , @input_data_1 = N'select PhoneId, IsCorporate, Size, ActionRoute
            , MonthAndYear, Units, Unit, RecomputeUnits
        from SourceData.viInputCalls where MonthAndYear > ''2017-01-01''
and Unit = ''min'''

with result sets ((PhoneId int, IsCorporate nvarchar(10), Size
nvarchar(10), ActionRoute nchar(1)
    , MonthAndYear int, Units int, Unit nvarchar(10), RecomputeUnits bit,
PredictedValue float))
```

This script sample gives us the whole solution of the prediction of minutes spent by voice calls every month. A where clause was added to a source query and the `WITH RESULT SETS` clause was added at the end of the stored procedure execution. Let's review the result of the preceding script:

Results | Messages

	PhoneId	IsCorporate	Size	ActionRoute	MonthAndYear	Units	Unit	RecomputeUnits	PredictedValue
1	74	Corporate	Middle	I	17712	1	min	1	23.402806910601
2	106	Private	Middle	O	17225	8	min	1	47.4034344186256
3	141	Private	Small	O	17347	49	min	1	51.7754194505695
4	119	Corporate	Middle	O	17197	153	min	1	77.115838800308
5	121	Corporate	Middle	O	17743	30	min	1	80.7972293971654
6	1	Corporate	Big	O	17500	243	min	1	70.2316793644633
7	49	Corporate	Big	O	17682	2	min	1	71.4588095634157
8	130	Corporate	Small	O	17256	44	min	1	81.063047994153
9	24	Private	Middle	O	17470	20	min	1	49.0553404556769
10	11	Private	Small	O	17256	39	min	1	51.1618543510932
11	61	Private	Middle	O	17531	1	min	1	49.4666313465346
12	40	Private	Middle	O	17562	23	min	1	49.6756480287738
13	1	Corporate	Big	O	17531	258	min	1	70.4406960467024
14	42	Private	Small	O	17470	37	min	1	52.6047437059054

The preceding screenshot shows a more readable result set with current as well as estimated values in the `PredictedValue` column. The estimation is still not too accurate, but estimated numbers became much more meaningful than in the first attempt at prediction.

As explained earlier in this section, the source data is very raw so at this moment we can decide that a better estimation is not reachable.

The last task we need to perform is to calculate predictions and store them in the `Models.ModelVersions` table. We will use most of the preceding scripts with several corrections:

- We will erase lines with the model evaluation
- We will add a serialization of the model
- We will return the model in serialized form and we will insert a new record in the `Models.ModelVersions` table
- We will encapsulate the script into a stored procedure

The core of the `sp_execute_external_script` stored procedure is the `@script` parameter. The following R script shows the final version of the R script, which will be used in the stored procedure:

```
#formula for linear regression
formula <- Units ~ IsCorporate + Size + ActionRoute + MonthAndYear;
actions <- InputDataSet;

#factorization of the date
actions$MonthAndYear <- as.Date.factor(actions$MonthAndYear);

#model from training data
model <- rxLinMod(formula, actions);

OutputDataSet <- data.frame(rxSerializeModel(model, realtimeScoringOnly =
TRUE));
```

This R script defines the regression formula, factorizes the `MonthAndYear` column, and then calculates the model over all input data. The output of this script is assigned into a `OutputDataSet` variable and contains the predictive models serialized as a binary string.

We know that we will calculate two predictive models: one for the voice calls, and one for the amount of text messages consumed by a customer. This is why we also need to parameterize our input data. The following SQL script shows parts of the script, which will be a part of a stored procedure that we will develop later. The stored procedure will then be executed regularly and it will train the model:

```
declare @sqlMin nvarchar(500) = N'select PhoneId, IsCorporate, Size,
ActionRoute
    , MonthAndYear, Units, Unit, RecomputeUnits
    from SourceData.viInputCalls where MonthAndYear > ''2017-01-01'' and
Unit = ''min'''
declare @sqlPc nvarchar(500) = N'select PhoneId, IsCorporate, Size,
ActionRoute
    , MonthAndYear, Units, Unit, RecomputeUnits
    from SourceData.viInputCalls where MonthAndYear > ''2017-01-01'' and
Unit = ''pc'''
```

This script contains two declared variables: `@sqlMin` and `@sqlPc`. Every variable stores one alternative of the input query. The only difference could be seen in the last condition ... `Unit = 'pc'` or ... `Unit = 'min'` in the query strings.

The next step in the further stored procedure is to create a temporary table for the result of the prediction. The `sp_execute_external_script` stored procedure will insert the model stream into the temporary table, then the new record will be updated with the proper unit. The following script shows the execution of the `sp_execute_external_script` stored procedure with erased R script:

```
create table #models
(
ModelStream varbinary(max)
, PredictedUnits nvarchar(10) null
)

insert #models (ModelStream)
exec sp_execute_external_script @language = N'R'
    , @script = N'         #shortened here     '
    , @input_data_1 = @sqlMin

update #models set PredictedUnits = 'min'

insert #models (ModelStream)
exec sp_execute_external_script @language = N'R'
    , @script = N'         #shortened here     '
    , @input_data_1 = @sqlPc

update #models set PredictedUnits = 'pc' where PredictedUnits is null
```

This SQL script shows us how to catch results from the `sp_execute_external_script` procedure in a temporary table, called `#models`, and how to correctly update the predicted units. When the script is executed (containing also the R part, however), we can query the `#models` table and we'll see two records with two binary strings; the first record with `MeasuredUnits` is set to the `min` value, and the second record with `MeasuredUnits` is set to `pc`.

The last task in the developed stored procedure is to insert data durably into the `Models.ModelVersions` table. This is very straightforward, and the following script shows us how to do it:

```
insert Models.ModelVersions (ModelStream, PredictedUnits)
select ModelStream, PredictedUnits from #models
```

Now we can plan the retraining of the model as a simple stored-procedure execution. The stored procedure can be executed every time new monthly data is uploaded to the `Phones` database. The schedule of the execution could be a SQL Server Agent job, or even an Execute SQL Task in SSIS.

The whole solution is provided to readers in the Phones database, which is accessible as a database backup on the GitHub repository of this book. Procedures calculating predictive models are `Models.procTrainModels` for the persisted models, and `Models.procTrainModelWithEval` for seeing the accuracy of the model.

The last but most important task that must be developed is to make predictions from the model. The following short section will show you how to provide the predictions to users.

Using the model in predictions

We have been through almost all of the steps of the resource-consumption-estimation project, but the last step is to prepare a comfortable way of making predictions to users. Let's reflect on which parameters the model depends:

- A customer can be `Private` or `Corporate`
- A customer can live in a small, mid-sized, or big city
- We can predict incoming (I) or outgoing (O) actions
- We make the prediction for a point in the future (the end of a predicted month)
- We are predicting voice calls (min) or text messages (pc)

This list is also a description of all parameters needed to calculate and return a predicted value to a user.

The most comfortable and secure option for making predictions is to develop a stored procedure executed by users. The following script shows a header of the newly-created stored procedures, called `Models.procPredict`:

```
create or alter proc Models.procPredict
    @isCorporate nvarchar(10)
    , @size nvarchar(10)
    , @actionRoute nchar(1) = N'O'
    , @monthAndYear date = '2019-01-31'
    , @predictedUnit nvarchar(10) = 'min'
as
-- TO BE CONTINUED
```

This script shows a header of new stored procedures with all the parameters that need to be set. The first two parameters, `@isCorporate` and `@size`, are always requested; the user must set their values using a proper word here (for example, mid-sized for the `@size` parameter, or *Private* for the `@isCorporate` parameter). The rest of the parameters are optional, but their values can also be explicitly set.

The `@monthAndYear` parameter is a little bit confusing. We are using the last day of a certain year and month here, but the trained model has factorized the value, so the value is an integer. We also need to factorize the value of the `@monthAndYear` parameter. We will do this using R, however. The following script shows how to factorize the date and how to bring it back from the `sp_execute_external_script` stored procedure:

```
declare @x table (x int)
insert @x
exec sp_execute_external_script
    @language = N'R'
    , @script = N'
        OutputDataSet <- data.frame(as.Date.factor(theDate));
    '
    , @params = N'@theDate date'
    , @theDate = @monthAndYear
```

This script will be used in the `Models.procPredict` stored procedure. The script prepares a table variable, called `@x`, with only an integer column. The `sp_execute_external_script` stored procedure uses the `@params` parameter to declare parameters used inside the R script. We will provide the date parameter to the `@theDate` parameter of the `sp_execute_external_script` stored procedure. The R script factorizes the `theDate` parameter and returns a result as an `OutputDataSet` variable. The result is then inserted into the `@x` table variable. We must not forget to adjust the values of user parameters to comply with a format of variables in the predictive model. In the case where we'll miss the adjustment of variable values, the prediction will fail.

The next step is to select the correct trained model. The following script shows the query for this:

```
DECLARE @model varbinary(max) =
    (SELECT ModelStream from Models.ModelVersions where PredictedUnits =
@predictedUnit
        and CreationDate = (select max(CreationDate)
        from Models.ModelVersions where PredictedUnits = @predictedUnit)
    );
```

This script uses the `SELECT` statement to find out the last version of a stored predictive model for a certain unit. The result is placed into a `@model` variable.

When all preparation steps are done, we can use parameters, adjusted parameters, and the model for the prediction. The following statement is the statement that returns new predicted value from the model:

```
WITH newData as (
    SELECT * FROM (values(@isCorporate, @size, @actionRoute, (select x from
@x)))
    as t(IsCorporate, Size, ActionRoute, MonthAndYear)
)
SELECT newData.*, p.*
FROM PREDICT(MODEL = @model, DATA = newData) WITH(Units_Pred float) as p
```

The preceding query uses a common table expression, called newData. The CTE uses the row constructor to make parameters as a new record. In other words, the newData CTE returns a result set with one record. The result set is then posted as a DATA parameter to the PREDICT function. The second parameter of the PREDICT function, called MODEL, has a variable with the model stream assigned. The predict function returns a new column named Units_Pred. This column contains the predicted value.

The whole stored procedure looks as shown in the following script sample:

```
create or alter proc Models.procPredict
    @isCorporate nvarchar(10)
    , @size nvarchar(10)
    , @actionRoute nchar(1) = N'O'
    , @monthAndYear date = '2019-01-31'
    , @predictedUnit nvarchar(10) = 'min'
as
declare @x table (x int)
insert @x
exec sp_execute_external_script
    @language = N'R'
    , @script = N'
        OutputDataSet <- data.frame(as.Date.factor(x));
    '
    , @params = N'@x date'
    , @x = @monthAndYear

DECLARE @model varbinary(max) =
    (SELECT ModelStream from Models.ModelVersions where PredictedUnits =
@predictedUnit
        and CreationDate = (select max(CreationDate)
        from Models.ModelVersions where PredictedUnits = @predictedUnit)
    );

WITH newData as (
    SELECT * FROM (values(@isCorporate, @size, @actionRoute, (select x from
@x)))
    as t(IsCorporate, Size, ActionRoute, MonthAndYear)
)
SELECT newData.*, p.*
FROM PREDICT(MODEL = @model, DATA = newData) WITH(Units_Pred float) as p
```

The preceding script contains the complete T-SQL code of the Models.procPredict stored procedure that was discussed in this section. Let's execute the stored procedure and observe the results, as follows:

```
exec Models.procPredict 'Private', 'Small', 'O', '2018-12-31', 'min'
```

The preceding stored-procedure execution calculates an estimation of minutes spent by voice calls consumed by a private customer from a small village. The result of this is shown in the following screenshot:

Results | Messages

	IsCorporate	Size	ActionRoute	MonthAndYear	Units_Pred
1	Private	Small	0	17896	56.1876425115802

This screenshot shows that we predicted up to one minute of out going text calls for a customer from a small village.

Summary

This chapter explained the creation of a predictive model. Here, we learned that the process is very iterative. Even though we initially explored data, we did it even more times after its transformation, looking for better corrections that will help to fit data better to a predictive model.

In the first two sections, *Assignment and preparation* and *Data exploration*, we described the physical structure of source data and used several techniques, namely T-SQL queries, the SSIS Data Profiling Task, and R scripts, to explore data and to uncover its hidden patterns.

In the *Data transformation* section, we made several T-SQL transformations and explored data once more to ensure that the transformations did not corrupt the data.

During the last section, we developed training stored procedures with an evaluation of the model quality, and we also created a stored procedure that will be used for regular training of the predictive model. In addition, we developed a stored procedure for making predictions.

This book is now approaching its end, but data science is a fascinating, never-ending story. The next chapter will inspire us with the many possible steps that we can make in the data-science domain.

Questions

1. Which SQL Server versions and editions have machine learning services?
   Machine learning services (formerly called **R Services**) are offered within SQL Server from version 2016. The machine learning services can be installed with every edition of SQL Server.
2. How do we configure machine learning services?
   Machine learning services must be enabled by an SQL Server administrator using the `sp_configure 'external scripts enabled'` stored procedure.
3. What is the best method of data exploration?
   There isn't a best option. Every developer prefers a different technology for basic exploration of the data. For example, descriptive statistics, and uniqueness of values. Alternatively, to look at the amount of NULLs in columns, T-SQL queries or the SSIS Data Profiling Task are very useful. For more sophisticated exploration, we will probably use languages such as R or Python.
4. My data is categorized using numbers. Is this correct for a predictive model?
   No, it is not. The predictive model will use numbers just as a numbers, not as factors. This means that, for instance, categories marked as 1, 2, and 3 will be used as numerical features. If we would like to have a special meaning for our numbers (1 small, 2 medium, and so on), we must factorize these numbers (remember the `as.factor()` R function).
5. Can the T-SQL `PREDICT` function be used with any trained model?
   No, this function can be used with models from a `RevoScaleR` library (for instance, the `rxLinMod` or `rxLogit` functions), serialized using the RevoScale `rxSerializeModel` R function.

12
Next Steps with Data Science and SQL

As we have seen throughout the book, data science is a very rich field of study that can be also considered as an entry point to other technology domains where we work with large or complex amount of data and need to find insights, or build patterns for additional usage. This book uses SQL Server 2017 as the baseline for all the tasks; however, by the time this book had been written, the first Community Technology Preview edition of SQL Server was released, introducing a very interesting path forward in the field of data science and SQL Server.

Data science next steps

Data science is a prerequisite for numerous other fields of study that closely relate to data that we have available including globally the following:

- Deep learning
- Reinforced learning
- Artificial Intelligence
- Big-data processing and many others

AI and machine learning are commonly interchangeable, although they are not the same thing and are usually applied differently based on the available data and expected outcomes. In general terms, AI is a larger concept than machine learning, which is trying to mimic cognitive behavior in humans.

A very frequent approach to training computers to think such as humans, or to implement AI, is the usage of neural networks. Same neural networks can be used also for deep learning, where the algorithm is mimicking the human neocortex in the human brain, allowing the algorithm to learn to recognize patterns in digital representations of sound, images, and other data. Such features however are not yet available in the SQL Server 2017/2019 version, but it can be very interesting follow up your data science study, if you would like to build on the current knowledge of data processing, math, and statistics.

Next steps with SQL Server

As the new SQL Server 2019 is being introduced by the time of the writing of this book, there are numerous new features that have links to the data science domain too. One of them is the availability of the big data clusters. Big data is a huge phenomenon, and SQL Server entered this world with the version of SQL Server 2016 and its PolyBase feature, which we have discussed in the previous chapters. The new version of SQL Server will allow you to access not only HDFS filesystem but also other external data stored in SQL Server - Oracle, Teradata, and MongoDB, expanding the reach of the SQL Server to other DMBS systems and big data storage systems.

Big data clusters

SQL Server big data clusters allow you to manage clusters of SQL Servers alongside containers with Spark and Hadoop HDFS orchestrated by **Kubernetes**. Kubernetes is an open source system, used for automating the whole life cycle which includes the following:

- Deployment
- Scaling
- Management

The SQL Server container capability is available since the Windows Server 2016 and SQL Server 2016. The container approach offers a higher level of isolation then normal processes running in Windows server, by using new operating system technologies such as namespaces and enhancements to technologies such as a job object. A container shares the host kernel but isolates the application from other containers and processes running on the server. This allows for a greater density of isolated applications running on a single host:

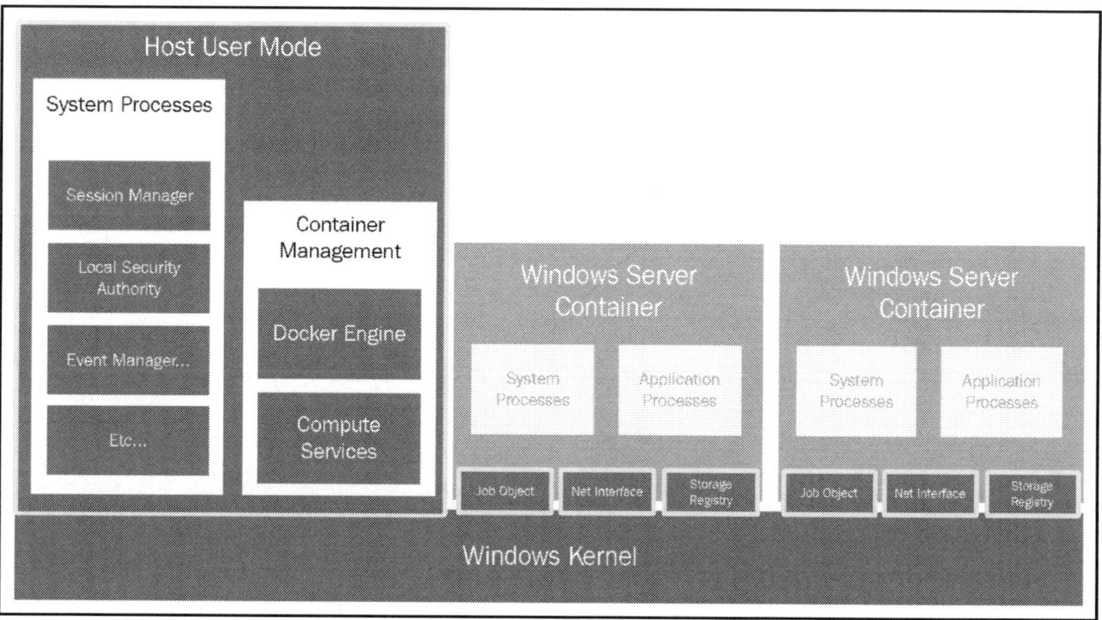

There are two types of containers, which you can use on the Windows Server 2016:

- Windows container
- Hyper-V container

Although the Windows Server containers and Hyper-V containers do the same thing and are managed the same way, the level of isolation they provide is different. Windows Server containers share the underlying OS kernel, which makes them smaller than VMs because they don't each need a copy of the OS. Hyper-V containers and their dependencies reside in special Hyper-V virtual machines and provide an additional layer of isolation. Although the Hyper-V isolation uses Hyper-V under the hood, you actually don't manage these types of containers via Hyper-V Manager or PowerShell.

Installing the feature on Windows Server is based on adding a Docker component via PowerShell environment. You can use following set of commands to install containers on to your Windows Server (providing all prerequisites are met):

```
Install-Module -Name DockerMsftProvider -Repository PSGallery -Force
Install-Package -Name docker -ProviderName DockerMsftProvider
Restart-Computer -Force
```

Once you have installed the feature itself, you'll need to download based images for your containers. The container OS image is the first layer in potentially many image layers that make up a container. This image provides the operating system environment. A Container OS image is immutable; that is, it cannot be modified.

Once a container has been started, all write actions such as file system modifications, registry modifications, or software installations are captured in this sandbox layer.

Any modifications which are made to a container filesystem or container registry is captured inside of the sandbox. As we would like to harden these changes and would like to use them for spinning up new containers we can create an image by converting the sandbox with the applied changes to the container image, which is stored in the image repository.

As example, consider you have deployed a Windows Server Core image for the container and installed SQL Server into the container. Creating new image from this container will allow us to rapidly deploy new containers with installed SQL Server.

Once the containers feature is installed on to your system, you can verify with a few commands what the available version and images are for you to use:

```
docker version
```

This will display the actual version of the Docker component available. There are two versions available as of now:

- 17.06 is the default version (Docker Engine, Universal Control Plane).
- 18.03 is used if only Docker Engine EE is used.

```
docker images
```

This will display all the images, which are present on your system. These images are used to start the containers. By default, there's no container image present after you install the feature to the system and you need to download those images from the internet. To download two basic images to run MS SQL Server you'll need the image for Microsoft SQL itself and the image for the operating system:

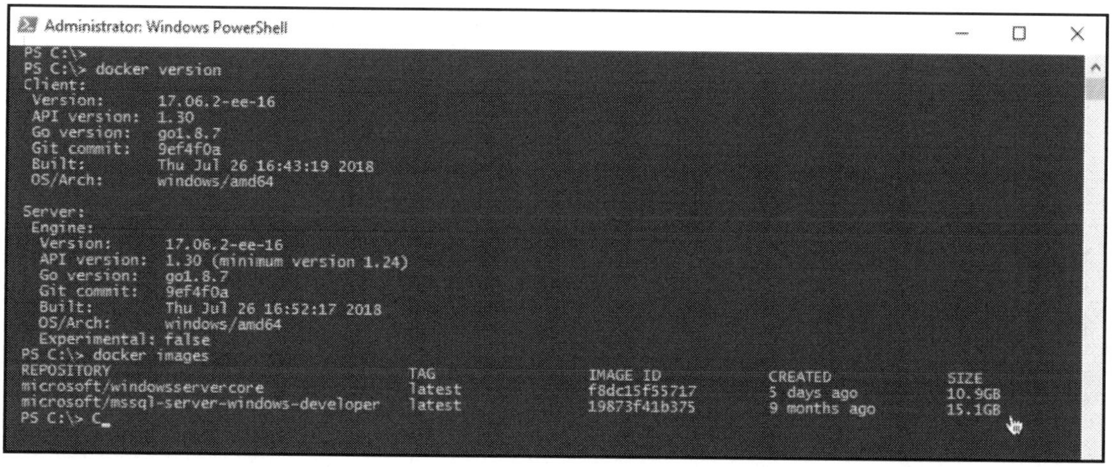

```
Administrator: Windows PowerShell
PS C:\>
PS C:\> docker version
Client:
 Version:      17.06.2-ee-16
 API version:  1.30
 Go version:   go1.8.7
 Git commit:   9ef4f0a
 Built:        Thu Jul 26 16:43:19 2018
 OS/Arch:      windows/amd64

Server:
 Engine:
  Version:      17.06.2-ee-16
  API version:  1.30 (minimum version 1.24)
  Go version:   go1.8.7
  Git commit:   9ef4f0a
  Built:        Thu Jul 26 16:52:17 2018
  OS/Arch:      windows/amd64
  Experimental: false
PS C:\> docker images
REPOSITORY                                TAG      IMAGE ID       CREATED        SIZE
microsoft/windowsservercore               latest   f8dc15f55717   5 days ago     10.9GB
microsoft/mssql-server-windows-developer  latest   19873f41b375   9 months ago   15.1GB
PS C:\> C_
```

To start a container with SQL Server, we'll use the **microsoft/mssql-server-windows-developer** image and add some port mappings so the container is accessible from the host with port forwarding:

```
docker run microsoft/mssql-server-windows-developer -p 1433:1433 -e
"ACCEPT_EULA=Y" -e "SA_PASSWORD=P@ssw0rd" --name SQL01
```

With Docker isolation and container density, one container host can run multiple containers; similarly, one virtualization host can run multiple guest virtual machines. Managing a large number of such hosts without any complex tool would be very hard and challenging, and here's where Kubernetes comes into play.

Kubernetes was originally from Google, and available as a service on your Linux, Mac, or Windows servers or as an **Azure Service—Azure Kubernetes Service** (**Azure AKS**). Such a tool is used to manage and orchestrate the whole ecosystem of the containers and is actually the center of the SQL Server big data cluster. Kubernetes uses the concepts of cluster, node, and pod where the following applies:

- A cluster is a set of machines, also called **nodes**. One node is a master node, controlling the whole cluster, and the other nodes are known as **worker nodes**. The master node distributes the work among the worker nodes and monitors the health of the cluster.

- A node is a host that runs the containerized applications (which can be based on several containers). Node can be either a virtual or a physical machine, depending on the environment design.
- A pod is a unit in Kubernetes describing logical grouping of containers and other required resources that build up the containerized application. The master node assigns pods to the nodes.

In SQL Server big data clusters, Kubernetes is responsible for the state of the SQL Server big data clusters. Cluster nodes are built and configured by Kubernetes, and pods are assigned to nodes. Kubernetes is also responsible for the health monitoring. Nodes in the cluster are arranged into three logical planes: the control plane, the compute pane and the data plane. Each plane has different responsibilities in the cluster. Every Kubernetes node in a SQL Server big data cluster is a member of at least one plane:

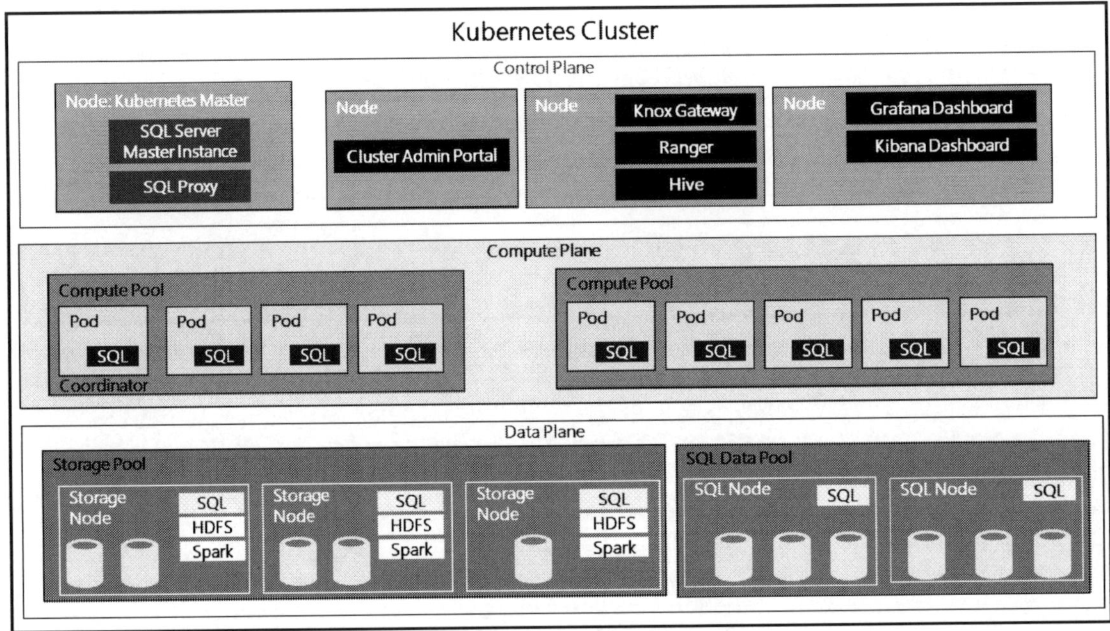

To manage a big data cluster, you can either connect to the master instance or the HDFS/Spark Gateway. For such a connection, you can use the new tool Azure Data Studio, with SQL Server 2019 extensions installed, and choose a relevant **Connection type**:

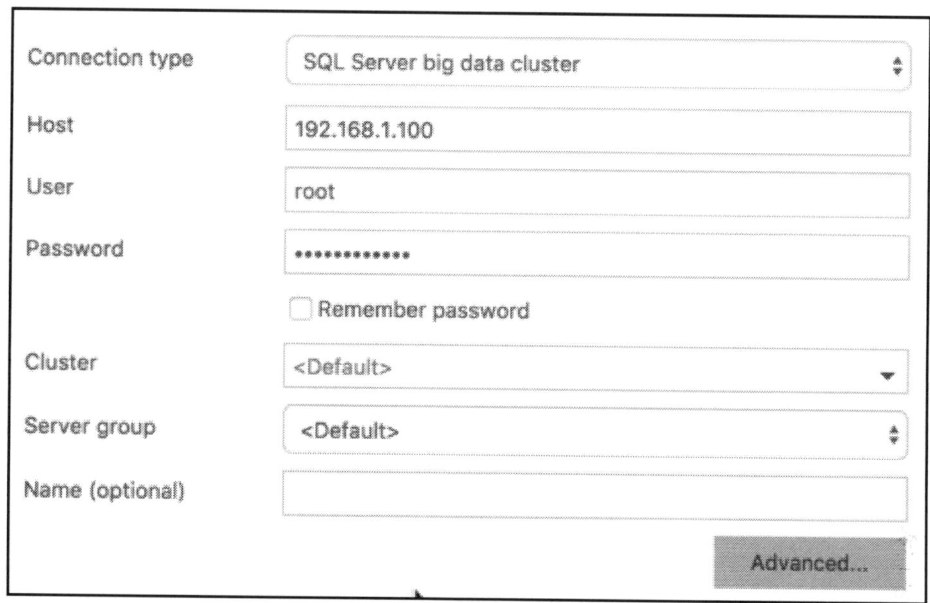

Azure Data Studio is the new name for SQL Server Operations Studio. It is a cross platform tool for working with SQL Server from Windows, Linux, and macOS. You can find more at `https://docs.microsoft.com/en-us/sql/azure-data-studio/download?view=sql-server-2017`.

After you connect to the big data cluster, you can browse the `HDFS` folders. WebHDFS is available after deployment completion and you can do the following:

- Create new directories
- Upload files
- Delete
- Refresh and browse

Not only can you can work with HDFS, but you can also work with **New Notebook** and **New Spark Job**. These Notebooks can use three different kernels as of now:

- PySpark, for Python code with Spark, compute on the cluster
- Spark, for Scala code with Spark, compute on the cluster
- Python, for Python code, local compute

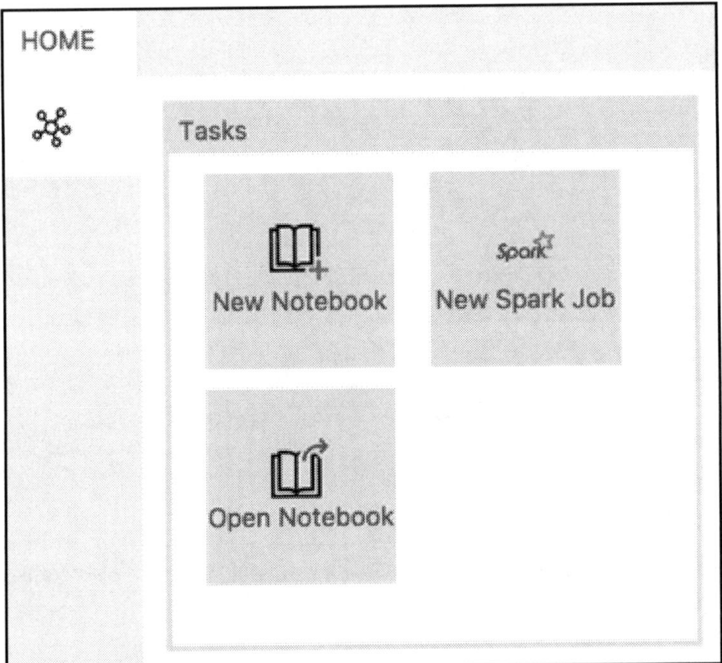

Spark jobs allow you to submit `.jar` or `.py` files with the Spark jobs for execution on the SQL Server 2019. Apache Spark is an analytics engine for processing large data. There are several big data frameworks available and used today, each with its advantages and disadvantages. Spark and MapReduce are the leading ones, where Spark jobs are currently only supported in the SQL Server big data cluster. Spark has some advantages over MapReduce, which would include the following:

- Fast data processing
- Iterative processing
- Near real-time processing
- Machine learning
- Joined datasets

The source files can be submitted either from local storage or the `HDFS` folder. In the case of any reference to additional files, you'll need to specify those in the configuration of the job. Azure Data Studio allows you to monitor the spark jobs and the spark job execution.

Machine learning

SQL Server machine learning services have several improvements coming up in the new release of SQL Server. One of the major improvements is the availability of the machine learning services on the Linux platform. With SQL Server 2017 and 2019, the choice of operating system is now more diverse than before, and you can run SQL Server on Windows Server, inside a container, and on Linux. With Linux, there are actually three distributions available, as follows:

- **Red Hat Enterprise Linux** (**RHEL**)
- SUSE
- Ubuntu

Installing SQL Server on Linux is a little different when compared to the installation on the Windows server. Based on the distribution, you'll need to update the repository for package management system, RPM, Zipper, or APT, to include the repository with Microsoft SQL Server and then just with the appropriate proper package management, you'll download the required packages.

Registering such a repository on Ubuntu is based on running these two commands:

```
wget -qO- https://packages.microsoft.com/keys/microsoft.asc | sudo apt-key
add -

sudo add-apt-repository "$(wget -qO-
https://packages.microsoft.com/config/ubuntu/16.04/mssql-server-preview.lis
t)"
```

Once the repository is added, you can install the SQL Server or additional packages with following commands:

```
sudo apt-get update
sudo apt-get install -y mssql-server
```

Such commands will install the SQL Server database engine. There are more available packages for Linux, and based on your needs you can add more if required. The list of packages would include the following:

- **mssql**: Server for SQL Server
- **mssql**: Server-agent for SQL Server Agent
- **mssql**: Server-**ha** for **High Availability**
- **mssql**: Server-**fts** for **Full Text Search**
- **mssql**: Server-**is** for **Integration Services**
- **mssql**: Tools for command-line utilities

If you would like to also install command-line tools, you'll need to update the repository information, since that's different from the other packages:

```
curl https://packages.microsoft.com/keys/microsoft.asc | sudo apt-key add -

curl https://packages.microsoft.com/config/ubuntu/16.04/prod.list | sudo
tee /etc/apt/sources.list.d/msprod.list
```

Once the information is updated, you can install command-line tools via the following:

```
sudo apt-get update
sudo apt-get install mssql-tools unixodbc-dev
```

Installing the SQL Server package will just bring the binaries and enable the service. You can verify the status of the service via the following:

```
systemctl status mssql-server
```

If the server is up and running, this will be shown in the output:

```
marek@server02: ~
marek@server02:~$ systemctl status mssql-server
● mssql-server.service - Microsoft SQL Server Database Engine
   Loaded: loaded (/lib/systemd/system/mssql-server.service; enabled; vendor pre
   Active: active (running) since Čt 2018-10-18 14:20:50 CEST; 18min ago
     Docs: https://docs.microsoft.com/en-us/sql/linux
 Main PID: 1095 (sqlservr)
   CGroup: /system.slice/mssql-server.service
           ├─1095 /opt/mssql/bin/sqlservr
           └─1889 /opt/mssql/bin/sqlservr
```

The configuration, however, is not part of the installation, but once the package is added to your distribution, you'll run the configuration script as follows:

```
sudo /opt/mssql/bin/mssql-conf setup
```

This configuration tool will help you configure the SQL Server on your host, starting with choosing a SQL Server edition, where you'll enter the number for a predefined list of choices, which are presented to you:

```
marek@server02:~$ sudo /opt/mssql/bin/mssql-conf setup
Choose an edition of SQL Server:
  1) Evaluation (free, no production use rights, 180-day limit)
  2) Developer (free, no production use rights)
  3) Express (free)
  4) Web (PAID)
  5) Standard (PAID)
  6) Enterprise (PAID)
  7) Enterprise Core (PAID)
  8) I bought a license through a retail sales channel and have a product key to
 enter.

Details about editions can be found at
https://go.microsoft.com/fwlink/?LinkId=852748&clcid=0x409

Use of PAID editions of this software requires separate licensing through a
Microsoft Volume Licensing program.
By choosing a PAID edition, you are verifying that you have the appropriate
number of licenses in place to install and run this software.

Enter your edition(1-8):
```

Afterward, you have to supply the password for the sa account and the SQL Server will then be started for you:

```
Enter the SQL Server system administrator password:
Confirm the SQL Server system administrator password:
Configuring SQL Server...

ForceFlush is enabled for this instance.
ForceFlush feature is enabled for log durability.
Setup has completed successfully. SQL Server is now starting.
```

When SQL Server is running on Linux, you might need to have local tool more powerful than just the command-line tools. In that case, you need Azure Data Studio.

Azure Data Studio, formerly known as **SQL Server Operations Studio**, is a free tool available from Microsoft, which runs on Windows, Linux, and macOS. You can get Azure Data Studio from `https://docs.microsoft.com/en-us/sql/azure-data-studio/download?view=sql-server-2017#get-azure-data-studio-for-linux`

For Linux, you have to download a package specific to your distribution, which will be one of the following:

- `deb` file for Ubuntu
- `rpm` for RHEL
- `tar.gz` for SUSE

On Ubuntu Linux, the tool to install such a package is `dpkg`, and the command you would use in such case is as follows:

```
sudo dpkg -i ./Downloads/azuredatastudio-linux-1.1.3.deb
```

This will install the Azure Data Studio, which you can later on start by calling `azuredatastudio` in the terminal window. The `dpkg` tool is actually used to install the single package, instead of the apt-get, which is more robust and can also install depended packages with MS SQL Server:

```
marek@server02:~$ cd ~
marek@server02:~$ ls
Desktop    Downloads          Music     Public     Videos
Documents  examples.desktop   Pictures  Templates
marek@server02:~$ sudo dpkg -i ./Downloads/azuredatastudio-linux-1.1.3.deb
[sudo] password for marek:
Sorry, try again.
[sudo] password for marek:
Selecting previously unselected package azuredatastudio.
(Reading database ... 212557 files and directories currently installed.)
Preparing to unpack .../azuredatastudio-linux-1.1.3.deb ...
Unpacking azuredatastudio (1.1.3-1539810663) ...
Setting up azuredatastudio (1.1.3-1539810663) ...
Processing triggers for gnome-menus (3.13.3-6ubuntu3.1) ...
Processing triggers for desktop-file-utils (0.22-1ubuntu5.1) ...
Processing triggers for bamfdaemon (0.5.3~bzr0+16.04.20160824-0ubuntu1) ...
Rebuilding /usr/share/applications/bamf-2.index...
Processing triggers for mime-support (3.59ubuntu1) ...
marek@server02:~$
```

Once the tool is installed, you can run Azure Data Studio and connect to your SQL Server. Azure Data Studio can be used to connect to SQL Server, but not to the big data cluster, right away. For the big data cluster, you'll need to download an extension to the Azure Data Studio and install the extension based on the operating system, where you run the Azure Data Studio:

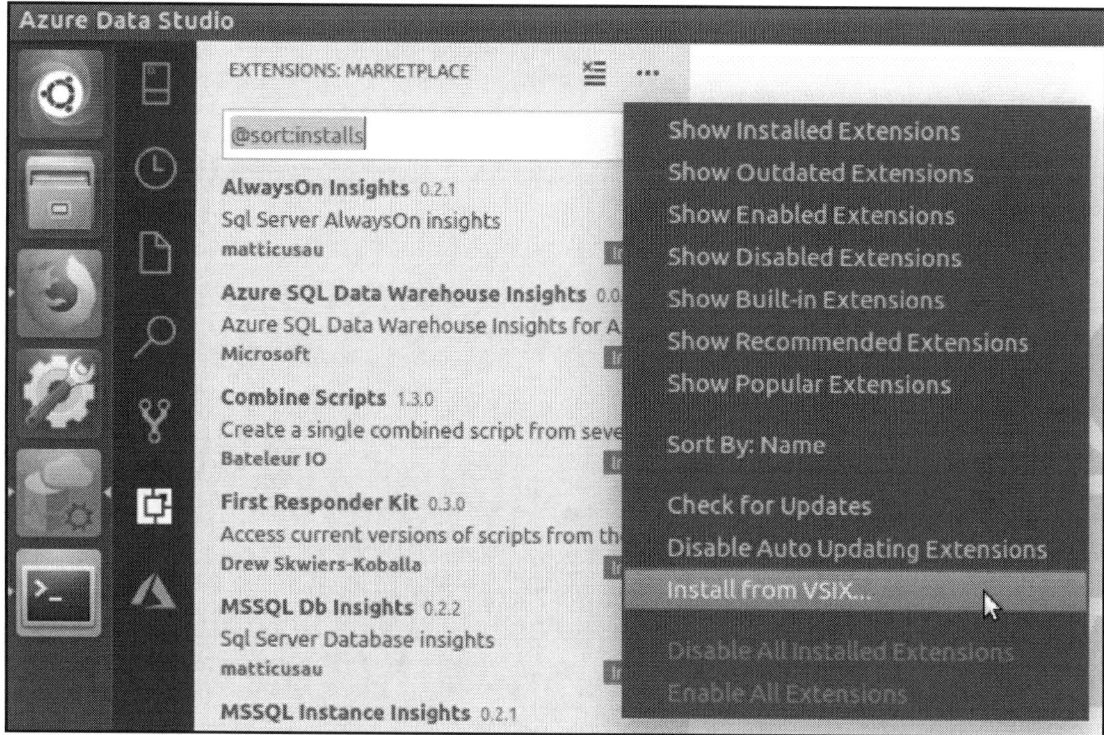

Once the extension for SQL Server 2019 preview is installed, and you relaunch the Azure Data Studio, you can connect to the big data cluster and start managing the cluster, HDFS, and notebooks:

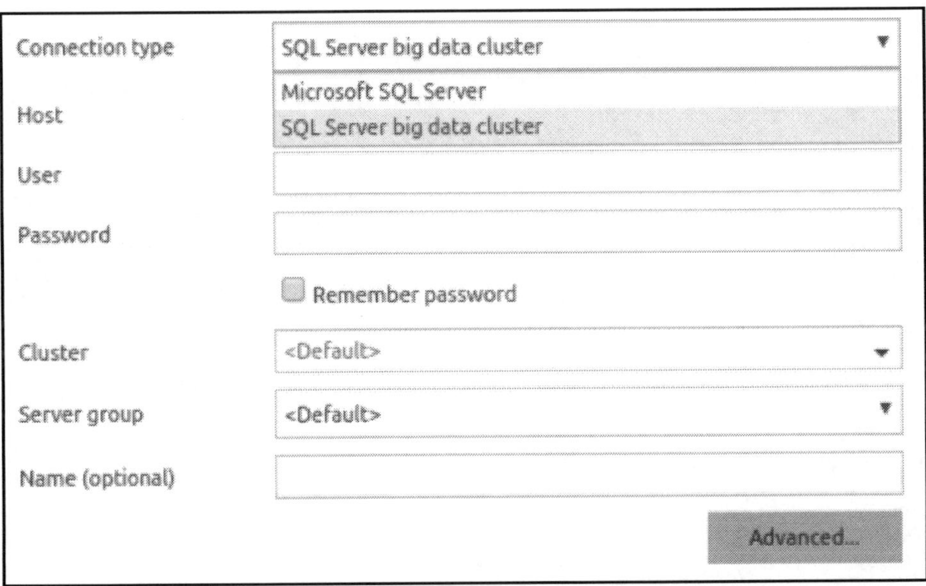

But that is not the only way for you to manage the **SQL Server big data cluster**; there's also the cluster administration portal available, which will display you the overall health of the cluster for monitoring purposes.

When you first enter the portal, you can quickly view the number of pods running in the following:

- Controller
- Master instance
- Compute pool
- Storage pool
- Data pool

Machine learning services on Linux

The packages which will install SQL Server 2019 Machine Learning Services are split into several components depending on the language support, which you'll like to have on your system. Those would include the following:

- R Language
- Python
- Java

There are variety of available packages, including or excluding the models, depending on the chosen language. There's a prerequisite for most of the R packages to run **Microsoft R Open** (**MRO**), which is required in version 3.4.4 and can be obtained from the `packages.microsoft.com` repository.

To install the support for Python language in ML Services, you can add it, just like any other package, with the following command:

```
sudo apt-get install mssql-mlservices-mlm-py
```

Machine learning high availability

While the machine learning services were already available on SQL Server 2017 with Windows Server operating system, the service did not provide any high availability. A major improvement for SQL Server 2019 on Windows Server and Linux is the option to add the machine learning services as a clustered resource, while configuring Windows Server Failover Clustering or the HA Linux package for high-availability deployments.

Data science in the cloud

We're focusing on SQL Server, but you need to be aware of the fact that machine learning as a service was first available in Microsoft Azure cloud before it was available with SQL Server. There are already seven services associated with machine learning available in Azure (two of them, however, are already retiring):

- **HDInsight clusters**
- **Machine Learning Studio web service plan**
- **Machine Learning Studio workspaces**
- **Machine Learning Studio web services**
- **Machine Learning Service workspaces**
- **Machine Learning Model Management (Retiring)**
- **Machine Learning Experimentation (Retiring)**

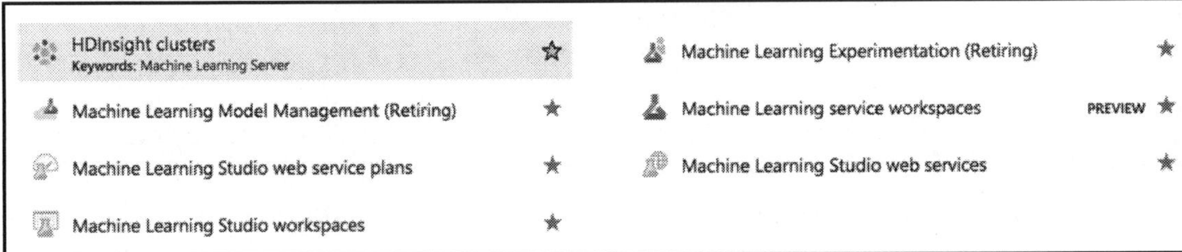

These services, together with the proper tools, can be another entry point to data science and working with your data. One of the tools you can use is Machine Learning Studio, a free online application, which you can use to create your experiments.

Azure Machine Learning Studio is available at `https://studio.azureml.net/`.
For login, you'll need a liveID account, which will be used to work with the experiments.

The web application will allow you to work with several different items; for those, you have a navigation menu on the left:

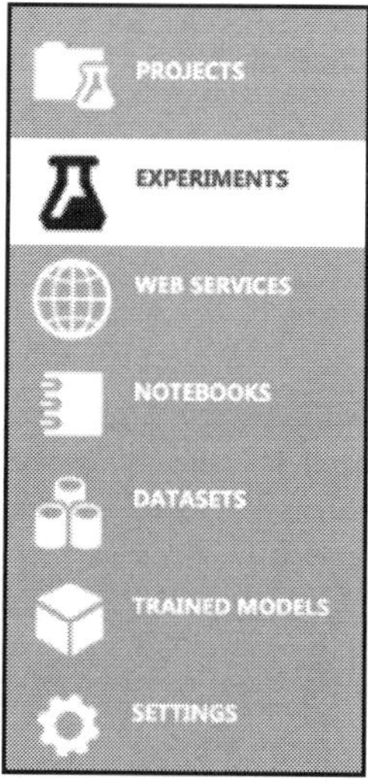

Before we start working on an experiment, you'll need to decide how to acquire your data. You can use a saved dataset, which is actually based on a file you have uploaded to the workspace, or directly in the experiment, you can import data from live data sources:

The files for the dataset can come in several different formats, as you can see in the following screenshot:

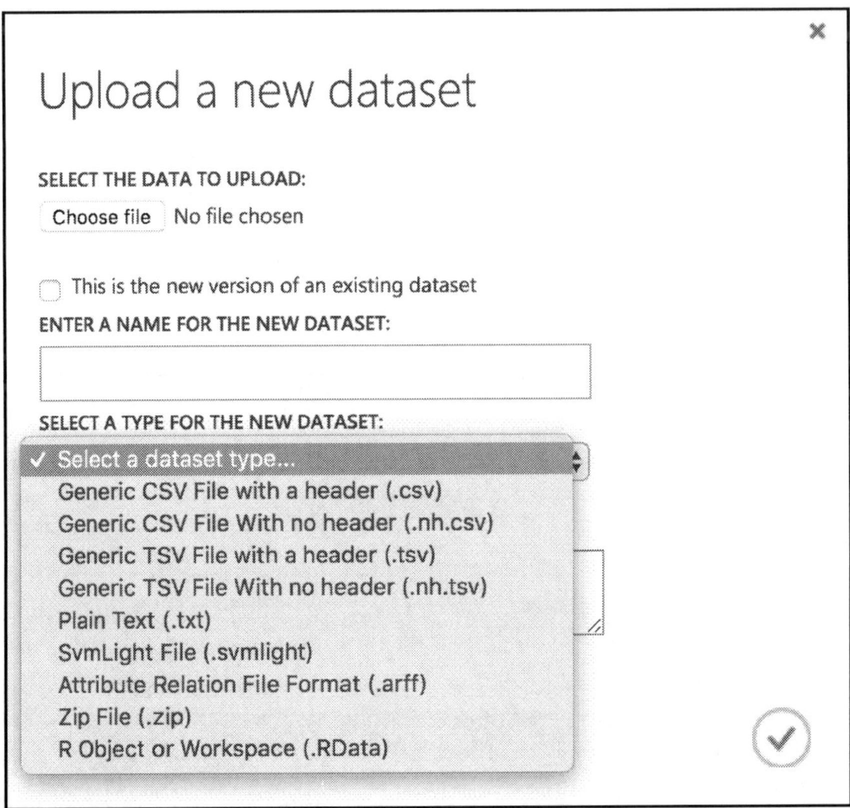

If you decide to work with data later in the experiment, then you have several different options. The experiment itself is a workflow of data processing and machine learning steps, which generate a machine learning model. This model can be then published via web services and used within your applications. Once you create a new experiment, you'll see a blank workspace to which you have to drag and drop actions to take (a similar approach to SQL Server Integration Services):

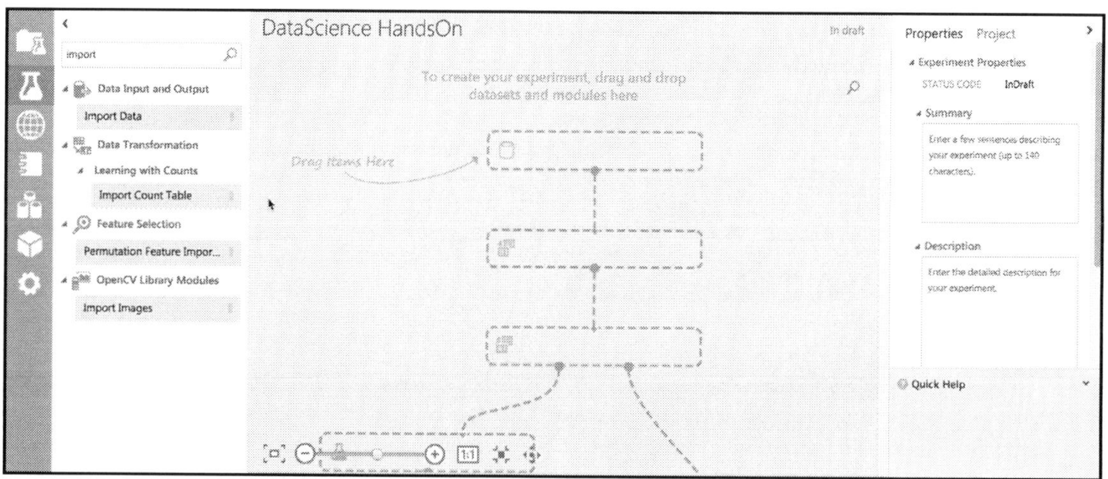

Since there's numerous actions to use, you can use live filtering in the search field, as in the screenshot, where import was looked for and the only items with import in their name are displayed; one of them being **Import Data**. If you have uploaded a dataset before, it will be available in the **My Datasets** category for you to drag and drop the dataset on the workspace.

Each item you'll use can have additional settings, which can modify the task outcome, such as when you're working with missing values, there are several options for you to choose. First, you need to select on what columns in the dataset to implement the task with column selector, and then you'll need to configure the action itself:

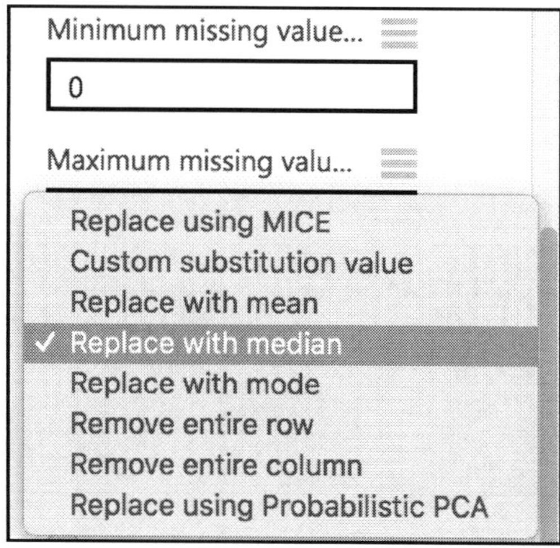

The way you deal with the missing value problem is dependent on numerous factors, one of them being the structure of the dataset and its size, and also the business question and the expected outcomes themselves.

The items that you'll use will depend on the task you're trying to achieve, but in most cases, they will follow a similar workflow:

- Import data
- Process data
- Train model
- Improve model

Data processing could include variety of steps such as these:

1. Clean missing values
2. Normalize the data
3. Remove rows or columns from datasets
4. Transformations with R, Python, or T-SQL
5. And many others

Machine learning will include just a few simple tasks such as the following:

- Model initialization (based on the selected algorithm)
- Train model
- Score model
- Evaluate model

Scoring the model is based on unknown data to the training part, so you'll usually split your dataset between a training subset and a scoring subset (usually with 70/30 or 80/20 ratio as a baseline). The evaluate model will then display the characteristics of the trained model, which we have introduced in the previous chapters such as AUC, F1 score, accuracy, and so on.

In the following diagram, you'll see the data import for the `Loan Data` dataset, which was imported into the machine learning workspace as a shared dataset for multiple experiments. The data-processing part includes transformations, missing value work, and other tasks.

The machine learning algorithm used here was a **Two-Class Bayes Point Mach...**, which gave the best results. As the model training is iterative work, you'll compare multiple algorithms to multiple settings to find the one that performs best and gives you the results based on your needs:

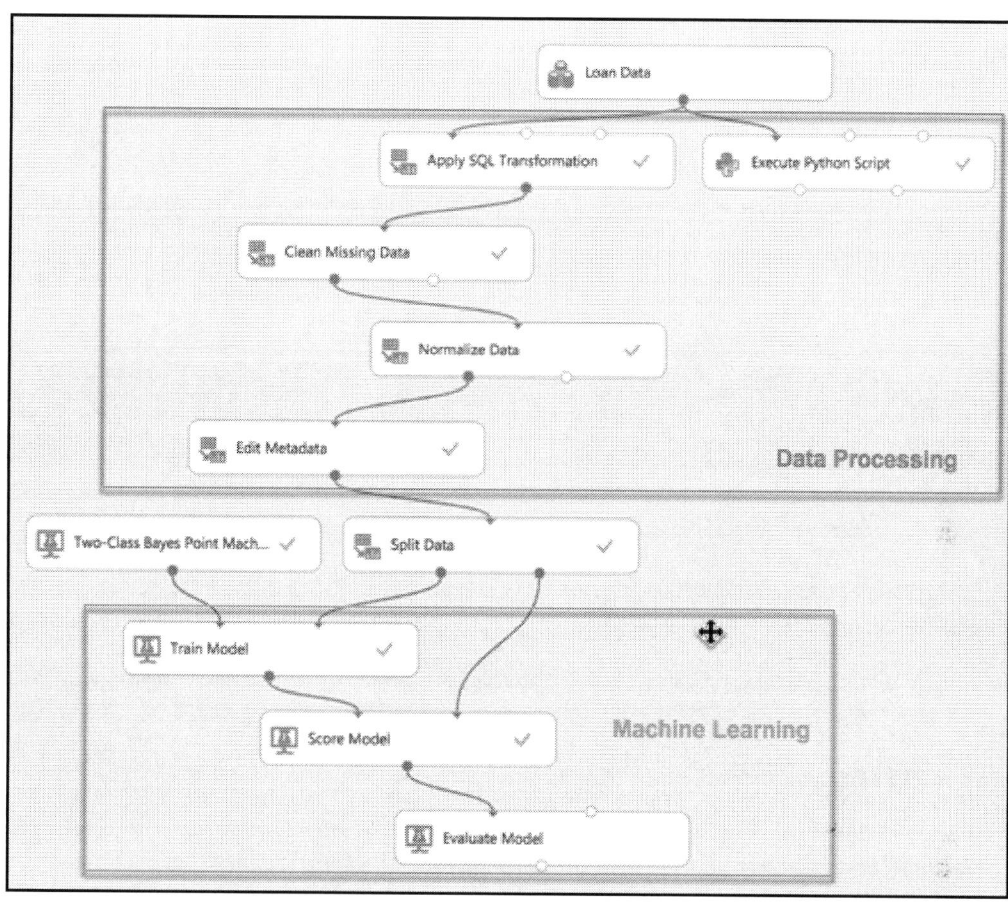

Azure Machine Learning Predictive Experiment Workflow

When you would like to see how the model is behaving, you can visualize on the Evaluate Model component to get the metrics as follows:

True Positive	False Negative	Accuracy	Precision	Threshold	AUC
8711	195	0.884	0.853	0.5	0.864
False Positive	**True Negative**	**Recall**	**F1 Score**		
1496	4160	0.978	0.912		

As we have already discussed the meaning of the metrics in the first chapters, you can see whether the model is good for your needs. When you've finished tuning the model tuning, you can publish the model as a web service. Such a web service can then be used in your application, or if you'll publish the model to the Office Marketplace, you can use the model directly in the Office applications:

Comprehensive coverage of the model is outside the scope of the book. However you can find more information in this book by Sumit Mund: *Microsoft Azure Machine Learning*, which is available at `https://www.packtpub.com/big-data-and-business-intelligence/microsoft-azure-machine-learning`.

Summary

We've reached the final chapter of the book, which took us on a long and rich journey into the field of data science and the Microsoft SQL Server. We have mostly focused on performing tasks in data science with the SQL Server toolset—either a T-SQL language, or additional services that are available with SQL Server, as the SQL Server is a important component of enterprise infrastructures based on Microsoft Servers. It's not the only choice for data science, and there are of course more tools available out there.

The aim of the book was to introduce a platform that can offer most of the tasks related to data science, and in this last chapter we have tried to uncover what's coming with the new version of SQL Server for data science and how to work with data science projects in Microsoft Azure.

Other Books You May Enjoy

If you enjoyed this book, you may be interested in these other books by Packt:

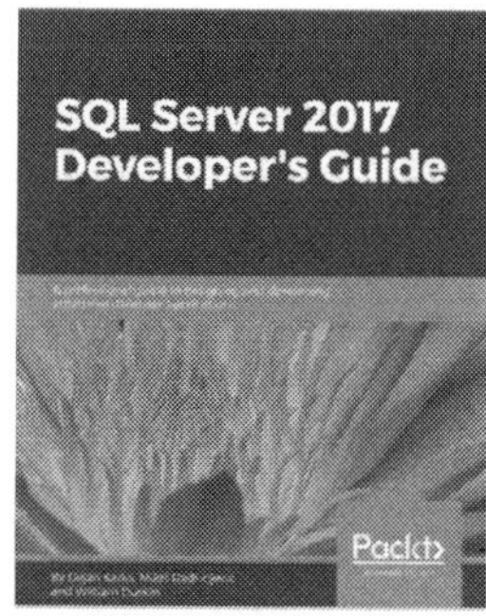

SQL Server 2017 Developer's Guide
Dejan Sarka, Miloš Radivojević, William Durkin

ISBN: 978-1-78847-619-5

- Explore the new development features introduced in SQL Server 2017
- Identify opportunities for In-Memory OLTP technology
- Use columnstore indexes to get storage and performance improvements
- Extend database design solutions using temporal tables
- Exchange JSON data between applications and SQL Server

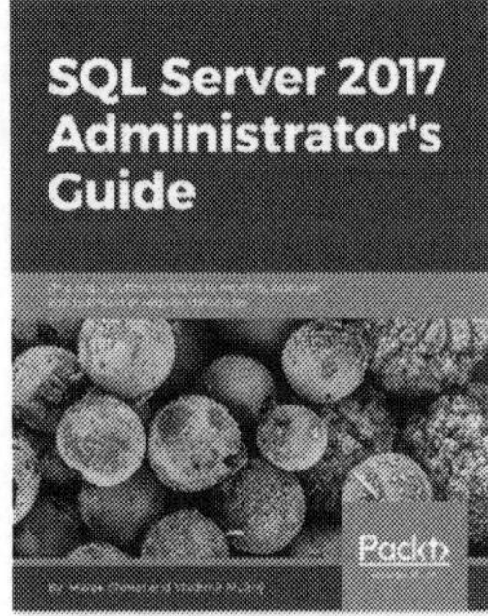

SQL Server 2017 Administrator's Guide
Marek Chmel, Vladimír Mužný

ISBN: 978-1-78646-254-1

- Learn about the new features of SQL Server 2017 and how to implement them
- Build a stable and fast SQL Server environment
- Fix performance issues by optimizing queries and making use of indexes
- Perform a health check of an existing troublesome database environment
- Design and use an optimal database management strategy

Leave a review - let other readers know what you think

Please share your thoughts on this book with others by leaving a review on the site that you bought it from. If you purchased the book from Amazon, please leave us an honest review on this book's Amazon page. This is vital so that other potential readers can see and use your unbiased opinion to make purchasing decisions, we can understand what our customers think about our products, and our authors can see your feedback on the title that they have worked with Packt to create. It will only take a few minutes of your time, but is valuable to other potential customers, our authors, and Packt. Thank you!

Index

D

E

F

G

H

I

J

S

T

U

Made in the USA
Middletown, DE
07 February 2019